P9-DZN-704

Siegfried Sassoon

BY THE SAME AUTHOR

NON-FICTION

The Cousins

Balfour

Under Two Flags:
The Life of Major-General Sir Edward Spears

FICTION

The Ladies' Man

Dear Shadows

Painted Lives

Second Spring

MAX EGREMONT

Siegfried Sassoon

A LIFE

FARRAR, STRAUS AND GIROUX / NEW YORK

Farrar, Straus and Giroux
19 Union Square West, New York 10003

Copyright © 2005 by Max Egremont
All rights reserved
Printed in the United States of America
Originally published in 2005 by Picador, Great Britain, as
Siegfried Sassoon: A Biography
Published in the United States by Farrar, Straus and Giroux
First American edition, 2005

Grateful acknowledgement is made to Charles and Lisbet Wheeler for permission to
reproduce the photograph of Weirleigh.

Library of Congress Cataloging–in–Publication Data
Egremont, Max, 1948–
    Siegfried Sassoon: a life / Max Egremont.—1st American ed.
        p. cm.
    ISBN–13: 978-0-374-26375-1 (alk. paper)
    ISBN–10: 0-374-26375-2 (alk. paper)
        1. Sassoon, Siegfried, 1886–1967.   2. Poets, English—20th century—Biography.
3. Catholic converts—Great Britain—Biography.   4. Soldiers—Great Britain—
Biography.   I. Title.

PR6037.A86Z66 2005
821'.912—dc22

                                                                          2005051629
                        www.fsgbooks.com

1   3   5   7   9   10   8   6   4   2

For George and Alison

CONTENTS

Preface

'THERE ARE SO many things I ought to tell you that I don't know how to begin,'[1] Siegfried Sassoon wrote to his friend, the poet Ralph Hodgson on 1 September 1930. He was in a quiet Wiltshire valley as summer changed into sharpening yet melancholy autumn, his favourite time of year.

Sassoon seemed to be extraordinarily fortunate: rich, a bestselling writer who had shaped people's view of the most important event of the European twentieth century (the Great War of 1914 to 1918) and now a man in love. He sat looking through the double doors of a manor house into its garden, past two round bushes of box to an old mulberry tree. Over the lawn skimmed swallows, wagtails, blackbirds and thrushes; further away in this 'little paradise' the River Avon ran through water meadows. Two miles distant was Stonehenge, a monument to England's prehistory; nearer were some tumuli of primeval burial sites, still safe from 'creeping motors going along the highways'. The landscape resembled that seen by the radical writer William Cobbett during his rural rides in the 1820s, even though its inhabitants had become much more prosperous since then, in spite of the present agricultural depression.

To Hodgson, Sassoon admitted the hardship endured by the farmers, comparable to the years after the Napoleonic wars, and said he had heard 'things may get much worse' because bad weather had wrecked the harvest. He lamented that the future would be more mechanized, that literature would descend into journalism, although his own reading was far from this: Lafcadio Hearn on Japan (where Hodgson was working), a chapter called 'The Dream of a Summer Day', and his friend Edmund Blunden's book on the romantic poet Leigh Hunt. He had been book-hunting in Salisbury and found a bargain: a large paper copy of the *History of Quadrupeds* by the artist Thomas Bewick. His next book, *Memoirs of an Infantry Officer*, had been serialized in the *Daily Telegraph*; over 15,000 copies had already been ordered although it was not to be published until 18 September, more than two weeks away. These slightly fictionalized autobiographies, of which there were to be three volumes, show innocence broken on the Western Front where their hero – George Sherston – endures a brutal, mechanical warfare quite different to his dream of chivalry and righteous battle.

Sassoon wrote to Hodgson from a ground-floor study. Fishing rods and nets leaned against the chimneypiece; on one wall was a bookcase full of children's classics, relics of the family who had grown up here, one of whom had been killed in the battle of the Somme. The scene could be a parody of a certain lost Englishness: the manor house, a yew-hedged garden, the reminders of a fortunate childhood that had ended in chivalrous sacrifice, a cultured country gentleman commenting on the state of agriculture. Sassoon's letter hints at present tragedy in the mention of a colliery disaster in Kent but goes quickly back to the past in a reference to the vicarage and church in the mining village.

The reality is different. Siegfried Sassoon was half Jewish, an uncertain Englishman. The manor house, called Wilsford, had been built at the start of the twentieth century in imitation-Jacobean style by a family rich through the manufacture of bleach in hideous, industrial Glasgow: the study was used still by a retired politician who, as Britain's foreign secretary in 1914, had taken the country into a war that Sassoon loathed. The person whom Sassoon loved, inside the house, was a man: Stephen Tennant. Even Ralph Hodgson (to whom the letter was written), although superficially steeped in

English tradition – an eighteenth-century world of prize fighters, mastiffs and boisterous talk – spent much of his life abroad, in Japan and the United States.

Unlike Hodgson, Sassoon stayed, trying both to escape himself and to catch his own instinctive vision. What makes him exceptional is that in all this he made a lasting version of history as well as a writer's world, reaching beyond literary achievement to a national myth. The tall, thin, shy, officer–poet with the Military Cross defying the old men who sent young heroes 'up the line to death' is as much a part of the tragic version of the First World War as Wilfred Owen's preface ('the poetry is in the pity') to his own poems – a preface which, ironically, Sassoon had not wanted published at all, feeling that Owen's poetry should speak for itself. Sassoon's war means a callous, out-of-touch High Command and the sacrifice of innocents in the apparently unceasing hell of the Western Front: a vision so haunting that twentieth-century British warfare still seems to be defined by futile offensives, exhausted men impaled upon wire or trapped in mud before an immovable enemy a mere few yards away across a dark, lunar landscape. More than anyone, even more than Owen, Siegfried Sassoon created this, through his poetry and his prose, turning it into one of the most resonant myths of our times.

Sassoon's importance, both literary and historical (rare in a writer), has led to many people going in search of him; since his death in 1967, there have been at least five full-length studies of his life and his work. So why add to an already crowded field? My answer is that, through Siegfried's son George – who has never co-operated so extensively with a biographer before – I have been shown much new material. The substance of this is the unpublished manuscript diaries from 1926 onwards, Sassoon's extensive notes for his autobiographies, and other correspondence and drafts of poems and prose books.

Rupert Hart-Davis edited three volumes of Sassoon's diaries, from 1915 to 1925, and these were published in 1981, 1983 and 1985. Then he stopped and the manuscripts for the later years have stayed unseen by biographers until now. Sassoon himself thought that his autobiography was in his poetry; that is why I have taken a biographical approach towards his poems and treated them extensively. But the diaries and drafts and notes for his three volumes of straight autobiography – *The Old Century, The Weald of Youth* and *Siegfried's Journey* – and a fourth volume that was started but never finished, give an astonishingly frank and revealing view of the man in what is, perhaps, one of the most extensive self-portraits of any twentieth-century British writer. Another extraordinary source is the journal that Stephen Tennant kept during his relationship with Sassoon, now in a private collection and used here for the first time. I visited Stephen Tennant towards the end of his life, some years before I began to write about Siegfried Sassoon. Tennant wrote many letters to me about earlier days, and I have drawn on these in my portrait of him. I knew Sir Geoffrey Keynes in his last years and heard him speak often of his beloved Siegfried. The late Dame Felicitas Corrigan, in an electrifying conversation at Stanbrook Abbey, talked very frankly about Sassoon and then let me read his letters to her. Adrian Goodman made available to me the journals of his grandmother Lady Ottoline Morrell. I am very grateful to him for allowing me to be the first person writing about Siegfried Sassoon to see these. The Morrell papers are now in the British Library, and Lady Ottoline's photograph albums in the National Portrait Gallery.

When George Sassoon asked me to write this book, he also offered me his own memories. We have spent much time together, in Wiltshire or on the island of Mull, discussing Siegfried Sassoon, and I am immensely grateful to him and to his wife Alison and his daughter Kendall. I cannot exaggerate the help I have had from George Sassoon and from his family – this book would have little point without it. Others who have helped me, with information, advice and hospitality, include: Bart Auerbach; Gabriel Austin; Ian Balding; the late Rolfe Barber; Nicolas Barker; David Behrman; Simon Blow who showed me his play, *Uncle Stephen's Lizards*, about the relationship between Stephen Tennant and Siegfried Sassoon; the late Claire Blunden and her daughters, Margi Blunden and Lucy Edgeley; the late the Hon. Raymond Bonham Carter; Michael

Borrie; Sir Henry Boyd-Carpenter; William Buice; the Marquess of Cholmondeley; Jenny Coutts; the late Lionel Dakers; Roy Davids; the late Ian Davie; Paul Delaney; the late Mary, Viscountess Eccles; James and Maggie Fergusson; Federico Forquet; Colin Franklin; Sister Jessica Gatty; Pamela Gatty; Milton and Monica Gendel; Lewis and Jacqueline Golden; Adrian and Shena Goodman; the late Beryl Graves; William and Elena Graves; Duff Hart-Davis; Lady Hart-Davis and the late Sir Rupert Hart-Davis; Selina Hastings; Simon Head; Lord Hemingford; Dominic Hibberd; Martyn and Joanna Hitchcock; Anthony Hobson; Haro and Elizabeth Hodson; Lynn Humphries; Rosalind Ingrams; Dom Philip Jebb; John and Victoria Jolliffe; Laurence and Linda Kelly; Stephen, Milo, Simon and the late Quentin Keynes; the late the Hon. Dame Miriam Lane; Mark Samuels Lasner; David Lloyd; the late Kenneth Lohf; Roger and Dagmar Louis; Ed Maggs; Alison McCann; Helen McPhail; Dom Sebastian Moore; Professor Masatsugu Ohtake; the late Rosemary Olivier; the Earl of Oxford and Asquith; Christine Parham; Peter Parker; Tim Penton; Jonathan Petropoulos; Andrew Pinnell; Nicholas Poole-Wilson; George and Jane Ramsden; William Reese; Sir Adam Ridley; John Stuart Roberts; Bill and Janice Rossen; Anthony Rota; the late Hamo Sassoon; Meredith Sassoon; John Saumarez Smith; Desmond Seward; Bruce Shand; Dennis Silk; Jon Stallworthy; Peter Stansky; Toby and Emma Tennant; Sir Simon Towneley; Hugo Vickers; Jonathan Walsh; Leslie Weller; Mrs Charles Wheeler; the late Laurence Whistler; Robert and Pamela Woof; Samantha Wyndham.

My research has led me to many libraries and I thank all those who helped me during my visits or answered my inquiries. In Britain: the British Library; the Bodleian Library, Oxford; Peter Fox, Patrick Zutshi, Kathleen Cann and John Wells at the Cambridge University Library; the library of the Craiglockhart campus of Napier University; Sue Usher at the English Faculty Library, the University of Oxford; Michael Meredith and the staff of the Eton College Library; Adeline van Roon at the Henry Moore Institute in Leeds; Simon Robbins; Christopher Rowling and Roderick Suddaby at the Imperial

War Museum; the King's College, Cambridge, Archives Centre; the London Library; Martin Evans and Terry Rogers at Marlborough College; the National Army Museum, Iain Brown at the National Library of Scotland; the Public Record Office at Kew; Norman James and Richard Olney at the then Royal Commission on Historical Manuscripts; Lieutenant Colonel Peter Crocker and David Bowness at the Royal Welch Fusiliers' Regimental Museum at Carnarvon; the Sheffield Archives. In the United States and Canada: Dr Howard Gottlieb of the Mugar Memorial Library at Boston University; the Special Collections at the Butler Library at Columbia University in New York; the Grolier Club in New York; the University of Delaware; the Lily Library at Indiana University at Bloomington; the Library of Congress in Washington DC; the Mills Memorial Library at McMaster University, Hamilton, Ontario; the University of Maryland at College Park; Stephen Crook, Isaac Gewirtz and Philip Milito at the Berg Collection in the New York Public Library; the University of Buffalo; the Special Collections at Rutgers University Library in New Brunswick, New Jersey; Southern Illinois University at Carbondale; Tom Staley and the staff of the Harry Ransom Humanities Research Center at the University of Texas at Austin; the McFarlin Library at the University of Tulsa; Washington State University at Pullman; Wichita State University; Vincent Giroud at the Beinecke Library at Yale University.

Some people have helped me consistently from the start of my researches and have read parts or all of my manuscript; to them I owe an especial debt: Carol Rothkopf; Brian Bond; Hugh Cecil; Peter Washington. To my publishers in Britain and the United States – Peter Straus and Jonathan Galassi who commissioned this book and Andrew Kidd who inherited it and Peter James without whose brilliant copy-editing it would have been much worse – and to my exemplary agent Gill Coleridge and her assistant Lucy Luck I am profoundly grateful for constant encouragement and patience. To my family – my wife Caroline, our four children and my mother – I owe more than I can say for help and tolerance during what has turned out to be a long journey.

The purchasing power of the pound

Money – both the possession and the giving away of it – plays an important part in this book and, to make the figures clearer, here is a comparison of the purchasing power of the pound at certain dates.

There was little price inflation between 1886, the year that Siegfried Sassoon was born, and 1914. Taking the pound at £1 in 1998, its comparable purchasing power is:

1914: £58.18
1920: £23.27
1930: £36.20
1938: £37.02
1946: £22.01
1955: £14.54
1965: £11.00
1975: £4.76
1985: £1.72
1998: £1.00
2002: £0.92

Source: *Whitaker's Almanack 2004*

ONE

'The daybreak world'

SIEGFRIED SASSOON DENIED that he was 'a typical Jew'[1] and disliked to be thought rich, but at the end of the nineteenth century, when he was born, the name of Sassoon meant great riches: a 'gilded'[2] Jewish family linked to the raffish Prince of Wales (later King Edward VII) and to an exotic, slightly mysterious past. If this eastern ancestry featured in his dreams, it usually took a more Arabian form, as 'processions, strange crowds of people, façades of oriental looking buildings with hieroglyphics on them – like racial memories',[3] nothing to do with trade. He made anti-Semitic remarks and mocked his family's 'Jewish gold' made 'in the east by dirty trading' to allow a snobbish life in England as cigar-smoking worshippers of 'German royalties and dissolute peers'.[4] Siegfried's cousin Philip Sassoon, the bachelor politician and host, was similarly uneasy about it and hinted that he was of Parsee stock,[5] aware perhaps how quickly the English could turn on Jews, how much they remained essentially outsiders.

The word Sassoon means 'joy' in Hebrew, and Siegfried thought the name came from a place in Mesopotamia called Sashûn and that his ancestors were 'partly Persian'. In fact they were Sephardim, descended from the Jews of Spain, Portugal and north Africa. By the eighteenth century the Sassoons were successful traders in Baghdad and prominent members of the synagogue, but it was

David, Siegfried's great-grandfather, born in 1792, who had a genius for business. He moved to Basra from Baghdad, and in 1832, having been harried by Ottoman officialdom, arrived in Bombay, then under British rule, in search of larger markets and stability. The fortune was founded upon trade in (among other goods) textiles, tea, dried fruit, metals and, when the link with China developed, opium, as well as property in Bombay, Shanghai and Hong Kong. The riches combined with piety and philanthropy: schools, synagogues, hospitals, orphanages, museums and a Jewish newspaper in Bombay and another synagogue in Poona. David was a patriarchal figure, naturally powerful, and the father of thirteen children by two marriages. After his death in 1864, contributions towards the cost of a statue of him to be put up in Bombay came from Jews, Parsees and Christians in India, Persia, China and Europe and included five guineas from the Liberal statesman William Gladstone.

David's son – and Siegfried's grandfather – Sassoon David Sassoon, who landed from Shanghai in 1858 to establish the family's business in London, was quite different. Tall and thin, sickly and shy, the scholarly, lisping 'S.D.' – collector of a library of Jewish books and manuscripts – had married Farha Reuben, the daughter of a rich and devoutly Jewish merchant in Baghdad. He seems to have been proud of his Sephardic inheritance, having a sense of being set apart from the more numerous Ashkenazim of the northern European ghettos like the Rothschilds,[6] but his father David dominated his life and S.D. also became eclipsed, at least in the public eye, by his more worldly brothers. Arthur, Reuben and their half-brother Albert (who changed his name from Abdullah) Sassoon in particular were voraciously social and sometimes mocked for this – as shown by verses in the racing paper *The Pink 'Un* about Albert, who had been made a baronet:

> *Sir Albert Abdullah Sassoon*
> *That Indian auriferous coon*
> *Has bought an estate called Queen's Gate*
> *And will enter upon it in June.*[7]

Albert, Arthur and Reuben joined the Prince of Wales's Marlborough House set and were no doubt graciously allowed to lend money to the heir to the throne. Later Siegfried Sassoon imagined the 'high minded' David's disapproval of his sons' Edwardian ostentation.[8] But the Sassoons remained devout Jews. At the Scottish estate of Tulchan, bought by Arthur Sassoon, the family spent Jewish holy days praying while their guests shot or fished without them.

The quiet S.D. had to work unexpectedly hard in London because the American Civil War had cut off supplies of raw cotton to English manufacturers, obliging them to turn to India and the east. He lived in a Georgian house overlooking Regent's Park with his small, sharp wife and their children, Joseph, Rachel and Alfred Ezra (Siegfried's father), who was born in 1861. Old David bought S.D. a Tudor house called Ashley Park (once owned by Cardinal Wolsey) by the Thames in Surrey, some seventeen miles from London, where the young family spent much of its time. Then, in July 1867, on a very hot day, Sassoon David Sassoon dropped dead in the foyer of the Langham Hotel while waiting for a cab to take him to the Victoria and Albert Museum, where he was to look at a model of the statue of his father David that was to be put up in Bombay.

David Sassoon's fortune was diluted among his many descendants, and S.D.'s children and grandchildren lost out further by their mother's decision to encourage her sons to avoid the family business and become aristocratic Englishmen. S.D.'s widow stayed on at Ashley Park and in 1884 followed several other Sassoons by buying a house at Brighton. She kept up the family philanthropy, even if she had trouble in paying for the upkeep of Ashley Park. Walton-on-Thames, the nearby town, was given a meeting hall, Hove received a public park and she once sent melons to Brighton police station when she saw a constable suffering from the heat. This cascade of sometimes eccentric giving accompanied an increasing isolation; she became preoccupied by her religion and the past, while the extravagance of the other Sassoons grew ever more ostentatious.

Sassoon David Sassoon's widow wanted her sons to avoid this crude display. The shy Joseph, the eldest, was a good linguist and followed S.D. in collecting books and buying antique furniture, but Alfred, Siegfried's father, seems to have worshipped little more than pleasure and, in a dilettante way, the arts. As a younger son (only six when his father died), he was spoilt by his mother who, thinking he might become a concert violinist, bought him two Stradivariuses. Thin, slightly less than average height, with dark hair and a moustache and a dimpled chin, Alfred stayed at Exeter College, Oxford, for only a few terms, leaving without a degree to become a rich, cultured amateur who sketched, sculpted, played cricket and the violin and rode well (although disliking the horse world). He took a house in Paris where he met Sarah Bernhardt who, in her unreliable memoirs, claims to have refused this 'rich nabob's'[9] offer to replace a lost bracelet once given to her by Victor Hugo after her performance in his *Hernani*.

To the world, Alfred Sassoon's identity was as the heir to a fortune rather than someone of individual achievement or merit. Siegfried Sassoon had little evidence of his father's tastes: merely a glass-doored cupboard at Weirleigh, his childhood home in Kent, and some unused instruments – lutes, guitars, a viola da gamba – and stories of Alfred's 'gypsy wildness'[10] in violin-playing, in which he had been taught by the master Sarasate. There was also a slapdash amateur watercolour of the local landscape, some books by Walter Pater and one particularly fine volume, FitzGerald's *Omar Khayyám*, bound in faded rose-coloured damask figured with old gold, redolent of *The Yellow Book*, that Bible of the Aesthetic Movement, and of Oscar Wilde.[11]

On 30 January 1884, in Kensington parish church, the twenty-two-year-old Alfred married Georgiana Theresa Thornycroft, aged twenty-nine, of Melbury Road, Kensington, the daughter of Thomas Thornycroft. The marriage met furious opposition from the bridegroom's mother, for Miss Thornycroft was a gentile. Mrs Sassoon did not go to the wedding, reputedly cursing any children of the marriage and entering into ritual mourning for her 'dead' son. The very English Thornycrofts, worried by the Jewish link, felt reassured when it seemed to have been at least partly broken. But Victorian materialism made them fear that Alfred might now forfeit the Sassoon money under the terms of his dead father's will. The prospective bride's brother Hamo inspected this document at Somerset House and was relieved to find that 'all seems right and the youth is free. He will be very well off.'[12]

*

GEORGIANA THERESA THORNYCROFT, known always as Theresa, came from Cheshire farming stock, reputedly reaching back to the thirteenth century. Indeed the Thornycrofts still had land near Congleton in Cheshire and it was said that Theresa Thornycroft had rushed into marriage to Alfred Sassoon after being jilted by a Congleton farmer who had run off with a barmaid. Her parents, though, were both sculptors, in a much more professional way than Alfred Sassoon. They had met when Thomas Thornycroft was studying with the sculptor Jack Francis in London and fell in love with Francis's daughter Mary, marrying her in 1840. The Francises were (like the Thornycrofts) originally a farming family, from Norfolk.

Although drawn to socialism and republicanism when young, Thomas Thornycroft had a style suited to the public pomposity of the Victorian age. He made busts for the House of Lords, a statue of Queen Victoria on a horse for the Great Exhibition of 1851, and, after 1861, three equestrian statues of the dead Prince Consort for Halifax, Liverpool and Wolverhampton. Thomas's most spectacular piece, however, is *Boadicea and Her Daughters*, a massively bombastic display begun in 1856, still in progress when he died in 1885, and finally put up on Westminster Bridge some ten years later. Mary worked more delicately. In 1843 she did the first of her royal commissions, a portrait of Queen Victoria's baby daughter Princess Alice as *Spring*, and soon the drawing room at Osborne filled up with cloying pieces like the young Prince of Wales as *Winter*, *Princess Beatrice in a Nautilus Shell* and *Prince Leopold as a Fisher*

Boy. Mary Thornycroft also gave lessons to her subjects and was partly responsible for Princess Louise becoming a sculptress. Both Thornycrofts were loving but firm parents to their seven children (five girls and two boys), who, when young, began letters to their mother, 'Honoured Madam'.[13]

In addition to his art, Thomas Thornycroft became interested in engineering and in 1862 bought land by the river at Chiswick. Here his elder son John founded the firm of John I. Thornycroft that later made warships for the Royal Navy. Frances, one of Thomas and Mary's daughters, married John Donaldson, one of John's engineering partners, but the rest of the family stuck to art, and three of the other daughters, including Theresa, painted and sculpted.

Siegfried Sassoon much preferred the Thornycrofts to the Sassoons (in whose remarkable history he took very little interest) and felt that he had inherited their respect for hard work, craftsmanship, dislike of flamboyance and sense that the ideal life was one lived simply in the landscape of rural England. But Thomas and Mary Thornycroft's younger son William was an example of artistic fame as well. By 1870, aged twenty, William had adopted the name of Hamo, derived from an early-thirteenth-century Thornycroft, and his sister Alice, echoing the romantic medievalism of Alfred Tennyson and the Pre-Raphaelites, changed her name to Alyce. Sent as a boy to his childless uncle's farm in Cheshire, with the idea that he should eventually inherit it, Hamo Thornycroft liked country life but returned to London to complete his education at University College School. In 1868 his sister Helen painted him as a knight in armour – athletic, powerful, with longish golden hair and a frothy moustache – representing the Tennysonian ideal.

Hamo also wanted to be a sculptor. He improved his talents and his body, attending classes at the Royal Academy, swimming and rowing and joining the Artists Rifle Corps, although admonished by his mother for taking time off from his art. In 1872, in competition with (among others) his father Thomas and G. F. Watts, he was chosen to sculpt the statue of the assassinated Viceroy of India, Lord Mayo; in 1873 he won the Royal Academy gold medal and in 1881 was elected an associate of the Academy. Among his supporters for this last honour was his new friend the writer Edmund Gosse, with whom (although they both married and had children) he had a relationship of such sentimental intensity that it seems like homosexual love. But the Thornycrofts were quietly wholesome, a little prim; Gosse's involvement with *The Yellow Book* shocked Hamo, and his sisters feared that the writer might have lured their brother away from their mother's High Church principles.

The family was also suspicious when Hamo took up with the agnostic Agatha Cox, whose beauty stunned Thomas Hardy and who may have been the model for the heroine of *Tess of the D'Urbervilles*. Fourteen years younger than Hamo Thornycroft, and with brothers who were Fabian socialists, she seemed unsuitable, and among other girls put in Hamo's path was Siegfried's aunt Rachel Sassoon. But in 1884 Hamo married Agatha and, perhaps under her influence or that of William Morris (the result of an early meeting with Burne-Jones), became even more contemptuous of 'the lazy do-nothing selfish' rich.[14]

A pioneer of the 'New Sculpture' which, under French influence, attempted to show natural movement, emotion and strength, Hamo created pieces like *The Sower*, examples of the 'democratic art'. But with this went a lucrative line in memorials to the great: gigantic figures of General Gordon, William Gladstone and Oliver Cromwell for London; King Alfred in Winchester; and icons for the Raj – Queen Victoria in Karachi, Lucknow and Ajodhya; King Edward VII in Karachi and King George V and Lord Curzon in Calcutta. These made Hamo Thornycroft one of the establishment's favourite artists, a communicator of imperial and patriotic ideals.

Hamo's sisters had been, by the standards of the time, quite free. Theresa – short, plump, red-haired, with large ears, and nicknamed 'Trees' – studied painting under Ford Madox Brown with her friend Nellie Epps (who married Edmund Gosse). She too went on to the Royal Academy Schools and, with her sisters, learned musketry drill from Hamo, as well as swimming and rowing in the healthy, country-loving Thornycroft spirit, and had High Church beliefs.

Alfred Sassoon, in contrast, was spasmodically energetic, a frustrated artist, essentially metropolitan. There was an age gap of eight years, with the older Theresa, at twenty-nine, embarrassed by this.

*

THEY BOUGHT WEIRLEIGH, a house just outside the village of Matfield, near Tunbridge Wells in the still unspoilt weald of Kent, within reach of London. Even though its garden and views inspired his poetry, Siegfried Sassoon came to dislike the tall, narrow, suburban-gothic building of red brick and tiles, crammed up on one side against a road and possibly designed to be the lodge of a much larger residence. Its original owner and builder was Harrison Weir, a popular children's illustrator and admirer of William Morris who lived on into the 1890s. He had added a sixty-foot-high tiled spire (taken down during the Second World War because of the danger to aeroplanes), where a lamp was lit at night if he was at home. Weirleigh is fake medievalism at its most gloomy, with narrow-paned windows, high gabled roofs, doorways that might have been designed for dungeons and prominent chimneys in the Jacobean style. There is even a Latin inscription over the front door by the road, 'Vero Nihil Verius', the motto of the aristocratic de Vere family to whom Weir thought himself related. The architect John Belcher, a friend of Hamo Thornycroft, added a two-storey studio, set back from the house on the garden side, the lower part red brick below white walls crossed with black-patterned beams. Weirleigh evokes that fairy-tale Victorian land of knights and castles, a small-scale dream-world of the sanitized but romantic past: that of Shalott or Tennyson's 'moated grange' yet more like 'the black bat night' than a visionary dawn.

Alfred and Theresa's first child, Michael Thornycroft Sassoon, was born at Weirleigh in October 1884, ten months after their marriage. On 8 September 1886 Michael was followed by Siegfried; and, in 1887, Hamo (named after his uncle Hamo Thornycroft) completed the trio of boys. Siegfried Loraine Sassoon's first name came from his mother's admiration for Wagner and the second out of her respect for a High Church clergyman, Canon Loraine. Although half Jewish, he was baptized and brought up in the Christian faith.[15] As an infant, he featured in a pious picture by Theresa of Christ with a fat baby and sensually curved children, a reflection of her continuing belief.

At Weirleigh, Theresa went on with her painting, although it seems to have made Alfred jealous, and worked on her huge picture *The Hours*, shown at the Royal Academy in 1889, in which twenty-four large Rossetti-like women in classical costume float across the sky from darkness into light, apparently in a state of heifer-like calm. All his life Siegfried Sassoon loved the work's poetic atmosphere and idealistic emotion, which owed much to the symbolism of Burne-Jones and Watts – Pre-Raphaelite precision merging with the romantic mystery of 'poems painted on canvas'.[16] Theresa knew Watts, who had his studio next to the Thornycroft house in Holland Park, and made him godfather to her youngest son Hamo; later she took the boys often to the Tate Gallery to see Watts's *The Happy Warrior*, in which a woman representing Death approaches a young man in armour. A reproduction of his famous *Love and Death*, thought by Wilde to be worthy of Michelangelo, hung at Weirleigh, its frightening depiction of the giant, sinister Death and the helpless boy-figure of Love bringing to Siegfried an early image of innocent and beautiful sacrifice.

Siegfried recalled his father as pale, moody and delicate-looking with a dark moustache, yet capable 'when in good spirits' of riotous joking.[17] There were stories of Alfred hitting sixes on the village cricket field and, in 1889, when the London Sassoons entertained the Shah of Persia, sending three camels and attendants dressed as Arabs to Sir Albert Sassoon's Kensington house ostensibly with gifts from the Shah that in fact were sacks of old newspapers and rags. But by 1890 Hamo Thornycroft wrote that Theresa's husband ('a madman') had revealed his 'eastern blood'[18] by abandoning his wife, probably for the independent, sophisticated American novelist Julia Constance Fletcher. Certainly in 1885, only a year after his marriage, Alfred Sassoon sent £50 secretly to the publisher George

Bentley as a contribution to Bentley's purchase of the rights of *Andromeda*, a two-volume novel by Fletcher, who wrote epigrammatic stories under the name of 'George Fleming', had lived in Italy, talked brilliantly and knew Oscar Wilde and Henry James.[19] Soon the liaison, possibly revealed to Theresa when they were all in Venice together, failed, reputedly because Constance found Alfred too poor. But he moved to London, away from his wife.

The boys were sometimes visited by their father, for whom they dressed up, to be first tickled by Alfred's moustache when he kissed them and then fascinated by his amber and gold cigar-holder, his two gold rings (one with a brown diamond) and his gold watch, which – anxious not to miss the London train – he repeatedly took out of his pocket. Alfred brought exotic presents of guava jelly, pomegranates and expensive toys, and smelt of cigar smoke as he romped with his sons and made 'screamingly funny jokes'.[20] One autumn afternoon, when he was pushing them in a handcart, they met Theresa in the garden and the laughter abruptly stopped. In the ensuing silence, Alfred looked obstinate and masterful, but Theresa was suddenly pathetic. 'I have never forgotten the look on her face,' Sassoon wrote: 'the first time I had seen life being brutal to someone I loved'. He longed to enjoy them both together.[21] Theresa never criticized their father to the children, beyond referring to 'poor Alfred',[22] but the separation preyed on her emotionally; she was a single, abandoned woman, a rare, pitiable and humiliating position in Victorian society. In revenge, she brought her boys up almost as if the Sassoons did not exist, to try to make them not only as English as her Cheshire ancestors but far in spirit from the unhealthy city to which her husband had fled. Pushed into the background by Theresa's silence about him, their father faded. Like Alfred, Siegfried experienced throughout his life outbursts of apparently uncontrollable high spirits and a very emotional response to music, but he lacked, to his occasional regret, that less rigidly English outlook that his absent, more cosmopolitan father might have given to him.

Theresa epitomized a certain kind of Englishness. A tremendous

Tory, an admirer of the statesman Lord Salisbury, she was a Victorian patriot, utterly confident that her country was by far the best in the world. Weirleigh became the centre of an almost aggressively English childhood, even though it could not quite fulfil the role to which those who lived there aspired. Sassoon admits that in his memoirs he gives Weirleigh, as part of an aesthetic exercise, 'an impression of charm' whereas in reality, uncertain of 'its social position', it 'lacked dignity'. Privacy was fleeting because the family's quarters were scarcely separate from those of the servants, and tramps and other unwanted callers often banged on the door. Above all, Weirleigh seemed very different to 'the mellow old mansion in a park' Siegfried longed for as a child, especially when he began to read Tennyson and *The Ingoldsby Legends* and went to some of the grander houses near by. Even so, he knew every corner of Weirleigh: the plaster casts of classical busts, the smell of oil paints in the Studio and of potpourri and beeswax polish in the drawing room hung with large etchings of Mason's *Harvest Moon* and Walker's *Harbour of Refuge*; the dining room and the bust of Hypnos painted green by Alfred; a Queen Elizabeth clock standing on an old oak cupboard. Then there were the books in the drawing-room bookcases: *Wuthering Heights*, a favourite of Theresa's, and the translated Russian novels bound in green cloth, among them one called *My Husband and I*. This last vaguely upset the young Siegfried for the word husband 'suggested antagonism between two people who had once been happy together'.[23]

Outside, however, was Theresa Sassoon's solace – her garden of Irish yews, climbing roses, apple orchards, wide lawns, peony walks, sloping paths, a quince tree by the pond and herbaceous borders that shone against the dark house. From here, Siegfried could see across the fruit orchards and hop kilns of the Kentish weald to an apparently illimitable land of mysterious possibilities hinted at by trains rattling through the stillness on their way to London or the coast. This brought about the feeling of wonder that he later dreaded losing.

When I have lost the power to feel the pang
Which first I felt in childhood when I woke
And heard the unheeding garden bird who sang
Strangeness of heart for me while morning broke . . .[24]

At the start he and his brothers 'all behaved as if we were the same age'.[25] They shared the gypsy-faced nanny Mrs Mitchell whom Siegfried never liked. Later (after she had left), when he caught pneumonia, he lied and said that she had brought it on by making him sleep in wet sheets. There were shared thrills, not least the aurora borealis, a 'great feast' on the lawn on Hamo's sixth birthday and later their hut known as The Build. The head gardener and Mrs Mitchell sometimes cursed the boys, but it was a protected world, far from the local labourers' broken-down cottages and hovels, isolated from the agricultural depression of the time by Sassoon money, and disturbed only slightly by the annual influx into the district of rougher Cockney hop-pickers.[26] Also living at Weirleigh was old Mrs Thornycroft, Theresa's frail mother, no longer the formidable sculptress. Dressed usually in a white shawl and long black silk dress with white ruffles, she stitched up Siegfried's collapsing cuddly toy, Moocow, for whom he created a 'dream' world of creatures of indeterminate sex called 'Mezenthrums'. Sassoon clung to Moocow until he was nearly nine. He found early on that he needed to be alone sometimes – dreamy and unpractical, sensitive and 'unmanly', easily humiliated.[27]

The boys called Theresa 'Mamsy' and later 'Ash'; a family legend has the latter name as a tease deriving from a chatty cleaning lady called Mrs Ash. Theresa's friends were mostly the neighbours, among them squires like the Marchants of Matfield; Sir James Stirling, a judge, and his wife; retired military men like Captain Ruxton and Major Horrocks; and the clever Florence Bramwell who lived further away. She tried to enliven this county life, little changed since Jane Austen, with *tableaux vivants* and a society to discuss poetry but must have been pleased when her brother Hamo, Nellie Gosse or Mrs William Morris brought news of the London artistic world. Generally Weirleigh was superficially calm except when Theresa's sister Alyce, known as 'Auntie Lula', came and made scenes, once taking a hammer to a bust she had made in the studio, often exploding with rage before softening into a disconcerting friendliness.[28] But the house could seem melancholy, Theresa telling a visitor about Alfred's bad health, how 'he had every quality she didn't expect and none of those she imagined he had',[29] herself enmeshed in 'a very quiet and monotonous' life, seeing little of the children who were looked after by the sly Mrs Mitchell (whom, in an effort at intimacy, she called 'Sweetheart').[30]

Alfred Sassoon was dying of consumption. In 1894 the children and their nanny went to Eastbourne to see 'pappy' to whom Mrs Mitchell was cringingly respectful. In a photograph taken there Hamo (Alfred's favourite), whom he called 'Doggie', sits on his knee,[31] the boys absurdly tidy, reality only in their father's face.[32] At Eastbourne, they met their Sassoon grandmother, who had relented towards her dying son – a small, lively, brown-faced, oddly laughing, foreign-voiced woman, apparently kind and 'rich in a quiet sort of way'. She showed her grandsons the family's printed pedigree while their shy uncle Joseph stood gloomily by in the sickroom.

The hard winter of 1895 brought two deaths: first, at Weirleigh, old Mrs Thornycroft, Siegfried's grandmother; then in April, at Eastbourne, Alfred Sassoon. Theresa thought Siegfried too sensitive to go to his father's funeral, so Mrs Mitchell took Michael and Hamo to it, but they (knowing nothing of their Jewish inheritance) were 'frightened' by the 'jabber-jabber-jabber'[33] of the rabbis and the strange ceremony during which flowers were stolen from a grave close by. No last message came from Alfred to Theresa, who had wanted an English burial for her husband under the yew trees at Brenchley.

Mrs Mitchell left, after receiving £100 a year in Alfred's will. Theresa had the contents of Weirleigh, becoming tenant for life of the house, its running costs to be borne by the income from his estate of which the trustees were John Donaldson (her brother-in-law) and Herbert Lousada (Alfred's solicitor). Weirleigh and

Alfred's capital were held in trust for his children at the discretion of the trustees, which would make it harder to sell the house. If not substantial by Sassoon standards, Alfred's estate had, by 1919, accumulated investments and cash of some £25,564. Of this, £10,245 seems to have been his personal estate and £15,319 Sassoon property in Walton-on-Thames (near Ashton Park), Hong Kong, Shanghai and Bombay. This, after funding Theresa's life, would have to be divided among his three sons.

Mrs Mitchell's successor was a friend of Theresa's called Ellen Batty, a daughter of the Raj who told the boys stories of heroes of British and imperial history. In the evenings a parlourmaid read to them, books of adventure like *Coral Island*, *Treasure Island*, *Tom Sawyer* or *Around the World in Eighty Days*, the comic *Diary of a Nobody*, or (the maid's favourite) *Golden Horseshoes*, about a poor young knight finding a beautiful, aristocratic bride. They went on trips, to the Isle of Wight to stay with Theresa's brother John, to the shipbuilding yards at Chiswick, to swim and go boating on the nearby Medway, and, in 1897, to the Old Rectory at Edingthorpe, Norfolk, rented for the summer. Meanwhile Sassoon's education passed into the hands of a gentle retired schoolmaster called Mr Moon. A more masculine influence, and a partial father-substitute, was the groom, Tom Richardson, captain of the village cricket team who, in his twenties, came closer to Weirleigh life by marrying Grandmother Thornycroft's maid. For Sassoon, Richardson became a 'paragon' who lifted Mr Moon's lobs high over the Studio during cricket games in the paddock with the boys. He also took charge of the pony on which the Sassoon boys were taught to ride.

*

As early as 1891, urged on by Theresa, Siegfried felt that, although trailing the others in strength, vigour and manliness, he was a poet, acutely conscious of the natural world. On his third birthday his mother gave him Coleridge's *Lectures on Shakespeare*, published by William Pickering in 1849. In 1894, Siegfried gave

Theresa coloured and decorated notebooks of stories about kings, princes and princesses marrying happily or about life at Weirleigh, including a true account of a shy young traction-engine driver blurting out to her at the Christmas party, 'I don't dance thank you Mam.'[34] But it was sickness that raised his poetic consciousness when, after a bout of pneumonia, he lay on a stretcher in early summer on the lawn where a small tent had been put up for him. Here, too weak to walk, he felt 'my first conscious experience of exquisite enjoyment' alone in these serene days when he was loved, listening to the sounds of Weirleigh in summer: birdsong, the gardeners' voices and their rumbling wheelbarrow, the sharpening of a scythe, Richardson bringing in the horses. With all this mingled dreams about his parents as a happily married couple, inspired by the smell from an empty scent phial borrowed from Theresa and given to her by Alfred. Siegfried imagined that, like the Sassoons, it had come from Persia and might bring together the disparate strains of his inheritance. Theresa had hung a small Aeolian harp in a crab apple tree and the instrument sighed in the summer breezes 'like poetry'. He read Longfellow, Shelley and Tennyson secretly, thrilled by Tennyson's 'many towered Camelot'.[35]

Theresa was vital in all this, and Siegfried Sassoon's notebook, which he called 'Complete Edition', has the dedication 'For Mamsy from Siegfried 1896'. Here his drawings, mostly of country landscapes, illustrate poems about the seasons, Kent villages, nightingales, dawns, thrushes, larks and 'solitary reapers'. Ghosts, however, flit through the night in gothic mystery, storms burst upon the gentle fields and 'the oak looks huge against the blackened sky'. One of the poems – 'The Spirit of Land and Water' – has been copied out by the poet's mother. He wrote fast, finishing eleven poems in March 1897 alone. These childhood verses show not only a sunny country life and jokey scenes but the land at twilight; death is there, as in the Symbolist pictures of Watts and Burne-Jones, but it is a romantic, sweetly shocking death, for instance in 'The Ripple':

There rose the sun without a shiver
On the brightly tinted earth.
Like a silver thread, the river
Prattled on, as if in mirth . . .
Came a ripple, moving slowly.
As it came, the rushes trembled.
'Crush us not, oh cruel ripple'!!
Said the ripple, 'I am death.'[36]

Theresa set one of the shortest poems, 'To a Wild Rose', to music and it was performed in front of guests at Weirleigh by Siegfried's cousin Mary. Animals feature in the early work: cats (which Theresa liked), cockerels, horses and dogs, usually foxhounds for Sassoon started to go hunting in about 1898, aged twelve. He also wrote two stories about cats in 1896–7 and 1897–8: 'The Story of Peter' and a first-person narrative called 'Something About Myself', featuring 'a very well bred' beautiful cat with 'common relations' who becomes less narcissistic and pretentious and more useful. The Thornycrofts would surely have approved.[37] Siegfried sometimes copied the same poems into new notebooks, a process he followed all his writing life, often making a few changes and adding illustrations or, later, decorations in coloured inks.

These notebooks were very precious. When his brother Michael jogged the table and made him smear a page of one, Siegfried punched him hard on the nose, drawing blood. He was proud to be a poet, and for Christmas 1898 prepared 'The Red Poetry Book' for his uncle Hamo Thornycroft – the same mixture of country scenes, ghosts and twilight and mysterious but thrilling death. Sassoon thought later that he saw a gradual change in these early poetry notebooks from innocence to a self-conscious poeticalness, perhaps partly brought about by Theresa reading Browning to him – those lines he never forgot about the artist set apart from, and above, the rest:

But God has a few of us whom he whispers in the ear;
The rest may reason and welcome; 'tis we musicians know.[38]

The greatest living poet, she said, was Swinburne, but she did not encourage her son to read his lush, high-flown, sometimes erotic work.

*

SOMETIMES IN THESE early poems there are signs of a world outside the weald of Kent or fairyland, including a poem about Westminster Abbey ('What is that towering pointed spire?'). Occasionally Theresa took the boys to London, perhaps to the Thornycrofts or to call on the only Sassoon whom she still saw, her dead husband Alfred's sister, Rachel Beer.

Eccentricity is often, in the rich, another word for madness and there was certainly a very strange atmosphere in the huge Beer house in Chesterfield Gardens, near Park Lane. Like Alfred, Rachel Sassoon had married outside the faith, though Frederick Arthur Beer may have had at least some Jewish blood through his father, Julius Beer, who had come originally, like the Rothschilds, from Frankfurt; Mrs 'S.D.' did not repeat her excommunication but disapproved. Perhaps partly because of this shared disapproval, Rachel visited Weirleigh, where she made the young Siegfried her particular favourite. The gentle, cigar-smoking, limp, brown-bearded Mr Beer had inherited a vast income from his father's stock-exchange dealings but suffered agonizing headaches, veering from extreme irritation to wild euphoria in symptoms of syphilis that Theresa passed off as a mysterious condition inherited from his opera-singer mother. Yet even when Mr Beer was mostly confined to his bedroom, paralysed and speechless, Rachel, while buying Siegfried a bat in Wisden's shop in 1897, ordered cricket stumps, balls and a practice net to be sent to their other house in Richmond where the footmen could bowl to her husband.[39]

Rachel Beer – small, dark-haired, pale and handsome – was editor of the *Observer*, a paper that Mr Beer had inherited from his father who had bought it to advance his own opinions on international affairs. In 1893 she bought the *Sunday Times* as well, which she also edited. Her scatty running of the papers made her a joke with journalists and Oscar Wilde's set[40] and in 1896 Rachel Beer made her nephews take part in the 'Press Bazaar' at the Hotel Cecil dressed as 'pages of the *Observer*' where they were presented to the Princess of Wales.[41] But in 1898 Mrs Beer had a scoop that, given her Jewishness, needed courage: her paper revealed Major Esterhazy's confession that he had forged the documents used to convict the French army officer, Dreyfus, of spying in the greatest European scandal of the decade.

To the young Siegfried, the immense house of 7 Chesterfield Gardens seemed dead behind the 'priceless' pictures and the oriental furniture, the only reminder of old David Sassoon's beginnings. The slow-moving footmen and grooms with their gilt buttons showing the Beer crest of a pelican feeding its young (a crest which was even clipped out on the back of Mrs Beer's black poodle) were attendants on a corpse, and, unlike the energetic Theresa, Auntie Rachel always seemed tired. In the hall, there was, however, a reminder of the Thornycroft taste: G. F. Watts's doom-filled study of *Orpheus and Eurydice*, a story told again for Siegfried Sassoon at an afternoon party given by the Beers when an act of Gluck's *Orpheus* was performed. Hundreds of unread books sent for review in Rachel's newspapers were stacked on the polished floors and dazzling electric bulbs lit the windowless dining room, but domestic tragedy was the background to many of his boyhood trips to London for treats of magic shows or the theatre. Chesterfield Gardens showed the strange unhappiness, suffocation and chaos that could come from too much money.

*

HAMO AND MICHAEL learned the violin and Siegfried the piano, and through music Siegfried found an early influence in Helen Wirgman, the sister of Hamo Thornycroft's artist friend Theodore Wirgman. Mercurial and passionate, she seemed to understand his inarticulate yearnings, those blurted-out thoughts and impressions that accompanied his poetic life, and her summer visits broke

through the rather bland calm of Weirleigh, where even Theresa
feared her moods. For 'Wirgie', as her close friends called her, music
was the outlet for what Sassoon called a 'touch of genius'.[42] From
a Swedish family that had moved to London, she spent some of
her childhood in Belgium and later travelled through continental
Europe, bringing a European intensity about art to a Weirleigh ruled
by the Thornycroft loathing of pretension. Born in 1842, she was
in her early fifties when she and Siegfried began their friendship.
Fascinated by the natural world, she walked with him in the
Weirleigh gardens or in neighbouring woods, perhaps 'just a little
mad' with her 'white hair and faded finery' and 'sidelong inquiring
expression in her eyes'.[43] Her memories of the Alps and the cities
of Europe were vivid and, to Sassoon, she played Chopin and
Beethoven more dramatically than Paderewski, whom he heard once
in Tunbridge Wells. Wirgie knew George Meredith well, perhaps
partly forming Sassoon's admiration for the novelist and poet.

The boys were slipping out of control. Reluctant to send them
to school, especially the delicate Siegfried, their mother brought in
more help at home: first, a Thornycroft cousin, an extrovert woman
called 'Piggins' who disliked (in Thornycroft style) 'humbug, arty
people and self-pity'[44] as much as Siegfried's 'emotional self-
indulgence';[45] then Fräulein Stoy, a cosy, dull German governess
who spoke longingly of the paragon children she had taught before,
Nevill and Janet Forbes. Sergeant Ryan came to the house for
sessions of gymnastics, but Tom Richardson, the groom, and horses
gave Siegfried Sassoon the physical exercise that he enjoyed most.

Theresa sold jewellery to give Richardson enough horses and
ponies to look after, but Michael and Hamo preferred the lathe in
the small workshop they had, fostered by visits to the Thornycroft
works at Chiswick. His brothers called the dreamy Siegfried 'Onion'
because he was 'off it', or odd, and they drew slowly away, leaving
him wistfully to imagine an ideal friend. Riding, then fox-hunting,
became his territory. Richardson, in contrast to the feeble Mr Moon
or the women who worked indoors at Weirleigh, came to seem the

only 'sensible' element in the young Siegfried's fatherless life. Eventually the groom suggested to Theresa that her son should try a day with the Eridge hunt.

It is hard now to imagine the importance of fox-hunting in pre-1914 rural England, a landscape still dominated by the landowning class. For the Sassoons at Weirleigh, the local grandees were the Marquess of Abergavenny, head of the Neville family at Eridge Castle, and the Master of the Eridge Hunt, Lord Abergavenny's younger brother Lord Henry Neville. Below these Himalayas of magnificence stretched the foothills of lesser landowners, then the yeomen and tenant farmers. Next came those dependent on hunting for their livelihoods: grooms and terriermen, keepers and earth stoppers, owners of livery stables and horses for hire, horse dealers and suppliers of feed. Further off, in London and towns in good hunting country, were the boot manufacturers, tailors, hatters and saddlers, to say nothing of the horse markets like Tattersalls and Newmarket where fox-hunters came to look for new mounts for the next season or to sell old ones from the last.

This self-contained world had its own values, language and standards. Fox-hunting was exclusive in that leisure and money or land were needed to gain entry to it. But, after the entry fee had been paid, the sport had a curious democracy of elegance and courage where feats of horsemanship and nerve were admired unstintingly as physical, sometimes beautiful, manifestations of human achievement. For many young Englishmen – not only aristo-crats but farmers and those who lived in a hunting country or worked with the hunt – fox-hunting could prove their manhood to each other and to women who often rode hard as well. In the British army, it was thought to be a useful preparation for war and did not count as leave.

At Weirleigh, Theresa hunted with the Eridge hounds and told her sons about her adventures,[46] and the young Siegfried Sassoon read Trollope's *Sporting Sketches* and the Victorian humorous novels about fox-hunting by Surtees. Early poems show that it was the landscape and the leaping 'over fields and brooks and hedges' or swooping 'like an eagle' rather than the kill that excited him.[47] He knew that hounds tore their quarry 'in two' and were 'whipped'[48] for disobedience, and that horses could suffer, yet throughout his life Siegfried Sassoon brought a tenderness to the sport, glimpsed in his elegy of 1898 'To Sylvia, a horse' ('So gentle and so mild is she').[49] Hunting also let him prove himself. As a boy, he read (or was read) the adventure novels of Rider Haggard, G. A. Henty and Stanley Weyman that glorified physical courage and chivalry – the ideals of Victorian boyhood. Because of his delicacy and his 'poeticalness', he felt 'unmanly', isolated by Theresa's wish to keep him from school.

The first days out must have intensified this isolation when he saw the skill of some of the other young followers. Then the ideal friend of his dreams became real in one boy who showed the masculine virtues of calm courage and watchfulness. 'Denis Milden' in Sassoon's autobiographical novel *Memoirs of a Fox-hunting Man* is based on Norman Loder who, as the younger son of a landowning baronet, had confidence founded on impeccable connections and quiet skill as a rider. To the shy Sassoon – schooled by Richardson in the hierarchy of the hunt ruled by the Nevilles, with whom Loder stayed – this boy, although only a year older, was awe-inspiring. His immaculate turn-out and 'steady, unrecognizing stare' somehow made Siegfried drop his own 'unpresentable old hunting-crop' and dismount to pick it up.[50] In a new world of anxiety and giants – the fiery master of the hunt, the unknown other riders, Richardson's palpable fear that his young charge might fail – this omniscient boy induced an obsessive admiration that verged on love.

Memoirs of a Fox-hunting Man shows the contrast between innocence and sophistication. At the end of the first day out, the Master, having heard that the newcomer has jumped a high hedge, says, 'I hear he's quite a young thruster', at which the uncomprehending George Sherston (Sassoon's alter ego in the book) flushes instead of taking a quiet satisfaction in praise. The next time, the 'ideal friend' shouts to tell the Master he has seen a fox, and Sherston blurts out, 'Don't do that; they'll catch him,' instantly realizing how childish, how 'unmanly', this must sound to his hero.[51] But soon the young Sassoon came to be known as a wild follower of running hounds, hanging back only when little was happening, 'so keen and yet so unobtrusive in the field'.[52] Henceforth early morning meant not only crowing cockerels and a brightening sky or a world free of people but the wordless adventure of hunting when aesthetic delight mixed with physical well-being to make 'manliness' realizable at last.

*

BY 1897, THE year of bonfires in the weald for Queen Victoria's Diamond Jubilee, Theresa felt she must find a boarding school for her sons. The next year Michael went off, first to 'an advanced co-educational' establishment that he found 'cranky',[53] then to a more conventional place. Siegfried and Hamo had a new tutor, Clarence Hamilton, a red-faced man, supposedly a brilliant cricketer although he was bowled out almost immediately on the bumpy Matfield pitch (at which a watching local said, 'Them toffs never do any good on the Green').[54] Hamilton, nicknamed 'the Beet', was a dull teacher, but feminine influence was on the wane as Fräulein Stoy slipped into the background. In 1898, while watching some older boys swim and fish in a mill pond, Sassoon yearned suddenly to escape 'prolonged' protected 'childishness' into freedom;[55] then in December 1899, as if to mark the end of the century and of their childhood, the brothers burned their hut, The Build. Finally, in the summer of 1900, Siegfried and Hamo set out for Sevenoaks to join Michael as boarders at the New Beacon School.

TWO

'Try to be more sensible'

SIEGFRIED SASSOON WAS nearly fourteen, by far the oldest new boy, when he started at the New Beacon. Recommended by Fräulein Stoy because her beloved Nevill Forbes had gone there, the successful school (quite small, with between sixty and seventy boys) had recently moved further out of Sevenoaks into new purpose-built premises. Theresa worried so much about giving Siegfried enough warm underclothes that she forgot to pack any shirts for him or Hamo.

Thus fussed over, with a slight sense of invalidism, he entered the world of late-Victorian preparatory and public schools, with its tribal atmosphere of nicknames, private languages, codes of behaviour and attitudes that lasted most of the pupils' lives. Food was 'grub'; instead of going somewhere you 'cut along'; Siegfried, because of his dignified manner, was called 'Dook Sieg' by J. S. Norman, the headmaster, himself known as 'Cockeye'. Games were very important and Sassoon found himself briefly one of the better cricketers, never forgetting one match that temporarily banished any sense of 'unmanliness' when he scored fifty runs. Friendly relations between the staff and pupils were such that one summer holidays he and his brothers went with two of the masters on a boating trip on the Norfolk Broads. But the New Beacon and the benign yet tough 'Cockeye' were overwhelmingly philistine. As a result he came to believe that to write poetry was shameful, so he stopped, feeling the loss of 'something wonderful'[1] but also, mixed with an outsider's anxiety, a certain martyred pride. Apart from the memory of 'Cockeye' reading the adventure story *Moonfleet* aloud, there is little evidence that Sassoon experienced any intellectual stimulation at the school, although in 1901, despite generally poor marks (except in English), he passed the Common Entrance exam for Marlborough.

Michael had gone on to Malvern but Mr Norman thought Marlborough would be better for Theresa's delicate second son. Believed then to be moderately progressive, the school (entirely a product of the Victorian age) was founded in 1843 in the Wiltshire market town of Marlborough on the River Kennet, notable for its eighteenth-century houses and massive prehistoric mound, reputedly the burial place of the magician Merlin. A separate entity to the west of the town's wide main street, Marlborough College has as its centre a low, long red-brick building of about 1700, once a private house of the dukes of Somerset and later a coaching inn. In Sassoon's day the other buildings were mostly in a nineteenth-century imitation of this Queen Anne style, with the occasional addition of Victorian gothic or grim fake Tudor. It is still easy, and in 1901 was even easier, to leave the school for the fields by Savernake Forest or to reach the nearby high downland, and in January 1902, 'without a friend in the world except the matron',[2] the fifteen-year-old new boy ate a bar of chocolate cream alone on the hill he had climbed above the town as a brief escape during his first day.

*

TO SOME EXTENT he found the same atmosphere as at the New Beacon, with a headmaster nicknamed 'the Druid' or 'the Tup' and Theresa fussing embarrassingly over the extra blankets she had brought for him. But Marlborough was much bigger, harsher, with agonies about stiff collars, ties that were difficult to tie and the impossibility of finding your way around when no one seemed to want to help you. He boarded at Cotton House, a bleak 1872 building of concrete faced with plaster, and, although the school year was some four weeks longer than it is now, there were few opportunities for leave out in term time. This self-contained, oddly protective but challenging world stayed with Sassoon for years in his thoughts and dreams. Marlborough was an early initiation into the rough, communal, all-male life of the trenches.

Boys were at the mercy of their capricious, sometimes mordantly bitter, occasionally sadistic teachers. Sassoon's housemaster, a bachelor of fifty with a booming clubman's voice and a military moustache called Marius Herbert Gould, seems often to have been drunk and made little effort with his dimmer charges. Some academic Marlburians found Gould, with his Oxford First in Greats, a good teacher;[3] to Sassoon, the housemaster spoke usually in a bantering, sometimes angry, often preposterously orotund manner, the aftermath of an earlier ambition to be a barrister and Conservative politician. Drink made him unpredictable. Early on, after Sassoon had opted to take organ lessons, Gould yelled at the new boy at lunch, in front of the rest of the house, 'I know why you play organ. You play organ to get out of playing games, you wretched brute!' Only at night, when he thought the boy was asleep, did Gould show affection, muttering a gruff 'Good-night, you Siegfried'[4] on his dormitory round. The matron was excited by Sassoon's possible link to King Edward VII, but Gould thought the name meant idle decadence. When the housemaster shrieked at him again, after Siegfried played a hymn at evening prayers whose words seemed to be a joke against the matron, there was muted laughter among the boys at this unusually old, unhealthy Jewish newcomer. A family story has it that Sassoon carried knuckle-dusters to protect himself from anti-Semitic attacks at Marlborough.[5]

Failure at games was often persecuted, the unathletic being 'ragged and despised and jeered'.[6] In the Cotton House books, written by successive Heads of House, the comments on the boys refer almost exclusively to games and say that Siegfried Sassoon showed some cricketing promise at first (although he was feeble at rugby), then declined into disappointment. Halfway through his first cold term, in a return to physical weakness, he caught measles that became double pneumonia. His life was prayed for in chapel and Theresa rushed down with steaks to make him the strongest beef tea and summoned a famous doctor from London. The school authorities disapproved but Gould thought she had saved the boy's life. Sassoon went home to recuperate, returning to Marlborough at the start of the summer term with his younger, much more self-possessed brother Hamo.[7]

Summers meant cricket, the elegant game that Sassoon came to love, and gradually Marlborough showed itself to be less philistine than the New Beacon School. That first summer term, one master, an Irishman called John or 'Pat' O'Regan, also a First in classics from Balliol, set his form to write poems, offering a prize of half a crown. Sassoon's verses for the first competition were hung up in the classroom and mix adolescent melancholy ('My life at school is fraught with care') with ambition, declaring at the end that not even 'extra lessons' and other school trials can kill this 'ambitious little bard'.[8] Poetry welled up again, self-conscious but not rebellious – odes, for instance, on the death of King Richard II or the illness of King Edward VII that delayed the coronation. In the library of Cotton House, he read Thomas Hood's 'Bridge of Sighs' whose music of rhythm and words brought 'goose flesh' and tears.

This was where he might excel; poetry, and writing, became a secret strength. Inspired also by 'music's poetic feeling', Sassoon practised the organ alone in the school chapel, a long, tall gothic building of dark stone decorated inside with Pre-Raphaelite murals by Spencer-Stanhope and bright stained-glass windows, ethereal in atmosphere, one of which had been designed by Burne-Jones. There were memorials to Old Marlburians killed in battle and, on the reredos above the altar, martial yet innocent youths in armour surround a crucified Christ. The emotional atmosphere was one of sexless decency, courage and patriotism – the moral edge of the sense of mission that marked the self-conscious height of Britain's imperial power. As if responding to this spirit, Siegfried Sassoon joined the school Rifle Corps but could not remember which eye to shut when firing his rifle.

His autumn term at Marlborough ended early in more weakness: a 'strained heart' and eye trouble perhaps brought on by exhaustion. Relieved to be missing rugby football, he went home to Weirleigh where the family doctor insisted on an invalid's existence stretching through the Lent term of 1903. 'The Bridge of Sighs' had heightened Sassoon's view of books and literature as a part of a secret life in a comforting past. Romantic, emotional poetry moved him the most; now he also wanted 'quaintness' and the aesthetic appearance, 'the look and smell', of old books.[9] Already, in Brighton in 1900, he had bought his first rare volume, a first (1833) edition of *The Young Cricketer's Tutor* by John Nyren, edited by Keats's friend Charles Cowden Clark. During the winter of 1902–3, he began to think about creating a library, an ideal repository of learning and literature, guided by the *History of Eighteenth Century Literature* written by his mother's friend Edmund Gosse.

Sassoon obtained a copy of the *Bookseller's Circular* and sent off for catalogues from dealers all over the country who responded quickly, perhaps impressed by his 'gilded' name and Weirleigh's crested writing paper. Some of the volumes for sale cost £500 or more when his capital stood at only £1. But Theresa let him sell his father's books, although he kept Alfred's 1883 privately printed quarto of FitzGerald's *Rubáiyát of Omar Khayyám*. Over the next year old volumes arrived at Weirleigh: an 1801 edition of Samuel Johnson, an eighteenth-century life of Queen Elizabeth, works by Adam Smith, Burke and Archbishop Ussher, mostly incomprehensible to the boy. The point was not their contents but their aesthetic arrangement on the shelves, the creation of a comfortable sense of age and stability, of merit increased by his brightening of the tooling and lettering on the labels with burnishable gold from the Army and Navy Stores.[10]

The diary that he kept for January 1903, interspersed with records of book-dealing, has details of golfing expenses and his reading: 'read March: Antony and Cleopatra, Pope's Homer's Iliad Bks I–II, Comedy of Errors, Pope's Rape of the Lock, Gray's Poems, Odes etc:, Shenstone's "Schoolmistress"', and on the 29th he 'read Byron's Don Juan I–II (quite enough)'. But many days have the words 'Nothing happened' against them. That same month he wrote the poem 'Fragment of an Allegory' in which melancholy adolescence imagines the journey towards death across 'Time's golden sands' where 'the flowers of life' fade 'all too soon'. His poetry, he thought, had improved 'in fluency and grasp'.[11]

The summer term at Marlborough meant more cricket and in the holidays Sassoon played for the village sides of Matfield or Brenchley or in a Weirleigh team against a scratch eleven put together by Tom Richardson. But he was bad at work, even bad at cricket, and very bad at rugby. The *Marlburian* refused to print his poems and when asked to recite some verses by Thackeray at the Cotton House leaving supper in July 1903 he broke down and had to refer to the book.[12] Longing for recognition, Sassoon sent a poem called 'The Extra Inch' to *Cricket* magazine which published it on 9 April 1903. The lines are a parody of Charles Kingsley's 'The Sands of Dee', telling how a batsman is bowled because he had been fooled by the wicket's 'extra inch'. *Cricket* then accepted 'Spring' and 'To Wilfred – Bowling' ('When Wilfred Rhodes [the great cricketer] a-bowling goes') but never paid him. An advertisement, 'Earn Money by Writing', which he answered turned out to be an attempt to recruit people to sell personalized rubber stamps.

Fearing pneumonia, Theresa kept Siegfried and Hamo at home in January 1904 and a shy young tutor from Oxford coached them. Favourite poems in the diary at this time include Emily Brontë's 'Last Lines', Arthur Clough's 'Isolation', Dante Gabriel Rossetti's regretful 'Parted Love', A. Shaughnessy's 'Song' on the return of an old romance and Byron's 'On This Day I Complete my 36th Year' – signs, perhaps, of a young poet's romantic despair.[13] There are extracts from Matthew Arnold's 'Rugby Chapel' on a son's thoughts of 'bygone autumns' with his late father without whom he feels 'bare, unshaded, alone'. Alfred Sassoon had now been dead for nine years.

In the summer of 1904, Sassoon left Marlborough, too old and too low in the school to give point to staying on for another year. His report noted poor concentration, little 'intelligence or aptitude for any branch of his work' and bad prospects for 'any special career'. Hamo, more successful, stayed until December. Gould's final advice to the departing boy – 'Try to be more sensible'[14] – was muffled by a sense of freedom. Sassoon looked forward to cricket at home in Kent before another winter's hunting and always the secret life of poetry.

*

SIEGFRIED SASSOON KNEW now what set him apart: his Jewishness, his delicacy and his homosexuality. At Marlborough, there were intense masculine friendships, yet the school scarcely acknowledged sex, apart from terrifying warnings against masturbation. Even in the 1920s, the headmaster warned Louis MacNeice, 'Self-abuse is adultery too; it destroys your body and your mind and you end in the madhouse.'[15] Sassoon wanted to conform and from this came affection, sometimes love, for a type he was drawn to all his life: the man of character, not intellect, whose conversation inclined towards sporting metaphors, who liked cricket or golf, who distrusted display and loathed conceit – the clean, decent man. Norman Loder, the modest but expert fox-hunter; Mr Jackson, a cheerful, golfing schoolmaster at the New Beacon; David Thomas, whose death transformed Sassoon's view of war – these friendships show his feeling for the values of a Victorian public school.

At Henley House, the nearby crammer's where he went to be prepared for the Cambridge entrance exam, there were several of these paragons, their nicknames once again showing their worth: 'the Boss' (Henry Malden, the headmaster) and his two assistant masters 'Uncle' and 'the Teacher' (a Mr Rawsthorne). 'Uncle' (Eustace Malden) and another master, George Wilson (whom Sassoon especially liked), were good games-players, particularly at golf.[16] When Henry Malden caught the boys throwing water at each other he said simply, 'Oh Sassoon, do you mind using the *metal* jugs? The earthenware ones are apt to come away from their handles.' In this gentler place Sassoon made greater friends than at Marlborough: Henry Thompson ('Tommy') from Cumberland, again a golfer with 'a delightful cronyish quality'[17] whom Theresa particularly liked; and, as if to emphasize Henley House's philistine air, Norman Loder, his hunting hero, was a fellow pupil. With some sadness, he left to go up to Clare College, Cambridge in the autumn term of 1905 with his brother Hamo. Poetry had stalled again. In the spring of that year, Sassoon had worked on an epic of twelve books of which the first was to be called 'The Awakening' but got no further than four lines about 'a soul', ending in:

> *Dim glades of ecstasy he trod alone*
> *And passed the gates of hope where fame is born.*

An advance at least on a love lyric of December 1904:

> *Love first conceived is like a distant view*
> *Of mountains – crowned by dawn's first tender hue,*
> *A tinge of gold athwart mysterious blue.*[18]

*

CHOSEN BY THERESA because several Thornycrofts had gone there, Cambridge offered academic study and a chance to meet other young writers. But at Clare, a small college founded in the fourteenth century and rebuilt in the seventeenth and eighteenth, next to King's and bordering the River Cam, Sassoon 'lapsed into day dreaming and Pre-Raphaelitism' and isolation. In his first term, during an unusually dry autumn and early winter, he felt ill, escaping into 'poetry writing and music' in a low-ceilinged room decorated with reproductions of pictures by Rossetti and Burne-Jones.

Then there was a crisis at Weirleigh. Siegfried's elder brother

Michael had left Clare without taking a degree and now had a girlfriend whom Theresa disliked. Already under strain from bringing up three sons alone, money problems and a sense that her beloved Siegfried was unhappy, she broke down completely, marking for the second youngest boy 'the end of my boyhood'.[19] A notebook dated 1905, dedicated 'To Ash' and filled with his poems, may have been a present to comfort her; certainly his devotion is clear in the elaborate decorations and use of coloured inks. The book, called 'A Pageant of Dreams', has Keats on the title-page ('Magic casements, opening on the foam . . .') and inside ('Beauty that must die') and quotations from Swinburne, William Watson and Dante Gabriel Rossetti. In his own poems, the tone is of romantic melancholy and word music. 'Dies Irae – Russia 1904' is about the political turmoil in Russia, with a quotation from Swinburne mocking human endeavour ('The wind has the sound of a laugh in the clamour of days and deeds') but most titles make clear the Pre-Raphaelite fairy-tale atmosphere of dream pictures: 'Slow Music (On a Picture)', 'Love Triumphant – On a Picture', 'Avalon', 'Rondel, Dawn Dimness'. Two are interesting autobiographically. 'Ambition' is a Tennysonian monologue, reminiscent of 'Ulysses':

> Far is the height toward which I have begun
> To toil, who, tho' the ascent seems ever higher,
> Would pass the mountain-barriers . . .

And 'Doubt' reflects the longed-for power he wanted for his own poetry:

> Doubt not the light of heaven upon the soul;
> Doubt not the lyric pattern, giving all
> Desire and hope and wonder to its thrall;
> Doubt not the goal:
> Doubt not the rapture of the smitten lyre . . .[20]

An anthology compiled and copied out in October 1905, the month he started at Cambridge, has Browning, Rossetti, Tennyson, Swinburne, Clough and Christina Rossetti. Modern poetry is

represented by W. E. Henley, James Elroy Flecker, Alfred Noyes, Stephen Phillips (from *Paolo and Francesca*), Austin Dobson and, as a sign of what might come after the 'lutes and nightingales', Robert Bridges. Later Sassoon saw the discovery of Bridges as a step towards Thomas Hardy.[21] He was oddly proud not to have mixed much with other poets, of having, as he said, done 'it all under my own steam'.[22] He believed always in magic coming from a poet's sensations in solitude.

Sassoon read law, partly at the urging of his uncle Hamo Thornycroft, who had become his trustee. Thornycroft accepted that Siegfried's future lay in literature yet thought a law degree followed by time in a barrister's chambers in London might give some mental discipline. But between golf and writing poetry Sassoon did little studying. To *Granta* and the *Cambridge Review* he sent parodies of Stephen Phillips, Browning and the psalms and a skit on heartiness called 'To a Blood',[23] and this more bubbly Siegfried, or 'Sig' or 'Siggy', appears in his correspondence with an older undergraduate at Clare, E. L. 'Gussy' Guilford: letters full of schoolboy humour and joshing self-deprecation, even about his poetry. In the summer vacation, he reported an 'uneventful existence' with no golf, only 'a dance in town' and trips to the Royal Academy, a performance of *The Taming of the Shrew* and playing cricket 'for Tunbridge Wells v: Lewes' when he scored no runs and took no wickets. He read Swinburne, 'with dire results for my adjectives', and by October 1906 mocked his preoccupation with nature and lack of inspiration, declaring that the god Pan 'must have missed his train to Paddock Wood [the nearest station to Weirleigh] for he hasn't turned up yet'.[24]

Sassoon lived idly and disjointedly. He bought nice editions of Swinburne and the Kelmscott *Maud*, read William Morris in a punt and went to the Trinity Boat Club Ball with a party of Thornycroft cousins. Entertaining his uncle Hamo in his rooms towards the end of the summer term, he laid on an 'overwhelming' lunch of lobster mayonnaise and the best college hock, and talked about his about his poetry. Thornycroft said, 'You should try for the Chancellor's Medal, old man.'[25] This university prize – previously won by Lord Macaulay (twice), Tennyson, Henry Malden (Sassoon's old headmaster at Henley House) and (in 1904) Lytton Strachey – seemed a way to get something serious out of Cambridge. When he dropped law and took up medieval history, inspired by a Pre-Raphaelite idea of the Middle Ages and the novels of Stanley Weyman, Sassoon had serious difficulties with some of the sources in Old French. Joan of Arc, however, he read about in detail, for a long poem.

'Gussy' Guilford had literary and artistic tastes and liked cricket, turning out once for Matfield while staying at Weirleigh. But, beyond vague idleness, there was no sign of rebellion in him or Siegfried. At Cambridge, some three or four years before, the young Bloomsbury group – Leonard Woolf, Lytton Strachey, Thoby Stephen and Clive Bell – had admired Hardy, Ibsen and Shaw for challenging the conventions of the age; Tennyson and Browning, Sassoon's favourites, seemed to them dully out of date. Sassoon had a link to Rupert Brooke through a brother, Hamo, and a cousin, Oliver Thornycroft, both of whom knew this young meteor, but he stayed well outside Brooke's narcissistic world of sexual experiment and pagan revolt, keeping love and passion for his poetry.

*

AFTER VISITING THE senior tutor at Clare, W. L. Mollison, to say that he wished to give up law for history, Sassoon fell downstairs; Mollison, a small, anxious man who stammered, made him jumpy. But the tutor asked to see some of his poems, then, surprisingly enthusiastic, urged him not only to enter for the Chancellor's Medal but to publish as well. So on his twentieth birthday, in September 1906, Sassoon decided to have his first volume of poems printed in an elegant edition of fifty at his own expense. The selection was influenced by Theresa's taste, reflecting the Thornycroft simplicity and love of country life, also the subdued yearning of her art. Later he detected in the book a religious tone, again derived from his mother, and more 'innocent youngness and aspiration' than in his other volumes that were privately published before 1914.[26]

None of these poems was included in his later *Collected Poems*, not even to show the irrecoverable 'Paradise felt in Youth'.[27] The main influences are Swinburne, Tennyson and Browning (in the long monologue 'Joan of Arc') and Dante Gabriel Rossetti. One poem, 'Sic Transit', is inspired by a Watts picture of a dead knight. There is a yearning for poethood, for romance, and a sense of words creating a colour that life lacks; 'Joan of Arc' evokes childhood as the ideal time and was written in 'rapture' at Weirleigh, at the end of June.[28] Throughout his life, Sassoon looked back longingly to the unknowingness of his first years.

Meanwhile he had fun imitating Swinburne (Sassoon had a lifelong gift for parody) but took Guilford's advice to stick to original work. The subject for the Chancellor's Medal was given out as Edward I. He read Tout's dry account of the king's reign, then became confused by research and about what style he should use; probably he should be 'very restrained and conventional' although, as he told Guilford (sending him extracts from a draft), this was 'a thing I abhor'. On his writing table, he had a photograph of Hamo Thornycroft's statue of the young King Edward I on a horse, removing it during some frustrating early stages of composition before producing a final version that Theresa liked. In December 1906, the piece went off to be judged. In the New Year, Sassoon, stricken by influenza, stayed on at Weirleigh, vowing not to go back to Cambridge until the winner was announced in February. Would the judges ('these dour scholars') bring 'radiant reward or desolately damn'?[29]

Like 'Joan of Arc', 'Edward I' is a long poem in what Henry James called the British 'anecdotical' style.[30] The old king, near death, soliloquizes at Burgh-on-the-Sands. The tone is that of Tennyson at his most stately, part the dying Arthur in the *Idylls*, part 'Ulysses', with a sense that there is no obvious reason why this poem should ever end. One line ('All the marching months have passed along') hints at 'the nobly marching days' of the war poem 'The Kiss'; a foreshadowing of religious feeling occurs in the king's prayerful 'strange spiritual drawing nigh to God' that takes him 'even further from the World'. As in 'Joan of Arc', 'unclouded' youth is a beautiful memory.[31]

The prize went to D. W. Corrie, 'a gushing youth from Eton', with Sassoon not even the runner-up. He tried to shrug it off – 'I never felt really confident' – and treated Guilford as a disciple, showing how, although the younger, he had dominated their friendship, finally admitting disappointment. 'I expect you will be more injured about it than I, oh faithful Griselda (entre nous) I do feel rather small . . . I suppose the rejected one is a little unconventional and emotional.'[32] What really hurt was that he had had no triumph with which to boost his mother after her breakdown.

Sassoon left Cambridge without a degree. Theresa seemed to understand but Uncle Hamo pontificated that 'the moral discipline of work we do not quite like is an excellent thing, and as Christianity gets less and less a guiding influence, will become more and more necessary',[33] and was further annoyed in April by his nephew's assurance that he was 'getting good golf'.[34] At Weirleigh, in beautiful May weather and surrounded by books, the walls of a private world, Sassoon read Laurence Housman's plays, a study of Shakespeare, some works on St Francis (possibly for another narrative poem) and (for the second time since Christmas) Browning's *The Ring and the Book*. He told Guilford he had left Cambridge 'with the degree (honorary) of R.I.P. (Retired Ignominiously (To) Paddock Wood). You know Cambridge didn't suit me in any way, and at the end of Oct: term I was a perfect wreck, and knew nought about my Tripos work. Therefore I have resigned myself to Poesy and Perdition amid a perfect storm of abuse and homilies from Mollison and Uncle Hamo. But what care I? I know my own mind better than they do.'[35]

He had written twenty short poems since being at home and

Theresa spoke comfortingly of 'The Chancellor's Muddle'.[36] Perhaps she was glad to have her second and favourite son with her. Certainly Sassoon's first mild rebellion that edged him further from timidity was made much easier by her love.

THREE

The weald of youth

BOTH OF SIEGFRIED SASSOON'S brothers broke away before
1914: Michael to Canada, to British Columbia, to work in remote
fish canneries and, later, in Vancouver, making parts for cars; Hamo
to be an engineer in Argentina. Sassoon did not miss the small,
jaunty Michael or Michael's wife Violet, whom neither he nor his
mother liked, Theresa wincing at what she called her daughter-in-
law's 'Gentlemen prefer Blondes'[1] jokes. Hamo, however, was different – imperturbable, a friend of Rupert Brooke while at Cambridge,
broad and tall, with dark wavy hair, scruffy on his motorcycle,
mocking Siegfried's exquisite hunting clothes. Siegfried confessed his
homosexuality to Hamo, who said calmly that he was the same.
Hamo laughed at Siegfried's vague mixture of belief in God and
superstition, his fear of the evil spirits[2] sensed during childish
experiments with automatic writing.

On his twenty-first birthday at Weirleigh, still feeling responsible
for Theresa after her breakdown and joined only by some elderly
neighbours, Sassoon wished again that his cosmopolitan father had
been there to break this sense of entrapment. Both he and his mother
wanted somewhere else, perhaps 'a Jacobean manor'[3] in Dorset,
better for hunting; another annoying feature of Weirleigh was that
its stables were situated down the road, far from the house. But they
knew that they could not afford to leave. One hope was the childless

Aunt Rachel Beer's fortune, still large in spite of the £45,000 taken from her by a confidence trickster, supposedly to help rescue Dreyfus. With Rachel's help they could have what they wanted. But after Frederick Beer's death in 1903 Mrs Beer had been certified insane, moving to a large house near Tunbridge Wells in the care of nurses and servants. When visiting Weirleigh, she veered between listlessness and 'vehement dementia', clutching Siegfried's arm once in the garden and 'raving wildly' about how she must go to London to burn some papers. Perhaps, he thought later, she, like her husband, had had syphilis;[4] surely this was the condition blamed opaquely, and ridiculously, by Theresa on Mr Beer's opera-singer mother. Hamo mocked their hopes, saying that Aunt Rachel would live for years and leave all her money to 'some dotty institution'.[5]

*

POETRY REMAINED SASSOON's secret strength. He admired C. M. Doughty's epic *The Dawn in Britain* and wrote to the author, who replied that on his eastern travels he had met some Sassoons in Poona. But, mixing aestheticism with sexual repression, his isolation found its true 'cloister'[6] in Walter Pater. In the spring of 1908, partly, Sassoon said later, to 'chaff'[7] himself out of this, he published privately, using his allowance of £400 a year, a one-act verse play, *Orpheus in Diloeryum*. The characters' names give the atmosphere – 'Epicurio, a patron of the arts', 'Dorgelian, a poet', 'Discordias, a musician', 'Time, disguised as an ancient husbandman' – and the dialogue creaks, even when attempting a joke (Time declares Orpheus to have 'Not glory, as you might call it, so much as a sort of mutuality'). Alongside the mockery of Paterian atmosphere and parody of Swinburne, there is a description of dawn by Orpheus that may be an attempt at heartfelt beauty:

> *Hush for the dawn grows red beyond the hills;*
> *The earth is awed with prayer.*

Theresa would not have been shocked. In this womanless universe, a hint of eroticism comes only in one copy when Sassoon inked in a change from 'arch-priest of the revels' to 'arch-priest of the orgies'.[8] On his uncle Hamo's advice, he sent one of the fifty-five copies to Edmund Gosse. Gosse commented on the 'richness of fancy and . . . melodious verse' and referred to this 'delicate and accomplished little masque', connecting it to 'the strange entertainments of the early renaissance and Italian humanism . . .', of which Sassoon knew nothing. Gosse said he hoped Sassoon would make 'a prolonged study of the art of poetry and advance in it from height to height';[9] in other words there was little point in them talking seriously about literature.

In the spring of 1909, having had poems in *Cricket* and the *Thrush*, Sassoon tried other journals without success until T. C. Crosland, editor of the *Academy* and always short of money, showed interest, perhaps attracted by the rich name of Sassoon. Excited, Siegfried Sassoon went up to London without telling Theresa why, to meet this cigar-smoking hack who wore a bowler hat in the office, had a heavy dark moustache, side-whiskers, a 'harsh' northern accent and flaring bloodshot eyes. Crosland offered Sassoon a guinea for each of the nine poems he had submitted, which delighted the young writer.[10] Lord Alfred Douglas's lieutenant in the crazy, homophobic persecution of Wilde's friend Robbie Ross and the author of bestselling racial diatribes like *The Unspeakable Scot* and *Taffy was a Welshman* and, later, of the anti-Semitic *The Fine Old Hebrew Gentleman*, Crosland, who called himself a poet, was Siegfried Sassoon's first commercial publisher and never paid him a penny.

The poems appeared in the *Academy* above the initials S.S., showing the same 'instinct for anonymity'[11] as Sassoon's privately printed and expensively produced volumes. There were some seven of these between 1909 and 1914 (following *Poems* of 1906 and *Orpheus in Diloeryum* of 1908). *Sonnets and Verses* of 1909 suffered from Helen Wirgman's reaction to it, in spite of a quotation on the title-page from her hero George Meredith, for, shocked by her silence after she read the book at Weirleigh, Sassoon burned all thirty-five copies[12] except the one he had given to her. Eleven of the

poems appeared again in *Sonnets* of the same year, with alterations
that did not make them noticeably stronger, together with six new
poems. *Twelve Sonnets* of 1911 had only two new poems, with the
rest either unchanged or slightly revised versions of those in *Sonnets*
and *Sonnets and Verses*.

The sonnets are aesthetic, often pastoral, with some dire phrases
('scythemen strong' trudge through 'daisy-speckled meads' and
'along the tufted dunes a throstle sings'), sometimes invoking music
(one has Grieg as its subject). There are lyres and a quotation from
Doughty, perhaps to raise the Sassoon inheritance, about evening in
an oriental encampment. More personal is a sense of shame about
homosexuality, of how taking 'a friend to-day' meant 'hell in thy
heart', so that:

> *Thy youth that was like April fresh,*
> *Through him, shall reckless years degrade . . .*

In 'Sunset', there is loneliness:

> *Out of the world, were it not well?*
> *Here have ye known infinite hell,*
> *Lost and alone.*

From the second book of 1909, *Sonnets*, 'Before Day', inspired by
dawn, love of nature and the Weirleigh garden, was reprinted in
his *Collected Poems*; the word 'clack' ('fieldward boys far off with
clack and shout') denoted, he thought, a loosening up. To Edmund
Blunden, much later, it seemed 'such a beautiful, natural song',[13]
but Blunden did not remark on the ending when this lone 'dweller
among men' yearns 'for what my heart shall never say'. The pre-
1914 poetry has signs of regret and shame over denied feelings, as
in 'Villon' (*Sonnets and Verses*, 1909) when the French poet's 'spent
frame' is rescued by one who 'used me with healing hands for all
my needs'. The 'spirit of purity' of 'At Daybreak' (*Poems*, 1911)
comes with 'music to awake me', but:

I may not hold him with my hands
Nor bid him stay to heal my sorrow;
Only his fair, unshadowed face
Abides with me until to-morrow.

There may have been a sense of heroism in being set apart, but there was much loneliness too during those evenings in the Studio at Weirleigh when he wrote by candlelight about solitary dawns and twilights.

Hamo Thornycroft quite liked the sonnets printed in 1909 and suggested that Sassoon should show them to a 'competent'[14] critic. In May of that year Edmund Gosse had advised that Hamo's 'most attractive and engaging'[15] nephew was not talented enough to become a full-time writer. But on 5 December, Gosse was gentle with Sassoon (who Thornycroft had told him was 'too much with inferior country intellects'),[16] saying, 'You have the sonnet spirit and something of the sonnet touch', but decrying his 'foggy allusiveness', occasional bad scansion and malapropisms like 'passional'.[17] Hamo Thornycroft had given up hope of Sassoon getting a job.

To Helen Wirgman, the robustness of George Meredith, who died in 1909, was what the young poet needed to counteract his precious, *fin de siècle* style. Sassoon, himself wanting grander themes, was 'overwhelmed'[18] by Thompson's 'The Hound of Heaven', and then discovered the poetic supernatural when in 1910 he read Walter de la Mare's 'All's Past' in the magazine the *Thrush*, and wrote admiringly to the poet. Shadows at twilight, strangely darkening moons, rustlings in thickets and some sense of evil crept into his verse.

The *Literary Post* attacked the *Academy* in May 1910 for calling 'Before Day' a sonnet when it broke from the octave of the Italian model. Crosland trumpeted in an editorial that 'Mr Siegfried Sassoon' knew 'quite as much about the sonnet form as *The Literary Post*', though he conceded that the poem wasn't 'flawless'.[19] Hester Brayne, on the letters page of the *Literary Post*, said she thought the *Academy* would have objected if 'this unfortunate variation on the

Italian form had appeared in the *Spectator* or *The Literary Post*.[20] Sassoon had at least become a poet of minor controversy.

*

HE LED A DIVIDED life, one moment poet and frustrated homosexual, the next a sporting country gentleman, guest in the local grand houses where he danced, waltzing eligible girls 'sexlessly' but 'with real ardour and enthusiasm'.[21] A 'swashbuckling'[22] golfer, he played on Squire Morland's links and toured courses in the south of England with his friend Thompson – a teasing, easy, sexless friendship. In the summer he played cricket for the Blue Mantles, a team based at Tunbridge Wells, where his team-mates nicknamed him 'Jane', sometimes singing softly as he walked to the wicket, 'My pretty, pretty Jane', not jeeringly but with affection for this gentle, immaculate, dreamy figure.[23] Matches often unfolded in quiet villages, beneath grey-stone churches; and to travel in a horse-drawn brake with a team that mixed all sorts of local characters through orchards and small fields to an away fixture, then to return home through a long, light evening, made for journeys of shared hope, of recollected success or mild disappointment – the comfort also of tradition and of belonging, a break in the walls of class and social convention. Talk was generally confined to the game itself, or to memories of other games, with little need for personal revelation, and women exiled to its edge.

In the winter Sassoon hunted. In December 1910, he bought a horse called Cockbird from Edgar Newgass of Frant, near Weirleigh, who had been at Henley House with him and had given up hunting because of a bad heart. Sassoon rode Cockbird in eleven point-to-points before the First World War, winning four, coming second once and third three times, unplaced in only three races. He built up a reputation for courage and skill, especially as Cockbird (bought cheaply for £50 thanks to the animal's slightly 'whistling' breath), although fast, turned out to be temperamental, occasionally dangerous, apt to run out at speed towards the edge of the course.

Sassoon had two main hunting companions: one from the past, the other a new, cheerful, 'strangely wise and good',[24] less daunting sporting friend, neither of them remotely literary although one read Surtees. Norman Loder – the hero of his childhood – had become an expert huntsman, first with a pack in County Galway, then for the Southdown in eastern Sussex, within reach of Weirleigh by a slow train. Tall, sandy-haired, authoritatively monosyllabic with a slight Irish accent picked up in Galway, amused by 'Sig's' gentle treatment of his horses, Loder, still a bachelor, asked Siegfried Sassoon to stay at his house by the hunt kennels. Soon the Southdown replaced the Eridge and the West Kent as the centre of Sassoon's hunting world; and among the followers were the Reverend Harry Harbord, rector of East Hoathly, and his family. Harbord had nine children and one of his sons, Kenneth, had been at Marlborough with Sassoon, although he was some two years younger. But it was Kenneth's younger brother, Stephen Gordon Harbord, born in 1890 and educated at Winchester, who, after they met in 1908, became 'the best sporting friend'[25] and 'the only proper brother I ever had'.[26]

East Hoathly's rectory and its large, clamorous family, very different to quiet Weirleigh, became Sassoon's second home in winter, and there the energetic Reverend Harry Harbord led long, loud discussions, with the aid of maps, about the activities of the Southdown hounds. For the tall Gordon, a graduate of London University who wanted to be an engineer, hunting was an obsession. He nicknamed his friend Sarsoon or Sarson (perhaps in imitation of how country people said the name or after the brand of vinegar) and joked about Sig's fabulous riches. But this dreamy poet could keep up as a horseman; to Gordon's younger brother Geoffrey, the visitor's courage made him 'a regular hero'.[27] Others recalled a distinctive figure, perfectly turned out, leading his horse on foot when going home to make it easier for the animal, and often taking 'his own line'[28] during the hunt, 'so keen, yet so unobtrusive'.[29] When Sassoon arrived at a Southdown meet, after a slow train

journey from Kent and then a bicycle ride to where the groom Richardson had Cockbird or another horse waiting, this shy young man was often cheered by the rest of the field.

*

SASSOON LOOKED BACK on the summer of 1911 as a time when he glimpsed what he might truly be. First, one afternoon he saw a much grander literary life than that of Crosland's Grub Street when, immaculate in a dark suit and buff linen waistcoat with spats to match, he went with Theresa, a great friend of Mrs Gosse, to the Edmund Gosses' house in Regent's Park, near the London Zoo. The moustachioed Gosse's quick movements through the crowd and glinting eyes behind gold spectacles belied his age. Sassoon associated him with genial advice, melodious verse, well-turned essays and critical influence, but Gosse was also librarian of the House of Lords, an expert on Scandinavian literature and, four years earlier, had published, in *Father and Son*, an autobiography of genius. At the party Mrs Gosse and her daughter Tessa pointed out various literary figures, Sassoon thinking that he recognized the artist Alma-Tadema. Gosse described Siegfried to the Dutch novelist for whom the party had been given as 'the very youngest of our unpublished poets, and a veritable centaur among them, since he bestrides his own Pegasus in hunt steeple chases'. The pompous words seemed patronizing but true. When they left, Theresa said delightedly of their host, 'He does trifle so perfectly!'[30] Two years passed before Sassoon saw Gosse again.

Sometimes that fine summer Weirleigh became 'a little paradise' – tennis, conversations in the garden, the slim elegance of Steenie, Theresa's white Persian kitten, the memory of a spring victory on Cockbird in the Southdown point-to-point. In July Wirgie arrived, slowed down slightly by a cracked rib, to be joined by Nevill Forbes, initially 'unassuming' as he giggled at Siegfried's jokes. Forbes, Fräulein Stoy's former pupil, had become a friend, a brilliant linguist and a good musician who had studied at Leipzig before becoming Reader in Russian at Oxford. As if to emphasize his studiousness, he wore convex glasses and had played duets with Tolstoy's daughter in Russia, bringing to Weirleigh a sense of intellectual adventure that impressed and diminished his host. On his second evening, Forbes played Reger's variations and pieces by Debussy, Ravel, Scriabin and César Franck. 'But this has been an orgy!' exclaimed Wirgie. Awestruck, Sassoon watched as Forbes blew out the candles on the piano, rubbed his spectacles, laughed shyly and put away his scores. Sometimes Wirgie tried to turn the instrument into a harpsichord by stretching some pages of newspaper across its wires. She and Nevill Forbes talked constantly: about Bayreuth or Leipzig, of Russia and Tolstoy, about Italy and her memories of the smell of cooking in the medieval streets of Italian towns. Sassoon, who had never left England, thought again of how his father might have introduced him to some of this.

After Forbes left, Wirgie reread the 'tremendous' *Anna Karenina*, but when Sassoon said he might try the novel, she declared, 'You are far too young for it, and I am too old and weary to be any use to you after such a wildly gifted young musician as your friend Forbes.' He persuaded her to play, and that July evening she gave a passionate rendering of Schumann's 'Warum?'. The days had been a glimpse of freedom, through music and in recollected voices – Wirgie's deep and slow (an andante), Forbes's fast and nervously fluent (an allegro) – unveiling a new romantic world. All he needed was the courage to break out. But, sitting frustrated at his desk, Sassoon found the reality of escape beyond him, adding to his self-contempt. He became obsessed by the novel *Peter Ibbetson* (to him 'a dangerous drug') in which the hero has a beautiful dream life running parallel to the dank truth.[31]

Oscar Wilde's trial had, only some fifteen years previously, shown how much the homoeroticism of *The Yellow Book* and Walter Pater hid danger, as homosexuality, even between consenting adults, remained a criminal offence in Britain until 1967. There were, however, a few people like Edward Carpenter who rejected concealment, British middle-class respectability and cant. Born in 1844, once an extension lecturer at Cambridge in the history of

music, Carpenter left the Church to take up communistic utopian-
ism, advocating his ideas in a series of books and poems. In 1911
he lived a simple country life at Millthorpe, near Chesterfield, and
made money from lecturing, farming and his controversial writings.

During discussions at Oxford (where Forbes lived) and at Weirleigh, Nevill Forbes (who was probably homosexual) must have
mentioned Edward Carpenter. Sassoon wrote to Carpenter ('a leader
and a prophet') and seems to have sent him *Twelve Sonnets*, the
first of his two privately printed books of 1911. He also enclosed
two photographs of himself (one 'taken at Oxford by Nevill Forbes,
who has spoken to me about you a great deal')[32] and another
sonnet, perhaps because of Carpenter's musical interests, called 'On
Music' whose ending shows a mixture of exaltation, shame and
isolation.

> *The rapture life acclaims, forgetting fear;*
> *Light in the night where I have dwelt alone;*
> *Forgiveness where the world has no forgiving.*[33]

Carpenter believed that homosexuals had greater imaginative
freedom than heterosexuals, who were constricted by their utilitarian, procreative role. His book *The Intermediate Sex* was a revelation for Sassoon, opening 'a new life to me, after a time of great
perplexity and unhappiness'. The letter shows agitation in its
unsteady underlinings. He admits his previous 'ignorance' of the
subject and declares himself a virgin, 'entirely unspotted'. 'What
ideas I had about homosexuality were absolutely unprejudiced,' he
wrote, 'and I was in such a groove that I couldn't allow myself to
be what I wished to be, and the intense attraction felt for my own
sex was almost a subconscious thing, and my antipathy for women
a mystery to me. It was only by chance that (when I had read your
book) I found my brother (a year younger) was exactly the same.'[34]
He mentioned his links to the rich Sassoons and to Hamo Thornycroft, also saying that he played cricket and hunted (which 'you may
not approve of'), proud to be 'as good as those others in their
sports, and have some of their strength and courage'. Music and

poetry were his 'other life'. The loss of his 'intensely musical' father led him to fantasize that Alfred may have 'had a strong strain of the homosexual nature in him'.

The answer came quickly from Millthorpe. 'It is good to feel one has been of help to people,' Carpenter declared on 31 July and from the poems singled out two sonnets ('A Melody' and 'Perilous Music'), making no mention of 'On Music': 'you have evidently some literary skill, *as well* as feeling.' He urged Sassoon on: 'I think the Uranians [another word for homosexuals] have a great work to do and some time I should like to have a talk with you about it. Do you ever come to the wilds of Derbyshire?' Carpenter mentioned that the Fabian socialists Sydney Olivier and his wife (Hamo Thornycroft's sister-in-law) had been staying with him. 'Hamo Thornycroft I only occasionally see. Is Nevill Forbes much at Oxford nowadays, or is he mostly abroad?'[35] He returned one of the photographs of Sassoon but kept the other. Sassoon, 'tremendously pleased to get a letter', said he could come next week yet after that would be obliged 'to wait until the middle of September', although he wanted to see Millthorpe in summer. He must be allowed to adopt Carpenter's principles while with him; 'Nevill Forbes told me you wouldn't let him help wash up the dishes. I do hope you won't think me as genteel as that.'[36] Carpenter advocated a simple life of physical labour and co-operation, of all-embracing socialism and rough experience. The visit never took place; again Sassoon failed to break away.

*

IN DECEMBER 1911, Gosse responded more encouragingly to the two privately printed 'pamphlets' of that year (*Twelve Sonnets* and *Poems*) yet was still schoolmasterly. 'Practise this delicate mode of writing more and more. In lyrics, do not leave yourself any laxities: I notice here and there a rhymeless ending where the ear calls for rhyme. Cultivate the beautiful richness of rhyme. I fancy you should work more. Write, write, write . . .'[37]

The divisions in Sassoon's life became more obvious. During this time, perhaps encouraged by the exchange with Carpenter, he wrote, as if operating behind the lines, some of his more overtly homosexual verse, notably the dramas *Hyacinth* and *Amyntas*, both privately printed (*Amyntas* was suppressed in proof). In December 1911 came a poem, 'suggested by the Balkan wars'. There are signs of what was to come in self-mortifying pity ('I should be nearer to them on my knees'), attempted realism in the descriptions of the dead or wounded ('Mangled and gashed and wild with terror') and the contrasting of an abstract vision of glory with the reality of pain. There followed an ironic, if clumsily expressed, end:

> *These, the victorious, the defeated,*
> *Whose groans shall sound through age and aeon.*
> *Glad be the nations that are greeted*
> *And crowned by such triumphal paean!*[38]

Hyacinth, written in November and December 1911, is a prose play with five passages of verse, of which only some thirty-five copies were printed. Like *Orpheus in Diloeryum*, it is a mildly homoerotic *fin de siècle* work, this time about the friendship of Prince Hyacinth for Pierrot that ends with them both poisoned. *Amyntas*, written early in 1912, tells of the nineteen-year-old dreamy Prince Amyntas who worships Apollo before meeting an ideal friend ('a naked figure that played on a lyre and made immortal music'). In both of these, fairyland is described in a style of tired preciousness, as in Amyntas's comment on his garden: 'I love the half tones; cool courts and whispers of fountains . . . Not death but life makes me afraid.' Sassoon's collection of 1912, *Melodies*, has fifteen poems, three of which are also in *Hyacinth*. As usual, the love lyrics are to people of an indeterminate sex; but he later thought two pieces worthy of his *Collected Poems 1908–1956*: 'Night Piece' (about dryads and fauns) and 'The Heritage' which portentously claims 'Death is our heritage' as much as life.

Gosse saw 'progress' in *Melodies* but urged the poet to 'take longer flight' away from 'moon beams and half-tones' and to 'go on writing hard and reading the old masters'.[39] Yet the more ambitious

Ode for Music – a long poem prompted by a surge of religious feeling brought on by 'The Hound of Heaven' and a session at the Ouija board – failed. Sonorously pompous, like an organ with the 'swell stops pulled out', the ode was privately printed in 1912 and published (and not paid for) by Crosland in the *Antidote* in February 1913. Gosse offered no opinion after Sassoon sent it to him; nor did Elgar, another recipient. The only notable result of the poem seems to have been that it prompted Crosland to introduce his young contributor to Lord Alfred Douglas. In February 1912, Sassoon wrote a fourteen-line Browningesque monologue by a woman who had murdered her lover ('Stab swift while he's asleep') called 'Two in a Garret',[40] and on 24 May sent 'two small volumes'[41] to Sidgwick and Jackson, who published Rupert Brooke, but they were turned down.

*

IN NOVEMBER OF the same year, he asked Gosse what the critic thought of 'John Masefield and his realism'.[42] The next month, sitting in the Studio, with rain and wind outside and a photograph of Burne-Jones's *Days of Creation* on the wall, Sassoon looked at Masefield's dramatic monologue poem *The Everlasting Mercy* which he had read the year before. Why not try to parody it, he thought, perhaps unconsciously exemplifying T. S. Eliot's comment that all art grows out of passionate boredom? He raced ahead, thrilled to find himself writing 'physically' at last, finishing over 500 lines by the next evening.[43] The result was *The Daffodil Murderer*, a breakthrough in technique and reputation and a move out of the confines of his upbringing.

Masefield, after growing up in rural Herefordshire, had gone to sea as a boy, lived rough in the United States and felt intensely for the underdog. By seeking a naturalistic, physical style, and writing about people and places of all types, he influenced the new school of Georgian poetry, whose first anthology was published in 1912, and *The Everlasting Mercy* had caused a sensation when it came out the year before. With no trace of homoeroticism, Watts, Burne-

Jones or *fin de siècle* decadence, the poem is a story of rural squalor and violence with flashes of apocalyptic chaos ending in mystical redemption, owing much to the novels of Thomas Hardy – an author Sassoon did not yet appreciate – in which individuals are trapped by circumstance in a harsh, if sometimes beautiful, world. Its brisk rhyming couplets spoken by the apparently damned narrator, Saul Kain, are different to the lyrical poetry Sassoon had previously yearned to write, but he found Masefield's voice and, within another poet's world and style, freedom. Calling his parody *The Daffodil Murderer*, he set it in rural East Sussex, in an atmosphere far removed from the East Hoathly rectory and the farmers and local gentry of the Southdown hunt, revealing instead wretched, inescapable, poverty-stricken lives.

Albert Meddle looks back from the condemned cell in Lewes jail, telling his story to the prison chaplain: how he killed Bill; how he had started life as one of a drunkard's nine children. He is sure, however, that 'there's dirtier rogues than me' – crooked lawyers, stockbrokers, hypocrites. He might have been 'a worse 'un' and had worked as a farm labourer, had married and had had seven children. Then one evening after coming back to their bleak but neat home (with a picture of the coronation and a biblical text on the wall), he went out to the Barley Mow where, inflamed by drink and rough talk, Ted Brown and he had a fight after beer had been spilt. Sassoon tries for the same colloquial language as Masefield's fight scene in *The Everlasting Mercy*, even if he makes it sound more like a 'rag' in Billy Bunter's public school:

> *Leggo my ear.*
> *If you must take and booze my beer,*
> *I'll pour it down your blanky neck.*

Bill, the chucker-out, evicts them both, to cheers from the other drinkers, but Ted stokes Albert up and they go to Bill's cottage to wait for him under stars that shine on everyone, from the lowest to (and here Sassoon mocks his own relations) the King.

They see the King and Queen at Windsor,
And hear the story that he spins 'er
Of how he's been to pheasant-shoots
With Jew-boy lords that lick his boots.

Albert also reflects on how he has known Ted and Bill since childhood, on how they fished and played together in innocence, that mythical time cherished by Sassoon:

I thought how in the summer weather
When Bill and me was boys together,
We'd often come this way when trudgin'
Out by the brooks to fish for gudgeon.
I thought, 'When me and Bill are deaders,
'There'll still be buttercups in medders,
'And boys with penny floats and hooks
'Catching fish in Laughton brooks.'

The church clock strikes eleven and Bill returns to his house. Ted has run off but Albert trips Bill up, kills him with a kick to the head, is arrested and later condemned to death. His story over, the murderer says goodbye to Sussex, the county he has never left, the poem's metre changing (as in Masefield) in a pastoral evocation:

O golden autumn weather,
And apples ripe to gather,
And white rime-frost at morn,
When huntsman blows his horn;
O all things I remember,
Who've seen my last September.[44]

The Daffodil Murderer does not have Masefield's sense of low life; 'whore', for instance, is a word still too strong for Sassoon, as is the brazen but doomed sexuality of *The Everlasting Mercy*'s barmaid 'Doxy Jane' or such stark similes as 'The room stank like a fox's gut'. He lacked also, as yet, the skills of dialogue and character shown in the urbane response of Masefield's parson to Saul Kain's abuse of the establishment, Mrs Jaggard's tirade when Saul tries to befriend her child or the Quaker Miss Bourne's rigid self-certainty. Also missing are Masefield's apocalyptic vision and the contrast of Kain's final redemptive calm with his brutal life. Sassoon sent the poem to Crosland, who agreed to publish it through his imprint John Richmond, a venture backed by a rich novelist called Irene Osgood, but asked for ten pounds to help with costs. At first the man of letters wanted to call the poem _The Gentle Murderer_ and its author 'Peter Expletive' before Sassoon and he decided on the pen-name of Saul Kain, the hero of _Everlasting Mercy_ and, for the title, a part of Masefield's recent volume, _The Daffodil Fields_.

An attempt to hint that the real author was a famous figure (perhaps Crosland himself) failed when Sassoon gave away Saul Kain's true identity to a Cambridge bookseller. Printed in a thousand copies as a small paperback of thirty pages, _The Daffodil Murderer_ had an orange-coloured cover and the title lettered in red above the false claim 'Being the Chantrey Prize Poem' (no such prize existed) and, in inverted commas (as if from an unnamed critic), 'Brilliant Beyond Belief'. A mock-serious preface by 'William Butler' – in fact Crosland making another literary joke, this time against Yeats – ended with a demand for a grant from the civil list for Mr Kain who had an intimate knowledge of 'the insides of various rustic public houses' and was living off a War Office pension. 'William Butler' claimed to have read _Daffodil Murderer_ nineteen times, weeping 'more copiously' on each occasion.[45]

Crosland hoped for a reprint and sales of at least 2,000 following the success of Masefield's original two years before, but the first public comment was disappointing. Sassoon, on publication day, had been hunting with the Southdown (going 'terribly sticky')[46] and, on the way back by an evening train, bought several literary magazines at the Lewes station bookstall to read some damning lines in the _Athenaeum_ on this 'pointless and weak-kneed imitation of "The Everlasting Mercy".'[47] Then, four days later, came much better news. Gosse wrote to him, delighted at 'this very clever brilliant thing' that showed 'powers which I had not expected from you'. The poem was, he thought, 'a pastiche' more than a parody where 'a tale of rustic tragedy is told with real pathos and power, only exactly as Masefield would tell it. The end is extremely beautiful.' Gosse had sent the work to 'Mr Edward Marsh, who . . . has published the interesting anthology of "Georgian Poets"'. Marsh had asked for more and Gosse suggested sending him 'a parcel of your pamphlets'. Sassoon should abandon his 'isolated life' and get to know 'this most charming man' who was 'the personal friend of all poets'.[48]

Some critics were kinder than the *Athenaeum*. The *Cambridge Evening News* welcomed this 'brilliant parody' (which it presumed was by Crosland); the *New Age* thought it 'perfect, down to the little farewell twiddly bits'; and the *Manchester Guardian*'s critic 'gladly read every line of it, undebarred by our knowledge that he wrote them with his tongue in his cheek'.[49] But the most important result for Sassoon was his introduction to Edward Marsh.

Born in 1872, Marsh was a civil servant, in 1913 private secretary to Winston Churchill, who was then First Lord of the Admiralty. But he also helped artists and writers, using what he called his 'murder money' – a small allowance granted to him by the state as a descendant of Spencer Perceval, the Prime Minister who had been assassinated in 1812. The son of an eminent surgeon, Marsh had a high-pitched voice, a relic of a youthful attack of mumps that had supposedly left him impotent but still prone to romantic homosexual attachments. He worked hard and was a good classical scholar, but adored the aristocratic world, society gossip and grand country houses, as well as his literary and artistic friends, and, hating to be alone, kept in touch with people constantly 'by voice or pen'.[50] With his urbanity came a slight primness, a slightly prissy upper lip 'a little odd'[51] between a firm masculine jaw and a strong, straight nose; people were surprised at how formidable Marsh could be. Sassoon, growing irritated by him, later called him 'hollow',[52] but was always a little in awe of this clever, precise, witty, snobbish and extraordinarily well-read man.

The first volume of *Georgian Poetry*, which Marsh edited,

combined pastoralism with down-to-earth language and a realistic, modern point of view. D. H. Lawrence was in it, alongside the more predictable Lascelles Abercrombie and John Drinkwater, as were Walter de la Mare, W. H. Davies and Rupert Brooke, with whom Marsh was in love. His response to Sassoon – sent on 22 February 1913 from the Lake District, where he was staying – was long and detailed: an example of why he was valued by many writers. Clearly Marsh thought that Gosse had held the young poet back through an admiration for past masters like Swinburne. 'It is certain that you have a lovely instrument to play on,' he began, adding that he felt poetry of the 'vague, iridescent, ethereal kind' had been worked out and now one should write 'either with one's eye on an object' or with 'a (more or less) definite idea'. He chastised Sassoon for poor technique, such as not attaching pronouns to nouns, changing metre and 'sometimes a want of fundamental brain work'. The poems – particularly the sonnets – were occasionally too derivative ('sheer Rossetti'). But Marsh liked some 'magical' lines, showing that he too was not immune to the aesthetic movement:

> *Fantastic shepherd, from your breezy winter*
> *Prithee some snatch of wayward April bring.*

'Goblin Revel' reminded him of the Russian ballet *Oiseau de Feu*, or *Firebird* (which Sassoon had never heard of), *Orpheus in Diloeryum* seemed obviously influenced by the Post-Impressionists (of whom Sassoon was also ignorant) and *The Daffodil Murderer* (with its 'capital'[53] preface, which Marsh didn't know was by Crosland), although good, fell between parody and imitation.

Sassoon was delighted. Answering, he admitted to having 'passed through most of the influences' but hoped 'to emerge into an individual style of my own'; he went on to say that the lack of reviews of *The Daffodil Murderer* ('such a good joke') had disappointed him. Sassoon told Marsh he found *Georgian Poetry* 'very interesting', especially 'Mr Abercrombie's work' and 'Mr de la Mare is delightful in a limited way'.[54] This slight denigration of de la Mare

– a poet who had greatly influenced him – may have been an attempt at sophistication.

The Daffodil Murderer sold badly, with no reprint. Edward Carpenter could not see its point and suggested that Sassoon, in order to experience life, should take a job as a stoker on an ocean liner. But Sassoon went on writing poetry. On 17 February, five days before Marsh wrote to him, came 'England 1913', which expressed the hope that a country defeated by 'enemies resistless' might find a new strength and humility alone – a hint perhaps of anti-imperialism. On 27 February there is shame at lust ('How with invisible demons your spirit was mated'). In 'Cortège Macabre', the dead become 'death's battalion of corruption branded', foretelling the processional

> *Battalions and Battalions, scarred from hell;*
> *The unreturning army that was youth*

of 'Prelude: The Troops' written in the autumn of 1917. 'Vision', dated 22 April 1913, describes a dissolving dream of 'Youth with his arms outspread', and evokes a sense of loneliness. 'Of a Lady Waiting to Be Wed' (written on 27 June) is stronger stuff, pointing to the woman-hating poems of the war in its depiction of a 'sleek' and crafty seductress whose 'flaunting feather' and 'crescent of that glimpsèd calf'[55] seem predatory. Then the old fairyland reappears in 'Nimrod in September' about 'Young Nimrod' up early on his horse while 'half the drowsy world's a-bed'.[56]

*

HE MET MARSH over lunch at the National Liberal Club where the urbane, surprisingly young 'Eddie' coped easily with Sassoon's inarticulacy, and the poet Austin Dobson – a particular favourite of Theresa's – joined them afterwards. 'We are all waiting for Mr Marsh to give us a volume of his own verses,' Dobson said teasingly, to which Marsh murmured mild dissent. At the House of Lords, where he was the librarian, Edmund Gosse was more daunting, asking Sassoon about Crosland, to be told, 'Oh, he's not a bad sort of chap,' at which Gosse said, 'Indeed! What I myself have heard of him has been altogether to the contrary.' They looked in on the chamber where most of the peers seemed to be asleep and the snobbish Gosse's smile was 'almost fraternal'.[57] Then came the first apparently insignificant meeting with Wilde's friend and lover Robert Ross on 5 June 1913, at a party at Gosse's house. Now Siegfried Sassoon had met the three guiding spirits of his early literary life.

Crosland disliked the Georgians, preferring W. E. Henley among modern poets. He asked for more poems, even suggesting a 'small volume', but Sassoon, perhaps emboldened by meeting Marsh, held back, offering instead the five-year-old *Orpheus in Diloeryum* which the editor agreed to accept in return for ten pounds. Sassoon changed the work in proof, at which Crosland protested and asked for another ten pounds; this letter Sassoon did not answer. Some months later, he tried to retrieve the proofs from the Conduit Street office of John Richmond (above a Rolls-Royce showroom), only to find that the firm's new owner had sacked Crosland and the proofs had vanished.

Marsh was now his chief mentor. To him, in May, he said he hoped to be in London in June and would like 'if possible' to stay a night with Marsh at Gray's Inn. 'Now the hunting is over I am making desperate efforts to produce vehement verse. Won two point-to-points this year!' The letter had a sketch of a man on a horse going over a jump with the sun rising or setting in the distance[58] but left out how, after his second victory, he had wandered off alone and thought, characteristically, 'Someone else is winning the next race now. I am forgotten now.'[59] Marsh disliked some 'cynical' poems Sassoon sent him in October 1913, decrying words like 'evotion' and 'artichoken'. 'You must come to London occasionally,' he said.[60]

But Sassoon, his chances of publication wrecked by Crosland's downfall, had followed Norman Loder to Warwickshire where his friend had become master of the Atherstone hunt. Lord Alfred Douglas, to whom Sassoon wrote in desperation, said that he would pass on a letter to Crosland, who 'has been very ill and away in the country. I hope you have been writing some poetry.'[61] Sassoon told Marsh of his despair on 23 October. 'I don't suppose I shall ever publish any poems. The stuff I wrote last summer was utterly hopeless. Perhaps I will begin fresh in the spring, but I feel very sad about my work the last few months.'[62]

Staying with Norman Loder was a life of 'purposeful simplicity'.[63] They lived in the village of Witherley, first in the huntsman's cottage, then in a larger house near by; once again the tall Loder was the dominant figure, his face 'like a boot', certain that all other local activities should be subordinate to fox-hunting.[64] Charles Wiggin, Loder's Old Etonian contemporary, joined them; with Sassoon also were his horses and Richardson, ecstatic to be in the English midlands, to him the best hunting country in the world. They all imagined Sassoon to be rich because of his name, although Wiggin (heir to a large neighbouring estate) and Loder were both richer and had more horses. On one occasion Sassoon deputized for a Miss Stubbs who wrote the Atherstone hunting reports for the *Morning Post* under the name of Tonio, and had his first piece of prose in print (its heading was 'A Good Day with the Atherstone').[65] Out hunting he met a girl called Dorothy Hanmer, the daughter of a clergyman from a local landowning family. She had a brother called Bobbie with whom Sassoon became infatuated, but Dorothy loved this tall, shy, brave and physically awkward friend of the master's, although her father didn't approve, perhaps because of his Jewishness; 'we never really knew why', Sassoon wrote later.[66] At meets he collected for the Royal Agricultural Benevolent Society, a charity that helped poor farmworkers.

Gradually the company of these philistine good-natured hunting types began to pall and he wanted to be alone. Above all, though, he dreaded a return to Weirleigh, to be 'bored, worried by suppressed sex', irritated by the fussy Theresa, who was cast down by the death of her faithful maid Miriam. The weald's 'haunting quality', he saw, belonged only to his 'poetical' side. Even the hunting there had been spoilt by 'the glories of the Atherstone'.[67] So Sassoon went to London. But a dinner with Gosse never left the ground, the host desperately getting Max Beerbohm's collection of parodies, *A Christmas Garland*, out of his bookcase to read parts of it aloud before glancing at a clock.[68] Then a blow-out lunch with Crosland (this time paid for by the man of letters) ended with a lecture. Sassoon's circumstances, Crosland said, were too comfortable. Life 'ought to be a Promethean struggle with adversity and injustice'.[69]

He never spoke to Crosland again, but those words went with him to his club, the Royal Societies in St James's, which Sassoon nicknamed The United Nonentities. Dissatisfaction seemed stifling in the silent, empty library of the dank, dark building for this was a Saturday and most of the members were out of town or with their families. An idle Sunday brought thoughts of wasted time, of dislike for his chameleon self, of a feared dead-end. Since childhood he had felt that 'I was a prophetic spirit,' waiting for an 'opportunity' to 'give myself to the service of my fellow men – and all I had hitherto done had been to hunt foxes and jump hedges!' Even cricket had let him down; he was simply too bad at it. Suddenly Sassoon saw himself among the poor, 'befriending grateful but indefinite unfortunates on the Embankment', but he did not know how to embark upon such work; in any case, 'it was the audience I wanted, not the social service'.[70] That night he wrote 'The Riverside' about how 'something snapped inside my head', releasing the idea of freedom in sacrifice where 'glory waits for me'.

> *Destiny calls me home at last*
> *To strive for pity's sake,*
> *To watch with the hopeless and outcast*
> *And to endure their ache.*[71]

He went back to the fox-hunters, and had a final success, winning the Atherstone point-to-point's heavyweight race on his beloved Cockbird; then, helped by Marsh, he found rooms in 1 Raymond Buildings, near Eddie's own Gray's Inn chambers. The white bedroom, newly done-up bathroom and sitting room (painted Sassoon's favourite peacock blue) above the lawns and plane trees of Gray's Inn and the distant rattle of trams in Theobald's Road surely meant hope. He had some furniture but only one picture: a colour reproduction of Titian's portrait of a young man with a glove. Theresa had insisted he should bring up lots of white lilac and some brown–gold curtains, the only additions from a Weirleigh that he wished to leave behind.

Marsh's servant Mrs Elgy had found Sassoon a housekeeper and his letters seem cheerful. But Eddie didn't like the 'invertebrate sort of poems fading away in a sigh'[72] and 'Rain in June', probably written in Raymond Buildings, has this feeling. The better 'South Wind', praised later by Virginia Woolf, he sent to Marsh, saying 'at any rate this has the virtue of being unemotional! And the name of God is absent!'[73] Marsh tried the poem on J. C. Squire of the *New Statesman*, who thought this picture of the weald on a blustery spring morning 'too much of an Exercise' and turned it down.

Sassoon went to the sale of the Atherstone hunt horses at Tattersalls to meet his hunting friends and yearned briefly for the simplicities of the previous winter. If only he could bring poetry and sport together in 'one grand sweet song' like Ralph Hodgson's *Song of Honour*. The poet W. H. Davies, whom he met with Marsh, gave him Hodgson's address in the King's Road, but when Sassoon went there one wet afternoon the sporting poet and connoisseur of boxing and bull terriers was out. Robert Ross he saw again at a party given by Gosse in March and sent him his poems; Ross wrote encouragingly, hoping they might meet for dinner, but nothing happened. He grew fonder of London, of sunsets above Holborn and breezes bringing hints of country life, and also of the imagined world of this vast city where he might lose his innocence at last. When Mr Lousada, the lawyer, lectured him on his extravagance, the picture of a cultured, sporting young man about town was almost complete.

Early in June, however, soon after the Tattersalls sale, came a chilling encounter. Eddie Marsh had rhapsodized about Rupert Brooke, so much so that, after Marsh had read from Brooke's unpublished 'Heaven', Sassoon had exclaimed in irritation, 'Why does he always write about fishes?' Marsh's eyeglass fell out. 'But

my dear, he *doesn't*! And the only other fish poem he wrote isn't in the *least* like this one!'[74] On his return from a journey to Tahiti and the South Seas, Brooke spent some days with Eddie in London; Marsh never introduced Sassoon to his more bohemian friends like Isaac Rosenberg or Mark Gertler or even to E. M. Forster, but Brooke he clearly felt was suitable.

Sassoon had glimpsed the golden-haired, hatless poet walking through Gray's Inn, and felt thrilled when an invitation to breakfast came, Eddie saying that another Georgian poet, W. H. Davies, would be there as well. Also present was the artist Paul Nash, who asked what Sassoon thought of the sculptor Gaudier-Brzeska, to receive the answer, intended to hide ignorance, that he liked neither Futurism nor Marinetti, thus 'clumsily revealing' conventional taste. While Davies spoke of his travels round America, Brooke – sun-burned, hair unbrushed, wearing an open-necked blue shirt, grey flannel trousers, sandals on bare feet – sat quiet, as if secure in his fame and beauty. Sassoon recalled Theresa's loathing of people in 'sloppily artistic' clothes who talked 'silly Fabian Socialism'; perhaps dragged down by this, he lapsed into the jargon of the hunting field. Nash and Davies left and Marsh got up to go to work for Churchill at the Admiralty, pausing to say to Brooke, mixing playfulness, avuncularity and the mention of a famous hostess and a cabinet minister: 'Don't forget we're lunching with Lady Horner to meet Mr Birrell, and *do* try to be on time.'

These two poets of the First World War were alone with each other for about half an hour. Brooke, sitting by a window where the light framed his famous head, was a year younger than Sassoon but years ahead in sophistication, learning and recognized promise. Groping for conversation, Sassoon said he thought they had been briefly at Cambridge together. Brooke reminded him of his role as the Herald in *Eumenides* that had transfixed the university and they spoke admiringly of Davies, of how accurate Brooke had found Conrad and Kipling on the 'tropics'. Anxious to be modern, Sassoon called Kipling's poetry 'terribly tub-thumping stuff', only to have Brooke say condescendingly that Marsh had made him see the worth of 'Cities and Thrones and Powers' which Sassoon had never read. Soon a sense of the other's boredom brought panic and the fear of lapsing again into hunting language that might even make him blurt out that Georgian poets were 'quite a cheery crowd'. Rupert Brooke failed to ask about his poetry and Sassoon felt unable to give yet more praise to Brooke's own 'Home Thoughts from Abroad'. While saying goodbye at Marsh's outer door, this brilliant figure seemed relieved at the prospect of being once again 'his unimpeded self'.[75]

Restless, humiliated, flattened by an extraordinary personality rather than by the 'radiant good looks', Sassoon went forlornly to the zoo. There, by chance, he met Wirgie, to whom he had written some months before to say he was in London, and gave her lunch, keeping quiet about his sense of failure. The next day he went back to the zoo, and again she was there; this time he was more forthcoming, and they went, a few days later, to an afternoon concert of some of Schoenberg's music. Wirgie assured him that artistic failure could be transformed into success. He talked only of himself, never of her own problems, living alone at the age of seventy on a pitiful income with no companion but her cat. Both of them were mystified by Schoenberg's *Verklärte Nacht*. But, to Sassoon, 'the message of that yearning exotic music' cried out with a sense of 'the unknown want', like a call to action that also touched his regret at never having known 'deep and passionate love'.[76] Back at Raymond Buildings, Wirgie chided him for not having a piano and for his self-imposed isolation 'in affluence among lawyers'.[77] He said despairingly that any development seemed impossible.

Some days later, dining alone in an Italian restaurant – where Crosland had given him that huge lunch – he talked to one of the waiters about Italy and suddenly yearned to go south. His great-aunt Mozelle (S. D. Sassoon's sister), whom he met for lunch, spoke about his father's family; and he thought again how Alfred might have taken him abroad. Schoenberg, Chaliapin at the opera, the Russian ballet (where he went night after night, alone, sometimes with Wirgie), Richard Strauss conducting *The Legend of Joseph* with Léonide Massine as the lead dancer: these show Sassoon's brief flaring of interest in modernism and artistic Europe, although, to Marsh, he mocked those rivals of the Georgians, 'Les Imagistes',[78] anti-Romantic, French-influenced poets like T. E. Hulme and Ezra Pound. Above all, though, he felt his isolation: laughing young society people at the Russian ballet and (even worse) meeting Mr Gould, his old Marlborough housemaster, in St James's Street (the drunken Gould said, 'Well, and are you still as silly as ever?') seemed only to emphasize his static, lonely life.[79]

Early in July, during a heatwave, he left a London preoccupied by the Ulster crisis and rioting suffragettes, for Selsey in Sussex, to spend a weekend in a hotel alone. Here a fellow guest spoke of the recent assassination of the Austrian Archduke Franz Ferdinand at Sarajevo; and Sassoon went to sit dreamily by himself on the beach. He had little money, his poetry had dried up and Norman Loder (now engaged to be married) was moving to the Fitzwilliam hunt near Peterborough, where Sassoon could not afford to follow him. He dreaded a return to Weirleigh, 'to the narrowing existence of an elderly person'. Perhaps Gosse might help him get a job on a literary journal in London and he could come to Kent at weekends for hunting or cricket or golf. But Sassoon thought Gosse and Marsh were bored of him. His literary earnings were so far less than £5 and he had spent well over £100 on his privately printed pamphlets. His life was emotionally and sexually unresolved, yet he felt 'in perfect physical health and youngness'. Perhaps he should enlist in a cavalry regiment and vanish into a simple army life. He wanted to test himself; 'like most of the human race I had always wanted to be a hero'.[80] Sunburned after hours by the sea, he returned to London; then, carrying the scores of some of the Russian works that had thrilled him at the opera and ballet, he left the city for Weirleigh. 'Just off to the country and bucolic delights,' he told Marsh, with false cheeriness. 'I hope to see R. Brooke again some day; he is absolutely delightful.'[81]

Staying at Weirleigh was Mab Anley, an old Irish friend of Theresa, married to a retired officer and with two sons in the army;

and she – a large, warm-hearted former beauty – spoke of the European crisis, thrilling Sassoon with these 'thunderstorms muttering beyond the Kentish horizon'. Mab Anley said, 'Where my two boys will be in a few weeks time, God only knows,' making him feel that 'courage was the only thing that mattered'. The longed-for change, he thought, had come at last. He played in a two-day cricket match at Tunbridge Wells and several army officers there received telegrams calling them to their regiments. Sassoon suddenly felt anxious as thoughts of an invasion of southern England jostled with memories of ineptitude in the Marlborough school Cadet Corps. He might fail this test of his manhood.

The next day, 31 July, he bicycled thirty sunlit miles to Rye, seeking relief in hard exercise, and, after tea in the town, rode back through the evening landscape of the weald. The *Times* leader of that morning had made clear that war was imminent; he felt magnificently well, with 'only that suppressed ache of desolation because I'd got to go and be a soldier and knew nothing about how to do it when I got there', but he was relieved by the decision. That evening, while his mother searched for the cats in the cool garden, he played the first act of *Prince Igor*. Mab Anley, praising his 'great feeling', could not know that 'so far as my mental processes were involved, I was already in the Army'.[82]

He went for a night to the Harbords at East Hoathly where Gordon, in the special reserve since 1912 and soon to be commissioned in the Royal Field Artillery, told him not to join the bone-headed rich in the regular cavalry. Finally, on 4 August, at the Drill Hall in Lewes, Siegfried Sassoon enlisted, aged twenty-seven years and ten months, as a trooper in the Sussex Yeomanry, a territorial regiment, signing on for four years. A medical report gave his height as 6 feet, 1 inch, girth as 38½ inches, vision 'sufficient' and physical development 'good'.[83]

FOUR

'Grief can be beautiful'

IN AUGUST 1914, while in other countries huge conscripted forces massed amid hysterical fervour, Britain fielded only a small volunteer army, and a French observer in London noted that one of the few outward signs of war was an unarmed policeman outside the German embassy.[1] Almost a century's isolation from European conflict led to a self-confident, perhaps more naive, nationalism based on imagined imperial and naval strength.

This was reflected by poets, many of whom tried to match the hour. On 5 August, the first poem about the war appeared in *The Times* – Henry Newbolt's 'The Vigil', written years before but suitably stirring – to be followed through the late summer and autumn by a torrent from (among others) Rudyard Kipling, Edmund Gosse, Laurence Binyon ('For the Fallen'), the Poet Laureate Robert Bridges, William Watson and Thomas Hardy. In the autumn of 1914, Gosse praised the possible cleansing quality of war; it was thought that this simple challenge might sweep away *fin de siècle* decadence or modernist 'caterwauling'[2] like the Schoenberg concert which had moved Sassoon. Patriotism made some Georgians leave realism for romance, as in Rupert Brooke's sense of the permanent, subtle conquest of foreign fields by the 'richer dust' of the decent British dead. This too became a theme of Siegfried Sassoon's war: the lasting victory of ostensibly defeated innocence, the victims' triumph.

*

As a trooper in C Squadron of the Sussex Yeomanry, Sassoon spent two nights on the floor of the Lewes Corn Exchange before 'an awful journey' to a camp in open country near Canterbury. Here he longed for a decent bath, speculated to Marsh about a short war, complained of the lack of 'gents'[3] yet refused to become an officer – perhaps because of that wish for self-sacrifice – staying apart from his old fox-hunting friends who had commissions. Sassoon volunteered for foreign service, shocked that only 20 per cent of the Sussex Yeomanry did so. He gave up his beloved Cockbird to an officer because the horse could not manage a trooper's heavy equipment. By September, he felt bored as the first thrill of feeling purposefully fit in cloudless weather and making friends with the hard-swearing troopers ebbed away in the dreariness of hard work previously done for him at Weirleigh by grooms and servants. He broke his arm when, on exercise, his horse tripped on some wire at a jump and Sassoon suffered agony when the bone was set and reset and a silver plate screwed in. He regretted missing the battle of the Marne that ended the German advance, but Gordon Harbord, an officer at the front in the Royal Fusiliers Artillery, begged him to stay out of the fighting.[4]

The poems of late 1914 and early 1915 mention the war only obliquely. The pastoral 'To-day' declares 'to-morrow might bring death', and 'Wisdom' looks 'to the edge of the dark'; in 'Storm and Rhapsody' a storm 'rides a hurtling legion'. Sassoon sent these and others to Marsh. At Weirleigh, early in 1915, while nursing his arm, he experienced a 'sort of farewell to poetry', and read books on mysticism and St Francis of Assisi.[5] The pastoral Georgian and *fin de siècle* phases continued – as the titles show – with

'Wonderment', 'Daybreak in a Garden' and 'Companions' in which a bird pipes a 'roundelay complete'. 'Morning Express', a 'verse exercise' describing a railway-station scene, came to him while travelling to Canterbury to have his arm examined. Praised later by Virginia Woolf, it is unusually realistic for pre-Western Front Sassoon. The hunting world still features, from a sense perhaps of its possible disintegration – hence 'What the Captain Said at the Point-to-Point', a poem in colloquial speech, and 'The Old Huntsman', over 200 blank-verse lines influenced by Browning's monologues and Masefield's colloquial style.

'The Old Huntsman', dedicated to Norman Loder, mixes demotic language and rueful sensibility. Sassoon later called the poem a 'self-interview',[6] although it is ostensibly the musings of a retired huntsman who looks back from poverty across romance, beauty and achievement against intimations of his own death and the prospect of a hell consisting of hard ground impossible for sport, or of a heaven with God like an old duke he once knew offering twinkling praise 'in a great room full of books'. Some have found a jarring tension between the sensitive poet's voice and the old huntsman's awkward uneducated sensibility that Sassoon had earlier tried to create in *The Daffodil Murderer*. But the description of the hunt's savagery foreshadows the later poet of the trenches; and the huntsman's regret for unappreciated days hints, probably unconsciously, at war's enlivening as well as terrible truth:

> *I never broke*
> *Out of my blundering self into the world,*
> *But let it all go past me, like a man*
> *Half asleep in a land that's full of wars.*[7]

Like pre-1914 Sassoon, the huntsman laments 'a power of sights I've missed, and foreign marvels', and the poem's moving nostalgia and delight in nature show his constant themes in this attempt to combine poetry and sport into 'one grand sweet song'.[8] This, however, is life recollected, overshadowed by the melancholy of age and regret, rather than the moment of living; here too the future Sassoon, this time of the autobiographies, dreams of a better past.

He wrote to Marsh and, in April, saw Gosse again – who spoke of Rupert Brooke as 'the best of the young bards' – and then published privately a thin green-covered pamphlet called *Discoveries* of which fifty copies were printed at the Chiswick Press. These thirteen poems, some written before the war, often have a euphoric note in the appreciations of nature, and a sense of longing for what he later called, quoting Walt Whitman, 'the unknown want', as in 'Alone':

> *I've looked: the morning world was green;*
> *Bright roofs and towers of town I've seen,*
> *And stars, wheeling through wingless night.*
> *I've looked: and my soul yet longs for light.*[9]

The book is less limp, more – as Marsh had taught him – expressive of a definite idea or object, yet the old tendencies remain, as in 'Romance', a poem about 'a duke in Olden France'.

*

SASSOON, FEELING THAT the real war might slip past him, took a commission in a regular infantry regiment, the Royal Welch Fusiliers, at the suggestion of a neighbour, Captain Ruxton, who had contacts there; the regiment was also the choice of 'Bobbie' Hanmer, his pre-war hunting friend and brother of Dorothy, whose family had Welsh estates. On 28 May his name appeared in the *London Gazette* as a second lieutenant 'on probation'. He was joining an infantry regiment with strong fighting traditions, including the right – confirmed by King William IV – to the 'flash', five black hanging ribbons attached to the back of the collar in imitation of the pigtail once worn by soldiers. Founded in 1689 and based at Wrexham in Wales, the Royal Welch Fusiliers had many Englishmen in its ranks and was sometimes, before 1914, called the 'Birmingham Fusiliers', although after conscription was introduced in 1916 the regiment received an increasing number of Welsh recruits. Before 1914, many of the officers were country gentlemen or from the professional classes of north Wales, but the war brought in less orthodox types like Siegfried Sassoon.

Sassoon was initially put into the Third, or Reserve, Battalion of the RWF. Advised by Gordon Harbord, he chose a regimental tailor and went to a fitting in London before going north by rail to the training depot of Litherland, a bleak industrial suburb of Liverpool, dominated by the huge Bryant and May match factory. Here, in huts near a stinking tannery, a TNT plant and a Roman Catholic cemetery, he learned how to be an infantry officer, looking out on 'stunted dwelling-houses, dingy trees, disconsolate canal, and flat root fields',[10] back in a public-school atmosphere of communal male living, forced exercise and hearty philistinism. There was a hierarchy: first the older reserve officers – some of them veterans of the Boer War – in charge of training, then the young men who had just joined up and who would do the actual fighting, themselves divided between boys straight from public school and those, like Sassoon, supposedly with some worldly experience. Over it all hung the British class system, the divide between officers labelled 'temporary gentlemen' and other, generally younger, men of more elevated social status. Letters from the front, like that from Geoffrey Harbord – Gordon's brother – echoed like distant artillery ('Good luck and don't come out here. It is a mug's game').[11] In May 1915 came the news of the heavy losses suffered by the First Battalion of the Royal Welch Fusiliers at Festubert.

The commanding officer was a Breconshire landowner, in charge of about 3,000 men and 100 officers. NCOs did most of the training, watched over by the senior officers. A soldier there who had joined up aged sixteen recalled Sassoon years later as 'very shy' but 'very kind'.[12] The poet began to meet the human background to his war writing, including the humorous 'Birdie' Stansfield, who had lived in Canada, and David Thomas, reticent and modest, whose fair good looks he saw for the first time after an evening's cricket practice on the local ground. To Sassoon, it was a glorious juxtaposition – the gentle game, then this glimpse of a physical ideal and a noble character.

Between April and September he wrote only one poem, begun in the spring and re-written in late summer. 'Absolution' is Brooke-like in its idealism – Rupert Brooke had died of blood-poisoning on 23 April, on his way to fight in the Dardanelles – and euphoric about a war where big decisions are made for you without bewildering, civilian choice, where in 'fighting for our freedom, we are free', as part of 'the happy legion' outside Time:

> *Horror of wounds and anger at the foe,*
> *And loss of things desired, all these must pass.*
> *We are the happy legion, for we know*
> *Time's but a golden wind that shakes the grass.*[13]

Such elation lit up convalescence at Weirleigh, drill at Litherland and the Officers' School of Instruction at Cambridge, where he shared rooms with David Thomas and walked with him through the oddly silent university and, again, played cricket. 'Absolution' has the sense of a drum banged before battle, of a 'scourge' of hopefulness driving him forward.

During the summer of 1915, Siegfried Sassoon was already in love when, at the end of July, he moved from Litherland to Cambridge, to the Officers' School of Instruction. Born in 1897 – some eleven years after Sassoon – David Cuthbert Thomas had been educated at Christ's College, Brecon, and lived at Llanedy in Carmarthenshire where his father was the vicar. Described patronizingly by Robert Graves as 'a simple, gentle fellow and fond of reading',[14] Thomas – an only son with two sisters – was fair-haired, 5 feet 10 inches tall, played robustly in inter-battalion rugby yet also read the *Iliad* in Greek and liked poetry. To judge from 'A Subaltern', Sassoon's poem about him written in March 1916, he had the shyness of emotion that afflicted many public schoolboys, a 'kind, sleepy gaze' and 'fresh face slowly brightening to the grin' when humour cloaked Sassoon's erotic interest or Thomas responded to his friend's 'stale philosophies'. In 'A Subaltern', Thomas seems the epitome of Victorian chivalry, a gentle, cricketing youth who dreams honourably of his girl while enduring the 'hell' of battle.[15]

At Pembroke College, Cambridge, for four weeks, Siegfried Sassoon and David Thomas shared rooms where Paradise, the name of the previous occupant, was written above the door. Less beautiful than Clare, Pembroke had a partly fourteenth-century Old Court, a chapel by Wren and some unexciting Victorian additions. But for Sassoon this was a better Cambridge with Thomas and cricket and introductions from Gosse and Marsh: to Sydney Cockerell, director of the Fitzwilliam Museum, and to Edward Dent, formerly a Fellow of King's College and, from 1926, the university's Professor of Music. He met Cockerell, then aged forty-eight, when asked to dinner by him on 1 August, when he enjoyed an evening steeped in late Pre-Raphaelitism and the rather old-fashioned literary world. Cockerell, before coming to the Fitzwilliam – which he transformed – had worked for William Morris at the Kelmscott Press and for the veteran poet and political idealist Wilfrid Scawen Blunt. Short and stocky, he could be pedantic yet revered artistic achievement and was a loyal friend. He had married a talented artist and bookbinder and their collection, ranging from early manuscripts to Kelmscott masterpieces and illustrated works by Rossetti and Burne-Jones, thrilled Sassoon. That first evening they sat at a dining-room table once owned by Philip Webb, the architect and disciple of Morris, and talked of poetry and books, Cockerell delighted to find this 'very nice fellow'[16] in a Cambridge emptied by war.

In Edward Joseph Dent, his senior by ten years and also a friend of Cockerell's and of Nevill Forbes, Sassoon found a greater challenge. Although a scholar whose field ran from obscure early Italian operas through Purcell, Mozart, Beethoven and Verdi to contemporary music, Dent was not at all the cloistered academic. A cosmopolitan Old Etonian who loved Italy, he came from a family of prosperous Yorkshire gentry and, quite blatant about his homosexuality (openly proclaiming himself 'with great fervour'[17] a disciple of Edward Carpenter), played Scarlatti to young officers at his

Cambridge house, showing them a statue – supposedly of Paganini – whose main feature was a huge erection. In London, where he kept a flat, Dent was seen often with rent boys. Beverley Nichols thought him 'a wicked old man in a withered sort of way'.[18]

Dent detested lazy sentimentality. In 1915 he published a memoir of Rupert Brooke, whom he had known and admired, in which he decried the war sonnets and emphasized Brooke's mocking wit, prompting the poet's furious mother to consider legal action. He and Sassoon met in August. Dent, writing of their first dinner together in his diary, noted that his guest ('whom Cockerell has discovered at Pembroke, training') was 'keen on artistic things, and music. We got on very well.'[19] A week later, Sassoon came again and this time 'opened out a good deal when alone' and Dent 'enjoyed my evening very much – he is a most delightful person'.[20] Sensing an uneasy personality, the musicologist found him, after several meetings, still delightful but 'a curious person. Also hunts a great deal, writes poetry . . .'[21] Sassoon gave Dent 'a little book of privately printed poems – rather in Mrs [Frances] Cornford's manner'.[22] They must have spoken quite intimately because Dent discovered Sassoon's friendship with Nevill Forbes and his admiration for Edward Carpenter, and on 22 August, Sassoon's last day in Cambridge, introduced the young officer to Theo Bartholomew, another homosexual, who worked at the University Library. Slight, spruce, shy behind thick spectacles, Bartholomew, born in 1882, came from a modest background – his father was a cabinet-maker – and saw a lot of Dent but disliked the musicologist's anti-war views, self-absorption and habit of comparing 'everything in this country with something "abroad" to England's immense disadvantage'.[23] Dent and Bartholomew were misogynists, Bartholomew thinking he would 'never get over my inherent dislike of the proximity of women'.[24] Sassoon thought the melancholy librarian, with his quiet humour and knowledge of book design, the more sympathetic of the two.

On 23 August, Sassoon left Cambridge for Litherland. Although Sydney Cockerell noted how hard Sassoon had had to work, the weeks had been an idyllic interlude and at the training camp Bobbie Hanmer sweetened the transition to a more intensely military life. On leave at Llanedy rectory, Thomas, now 'Tommy' – to whom Sassoon had given some of his privately printed pamphlets – wrote, in a hint that the poet may have revealed his homosexual feelings, about 'lovely . . . splendidly lyrical' poems, of how the homoerotic *Hyacinth*'s 'real poetry' moved 'one who has been privileged to know a small part of your mind . . . I even recognise old Sassons himself, as it were, living in the piece, as things are introduced which I know to be your own experiences.'[25] By now Dent too had read the poems, thinking them 'nothing very marvellous, but quite good in their way'. By September, however, he recalled Sassoon as 'the most agreeable thing' of the summer 'with the vitality and artistic enthusiasm of his race and without their bad qualities'.[26]

*

IN MARCH 1915, Norman Donaldson, a Thornycroft cousin, had been killed in action. Now the war struck again at Weirleigh. At its outbreak, Hamo, Siegfried's younger brother, came back from Argentina to be commissioned in the Royal Engineers, unlike the older Michael who stayed in Vancouver. Serene and strong, always 'smiling at himself and at the queer ways of the world', he was a distant ally for Sassoon with an adventurousness envied by the more timid Siegfried, travelling to Mount Athos before leaving for South America.[27] On 17 August 1915, Theresa told Siegfried how she had driven with her third son to the nearby port of Chatham – 'a most miserable Ash' – but did not see his troopship leave for the Dardanelles.[28] There, like Siegfried later in France, Hamo often crawled alone into no-man's land and did 'the most daring things in a cool, quiet and unassuming way'.[29] But on 28 October, at Gallipoli, while putting out wire, he was hit in the leg by a sniper's bullet, not calling for help in case a rescue attempt attracted enemy fire. Carried eventually to a dressing station, where his stoicism impressed the doctor, he seemed out of danger, but the wound turned septic. On

1 November Hamo Sassoon was buried at sea from a hospital ship on the way back to England.

From Litherland, Siegfried wrote, 'My dear dear Ash, I can't write anything. We must just keep our chins up, that's all.' A few days later, he added, 'Now you have got over the worst of it, and you must be a brave Ash and proud of what everyone will say about him. I am lucky to be here where I have to keep on as if nothing was wrong, but I long to be with you . . . You still have got Michael to live for, and he would be absolutely alone in the world without you. Everything I write seems futile. My brain won't work. God bless you, my dearest, for all you have done and all you have endured for us.'[30] The grieving was interrupted when on 17 November Siegfried Sassoon left Folkestone by boat with David Thomas, leaving Bobbie Hanmer behind, to join the regiment and the war in France.

On 25 November he reached the ruined village of Festubert, three miles south of Neuve Chapelle: a second lieutenant now transferred to C Company of the First Battalion of the Royal Welch Fusiliers, within sight and sound of shells and flares, moving among sodden trenches. On the 28th, his diary, begun nine days before, records, 'Walked into Béthune for tea with Robert Graves, a young poet in Third Battalion and very much disliked.'[31]

*

SASSOON ARRIVED AT the Western Front at a time of confusion and disappointment. The recent battle of Loos – a British attempt to storm the German line – had ended in defeat and high casualties; and the generals, faced by deadlocked trench warfare, did not know what to do. The old regular army had suffered great losses since August 1914 and the Territorial soldiers and those who had joined through Secretary for War Lord Kitchener's recruiting campaign were, in the words of a veteran observer, 'raw enthusiasts . . . ideal for a dashing attack, but when they've got to the limit they don't know what to do next'.[32] The French, with their much larger army, had done more of the fighting, principally in the battle of the Marne in September 1914 when the German advance that almost captured Paris had been halted and the long, bloody stalemate on the Western Front began. Throughout 1915, under the uninspired command of Sir John French, a small number of experienced officers in the British Expeditionary Force tried desperately to train new recruits, adapt to trench fighting and break the enemy's line – in a war that greatly favoured the defender – while the Germans occupied swathes of northern France. By the end of 1915 casualties had reached half a million on the British side, admittedly a fraction of the nearly two million French, of whom one million were dead or missing. In the east, at Gallipoli, a seaborne attempt to knock out Turkey, Germany's ally, failed when forces had to be evacuated, the defeat costing Winston Churchill his position as First Sea Lord and – closer to Sassoon's heart – moving Churchill's private secretary, Edward Marsh, to a less influential job in charge of Civil List pensions.

At the start of his diary Sassoon copied out Walter de la Mare's lines about music's mystical power:

> *When Music sounds, all that I was I am*
> *Ere to this haunt of brooding dust I came,*

as well as lines by the Georgian Gordon Bottomley, on regret for 'the things I have not done' and youth's passing.[33] His new friend, the 'very much disliked' broken-nosed young poet, was more vigorous than this. Another of Marsh's protégés, Robert Graves, nine years younger than Sassoon, had already seen battle, writing of his shredded nerves after Loos. A big man, with large head, hands and feet, Graves despised tact; and this, together with his clumsiness and disinclination to wash, made his brother officers think him eccentric or bumptious. Physically strong – at Charterhouse school he had won the middleweight boxing cup, which he kept by his desk until the end of his life – he could be aggressive, though often this hid vulnerability, particularly in his youth.

Graves had grown up mostly at his parents' house in Wimbledon. His father, an inspector of schools and collector of Celtic verse, was the son of an Anglican bishop, and his mother was from the aristocratic German family of von Ranke, Graves's middle name for which he was teased at school (Sassoon and others turned this into von Rubberneck, sometimes von Runicke). The puritanical Mrs Graves wanted her children to be innocent yet successful; from their gentler father they learned to revere literature. Childhood visits to the Rankes' Bavarian estate had shown Graves a Europe different to Weirleigh's gentility – raucous Munich beerhalls, wayside crucifixes bright with painted blood, wall pictures of souls burning in hell, peasants feasting off raw fish – and the beautiful but barren land round the Graveses' country home near Harlech was harsher than the soft weald of Kent. Young Robert had already been to France, Germany, Belgium and Switzerland, whereas Sassoon, before 1915, had never left England. Most important of all, Graves knew the reality of war. There was, however, something that they shared: as Sassoon loved David Thomas, so Graves, at Charterhouse, had adored a boy called Peter Johnstone and had also written to Edward Carpenter about his 'great elation' at Carpenter's writings.[34] Graves was a strange mixture: slightly prudish, a schoolboy pacifist but militant when war began, a poet who – on the advice of Marsh – dropped old-fashioned language for a more colloquial style than Sassoon's, sensitive yet arrogant, humorous but idealistic.

In France that November Graves saw a book of Lionel Johnson's poems, and then met the tall, thin, shy officer to whom it belonged. Both reported the encounter to Marsh, each decrying the poetry of the other, although Sassoon wrote later that he did not show Graves his poems until 'some time afterwards' and 'when I did I was much more modest than I need have been (or than he was!)'.[35] Yet of the months from November 1915 to July 1916, he declared, 'The main thing here is the influence of Robert Graves. This amounted to little more than forcing me from cliché writing, posturing. He taught me to be natural and idiomatic . . .'[36]

The poetry came again, after a barren Litherland, partly because of the stimulus of another poet. 'The Redeemer', Sassoon's first front-line poem, begun in November and finished in March 1916, reflects the working parties at Festubert and the snow, sleet and rain. 'I have never before experienced such cold,' a fellow officer wrote.[37] The Christ-like soldier 'white and strong' with his 'cross' (a 'load of planks') evokes an imagined pre-war life ('good days of work and sport and homely song'), Sassoon's version of Housman's working-class lads' muscular innocence (he had *A Shropshire Lad* with him throughout the war).[38] In the first draft, which was apparently unamended until March 1916, the soldier 'hopes to die / That Brummagen [because so many Royal Welch Fusilier recruits came from Birmingham] be safe beyond the seas'. The poem's Pre-Raphaelite precision of detail ('we lugged our clay-sucked boots', 'a rocket fizzed and burned with blanching flare'), use of short, strong words and concentration on objects rather than cloudy 'iridescence' show that Sassoon had taken Marsh's advice; yet he kept the old romance. The final printed version has:

> *not uncontent to die*
> *That Lancaster on Lune may stand secure,*

– a sign of a darkening reality because Sassoon's soldier servant Molyneaux came from Lancashire. At the close, rather than the grimly realistic last two lines of the final printed version:

> *And someone flung his burden in the muck,*
> *Mumbling: 'O Christ Almighty, now I'm stuck!'*

an early draft reflects a Brooke-like sacrifice:

> *But in my heart I knew that I had seen*
> *The suffering spirit of a world washed clean.*[39]

Officers, according to the public-school ideal, should not only lead but show their soldiers how to die: a debt payable for inherited advantages, an absolution for privilege. Sassoon's 'The Young Men', an unpublished poem of this time, declares:

> *In Hell we seek for Heaven*
> *The agony of our wounds shall make us clean . . .*

This is in the service of:

> England, our June of blossom that shines above
> Disastrous war; for whom we have forsaken
> Days that were rich and gleeful and filled with love.[40]

For Sassoon the idea of blessed civilian life contrasted with 'disastrous war' was not true in reality – hence his easy surrender to the army, almost as if he resembled one of those drifting, passive figures in pictures by Watts or Theresa. The diary, amid descriptions of Picardy ('more like Arcady than anything I saw'),[41] speaks of 'peace unbelievable in this extraordinary existence'; it also contains the austere line, 'I ask that the price be required of me. I must pay my debt. Hamo went. I must follow him.'[42] Out of this came the poem, written at Montagne, called first 'A Man's Faith', then 'To My Brother', not quite a memorial to Hamo – it had an earlier, more impersonal title of 'Brothers' – more a wish for personal purification, to be worthy of the 'laurell'd head'. Death and sacrifice were linked, as in the chapel at Marlborough, to religion, but only in poetry, for Sassoon never prayed during the war. In the unpublished 'A Simpleton', a strong God is a comfort in loneliness and 'triumphs' in wounds and war as well as laughter.[43] 'The Prince of Wounds', originally entitled 'The Prince of Peace', also has Christ on the cross watching over 'the spirit of Destruction'; it ends with an image of unbelief at 'warfare's altar' before 'a God of wood and stone'.[44]

*

In Montagne, eighteen miles from Amiens, Sassoon was billeted in a cottage with a tiled kitchen, an open log fire and an old oak dresser. He found an obstinate black pony to ride, imagining himself out hunting, and Theresa sent torrents of warm underclothes. How much better it was than the 'old inane life of 1913–14'.[45] Christmas night by the log fire held hopes of poetry, of 'flights into the dawn, across the cold hills',[46] in spite of the drunken soldiers outside. Since the middle of December, the British army in France had a new commander, Sir John French having been replaced by Douglas Haig, a neat, optimistic, doggedly inexpressive Scotsman. The war in 1916 must go better, and Sassoon summoned up, almost as if to prove that he had something worth losing, an idealized, idyllic Weirleigh. He knew that he was now doing what most people admired, that to Gosse and his uncle Hamo and Marsh, he must now seem more substantial. Even to Dent (addressed as 'Dear Bolognese' because of the musicologist's love of Italy), who loathed the war and its jingoism, his letters show elation.

By January 1916, he had still seen no fighting, just moving around the Somme valley, watching birds near Montagne, going on a brigade field day and a trip to Amiens, its cathedral full of British troops. Then on 1 February his battalion (nearly a thousand strong) marched ten miles to Morlancourt before taking over front-line trenches formerly held by the French at Bois Français, about three miles east of Albert, facing the ruined German-occupied village of Fricourt. The First Battalion Royal Welch Fusiliers and three other battalions made up the Second Brigade, in the 7th Division. Only one other battalion in the Second Brigade came from the old regular army (the Second Royal Warwicks); the others were composed of those who had joined up during Kitchener's great recruiting drive launched in 1914. The brigade's front line ran for about 500 yards along a bare chalk ridge pitted with mine craters. In some places the German trenches were only forty yards away.

Partly because of his skill with horses, Sassoon had been made temporary transport officer, at first to replace an officer away on leave, then more permanently when the man stayed in England, and he helped the quartermaster, Joe Cottrell, get the rations out, a dangerous journey when the battalion was in the front line. In the back of a notebook, after veterinary notes for use as a transport officer, some lines of poetry reveal him not so ecstatic:

> The silver moment showed him lashed with rain,
> Unhappy in his labour: one whose voice
> Must swell the dying roar of legions slain,
> That in the end, bright victory may rejoice.[47]

Joe Cottrell, the quartermaster of the First Battalion, was in his mid-forties in 1916 and had been with the regiment for twenty-eight years. Awarded the DSO in March for unfailingly getting the rations up to the front, Cottrell came from the slums of Manchester and had been promoted from the ranks. Small, red-faced, fond of warm rum and the brothels of Amiens, an 'arch pessimist' prone to 'red talk', his railing against staff officers provided 'the greatest entertainment the battalion could offer'.[48] Sassoon liked his humour and humanity, having never met anyone quite like this 'old sweat' who questioned authority yet loved the army. The Kiplingesque poem 'The Quarter-Master' of March 1916 shows the affection:

But when the rum is hot his eyes will kindle,
And all that nearest to his heart he'll speak,
Lifting his banner over the tired and humble
Who toil and die with nothing good to seek.[49]

Sassoon learned from Cottrell how the volunteers replacing the old destroyed regular army seemed to the veterans, as another officer wrote, like scarcely trained 'children', their obscene banter often disguising innocence.[50]

Inevitably Sassoon came to know the officers much better than the men. The commander of C Company, Jack Greaves – 'cheerful, chatty, rather silly' but very kind,[51] an acquaintance from pre-war hunting in Kent – became old man Barton in the Sherston memoirs with his pince-nez, his unearned income, his wish to be a cathedral organist and his surrealistically nostalgic remarks such as, 'Do you remember the five-thirty from Paddington? What a dear old train it was.' 'Birdie' Stansfield, his first friend at Litherland; 'little' Orme, the inspiration of the 1917 poem 'To Any Dead Officer'; the Dadd brothers, great athletes, 'splendid fellows',[52] sons of a sporting artist, related to the mad Victorian painter Richard Dadd: the decency of these men contradicted Joe Cottrell's view that the middle classes had not done enough in the war. Sassoon was nicknamed 'Kangar' because of his tall, lolloping likeness to a kangaroo. Many of the First Battalion had, unlike Robert Graves, seen little or no action.

In February their commander, Minshull Ford, was replaced by Major Clifton Inglis Stockwell, described by one of his officers as 'a really great soldier' and by Sassoon as 'aggressive efficiency, very blatant, but knows the job'.[53] The son of a major general and a regular since 1899, Stockwell – who, incongruously, was reputed to be a keen rose-grower – threatened laggards with a revolver, thus earning the nickname 'Buffalo Bill',[54] and declared, 'No Man's Land belongs to *US*. If the Boche dare show his face in it, he's going to be d—d sorry for it.'[55] For his officers, if things went wrong 'there was the devil to pay', otherwise they were left alone; and in action Stockwell's orders were quick and clear, qualities 'worth almost anything'.[56]

*

THIS WAS THE atmosphere Sassoon found in the battalion. Stockwell's strictness, Cottrell's bleak humour, friendships with the Dadds, Greaves and the others, and the secret life of poetry that Robert Graves and he hid from the philistines in the mess. And now the poetry of war was changing. In October 1915 Charles Sorley, a classical scholar at Marlborough who had studied in Germany, died at Loos, and in January the following year a selection of his poems and letters appeared. These showed nature as chillingly indifferent to suffering rather than as a source of inspiration and patriotism, and they revealed sympathy for the enemy, even doubt about who deserved to win the war. On 24 February 1916, Graves wrote to Marsh about Sorley, 'It seems ridiculous to fall in love with a dead man as I have found myself doing.'[57] By July, Sassoon was reading Sorley and must have discussed him earlier with Graves.

At first his 1916 poems do not reflect this change. On New Year's Day Sassoon recalls weeping for England's 'joy of loveliness' and experiences the premonition of 'a sundown spilt with glory'. This poem, 'A Testament' – unpublished during Sassoon's lifetime – has additional lines partly crossed out in his notebook that identify death with welcome sacrifice ('And is there much to lose?'). Then come the tritely pastoral 'January' and the processional 'Druids', perhaps inspired by his new regimental Welshness. In 'The Silver Stem' he has, while riding, premonitions of an 'age-long peace' and in 'Glory' a young figure rides like the Arthurian Sir Galahad.[58] More important for the future was 'To Victory', written on 4 January and owing much to Swinburne in the 'woeful crimson of men slain', where the poet expresses a longing 'for lustre', for the grace of the pre-war Russian ballet ('I would have hours that move like a glitter of dancers'), yet declares defiantly, 'I am not sad':

> *Return to greet me, colours that were my joy,*
> *Not in the woeful crimson of men slain,*
> *But shining as a garden; come with the streaming*
> *Banners of dawn and sundown after rain.*[59]

Sassoon sent this to Gosse who passed the poem on to *The Times*, where it appeared on 15 January, signed 'S.S.', wrongly described as being 'By a Private Soldier at the front'.

Among those who read 'To Victory' was Lady Ottoline Morrell, who traced the author through *The Times* and Gosse. Soon a letter of admiration went out from The Manor House, Garsington. How wonderful, she told Sassoon, to find 'in the dark prison-like days a sympathetic desire – to fly out beyond into the beauty and colour and freedom that one so longs for. It is only thro' Poetry and wild days in the country that one can escape.'[60] She was not the poem's only admirer. Graves, although he mocked it in his autobiography *Goodbye to All That*, told Marsh, 'It was very good I thought. It couldn't have been better if he'd been actually in the trenches . . .'[61]

The war came closer. Graves had left the battalion on 14 January to be an instructor at Base Camp, but on 6 February, still transport officer, Siegfried Sassoon saw the Royal Welch Fusiliers' trenches knocked about by German bombardment. Lewis guns and steel hats reached his unit for the first time; the British were waking up to the new warfare. On 10 February, a cold morning at Morlancourt, by the fire in the quartermaster's billet, with an alcoholic machine-gun officer shivering in blankets on the floor, Sassoon wrote what he called 'the first of my "outspoken" war poems', 'In the Pink'.[62] Davies, a soldier in France briefly happy after rum and tea, writes to his sweetheart ('So Davies wrote: "This leaves me in the pink"'). He yearns for those Sunday walks 'at the farm' instead of probable death after tomorrow night's march to the trenches ('Five miles of stodgy clay and freezing sludge') in leaking boots. The poem, ending with a sense of exploited innocence ('And still the war goes on – *he* don't know why'), is an idealized view of working-class love – 'stiff in the dark' almost certainly has no erotic connotation – with misogynist hints at feminine silliness. But it aims, under Graves's influence, at accurate physical description, and, like 'The Redeemer', contrasts human pre-war country life with dehumanizing war, a theme that occupied Sassoon for years.

> *But he couldn't sleep that night; stiff in the dark*
> *He groaned and thought of Sundays at the farm,*
> *And how he'd go as cheerful as a lark*
> *In his best suit, to wander arm in arm*
> *With brown-eyed Gwen, and whisper in her ear*
> *The simple, silly things she liked to hear.*

The *Westminster Gazette* refused 'In the Pink' because the poem might damage recruiting, and it did not appear until October 1916, in the *Nation*. Meanwhile there was still the gentle homoeroticism of 'Love', also written early in February:

> *I find a clear blue morning in your looks*
> *And youth, who comes and goes, but never dies . . .*

Or the old observation of nature in 'The Rainbow' and 'Pastoral', the latter about a shepherd in winter in the rather bleak company of 'two dogs, a ram, and many a nibbling ewe'.[63] The war could merge with his poetic past, as in 'The Dragon and the Undying' where the dead are absorbed into the natural world as 'dawn-lit trees, with arms up-flung' hailing 'the burning heavens they left unsung'.

On the evening of 22 February, still a spectator of war, Siegfried Sassoon went up with the rations to the front line and the roar of gunfire and shells bursting through the cold, dark sky. He saw a star, thought of Blake's 'fair-haired angel' and came back to bed, to be woken at midnight by Cottrell who told him he was to go on leave in the morning. Through the new friendships, the love for David Thomas – they now went on mock fox-hunts together on horses borrowed from Transport – and Graves's challenge to his poetry loomed rumours of an offensive in the spring or early summer. Yet the frost brought other thoughts as he arrived in Southampton from Le Havre: 'Very poor prospect for getting a hunt.'[64]

*

HE SENT LADY Ottoline Morrell one of his privately printed books of poetry and a photograph of himself, perhaps sensing that her interest in him was not purely literary. Edward Marsh and Dent now wrote to each other possessively about Sassoon. 'I had two very pleasant meetings with him in spite of you,' Marsh declared archly, hoping Dent agreed that the 'gift of melody' in Siegfried's poetry should not be entirely sacrificed in the desirable switch to 'a more direct and simple manner'.[65] At Weirleigh, Theresa tried to hide her anxiety about the rumoured offensive and, intensely patriotic, only wanted to hear good news about the war.

London opened further through another friendship: that with Robert Ross, a connoisseur of literature and art whom Sassoon had met before the war with Edmund Gosse. By 1916 Ross, at forty-seven, had lost most of his hair and often wore a small black silk skullcap indoors which, with his thick moustache, short stature, epigrammatic conversation and round, careworn face gave him an appearance and manner that mixed melancholy and humour. Although from an establishment background – his grandfather had been Prime Minister of Canada and his father the Canadian Attorney General – like Dent, he did not disguise his sexual tastes and, when only seventeen, had seduced Oscar Wilde. In 1893, a sixteen-year-old schoolboy supposedly under Ross's care was taken to bed by Lord Alfred Douglas and Wilde, then led by Douglas to a female prostitute; the boy's father threatened prosecution before realizing that his son might go to jail as well. Hearing of the affair, Ross's relations disowned him and he left the country, returning in 1894, to have his reputation further blackened by the arrest of Wilde in 1895 while they were together in the Cadogan Hotel. Ever loyal, he was at Wilde's death-bed in Paris in 1900.

Helped by friends like the Prime Minister, Asquith, and Asquith's wife Margot, he recovered, to work as a critic, as the London director of the Johannesburg Art Gallery and as art valuer for the Inland Revenue. But a new torment came when Lord Alfred Douglas, having converted to Roman Catholicism, became horrified by his own homosexual past. Aided by Sassoon's early mentor Crosland, Douglas wrote viciously about Ross who unsuccessfully sued him, enduring in the courts a public airing of his promiscuous life. Ross resigned from the Inland Revenue, but in March 1915 a group that included Gosse and the Asquiths presented him with £700 and a public declaration of support and he continued to live at 40 Half Moon Street, under the supervision of the Cockney Nellie Burton, formerly Ross's mother's maid. 'Burton', as she was known, was a huge, forthright woman whom Sassoon came to adore – she called him 'my beloved Saint Siegfried'[66] – and a fierce protector of her 'gentlemen' lodgers (many of whom were homosexuals), not least from other women.

Ross's drawing room on the first floor, decorated in tones of muted gold, mixed the Italian and the oriental with a Roman landscape by Richard Wilson, Chinese prints and faience and, over the fireplace, a dark fifteenth-century 'Cassone front' whose panels inappropriately depicted incidents in a girl's betrothal. A glass-covered bookcase contained poetry and *belles lettres*. The address was handy for the homosexual hunting grounds of Piccadilly and Green Park and guests were usually artistic or literary, often eccentric, sometimes crazy. Alec Ross, Robbie's elder brother, later a stockbroker, was a heterosexual bachelor, blind in one eye since childhood, a small, bow-legged habitué of the Savile Club, soberly dressed, but tolerant of his sibling's promiscuity. William More Adey, with dark eastern looks – a connoisseur of painting, translator of Ibsen and friend of Wilde – had his country house pulled to pieces in search of buried treasure before being certified mad. Roderick Meiklejohn, a bleak Scotsman, a Treasury civil servant and Prime Minister Asquith's secretary, was a homosexual sustained by food, wine, bridge, the classics and obscene poetry. All these were older than Sassoon, Meiklejohn by ten years, Robbie by some seventeen, Alec and More Adey by almost three decades.

Before the war, Ross had been too harassed by persecution to do anything for Sassoon; in 1916, when their friendship truly began, he still felt threatened, if marginally less so – an aesthete out of his time. But Sassoon saw, like many others, one quality: 'his marvellous kindness of heart'.[67] This mixture of charm, good taste, loyalty, quite open (if necessarily discreet) homosexuality and quiet rebelliousness changed Siegfried Sassoon's life. For Ross, again like Dent, detested the war and militarism and those in Britain whom he thought were encouraging it – the old guard who had persecuted Wilde and himself.

*

ON MARCH 5, Sassoon set off again from Southampton for the front. Back as transport officer in the snow-covered fields by Morlancourt, he recalled his leave, the smiling friends, the fire-lit rooms, the London streets at night, hunting in Sussex, a violinist at a concert, 'an austere Apollo in a black coat'.[68] The war had blown much of his old life apart. Norman Loder was in the cavalry in France, Gordon Harbord in the artillery, Richardson also at the front, Hamo dead and Weirleigh tense with anxiety. He rode towards Albert and Méaulte, the road winding towards German territory, 'unexplored and sinister', and read Robert Bridges's anthology *The Spirit of Man* and Shelley. Joe Cottrell was still cursing the parasites in England, the middle classes: 'This war is being carried out by the highest and the lowest in the land...'[69] Robert Graves told Marsh on 15 March, 'I think S.S.'s verses are getting infinitely better than the first crop I saw, much freer and more Georgian. What a terrible pity he didn't start earlier!'

What Graves particularly liked was 'a perfectly ripping'[70] sonnet, 'A Subaltern', which depicts Sassoon's beloved David Thomas as a public-school hero: kind, modest, awkward with emotion, fresh-faced, redolent of cricketing summers, speaking of his 'bloody time' in rat-seething trenches and dreams of 'his girl'. The poem shows the subaltern's physical charms, 'a kind, sleepy gaze' and 'fresh face' ('blonde face' in one draft), an earlier version ending as Sassoon's 'heart rejoiced and crowned him king'. The final version finishes with an English retreat from intimacy:

> *But as he stamped and shivered in the rain,*
> *My stale philosophies had served him well;*
> *Dreaming about his girl had sent his brain*
> *Blanker than ever – she'd no place in Hell . . .*
> *'Good God!' he laughed, and slowly filled his pipe,*
> *Wondering 'why he always talked such tripe'.*[71]

This poem again contrasts a pre-war idyll – and perhaps the type of man Sassoon yearned to be – with the trenches. At the same time came 'Up in the Sky' and 'The Edge of the Sword', about solitude against the noise of distant guns.[72] To Marsh on 16 March Sassoon wrote of wanting action ('this horse work is too slow for me') and his poems in print. 'O Eddie, you *must* get my poems printed soon; it will be such fun to think of them when everything becomes horrid and people begin to be sent away hurt.'[73]

That same day Siegfried Sassoon saw David Thomas in the moonlit trenches, reading a poem from Sassoon's notebook. Two days later, news reached Morlancourt that Thomas had died after being hit in the throat by a stray bullet. To Graves it meant the war's first great personal grief and for Sassoon a larger tragedy, worse because his strongest feelings had had to be contained. Graves believed one of the boy's last acts was to ask a medical orderly to post a letter to a girl in Glamorgan. Now this comrade who had combined the admired attributes of his type with some sensibility crumbled terribly in pity and hopeless physical desire.

The next afternoon Sassoon rode, then walked alone in the

woods above Sailly-Laurette. Here he wrote Thomas's name in chalk on a beech-tree stem and left a rough garland of ivy and a yellow primrose, remembering the dead man's fair hair and kind grey eyes. 'Grief can be beautiful,' he thought, 'when we find something worthy to be mourned.' 'Tommy' and two other officers of the battalion were buried in the moonlight with a flag draped across them. Next to Sassoon stood Robert Graves, 'his white whimsical face twisted and grieving', the clergyman's words blurred briefly by a rattling machine gun. The burst of a canister bomb a few hundred yards way gave the service a cataclysmic end.[74]

At the end of March Sassoon went for six days with C Company in the trenches, having talked his way out of transport duties, and began his trips into no-man's land by night to bomb the enemy's working parties. 'I want to get a good name in the Battalion, for the sake of poetry and poets, whom I represent,' he wrote. But since David Thomas's death, there was another motive: 'hate' and 'the lust to kill'.[75]

From this came 'A Working Party' with the trenches a darker world where men lose their identities, a world precisely described in physical details like 'sodden bags of chalk', 'the drum and rattle of feet', 'ankle-deep' sludge, a flare's sudden whiteness, the 'split and crack' of rifle shots, the wind and 'calm' descent of shells before explosion. 'A decent chap' from the midlands who laughed at others' jokes 'because he hadn't any of his own' stumbles through this, a victim not only of war but of his 'meagre' wife, two children and small expectations. He thinks of his dug-out, tot of rum and sleep; then, pushing a bag up into its place, sees 'No-Man's Land and wire' before a bullet ends 'his startled life'.[76] The unpublished 'Memory' of the same date is about Tommy, whose blood is no longer that of Swinburne's poetic agony or beautiful sacrifice but that of true, wasteful death.

> *I thought of him, and knew that he was dead;*
> *I thought of his dark hour, and laughter killed;*
> *And the shroud hiding his dear, happy head;*

And blood that heedless enemies have spilled,
His blood.[77]

Sassoon's short poem 'Blind', perhaps pre-war in origin, appeared at this time in the *Westminster Gazette* – an image of pitiable loss but with no mention of the trenches.[78] Such pity was now mixed with rage; 'since they shot Tommy I would gladly stick a bayonet into a German by daylight'. The poem 'Peace' (2 April) has a lyrical longing for the tranquillity of death sharpened by images of 'bleeding bodies' and 'bitter lust' for revenge.[79] Around this time also he wrote the unpublished 'To a Citizen Soldier' – reflecting the introduction of conscription in January 1916 – and sent it to Dent. In spite of tragedy, the war – 'Crowds of luckless bodies' and 'writhings on the rack' – still seems nobler than the 'citizen soldier's' imagined home of 'frowsty parlours of familiar bliss', a pointless life with little to do except:

> *To boast and wrangle, loaf and sleep and kiss*
> *And grow ignobly sterile, gorged and slack.*[80]

The misogynistic, scornful Dent must have approved.

The war had pushed the apparent irreconcilables of peacetime – his frustrated literary ambitions, doubts about 'manliness' and a divided life – into the shadows. All that mattered now was courage and the ability to lead and to sustain comradeship. He found he had these, and a new Sassoon appeared, who told Marsh, 'I did get among them in a crater with six bombs and a revolver and I don't think they liked it a bit'[81] – combined with the poet of angry compassion. He found release in his nocturnal patrols, and Corporal O'Brien, an Irishman with a 'rather ape-like face and mat of dark hair over his forehead',[82] a survivor of Neuve Chapelle, Festubert and Loos who had been with the battalion since November 1914, was one of those who accompanied him. On 11 April 1916, after chasing Germans away from the British trenches, Sassoon and three men – one of whom was O'Brien – brought back the boots of a French corpse, one with half a leg attached. 'O yes, this is some life,' he told Marsh. 'The men almost make me weep sometimes, so patient and cheery and altogether dear. And chasing Germans in the moonshine with bombs is no mean sport.'[83]

He dreamed of an English spring, thought of a tragic Theresa when she opened the telegram at Weirleigh announcing his death. But, as the poem 'Battle', written on 12 April, declared, 'Here life is good, poised on the edge of doom.'[84] 'Home' must be about Theresa alone in an English garden; from the house, the piano sounds 'one smouldering chord' and his spirit moves invisibly across the lawn, causing her to sigh 'and wonder if my music's dead'.[85] The trenches, where he stood knee-deep in rainwater on Easter Saturday, remembering a fine Good Friday dawn, still had images of his country childhood: larks, nightingales, the sounds and feel of the rural landscape. In the epigrammatic 'Stand-to: Good Friday Morning' a soldier on duty, as Sassoon had been, from two to four in the morning hears singing larks; then, splashing up 'to our bogged front line', thinks,

> O Jesus, send me a wound to-day,
> And I'll believe in Your bread and wine,
> And get my bloody old sins washed white![86]

The poem is realistic, yet also a comment on how the religion taught in his childhood seems inadequate in an earth-bound war. It is an attack too on those who claimed that God was on the British side.

*

ON 23 APRIL Siegfried Sassoon went for a month out of the line for a course at Flixécourt, the Fourth Army School. Leaving the trenches in bad weather, he travelled by bus through the sunny spring landscape, past Amiens, glad to be alone; loss of privacy was another offspring of war. Then he experienced the delight of waking up in a clean, small room with shuttered windows looking out on an angled street of a 'pleasant little town' in wooded country alive with nightingales.[87] Not far away were flax mills and three vast, hideous châteaux.

The hundred or so officers at the school seemed friendly, half of them from the cavalry, who were not as experienced in trench warfare as their infantry equivalents. After the day's instruction, he walked alone through the country, then sat in his room with his *Concise Oxford Dictionary* to write. On 25 April a lecture, 'The Spirit of the Bayonet', and a walk afterwards to an already cherished place – a half-built house in a wood – brought on a poem. Phrases from the lecturer, a choleric Highland Scot called Major Campbell, who had used a fierce-faced sergeant as a demonstrator, came back to him. 'Quickness', 'the slowest man gets killed', 'the bullet and the bayonet are brother and sister', a story of a brave man 'sitting on Hun's chest and biting his nose', 'places to go for: small of the back, kidneys, go in as easy as butter' – certainly 'not up the backside and pull the trigger'. To 'hit a bone' was 'no good. Don't waste steel: 3 inches sticking out the other side is good fury wasted.' More places to go for: 'between eyes, throat, abdomen, below equipment. If he coughs, he's done – go on to the next. Importance of quick withdrawal. Don't waste time stabbing.' Campbell won the DSO for lecturing. The German deserves anything ('only one sort of good German – a dead one') as he comes 'at you licking his lips' if you drop your bayonet. The class was told to deflect the enemy's bayonet ('don't grab it') with the right hand, seize his rifle butt with the left and 'try the quick twist over or a trip'; Campbell illustrated this with 'story of man with fork'.[88]

Sassoon must have seen the sexual imagery, although he later claimed the poem inspired by the lecture was a mere exercise in the use of short Anglo-Saxon words. He certainly admitted to feeling bloodthirsty after Campbell's talk, as well as being shocked by the Scotsman's crudeness. In 'The Kiss', critics have seen sadism, masochism, hatred of women and tortured sexuality. The brutality does slide into equally chilling but picturesque destruction as the male bullet 'spins and turns and loves the air' before splitting a skull 'to win my praise'; the female bayonet like ice, 'naked, cold and fair'; then the unforgettable last verse:

Sweet Sister, grant your soldier this:
That in good fury he may feel
The body where he sets his heel
Quail from your downward darting kiss.[89]

After Freud – of whom Sassoon knew nothing in 1916 – this seems to be the poet codifying his own violent feelings. But the poem has predecessors, also bloodthirsty but in loftier language, some of which he must have read: Bret Harte's 'What the Bullet Sang' (in the *Oxford Book of English Verse*), Henley's 'Song of the Sword', where weapons – Harte's exultant bullet and Henley's virile sword – kill and caress their victims. As in so much of Sassoon's war, there is an ambiguity in 'The Kiss'. In strange contrast is the pre-war style of 'Children' of 28 April where 'strong' soldiers pass children in a village and are reminded of childhood innocence ('when elves were dancing, rayed among the leaves')[90] after battle.

Flixécourt was a break: more than thirty miles from the front line, he had his soldier servant Molyneaux to look after him, a routine of parades, lectures on gas and tactics and good spring weather, and letters from Cottrell about the battalion, though rumours of a major offensive were still circulating. The place made him think of Marlborough, and another reminder was Marcus Goodall, a birdwatching Old Marlburian ten years younger than Sassoon – good-looking, gentle, a classicist who had hoped to go to Cambridge and, like Charles Sorley, study in Germany. Goodall sometimes had a look of distant melancholy, perhaps (Sassoon thought romantically) from a premonition of death. At Flixécourt, the agony of David Thomas seemed to slip away, to become material for poetry. 'These last six months have been miles the best I have ever struck,' Siegfried Sassoon told his uncle Hamo Thornycroft on 18 May. 'In fact I find it very hard to take it all in; there is so much, and it is mostly beautiful or terrifying, or both. And the excitement of things bursting is positively splendid: I had no idea I should enjoy it so much.'[91]

This would have shocked C. K. Ogden, the editor of the daringly anti-militarist *Cambridge Magazine* – it carried articles from the German papers – to whom Dent had sent Sassoon's poems. On 29 April Ogden published 'The Redeemer', followed by 'The Kiss' on 27 May, and that month also brought out, in a production arranged by Theo Bartholomew, 'The Redeemer' as a single reprint (price twopence). But, as often with Sassoon, anger and energy were joined by nostalgia, a yearning for country life that turned him towards one of his greatest idols: Thomas Hardy. 'Books about England were all I wanted,' he wrote later of his time at Flixécourt. Among these were Surtees's celebration of fox-hunting in *Mr Sponge's Sporting Tour*, the *Essays* of Charles Lamb and Hardy's *Far from the Madding Crowd* and *The Dynasts* ('what enormous minds these men have got').[92] He also had Gosse's essays on French themes, *Inter Arma*, but spring brought 'dreams of English woodlands and orchards'.[93] In his room, reflecting this mixture, he wrote 'France', a tribute to 'radiant' landscapes for which it was 'fortunate' to fight, as well as 'A Poplar and the Moon' and 'The Wind in the Beechwood', neither of which has any hint of battle.

More personal is 'The Last Meeting', written at Flixécourt perhaps before 'France'. The longest of Sassoon's war poems, it has the poet searching for David Thomas through a darkening small town (Flixécourt) and then in a big empty house above it. Here in a de la Mare setting of owls and shadows he whispers Tommy's name, but not until the poet is in a wood, apparently at dawn, does the dead man speak – as in Owen's 'Strange Meeting' two years later – of a pantheistic union of the human soul, nature, power and beauty. Tommy seems inviolate in ideal memory, and homoerotically recalled 'with lifted arms and body tall and strong', though an earlier version is even more daring, with the poet feeling the victim's face and memories of lips touching in Paradise, the rooms they had shared at Cambridge.[94] The much terser 'A Letter Home' of the same time, addressed to Robert Graves, evokes their laughter together – the Celtic Graves wilder than Sassoon – and their scorn for the war. It is another glimpse of purifying memory:

Back to hell with Kaiser send it,
Gag the noise, pack up and go,
Clockwork soldiers in a row.
I've got better things to do
Than to waste my time on you.

Tommy is recalled ('like the prince in fairy story') with nature's revelation of him ('blossoms bring him home with May'). The happiness of the Flixécourt interlude imbues this record of a friendship made permanent in poetry.

War's a joke for me and you
While we know such dreams are true![95]

On the cloudless last day at Flixécourt, about a hundred British and French generals, led by the red-faced Sir Henry Rawlinson, commander of the Fourth Army, watched bayonet work, wiring and other techniques before a march-past. The occasion resembled a school prize-giving, except for the show explosion of two enormous mines before the top brass left for lunch in a nearby château. Then Sassoon went by bus with Marcus Goodall through sunlit open country to Abbeville, which seemed like an English market town or Oxford, although its river was the Somme, and he thought of Debussy's *Cloches à travers les feuilles*. They dined at the Tête Boeuf among 'utterly commonplace and self-satisfied, or else tired-looking'[96] officers. It was an evening like those he had shared with Tommy in Cambridge. Back at Flixécourt, after they had said goodnight, Sassoon felt surprised at his power, his apparently easy dominance, in such a friendship.

*

AT MORLANCOURT, IN a communication trench on the way back to the battalion, he entered a dusk of voices disembodied except for that of a Northumberland Fusilier 'who drops aitches'.[97] Throughout his war diaries little grenades of Edwardian snobbery explode with invidious frequency, sometimes loaded with the nasty kick of anti-Semitism: 'low class Welsh officers', 'Jew profiteers', jibes at 'suburban manners' or those who lick their fingers when playing cards. With this went, as in the poem of 23 May, a world of 'muffled crying' and the ultimate peace of death which 'cannot fail to bring good rest'. Such thoughts point to what Sassoon called his Enoch Arden complex: a wish invisibly to watch others, preferably those to whom he was close, and the consequent narcissistic self-consciousness. Getting the idea from Tennyson's poem about a sailor thought to be dead who returns, unknown, to observe his wife's happiness with another man, he seems to transmute this into a vision of death – or reputed death – as the ultimate refuge, the place of freedom and power. One feels sometimes also, with the fastidious Sassoon, that it is somewhere that his social sensibilities can no longer be offended.

The battalion was out of the line. Sassoon's old comrades in the officers' mess – Stansfield, Julian Dadd, Orme – spoke of a raid, already in the air before Flixécourt. Greaves, their easygoing company commander, had promised that the Kangaroo might lead this because of his enthusiasm for exploring no-man's land. They joked that Greaves hoped to get a DSO for his part in its planning, and Sassoon thought how a Military Cross could show his own courage to the world. A raid was a rare chance for individual initiative on the deadlocked front where mass attacks swallowed up personality – a boy's fantasy of adventure from before the machine age. But Stockwell (Cottrell told Sassoon) did not approve of the raid and put Stansfield in charge of it. Perhaps he wanted to curb Sassoon's increasing assumption of nocturnal freedom, or was reluctant to risk losing someone whom he described later as one of his bravest officers. Cottrell said it was always the best men who volunteered for a raid. Sassoon thought Stansfield too large and inexperienced at night patrols to crawl unnoticed through shell holes and considered setting out on his own. He wrote a farewell letter to Theresa, giving it to Julian Dadd on a rainy night to post; she still thought he was transport officer, away from the front line. The letter was in the 'happy warrior' style, fuller of his own fine feelings than sympathy for hers, partly because he hated imagining her anxiety.

The raiding party – twenty-seven men with blackened faces, festooned with bombs, hatchets and knobkerries – assembled in a dug-out in the reserve line. Greaves gave each one a nip of whisky, before, with Siegfried Sassoon as an escort, they set off to battalion HQ where, confronted by Stockwell, Sassoon asked if he could go out as well. 'Certainly not,' the colonel snapped. 'Your job is to stop in our trench and count the men as they come back.'[98]

Four parties, each of five men, were to enter the German trench at two points. The aim, absurd against the strong, wire-protected enemy positions, was to throw bombs, size up the opposition and take prisoners. An evacuation party of seven men with ladders and a red flash lamp would follow the attackers. The German wire was only sixty yards across no-man's land, the way interrupted by two large mine craters that had become browny-grey pools of shallow water after some late spring rain.

At midnight Sassoon waited in the wet, after the raiders had left. He heard a sentry say, 'They'll never keep that —— inside the trench' and felt proud. There were few sounds – the hiss of a flare showing rain against the dark, droning shells – before he crawled out with the evacuating party, disobeying Stockwell. Some whizz-bangs arched over near to them, and suddenly silence enveloped the German side. He knew the raiders must have been held up by stronger than expected wire. A message came back to him, from O'Brien through the evacuating party: they can't get through the wire, the raid has failed, they will throw their bombs and return.

The enemy rifle shots began, followed by exploding bombs thrown by both sides – the noises of trench, as opposed to artillery, warfare. The raiders ran back. Sassoon counted sixteen in and went out, finding Stansfield wounded and two men helping him. 'Mick O'Brien is somewhere down the crater badly wounded,' someone said. Sassoon crawled out again, so near to the Germans that he heard the clicks of their rifle bolts as they reloaded. He came under

fire ('the bloody sods are firing down at me at point-blank range . . .
I really wondered whether my number was up'), then found O'Brien
moaning, badly hit in an arm and a leg at the bottom of a crater,
twenty-five feet deep, with another less seriously wounded man. He
went back to the British trench where a lance corporal with a foot
almost blown off was thanking God for a wound that would send
him home. Sassoon collected a rope and, helped by two men, slowly
hauled O'Brien up and, as the sky lightened after one o'clock, the
Germans, who must have seen what was happening, stopped firing.
The courage needed – steady and patient – was the opposite of that
later apparently given to Sassoon during the war but which Julian
Dadd said he had never heared used.

The rescued man's limp body, with pain-torn face and matted
hair, came heavily up the side of the crater, the wet earth crumbling
beneath his rescuers' feet. Two raiders had been killed and ten
wounded, and O'Brien was dead when they got him back to the
British lines. Not far away to the left, thirty tunnellers were gassed
or buried in an explosion set off by the Germans. Reporting to
Stockwell on this grim night, Sassoon, for the first time, sensed
vulnerability in that exhausted figure in an absurd woollen cap with
a tuft on top. This, and his own proved courage, made him feel
elated, in spite of O'Brien's death, when the 'Colonel spoke to me
kindly in his rough way'.[99] The larks sang as he returned through
the drizzling rain. There had been no terror, more a delight in
danger. And he still had not seen the enemy face to face.

On 30 May Sassoon told Marsh of 'a dead secret; my name has
gone in for a Military Cross. Probably shan't get it, so don't tell
Robert, or it may get round the Depot that I told someone . . .'[100]
He resumed his night-time patrols and just escaped a German bomb
while collecting the debris of the raid, three axes and a knobkerry.
'Still my luck seems to hold.' Stansfield was out of danger. Two new
officers joined C Company, 'neither of them at all interesting'.[101]
In the first week of June, Sassoon was given the job of sniping
observing officer ('knowing nothing about sniping or map making').
Orme and a newcomer Morris were hit in a night of explosions, and

he felt a loss of courage. Kitchener had drowned on the way to Russia. On 7 June Sassoon wrote, 'Why shouldn't he die? We're all dying,' partly from a loss of poetry, beauty and music.[102]

His leave might break this mood. On the way home on 9 June he saw the crowd at Amiens station – some Frenchwomen in mourning, girls collecting for the Red Cross, elderly French officers with monocles, neat figures from the British Staff, some priests. In his carriage were four other officers, 'the last word in nonentitude and flatness and commonness',[103] low compared to the men he had commanded. At Rouen the evening filled with the sound of bells; then the boat and arrival exhausted at Southampton before London and a summer evening in Holland Park, with the Donaldsons and the Thornycrofts at their house in Melbury Road, and the sound of a piano from across the street.

FIVE

'I am sure I shall get blown to shreds'

SIEGFRIED SASSOON'S LEAVE that summer of 1916 was overshadowed by rumours of the coming battle, supposedly the last before
victory. At Verdun, the French army held out against a German
onslaught; now, on the Somme, Haig, under pressure from the
British War Cabinet and the French High Command, was to mount
the first great British offensive of the war. There was anxiety for
individual lives, yet also a quiet self-confidence.

In London, Sassoon's literary friends were welcoming: Marsh
and Gosse proud of their protégé, now a brave young officer; Dent
more circumspect, mocking 'Eddie's' infatuations yet interested in
Sassoon and this 'splendid creature's'[1] growing devotion to Robbie
Ross. At Weirleigh, pride in his having been recommended for a
Military Cross mixed oppressively with Theresa's anxiety, for she
knew that he was no longer in comparative safety as a transport
officer. On Sassoon's last evening at home, the cook made two of
his favourite puddings and his mother and he played cribbage, as
they had during his schooldays, watched by the Persian cat and a
caged parrot brought in from the kitchen. Knowing how agonizing

it would be for them both, Theresa did not come up to London to see him off to France.

*

ON 19 JUNE Sassoon reached Le Havre, to be told to get the train to Corbie and then walk to Bussy, a village on a tributary of the River Ancre. Here he found the First Battalion and his own C Company, the men bathing under some poplars, Greaves fussing, anxious that they should have their sports day the next day, before the battle. Stockwell was confident, encouraged by the French success in holding the Germans at Verdun. On 26 June the battalion went up to Morlancourt again, to prepare for the front line. The night before, Molyneaux, his soldier servant, slightly drunk, had said that the company only felt confident if Sassoon was with them and that he loved his officer 'like a brother'.[2] Sassoon hoped he might now get to know the men better, but the silence imposed by rank and discipline returned, making him wonder if any officer's understanding of them could go further than sentimental compassion. At Morlancourt, in a room with pictures of the Eiffel Tower and a cheerful Jesus preaching from a boat, he fell asleep to the sound of rain. The poem of 25 June, 'Before the Battle', mixes scorn of fear with the hope of comfort from nature's deathless mystery: 'O river of stars and shadows, lead me through the night.'[3]

Corps Intelligence spoke of a British artillery triumph, but then the troops heard the attack had been postponed. Sassoon had his usual feelings about some of the other officers, with their 'commonplace talk, girls and silly second rate vulgarity, eating and drinking' – but behind these lurked an immense unifying terror.[4] The battalion went into the front line to relieve the Border Regiment, C Company and Sassoon taking up muddy positions opposite the cemetery by the station of the ruined Fricourt. He had *Tess of the D'Urbervilles* and thought of the Sussex landscape round Ringmer as the bombardment intensified.

Stockwell wanted the British wire to be more thoroughly cut, to allow the troops through when the assault began. Sassoon went out at night with his new wire-cutters, to be driven in once by German shelling. He watched the men: the jaunty Lance Corporal Gibson at dawn, good brow and eyes, the rest of his face weak beneath the cheery attempt at fearlessness, the fussy Greaves urging them to get back before the snipers started. The next morning, in daylight, as his company was leaving the line, Sassoon and Jordan, one of his soldiers, went out unnoticed for an hour to finish the wire-cutting, excited, oddly without fear.[5] Then the Manchester Regiment replaced them and he heard that his Military Cross had been confirmed. With this came an omen of chaos. From outside his dug-out in the lines of support Sassoon heard the clamour of troops obviously uncertain of where they should be. The next day these attacked at the wrong time, to be hit by their own artillery support.

After a morning mist, 1 July was bright and clear. A final bombardment preceded the great assault, in which the lines of attacking troops were meant to walk virtually unopposed into the smashed German trenches. In reserve, safe in a dug-out, Greaves thought cosily of 'carpet slippers and kettle-holders' while Sassoon could not rid his mind of an advertisement, often seen at railway stations:

> They come as a boon and a blessing to men,
> The Something, the owl, and the Waverley Pen.[6]

C Company was in support as a carrying company, allowing Greaves and Sassoon to watch the first day of the Somme from what Greaves called 'our opera box' on Crawley Ridge about 500 yards behind the British trenches. Eating oranges, Sassoon saw a lark, heard the cry of birds as the explosions died out and imagined 'a sunlit picture of hell'. The Manchesters walked out of their trench, and news came through in the evening that Montauban and Mametz had been taken. The night was quiet,[7] and the next day, still in reserve, Sassoon heard from the excited adjutant that Fricourt had fallen. 'Everywhere the news seems good,' he noted, adding, 'Next thing is to hang on to the country we've taken' – a difficult task as the Second Battalion the Queen's Regiment was 'said to have legged it as usual when the Bosche made a poorish counter-attack'.[8]

*

WITH THE FRENCH still overwhelmingly engaged at Verdun on their eastern frontier, the Somme was a British battle, planned by the commander-in-chief Sir Douglas Haig and Henry Rawlinson, commander of the Fourth Army. A colossal artillery barrage was to precede an offensive of massive dimensions, leading – it was hoped – to a breakthrough exploited by cavalry following the infantry. Haig had wanted the battle to be delayed at least until August, fearing that his untested volunteer troops were not ready, but he had been overruled by the War Cabinet under pressure from the embattled French.

Haig ordered a front of twenty miles, although Rawlinson had advised more limited attacks. Sir Douglas, present at all the battles of 1915, failed to realize that only exceptionally concentrated artillery fire could destroy the strong German defences. Even his 400 heavy and 1,000 light guns and vast stockpile of shells were not enough on a front this long, especially as almost a third of the shells turned out to be duds. So the German batteries stayed comparatively unaffected, with well-dug-in machine guns ready for the waves of infantry who came across no-man's land on 1 July. The British made another mistake. Fearing that quick, concerted movement was beyond the only briefly trained troops, Haig sent them forward slowly in flat, open country, showing that another lesson unlearned was the need for speed and the use of cover in attacks on the Western Front. In the southern sector, the French, helped by their more concentrated artillery, had more success, but were held back by the slow British progress in the north and centre, Sassoon's part of the line. That first day was, inevitably, a disaster.

The First Battalion of the Royal Welch Fusiliers stayed in reserve to the attacking Twentieth Battalion of the Manchester Regiment, mostly volunteers or 'Pals', many from the same street or district. Sassoon's view inevitably hid truth behind confusion. First the Tenth

West Yorkshires went across no-man's land, entering the German trenches from where he could hear their cheers. But a German machine-gun post at a strongpoint known as Wing Corner wrecked the celebrations, practically wiping out the battalion. A company of the Green Howards, although ordered to attack at 2.30 in the afternoon, went out earlier at 7.45 a.m. to try to silence the machine gun, only to be mown down. At 2.30 p.m. the Seventh Battalion the East Yorkshires attacked over the same ground, again suffering heavy casualties, British artillery now not firing on the machine-gun post for fear of hitting the attackers, many of whom sheltered in no-man's land. In three minutes, the East Yorkshires suffered 123 casualties. The German machine-gun post was still lethal, as the Twentieth Manchesters discovered when they went over the top at the same time, losing their commanding officer. At 5 p.m. the First Royal Welch came out of reserve to help the Manchesters, with Sassoon still kept back, although his friend Julian Dadd was in action. Bombing their way across craters and down trenches they took Wing Corner, knocking out the machine gun. The next morning, 2 July, Sassoon reported that the British were 'everywhere' in Fricourt, although the Yorkshires appeared 'to have made a mess' of clearing the village. His battalion had suffered less than many others: four men killed and thirty-five wounded. Sassoon could not know that Stockwell, by ordering his bombers up into Fricourt, had grabbed success by going against orders.

Further orders came to move up towards the next objective, Mametz Wood, which lay just beyond the town of Mametz, and Sassoon dozed in the sunshine. That afternoon, Kelsey Fry, the battalion doctor, unstitched his own MC ribbon and sewed it on to Sassoon's tunic. The Twenty-Second Brigade, of which the First Royal Welch was a part, assembled at a concentration point between Mametz and Carnoy, apparently cheerful. As yet Sassoon's own battalion had had no officers killed, not least because most of C Company, including Molyneaux, had been given safer duties like carrying. The rumour was that the battalion, including Sassoon, would attack Mametz Wood the next day. A and B Companies had

had no sleep for two nights. Stockwell shouted at the soldiers to lie down while they could. Voices murmured, the sound of mouth-organs mixed with the guns, and Sassoon's poem of 3 July – 'At Carnoy' – has a sense of comradeship at twilight, a flaring sunset, tufts of thistles in a hollow, harmony of sorts, then a grim end:

> *Tomorrow we must go*
> *To take some cursèd Wood . . . O world God made!*[9]

On 3 July Sassoon marched up to the front line with the battalion, through Mametz to a trench opposite Mametz Wood, passing the 'terrible undignified' British and German dead. The mauling of the Royal Irish and A Company of the Royal Welch showed that the Germans were still in the wood. A mass of oak and birch trees and dense undergrowth a mile long and three-quarters of a mile wide, vulnerable to enemy machine-gun fire on its exposed high places, it would be very difficult to take. Artillery shrapnel forced the battalion to march back to its camping ground: 'great fun these last two days', Sassoon noted ironically.[10] The next day, in mud and rain, they went up to Mametz again, to a position opposite the wood. Sassoon and C Company sat in reserve; at 2.30 a.m. he and his bombers were sent for, then ordered back. He went to try to find out what was happening. A and B Companies had attacked and occupied the half-finished Quadrangle Trench against little German resistance. Several men had been killed by enemy sniping.

This was Sassoon's first big battle. He saw officers panic (he threatened one with his revolver) and men whom he knew well were shot in front of him. In an act of solitary courage – and in daylight – he charged a German trench, throwing bombs, scattering its fifty or sixty retreating occupants and shouting the hunting cry of 'View Halloa!' Alone, he sat on the fire step, looking at the packs left by the enemy, for the Germans had fled, pushed out also by a Lewis gun fired from the British lines. Sassoon realized slowly that there was nothing else he could do on his own because the Germans would return and overwhelm him. Graves, some twelve years later, called the charge 'a pointless feat'.[11] From the British trenches a party could not be sent across to hold what Sassoon had taken as the enemy was now alert and using a machine gun. Ignoring a written order from Greaves, he stayed in the Quadrangle Trench, the most advanced position held by the XV Corps of which his battalion was a part, noting, 'I definitely wanted to kill someone at close quarters.'[12] Overcoming the individual tragedies of his comrades' deaths, a thrill seized him: addictive, heroically solitary, without introspection or regret.

Sassoon went later that day to report, finding a furious Stockwell. Why hadn't he obeyed an original order and come back with his bombers? Why hadn't he reported the capture of the trench so that it could be consolidated? The corps artillery bombardment had stopped for three hours because Stockwell could not say that Sassoon's 'patrol' was back. Having expected praise, Sassoon's spirits collapsed even further that evening on the arrival of the relief: an RWF battalion of the New – or recently recruited – Army that was obviously only half trained. He and the First Battalion, now down to fewer than 400 men, withdrew to camp at Heilly, on swampy ground by the River Ancre, which rain soon turned into a place of mud and discomfort. At an officers' conference, a calmer Stockwell joked of keeping him out of 'the next show' as a punishment[13] and there seemed a chance Sassoon might get another medal, but the failure to consolidate the captured trench put paid to this. The battalion had gained its objectives with 130 men and 2 officers as casualties, of whom 14 were dead. The Manchesters had lost 16 officers and the Royal Irish 250 men and several officers. When Rawlinson, the Fourth Army commander, visited them, his congratulations carried a sense of temporary good fortune.

*

On 7 July, as an interlude, Sassoon went with Greaves, Cottrell, Julian Dadd and another officer called Reeves into Amiens, partly by riding and partly getting a lift in another quartermaster's car, and ate a large lunch. When Cottrell said that he wanted a woman, Sassoon suggested they might look at the cathedral instead. He rode over to Corbie to call on Norman Loder, who now had a comfortable staff job as an assistant provost marshal at a corps HQ, different from the pre-war years when Loder had been his mentor in physical daring. Then on 10 July the battalion marched up the line again, passing Sir Douglas Haig in his car between Méricourt and Treux. As if carrying out his threat, Stockwell kept him, Julian Dadd and six other officers in reserve in the transport lines near Méaulte where Sassoon read Hardy – *Tess of the D'Urbervilles* and *The Return of the Native* – suitable for the damp landscape and his nostalgia for rural England.

Robert Graves, who had returned to France in the last week of June after an operation on his nasal passages, was near by with the Second Battalion and they talked of the war and what they might do after it. Sassoon heard that his comrades had reached their objective with Greaves slightly wounded and two men he knew well killed. Still he was kept in the rear while they attacked in Mametz Wood, which was not taken until 12 July after fierce hand-to-hand fighting. Graves had made him think of life 'aprés la guerre': poetry, travel, adventure, his dead father's world, not 'the old groove' of cricket, hunting and Weirleigh; honesty too about love and the absurdity of his unofficial engagement to Dorothy Hanmer. How could she know that his feeling for her brother Bobbie had led to the 'mistake'? He longed for a room full of books, for music and for time to write poetry, but 'the men love me, that's the one great consolation'. Meanwhile the other officers were puffing their pipes and talking rubbish.[14] Graves, in a verse letter, had imagined their post-war world, first in Harlech, then in 'the great greasy Caucasus' and Baghdad (and 'the Sashuns' ancestral vault') and Tibet, mentioning his love from his schooldays at Charterhouse, Peter Johnstone, and David Thomas:

> *(This Peter still may win a part*
> *Of David's corner in your heart*
> *I hope so). And one day we three*
> *Shall sail together on the sea*

For adventure and quest and fight –
And God! What poetry we'll write.[15]

Two days later news came that Graves had died of wounds after an attack on High Wood. 'Won't they leave us anyone we are fond of?' Sassoon asked Marsh.[16] 'So I go my way alone again.'[17]

*

THE BATTALION RETIRED to La Chaussée where he fell ill in his billet with dysentery and a fever; and was taken to the New Zealand Hospital in Amiens. In the hospital ward, he lay listening to a dying young officer: 'all the horror of the Somme attacks was in that raving: all the darkness and the dreadful daylight'.[18] From this came the poem 'Died of Wounds' which starts laconically before breaking into the wrenching direct speech of the middle stanza which, Graves wrote later, 'knocks me more every time'.[19] The officer's public-school tone shows the shattering of a once-protected life, and a hint of the ideal friend in 'Dickie':

> *The ward grew dark; but he was still complaining*
> *And calling out for 'Dickie'. 'Curse the Wood!*
> *It's time to go. O Christ, and what's the good?*
> *We'll never take it, and it's always raining.'*[20]

At the last cry – 'They snipe like hell! O Dickie, don't go out' – the poet, calm again, falls asleep; and by next morning the man has died, replaced by 'some Slight Wound . . . smiling on the bed'. 'A Night Attack', unpublished until 1970, shows German corpses, particularly 'a Prussian with a decent face' who no doubt 'loathed the war'. Here Sassoon is, for the first time, pacifist in tone; both sides kill and are killed under orders during this machine-age war that leaves the decent 'young, fresh and pleasant' soldier's 'sturdy legs' bent beneath his body. In another manuscript version dated 6 July, the Prussian has a 'blond head' and a pre-war life of walking in parks, listening to bands, 'wondering if all women are such fools'. Sassoon lifts him up and, as in a passage in his autobiographical novel *Memoirs of an Infantry Officer*, wipes mud from his face, returning later to find the corpse disfigured after a British boot had trodden 'his skull deep into the grey ooze'.[21] But, two days later, a poem called 'The Crown' showed he wanted only to be at the front, not in safety away from the war.[22]

At Amiens, he heard that Marcus Goodall, his companion at Flixécourt, had died of wounds. The 'Elegy for Marcus Goodall' mixes pastoral charm with the reality of Goodall's body tipped 'into a shallow pit' before a bursting shell brings thoughts of resurrection and a 'dear, red-faced father God' who seems more like a hunting squire than a deity. Lines from this – and from a version called 'The Traveller – to M.H.G.'[23] – are in 'To His Dead Body', his tribute to Robert Graves, written with Sassoon now perhaps feeling guilty at being 'safe quit of wars'.

He was moved to a hospital in Rouen, apparently suffering from a form of enteritis. Here a doctor saw his name in a *Times* list of recent recipients of the Military Cross and, patting him on the shoulder, said he should go back to England, implying that he had done his bit, possibly saving his life by sparing him the rest of the Somme battle. A hospital ship took him to Southampton, where he boarded a Red Cross train for Oxford, people waving at the carriages supposedly full of heroes. 'Everything seemed happy and homely,' he thought. 'I was delivered from the idea of death and that other thing which haunted me, the dread of being blinded.'[24] He slept on the train, then was taken to a small white room on the ground floor of Somerville College, Oxford, where he could see chestnut trees and hear distant bells and, once more, a piano.

*

AT SOMERVILLE, THE conflict in his poetry between the warrior and the humanitarian shifted to satirical anger. In these weeks, he found a style for this, and a new elation at becoming a writer not merely up with the spirit of the time but ahead of it. Somerville mixed the old and new worlds. He shared his room with a dull Old Marlburian and was visited by a friend of Theresa's, a burbling old

India hand called Mr Forrest.²⁵ In his diary, however, Sassoon compiled 'notes for Satire', in which he wrote of 'boring, 2nd rate' officers obsessed by racing, hunting and snobbery who spoke of men being used to hardship, and in which he recorded 'vivid' incidents like 'collecting souvenirs from dead Germans, men dying from bullets in the head.'²⁶ In hospital, the only music was songs about 'my girl', apparently comforting for patients who were visited often by proud relations. He found his own comfort in reading Edward FitzGerald's letters about the quiet, Victorian Suffolk country world of this friend of Tennyson and translator of *The Rubáiyát of Omar Khayyám*.

His 'chameleon' self showed another side to his uncle Hamo Thornycroft, whom Sassoon went out to see at Burford where he was helping a farmer with the harvest while staying at the Bull Inn. They spoke of Thomas Hardy and Hamo told of how he had bicycled with the novelist and done a bust of him in 1915. Over tea at an old priory, it was hard to be the angry poet, especially when Thornycroft spoke proudly of Sassoon's medal or 'his cross'. Many of the 'stooks' of wheat made by Thornycroft collapsed, but the sculptor's joy in catching a trout in a nearby stream seemed so English, an absurd contrast to the Somme. Surely this was worth fighting for: the priory, picturesque Burford, local people like the driver of the horse-drawn bus, the homely inn which Hamo wanted Hardy to see. Yet when Uncle Hamo and the owner of the priory talked about glorious battle, their blind patriotism – like Theresa's – seemed at odds with the grim reality of the front line. Sassoon reported to Cockerell that Dent 'laughs at decorations – or pretends to – but I cannot help being intensely satisfied with mine!'²⁷ He told Marsh that he doubted if he was 'brave enough' to go back to the trenches unless stirred to anger by the death of a friend. 'All my military virtues seem to have gone phut!'²⁸

When Robert Ross came to see him, he inspired a different mood: that of the rebel. Early in August Robbie took him to The Manor House at Garsington, apparently like that England seen with Hamo Thornycroft, until Sassoon realized that their hostess, Lady

Ottoline Morrell, a tall and oddly dressed woman – her clothes (including a pair of pale pink Turkish trousers) and her manner artificial – lived in an artful landscape. To her, it was the visit of 'an angel', longed for since their first exchange of letters after his poem of early 1916, 'To Victory', had appealed to her romanticism. But if she found in the war and its heroes a certain excitement her attitude was not jingoistic. A half-sister of the Duke of Portland, born in 1872, she had married Philip Morrell, who came from a family of Oxfordshire solicitors. In August 1914, both of them had spoken against the war, Philip in the House of Commons, where he sat as a Liberal MP, and Ottoline by calling on the departing German ambassadress. Shocked by the patriotic hysteria even of the left-wing *Nation*, the Morrells made Garsington a refuge for conscientious objectors.

Yet to some, like D. H. Lawrence, the idyllic medieval manor house seemed to represent the death-throes of an ancient, structured England, and even for Lady Ottoline the idyll was tainted. Her marriage had become one of affection rather than passion and she felt 'too stupid to be in touch with those intellectuals and too clear-headed to be in touch with the crowd'.[29] The hard intellect of Bertrand Russell, who became her lover, could repel her. Ottoline Morrell longed to meet 'someone full of life and quivering to all beauty and interest like Keats'. With this came a sense of dwindling powers: 'I am no longer attractive. I am too old and too intellectual now – that doesn't attract men.'[30] Secretly she despised the Bloomsbury conscientious objectors, some of whom the Morrells employed on their farm, and she found Philip Morrell too monochrome for romance: each was unfaithful to the other. Sassoon's arrival, as she descended a ladder from the room where Dorothy Brett was painting her, seemed like 'a quick gay dream' yet 'so natural'. She found him 'very easy to talk to – hesitating in talk but always sympathetic and full of humour', and they had tea on the lawn, the urbane Ross lightening the conversation. Sassoon, on a walk round the garden, found himself alone with her; they discussed Robbie's kindness, how he had once jumped into the Garsington swimming pool to rescue a young girl. Only later, in her edited journal – after he had disappointed her – did Lady Ottoline say that she could see cruelty in the poet's face. Ross told Sassoon to cultivate this strange figure, who had good connections in the literary world.

On Sunday Sassoon came back to Garsington for tea: 'tall and thin and wonderful', his hostess thought, 'he thrills me.' The next day she and Brett bicycled into Oxford but missed a rendezvous with him and he followed them to the Ashmolean Museum. Soon Ottoline was writing that she feared her lack of attraction for men ('unless they get into my inner self') might frighten this new friend: 'I love him – and long and long for him – but he cannot feel it or he would come.'[31]

*

ROBERT GRAVES WAS alive. From Queen Alexandra's Hospital in Highgate, he wrote to Sassoon on 7 August, 'Been collecting any more VC's lately? I feel a rotten fraud with 12 months service in France and not even an MC . . .'[32] Graves suggested they do a book together called *Two Fusiliers*, and sent some poems, including one about his 'death'.[33] While at Somerville, Sassoon at last had time for poetry. A father pushing his wounded son in a wheelchair prompted the idea of a pitiful reconciliation ('I loathed my sallow son till he went fighting') followed, when the war is over, by a return of loathing; the end even hints at paternal triumph in the boy's permanent disablement. He scribbled on the manuscript sent to Marsh, 'Isn't this ill-natured?'[34] In 'Christ and the Soldier', not published in Sassoon's lifetime, Christ revealed through a crucifix on a French road has an exchange with a soldier who envies wounds that 'would shift a bloke to blighty' – 'Blighty' being slang for England. Asked to stop the fighting, the roadside Calvary seems powerless, useful only as an observation post, another sign of Sassoon's scorn for religion's inadequacy in war. 'Night and Rain' evokes the 'God made' weather of Flanders and a Jesus who 'never dream't there'd be such mud'.[35] 'For England' shows how war, through death, transforms 'a bore' into the reason his family mourns.[36] 'The Stunt' has an officer winning the DSO by killing three 'Saxon peasants half-asleep' and wounding others, basking in his relations' pride.[37] He still felt childlike joy in religious symbols, as in 'Morning-Glory', inspired by a Madonna and Child seen in the Ashmolean Museum, and on 7 August, amid pity for dead 'lads that I've loved', pride in the soldiers he commanded.

> *But, oh my dears, did you know I was proud as a King*
> *When I heard you grumble, and joke, and chatter and sing?*[38]

The new style – which Sassoon said he owed to Thomas Hardy's *Satires of Circumstance*, read in 1914 – developed with a 'knock-out blow' at a poem's end, often in direct or colloquial speech. In 'The One-legged Man' a soldier with a stick looks across the Kentish weald, anticipating 'comfortable years', before the last line explodes in gratitude for a 'blighty' (a wound serious enough to send him back to England): 'Thank God they had to amputate.' 'The Hero', which was almost immediately controversial, has an officer bringing a letter from the regiment's colonel to a dead soldier's mother:

> *'Jack fell as he'd have wished,' the Mother said,*
> *And folded up the letter that she'd read.*
> *'The Colonel writes so nicely.' Something broke*
> *In the tired voice that quavered to a choke.*
> *She half looked up. 'We mothers are so proud*
> *Of our dead soldiers.' Then her face was bowed.*[39]

But the officer recalls a different scene – Jack ('cold-footed, useless swine') panicking in a mine-blown trench – and knows the comfort of these 'gallant lies'. Realizing the willing sacrifice articulated by some non-combatants, particularly women, Sassoon writes of deluded home-front courage contrasted with front-line reality and treats it tenderly as well.

There were also the poems of description. In 'Stretcher Case', dedicated to Marsh, a wounded soldier wakes on a hospital train wondering if he is dead. He then drowses through front-line horrors before noticing the 'serene, the prosperous' England. Sassoon moves from pastoral to contemporary materialism: first the war, then 'trees, cows and hedges', then the 'large, friendly' advertised names ('Lung Tonic, Mustard, Liver Pills and Beer') more familiar and soothing to most people than poetry.[40] In 'The Road' he goes back to the Somme and 'big bellied' horses, 'bloody-fingered' corpses and a sleeping Scotsman, a 'poor sprawling Jock' too exhausted for lustful thoughts of women or 'home and love and ease'.[41]

At Weirleigh towards the end of August, he was bored and agitated by Theresa's attempts to reach the dead Hamo through automatic writing. Sassoon had left the Studio for a small front room off the hall where he had worked early in 1915. Now the dull, melancholy house and its empty stables spurred his writing. Here the recollection of hospital at Amiens, trips on the river at Oxford, death's terror and relief at having survived merge in 'The Death-Bed'. Late at night, over about four hours, the forty lines came to him as a result of 'great intensity',[42] heightened by the deaths of Tommy and Corporal O'Brien and Graves's reported death and infused with memories of a darkened ward, distant gunfire and a delirious officer screaming – as in 'Died of Wounds' – about the Somme. In the poem, Sassoon uses memories of canoeing on the Cherwell ('Water – calm, sliding green above the weir', the calm concealing dangers) to show a drift from life checked briefly when a nurse offers a drink. The victim forgets his wound and, although blind, is free to imagine peaceful landscapes washed by rain; then he moves and pain leaps 'like a prowling beast' while Death waits. There is a brief bargaining for his life ('He's young; he hated war'), but Death replies, 'I choose,' and the soldier dies, among the alliterations and assonances increasingly typical of Sassoon's musical language.

> And there was silence in the summer night;
> Silence and safety; and the veils of sleep.
> Then, far away, the thudding of the guns.[43]

The next morning, reading it through, and feeling 'a dull ache low down at the back of my head', he thought the poem 'the best thing' he had done since 1914, 'with all respect to my Military Cross of which I was pardonably proud'. Ross had told him he was 'one of those people who only write well when they are strongly moved'.[44] Too strong for some: the *Westminster Gazette* turned 'The Death-Bed' down without comment. But to Wilfred Owen, writing to his father in August 1917, the poem was 'a piece of perfect art'.[45]

*

As A BREAK from Weirleigh, Sassoon went first to London to see the Gosses, then to the Graveses' house near Harlech. Edmund Gosse reported to Hamo Thornycroft, 'He looks fine, but not quite strong. He was most charming, as he increasingly is . . .'[46] Robert Graves's father thought his son's friend 'a fine tall, manly modest fellow' and was beguiled by Sassoon's terrier Topper, while Robert's brother John listened to Siegfried tell stories, many of them about hunting, 'in a nervous but entrancing way'.[47] Graves's *Over the Brazier* had been published by Harold Monro of the Poetry Bookshop in May; and Sassoon and he talked more about doing a book together and what they longed for most in peace – hunting, nature, music and pastoral scenes for Sassoon, children for Graves. Graves's love for Peter Johnstone was still bright. Sassoon tried out the local golf courses and had picnics with the family. On 11 September they went to London where both men saw doctors.

News came of the most recent Somme battle and an attack on Ginchy on 2 and 3 September in which Edmund Dadd, Julian's brother, had been killed. The assault seemed suicidal, at least in hearsay; Julian Dadd, in charge of C Company, was badly wounded in the neck and chest. The Dadd brothers had shaken hands before going over the top and Cottrell wrote to Sassoon, 'It is terrible to think of those two splendid men being sent off.' Some two weeks later, the quartermaster was still seeking a response from his old comrade ('How are you? I haven't heard of or from you for weeks'), imagining the misery of the Dadds' father who had already lost one son at Gallipoli. Stockwell was moving on ('a great loss', Cottrell thought), having been given command of a brigade, to be replaced by a Colonel Holmes. The quartermaster could see little progress as they rested 'about 10 kilos from the place we were at last Xmas – further back'.[48]

Now Robert Graves and Sassoon were back at Weirleigh, Graves hearing Theresa's cries in the night as she tried to reach the dead Hamo. A medical examination which Sassoon had undergone, on 14 August, had reported continuing diarrhoea and stomach trouble, rendering him unfit for another four weeks, even for service at home. On 18 September a specialist in Harley Street found 'some doubtful sounds' in the lung and, in the light of Alfred Sassoon's death from tuberculosis, recommended 'another month's holiday'.[49]

Ottoline Morrell asked them both to Garsington where, in an atmosphere heightened by the conscientious objectors who were working on the farm, old shibboleths about which the soldiers grumbled but did not dream of overturning came under attack and a surprised Sassoon heard of the supposedly disgraceful political motives behind the fighting. Garsington was an odd combination, Lady Ottoline's theatricality – she presented a peacock feather to Ross and Sassoon on their first visit – amid the 'sumptuous homeliness' of the dark-roomed manor house[50] allied with the way that, as a poet and decorated soldier, he felt the company rise to him in instinctive admiration for his brave and sensitive response to the battles that these people had never known. The violinist Jelly d'Aranyi, an 'enemy alien', played Bach one evening; when Sassoon and Ottoline walked through the gardens, she gave him some 'touchingly amateurish' pages about turning the place into a refuge for creative and intellectually daring spirits and the nurturing of truth and sympathy and love.[51] The music and beauty of Garsington made Sassoon angry at what the army was making him miss. But then, in another sign of his chameleon self, came sport: cub-hunting in Kent and East Sussex and near Peterborough where he stayed with Norman Loder's wife Phyllis. He sent Ottoline another photograph and asked if Brett might paint him in his hunting clothes. This self-centredness disappointed her 'after he was friendly here – but after all it was I who made advances to him originally. I will go on giving him what I can.'[52]

In September Sassoon reverted to his pre-war habit, publishing, at his own expense, eleven finely printed copies of a pamphlet containing eleven poems: the same number, he pointed out, as a cricket team. *Morning-Glory* is a mixture of his old and new selves. There is the cherishing of innocence in 'A Child's Prayer'; and the dreaminess of 'A Poplar and the Moon', sharpened by the paganism of 'Wind in the Beechwood' and its overtones of the Russian ballet. 'To Victory' shows both the first thrill of war and, as in the poem originally written for Graves ('To His Dead Body'), its darkness. In 'Dream Forest', there is heroic isolation, followed by childlike sweetness again in the title poem 'Morning-Glory', inspired by an Ashmolean nativity scene; and the cleansing effect of war is shown in 'Brothers'. 'Blind' has a more realistic romanticism. One poem, 'Ancestors', looks further back, pointing to his family's exotic history ('jewelled' merchants bartering 'monstrous wealth with speech subdued' in 'glimmering halls'). The pamphlet has no hint of satire.

Ross now had the publisher Heinemann lined up for a commercial edition of Sassoon's work. The poems needed careful selection, in which Ross – who gently mocked some of the pre-war work – Marsh and Graves helped. The prospect of commercial publication made him scorn the pamphlet *Morning-Glory* and he told Marsh, dismissively, that it was merely 'my mother's favourites'.[53] Meanwhile there was a suitably patriotic view of the Germans for Uncle Hamo: 'Isn't the news good? They are on the downward grade at last, but it will be a slow descent.'[54] Yet, on a visit to Cambridge, Sassoon was fascinated to meet Professor Sorley, the father of the dead Charles, one of the first poets to write critically of the war; and, perhaps taking pleasure in shocking the home front, he told Dent stories about the trenches that made the musicologist's 'hair curl! Officers who drink 2 bottles of whisky (neat) a day . . . etc.'[55]

On 18 October, Sassoon came before a medical board in Northampton and was thought still to look anaemic; he also complained of a cough, and the board recommended two months' further relief from 'General Service'. On 23 November, giving his address as 40 Half Moon Street, Ross's rooms, he was examined at Caxton Hall in London where the board advised another two months away from the front, with only 'light duty' at home.[56]

This gave him more time for poetry. In 'The Tombstone-Maker', rejected as too strong for the 'respectable' *New Statesman* by its literary editor J. C. Squire,[57] a tombstone carver complains that he makes no money as the dead are now buried in France, to which the poet replies, shaming the non-combatant with an apocalyptic vision of Germans boiling British bodies down 'for fat'. The sonnet 'Two Hundred Years After', inspired by a diary entry of 3 June 1916, imagines the ghosts of the Great War dead ceaselessly haunting the old front line. In 'A Ballad' a fire-eating officer cannot stand the trenches, shoots himself in the foot and ends up teaching recruits 'the way to blood and glory'.[58]

'They', one of the most famous anti-war epigrams, is perhaps the clearest example of the influence of Ross's loathing for the jingoism of a society that persecuted him. One November evening in Half Moon Street, Robbie read out extracts from a sermon preached by the Bishop of London, Winnington-Ingram (who, years earlier, had confirmed Sassoon), about soldiers having their souls purged by the war. Two of the other eccentric members of the Half Moon Street circle, More Adey and Meiklejohn, were there, and when the exhausted Sassoon went to bed some lines of the poem, almost all in dialogue, came to him. He got up and scribbled some words, spoken by a 'vicar' in the first draft, on the transformation of 'the boys' after their fight 'in a just cause' for 'they have challenged Death and dared him face to face'. This is perhaps too easy a target – or seems so now – weakening the soldiers' imagined reply. But the answer is a 'knock-out blow': the first time also, as Sassoon later claimed, that 'syphilitic' had been used in a published poem.[59]

'We're none of us the same!' the boys reply.
'For George lost both his legs; and Bill's stone blind;
Poor Jim's shot through the lungs and like to die;
And Bert's gone syphilitic: you'll not find
A chap who's served that hasn't found some change.'
And the Bishop said: 'The ways of God are strange.'[60]

He took it to Marsh, who gasped, 'It's too horrible.'[61] In the street on the way back – in an extraordinary irony – Sassoon passed Winnington-Ingram, who smiled on seeing the MC ribbon on the officer's tunic.

*

BUT THE WARRIOR was not dead. On 2 November, over lunch in London, Sassoon told Robert Graves and Robbie Ross that poets must be seen as 'men of courage'. The best place for them, he thought, was 'back in France away from the more shameful madness of home service. Our function there was not to kill Germans, though that might happen, but to make things easier for the men under our command.'[62] This dislike of home-front jingoism, perhaps added to by shame that he had missed his old battalion's bad time on the Somme, is shown in some of the November poems. In 'Decorated' a 'jostling mob' acclaims the homecoming 'Corporal Stubbs, the Birmingham VC', for having killed five Germans. Sassoon rightly thought this below his usual form. 'Arms and the Man' shows 'Captain Croesus', presumably the rich Sassoon, seeing 'Colonel Sawbones', an army doctor, at Caxton Hall and hoping, guiltily, for an extension of leave. 'A Mystic as Soldier' is narcissistic as Sassoon recalls pre-war days lived apart, 'dreaming fair songs for God' and walking 'the secret way', perhaps a euphemism for homosexuality. 'The Poet as Hero', similarly narcissistic, tells why he has exchanged his 'old, silly sweetness' for 'an ugly cry', why a search for 'the Grail' has become 'lust and senseless hatred' and revenge. His poetry can, he hopes, absolve this brutality through its truth and compassion.[63]

Not everyone agreed. The barrister and Liberal journalist Charles Geake – once a Fellow of Clare, Sassoon's old college – publicly declared himself 'disgusted' by an earlier poem, 'The Hero', because mothers 'in the hour of bitter grief' might now wonder if their dead son had been a 'cold-footed, useless swine'. His letter to the *Cambridge Magazine* – where the poem had appeared – ended, 'Believe me, sir, the average Englishman does not like it, and as an old Cambridge man I sorrow to find this sort of thing in the *Cambridge Magazine*.'[64] The magazine's editor C. K. Ogden printed the later poem, 'The Poet as Hero', on the same page as Geake's letter.

Sassoon's leave was coming to an end. From Litherland, Robert Graves wrote that Bobbie Hanmer ('your particular intimate') was there, 'one of the dearest people I've ever met' and 'extraordinarily like' David Thomas – not conventional but charmingly naive.[65] Back at the training depot, Sassoon found Litherland unchanged: the factory sirens, ships' foghorns from the Mersey, the camp's bugles sounding across flat country and heavy skies, none of it conducive to poetry. At least there were no women and he could get away to hunt with the Cheshire hounds, play golf at Formby and eat well at Liverpool's Adelphi Hotel, about which he felt guilty. Graves and Hanmer made things better before, on 22 December, Graves went on leave. Julian Dadd came to visit, his whispering voice – stricken by the throat wound – rising as, after dinner at the Adelphi, he described the deadly Ginchy attack. Sassoon read Donne (where Death speaks, as in 'The Death-Bed'), Charles Sorley on the 'millions of the mouthless dead' and George Moore's 'beautiful' novel about Christ, *The Brook Kerith*. On 27 December a medical board gave him another month away from the front ('He is gaining strength but requires hardening').[66] Next Bobbie Hanmer went off to the Clapham Bombing School, leaving his pipe in Sassoon's hut and a note: 'with love: just off to bloody Clapham. R.H.H.'[67]

While Robert Graves was on leave, solitude broke the Litherland poetry block. 'Secret Music' reaches that part of Sassoon where 'glory' conquers pain and his 'dreaming spirit' hears 'proud-surging melodies of joy', all tensions fused in narcissistic isolation. Music's worldless ecstasy, to the unanalytical Sassoon, meant forgetting and solitary peace. 'A Whispered Tale', an ode to gentlemanliness, is addressed to Julian Dadd, whose account of the Ginchy battle lifts his faltering voice through 'those horrors left behind'. In 'The Distant Song', versified from a diary entry that was used later in *Memoirs of a Fox-hunting Man*, a blackbird singing from beyond the German lines on a dank morning makes a soldier think of spring and 'Paradise'. 'The March-Past' is a not quite sharp enough satire on a parade – probably that taken by Rawlinson at Flixécourt – where a bemedalled general (a hunting man, 'a damned good sort') takes the salute with Death leering behind him.[68] After Graves's return, they discussed poetry and life, Sassoon reeling before the younger man's iconoclasm as Milton was demolished, classical music scorned in favour of north-country or Scottish ballads, and fox-hunting condemned as snobbish. Graves, still only twenty-one, seemed astonishingly sure of himself, a mixture of priggish puritan-ism and obsessive speculation on what Sassoon called 'anything nasty',[69] but making everyone else at Litherland seem nonentities. Then on 20 January 1917, the weather raw and drizzling, he noted, 'Robert left for France to-day' – his third time out.

The soldiers were told that another Big Push would end the war by the summer, just as they had heard the previous year of certain victory on the Somme. Joe Cottrell wrote of the harshest winter ever seen in northern France. At Litherland, Sassoon read Wells's vision, in *Mr Britling Sees It Through*, of how the hopes of 1914 had turned into 'a war without a point' and a very fierce piece in a Danish magazine about the crucifying of the 'sons of Europe'. At the end of January, he wrote to Ross, mixing excitement at Heine-mann's publication of his poems with anxiety at what awaited him in France where 'I am sure I shall get blown to shreds in the spring offensive; which will be a good advertisement for the book, though I fear that wheeze is rather played out among the hero–poets now – they *all* do it. Do you think a general court-martial for cowardice would make a better paragraph? It's all the fashion *here* now, we've got two this week. They always bring these things up against people about 6 months after the episode, which is characteristic of their methods!'[70] By then he had proofs of the first twenty pages.

In the mess, hearing someone talk of how he had had his leg cut off, Sassoon staggered out and fainted and told Ottoline Morrell he was sure most soldiers wanted an immediate peace.[71] A revue at the Liverpool Hippodrome with its jingoistic jokes and songs gave rise to the satirical 'Blighters'. In his diary, he blamed women for their pride in having a child by a warrior and vicarious joy in bloodshed.[72] For Sassoon, they represented marriage, domestic conformity, what his mother wanted from him, a way barred by his sexuality. Many women would despise the truth about Siegfried; he hated them for this and struck first in subconscious consolation.

He spoke to Bobbie Hanmer (now back and 'not *quite* so adorable') about religion, self-sacrifice and war,[73] Hanmer's 'kind eyes and ingenuous looks' making him 'a good person to die for, and suffer with', and this led to a resolve to be reckless when he went out again.[74] In Liverpool on 22 January he heard Elgar's violin concerto for the first time, imagining he might never hear again this 'melody of an average Englishman'[75] with which he 'more or less' identified – once more ignoring his Jewish roots – and in a poem linked the slow movement to Christ 'bowed with pain', and later, in his diary, to himself, 'the suffering mortal figure on a cross'.[76] Memories of the dead Hamo in the garden at Weirleigh merged with Bobbie Hanmer and dread of the front. It was almost hysteria. On 27 January he was passed fit by a medical board of two elderly officers, one of whom snapped at him for nervously tapping the table. There was one consolation: *The Old Huntsman*, his book's title, looked 'first class' in proof. But 'now the wings of death are over me once more'.[77]

One of the Litherland poems, 'Enemies' – written after a day's hunting – imagines, through the dead David Thomas, a soldier after death meeting the German that Sassoon has killed, foreshadowing the post-battlefield hell of Owen's 'Strange Meeting'. 'When I'm Among a Blaze of Lights' shows up coarse 'women dawdling through delights' and 'officers in cocktail bars' in contrast to his 'kindly' candlelit room at Weirleigh. 'England Has Many Heroes' says he would rather shoot one 'General Dolt' than 'fifty harmless Germans', and damns staff officers who get medals 'from their German King'. This jibe at George V's Teutonic descent may explain why the poem stayed unpublished during Sassoon's lifetime. Two other poems came near the end of this spell at Litherland. The two-verse 'Blighters' is about wanting a tank to lurch down the stalls to stifle the jokes, the Hippodrome's dancing girls ('prancing ranks of harlots') and the jingoism that 'mock the riddled corpses round Bapaume', an ironical farewell to the home front. 'Conscripts', a longer poem with five verses of six lines each, stems from his drilling of new soldiers – gasping, sweating young marching men ('Left, right! Press on your butts!' might be sexual innuendo). The poem combines *fin de siècle* sentiments about Love, Rhyme, Wisdom, Rapture, Pale Enchantment and Young Fancy ('how I loved him all the while') with drill commands and guilt at preparing young men to be killed. Finally it claims that the beautiful, favoured ones ('many a sickly, slender Lord') could not stand the trenches whereas the 'kind, common ones that I despised' – the simple soldiers – became heroes.[78] When the poem appeared in the *Spectator*, Gosse complained about its slur on the aristocracy's martial spirit. The poet answered that 'such a thing had never entered my head'.[79]

Sassoon wrote to Thomas Hardy to ask if he might dedicate *The Old Huntsman* to him. On 5 February, Hardy sent a cautious answer, giving his permission and thanking him for the proof of 'On Corbie Ridge' ('I don't know where that is'). 'I hope the weather will be milder before you go back to France,' the septuagenarian poet wrote, 'and that you may have good luck over there.'[80] On 7 February, Sassoon was back at Weirleigh with Theresa and Topper before a last few days in London with Ross, Meiklejohn, Heinemann and Gosse that mixed light and serious talk. In the National Gallery, Ottoline Morrell revealed her 'inner life'[81] and gave him a little opal on a chain as a talisman; she also asked Lytton Strachey to get Virginia Woolf to review *The Old Huntsman* 'kindly' because if its author 'heard his work had "Promise" it might make him want to live.'[82] Julian Dadd wrote to thank Sassoon for some poems that he had sent him, saying, 'As you know I hate displaying feeling and anything of that sort,' but 'I do very much appreciate them' – particularly, Dadd thought, the effort 'to see and write the truth', for 'few people would have had the pluck' to write 'The Hero'. Dadd declared, 'it seems difficult to say anything adequate to a friend going out again to the front . . . My idea, as you know, is that you want to be a d—d sight more careful – the Boche is devilish cunning and nearly always gets his own back on anyone who despises him too much . . . I must shut up now: this letter shows a dangerous tendency to become serious.'[83]

On 15 February, a 'nervous and rattled'[84] Sassoon left for France from Waterloo station. Seen off by Theresa and Ross, he wondered what they could have found to say to each other after he had gone. The nerves wore off on the crossing – at the front there was only one real anxiety: that of being killed – and most of the boat's cargo, he felt sure, dreamed of girls, hoarded pay or 'peace next year', as Sassoon wrote in a pitying poem 'Life-Belts (Southampton to Le Havre)'.[85] He took books with him: Shakespeare's tragedies, Conrad's *Nostromo* and *A Set of Six*, Lamb's *Letters and Essays*, Chaucer, Thomas Hardy's *Dynasts* and a selection of Hardy's other poems. Into his diary went some lines of Hardy from *Time's Laughingstocks*:

> And some day hence, toward Paradise
> And all its blest – if such should be –
> I will lift glad, afar-off eyes,
> Though it contain no place for me.[86]

*

FROM LE HAVRE, Sassoon took a boat up the Seine to Rouen and the Infantry Base Depot. Here, looking for blankets, he blundered into a guardroom to see a kneeling man naked to the waist weeping uncontrollably. In detention for assaulting a military policeman, the soldier had just heard that his brother had been killed; and outside, on a noticeboard, Sassoon saw the names of three private soldiers recently shot for cowardice. The coarse talk of other officers brought him further back into the war, far from the comfortable, fastidious London he had just left. Two days later, again offended by 'obscene' talk and despising the other patients, especially the Jews, he lay at night in a hospital room with German measles, as he told Ross, 'in unholy terror at the thought of losing my life in that organised inferno of mud and misery up the line . . . I haven't met anyone yet who has any faith in "the purpose of war".'[87] A short poem showed yet another premonition of death:

> *Soon he'll make of me*
> *A grinning carcase in the trench . . .*[88]

'Old England with her cant and shame' was not worth this.

From the hospital, he walked in the pine woods, wanting simplicity, to be an accomplished patriot, to sleep and pray contentedly like Bobbie Hanmer. In Rouen, he admired the church of Saint-Ouen and the cathedral but loathed the staff officers guzzling in a hotel restaurant and the rich cavalry subalterns who had not served their time in the trenches. Back at the Infantry Base Depot, he complained to Theresa that 'most of the Welsh officers here are common and repulsive',[89] and to Ross he wrote, 'Poor weary old harlots, how weary they must be of the Welsh dialect . . . !'[90] While at Rouen, Sassoon wrote down some thoughts on the war and saw these later as one of the origins of his Sherston books and their themes of futility, pathos, irony (learned from Hardy) and a deluded High Command. 'I have no use for Generals,' he wrote, 'but I am a pacifist; and man is born to prejudices and distorted views.' The terrible feature of 'prolonged campaigning' was, he thought, that it 'deadens all the fine and sensitive instincts of men, till nothing survives but animal cravings for warmth and food and sleep'.[91]

The poetry of this return was predictably sharp. 'Base Details', ten lines written at Rouen on 4 March, features what Robbie Ross had called 'screaming scarlet Majors' (also reflecting the red flashes of the staff) when Sassoon imagines himself a staff officer in the city's best hotel, breaking into public-school direct speech over the roll of honour. At the end comes the 'knock-out blow' about a safe death in bed:

> *If I were fierce, and bald, and short of breath,*
> *I'd live with scarlet Majors at the Base,*
> *And speed glum heroes up the line to death.*
> *You'd see me with my puffy petulant face,*
> *Guzzling and gulping in the best hotel,*
> *Reading the Roll of Honour. 'Poor young chap,'*
> *I'd say – 'I used to know his father well;*
> *Yes, we've lost heavily in this last scrap.'*
> *And when the war is done and youth stone dead,*
> *I'd toddle safely home and die – in bed.*[92]

'The Optimist', sent to Ross with 'Base Details' in a letter of 8 March, again has an ironical title. The speaker says he is sure 'We'd got the Germans absolutely beat,' before the poet notices a head wound that shows possible craziness. The final Rouen poem, 'In the Church of St Ouen' – not published until 1973 – seeks a higher peace ('lost to God, I seek him everywhere') with organ music at sunset, away from the spring offensive. 'Return', written in a train from Rouen on the night of 11 March on the way to his regiment, hears whispers from the dead in three curiously lifeless verses.[93]

On 11 March, Siegfried Sassoon was turned out at Corbie station from where, after a night under a blanket on the floor, he walked with two other young RWF cadet officers ('quite dull')[94] seven miles to Camp 13, itself about two miles from Morlancourt. Here he joined the Second – instead of his old First – Battalion of the Royal Welch Fusiliers. His luggage had been lost.

Graves and Sassoon both thought the Second Battalion more irritatingly traditional than the First, partly because it had not seen as much action and its eighteen years' imperial service overseas before 1914 had induced a stiff atmosphere. But some friends were there: young Orme, once of the First Battalion, and Ralph Greaves,

brother of E. L. Greaves, Sassoon's former cosy company commander (later he thought Ralph the better of the two). The camp
had a gloomy atmosphere, partly because of cold weather and partly
because of the loss of a popular colonel, who had been replaced by
a Colonel Garnett, a 'decent old stick' but not the same.[95] There
was contemptuous talk of Major General Pinney, the general commanding the division, who had cut the rum ration, disapproved of
smoking and, earlier in the war, had forbidden the wearing of steel
helmets. Sassoon met the man viewed by some as the true commander of the battalion, its medical officer Dr James Dunn, then
aged forty-six and a decorated veteran of the Boer War, often dour
and cantankerous but exceptionally brave under fire. 'Toughest skin
of the lot, but you're a tough character, I know,' Dunn said to
Sassoon as he inoculated him against typhoid.[96]

The recent draft of dim recruits and the draughty, smoke-filled
huts made him think that 'I could scarcely have begun my acquaintance with the battalion under worse conditions.'[97] At least his
forthcoming book seemed to offer some hope, and reminders of
support at home came in still-scented silk scarves despatched from
Garsington by Lady Ottoline Morrell. But to Ross he wrote, 'My
companions here seem incredibly dull.'[98]

*

VICTORY SEEMED NO nearer since Sassoon's departure from the
front in July 1916. After the losses of the first day of the Somme on
1 July, Haig and Rawlinson's grand plan dwindled into a series of
attacks in different places, generally rebuffed by the Germans. By
the end of August the British had suffered 82,000 casualties for little
ground gained, but Haig went on, bound – he felt – by commitments
to his allies. In September the creeping barrage, with shells preceding
the advancing infantry, mauled the German trenches but not their
artillery. Tanks, used for the first time, showed their limitations
when several broke down and the gaps made for them in the barrage
left the infantry exposed. Haig's artillery was still not concentrated
enough. Then came the rain and slush of October and November.

By 14 November the offensive had stopped six miles short of Bapaume, one of the objectives of that first July day.

The estimated casualties of the Somme were grim: 450,000 British, 200,000 French. Yet the German army also lost around 400,000 men, and even such a dedicated warrior and nationalist as the writer Ernst Jünger commented on his own side's weak firepower and his admiration for the British logistics, courage and offensive strength. The battle was a terrible baptism for Kitchener's New Army, those thousands of enthusiastic volunteers, but to one subaltern, Charles Carrington, aged nineteen-and-a-half in 1916, 'The Somme battle raised the morale of the British Army.' Although not an outright victory, it gave the British, Carrington thought, a sense of superiority over their opponents, 'man to man'.[99] Edmund Blunden, no admirer of the High Command, wrote of a November 1916 'feat of arms vying with any recorded' and expressed the 'exaltation'[100] of thinking that after the Somme anything might be borne. For Carrington 'the further from the sound of guns, the lower was the morale'.[101] That mirrored the change of mood Sassoon sensed as he crossed from Southampton to Le Havre, to the reality rather than the second-hand accounts of the hells of Bazentin, High Wood, Delville Wood and Ginchy in letters from Cottrell and Julian Dadd.

During the winter of 1916 and early 1917, the coldest in living memory, both sides tried to recover. For the spring offensive, Lloyd George, the British Prime Minister, had affronted Haig by placing the army under the temporary control of the confident new French commander General Nivelle, who had impressed him by his good English and his record at Verdun. The British part in this, small compared to the huge French movement at the Chemin des Dames, was to attack a front that went from Bapaume north to Arras. The Germans disrupted the plans by an unexpected withdrawal in February and March to the so-called Hindenburg Line of linked fortifications, leaving behind a country devastated by their policy of 'scorched earth'.

The Second Battalion of the Royal Welch Fusiliers moved into the recently destroyed area in a series of marches that began on 3

April, first from Camp 13 to Corbie, with the company commander, Kirkby, at the head on a horse and Sassoon, as second-in-command, on foot at the column's rear. Three hundred strong, the battalion formed part of VII Corps under Lieutenant General Sir Thomas Snow. Kirkby, a Welsh landowner who was unpleasant to any new junior officer, relaxed; the dark-haired, monocled, musical Ralph Greaves was funny (sometimes crudely) and attractive with his slight stammer; the quartermaster 'Papa' Yates proved to be an old sweat like Joe Cottrell. After getting drunk with Kirkby and Greaves on bad champagne in a wine merchant's house in Corbie, Sassoon thought that 'The Second RWF are gradually taking me to their bosom,'[102] although, predictably, he despised the other B Company officers. The men were different, inspiring the old compassion. Inspecting their feet moved him to poetry, to say of one of them, 'How glad I'd be to die, if dying could set him free,' sensing that the soldier might think, 'Our officer's a decent bloke.'[103] But there was someone he missed more intimately, and, thrilled once more by the idea of sacrifice, he told Graves, 'If only Bobbie [Hanmer] would come here! And let me save his life.'[104]

They went from Corbie to Villers-Bocage, about fourteen miles, and the next day moved on to Beauval, eight miles along the main road between Amiens and Saint Pol, with snow falling all the way. Their former corps commander, Lieutenant General Sir Ivor Maxse, humiliated Colonel Garnett, publicly abusing him for not getting off his horse to salute, for leaving the muzzles of the troops' rifles uncovered and for carrying brooms and 'other utilitarian objects' on the cookers[105] – a futile display of discipline. After a night at Beauval, they marched another seven miles to Lucheux, hearing the enormous artillery barrage that was taking place at Arras. The weather had improved, and the troops felt sure that this offensive would win the war, a feeling Sassoon remembered from the Somme.

On 7 April, Easter Saturday, they were at Saulty, about twelve miles from Arras, where Sassoon sat alone in the park of a big white château watching deer and listening to birdsong and the distant guns. On the 8th, Easter Day, at Basseux, some three miles nearer

Arras, he looked down from a sunlit attic with his feet dangling out of the window, watching other officers play cricket. Later he inspected the enemy's old trench line, struck by 'the appalling inferiority of our position to that of the Germans'.[106] They had passed the cavalry massing for the hoped-for breakthrough, but Sassoon's excitement faltered as he noted the unpreparedness and poor physical state of his men. He was also experiencing gastritis, a sore throat and festering scratches on his hands.

On 9 April, Easter Monday, the battle of Arras, Britain's contribution to Nivelle's offensive, began. Good news drifted back to Basseux, where the Second Battalion remained, cricket continuing until 11 April when the order came to pack up quickly. More snow, heavy this time, fell as they marched through devastated villages, reaching a sunken road near Mercatel after eight miles; and here he shared a small dug-out with a young officer called Casson amid stifling coke fumes. Ottoline Morrell's literary efforts – which she had sent him – seemed out of place, far too diffuse, but with them came another opal to replace the first which had been stolen. 'I shall take it into battle,' Sassoon wrote on the 11th. 'I think they will kill me this time.'[107] He heard that the binders had delayed the publication of *The Old Huntsman*.

On 12 April they moved on through thawing snow, another four miles, to Saint Martin-Cojeul, a village levelled by the retreating Germans, and corpses showed the nearness of the front line. Near Saint Martin, the Second Battalion relieved the Second Manchesters in reserve and Siegfried Sassoon and B Company occupied the old German third-line trench, less than a mile behind the front line. He shared a dug-out with Casson, Evans (another young officer) and Kirkby, who, unlike Sassoon, slept through the freezing night. An underground dressing station had failed to help his suppurating fingers.

The next day, Friday 13 April, they waited in fine weather while the 62nd Division unsuccessfully attacked the village of Fontaine-les-Croisilles from a hill about three-quarters of a mile away. After tea, Sassoon took the twenty-three-year-old Casson to the hill to get him used to seeing the dead, mostly shot in the head, still laden with equipment, put in lines by stretcher bearers trying to identify them; and the sensitive boy did his best not to appear shocked. A tank had got stuck while trying to cross a wide trench, showing the limitations of this wonder weapon.

On the night of 15 April, when B Company was ordered up to the front line to relieve the Northumberland Fusiliers, the Northumberland guides had the wrong map references and Kirkby mistakenly shook a dead German's shoulder to ask him for directions; Sassoon, going on alone, found some Sappers who knew the way. On arrival in the trench, Kirkby told him to put out sentries and disappeared down a shaft to company headquarters. Sassoon, with no idea of the deep trench's geography, searched for the company on their left and met 'a panic party' of recent recruits vanishing through a narrow doorway into 'the bowels of the earth', herded by their two officers. One of them told him, 'The Germans are coming over.'[108] Then, alone, he crept along, as on his solitary patrols on the Somme, but found no sign of the enemy. At 4 a.m. he got to bed, in a passage under the trench, still too cold to sleep, rising at 9.30 to supervise the bringing up of bombs and ammunition all day in the rain.

Kirkby ordered Sassoon to take command of 100 bombers – out of a battalion of 270 – in support of an attack by the First Cameronians, a move ordered by General Pinney. After dark, a cheery guide took him to the Cameronian Company commander in a front-line dug-out where he heard that the attack would be across the barrier in the tunnel trench that cut them off from the enemy, a hellish place full of mangled German corpses twisted by shell explosions. Sassoon had slept no more than an hour at a time for the previous three nights and came back confused in the chilling rain, thinking he would be killed. He asked Ralph Greaves to put a plan of attack down on paper for battalion headquarters, comforted briefly by talk of pre-war days in Kent and by Greaves's 'whimsical debonair looks', eyeglass and gentle stammer and the homely mirror and clock in his chamber off the underground trench. At zero hour of 3 a.m., he sat in the Cameronians' headquarters, eating cake with the Scottish colonel and adjutant, with a hundred men on the stairs down to it, their chilled state a reminder of Pinney's cutting of the rum ration.

Shells exploded outside, communication with the attacking company soon broke down and, three hours of suspense later, a dishevelled sergeant burst in, almost incoherent, to say they had 'been driven back after advancing a little way'.¹⁰⁹ Sassoon stood stiffly. As officer in command of the supporting party, his moment had arrived. The Scottish colonel and the adjutant looked at him in sympathy, muttering, 'Well, old chap, I suppose you're for it!' He put on his helmet, told his two junior officers that he was taking twenty-five men 'up to the show' and went out into a morning of noise and sunlight.

His contingent, all private soldiers with the exception of a Sergeant Baldwin, followed him ('I hadn't the slightest idea what I was going to do') and a hunched Cameronian guide. They reached the wide main trench, to be met by the retreating Cameronians and their leader's breathless excuse that the Germans were all around them and they had run out of bombs. 'But where are the Germans?' Sassoon asked, tossing his own bomb from one hand to the other, affecting nonchalance. 'I can't see any Germans!' This steadied the other officer, and Sassoon said contemptuously, 'You needn't bother – we'll see to this' – or, as he later wrote, 'words to that effect'. He led his party on a bit, then told them to wait, and went forward a further hundred yards along the trench with Sergeant Baldwin ('an admirably impassive little man'). Then, telling Baldwin to go back and arrange for the collection of the Mills bombs that had presumably been dropped by the panicking Cameronians, he went on alone, round a corner, to find a small Cameronian corporal standing with a bag of bombs over his shoulder. Neither spoke to the other. Sassoon also had a bag of bombs and they went round the next bay together, to find the bloody corpse of a young, fair-haired Cameronian private propped against the trench wall, eyes staring from a calm, grey young face. A few yards further on lay the crumpled body of a German officer.

The dead Cameronian made Sassoon angry, prompting him to throw bombs at the invisible Germans ahead. The enemy retaliated so weakly that he advanced with the corporal, who, more cautious, sometimes sheltered in one of the small side trenches. They saw the retreating Germans, but Sassoon had no idea of his objective until, all of a sudden, the corporal said they had reached it. Very excited, he told the corporal he would explore one of the side trenches alone and finding nothing, paused, listened, heard a machine gun, saw an aeroplane overhead, thought 'what a queer business it all was' and 'decided to take a peep at the surrounding country'. Raising his head, he looked above the parapet and at once felt 'a tremendous blow in the back, between the shoulders'. He imagined that he had been hit by a bomb from behind, but in fact a sniper had shot him from the German lines. Leaning against the trench wall, Sassoon shut his eyes. A short while later Sergeant Baldwin was with him; 'to my great surprise, I discovered I was not dead'. Baldwin, who exclaimed, 'my officer's been hit!', was cool, 'like a well-trained footman', and helped Sassoon back to the main trench, looked at the wound and went back to get some more men.[110]

After fifteen minutes, Sassoon wanted to go on, for 'I was now not only a hero but a wounded hero.' Other soldiers came; then he spoke excitedly to an officer in charge of a mortar about renewing the attack: 'I felt capable of the most suicidal exploits.' He had been in action for four hours, with the Second Battalion for thirty-six days, in the battle of Arras for five of these – a short yet enduringly intense experience of war.

Another officer arrived to relieve him. Next a written order came from the Cameronian Colonel Chaplin saying that the attack had failed elsewhere, they should advance no further and Sassoon must come back. He left at 9.45 a.m., glimpsed a nonchalant Dr Dunn and had his wound seen to in a first-aid post in the tunnel. There he was told to walk about three miles through the mud, first to

Hénin, then to Boyelles, where a bus took him on a jolting ride of an hour and a half to the Casualty Clearing Station at Warlencourt. Exhausted, he heard that he could expect to go back to England. The sound of wind and rain made him pity his battalion. Meanwhile a tetanus injection had made him feel cold and odd, and the wound hurt 'like hell'.[111]

SIX

'The heroics of pacifism'

Sassoon slept for eight hours, read *Far from the Madding Crowd* and was put on a Red Cross train with 500 men and 32 officers, among them a Cameronian officer and one from the Northumberland Fusiliers who had a slight wound in the backside. He thought, 'My luck never deserts me,' and from the General Hospital in Camières wrote to reassure Theresa that the bullet had gone 'straight through without touching a nerve or blood vessel'.[1] In fact it had narrowly missed the jugular vein and the spine. On 20 April 1917, he arrived at the Fourth London Hospital at Denmark Hill, having been given flowers by a woman at Charing Cross station and a leaflet written by the Bishop of London advising a clean life and attendance at holy communion.

Robbie Ross came as soon as possible. Sassoon felt too exhausted to see Lady Ottoline Morrell; Edmund Gosse, who did go – with Meiklejohn and, again, Ross – detected 'severe shock'.[2] But Robert Graves's father, alerted by his daughter, a nurse at the hospital, called on the 28th and thought the patient seemed 'in some pain but very cheerful'.[3] In fact Sassoon dreaded all options – a convalescent home, Litherland, France or a job in England – but told Robert Graves that his 'reputation as a hero' demanded that 'I must go back *as soon as possible*'.[4] He dreamed of corpses and mutilated men, telling Bertrand Russell who, at the suggestion of

Ottoline Morrell, had sent him his anti-war book, *Justice in War-time*, that 'the horrors I saw last week were enough to drive any reasonable poet off his head'.[5] He put on good humour for senior officers, nurses and hunting friends, but confessed to Uncle Hamo, who usually experienced Sassoon's bluff side, that another dose of war might send him 'dotty'.[6] Theresa, suffering from rheumatism, did not come up from Weirleigh.

Wounded officers played cards, a gramophone ground out popular tunes, the newspapers seemed ludicrously optimistic and, in the ward, the talk was all about the war. Russell's book, Sassoon told Ottoline Morrell, 'makes me feel worse than ever about the senseless slaughter which is going on. *O it's monstrous!*' As if in protest, he had written 'the best "horrible" poem I shall ever do',[7] almost certainly 'The Rear-Guard', drafted in hospital in France and subtitled 'Hindenburg Line, April 1917', its subterranean scenes redolent of Doré's illustrations for Dante. Probably based on the incident when Kirkby shook a dead German to ask the way – in *Memoirs of an Infantry Officer* it is Sassoon who shakes the corpse – the poem is a descent into hell. The details of the trench – rotting bodies, 'Tins, boxes, bottles, shapes too vague to know' – lead up to the corpse being mistaken for a sleeping soldier:

> *Tripping, he grabbed the wall; saw some one lie*
> *Humped at his feet, half-hidden by a rug,*
> *And stooped to give the sleeper's arm a tug.*
> *'I'm looking for headquarters.' No reply.*
> *'God blast your neck!' (For days he'd had no sleep,)*
> *'Get up and guide me through this stinking place.'*

At the poem's end, Sassoon staggers past 'the dazed, muttering creatures underground' into the twilight, 'Unloading hell behind him step by step', the jarring adjectives and nouns ('patching glare', 'rosy gloom') reflecting a chaotic world.[8]

'The Rear-Guard' is dated 22 April. On the 23rd he produced 'To the Warmongers', a thrust at the home front by one feeling a survivor's guilt ('a curse is on my head'). The language tries to show the Hindenburg trenches: 'young faces bleared with blood', 'limbs that twist awry', the mud and moans of 'brutish pain'. 'Wounded' – expressing relief at being amid silence, sunlight and flowers and written on 24 April – was unpublished during his lifetime, perhaps because of lush *fin de siècle* phrases like 'the sombre evening dyes my glowing dreams'.[9]

Of the hospital poems, the best known is 'The General': seven lines portraying affable incompetence and the gulf between fighting soldiers and their commanders, an inspiration for the idea that the First World War was directed by château-based, stupid, callous old men. Triggered by Major General Sir Reginald Pinney – whose inept tactics, Sassoon told Florence Hardy, 'very nearly lost me my life'[10] – yet with overtones also of Rawlinson at Flixécourt in 1916 or Maxse more recently, the lines seemed to Dr Dunn, who recalled Pinney at the roadside as they went up to the Hindenburg trenches, to 'hit him to the life'.[11]

> '*Good morning, good morning!*' *the General said*
> *When we met him last week on our way to the line.*

The soldiers, Harry and Jack – good-natured, deferential – like this 'cheery old card'. Then Sassoon delivers his knock-out blow, a one-line verse: 'But he did for them both by his plan of attack.' At Marsh's suggestion 'did for' replaced the word 'murdered' of an early draft, as 'Harry' replaced 'Johnny'.[12] The poem may reflect news of the Second Battalion's attack on 23 April and a visit to its rest-billets by Pinney after Ralph Greaves had lost an arm for a gain of only a few hundred yards, during which attack Bobbie Hanmer had been wounded.[13] To Ottoline Morrell, Sassoon wrote of being recommended for a DSO and of how the medal 'will all help to make my position stronger when I start playing hell with the British smuggery'.[14]

Allowed now to leave the hospital during the day, he saw Ross, Meiklejohn and Julian Dadd, whose 'haunted unhappy look' still showed the aftermath of Delville Wood.[15] Everyone advised him to stay in England. Ross promoted *The Old Huntsman*, published on

8 May, giving away copies and trying to fix reviews. At the Reform
Club, with Ross, Sassoon saw H. G. Wells, Arnold Bennett and
J. C. Squire. Now he was the brave soldier–poet, a spokesman for
his generation. On 9 May he moved to a London hotel that had
been taken over by the army, having to attend lectures on trench
warfare, and was accused of malingering when he asked a doctor if
he might go to the country to recuperate. The request, however, was
granted. On the 12th Sassoon went to Chapelwood Manor at Nutley
in East Sussex, home of Earl and Countess Brassey. The previous
day the *Morning Post* had carried a review of *The Old Huntsman*:
'unqualified praise all the way through. There is no doubt the book
will be a huge success,' he told Theresa, ending with a request
appropriate to his new grand surroundings: 'Please send me a pair
of patent leather shoes.'[16]

Chapelwood, a grey-timbered, gabled country house built only
twelve years before in a pastiche of a medieval manor, certainly
seemed far from the Western Front as Sassoon, after dinner, watched
his host, the ancient Lord Brassey, reading Kipling's poem 'Sussex'.
The 1st Earl Brassey, born in 1836 and with only a year more to
live, had been a Liberal politician and a colonial governor, marrying
in 1890 as his second wife the younger Sybil de Vere, daughter of
the 7th Earl of Essex. To Sassoon, Brassey seemed often 'a pathetic
figure', occasionally muttering about ignorant guests, who included
several other officers and family friends, 'What do *they* know about
it?', before returning to solitary brooding. Sometimes he managed a
long pontification about Church Disestablishment or the uselessness
of Britain's smaller colonies, a whiff of the political world; one
evening, the old man went to a dinner in London for General Smuts.
Yet, although calling to his wife like a child, he showed courage,
pulling himself about in a chair, bent double with rheumatism.[17] At
first, Sassoon thought Lady Brassey 'a good specimen of her type',
the war having softened any haughtiness. She asked him if he
'enjoyed writing poetry very much' for she had read the *Morning
Post* review of *The Old Huntsman* which called its author 'a great
poet'.[18]

A sleepless Sassoon heard the birds at dawn and saw the sun creep over the garden as he read Andrew Marvell. He sought a bridge to these friendly people, telling Meiklejohn that 'No doubt hunting will save the situation, as usual,'[19] but felt overcome by fantasies of affronted innocence, of himself as a rescuer of beauty. 'It is my task to guard his beauty from wrong & so I bring him wounded home from war and love surrounds us both like sudden flowers,' he wrote in his diary, possibly of Bobbie Hanmer or an ideal friend, with 'body and spirit wrought to a single heart of unison, like the embrace of lovers'. Sassoon addressed this inspiration in the spirit of his pre-war writings, *Amyntas* or *Hyacinth*. 'It was not well to sleep, sleeping lost the perfect hours . . . Only when dawn comes in put out the light and let the light begin with madrigals. Sleep well, hurt heart that God has given me whose death is mine, and all his happiness mine, to be washed with . . . laughter and surge of tears when he must weep for joy that knows no other way of passion – only this that is not grief but merciful release.'[20]

He had been offered a job as an instructor to a cadet battalion at Cambridge but doubted if he should take it. His army comrades wrote with mystified respect about *The Old Huntsman*, Julian Dadd thinking the poems 'absolutely first rate' although they had 'made me feel a bit of a d—d worm. I did not realise before what a real, pukka poet you are.' Old Joe Cottrell heard from 'my Mrs' that the book had arrived at the Cottrell home in Chester. Cottrell, Dadd and 'Birdie' Stansfield praised his record, urging 'a b—y long holiday'.[21] *The Old Huntsman* brought a letter from the Reverend Harry Harbord, the father of Gordon, who had two sons in the army, sympathizing with Sassoon's 'terrible experience'. But, Harbord said, this life was 'only a beginning, a training' and, in Christ's words, 'What I do thou knowest not now, but thou shalt know hereafter.'[22]

The Brasseys' guests brought war gossip and attempts to understand his poetry, the women deflected, he hoped, by his silent contempt. Absurd, yet also upsetting and reminiscent of Theresa's search for the dead Hamo, or even Gordon Harbord's father's

Christian fatalism, was Lady Brassey's combination of spiritualism and Christian Science – something that tainted this beautiful part of southern England for whose pre-war simplicities Sassoon had hoped he was fighting. Death is nothing, she said, and those killed were still helping with the struggle from the next world. Since he was not an only child nor heir to a great name or estate, Sassoon should go to France, she implied, not stay in England 'dangling about and writing poetry'.[23] Maybe she was right. Sassoon thought he should return to the First Battalion, his original unit, unless he could make a protest. Even Lord Brassey doubted a military victory: better to negotiate, offer Germany some of the smaller British colonies, even abandon Belgium. Now Sassoon dwelt more and more on the futility. 'Expect I'll go back to France about August,' he wrote to Henry Festing Jones, Samuel Butler's old companion and friend of Robbie Ross, on 23 May, 'though I hate the show and am convinced we are losing and that all this loss of life is sheer waste.'[24]

Letters about the book kept coming – those from Gosse and Hamo Thornycroft particularly fulsome, Thornycroft liking the title poem and the softer poems of the first half, even some of the harsher war ones, although he later loathed 'Base Details'. Thomas Hardy admired 'When I'm Among a Blaze of Lights', 'Blighters', 'the grim humour' of 'The Tombstone-Maker', 'They', the 'pathos' of 'The Hero' and the 'reticent poignancy' of 'Working Party'. Bridges, the Poet Laureate, told Gosse he thought the poems had 'more of the real stuff' than 'almost any other' of Sassoon's generation.[25] Praise came also from Arnold Bennett and John Drinkwater, a poet of the Georgian school at its most insipid. The reviews were not all so pleasing. The *Times Literary Supplement* said that sometimes the collection seemed 'almost too naive and slender', although the mixture of 'stark realism' and 'the invisible presences' of rural life and landscape interestingly linked two contrasting worlds.[26] The critic then quoted from 'Morning-Glory', inspired by the Madonna at Oxford, a poem like 'the song of a child-like devout heart'. Sassoon complained to Theresa of this '*very bad*' review, adding that 'the poem they quote is one of the weakest, though quite pretty.

I am afraid it will make a good deal of difference to the sale of the book.' To Hamo Thornycroft, he said, 'Never mind; I will be a wicked poet, I will! Just to spite them.'[27]

It was a bad moment. Theresa revealed that she could not pay her bills and was threatened with a summons from the county court. Sassoon's underlinings and wild handwriting show his strain as he asked her for the details, seeking relief through a joke. 'Why should you worry about things which don't matter a damn? The County Court is, I believe, quite an amusing place to appear at.'[28] Dent was told on 29 May, 'The reviews are very perfunctory and disappointing.'[29]

On the 28th, thanks to Ottoline Morrell, the *Times Literary Supplement*, unusually, printed another review, this time by Virginia Woolf – unsigned, as all *TLS* reviews then were – praising the book's courage, vision and power. She wondered, however, if the realism had come too early, to judge by the 'not so effective' pre-war work that also had 'a rarer kind of interest', possibly 'full of promise'; 'South Wind' for instance showed 'the gift of being a poet'. It is an early sign of the view that Sassoon's war poems are journalistic, that these 'sordid and horrible' experiences blocked the development of an earlier, more poetic talent. On 2 June Dent said in the *Cambridge Magazine*, with characteristic mordancy, that, unlike many books of war poems, the author of this one had lived to choose its contents himself, thus cutting out 'pathetic' juvenilia. To Dent, the title poem was 'perhaps the best', these pre-Western Front lines showing Sassoon's 'broad humanity and sympathy' and sense of the poetry of country life. The war poems he liked for their lack of 'glaring heroics or cheap patriotic sentiment'.[30] The Graves connection helped when Robert's uncle, the journalist C. L. Graves, reviewed *The Old Huntsman* in the *Spectator*, whose editor St Loe Strachey changed the text in proof to express more enthusiasm for the title poem. The book showed, Graves thought, above all 'a generous indignation'.[31] On 9 June, in the *New Statesman*, Edward Shanks wrote of the book's beauty and humour and 'an agile, if not demonstrably profound, intelligence'. Shanks liked the war poems best but thought that when peace came their author 'may do still better work'.[32] On 16 June, the day before Sassoon left London for Weirleigh, the radical journalist H. W. Massingham wrote at length in the *Nation*. The war poems, he said, were not realism or even poetry but epigrams ('by no means the fruit of genius') well suited to 'honest rage and scorn, heartfelt bitterness and indignation'. Sassoon's other work he thought merely typical of 'an intelligent and promising young poet'.[33] Massingham loathed Gosse's idea of the war's cleansing qualities and seized on Sassoon's work to counteract this, pointing to a move from literature to political protest.

*

'FEELING QUITE FIT again now, and have done several wicked little poems in the usual style!' Sassoon told Robert Graves from Chapelwood Manor on 29 May.[34] 'The Hawthorn Tree', written on 25 May, is a sympathetic view of a mother walking in a country lane while her son is 'out in France' and seeing in the blossoming hawthorn tree, birdsong and rain, symbols of his life and longing for home and her tearful foreboding. 'Death in the Garden', on the same day and reminiscent of the elegy for David Thomas, is a sighting at dawn of a dead comrade. Then comes the contemptuous 'A War Widow' in which a woman, probably one of the Brasseys' guests, says 'vast' life is too wonderful to 'waste' in 'senseless war', and the poet thinks of the 'chattering comfortable years' ahead of her, dulled by diminishing sexual powers. In 'A Quiet Walk', on 1 June, a sleeping tramp in a lane three miles from Chapelwood makes Sassoon think of a body with 'some hideous wound'. The next day he finished 'In an Underground Dressing Station', begun at the front in April where a man shot 'horribly though the guts' asks the doctors to be careful of his much less serious ankle wound. On the same day, in 'Supreme Sacrifice', he attacked Lady Brassey's dreamy notion of an afterlife; if only, he writes sarcastically, sergeant majors could teach theosophy to comfort the troops.[35] He told Dent that the news from the front made the printing of his startling war poems even more important. 'The 2nd RWF have lost 25 officers since I left them – (11 killed). They had 6 killed on May 28th, and the show was a hopeless failure.'[36] One of the dead was Orme, an old friend from the Litherland days.

On 1 June there had come an extraordinary reminder of a dead past: a poem in two stately verses sent to him by his father's elder brother, addressed to 'my kinsman true!':

> *O piteous grave! – and black, untimely loss! –*
> *And laughing eyes, too soon acquaint with tears!*
> *Still the loved greetings faintly steal across*
> *The waste of years.*
>
> *A hero's shade now takes the grand adieu;*
> *His meed of praise in stately numbers ranged:*
> *And 'there's a war in France,' my kinsman true!*
> *And 'men are changed'.*[37]

This, the only communication Sassoon ever received from Joseph, demonstrated his reputation; it also showed, by its rarity, how completely he had been cut off from his father's family.

On 4 June, Sassoon left Chapelwood Manor for his club in London where Robbie Ross was waiting for him. A medical board, two days later, described his 'general condition' as 'good' but recommended three additional weeks' leave.[38] One piece of news further indicated the war's powers of transformation. His pre-war hero and leader, the Olympian Norman Loder, had collapsed, the army revealing a latent fragility and hypochondria. In May and June Sassoon visited him in a London hospital to find the great Nimrod worried 'to death' about his health.[39]

On 9 June, he had lunch with the novelist Arnold Bennett, who noted that Sassoon 'expected some decoration for admittedly fine bombing work' but it could not be granted because 'that particular push was a failure'. The war, Sassoon told Bennett, was mostly 'a tedious nuisance, but there were great moments and he would like to have them again'.[40] At Garsington, a day later, Lady Ottoline thought him 'very vain – and his nerves are in a terrible state from the war. It makes him violently self-centred.'[41] On 12 June, Theo Bartholomew noted, before Sassoon's interview with the colonel of the Cambridge University Cadet Force for a home-front job training cadets, 'I feel a good deal drawn to Siegfried: but he is not himself just now . . .'[42] To get up to Cambridge he had had to pass through London; Dent arranged to meet him at Liverpool Street station but there was a German bombing raid near by which killed 162 civilians and severely disrupted travel. They went to King's Cross and took another Cambridge train, Dent noticing, with characteristic mordancy, that 'S. was in a v excited and nervous state – the heroics of pacifism – and evidently a good deal upset by this air-raid'.[43]

*

SASSOON'S SENSE OF a heroic role was plain when he sat, at Ross's suggestion, to be painted by the artist Glyn Philpot. At first it was to be a drawing, but it became a full-scale portrait in oils and, out of affection for Robbie, Philpot waived the additional fee. Sassoon spent many afternoons in a Tite Street studio with the gentle and admiring artist who, having been invalided out of the army early on, tried to exclude war's ugliness by an absorption in work. Quite tall, dark-haired, dandyish and monocled, an unashamed aesthete, Philpot seemed to point back to Sassoon's *fin de siècle* youth, although his work mixed a polite, rather Georgian spirit with slightly more daring Post-Impressionism. 'It was the sort of thing I'd longed for in 1914,' Sassoon wrote of these sessions during which the artist's incomplete attention let his sitter voice many half-formed thoughts or silently settle matters in his own mind: his wish, for instance, 'to be well-known and talked about' for 'no-one wanted easy success more than I did'.[44] The result was a head-and-shoulders study, the head turned in profile, sensual lips slightly parted, a grey shirt open at the neck, a dark jacket adding a sombre note, leaving the sense of a fine, formidable, even wild creature. At the end, Sassoon told Philpot the picture was 'rather Byronic', to which Philpot answered, gazing from 'dark, heavy-lidded eyes', 'You are rather, aren't you?'[45]

While at Chapelwood, Sassoon had decided that he should write something more likely to reach a large audience than fierce poems published in small-circulation journals. At Garsington, Ottoline encouraged him but Philip Morrell – 'defeated and ineffective, a compromising pacifist' – believed any such gesture would be not only useless but painful and humiliating for Sassoon himself. In London Sassoon, at the suggestion of the Morrells, saw the journalists Middleton Murry and H. W. Massingham. He wrote his now famous statement, the final draft of which is dated 15 June, with the help of Murry and Bertrand Russell.[46]

Russell and Murry thought that a statement against the war from a serving officer decorated for bravery would help the pacifist cause. Russell, far more outspoken than the Garsington conscientious objectors such as Clive Bell and Lytton Strachey, went to jail early in 1918 for beliefs which had also cost him his lectureship at Trinity College, Cambridge, and his ruthless lucidity at Garsington, where Sassoon went after Chapelwood and London, kept up the pressure. Ross, Graves, Marsh, Gosse and other friends were excluded. When in London, Sassoon now stayed not at Half Moon Street but at his club. It was here, in the library, the background of his emotional crisis of 1914, that he stared at the fair copy of his protest against the war:

I am making this statement as an act of wilful defiance of military authority, because I believe that the War is being deliberately prolonged by those who have the power to end it. I am a soldier, convinced that I am acting on behalf of soldiers. I believe that this War, upon which I entered as a war of defence and liberation, has now become a war of aggression and conquest. I believe that the purposes for which I and my fellow-soldiers entered upon this War should have been so clearly stated as to have made it impossible for them to be changed without our knowledge, and that, had this been done, the objects which actuated us would now be attainable by negotiation.

> *I have seen and endured the sufferings of the troops, and I can no longer be a party to prolonging those sufferings for ends which I believe to be evil and unjust.*
>
> *I am not protesting against the military conduct of the War, but against the political errors and insincerities for which the fighting men are being sacrificed.*
>
> *On behalf of those who are suffering now, I make this protest against the deception which is being practised on them. Also I believe that it may help to destroy the callous complacence with which the majority of those at home regard the continuance of the agonies which they do not share, and which they have not sufficient imagination to realise.*[47]

Russell had taken him to see a Labour Member of Parliament, H. Lees-Smith, who promised to give the statement publicity in the House of Commons. The socialist journalist and publisher Francis Meynell agreed to print it.

Sassoon's motives were very personal. He found the news of the war unbearable as it came to idyllic Chapelwood from the front: the British assault at Arras, initially successful – as he had heard in France – had slowed down. On 23 April, the Second Battalion's attack towards Fontaine-lès-Croisilles had led to casualties of 120 other ranks and 13 officers, among them the wounded Bobbie Hanmer. The dead of the First Battalion of the Royal Welch Fusiliers included more friends, and then, on 27 May, Orme of the Second Battalion. He felt he could do more for those still enduring what he had suffered during his own short time in the trenches. 'How could I have accepted such a compromise when I was writing poems – a platoon commander in the O.T.C.!' he wrote later of the Cambridge job. 'Not exactly "Byronic"!'

Then he examined his own fears. 'I now wonder', he wrote in the 1940s, 'how much I was influenced by the fact that by protesting I was – as it seemed then – making it impossible for me to be sent to the front again.' Protesting could mean prison and martyrdom, an escape from the fear that he might break down in France, and would be better than a soft job at Cambridge: 'the idea of being martyrised appealed to me emotionally as a form of "heroism"'. Philpot's Byronic picture created an idea that 'remained with me for several years . . . If I looked Byronic, should I behave as such? And do something spectacular.' Sassoon dramatized himself as 'poetically picturesque' or a 'minor prophet', 'an elected spirit whose vocation was to stand apart'.[48] The only recognition of his bravery in the Hindenburg trenches had been a card of printed thanks signed by General Pinney, the man whose plan had almost led to him being killed.

*

AS A POLITICAL document, the statement is quite startlingly naive. Sassoon made several charges: first that the war had become 'one of aggression and conquest' – surely words heard from Russell – rather than one of 'defence and liberation' which he could support. The troops were suffering for 'evil and unjust' ends and there should be peace negotiations. He loathed too 'the callous complacence with which the majority of those at home regard the continuance of the agonies which they do not share, and which they have not sufficient imagination to realise'.

This seems muddled. Certainly the British had made secret treaties with their allies, to add to their colonies in the event of victory; but this remained secret until the Bolsheviks revealed it after October 1917. Nor was it a reason for the Allies' continuation of the war. The Germans, after all, still occupied neutral Belgium – the reason for Britain's involvement in the conflict – and much of northern France. In December 1916, the German Chancellor, Bethmann-Hollweg, had called for peace, partly to curb the Supreme Command's influence over the Kaiser, but there was no mention of terms or of abandoning conquered territory, and the Allies rejected his offer. President Wilson's Peace Note of the same month, which failed to mention the German statement, superseded this; then in January 1917 the Kaiser's proclamation of unrestricted submarine warfare showed Germany to be fighting with renewed ruthlessness.

In July 1917, the Socialist and Centre parties in the Reichstag carried a demand for peace without annexations or indemnities. Bethmann Hollweg, caught between the resolution and its opponents, resigned, to be replaced by a nominee of the Supreme Command; the Generals ignored the Reichstag. The military was still dominant in Germany, especially since the upheavals in Russia and successes on the Eastern Front, and was determined to go on the offensive before American troops arrived in large numbers. The ascendance of Generals Hindenburg and Ludendorff over the Kaiser continued.

Under these circumstances, the jingoistic patriotism of the home front, however brash and aesthetically unpleasing, was a sensible response to the war. In the summer of 1917, the Allies would have been negotiating from weakness after the failed Nivelle offensive and French mutinies. British shipping was still menaced by U-boats and the Americans were sceptical of Britain and France – imperial powers historically distrusted in the United States. Against this background, Sassoon's well-meaning protest appears ill-informed. He seems to have made it from a mixture of emotion, compassion, vanity, guilt and the trauma of his own battle wounds. Over-whelmed for the first time in his life by a sense of his own powers, he had felt surprised, and disappointed, that his poems and strong feelings – close to hysteria after the Hindenburg trenches – seemed, in the summer of 1917, to be having little effect. Now, away from the war, not sharing the suffering of his beloved men, he had perhaps found an effective way of pointing to its horrors and becoming a public martyr as well.

He saw Russell again in London, listening to the assured voice, 'precise, rather pedantic, fairly high-pitched, slightly harsh in tone'.[49] Russell, ruthless in his idealism, had been doubtful, perhaps sensing vanity or instability, but reassured Ottoline. 'You are quite wrong in thinking I don't like him. I thought I saw some faults, but not of the kind I mind, and his courage is wonderful.' He wanted the protest to be raised in the House of Commons, where parliamentary privilege should avoid censorship. 'S.S. had *quite* decided, and has now taken the irrevocable step – at least he was going to when I left him yesterday. So now the matter should be spoken of everywhere – the more the better. I think he is happier than he was . . .'[50]

*

MEANWHILE SASSOON'S BROTHER officers wrote to him about *The Old Huntsman*, 'Birdie' Stansfield saying on 15 June that he thought the book 'magnificent', particularly 'Blighters', but not 'The Hero' because 'it will cause many poor mothers to have doubts and unnecessarily so'.[51] Joe Cottrell wished Sassoon the best of luck in telling the truth, for 'the public have been fed for too long on their special pap . . . Men are beginning to ask what are they fighting – whilst they are fighting and struggling wearily out here day after day – night after night (especially night) their unfortunate dependants are being slowly starved to death at home – not because food is scarce but because they cannot pay the price a wise "Controller" in the interest of profiteers lays down.' Colonel Holmes had come back from leave with a copy of *The Old Huntsman* and had taken it up the line, 'so the boys are enjoying it'. Cottrell expected that Sassoon would be back with them for the next push. 'After all this is the best and only place for a man to be.' He also thanked him for 'the verse' about 'young Orme's death'.[52]

This was 'To Any Dead Officer', written quickly in the middle of June at that desk in his club's library after pondering over the statement of protest – an almost unbearably pathetic poem, with its telephonic dialogue ('How are things in Heaven? I wish you'd say'), the sense of a bad line ('Are you there? . . . Yes') and the dead man as a victim, dutiful but hating the trenches, tragically young. The stumbling speech and emotional awkwardness, even the sense of amateurism of composition, so different to Rupert Brooke's smooth verses, imply a childlike freedom from sophistication or artifice; it is always worse, Sassoon thought, when the unintellectual ones go. He valued the poem so highly that he was prepared to pay for its printing as a *Cambridge Magazine* pamphlet, adding 'who left school for the Army in 1914' to the title and a quotation from the pacifist writer Goldsworthy Lowes Dickinson about 'old men' who had caused the war. Robert Graves, although doubtful about the slang, thought it 'a great poem',[53] and Hardy wrote in August, 'I need not say how much I like the poem.'[54] Later Sassoon cited it to deny that his best war poetry had been 'savagely satirical'. He had never been 'an angry young man', he wrote. 'Only a hurt and indignant one – speaking for those with whom he had endured the trenches . . .'[55] 'To Any Dead Officer' may also hint at a belief that recklessness, like his own, could defy death.

> _Somehow I always thought you'd get done in,_
> _Because you were so desperate keen to live:_
> _You were all out to try and save your skin,_
> _Well knowing how much the world had got to give._[56]

Robert Graves was convalescing at Osborne on the Isle of Wight, in a state of disillusion, having heard that his great love Peter Johnstone had been had up for importuning a soldier. From Weirleigh, Sassoon reported to him, on 24 June, that 'the excitement of the book has mostly died away as far as I am concerned' and he did not know if he wanted 'to rush back and die with the 1st battn, or stay in England and curse everyone to Hell for their stupidity'. If only Hardy – 'the only honest _great_ writer in England now' – would speak out against the war. At least 'darling' Bobbie Hanmer had the MC. 'Isn't it nice for him? Now he will have something else to polish beside his hair, his pipe and his nails.' As for himself, 'I've got other things in my head – _not_ poems.'[57] Then Sassoon wrote to Graves again: 'I wish I could see you, Robert, because I've got something fearfully important to tell you,' of which he thought Graves might not approve ('I'm not engaged to be married').[58] He was upset about a recent review of _The Old Huntsman_ in the _New Witness_ by C. K. Scott Moncrieff, a friend of Robbie Ross, a homosexual, winner of the MC and future translator of Proust. Scott Moncrieff praised the poems of peace at the end of the book like 'Morning-Glory' but said of the satirical war poems, 'the cleverer his effect the more I regret so young a man's having made them'. 'The Hero' Scott Moncrieff thought 'disgusting'; 'They', although clever, 'adds precisely nothing to the corpus of English poetry' and 'The One-Legged Man' was 'too obvious to be effective'. Scott Moncrieff, recently wounded, declared, 'I have saved a leg of my own from destruction; but, in the other event, I think I should not have made a song about it.' The reviewer descended into anti-Semitism, saying the only line he could think of similar to the unpoetic 'Then he remembered that his name was Brown' of 'Stretcher Case' was Flecker's 'But you are nothing but a load of Jews.' To Scott Moncrieff, the war poems were, ultimately, no more than 'a regrettable incident', better forgotten.[59] This further showed that, even in literary circles, these offspring of his deepest emotion and feelings were not having the cataclysmic effect that Siegfried Sassoon, the new Byron, wanted.

At Weirleigh, Sassoon brooded on the way the Jingoes stoked up war fever. He wondered if women secretly gloated 'over the wounds of their lovers. Is there anything inwardly noble in savage sex instincts?'[60] He felt that the politicians should proclaim peace terms that would get a response from 'the German people' for 'nothing could be worse than the present conditions under which humanity is suffering and dying'.[61] By 4 July, he had overstayed his leave by a week. The adjutant of the Third Battalion the Royal Welch Fusiliers sent him a telegram: 'Join at Litherland immediately.' Sassoon noted in his diary that this marked 'the first step'.[62]

A poem written during these days of waiting shows the tension: 'Repression of War Experience' – thought by Marsh to be 'quite wonderful'[63] – dates, according to the poet's notebook, from June 1917 when, as he told Graves, the sound of the far-off guns, audible at Weirleigh, 'nearly drives me dotty sometimes'.[64] Its title, taken from a paper of December 1917 by his psychiatrist, W. H. Rivers (whom he did not meet until July), came later. The poem is, for Sassoon, long: thirty-eight irregular lines that do not rhyme. The scene is a summer night at Weirleigh – mothy, humid, quiet, with candles, books, a pipe to hand, the garden crowded with ghosts of old men who had died 'slow, natural deaths', wrecked by the 'nasty sins' of heterosexual passion. Tight with contrasts as tiredness breaches repression, the poem mutates the books and garden into lines of 'quiet and patient soldiers', death-like roses with impotent 'hanging heads', moths fluttering danger-ously near candles, dark thoughts of war, sexual doubt and shame. It ricochets from the real to memory, until the end when artillery blows Kentish stillness and personal secrets apart, forcing the cry of its final line.

> *You're quiet and peaceful, summering safe at home;*
> *You'd never think there was a bloody war on! . . .*
> *O yes, you would . . . why, you can hear the guns.*
> *Hark! Thud, thud, thud, – quite soft . . . they never cease –*
> *Those whispering guns – O Christ, I want to go out*
> *And screech at them to stop – I'm going crazy;*
> *I'm going stark, staring mad because of the guns.*[65]

In early July, Sassoon hinted to several people that he might surprise them, telling John Bain – a Marlborough schoolmaster who wrote mawkish poems about former pupils who had been killed, including Hamo – about his rejection of the Cambridge job. 'I have made up my mind to do something else. But that is my own affair and would not interest you.' He also tried to shrug off the Scott Moncrieff review. 'I don't mind what they say as long as they write a good fat column!'[66] Graves, from Osborne, asked Sassoon to come and see him: 'I want to know what characteristic devilment this is. Are you standing as a pacifist M.P.?'[67] On 13 July, Graves said he had heard Sassoon was taking the job at Cambridge.

Sassoon wrote to Russell when the telegram came from Lither-land. 'We must get the Statement published as soon as possible, and all will be over but the shouting. I shall probably have to go up there (to the R.W.F. depot)' to see 'all the people who know and respect me. It's pretty bloody; but – I shall be in town to-morrow, and will come and see you on Friday morning.'[68] He believed years later that 'the impulse which caused me to perform the protest exploit was identical with that which led me to behave with reckless daring in the front line'.[69]

On 6 July he sent the statement to his commanding officer, with this covering letter:

I am writing you this private letter with the greatest possible regret. I must inform you that it is my intention to refuse to perform any further military duties. I am doing this as a protest against the policy of the Government in prolonging the War by failing to state their conditions of peace.

I have written a statement of my reasons, of which I enclose a copy. This statement is being circulated. I would have spared you this unpleasantness had it been possible.

My only desire is to make things as easy as possible for you in dealing with my case. I will come to Litherland immediately I hear from you, if that is your wish.

I am fully aware of what I am letting myself in for.

Copies of the original statement went to friends and people he admired, including Lord Brassey; H. W. Massingham; some Members of Parliament (among them Lady Ottoline Morrell's fox-hunting brother Lord Henry Bentinck); Arnold Bennett; such mentors as Edward Marsh, C. K. Ogden and Robbie Ross; and his heroes Thomas Hardy, Edward Carpenter, H. G. Wells (a sign of his politicization) and the amateur golf champion and sportswriter Horatio Hutchinson.

Sassoon waited for the response, amused to get a letter from Edward Marsh, before Marsh had received his, saying he wanted at least ten of Sassoon's poems for the new *Georgian Poetry* collection. '*You think* I don't like your poetry,' wrote Marsh, who disapproved of anti-war sentiment, 'but I do now (*Not*, as you may think, because it's been reviewed well!).'[70] Sassoon knew he would shock many. Meiklejohn to whom he had spoken 'for hours thinks me utterly irresponsible'. To Marsh, he wrote, 'I could do nothing else,'[71] and he told Ogden, 'I suppose someone has to do it.'[72] To Harold Cox, the Liberal journalist, MP and Hamo Thornycroft's brother-in-law, he said, 'No doubt I am entirely wrong. Poets usually are! I hope you will forgive me for being honest, anyhow.

I am afraid Uncle Hamo will never forgive me' (kind old Uncle Hamo eventually did).[73] Later he described his feelings after sending the protest off: 'thus ended a most miserable morning's work',[74] made more difficult by his wish to keep up a charade with Theresa and her patriotic neighbours.

His friends responded before Sassoon went north. Edward Carpenter, the not-quite liberator of his youth, declared, 'Well done, good and faithful!',[75] but others were horrified. Marsh thought it 'intellectually wrong'[76] and Ross was 'quite appalled by what you have done'.[77] Harold Cox disagreed with it 'except in the last paragraph',[78] and for Arnold Bennett – then head of French propaganda at the Ministry of Information – the points could not 'survive argument'.[79] Graves told Marsh that the protest was 'completely mad', that in the regiment, 'they all think he's mad'. It could have been stifled, Graves thought, 'but I don't think S.S. will let them hush it up . . .'[80] Cottrell, who had shown the statement to several other officers, thought it misguided, although brave, for 'this war has shown what a lying underhanded swine the Bosche is – that no Peace now would be of any use'.[81] But there was a group that now wanted maximum publicity, if possible a full-dress court martial: Russell, Lees-Smith, Middleton Murry and Ottoline Morrell.

To Marsh, Sassoon was wrong to say that Britain's war aims had changed; and the entry of democratic America on its side and the continued support of the newly 'democratised' Russian army showed this. 'The Prussian autocracy' must be beaten and 'nothing that you can do will really affect the situation'.[82] Harold Cox thought it madness to negotiate when the Germans still occupied much of northern France, Belgium and central and eastern Europe.[83] To this, Sassoon answered that there was no hope of a German collapse, but 'Prussian autocracy' must be doomed in the long run by 'the social upheaval in Europe'. He then used a phrase of Middleton Murry's: 'nothing seems worthwhile except the truth of one's actions', adding, 'whatever their result may be'.[84] Robert Graves told Marsh, 'Personally I think he's quite right in his views but absolutely wrong in his action.' His own opinions, Graves said,

were those of 'a sound militarist in action however much of a
pacifist in thought'. In theory, the war should end tomorrow but it
must continue 'while a dog or a cat remains to be enlisted'.[85] For
Cottrell, 'war is hideous' but 'fighting the swine' must go on; the
newspapers said Germany was 'in the throes of unrest socially', its
people 'fed-up', and this gave hope, even if, for the battalion, 'things
are as bad as ever'. Cottrell warned against pacifist allies: 'They may
be pro-Germans – one never knows.'[86]

The day before he reported to Litherland, Sassoon wrote to
Bertrand Russell, 'The only thing to do is to force them to take
action, if it can be done without endangering the effectiveness of the
show.' Again, he repeated Murry's words, 'The only thing worthwhile is the honesty of one's actions.'[87]

His journey north on 12 July was bleak, broken in London
for one anxious night when he called on Bertrand Russell and
stayed at Half Moon Street with Robbie Ross away. Russell told
Ottoline that Sassoon was 'hating the prospect of painful interviews
with people he is fond of' yet 'much happier inwardly than before
he took the plunge. Yes, he is wonderfully brave. I admire his
courage more than I can say.' Russell, who realized how well
known his own anti-war views were, wrote, 'I don't want to appear
in the matter myself'; in any case 'S.S. is not an out-and-out pacifist.'[88] To raise the case politically, he had turned to other critics of
the war like the Labour politicians Arthur Ponsonby and H. Lees-
Smith.

The army adopted a soft approach, a brilliant ploy if it had been
planned – but this may be over-estimating military deviousness.
Colonel Jones Williams was on leave so his deputy, the bumbling
Major 'Floods' Macartney-Filgate, received Sassoon while another
deputy, who had lost a leg at Gallipoli, shuffled papers in the
background. The 'delightful' but embarrassed Floods took Sassoon
into another room, offered him a cigar – which he decided, tactic-
ally, to refuse – and said there was still time to forget the statement
of protest. Feeling impolite rather than rebellious, Sassoon declined
to do this. Shouldn't the major have him arrested? Floods looked

mortified. 'I'd rather die than do such a thing.'[89] He suggested that Sassoon go to the Exchange Hotel, Liverpool, and reflect upon his actions.

At the hotel, several subalterns, who knew nothing of his case, greeted him cheerfully. The one-legged deputy adjutant came round, passed on some gossip, made no reference to the protest but left an envelope containing instructions to go to Chester, headquarters of Western Command, for a special medical board. Sassoon told Russell, 'No result so far except tolerant kindness and amiability, and extreme unwillingness to take action.'[90]

Graves obtained permission to leave Osborne, consulted Marsh on the way north and wrote to the colonel at Litherland asking him to be sympathetic to Sassoon. He also wrote, some days later, to Evan Morgan, private secretary to W. C. Bridgeman, the Minister of Labour, suggesting that Morgan should encourage the War Office not to take disciplinary action and to offer a bland response in Parliament. A medical board must be the best way out; Marsh said that Sassoon shoud be told that he would never have the chance of public martyrdom at a court martial but simply be declared insane and put in an asylum. But Sassoon tore up the instructions to go to Chester and began learning poems from Palgrave's *Golden Treasury* to console him while in prison, where he would probably not be allowed books. More letters came, mostly against what he had done. Bobbie Hanmer, who had heard from Graves, said, 'What is this damned nonsense. Don't disgrace yourself and think of us before you do anything so mad. How do you propose to get out of the Army for the first thing? You are under-age and will have to join the ranks unless you become a Conscientious Objector, which pray Heaven you never will.' To Ottoline Morrell, it looked very different: '*tremendously fine*' and 'a True Act'.[91]

In the Exchange Hotel, after two or three days, he had an encouraging letter from Lees-Smith. Then, one afternoon, Colonel Jones Williams walked in while Sassoon was learning Keats's 'Ode to a Nightingale'. At first friendly, the colonel explained that the medical board had been especially set up. Why had he cut it? An argument about the war then began, a briefly buoyant Sassoon realizing that he faced someone even more inarticulate than himself. Eventually Jones Williams said angrily, 'Well, I've done all I can for you,' hinting at the interest taken from on high. The next day Sassoon took the train to Formby and wandered through the sand dunes, avoiding the golf course. He must either hurt his friends and comrades or betray Russell and his new cause. He shook his fists at the sky, then ripped the ribbon of the Military Cross off his tunic and flung it into the waters at the mouth of the River Mersey. The ribbon floated away but did not sink.[92]

Ross was doing his best to plead for leniency, through his links to the Asquiths and others and promises of 'powerful help at the War Office'.[93] Marsh too had been to the War Office, to ask for understanding treatment of Sassoon; then, on 16 July, he found himself nearer to real power when Winston Churchill, called back to the government by Lloyd George to be Minister of Munitions, asked Eddie to be his private secretary again. Meanwhile Robert Graves had arrived at Liverpool. Julian Dadd, also at the base and about to get his discharge, recalled later how Graves had been 'master of the situation, and I thought that, for a man of his age, his ability and tact [presumably with Siegfried] were wonderful'.[94] Sassoon hated to go against all this kindness. 'I wish you were here to buck me up,' he wrote to Ottoline on 17 July, after his talk at the Exchange with the colonel. 'It's very inconvenient being so popular! . . . You see I don't like hurting people's feelings when they are so kind.'[95] If only the case could come before hard-faced officialdom in London, public martyrdom would be easier.

Graves told Ross that Sassoon's colonel had wanted a court martial; it was 'the deputy commander' who showed more leniency. Ross, perhaps dreading publicity similar to that of his earlier ordeal at the hands of Lord Alfred Douglas, seemed frightened. 'One man can do so little,' he told Herbert Farjeon, another peace campaigner, and 'a man with a Christian name such as "Siegfried" is particularly not the man to do good by a protest of this kind'. To Farjeon, Ross seemed to think 'respectability is a better god than truth to one's ideals'.[96]

Graves came to the Exchange Hotel and walked with Sassoon along the shore at Formby. He took the line that 'everyone was mad except ourselves and one or two others' and it was useless to offer 'common sense to the insane': they must 'keep on going out until we got killed'. Graves himself expected to go to France soon, 'for the fourth time'. What 'would the First and Second Battalions think' of Sassoon? He would not be court-martialled, just shut up in an asylum until the war ended, his statement ascribed to shell-shock. Sassoon got Graves to swear 'on an imaginary Bible' that this was true. Then he agreed to go before a medical board.[97] In fact Graves had no grounds for denying that there would be a court martial. His oath was a lie, sworn to save his fragile friend from possible public humiliation, disgrace and further exploitation by anti-war campaigners.

The board met the next day, 20 July. Graves gave evidence to it, breaking down in tears three times, and was told he should go before the board himself, seeming to Sassoon 'much more jumpy and over-wrought than I was'. Sassoon faced three officer doctors, including 'a very sensible nerve specialist who had difficulty in dissuading them from treating me as (a) insane (b) pro-German'.[98] The doctors commented on the 'strongly pro-German tendencies' of some of his *Cambridge Magazine* poems;[99] then the nerve specialist mentioned Craiglockhart, a sanatorium in Edinburgh, and a doctor there called Rivers. Their report said, 'His mental condition is abnormal. His conversation is disconnected and somewhat irrational, his manner nervous and excitable. In addition to this his family history is neuropathic. He is suffering from a nervous breakdown and we do not consider him responsible for his actions.' His 'disability', the doctors thought, was caused by 'the strain of active service, acting on a nervous temperament'.[100]

Two days before, Graves had written to Bertrand Russell, saying that anyone could see Sassoon was suffering 'from nerves' and that the pacifists had been wrong to exploit him. 'I blame you most strongly for your indiscretion in having allowed him to do what he has done, knowing what state of health he was in after his damnable time at Arras.'[101] But, on 20 July, the day of the board, Russell, to another correspondent, repeated his admiration of Sassoon. 'He is altogether splendid, physically, mentally and spiritually . . . There is nothing in the faintest degree hysterical or unbalanced in his attitude, which is the inevitable development of the thoughts and feelings expressed in his poems.'[102] Russell had spoken again to Lees-Smith. 'S.S. remains absolutely unshaken. We have to see there is scandal and no "hushing up" . . .'[103]

The protest irrevocably disrupted the friendship between the 'two Fusiliers'. Graves went back to public-school definitions, nagging about 'good form', writing, while Sassoon was at Craiglockhart, that other officers in the regiment thought the 'invalid' was not acting 'like a Gentleman', that Bobbie Hanmer or 'Tommy' types – 'the exact people whom you wish to influence and save' – would see the protest as 'the worst accusation they can fasten on a friend', a breach of his officer's contract. The only way to their respect was to 'share their miseries' yet 'all the time denouncing the principles you are compelled to further'.[104] Sassoon's answer, more devastating, was to accuse Graves of cowardice by not speaking out much more strongly against the war.

Years later, Winston Churchill, sitting next to a friend of Sassoon's at lunch, made the dramatic claim that he, no doubt urged by Eddie Marsh, had saved the poet from possible execution for mutiny by persuading the War Office that there should be no court martial.[105] But if a court martial had been set up, what might have happened? In January 1918, Max Plowman, the socialist poet and writer, resigned from his regiment, saying he opposed all war – not merely, like Sassoon, British war aims. In April he was court-martialled and dismissed from the army. He then saw Rivers, who had been given a letter from Plowman by Sassoon, to whom Plowman had written. But Plowman was too determinedly political to be receptive to Rivers's attempts at persuading him to conform to the doctor's idea of what war required from an individual. Max

Plowman remained a radical and a pacifist, his First War martyrdom largely forgotten. It was the later literary elevation of Sassoon's actions that gave them such resonance and an excuse for Churchill's exaggeration of what might have become of the soldier–poet. The creation of a myth was only just beginning when on 23 July, supposedly escorted by Graves, who missed the train and arrived four hours late, Sassoon reached Craiglockhart to begin his cure.

SEVEN

'Dottyville'

SASSOON HAD BEEN away from the front since April 1917. While he was in England during the summer, the British successes round Arras faltered, the huge French attack on the Chemin des Dames failed, the lethal German U-boat campaign continued and mutinies spread through the French armies, to be calmed by their new commander, Philippe Pétain, who succeeded the humiliated Nivelle.

Any further offensive in 1917 would have to be a British affair. In June one began at Ypres; the British captured the Messines Ridge and on 31 July gained ground against strong German defences after a massive bombardment. Then the rain came, hardly ceasing for most of August. By the end of the month, after 60,000 casualties, the advance stopped. During a dry September, it resumed; then rain started again, and the mud and slaughter of Passchendaele ensued. Again pleading commitment to Britain's allies, Haig, and his more reluctant subordinates, Generals Gough and Plumer, pushed doggedly into a grim November. Throughout the summer, autumn and first winter months of 1917, news of death and disappointment on the Western Front seeped into Siegfried Sassoon's safe invalid life.

*

FROM EDINBURGH'S WAVERLEY station, in a ravine at the foot of the castle, he went on 23 July, presumably by taxi – and without his escort Robert Graves – to Slateford, a south-western suburb, and a long, dark, stone building under a high rock with a view over the city to the grey North Sea. Here he found himself a patient of Dr William Rivers, a captain in the Royal Army Medical Corps.

Sassoon scorned the other inmates of Craiglockhart, who were mostly, he told Ottoline Morrell, 'degenerates';[1] 'dottyville' he called the place, as if to emphasize his unnecessary presence at this gloomy Victorian hydro that had been requisitioned as a military hospital. He knew that he had disappointed her and Bertrand Russell. The drama of the statement had ended in this place, a retreat for those who might be said to have failed the test of the trenches. If he was like them, he had shown mental and physical weakness. These were the anxieties that Rivers worked on, making Sassoon see that redemption meant going back, probably to be killed.

Rivers, as Sassoon called him, had also been transformed by the war. Born in 1864, some twenty-two years before his most famous patient, Dr W. H. R. Rivers was the son of the Reverend H. F. Rivers, once the vicar of St Faith's church, Maidstone, near Sassoon's weald of Kent. Adored by his two sisters, he missed a Cambridge scholarship from Tonbridge, a public school in Kent, because of a bad fever, possibly typhoid, so went straight to train at St Bartholomew's Hospital in London. The shy, stammering Rivers was adventurous and travelled to Japan and America as a ship's surgeon after qualifying as a doctor, aged only twenty-two. He had wanted to join the Royal Army Medical Corps but was barred by poor health. Instead, on his return to England, he worked briefly at a hospital in Chichester before going back to Barts as house physician in 1889.

In 1891 Rivers moved to the National Hospital for the Paralysed and Epileptic in Queen's Square, London, to specialize in neurology and, eventually, psychology. A year later, he went to Cambridge as a lecturer and began physiological experiments with Henry Head, later one of Sassoon's most trusted older friends; he then worked at Jena and Heidelberg for several months, greatly admiring German medical and scientific achievement. In 1898, he joined, out of curiosity, a Cambridge anthropological trip to Torres in the Pacific and found the fieldwork immensely exciting. Other expeditions to south India and, again, to the Pacific islands led to investigations into kinship and varieties of colour identification that made Rivers a respected anthropologist. In the summer of 1914, when war began, he was in Australia at a conference attended by German scientists. But the war and work on battle-related mental problems at Maghull Military Hospital, Liverpool, brought him back to psychology, and in 1917 he came to Craiglockhart to help to turn the place into a centre for the treatment of shell-shock.

Rivers's looks were unmemorable, friends even disagreeing after his death as to whether he had been short or tall. Broad-shouldered, bespectacled and balding, with a dark moustache, and slightly over-weight, he seemed sympathetic, creating what Arnold Bennett called 'fallacious but charming equality'.[2] At Craiglockhart, where Major Bryce, the games-playing commanding officer, created a relaxed regime, Rivers disregarded military etiquette, forgetting to return salutes or carry his officer's stick. Thought to be timid until his few sharp words silenced the fiery matron, he had a monkish air, never marrying, dedicated to his work, strong, even ruthless, although the wish for adventure pointed to a quiet romanticism; it was rumoured that Rivers chose to treat only the most interesting cases, defending these fiercely from outside interference. Possibly a repressed homosexual, he and Sassoon established an immediate spoken and unspoken emotional intimacy.

Rivers knew about the Western Front from its vict like the man who, after being knocked on to a corpse by a shell's blast, regained consciousness with his mouth full of the contents of a dead German's stomach. He believed in coaxing these patients into realizing why they had collapsed, then building up their power to handle stress, a treatment he called 'autognosis'. Although influenced by Freud, Rivers doubted Freudian theories of infant sexuality and of the Oedipus complex, seeing – as a twist of Freud's idea of self-censorship – hysteria as a return to an infantile stage of development. Traumas, he thought, were consciously put into the unconscious and should be confronted through treatment even if this repression was desirable for civilization. He believed that the repression of instinct became more difficult in the infantile, or primitive, behavioural climate of war. Sex, he thought, had no part in war neuroses, which came from an urge just as deep: that of self-preservation.

Rivers may have joked that Sassoon was suffering from 'an anti-war complex',[3] but the doctor treated his new patient seriously, with gentle firmness. Rivers became not the ideal friend but an ideal father, discovering someone shocked by war – as those dreams showed – and gripped by two fears: of returning to the trenches and of failing the test of manliness, an anxiety since a boyhood suffused with sexual doubt and romantic notions of chivalry. To the doctor, there was only one cure. He saw Sassoon every day at first, then three times a week, in the early evenings; and started, at first indirectly, to try to persuade him to go back to the front.

*

MAJOR BRYCE BELIEVED in the therapeutic power of activity, and Craiglockhart was bustling and cheerful by day as patients played golf, tennis, croquet, billiards, cricket and badminton, swam or kept hens and bees. They joined the camera or gardening or field clubs or an acting group, the model-yacht club, music groups or a debating society, or helped on neighbouring farms. At night, however, the barriers against hysteria crumbled. 'One became conscious that the place was full of men whose slumbers were morbid and terrifying,' Sassoon wrote later. 'Men muttering uneasily or suddenly crying out in their sleep.' This 'underworld of dreams' lay beneath Craiglockhart life, giving it a sense of fear and defeat, of weak willpower fighting an uncontrollable subconscious.[4]

There were about 150 officers in the hospital, and at first Sassoon shared a room with a cheerful Scottish captain. But the more obvious craziness of some of these men made itself clear in his next room-mate, a theosophist who reacted to news of casualties by saying, 'Yes, Sassoon, it is the celestial surgeon at work on humanity.'[5] When not with Rivers, Sassoon walked in the Pentland

Hills, remembering Theresa reading Robert Louis Stevenson to him
on childhood evenings at Weirleigh, and played golf on the nearby
courses, taking no part in Criaglockhart's clubs and societies. To
Ross, he wrote that he found Rivers 'very nice' and that he was
'very glad to have the chance of talking to such a fine man', and he
joked about his own reputation: 'hope you aren't worried about my
social position'.[6]

This may refer to the public airing of his protest. On 30 July, H.
Lees-Smith raised Sassoon's case in the House of Commons, reading
out the statement. The Under-Secretary for War answered that the
officer in question was now being treated for a nervous breakdown
and shell-shock. On the 31st, the debate was reported in *The Times*
and other papers which resulted in Sassoon receiving several aggressively unpleasant letters. On 1 August the police raided the Non-
Conscription Fellowship office and seized a hundred printed copies
of Sassoon's statement before they could be distributed. Then the
furore subsided, stifled by Craiglockhart. Gosse put it all down to
'insensate vanity' and 'self-conceit',[7] Julian Dadd advised 'a little
real rest of mind and body',[8] and Dr Dunn noted in his diary that
'a great many are saying the same thing . . .'[9] H. G. Wells advised
patience and a refusal to stay quiet yet also an avoidance of 'mere
shrieks of protest'.[10]

To Rivers, Sassoon's rank made him prone to a particular neur-
osis: that of English public-school paternalistic anxiety. He dreaded
letting his men down or collapsing in front of them, destroying a
delicate mutual respect. In Sassoon, the wish to protect, then
strengthen and change a weaker person – usually a man – was very
strong, taking the place of robust, equal friendship or love. With
Rivers, there was no equality; Siegfried was first a patient, then a
disciple. But the doctor did not make Craiglockhart into a prison.
'I am perfectly free,' Sassoon told Meiklejohn on 1 August, 'and
there is no pretence made of anything being wrong with my health
. . . Anyone who says I'm "not responsible for my actions" is a
sanguinary liar.'[11] He started to read Henri Barbusse's realistic
book about the front, *Le Feu*, recently translated from French, and

he and Rivers debated the justness of the war. The influence was not all one way – later the doctor wrote of having had a 'pacifist dream' – but Rivers easily dominated their sessions, reducing the patient to exclaiming, 'It doesn't seem to matter much what one does as long as one believes it is right!'[12] Rivers, a socialist, brought up politics and the question of how one might define an officer's responsibility, and by his second month at Craiglockhart, Sassoon felt a growing 'sense of humiliation' at being 'healthy' and 'young' yet 'dumped down among nurses and nervous wrecks'.[13]

Golf, train or tram trips into Edinburgh or to the sea at North Berwick, visits to people to whom he had introductions – the Astronomer Royal for Scotland, the aristocratic poet Lady Margaret Sackville, the Vice-Chancellor of Edinburgh University ('I expect he will bore me stiff')[14] and a professor of literature: these filled time but the war never left him. 'What do you think of the latest push?' he asked Robert Graves on 8 August. 'How splendid this attrition is! As Lord Crewe [the Liberal politician] says, "We are not the least depressed."' Two days later he told Graves that Rivers was going to Cambridge on leave. 'He is an absolute dear and has been a most delightful companion in our evening talks about literature etc. . . . My opinions remain four-square.'[15] A pacifist visitor urged him to desert and come to London to challenge the authorities; Rivers's absence and this reminder of abandoned ideals made Craiglockhart bleaker. 'I'm left entirely to myself now,' Sassoon told Meiklejohn. 'No one interferes at all and as long as I'm in by 10 o'clock at night, they are quite content. However I usually sit in my room and try to write poetry after dinner. The food is beastly, and the patients very unexciting and pathetic . . .'[16] On 14 August, Gordon Harbord, the companion of pre-war Southdown days, was killed in France. Sassoon and he had written to each other often – exuberant letters in the spirit of the hunting field but mentioning the horrors of war – and Harbord had also won a Military Cross. The news took some days to reach Edinburgh, for on 17 August Sassoon wrote to Robbie Ross of 'having a very nice time' and being in 'glowing health', while 700 copies of *The Old Huntsman* had been sold.[17]

*

ON 15 AUGUST, a day after Gordon Harbord's death, another patient at Craiglockhart wrote to his mother about reading some poems that made Shakespeare seem 'vapid'. To meet the man who had written them, he thought, would be better than 'making friends with Tennyson'. The young officer knew that the poet, Siegfried Sassoon, was in Craiglockhart, but awe had so far stopped any approach.[18]

Soon afterwards, Wilfred Owen knocked on the door of Sassoon's room, entering to find, in the startling sunlight, a tall man sitting on a bed, cleaning some golf clubs. Carrying several copies of *The Old Huntsman*, Owen stammered out his admiration and asked for the books to be inscribed. Slowly Sassoon wrote in them while the visitor, 'modest and ingratiating', stood at his side. This new admirer was a small man with thickish dark hair parted in the centre like Wilde's, a moustache and a velvety, emotional, deferential voice with the 'texture of soft consonants and suggested crimsons', a hint of the 'sumptuous', hampered by a temporary stammer. After giving his own name for one of the inscriptions, Owen spoke with his idol of Sassoon's poetry for half an hour, the older man responding to the younger's courtesy and intelligence. 'The Death-Bed', Owen thought, was the finest poem in the book with its double evocation of boating at Oxford and agony in an Amiens hospital. The choice must have pleased Sassoon, who valued his lyrical works more than the epigrammatic satires. As he left, Owen confessed that he too was a poet, as yet unpublished. Turning back to his golf clubs, Sassoon wondered vaguely about the poems of this 'perceptively provincial' fellow patient, an 'interesting little chap'.[19] Later he remembered the embarrassment of Owen's accent.[20]

The differences, both obvious and hidden, were great: Siegfried Sassoon was six and a half years older and Wilfred Owen only 5

feet 5½ inches to Sassoon's 6 feet 1. Then came the abyss between
their backgrounds and experience. The son of a railway official,
Owen had grown up in Shropshire – where his mother's father was
an ironmonger and former mayor of Shrewsbury – and in Birkenhead, following his father Tom's different postings. The family had
a sense of pride, of being set apart from others; Tom Owen claimed
descent from a sixteenth baron, a sheriff of Merionethshire, and
Susan's childhood fostered expectations only partly dashed when
her father, on his death in 1897, left less money than had been
anticipated. Wilfred, educated at the Birkenhead Institute and the
Technical School at Shrewsbury, would have needed a scholarship
to go to university. He saw Oxford as an unreachable utopia, in
contrast to Sassoon's dreamy idleness at Cambridge.

Susan Owen adored Wilfred, her eldest child (she had two other
sons and a daughter). She was dominant in his life, sweet but also a
spur for he must have sensed that for her he represented hope and
vicarious fulfilment, as Siegfried did for Theresa. In 1911, he teasingly wrote of a vision 'cherished from my earliest remembrance', of
Susan in an elevated social position at last: a glimpse of Edwardian
country-house grandeur and 'my sweet Mother, in a delightful
garden, passing a bland old age among her greenhouses, and in a
small carriage drawn by an ambling pad-pony'.[21] Owen felt nostalgia for his grandfather's large house in Oswestry which the family
left on the old man's death, when Wilfred was four years old – an
abandoned paradise. When working in Bordeaux, he put it about
that he was the son of a baronet.

Like Siegfried Sassoon, Wilfred Owen began to write poetry
early, urged on by his mother. Also like Sassoon, he had an early
sympathy for the less fortunate, gained, as with Sassoon's reading
of Edward Carpenter, mostly from books rather than from experience. Susan Owen was an evangelical Christian; and her son worked
as an unpaid assistant to the vicar of Dunsden, a village near
Reading, while striving to matriculate at London University – which
he did in 1911, without the hoped-for honours. His only significant
early literary confidant, apart from his mother, was a first cousin,

Leslie Gunston, who also wrote poetry. In 1912, unhappy and ill, Owen left Dunsden, having lost his evangelical faith. The next year he went to Bordeaux to teach English and when the war began he was on holiday with a French family in the Pyrenees.

In France, Wilfred Owen found freedom, as well as literary encouragement from the French decadent poet Laurent Tailhade and possibly homosexual experiences in Bordeaux. His poetry, like Sassoon's pre-war work, had a *fin de siècle* sense: colourful, homo-erotic, languorous, romantic. Owen, however, was careful of strong feeling, perhaps because it might reveal a regrettable self. 'I love Music,' he wrote to his mother from Bordeaux on 24 May 1914, 'Violin first, Piano next, with such strength that I have to conceal the passion, for fear it be thought weakness . . .'[22]

Owen's first reaction to the war was different from the concern, even love, that he and Sassoon showed later for their men. Although 'furious' that 'the finest brains and temperaments' were at risk, he thought that the guns 'will effect a little useful weeding' and the volunteer British ('poor fellows') should be mourned less than the conscripted continental armies that embraced all the ablest young men.[23] What he would fight for was the sense of 'perpetuating the language in which Keats and the rest of them wrote! I do not know what else in England is greatly superior, or dearer to me, than another land or people . . .'[24] As with Sassoon, his poetry was a refuge from personal disappointment and forbidden sexuality. 'I seem without a footing in life,' he told his mother in February 1915, 'but I have one . . . I was a boy when I first realised that the fullest life liveable was a Poet's.'[25] In October 1915, Owen enlisted in response to the wave of recruiting publicity and while in London met Harold Monro, owner of the Poetry Bookshop and the only English poet of conse-quence to whom he showed his work before Siegfried Sassoon.

At first, he liked the army; but then, commissioned as a second lieutenant in the Manchester Regiment, he suffered fierce shelling on the Somme and the horror of battle, his first experience of the front line ending in nervous collapse, even possible imputations of cow-ardice. Towards the end of June he arrived at Craiglockhart, to be treated not by Rivers but by the psychiatrist Captain Brock who believed in activity, physical exercise and contact with the natural world, from which he thought civilization had drifted disastrously away. In his last volume of autobiography, *Siegfried's Journey*, Sassoon describes a modest, docile young man. Owen's brother Harold, however, recalled how Wilfred 'could be extremely bad tempered and at times almost violent'.[26] But, for the author of *The Old Huntsman*, there was in 1917 an immense reverence, open enough to be embarrassing in its 'Border-Welsh'[27] emotion.

Unlike Sassoon, Owen had involved himself, at Brock's instigation, in many of the activities at Craiglockhart. He became editor of the hospital's magazine, the *Hydra*, for which he wrote facetious editorials, and he might have raised this when he called on Sassoon for a second time on 21 August. Sassoon looked up from a letter he was reading from H. G. Wells, and asked for help in deciphering it, his eyes scarcely meeting his visitor's during a conversation that took place in the shadow of the death of Gordon Harbord – an uncomplicated, joyful young man. This time Owen had brought some poems and the next day they talked about them, Sassoon criticizing old work, praising others like 'Antaeus' or the musical tone of 'Song of Songs'. He advised against early publication, ending with the words, 'Sweat your guts out writing poetry.'[28]

Until Owen left Craiglockhart in November, the two men saw each other often and by early September the relationship had clearly deepened. Allowing the *Hydra* to publish his 'Dreamers' on 1 September, when Owen printed his own 'Song of Songs', Sassoon sent a copy to Ottoline Morrell, writing under the Owen piece, 'The man who wrote this brings me quantities and I have to say kind things. He will improve, I think!'[29] But soon they felt bound by their isolation, perhaps heroic isolation, as homosexuals and as poets. Owen's letters to Sassoon after Craiglockhart – as when he also mocks Leslie Gunston's love poetry because of Gunston's inexperience or in October 1918 writes how 'I desire no more exposed flanks of any sort for a long time'[30] – hint at past intimacy.

At first, however, Sassoon, although youthful in appearance, seemed remote. 'He himself is 30! Looks under 25!' Owen told his mother. But he 'talks about as badly as Wells writes' and is 'very tall and stately, with a fine firm chisel'd (how's that?) head, ordinary short brown hair. The general expression on his face is one of boredom.' Sassoon praised Hardy as the greatest living poet; Owen thought, 'I don't think much of what I've read.'[31] By 29 August, Owen reported that 'a word from Sassoon, though he is not a cheery dog himself, makes me cut capers of pleasure'.[32] On the night of 7 September, Sassoon talked to Owen again about poetry, praising and criticizing his work, and then read his own recent poems: 'superb beyond anything in his Book'.[33] These readings continued over the next two months, a selection from the *Counter-Attack* notebook that might have included the sonnet 'Dreamers' with its lush first verse and contrast between trench life and dreams of home, 'Does it Matter?' ('Does it matter losing your legs?') about physical and mental mutilation or 'Banishment', which shows the dilemma of choosing between rebellion on behalf of his men and sharing their martyrdom in France:

> *Love drove me to rebel,*
> *Love drives me back to grope with them through hell.*[34]

At the golf club once, Owen told his mother, 'my discipleship was put to a severe fleshly trial' when 'the master' failed to return to the club house for lunch, where Owen was waiting, until quarter-past two. Afterwards, Owen suggested Sassoon should write a poem in three minutes in the style 'of those in the *Graphic* etc:'; the twelve lines (written in four minutes) were a perfect parody. They visited the Astronomer Royal for Scotland, planning to tease him 'but it didn't come off',[35] and Lady Margaret Sackville. Owen, on 12 September, described his new friend again for Susan Owen: tall, 'noble-looking', eyes brown or blue, sympathetic but keeping 'all effusiveness strictly within his pages' and (in this) 'eminently English', more 'restful after French absurdities'.[36] Now when Sassoon read his latest poems to him, Owen held back hero-worship and criticized, impressed when the poet said he would make changes. He expected little for the *Hydra*: 'Sassoon is too much the great man to be bothered with it.'[37]

Sassoon introduced 'little Wilfred' to Bertrand Russell's books, to the *Cambridge Magazine* and the *Nation*, to Henri Barbusse's descriptions of trench life. They laughed and talked more about literature than about the war, the older man looking through his new disciple's poems in a corner of the Hydro's dark hall. Their relationship was 'curiously isolated'. Sassoon discussed Owen with no one else in the hospital apart from Rivers, yet soon the awe relaxed enough for the young man to smile at his hero's incoherent 'outbursts of intolerance and enthusiasm'.[38]

From Siegfried Sassoon, Wilfred Owen learned to use looser language, to write more directly from life. Sassoon had dismissed some older sonnets yet praised the lush 'Song of Songs' about dawn singing, love, dying viols, 'voluble leaflets' and a 'murmurous heart', reminded perhaps of his own 'lutes and nightingales'. In 'Inspection', based on an exchange in direct speech between an officer, a soldier and a sergeant over a 'damnèd spot' of blood from a hidden wound, Owen tries Sassoon's shocking realism. The first draft of 'The Dead-Beat', criticized by Sassoon for its jarring mixture of the serious and the facetious, also demonstrates his influence and the humour which Sassoon used both to fend off and to deepen intimacy. When Wilfred Owen showed him the sonnet 'Anthem for Doomed Youth' in October, Sassoon, although suggesting changes, realized its power and tried to get it into the *Nation*. Owen's editorial in the *Hydra* for 1 September uses part of 'The Dead-Beat' ('Who cares the Kaiser frowns imperially?'); he and Sassoon agreed about the 'apparent indifference of the public and the press' and the 'piquancy of smart women', even if Owen told his mother on 27 September, 'I hate washy pacifists as temperamentally as I hate whiskied prussianists.'[39] Many of Owen's poems of the last year of his life were drafted at Craiglockhart: 'Anthem for Doomed Youth', 'The Chances' (in Sassoon's style, with a knock-out last two words – 'Jim's mad'), 'Dulce et Decorum Est' (a reaction to the popular, jingoistic verse of Miss Jessie Pope), 'Disabled'. But not until the 'following summer',

Sassoon wrote later, when some new verses arrived from France, did he begin 'to suspect that my little friend Wilfred was a potential Keats'.[40]

*

Sassoon complained to Meiklejohn on 9 September of insomnia, describing how he indulged his Enoch Arden side – that intensely self-aware person who liked 'stealing into deserted places' – outside Edinburgh, near Roslin, in spite of the 'amorous soldiers and their doxies among the ferns'. On 4 October, he told Graves he hoped to write 'a good, long poem in blank verse' about the heroism of his soldiers, but he could not get a room alone for those late-evening hours when writing came best for him, so instead he would go 'to bed every night tired and irritable, and write querulous peace poems'.[41] He tried to console himself with Norman Douglas's epigrammatic novel *South Wind*; at last, though, he obtained a room to himself and wrote many of the *Counter-Attack* poems, for October was 'always a creative month for me'.[42] On 6 October, the *Cambridge Magazine* printed two of his 'querulous peace poems', 'Does It Matter?' and 'How to Die'.

Bad news came from Cottrell at the front: of Julian Dadd's breakdown, that Ralph Greaves might lose his other arm. Even the stoical quartermaster despaired now in the quagmire of Flanders: 'I am perfectly certain now that I can't carry on. I am far too weak to stick this . . . Truly we shall all be mad or dead presently.' He urged Sassoon to do something. 'Buck up and get into parliament. Surely they can't keep you there against your will . . .'[43] Rivers, back from leave in the first week of October, got tough, 'very war-like', saying that the Germans would crumple suddenly before the 'menace' of American manpower; 'he practically told me to-night that I am a pernicious person', Sassoon complained to Ottoline Morrell. He found himself itching to get back to his old battalion.[44]

Robert Graves came at the start of October. Sassoon, who had paid his fare, directed him to a golf course two-and-three-quarter miles' walk from Craiglockhart because he couldn't get out of his game, and Graves met Wilfred Owen ('a quiet round-faced little man')[45] who showed him 'Disabled', about which he wrote, a few days after leaving Edinburgh, 'Do you know, Owen, that's a damn fine poem of yours, that "Disabled". Really damn fine!'[46] To Graves, Owen was too lax about metre and rules, and 'too Sassoonish', a poet but still 'very careless'.[47] Graves's robust comments seem to have stirred Owen to write six poems in the following week, including 'Dulce et Decorum Est'. Sassoon clearly felt that this more bracing approach was what the young man needed. 'I will tell him to send you any decent stuff he does,' he wrote to Graves on 19 October. 'His work is very unequal, and you can help him a great deal.'[48] Two days later, he had changed his mind about publication. Owen told his mother, 'He . . . said I must hurry up and get what is ready typed. He and his friends will get Heinemann to produce for me.'[49]

On 28 October, when they spent all day together, chiefly at the Scottish Conservative Club, Sassoon gave Owen a book of absurd verses by Aylmer Strong, *A Human Voice*, with its introduction declaring that 'the proceeds (if any) are intended to swell the funds of the Recuperative Hostels (Hampstead and Romford), established for the care of critical nerve-cases from the fronts. Be this the justification of the marketing.'[50] Three days later a more serious gift was a realistic account by Bernard Adams (killed in 1917) of the Royal Welch Fusiliers in the trenches, *Nothing of Importance*. Discharged from Craiglockhart on 30 October, Owen stayed with friends in Edinburgh and on 3 November caught a late train south. That last evening Sassoon and he had dinner at the Scottish Conservative Club and laughed over another book of bad poetry. Sassoon left first, for Owen was to go direct to the station and, as they said goodbye at the door in Princes Street, handed to the younger man a sealed envelope. When the master had gone, the disciple sat on the stairs and opened it, finding a £10 note and Robert Ross's address in London, with the message 'Why *shouldn't* you enjoy your leave? Don't mention this again or I'll be very angry.'[51] At first upset by what seemed like a tip, Owen then felt so moved that he wrote a quick letter from the club too strong, or intimate, to send before walking to the midnight train.

Two days later, from his parents' home in Shrewsbury, 'little Wilfred' poured out thanks to 'Keats + Christ + Elijah + my Colonel + my father-confessor + Amenophis IV in profile'. Sassoon had given him so much: the envelope, Ross's address, the chance to spin 'round you like a satellite for a month', the prospect of becoming 'a dark star in the orbit where you will blaze'. There was a slight holding back: 'you did not light me: I was always a mad comet; but you have fixed me'. Then the 'Border-Welsh' emotion spilled over: 'I love you, dispassionately, so much, so very much, dear fellow, that the blasting little smile you wear on reading this can't hurt me in the least.'[52] Sassoon clearly thought Robbie a better, perhaps more daring – and less busy – guide to literary London than the celibate Marsh. On 10 November, Owen told his mother of meeting Ross, H. G. Wells and Arnold Bennett at the Reform Club, and on 31 December claimed, 'I go out of this year a Poet, my dear Mother, as which I did not enter it. I am held peer by the Georgians; I am a poet's poet.'[53]

*

IN SPITE OF Sassoon's gentle efforts to put her off, Lady Ottoline Morrell came to Edinburgh. Buoyed up by praise in Gosse's recent article on 'Soldier Poets' in the *Edinburgh Review*, he did not meet her at the station and she took a taxi alone to the hotel. At dinner, Sassoon, having turned up late from the golf course, inveighed against women in furs ('primitive savages hanging skins around them') and afterwards, in her sitting room, said the troops at the front haunted him. The next afternoon, late again, he took her out to Rosslyn chapel, and the clear autumn day and his halting words seemed to her 'very dream-like'. His brief engagement to Dorothy Hanmer had come, he said, from convention, not love, because 'all his brother officers had a girl'. He only liked men, finding women 'antipathetic', and this had been a torture to him until Hamo, his brother, had said he was the same. Then, irritated by an overblown sentence, Sassoon told Ottoline she should become 'simpler'. The visit left her 'desolate'. At its end, he played golf rather than come to the station to say goodbye and she wept in the train on the way south. On 13 November, Sassoon wrote to tell her that nightmares about the war made him feel even more certain that he should go back. He was not going to be her pacifist martyr.[54]

When he had told Rivers that he wanted to go back to France, the doctor said he could do nothing more than pass him for General Service. But at least this might calm the guilt set off by letters like that written by Cottrell on 6 November about having 'an exceptionally rough time in the "push" area' in 'terrible' conditions, although casualties were fewer than in some other battalions. The quartermaster declared, 'We were glad to hear you will soon be out again. That shell shock retreat must have bored you stiff,' and Holmes, the commanding officer, wanted him back. Cottrell dreaded the next year, with Russia out of the war 'and Italy finished absolutely'. The only hope seemed to be 'the Yanks'.[55]

First, however, Sassoon had to cope with London where he was allowed to go from Craiglockhart for a couple of nights on 13 November. There to call on a pre-war friend, a Conservative MP who might 'put in an influential word' at the War Office,[56] he joined Ross and Meiklejohn at the Reform Club for dinner and met the poet Robert Nichols (he was struck by Nichols's good looks and his gushing remarks about *The Old Huntsman*). That evening, Nichols, a bestselling writer of vainglorious verses about a war he had been invalided out of after a few weeks because of a nervous breakdown and syphilis, played a trick, for nothing had been said about going on to the house of the hostess Mrs Colefax in Onslow Square. When Ross raised the idea, Sassoon protested at being exhibited as a literary lion, then agreed when Robbie half humorously pleaded that he did not want to lose his reputation as 'a chaperon of soldier poets'.[57] At Onslow Square, he found a party mostly of women and spoke to the artist Sir John Lavery and the American writer Logan Pearsall Smith. Then the armchair and small table in the middle of the room – and a histrionic recitation by Nichols – showed that he was trapped. Mrs Colefax led him to the chair and a copy of *The Old Huntsman*.

He read 'The Hero', 'They' and 'The Rear-Guard'. After this, his first public reading, a guest, Lady Cynthia Asquith, contrasted the two poets: Sassoon 'very shy' and Nichols 'very much at his ease'. She noticed Sassoon's large ears and embarrassment and did not speak to him but saw 'a great charm and a certain sweetness and grave strength in his countenance'. To Lady Cynthia, Nichols praised Sassoon 'as a poet and soldier' of 'astonishing valour', saying they had both suffered from shell-shock. Nichols read 'raptly and passionately', whereas Sassoon's 'terse, laconic style' was suited to his poems' 'brilliant, grim irony'.[58] In between the readings, the actor and composer Ivor Novello played ragtime, the music adding to Sassoon's discomfort. On 12 December Nichols read again at Mrs Colefax's, this time with Gosse in the chair, joined by Osbert, Edith and Sacheverell Sitwell, T. S. Eliot and Aldous Huxley with the absent Sassoon's poems read by another poet, a girl called McLeod.[59] Four days later, Bernard Freyberg, a New Zealander who had won the Victoria Cross in 1916, told Lady Cynthia that it was 'offensive to come back and say, I can't lead men to their death any more' which implied 'a monopoly of virtue, as if other officers liked doing it, because they acquiesced in their duty'. Freyberg thought 'The Hero' 'caddish, as it might destroy every mother's faith in the report of her son's death'. But, to Cynthia Asquith, Sassoon's poem 'broke the conspiracy of silence' that prevented 'those at home' from learning the truth about the war.[60]

The Colefax evening had at least made Sassoon feel the world was interested in his poetry. And he was now prominent in the anthologies, if not always in the way that he would have wanted. That month, E. B. Osborne's bestselling collection, *The Muse in Arms*, an attempt to show 'the British warrior's soul', had only 'Absolution', that call to arms of 1915, and 'The Redeemer', Sassoon's first front-line work: not the satirical 'They' or 'Blighters' or 'The Hero'. Marsh, more daring in his *Georgian Poetry* of the same month, even though he disapproved of the protest, used 'They', 'In the Pink', 'The Kiss', 'The Death-Bed' and 'Haunted', written under de la Mare's influence and tense with terror. Only 'To Victory' showed Sassoon as a happy warrior, before he went to the trenches. He wrote to Dent from the Scottish Conservative Club ('I am not Scottish or Conservative, thank God'), saying that, if the War Office did not let him go to the front, he would leave the army.[61] A medical board on 8 November had noted 'a general improvement';[62] then on 26 November, passed fit for General Service, Sassoon left Craiglockhart for Litherland, having been told to report to the Third Battalion of the Royal Welch Fusiliers.

*

ON 29 NOVEMBER, he went on leave for almost two weeks, to Weirleigh, where Nichols came to stay, less histrionic in the country.[63] Theresa did her best, ordering steaks and onions for them, but 'her tired face' and her disapproval of Siegfried's protest restricted talk to the excellence of the Edinburgh golf courses.[64] Neighbours in Kent had lost relations, Theresa served only 'Empire' wines, out of patriotism, and this added to the gloom. He hunted and went to London, where he saw Ross and showed Eddie Marsh his latest notebook of poems. Marsh was overwhelmed, weeping as he read them, but wondered if Sassoon had thought of its effect on morale. 'Your verse is a powerful weapon, but not powerful enough to stop the war – and that being so, it's rather a responsibility to publish things like the poem about the Major and the General . . . Will Heinemann face it?'[65]

Bad war dreams and an air raid disturbed him. Dent wrote, wondering if Weirleigh might be close enough to Margate for Sassoon to meet Gabriel Atkin, a young artist serving in the army there, and was told, 'Gabriel Atkin sounds all right. I wish Margate was nearer.'[66] Now he feared a return to the trenches. 'I don't think I'll be any good when I get to the war,' he told Graves.[67] Owen reported to his mother that Sassoon felt 'like a condemned man, with just time to put things straight'.[68] One of his last acts before the end of his leave was to ask Robert Nichols to write to Owen.

On 29 November, three days after Sassoon left Craiglockhart, the *Daily Telegraph*, mouthpiece of Conservatism, published a letter calling for a negotiated peace from the Marquess of Lansdowne, a former viceroy of India and foreign secretary at the time of the 1904 Entente with France and the alliance with Japan in 1902 that had ended British isolation. Lansdowne had lost his second son in the fighting of 1915, but other establishment figures also were worried. The constitutional historian Professor Alfred Pollard had complained in August that the 'Prussianisation' of wartime controls had destroyed the freedom for which so many had been killed. Aubrey Herbert, a Conservative who had fought at Mons and Gallipoli, defended Lord Lansdowne in the House of Commons. 'The Lansdowne affair has given us all a feeling of hope, hasn't it?' Sassoon wrote to Lady Ottoline Morrell on 4 December.[69] These doubts about the war came from sources very different from Garsington and Bertrand Russell's anti-conscription campaign.

How realistic were they? For negotiations, there had to be compromise from the other side. In December 1917, after the collapse of Russia and the stalemate of Passchendaele, the High Command hoped for a German victory before enough American troops arrived in Europe. Not until the offensives of early 1918 had failed, with Germany close to revolution, did Hindenburg and Ludendorff call for an armistice, indicating how much the warlords ignored German public and parliamentary opinion. This is one of the tragedies of the First World War: once begun, given the power and political character of Germany, it could end only in surrender or revolt on one side.

From Italy, where the Second Battalion Royal Welch Fusiliers had been sent, Joe Cottrell wrote that at least Limerick, where Sassoon was bound, seemed 'quite out of the way', although Colonel Holmes would be 'specially glad ... to get you back'.[70] On 11 December, Sassoon arrived at Litherland, having stopped in Northamptonshire on the way north for a day's hunting with his pre-war friends at the Atherstone. 'I intend a life of light-hearted stupidity,' he wrote at the depot, having done 'all I can to protest against the war and the way it is prolonged'.[71] Healthy 'beyond measure' and getting some golf at Formby, Sassoon felt relieved that the test of France had been postponed, 'extraordinarily happy', as he told Marsh, although as usual depressed by 'low class Welsh officers . . . I hate them . . . suspicious, greedy, and superstitious'.[72]

Sassoon had written 'nothing for weeks' but felt the poems piling up inside his head. He went to Rhyl, where Robert Graves was stationed, to find Graves 'so funny with his apologetic air about his engagement to Nancy Nicholson'.[73] This outburst of heterosexuality had further complicated their relationship, already in trouble after the protest and Sassoon's lending of money to Graves, the start of many such borrowings. Graves tried to explain the romance: Nancy, the seventeen-year-old daughter of the painter William Nicholson, and sister of another painter, Ben, dressed like a boy, he said, in heavy boots and breeches and had 'a child's heart' and 'a man's brain'.[74] Sassoon should emphasize her masculine qualities to Ross and others: 'young, kind, strong, nice looking and a consummate painter as well as a capable farmer's boy'.[75] Cottrell wrote again from Italy: 'Hope you manage to get back to us. You must pull strings at the W.O. [War Office].'[76]

The Graves engagement led Sassoon to say tactlessly to Ottoline, 'I wish I was in love',[77] but December was not too solitary with Graves at Rhyl and Dent visiting Manchester, where he introduced Sassoon to E. M. Forster's friend, the writer Goldsworthy Lowes Dickinson. To Dent, he seemed 'much more nervy than before he went into hospital', saying that the experience of the air raids in London had 'upset him very much'. Dent hoped 'he will not be sent out to the front again', for he did not seem up to it.[78] On Christmas morning Sassoon played golf at Formby and sat alone in his hut before going to dinner at Colonel Jones Williams's with plum pudding, crackers, games, giggling daughters and the colonel's wife saying that she'd like to see tanks mow down the Irish Fenian rebels. There were some consolations: Bobbie Hanmer, estranged after Sassoon's protest, had sent him a Christmas card, and Marsh's *Georgian Poetry 1916–17* had sold more than 3,000 copies. Yet still he had that dread of how he might cope with the war, of a failing manliness.

*

MARSH AND OWEN had been overwhelmed by Siegfried Sassoon's Craiglockhart poems, and Maurice Baring, to whom Marsh had shown these, thought them too strong and terrible to publish. In fact they are a mixture of the old and new styles. Owen and Lionel Johnson, one of Sassoon's 1890s mentors, may have had a hand in the heightened imagery ('citizens of death's grey land' or 'some fatal flaming climax') of the first verse of the sonnet 'Dreamers' – although Owen and Sassoon had only just met when it was written – that contrasts soldiers' simple yearnings and reality with grand ideals. 'A Wooden Cross', probably the first Craiglockhart poem and written to Gordon Harbord, mixes nostalgia and protest, foreshadowing the Sherston memoirs, and looks back to the innocent sexless pleasures of peace. But the exclusive, tremendous experience of war dominates: painful but elevating to those who had known it. 'Editorial Impressions', begun in May or June but finished at Craiglockhart, shows a young soldier experienced in battle to be much wiser and stronger than his older journalist interlocutor. 'Wirers' – praised by Edmund Blunden as an example of Sassoon's skill with twelve-syllable alexandrines – experiments with rhyme, perhaps influenced by talks with Owen, and 'Does It Matter?', written in depression when Rivers was away from Craiglockhart, again contrasts wounded veterans with home-front fantasies. 'How to Die' also pits truth against fantasy, this time an ideal of gentle death against reality's 'sobs and curses'. In 'The Fathers' the proud talk of 'impotent' old men about their sons also seems false to reality.

Marsh wrote of 'Sick Leave', a Craiglockhart poem, that the Foreign Secretary, Arthur Balfour, was 'deeply impressed by it'. Eddie suggested a change; Sassoon had altered 'from Ypres to Frise we sought you in the Line' to include the phrase 'craters of the line' whereas he preferred the old wording with its 'real'[79] monosyllables in this evocation of hospital nightmares about the poet's duty.

When I'm asleep, dreaming and lulled and warm, –
They come, the homeless ones, the noiseless dead.
While the dim charging breakers of the storm
Bellow and drone and rumble overhead,
Out of the gloom they gather about my bed.
They whisper to my heart; their thoughts are mine.
'Why are you here with all your watches ended?
From Ypres to Frise we sought you in the Line.'

'Attack', in whose lush images some have seen hints of Owen, comes from memories of the Hindenburg Line ('O Jesus, make it stop!'). The oddly fascistic 'Fight to the Finish', which Rivers thought dangerous, compares Members of Parliament to German Junkers – 'Prussians' in one draft, 'butchers' in another – who should be deposed in what sounds like a military coup. 'Survivors' is kinder about the Craiglockhart patients than Sassoon's earlier comments, describing 'children with eyes that hate you, broken and mad'. Gordon Harbord returns in 'The Investiture' where youthful memories dissolve into pity, written with Owen 'practically in the room'.[80]

'Thrushes', in the *Hydra* in November, contrasts man with the soaring thrush, like Meredith's or Shelley's skylark. Two poems pillorying women's obsessive love and bloodthirstiness appeared together in the *Cambridge Magazine* in December: 'The Glory of Women' and 'Their Frailty'. The *Hydra* December issue carried 'Break of Day', in which war collides with a Georgian vision of an English earth's 'old peaceful tale'. The poet hears the hunting horn, sees a fox-cub, shouts to the huntsman and cracks his whip like a rifle shot, the war 'forgotten' through sport in 'the quiet weald'.

'Prelude: The Troops' was written in September 1917. Owen thought the last stanza wonderful with its Whitman-like first line ('O my brave brown companions') addressing the soldiers who march from Georgian-like safety ('bird-sung joy') towards 'ruin'; Blunden likened the poem's beginning to a Greek drama or Keats's first lines in *Hyperion*.[81] Its end – evoking the dead passing through 'some mooned Valhalla' – recalls the earlier 'Two Hundred Years After', as well as Sorley's 'millions of the mouthless dead', in the 'unreturning army that was youth'.

> *O my brave brown companions, when your souls*
> *Flock silently away, and the eyeless dead*
> *Shame the wild beasts of battle on the ridge,*
> *Death will stand grieving in that field of war*
> *Since your unvanquished hardihood is spent.*
> *And through some mooned Valhalla there will pass*
> *Battalions and battalions, scarred from hell;*
> *The unreturning army that was youth;*
> *The legions who have suffered and are dust.*

'Prelude: The Troops' became the first poem in the 1918 collection, *Counter-Attack*. But the most effective is 'Counter-Attack' itself. First drafted in July 1916, partly worked up from his diary, this is the realistic Sassoon, with drenched trenches, men at dawn, a 'blundering officer', corpses' 'naked sodden buttocks', shells lobbed over by the 'Allemands', possibly a tribute to Barbusse.

> *We'd gained our first objective hours before*
> *While dawn broke like a face with blinking eyes,*
> *Pallid, unshaved and thirsty, blind with smoke.*
> *Things seemed all right at first. We held their line,*
> *With bombers posted, Lewis guns well placed,*
> *And clink of shovels deepening the shallow trench.*

Rain, 'the jolly old rain' – the phrase not perhaps a take-off of establishment-speak but of ineffectual English gentleness – blurs everything, appropriate to the poem's ambiguity. Does the German counter-attack fail? Can this be linked to the failure of the soldier's own counter-attack against death?

In 'Twelve Months After', Sassoon recalls his platoon of the previous year, most of them dead; 'old soldiers never die' is ironical. The Petrarchan sonnet 'Banishment' also evokes his love for his troops and the sense that, having rebelled out of pity, or love, he should go back for the same reasons. 'Autumn' sees the men's lives as 'the bronzed battalions of the stricken wood' and shows guilt at his own failure to do more: 'the burden of your wrongs is on my head'. Robert Graves had urged Sassoon to look to a better world after the war, to break out of this perpetual horror, to 'cheer up', and remember when war had seemed 'a joke for me and you'.[82] But the 1890s were still with him: the narcissism, extravagant language, beauty mixed with pain. In October, Sassoon abandoned realism in 'The Triumph', moving from dawn beauty to sadistic impulse ('I was cruel and fierce with despair') and masochism ('I was naked and bound') before his wartime comrades' faces bring beauty back. The 1890s feel comes also in 'Invocation', apparently an early Limerick poem, mixing Georgian sentiment with Swinburnian language: dawn's 'lakes of fire', 'heaven's bright hill', 'glades deep-ranked with flowers', 'remembrance of all beauty that has been', 'stillness from the pools of paradise': reminiscent of those privately printed collections of his youth.[83] He sent it to Lady Ottoline Morrell. In January 1918, Siegfried Sassoon went to Ireland – still, in part, his pre-war poetic self.

EIGHT

'I must be strong'

ON 7 JANUARY 1918, Sassoon reached Limerick where the New Barracks, River Shannon and green hills were an improvement on bleak Litherland – although potentially more dangerous, for there had been a surge of violent nationalism in Ireland with the Easter Rising of 1916 and subsequent execution of its leaders. Yet the town seemed calm with only some shouts of support for the Sinn Fein, or nationalist, leader Eamon de Valera. Sharing a room with 'little Billy Morgan', who had won the Albert Medal after twenty-three months' service in France and four wounds, he supervised the drilling of recruits, gave lectures on subjects like patrolling and felt proud when his pupils looked smart: 'a very blameless young officer again', as he reassured Gosse.[1] In his diary, he noted his ease of mind yet thought, 'It is a drugged peace, that will not think, dares not think. I am home again in the ranks of youth – the company of death.'[2] Four officers at Limerick had been in France with the First Battalion in 1915 and 1916 and spoke almost nostalgically of Mametz.

Sassoon had time to write poetry, less sharp than that written at Craiglockhart, though he still wanted to infuriate the 'Jingoes'.[3] A dreamy view of Billy Morgan is given in 'Journey's End', written the day after his arrival at Limerick; 'A Moment of Waking', of the same day, describes the ending of a nightmare about death, inspired perhaps by waking on the boat. 'In Barracks' is even more passive,

with its Housman-like lines about a 'bugle's dying notes' declaring
'Another night, another day' to the 'lusty Fusiliers' on 'the barrack-
square, washed clean with rain'. Gosse and Ottoline Morrell were
sent the *fin de siècle* 'Invocation' about escape into dawn's beauty;
in 'The Dream' a summer garden darkens into drizzly dusk reminiscent of the French village where he had inspected soldiers' feet,
wondering if they guessed his 'secret burden' of regret at taking
them into the front line. 'Dead Musicians' is about composers – all
German or Austrian (Beethoven, Bach, Mozart) – who 'built
cathedrals in my heart' but now seemed remote from the 'slangy
speech' of the soldier 'lads' and the mess gramophone's ragtime.
War killed not only friends but artistic appreciation. Then on 30
January came the last of three poems about Gordon Harbord,
'Together'. Sassoon may also have written 'Suicide in the Trenches'
at this time: a return to bitterness about 'a simple soldier' shooting
himself in the winter trenches:

> *You smug-faced crowds with kindling eye*
> *Who cheer when soldier lads march by,*
> *Sneak home and pray you'll never know*
> *The hell where youth and laughter go.*[4]

In 'The Noble Art' he conveys the absurdity of an army boxing
match ('let's box the Boche with gloves and then we're safe to win'),
so different to the reality of the Western Front.[5]

On 21 January, his name came through on a list of those going
to Egypt. Instinctively he wired Major Kearsley of the Second
Battalion in France asking to return to the Western Front. As Private
Frank Richards handed the telegram to Kearsley, Richards reflected
hopefully that 'it was only once in a blue moon that we had an
officer like Mr Sassoon'.[6] Sassoon enlisted Marsh in these attempts,
but Eddie answered, 'My dear, you can't expect me to help you go
to a place where you'd be more likely to be done in . . . I hope you
do go to Palestine.'[7] Rivers too favoured the safer front. Sassoon
went to Cork for an anti-gas course and, in the Cork County Club,
met another reminder of the war: an old clergyman who revealed

that his son, in the First Cameronians, had been in that hellish Hindenburg Line dug-out in April 1917.

He was on the gas course when Robert Graves got married on 23 January, an event that (as Graves had foreseen) caused much backchat among the bridegroom's homosexual friends. Marsh commented on an 'uncommonly plain' bride (although admitting that she seemed 'nice, honest and intelligent' and 'a good artist')[8] and Ross said that the couple might have a 'coal-black'[9] child because of the Nicholsons' reputed negro blood. Sassoon, who had already lent his fellow Fusilier money, offered a wedding present of a Rolls-Royce or a Crown Derby dinner service after the war. Graves, never bashful about borrowing, counter-attacked, writing, 'Please henceforth regard Nancy as your mother: she'll play the part much better than most.'[10] Wilfred Owen went to the wedding, in the hope of seeing Siegfried. Thought likely to break down at the front, Graves, after a short honeymoon, went back to the barracks at Rhyl, never returning to the trenches.

At Cork, on the course's last day, Sassoon played truant to go fox-hunting in a haunted, empty land that 'seemed to go deep into my heart'.[11] There were also days with the Limerick and other packs and Mr Harnett, an old character known locally as 'the Mister' who had made money in the United States and spent it on horses, drink and generosity – the sort of chaotic innocent that Sassoon liked. The wild country had deep ditches and high banks surmountable only by locally hired horses in a sporting world buoyed up by drinking in pubs and gargantuan alcoholic meals in the houses of the local gentry. The good humour could crack – as when a pub-keeper prophesied mayhem and murder and 'you officers', even if friends of the popular Mr Harnett, had better leave Ireland 'if you set value on your own skins'[12] – but in this landscape Sassoon felt that true poetry could come from what lay deepest in his heart: the mysterious, silent, natural world. Yet he knew that he must write again about the war.

The protest still had a flickering life. On 18 January, a Mr Sullivan of Birmingham, travelling north by train to Preston, found a document in the luggage rack of his compartment which turned out to be Sassoon's statement against the war, dated July 1917, perhaps one of those printed up at Russell's instigation and left there by an unknown person. Shocked, Sullivan sent it to the War Office, where an official passed it to the Intelligence section, noting, 'I think you wd like to see this. Lt Sassoon was undoubtedly the author but when it was written he was a lunatic vide medical board . . . and it seems that it is possible that some pacifists are circulating Sassoon's insane effort.' An Intelligence officer responded, 'I am informed [that the document] is not now circulating to the same extent as formerly.'[13]

*

HEINEMANN WAS BEING difficult, admitting to Ross that the new poems' 'haunting quality' made up for 'the horror of some of them', but there were not enough for another book and he wanted less on the trenches. He did not like 'Dressing Station'; the last line of 'The Effect' was 'quite impossible'; another poem ('Seventeen') was so 'horrible' that it might be used as evidence of British atrocities for which the Germans could take reprisals. 'To Any Dead Officer' offered propaganda to the enemy and might lead to the publisher being prosecuted under the Defence of the Realm Act. Of 'Banishment' he wrote, 'Is this not a little too personal?'[14]

Sassoon declared that he would change nothing. Surely the shortness of the collection, and its single theme, added to its impact? He might have to find another publisher. Marsh also opposed changes and liked a short book even though he doubted 'whether it is right from the national point of view to publish the book at all, but I have assumed all along that you've made up your mind about that'.[15] Marsh wanted 'Repression of War Experience' included and 'Atrocities' omitted. To him, the new poems were wrong in implying that peace was 'necessary at almost any price, to stop the horrors', for 'I am convinced as ever that we are in the right, and that we ought to carry on at whatever sacrifice'[16] while there was some hope of victory. Sassoon told Ross he would omit 'Atrocities', which had apparently shocked some of his brother officers, and had doubts about 'Repression of War Experience' because Robert Nichols disliked it. In his diary for 29 January, he drafted a blander poem called 'Beginnings', which might satisfy Heinemann: an evocation of grey faces at dawn, perhaps of dead comrades: then three lines from his pre-war self:

> *Set forth, my song and at your journey's end*
> *Be laden with the light that climbs and fades*
> *And pinnacles with stars the soul of man.*[17]

'Memory', written on 1 February, a day bleak because of wet weather and a long journey to a cancelled hunt, evokes carefree youth, a grimmer present, then sees the past as permanently enriching ('I am rich in all that I have lost') and ends in nostalgia, perhaps inspired again by memories of Gordon Harbord.

> *O starshine on the fields of long-ago,*
> *Bring me the darkness and the nightingale;*
> *Dim wealds of vanished summer, peace of home,*
> *And silence; and the faces of my friends.*

The same day he wrote 'Idyll', describing a meeting of lovers rather than of friends. More sensual than 'Memory', the 'you' of the poem comes not from the past but from that ideal 'where beauty murmurs to the soul asleep'.[18] On 3 February 'Après la Guerre', dedicated to Ottoline Morrell, declared that 'I could be happy' in a peacetime spring with loneliness abated by bird song and God 'in the air', yet the old 'cry of pain' awaited him: 'I must be strong.'[19] In 'Remorse', written on 4 February, he returns to the rain-swept Western Front and to 'screaming' Germans running away, chased by 'our chaps' intent on 'sticking them like pigs', and asks, 'Could anything be worse than this?'[20]

*

ON 7 FEBRUARY, ordered to embark for Egypt from Southampton on the 11th, Sassoon made a list of books to take: *The Oxford*

Book of English Verse, Keats, Wordsworth, Shakespeare's sonnets, Hardy, Crabbe, Browning, *A Shropshire Lad*, Meredith, Barbusse's *Le Feu*, Pater, Trollope, Surtees, Bunyan, Plato, Scott's *The Antiquary*, Tolstoy's *War and Peace*. The next day he had a last hunt with the Limerick, a generous late lunch and champagne with the Mister and his friends, then 'a mad rush' to the station.[21] Some Fusilier officers and hunting people were on the platform to give a cheerful farewell; at Dublin he caught the ferry, sailing through waters made dangerous by German U-boats, arriving at 40 Half Moon Street on the morning of 9 February. He lunched with Marsh and Ross, talked about Heinemann's obduracy, went to a Queen's Hall concert that included Beethoven's fifth symphony and the pianist Myra Hess playing César Franck and, having dined quietly with Robbie, saw Rivers. Then, after Heinemann, came Thornycroft life at Melbury Road and Theresa, 'brave as usual'.[22] On 11 February, he left Waterloo at noon, seen off by Ross and Meiklejohn. His boat from Southampton reached Cherbourg at eight o'clock the next morning, before, following a night in the rest camp, the long train journey began. Sassoon was joining the Twenty-Fifth (Montgomeryshire and Welsh Horse Yeomanry) Battalion of the Royal Welch Fusiliers, in the 231st Brigade of the 74th (Yeomanry) Division in Palestine, part of the Egyptian Expeditionary Force under the command of General Allenby.

He read *Barchester Towers*, Hardy's *The Woodlanders* and *The Renaissance* by Walter Pater, feeling feverish as the train edged southwards through bright days and cold nights. His companions – one had been an escort on his journey to Craiglockhart in July – were 'all decent chaps',[23] one only mildly irritating. Near Bologna, he tried some George Moore, found it unpleasant and went back to Hardy, Pater and Barbusse; Pater seemed to be in tune with the Italian landscape and with an awareness of his own Paterian 'hard, gemlike flame' of creative force.[24] Turned out at a sunlit Faenza, they washed and had coffee at a hotel, then left the next day, travelling along the Adriatic shore among olive groves, fig trees and the vine-pergolas and almond blossoms of Brindisi before reaching Taranto at nine o'clock in the moonlight on 21 February.

In the camp, Sassoon listened to the sea, then slept on the train and had his watch stolen. The place was full of officers, many on their way home – mostly coarse-looking except for the doctors. After dinner, while walking alone, he heard a piano and peered into a marquee to find some Jewish soldiers from an entirely Jewish volunteer battalion, one 'with his curved Hebrew beak' and 'thin-lipped mouth', another 'little Jew' identifying the performers for Sassoon – who, as usual, seemed oddly oblivious of his father's ancestry, preferring the language and thoughts of an English gentleman.[25] Three days later they left Taranto in the liner *Kashgar*. 'I realise now that I couldn't have stood any more French horrors without breaking down,' he told Meiklejohn. Gordon Harbord's brother Geoffrey, usually cheerful, wrote wondering if self-determination for 'bloody Belgium' was worth the loss of friends, several seasons' hunting and his father's misery after Gordon's death.[26] From Dent came different news: another mention of the artist Gabriel Atkin at Margate, then of the writer Osbert Sitwell in London wanting 'revolution' – a foretaste of post-war radical chic.[27]

On 28 February they reached Alexandria. Weak after fever, Sassoon felt no poetry ('I *must* have the heroic'), thinking, as he approached the war again, that he must abandon 'nature-poems'.[28] On 2 March, he was at the base camp at Kantara, enduring the same inane mess talk and sentimental songs or ragtime. There were consolations: onions for lunch, a garden in Ismailia, the romance of the Suez Canal, two Irish officers talking about the writers Francis Ledwidge – a poet killed in Flanders in July 1917 – and Lord Dunsany. These were glimpses of what mattered. But he felt ill, bored while his fellow soldiers seemed obsessed by lust; at least there had been plenty to do on the Western Front. In Port Said, Sassoon bought some books on the list made before leaving Ireland – *War and Peace*, Scott's *The Antiquary*, Meredith's poems – and thought of Rivers, an absent guide. Then he shared a cattle truck with thirteen officers, disembarking at Ludd, the railhead built to take troops and supplies into Palestine, after passing biblical scenes of camels, donkeys, villagers among crops – all this prompting thoughts of his Jewish origins at last, although the larks brought back an English summer.

But the rocky hills were desolate; an artillery major, speaking of Jerusalem, called the garden of Gethsemane 'the dullest show I've ever seen!'; and eight miles north, on a hilltop at Ramallah, the divisional HQ, a sergeant spoke of the hardships endured by the troops in Palestine. Sassoon, however, cheered up as the sun lit the landscape of Doughty's *Arabia Deserta*, although rain had turned the roads to mud, as in France. On 14 March, he left Ramallah, walking six miles to the Divisional Supply Dump, before moving on to the Twenty-fifth Battalion of the Royal Welch Fusiliers, a unit of territorial – yeomanry or hitherto part-time – soldiers, lower in the military hierarchy than the regular army, rather 'a rag time show'. His battalion, commanded by Lord Kensington, a Pembrokeshire landowner, mixed soldiers from the Welsh Horse, the Montgomeryshire Yeomanry and the Royal Welch Fusiliers. Sassoon commanded C Company with the temporary rank of captain.

Since Allenby's arrival from the Western Front, the British had captured Jerusalem and Jericho; Sassoon's company, with only one other officer, had recently had two killed and one wounded, and looked exhausted. His first task, however, was road-mending in the rain, after an idiotic speech from the brigadier, praising them for chasing 'Johnny Turk' and saying he hoped soon to command a division. Sassoon appraised two officers from B Company sharing his tent, as usual rather scornful: one an amusing 'commercial gent' from Welshpool, the other a well-read Oxford man ('a sentimentalist – not strong'). He wondered if his own death might come here, but thought 'a wooden cross in France' more likely.

As if to echo this, on 21 March a huge offensive began in the west. Reinforced by troops from the Eastern Front, the Germans smashed into the British line near Arras, forcing General Gough's Fifth Army into retreat, German forward units advancing some fifty miles. While Sassoon listened to the medical officer talk about pre-war birdwatching, news reached Palestine that most of the gains made since the Somme had gone – a further sign, he thought, of the war's futility. On 30 March, his glum little poem 'In Palestine' contrasts the natural world with 'the anger of the guns' that made him feel 'scorn for the deeds of men'.[29] On Easter Sunday he and Captain Bigger, the birdwatching doctor, were out on green hills reminiscent of Ireland, while reports from France grew worse.

The German gains sparked rumours of a move to the Western Front, and again he wondered how he would stand the trenches. Transferred to A Company as second in command – C Company's commander having returned from leave – Sassoon moved his soldiers down to the railhead at Ludd as the rumours became a reality. He sensed an air of dissolution: a padre drunk on communion wine, an after-dinner sweepstake organized by Lord Kensington – an 'odiously vulgar and snobbish' man and 'a very bad type of British nobleman', apparently 'windy and incompetent'[30] – a misguided attempt to relieve fear that took money from the poorer junior officers. On the way to Ludd, they passed General Allenby, then some Turkish prisoners guarded by Highlanders; 'Make the fuckers work, Jock,' someone shouted. At lunch Lord Kensington, to syco-phantic laughter, told how a friend of his had machine-gunned 280 troublesome Turkish prisoners. The poem 'Shadows', written on 10 April, has darkness following the marching column with real war 'at our feet like toads', and the diaries, reflecting his heightened feelings and perhaps the liberating influence of Rivers, become more frankly sexual, describing a man dozing on the train to Kantara, a foretaste of the July poem 'The Dug-out';[31] 'young Roberts' – 'a sort of Apollo' – at a football match, wearing only tight shorts; and the handsome Jim Linthwaite[32] who is probably aware of Sassoon's interest.

Back at 'beastly'[33] Kantara, he escaped to a lake in some salt marshes about a mile away, alone except for an aeroplane overhead and a flock of flamingos, to bathe in the shallow salt water and run in the desert, happy in solitude. There was a concert party – the singer Lena Ashwell and other performers, a 'jangling rag time piano', footlights under the night sky. Sassoon, after stout and champagne at dinner, became moved by these rows of soldiers under possible sentence of death, their choked tears at visions of Blighty, of the past, the popular music bringing nostalgia and memories of the dead. He left – it was too much, stronger than anything he had seen since leaving England; and from this came, two or three days later, the poem 'Concert Party (Egyptian Base Camp)', using the names of some of the songs ('God Send You Home', 'A Long, Long Trail', 'I Hear You Calling Me', 'Dixieland') in a mixture of melancholy and consolation. In the vision of 'low-jargoning men' drawn like moths to the faded gaiety of the singers and 'some actor bloke from town', sentimentality fools victims of dying innocence:

> O sing us the songs, the songs of our own land,
> You warbling ladies in white.
> Dimness conceals the hunger in our faces,
> This wall of faces risen out of the night
> These eyes that keep their memories of the places
> So long beyond their sight.

His other poem of this date, 'Flamingos (Imitation of T. Hardy)', is less ambitious: a description of the bare desert – contrasted with green England – interrupted by the beautiful flying flamingos.[34]

When Dr Bigger – his one friend – joined another division that was staying on in Palestine, Sassoon felt set up for solitary greatness on the Western Front, if his fragile mind could last. And death in France at least meant freedom. Only the 'simplicity' of the men and those other worlds of great writers like Tolstoy (he was reading *War and Peace*) and Hardy kept him going – secret worlds kept from Charles Wiggin, a pre-war hunting friend, who was on his way to join his regiment in Jordan. Sassoon spent a jovial evening with Wiggin and four other Old Etonians who spoke of the 'Yankee'[35] army, fox-hunting and the next year's offensive. Other officers were much worse: Lord Kensington, Bardwell ('a half-baked product of Eton and Sandhurst'), Ellis ('a suburban snob'), Stable (a bit better but still a snob), all warped by the war, with just one shy major quite decent.

The ship, SS *Malwa*, left Alexandria on 1 May in a convoy with six other vessels, escorted by nine or ten destroyers. While in the port, Sassoon had tried, and failed, to see Dent's friend E. M. Forster, who was working there for the Red Cross – someone else who felt nostalgia for the pre-war world, loathed jingoism and dreaded post-war Britain. Sassoon wrote to Forster from on board, saying how sorry he was his division had not been allowed ashore because the previous one to leave for France had behaved so badly ('it is indeed a disaster that two eminent authors must be so cruelly isolated'). Of the officers he said, 'I simply loathe them as a class,' and the troops, asleep and patient at night on deck, 'make me hate being an officer'. Then came the hint of martyrdom: 'I fear they'll do me in this time, or else send me off my chump.'[36]

There were three battalions on board – about 3,300 men on deck in the sun, mostly longing to get to France because it was nearer home – with a divisional general, four brigadiers and numerous staff officers. The soldiers lay sometimes with their arms around one another, 'pathetic and beautiful and human', arousing 'a sexual emotion in me',[37] and this journey towards the trenches inspired the poem 'Night on the Convoy', in which 'lads in sprawling strength' sleep on deck as still as the corpses round Arras. The inarticulate patience of the men, those victims, joins the mystery of his own lonely but thrilling tragedy:

> We are going home. The troop-ship, in a thrill
> Of fiery-chamber'd anguish, throbs and rolls
> We are going home . . . victims . . . three thousand souls.[38]

From *Howards End* he copied out Forster's words on the certainties of rural peace and an English spring and felt awed by the book's end, 'that wonderful and terrible finish, with its sunset glow of tired tranquillity at the last'. On the morning of 7 May, they reached Marseilles.

On the ship, Sassoon wrote 'Testament', a poem that condemns

the sending out of 'lads', but ends in personal consolation that he
had 'cried his cry' of protest: 'you have played your part' (the last
two lines were used again, slightly differently, later that year in 'To
Leonide Massine in "Cleopatra"'. His pity, he thought, should be
vast enough – like the Spirits in Hardy's *The Dynasts* – to include
even red-faced drunken officers, but another shipboard poem –
'Civilisation' – shows contempt as an officer relaxes, his hair bright
with oil, with drinks available, the war forgotten: 'civilisation at
last' and its anthems, the popular songs. Sassoon wanted another
book, as if in anticipation of what he expected for himself: 'send me
the English edition of Duhamel's *Vie de Martyrs*, please',[39] he wrote
to Lady Ottoline Morrell, to whom he posted a poetry notebook so
that it might survive his death.

NINE

'Threshold of the dark'

AT A REST CAMP outside Marseilles, everyone seemed happy to be back in Europe, and to have avoided the enemy submarines, in spite of reports that the British had lost more ground and another ship had hit a mine outside Alexandria with most of those on board drowned. Sassoon and some officers, including Lord Kensington, had dinner in the town, went to a music hall and then, the next day, to the zoo. Some relief came with the arrival of letters and a cheque from Heinemann before, on 9 May 1918, they left Marseilles by train.

Sassoon read H. G. Wells's *Kipps* on the journey north and three days later they reached Noyelles-sur-Mer, marching another eleven miles to the village of Domvast, about eight miles from Abbeville, near the battlefield of Crécy, some fifty miles from the front. Sassoon's job was to train inexperienced troops, and in his copy of a training manual the only marked passage is the injunction that the first duty of young officers should be 'to look after the comfort and well-being of their men at all times, and that it must be a point of honour to do so before thinking of their own needs'.[1] In April the enemy had struck again north of La Bassée, along a front that included Festubert, and Sassoon and the battalion moved to this sector, near Saint Floris, in July. First, however, he had some peaceful, fine days, buying food from the locals and seeing the men settle in their billets near Domvast. The landscape of beechwoods, flowering hawthorns, fading bluebells and lush orchards seemed to foster an even greater romantic fatalism in which he told Robert Graves not only that he had left him £250 a year in his will but that Robert Nichols ('the best poet of the three') must write an elegy about him if he was killed.[2]

Meanwhile prospects for British homosexuals looked particularly bleak, another reason to doubt the cause for which he was fighting. In London Robbie Ross felt harried again: first through the prosecution of his secretary Christopher Millard for homosexuality, then by more public abuse from Lord Alfred Douglas. In March the police had raided Half Moon Street under the Defence of the Realm Act because Ross was 'an art critic, a pacifist, a consorter of the company of conscientious objectors, a sympathiser with and visitor of German prisoners, a former professed Roman Catholic and now a professed and militant atheist'.[3] In June, Pemberton Billing, a Member of Parliament who had been sued for criminal libel, claimed in court that the Germans had a Black Book of 47,000 British homosexuals whom he threatened to name. When Asquith ceased to be prime minister in December 1916, Ross had lost a protector. Sassoon confided in Graves, 'I am very worried about dear Robbie.'[4]

*

ON 15 MAY 1918, another golden day, the inspiration of 'The Kiss', that 1916 poem of brutality and doubt, reappeared: Colonel Campbell and his lecture on the use of the bayonet. Standing on a farm wagon, Campbell put on his stunt which seems to have oddly impressed Sassoon, even though he condemns it in his diary. The colonel declared it an illusion that warfare no longer relied on human force; to him, battles were won not by artillery but by men who, in hand-to-hand fighting, overcame the enemy by 'guts!'. In his copy of *The Tactical Employment of Lewis Guns*, Sassoon wrote down 'six Cs and their consequences', partly ironically but knowing he must encourage the offensive spirit: the care of men, concentration, confidence, clear commands, co-operation, and 'consolidation = counteracts crumps; causes Kaiser casualties; and constitutes – The Big Campbell – (common-sense and the offensive spirit)'.[5] With all this went a pastoral dreaminess as nightingales sang between bombardments over distant Amiens and Albert.

Sassoon took his men eight miles to the brigade baths, through Crécy forest. Censoring letters about sore feet, fine weather, the wish for leave, pleasure at being nearer home after Palestine, the prospect of fighting soon, he thought he had never worked harder for his soldiers.[6] The company commander was useless, but 'O these men, they wring my heart' and 'then they get killed . . .'[7] Tired, worried about Robbie, he asked Meiklejohn for a bottle of eau de cologne as 'you know how I enjoy nice smells'.[8] The *Nation* reported not only the Russian Bolsheviks' revelation of secret treaties that divided conquered territory between the Allies after victory, but also Major General Sir Frederick Maurice's charge that Lloyd George, the Prime Minister, had lied to the nation about the number of troops in France. But Sassoon admitted that 'War has its compensations – for the happy warrior type.'[9] Among these were the handsome Jowett and 'Stiffy' Phillips, another young officer, lazy but charming. The best soldiers, Sassoon thought, were those with the most limited view, those who could be patient with the small world of army life. He still enjoyed the effect on them of his kindness: the sexual thrill, for instance of Jim Linthwaite breaking down in tears when Sassoon had given him an emotional but severe warning on drunkenness after Linthwaite had been punished for breaking into the bar on the ship from Alexandria to Marseilles.

They marched two miles to Cauchy, where the divisional general Sir Eric Girdwood pinned the Victoria Cross on Corporal Harold Whitfield, who had captured a Turkish machine-gun post single handed. To Sassoon, the stunt seemed too obviously aimed at raising morale; General Maurice should be honoured for his courage as well. The news came that they were to move nearer to the front. Work failed to cure his insomnia and he now had an English translation of Duhamel's *Vie des martyrs*, these descriptions of soldier–patients by a French surgeon moving him as much as anything he had read about the war. Unlike Henri Barbusse, Duhamel was not didactic, simply describing human suffering and the nobility given to those who endured it. Sassoon, in his diary, wrote the lines from his own 'Autumn': 'O martyred youth and manhood overthrown, The burden of your wrongs is on my head.' He then added an extract from Duhamel, about inarticulate victims: 'It was written that you should suffer without purpose and without hope. But I will not let all your suffering be lost in the abyss.' Before they left Domvast, he recalled his march through this country in April 1917, how 80 per cent of those officers with him then had since been killed.

After starting at 2.30 a.m. they reached Magnicourt, by road and train, at 11 p.m. The weather had changed to rain and Sassoon, thinking still of his probable death, wrote a good reference for his servant John Law. He got some tea for five of his men who came late to the serving point, then looked into himself. Was he 'a good chap' or 'only rather a humbug'?[10] There is a touching, if narcissistic, precision to the recording of his efforts to be a good officer: the need, for instance, for tact and care and to avoid over-excitement. On 25 May the battalion was at Habarcq, eight or so miles west of Arras, only five miles from Basseux, where he had been for three days in April 1917. He and the company commander Bardwell were in the château; Bardwell then went on leave so Sassoon took over command. He read Lamb's letters – their gentle good humour so different to Duhamel's evocation of agony – and heard the guns, now only eight miles away.

On 29 May, at an inspection, the divisional general praised Sassoon's company. Sassoon felt proud, telling Robert Graves that, thanks partly to the 'admirable' new training manuals, the battalion was first rate, although 'in 6 months they'll have ceased to exist'. For Graves, still in Britain, he felt a certain contempt and mentioned men who had not had leave for many months. He then referred to Owen: 'didn't know he's been ill again. Look after him. Love to Nancy the unknown' (or unknown to him).[11] Graves, Sassoon thought, 'doesn't suffer deeply'.[12] The Germans were back on the Marne, claiming thousands of prisoners. The brigadier said that Paris might fall.

Sassoon read Walter de la Mare's poems (including 'Motley', a simpleton's cry against the war) while sitting by some French graves and wrote a few thankful lines:

> *When the hard day is done, I read your book,*
> *Deep in the haunted forest, where the brook*
> *Sings, betwixt day's last dream and dawn's first spear*
> *You hushed me with your dreams and peace draws near.*[13]

He dreamed he was leading his company into battle, frightened that they would not follow him, and he lost them, the dream changing to a search for the hounds out hunting. Soon after this, on 5 June at Habarcq, he wrote 'Reward', a poem declaring it best to die with his men.

> *From their eyes I hoard*
> *My reward . . .*
> *O brothers in my striving, it were best*
> *That I should share your rest.*[14]

Sent with some other officers for three days' observation to a part of the front line near Mercatel held by the Canadians, he grumbled with a Canadian Captain Duclos about the Billing case, people with cushy jobs at home and the route of General Gough's Fifth Army. After a deafening bombardment, the Germans raided the ground to the left, killing two Canadians and wounding eight. Reminders of England seemed to taunt him: at headquarters, a page of the *Sussex Express*, with reports of whist drives and the prosecution of farmers for selling weak milk; the arrival of the Southdown hunt balance sheet (recording a £10 donation from the now dead Captain G. S. Harbord); a *Times Literary Supplement* article about Walter Scott's Edinburgh, bringing memories of Craiglockhart, the Pentland Hills and his need for Rivers. Back training again, Sassoon sat on a tank as it moved slowly through sunlit fields. After lunch, he glanced at *The Times*: Lieutenant 'little Colin' Dobell had been killed, a comrade from the Somme and Limerick (where Sassoon had introduced him to fox-hunting) recalled in the poem 'Colin', a Housmanesque elegy for his 'cheery friend'.[15] The waiting got him down. In the mess he stood up and said, 'I want to go up to the line and *fight*!' 'Handsome'[16] Jowett agreed. Then in the château his night-time anxiety began.

His servant John Law – who had not seen his wife and children for three years – was going on leave and Sassoon asked Nellie Burton to look after him on his way through London. He also gave a recent notebook to Law to hand over to Ross so that it could survive his death. He begged Ross not to worry about the Billing case (*'Please, please Robbie, don't'*) and complained to Ottoline's brother, the MP Lord Henry Bentinck, about the men's lack of leave. Reading Walt Whitman's poems, he recalled Delius's setting of them in *Sea Drift* and 'a passion for poetry' came back with Whitman's words, which seemed to speak straight to him, 'the unknown want, the destiny of me'.[17]

Dreaminess and intimations of death returned as training slackened before they went into the front line. Full of bodily energy, Sassoon yearned for mysterious fulfilment, and this surging inner music became his poetry. He dedicated and gave three poems to a brother officer from the months in Palestine, Captain Archibald Francis Freeman, also a holder of the Military Cross, a qualified chartered surveyor, probably far in spirit from Garsington or Graves yet perhaps, like Cottrell, contemptuous of bellicose civilians.[18] One mocked the fire-eating brigadier, another was scathing about the High Command, a third – 'The Patriot' – was a satire on the smug home front. Also written at this time, and sent to Robert Nichols, is the awkward, declamatory, Whitmanesque (although not in Whitman's free verse) 'I Stood with the Dead' where the poet, overcome by rain-sodden corpses at dawn, regrets having trained them to fight:

I stood with the Dead, so forsaken and still:
When dawn was grey I stood with the Dead.
And my sallow heart said, 'You must kill, you must kill:
Soldier, soldier, morning is red!'[19]

On 20 June the company left Habarcq for Saint-Hilaire, near Lillers. Just before the move, a young officer called Vivian de Sola Pinto, an undergraduate at Oxford for a year before the war, joined the Twenty-fifth Battalion. Pinto – tall, dark, bespectacled, humorous – was of Sephardic descent and a poet who read Flecker's *The Golden Journey to Samarkand* to his troops, knew Sassoon's work and felt lucky to be near him; 'he is a fine chap', he wrote to his sister on the 21st, 'and we are great friends already'.[20] Later, he described their meeting: Sassoon shaking hands rather than returning his salute, the self-deprecation ('I suppose you're my new second-in-command. I've never had one before') and commanding aspect ('the noble head, mane of dark hair, piercing black eyes and strongly sculpted features').[21] When they read Flecker together, Sassoon said poetry should be much more plain and direct. He took to Pinto, found his poems pompous but copied two of them – 'In the Line' and 'The Listening Post' – into his notebook. Like Owen, Pinto was entranced by this warrior–poet who in the summer of 1918 hated war but wanted passionately to beat the Germans.

The poem 'The Spirit of the Bayonet' described a version of Campbell's lecture Sassoon had delivered to his men, imagining how they must think that he knew no fear or shame. 'To Any Father (Who Thinks War Splendid)' has 'clumsy pale recruits' on their way to death partly because of the militarism of the older generation – Sassoon was reading Strachey's *Eminent Victorians* – and the way he had trained them ('I too must share your shame').[22] *Counter-Attack* was coming out at last, delayed because the government had commandeered the printer's presses for three weeks. 'Do, for God's sake, take care of yourself,' wrote Osbert Sitwell, whom he had met in London between Craiglockhart and Ireland. 'We cannot afford to lose a poet – and especially you.'[23] Sassoon and Pinto had ridden up to Saint Hilaire as the company recovered from a bout of the virulent flu epidemic that engulfed Europe in 1918. Nine miles from the line, the stately Deputy Chaplain General, L. H. Gwynne, Bishop of Khartoum and brother of the editor of the *Morning Post*, spoke to them, saying that Christ was a warrior and British soldiers comparable to early Christians facing the lions; the odd thing was that the troops liked it.

Siegfried Sassoon reported on 8 July to the First Battalion of the East Lancashire Regiment to arrange the takeover of trenches in the Saint Floris sector. Bardwell returned, saying he longed for the courage to shoot himself in the foot and escape the war; at least Sassoon was to command the company in the trenches. Inspecting the area they were to occupy, he found marshy ground where defences had to be breastworks rather than deep trenches, far less secure than the Canadian section, and noted that the East Lancs men talked too much before setting out on a raid, probably drunk from rum. Then, early in the morning of 10 July, Sassoon went into the front line. Here he found the old excitement: the thrill of crawling through a cornfield in daylight into a deserted enemy trench, the night patrols, shadowy encounters with unaware or frightened Germans. The poem 'Battalion-Relief' evokes the muttering front-line troops – thrilled and fearful – and the sense of an endless war. 'The Dug-Out' is based on Jowett asleep 'with that queer half-sullen look on his face':[24] eight lines ending in Sassoon's waking of the corpse-like, exhausted boy:

> *You are too young to fall asleep for ever;*
> *And when you sleep you remind me of the dead.*

According to Wintringham Stable, a brother officer, Sassoon came to battalion headquarters the morning after the takeover with a sketch of the German line opposite, showing that soon after arriving he had gone out on nocturnal patrol. Stable sent the sketch to the brigadier, who declared angrily that no company commander should go 'outside his wire' without brigade orders. Stable passed this on in writing to Sassoon, who he recalled years later was wearing the MC ribbon – perhaps a replacement for the one thrown into the Mersey – and had been a 'most delightful companion': no Mad Jack but someone who showed 'dedicated courage of the highest order'.[25] A part of this was leading patrols – usually the task of young second lieutenants, not of company commanders – to show inexperienced officers like Jowett or NCOs what to expect.

On 11 July there was a direct hit on Sassoon's dug-out. On the 12th, ignoring the brigadier's orders and Pinto's advice (and touching Ottoline Morrell's fire-opal beforehand), he went on one last patrol before they were relieved the next day, going out for over two hours with a corporal to crawl within fifty yards of a German machine-gun post that fired at them before they flung all their grenades towards it. His nerve had held, proving his courage and his manliness to Rivers and to others he admired. Perhaps hubris made him stand up to look back towards the enemy's lines in the early hours of 13 July as he returned. In any case, he was mistaken for a German and shot either by a sergeant in his company or by a young recruit who may have had his rifle knocked up too late by the sergeant. Robert Nichols, with typical melodrama, claimed later that it had been a plot by the High Command to kill this inconvenient rebel.

As blood cascaded from the head wound, he dreaded losing life's magnificence, then laughed at the idea of memorable last words before Pinto brought him in. Hating to abandon his company, he called out, 'I'll be back,' as he walked off to get his wound treated, saying at the Australian casualty clearing station that he did not want to go to Blighty. But John Law, his servant, loaded Sassoon's kit on to an ambulance. He went first to a place near Saint Omer, then on 14 July to the British Red Cross Hospital in Boulogne, consoling himself that leaving the line was not his fault. The nurses fussed sweetly over this 'bit of a celebrity'[26] and poet, and he thought again that he would refuse to go home, only for his determination to crumble into a dream of the garden at Weirleigh, Theresa with a basket of roses, his terrier Topper, the piano. On 18

July, he crossed from Boulogne to Dover, and travelled by train to London and the American Red Cross Hospital at Lancaster Gate. Pinto wrote, 'I am terribly sorry to lose him only for a short time and so are all the men.'[27]

Siegfried Sassoon's time as a fighting soldier was over. By leaving the front on 23 July, he missed the last four months of the war when the Allies launched the counter-offensives that ended in a German defeat. The French began these on the Marne on 18 July, with the British, Australians and Canadians following at Amiens on 8 August. The enemy retreated, demoralized by cumulative losses, the prospect of huge American reinforcements, Allied superiority in material and supply, an economic crisis at home and the eventual perfecting of combined artillery, tank and infantry attacks. The last months of fighting were severe, perhaps the hardest of the war, but had the sense of a final push towards victory, whereas Sassoon's time in the trenches came during the bloody disappointments of 1916 and 1917 – as promise and success quickly faded – and in July 1918 before the end of the apparently overwhelming German advance. When he came to write about it, this shaped his view of a calamitous Western Front.

*

ON 27 JUNE, *Counter-Attack* had been published – the second collection of a poet known now also for his Military Cross and pacifist protest. Even more consistently realistic about the trenches than *The Old Huntsman*, and strongly emphasizing their horrors, the volume mixed realism, satire, lyrical dreaminess and wistful glances back to a peaceful Arcadia. In Edmund Blunden's words, it was both a 'portrait of war' and 'the recollected charm of Peace'.[28] For Blunden the poem 'Dreamers' exemplified this, as soldiers think of home, of humdrum work and play, bank holidays and journeys to an office by train.

Several earlier poems appeared first in *Counter-Attack*. The sonnet 'Trench Duty' evokes nocturnal death and bombardment; 'Joy-Bells' is another attack on bellicose bishops, through a metaphor of church bells of peace melted down into material for guns. 'Song Books of the War', memorized by Winston Churchill, voices the dread that fifty years on young people, thrilled by the war's music, might imagine it as an adventure and poetry might ignore some veteran talking about the hell of 'Haig's last drive'. 'The Triumph' contrasts pastoral beauty with the thrill of battle – the finding of 'triumph' (or romantic fulfilment) in a rural idyll and also in homoerotic comradeship and sadomasochistic danger, bringing Swinburne's romantic pain to the Western Front.

Counter-Attack was a small book – some fifty-four pages of text bound in orange paper wrappers. Dedicated to a reluctant, embarrassed Robert Ross and published in a first edition of 1,500, it contained thirty-nine poems, many written at Craiglockhart. Those who were sent early copies wrote enthusiastically to the author. Gosse, who sometimes disapproved of Sassoon's realism and satire, said, 'You have certainly been writing admirably.'[29] Dent regarded the effect as cumulative, a technical advance on *The Old Huntsman*; the poems together were devastating. Rivers could not 'imagine any instrument more potent against the war' although he worried about Sassoon's 'damned hankering after death'.[30] Ottoline Morrell was 'overcome'.[31] Arnold Bennett 'gulped it down' yet wondered if the material had been 'sufficiently transmuted'.[32] The poems even made the recently knighted Hamo Thornycroft feel indulgent towards 'the young thing in its gambols and enjoyment of being naughty!', although he regretted the influence of Walt Whitman ('Hardy's the chap for me, and I'm delighted you keep him on top').[33] Russell liked the truth, the passion, the unremitting 'bitterness'.[34]

In hospital Siegfried Sassoon thought about *Counter-Attack*. His regimental comrades to whom he had shown the book judged it to be 'what *soldiers* like',[35] which pleased him, and Hardy, reading the poems slowly, had so far particularly admired the title piece and 'To Any Dead Officer'. But praise for his poetry was not universal; he had reason to be anxious about the critics. In November 1917 J. C. Squire had written, in the *New Statesman*, that Sassoon didn't 'produce durable poetry', and in February 1918 the critic Middleton

Murry had deprecated his 'epigrams of war', wanting 'a deeper expression for your experience' and 'a bigger theme', not exclusively about battle.[36] The *Times Literary Supplement* in a review of *Georgian Poetry* wanted from Sassoon fewer 'realistic and dashing' or 'elaborately "creepy" poems' and more like the early, gushing 'To Victory'.[37]

There were detailed, thoughtful reviews of *Counter-Attack*, reflecting the author's high, or controversial, reputation. The *Times Literary Supplement* on 11 July considered that if the poems were 'too much in the key of the gramophone at present, too fiercely suspicious of any comfort or compromise', their 'contempt for palliative or subterfuge gives us the raw stuff of poetry'.[38] On 13 July in the *Nation*, Middleton Murry followed up his earlier doubts, in a review that hurt although he had been asked to write it by Ottoline Morrell. To Murry, Sassoon's torment – his 'incoherent' and 'inhuman' cry – was much more significant than his poetry, for these were 'verses', without that 'harmony and calm' of the soul essential to the true poetry of 'emotion recollected in tranquillity'. To compare them with Hardy, Murry thought, was wrong; Hardy's poems had the 'philosophic background' lacking in *Counter-Attack*, and, unlike Hardy, Sassoon had no calm, therefore he conveyed no terror. His artistic feat was 'the irony of epigram' as in 'The General' – 'rather a device of technique than a method of real expression'. Duhamel says 'far more terrible things than Mr Sassoon has to tell, but they were made terrible by the calm of the recording mind'. To Murry, 'Mr Sassoon's mind is chaos', making his own suffering, the spectacle of himself, 'so much more impressive than his verses'. As if to show its continuing interest in him, the *Nation* printed, in the same issue as this review, Sassoon's poem 'I Stood with the Dead'.[39]

Prodded, no doubt by Ottoline, Philip Morrell wrote to the *Nation* to protest about Murry's review, and Bertrand Russell exploded angrily against 'the reviewer's safe smugness', reminiscent of the comfortable conscientious objectors at the Garsington farm. 'Ouf! I hate all the Bloomsbury crew, with their sneers at anything that has live feeling in it,' Russell wrote to Ottoline Morrell. '*Beastly* of them to be down on S.S.'[40] Writing to the *Nation* under the name of Philalethes (to disguise his well-known opposition to the war), Russell declared that art 'to remain living'[41] must be combined with truthfulness and set above 'ancient' rules and dogmas. Murry protested that he had meant no criticism of Sassoon or of his views: merely of his poetry. Ross thought the review's 'high seriousness' might help the book, and Virginia Woolf told Ottoline Morrell, 'I believe Sassoon has got far more praise' because of Murry. But by 15 July, the critics seemed to have fallen silent. 'I fear Siegfried may be disappointed,'[42] Ross observed.

As if in answer, a notice by Robert Lynd appeared in the *Daily News* on 16 July, complaining that *Counter-Attack* was not poetry but 'a book of the protests of a tortured spirit'. On the 21st, the *Observer*'s critic wrote that the poems were 'grotesquely horrid', yet 'Mr Sassoon creates beauty simply by the hunger for it he arouses . . .' *Everyman* on the 27th declared that Sassoon had 'an irrepressible vitality and depth of feeling that perhaps only those who have served in the war can understand', although he might have an uncertain 'place in poetry'. In *Today*, S. P. B. Mais liked the aesthete's eye for the beautiful and love of life that promised well for when peace came. On 21 August the *Tatler* commented that the more colourful women's fashions seemed to show that people had taken Sassoon's advice of 1915 in 'To Victory': 'Return to greet me, colours that were my joy.' The conscientious objector Max Plowman in the *Labour Leader* on 25 July urged that the poet be made a Knight of the Garter for telling '*the truth about the war*'. At last Britain had its Henri Barbusse.

Now the reviews kept coming. On 3 August, that pillar of Georgianism J. C. Squire wrote in the *New Statesman* that *Counter-Attack* was better, less journalistic, than *The Old Huntsman*: the title poem 'astonishingly vivid', the 'propaganda' not too strident, the whole promising an improvement after the war when 'he can turn to write of the things he loves instead of the things he hates'. Scott Moncrieff, characteristically, wrote in the *New Witness* of how 'the clever writing' was 'too colloquial' and would improve in peacetime. In the Labour-supporting *Herald*, C. E. M. Joad compared Sassoon to Barbusse; Gosse in the *Daily Chronicle* suggested that poets like Sassoon now needed the calm of peace to produce longer poems, for 'size counts in the impact made by poetry'. In the *New Age*, Stephen Maguire prophesied that Sassoon's next collection would 'revert to the pleasures of the English country gentleman, Tory mild'. If this happened it would disappoint H. G. Wells, who hailed the brave young soldier's attacks on old men and 'the whole elaborate rottenness of the European system'.[43] The *Westminster Gazette* complained of 'a monotone of protest' drowning the poetry. Sassoon told Cockerell, 'People complain of the 'lack of beauty' and 'excess of epigram', but I don't see how I could have said those particular things in any other form. And I had to say them.'[44] From the Middle East, where he was an artillery officer, Geoffrey Harbord showed concern for 'old Sig', writing, 'You poor old devil, I never realised . . . how much some people feel the horrors and bloodiness of it all more than I do.' He found the book 'too damn true', the title poem particularly bringing back 'the smell of the dead and mud and that horrible pit of the stomach feeling too vividly'.[45] But much was expected of Siegfried Sassoon's poetry when peace came – indeed too much, and with too many varieties of hope.

*

AT LANCASTER GATE, Sassoon found himself in an 'apotheosis of physical comfort'[46] but again without Ottoline Morrell's opal talisman, which had been stolen from the post of his hospital bed in Boulogne. He asked one of his visitors to arrange for a gramophone and other 'comforts' to be sent to his men in France. And the visitors threatened to become a torrent: members of the royal family on a tour of the hospital, Lady Randolph Churchill (Winston's mother and 'a decent old soul'),[47] then the friends old and new – Meiklejohn, Ross, the Sitwells, Nichols, Ottoline, Rivers. The medical report noted on 6 August that there was 'no concussion' and 'some indications of neurasthenia . . . but this condition has improved'.[48]

He could not sleep. This wound probably meant the end of the war for him and no chance now of making things better for his men, for the world, in a Byronic fusion of poetry and change, even revolution. But the authorities were still worried. On 20 July Brigadier General George Cockerill, Deputy Director of Military Intelligence, wrote to the editor of the *Nation* about Sassoon's poem 'I Stood with the Dead'. After mentioning the poet's 'nervous breakdown' of 1917, Cockerill asked Massingham, the editor, when Sassoon's poem had been written 'for it would appear that his mind is still [in] chaos, and that he is not fit to be trusted with men's lives'. Massingham answered, 'I have no clue to the date of the verses' and 'Poems are often sent to editors long after their composition.'[49] The correspondence went no further.

Now with a room to himself, and sleepless at night, Sassoon thought of possible poems of war, of attack, defeat and mutilation, of corpses, bodies like the war dead packing the London streets. 'The Dug-Out' emerged from this, but first came the agonized verse letter to Robert Graves.

> *Dear Roberto,*
> *I've timed my death in action to the minute*
> *(The* Nation *with my deathly verses in it).*
> *The day told off – 13 – (the month July)*
> *The picture planned – O Threshold of the dark!*
> *And then, the quivering songster failed to die*
> *Because the bloody Bullet missed its mark.*

Frank in its homosexual references ('O Rivers please take me') and about his platoon ('I make them love me' and 'what lovely faces were / The soldier-lads he sang'), the letter, its rhythm like the irregular explosions of a barrage, reports his state – no visitors allowed after so many had disturbed him, the comfort of Rivers, the loan to Graves ('why keep a Jewish friend unless you bleed him?'), a letter from Stable about the brave men, the gramophone sent out – before speaking of his shame ('And I'm ill and afraid to go back to them because those five-nines are so damned awful') and, finally, of a wish to return to be broken.

O Rivers please take me. And make me
Go back to the war till it break me.
Some day my brain will go BANG,
And they'll say what lovely faces were
The soldier-lads he sang.

Confusion – what doctors called 'neurasthenia' – led to an almost modernist clash of impressions, then a spinning free from orthodox vocabulary.

No visitors allowed
Since Friends arrived in crowd –
Jabber – Gesture – Jesture – Nerves went phut and failed
After the first afternoon when MarshMoonStreetMeiklejohn-
    ArdoursandenduranSitwellitis prevailed,
Caused complications and set my brain a-hop
Sleeplesse asperuicide, O Jesus make it stop!

Above the poem Sassoon wrote, 'Sorry about Mrs Nicholson [Graves's mother-in-law had just died]. Nuff said? And "same here, ole man", as Bobbie [Hanmer] the Beautiful used to say.'[50]

For some, he displayed cheerfulness. 'I'm still alive and praising God and Thomas Hardy,'[51] Sassoon wrote to Hamo Thornycroft, but he told Meiklejohn that he had been feverish 'and horribly depressed in consequence . . . Your face haunts me, you are so faithful . . . I don't know what I should do without Rivers.'[52] To Marsh on 18 July he said he was 'much stronger' and should be out in ten days. He wanted to go back for the men's sake, perhaps as 'a sort of official artist in words', writing not 'little epigrammatic poems' but 'large canvases, sort of Whitmanesque effects of masses of soldiers' as an observer. 'Damn it, I'm rather weary of proving I'm not afraid to die.'[53] John Law wrote to say that he 'never saw a company so upset at losing an officer'.[54] Marsh thought the anti-war tone of *Counter-Attack* made it unlikely that its author would be sent back to France as an 'official' recorder of what was happening there.[55]

On 1 August, Ottoline Morrell came from Brixton prison where she had been visiting Russell, inside for his anti-war campaign, to find Sassoon alone in a room with two beds. They talked about his soldiers and Murry's wounding review; then he got angry about the 'sex and constant appeals to sex in men' of women, especially the nurses. She found it 'impossible to leave' because he kept on showing her books and drafts of poems, and 'I feel much more separated from S.S. now than when he was abroad and far away.'[56] Sassoon had told her that he had written 'one great new poem' in hospital, like 'The Death-Bed', called 'The Vigil': 'Vigil of silence, love and death, vigil for you my son and my soldier'. But this seems to have gone no further.[57]

The day before he had diagnosed his condition in his diary:

1. *The angry, arrogant, secret pride of youth says, 'I'll go back and get killed' – just to spite these old men. How can they understand what I've suffered and seen? The gulf of hell divided me from them. Damn them. How dare they come and ask me what I feel like. What would they feel like if they'd been there? (Exit indignant victim). (Then of course there's always contempt for those numberless, pathetic 'lead-swingers'. These doctors are sure to class me with the 'wranglers'. I'd rather be mad or dead).*

2. *Sex says, 'Go back and play the hero and indulge in noble feelings of sympathy for your men.'*

3. *Vanity says, 'O hell, I don't want to die! When everyone's making a fuss of me.' Death would be highly effective, but is getting rather démodé as an incentive to the sale of soldier–poets.*

4. *The whole thing is a combination of sex-repression, warweariness, vanity and pride – with a little 'decent feeling' and a touch of nerves chucked in. A war-cocktail. And above all – that eternal, insane hankering for death.*[58]

By August, the restrictions on visiting had eased. Dent took fright at the crush when told that on one day Marsh, Theresa, Meiklejohn, Nichols and the Sitwells were expected. Then visitors were banned again because the patient had a headache and couldn't sleep. He was soothed slightly, however, by E. M. Forster's *A Room with a View* whose 'conversations of foolish women are quite unequalled in fiction'.[59] Marsh had come up with a job at the Ministry of Munitions where he now worked for the minister, Winston Churchill, but Sassoon turned it down, adding, 'Can't you find me a nice wheel to be broken on?'[60]

*

ANOTHER WARTIME FRIEND came back into his life. While out of England, Sassoon had asked Robert Graves to look after Owen, complaining on 28 June, 'Wilfred Owen hasn't written to me since December.'[61] Perhaps the changes in Owen's life brought about by Ross and others had momentarily dimmed his devotion, or letters may have gone missing on the way to the Middle East or the Western Front, for he had ignored Sassoon's advice to get a job out of the line, in Intelligence. He had been stationed at Ripon – where many of his greatest poems were written – then at Scarborough, with occasional visits to London. At the end of July, before seeing Sassoon, he told his mother that 'it was Siegfried's condition [revealed in their renewed correspondence] and not my own that made me so wretched', and, on 8 August, 'I can tell by many signs that Siegfried has been really unnerved this time.'[62] In London, while Owen was on leave, they met, for the first time since Edinburgh, on 15 August with Meiklejohn over dinner in the Reform Club, then, two days later, at Osbert Sitwell's house in Swan Walk, as Siegfried was now allowed to leave the hospital during the day. Sitwell, who had spent two winters at the front as an officer in the Grenadier Guards, banished the war that day, first through a concert given by the exotic harpsichordist Violet Gordon Woodhouse, then at a 'sumptuous'[63] tea, after which the guests walked in the Chelsea Physic Garden. Wilfred Owen and Siegfried Sassoon's only chance of a talk alone came when Owen went back with him to the hospital, Sassoon not realizing it was Owen's last leave before a return to the Western Front.

The correspondence resumed its old intimacy; Sassoon had said he would stab Owen in the leg if he went back to the war. On 31 August Owen wrote, 'Goodbye, dear Siegfried . . . I'm in hasty retreat towards the Front. Battle is easier here; and therefore you will stay and endure old men and women to the end, and wage the bitterer war and more hopeless . . . What more is there to say that you will not better understand unsaid.'[64] His last hours in England were lit up by a swim in the Channel with a boy from Harrow school of 'superb intellect & refinement' who had spoken of his hatred of war.[65] Like Sassoon, Owen was dazzled by aspects of the English public-school ideal, in his case encouraged by Vachell's *The Hill*, a 'lovely, melancholy' novel about boyhood at Harrow on whose slopes he would never lie. On 1 September, to 'dearest of all friends' from a depot in France came the affirmation that 'Serenity Shelley never dreamed of crowns me'; he also remembered 'the shape' of that Harrovian. On the 22nd he sent some poems, complaining about not having heard from Sassoon for some time and adding, 'You said it would be a good thing for my poetry if I went back.' He gave his mother's address, saying, 'I know you would try to see her, if – I failed to see her again.' Six days later, the Second Battalion of the Manchester Regiment, with Owen, moved forward to Vendelles for an attack. There was fighting during the first three days of October and Owen took command of a company, banishing all suspicion of cowardice, telling Sassoon on 10 October that 'your Counter-Attack' was more frightening, even though the boy soldier at his side had collapsed, shot through the head, soaking the poet's shoulder with blood. He said he had been recommended for the MC, and teased Sassoon about sheltering from gunfire behind a poppy. He offered a hint of homoeroticism: 'I desire no more *exposed flanks* of any sort for a long time.' Owen enclosed a copy of a Special Order for the Day that forbade peace talk ('the choicest of specimens'),[66] with this, his last letter to 'very dear Siegfried'.

*

ON 3 AUGUST, still in hospital, Sassoon went back to Palestine for the poem 'Jesus in Heaven' about Christ on a hill, 'Brown limbed and fierce like flame against the sky', among animals in spring and circling vultures that vanish like a threat removed. By the 8th he was sharing a room with an Indian Army major involved in Intelligence who read the newspapers all day, joyfully shouting from behind his screen at the good war news. Two days later he sent Ogden of the *Cambridge Magazine* 'some bad-tempered verses' – 'Great Men' inspired by a hospital visit of the royal Duke of Connaught, about the 'smiles and bland salutes' being more appropriate if 'the great ones' visited the graves of the victims of 'the war they wage': 'it isn't one of my best'.[67] *Counter-Attack* had sold 1,000 copies in July and was reprinting. 'My wound is healed,' he told Ogden, 'but my soul is scarified for ever.'[68] Nichols declared, 'this writing of poems did much to save S.S. from a temporary mental collapse' and on 15 August Sassoon sent him some examples. Among the batch are 'The Dug-Out', 'Butterflies', 'Dedication' and 'Via Crucis'. 'Dedication' ('to your blithe limbs, your steadfast gazing eyes') is mawkishly homoerotic, another return to Swinburne.

> O body's loveliness that leap't for joy!
> O spirit that burned within, a rose of fire!
> They have murdered the voice that was you; and the dreams of
>   a boy
> Pass to the gloom of death with a cry of desire.

Then the sight of a dead soldier, 'like a lover slain in sleep'.[69]

Winston Churchill planned – but failed – to visit him at Lancaster Gate. Churchill knew about Sassoon through Marsh, and Lord Esher, then at the War Office and a discreet fixer since the 1890s, became aware of *Counter-Attack* in the same way. Perhaps because of the urbane, obviously unthreatening Eddie, Esher took an indulgent view of 'your Siegfried' and the 'rough splendour' of his poetry, a splendour which the oily *éminence grise* stifled with condescension, writing, 'It is good for the character of our people that a picture of war should be represented by a man so close up against it in the crude manner of El Greco,' although he was surprised that 'the molly coddling censor permitted the publication of these poems'.[70] The establishment was not as shaken by Siegfried Sassoon as he might have liked to think. The poet, however, still had flashes of radicalism, if more in intention than reality. In August, he asked Edward Carpenter about something Carpenter had suggested to him before the war – a job as 'an ordinary worker in some big works in a large town (I have Sheffield in my mind's eye)'. The men in his company had made him think about 'labour', about how 'the whole world depends on it'.[71] Carpenter called at Lancaster Gate to find that Sassoon had been 'whisked off', but wrote to say that he could fix a job at a 'large steel works with a democratic and sensible management – a rare combination!' within reach of Carpenter's own home. He added that he found *Counter-Attack* 'jolly concrete and not bookish'.[72]

A medical board at the Prince of Wales Hospital for Officers at Marylebone on 6 August reported that Sassoon's 'slight'[73] injury meant probable absence from military duty for two and a half months. Doubt about his mental state led to him leaving Lancaster Gate for Craiglockhart eleven days later, because Rivers wanted him for another medical board. What had been supposed to be a brief visit dragged on for three days, and his sense of the place's gloom returned. Sassoon told the doctors he had no symptoms of neurasthenia and needed a rest. When Ottoline Morrell suggested a job on the Garsington farm, he refused: 'It must be either Sheffield or the Hindenburg line.'[74]

For the moment he endured neither: merely a country house in Berwickshire called Lennel, lived in by Lady Clementine Waring and in temporary use as a convalescent home for officers. He arrived at Lennel on 20 August to find fifteen officers in residence, books of his poems left about by the literary Lady Clementine, whose husband was on active service in Morocco, and again an atmosphere of nervous failure, this time at odds with the calm order of a terraced garden, a view across the River Tweed and a link to the hunting novelist Surtees whose rollicking, not at all neurotic, *Mr Sponge's Sporting Tour* had been partly set there. The library was said to have some Oscar Wilde, but Sassoon could not find it so he read Hardy's *Two on a Tower* and the Jacobean playwright Fletcher in pre-war comfort. Fourteen books of poetry were on his table, as well as prose by George Moore, D. H. Lawrence (*Sons and Lovers*), Carlyle (*Sartor Resartus* – 'it bores me to tears'), a biography of Whitman and Churchill's life of his father ('too political to hold my attention'). He had a sense of imminent cub-hunting and sexual barrenness, 'the only decent looking person in the place'[75] being the second footman.

Then he met a young Canadian called Frank Prewett, nicknamed Toronto, who had been in the Ypres Salient before a breakdown and was some seven years younger than Sassoon. Prewett was a poet, someone flitting between liveliness and depression, perhaps with 'a streak of genius', Red Indian blood heightening the romance when, on a fancy-dress evening at Lennel, he appeared in a head-dress and warrior kit. Aware of Sassoon's sexual interest, Prewett was at first 'horrified', but grew to accept a platonic friendship. Sassoon began to like Lennel. Lady Clementine had good taste 'of a rather superficial kind'.[76]

On 19 September, his hostess took Sassoon into Edinburgh for a medical board at Craiglockhart that led to him staying at Lennel for another four weeks. He had lunch with Rivers, who persuaded him to go for an interview, set up by Eddie Marsh, with Winston Churchill at the Ministry of Munitions. Prewett and he bicycled through the Border country, the Canadian – more easily exhausted than the fit Sassoon – talking about poetry, how he wanted to go to Oxford. Heinemann was at Lindisfarne staying with its owner Edward Hudson, the proprietor of *Country Life*, and asked Sassoon over to the island. But when he and Prewett went across the wet sands at low tide, this time by car, Heinemann and Hudson had returned to London, leaving behind the cellist Madame Suggia, who played for them, the sound of the waves mixing with her rendering of Bach to make Sassoon think of the end of a pilgrimage, the music calming his memories so that the war seemed remote at last.

In his poetry of August and September there is a searching for post-war themes of nature, place and serenity. To Robert Nichols he sent 'Beauty' with its thous and thees ('o never hast thou shone before my gaze') and 'Flodden Field', describing the landscape of the Border battle. The war looms here and in 'God in Battle', sent also to Nichols, about soldiers praying for 'a little of this ancient tenderness'; Nichols also received the homoerotic 'Dedication' and 'Butterflies'.[77] 'Can I Forget?', written at Lancaster Gate, shows the agony of a war memory of a dying soldier crying 'for me to save him'; Sassoon's consolation is 'that I have been your Captain and your friend'.[78] At Lennel came 'Vision', a Keatsian affirmation of love for 'all things that pass'. Robert Graves liked 'Ancient History', about Cain and Abel (perhaps inspired by Palestine), especially the way its language conveyed Abel's weakness ('a lover with disaster on his face') and Cain's strength ('hungry and fierce with deeds of huge desire') – symbols perhaps of Siegfried Sassoon's own two sides, the contemplative peaceful poet and the warrior. 'Wraiths' goes back to Walter de la Mare, and in 'Limitations' Sassoon writes of his own poetic method, the heart inspiring the head: an open window in dawn's half-light, a child's mind, birdsong, a dream of death, then soaring rapture:

> *I told you it was easy . . . Words are fools*
> *Who follow blindly, once they get a lead.*
> *But thoughts are Kingfishers that haunt the pools*
> *Of quiet; seldom-seen: and all you need*
> *Is just that flash of joy above your dream.*

'Fancy-Dress' evoked Toronto Prewett dressed as an Indian brave, 'Sunset at the Borders' nature's beauty.[79] In the *Cambridge Magazine* on 14 September came a return to war satire with 'Trade Boycott':

> *General Currycombe (half pay)*
> *Toddles round, and day by day*
> *Swears he'll boycott (if he can)*
> *German merchants to a man.*

This kind of poetry, and his 1917 protest, brought a letter from the secretary of the Hampstead Labour Party asking if he might stand as its candidate for the safe Conservative seat in the forthcoming election. Sassoon, mocking his unsuitability as 'a dithering poet', asked Ottoline Morrell to consult her brother, the MP Lord Henry Bentinck.[80] Then on 30 September he set out for London to meet Winston Churchill.

*

THIS WAS THE start of those post-war years of rush and occasional chaos, with people coming in and out of his life like the flickering disjointedness of early cinema. Staying with Eddie Marsh in Gray's Inn for four crowded days, Sassoon met, for the first time, Lytton Strachey, Maurice Baring, Edith Sitwell and Desmond MacCarthy, and saw an exhausted Robbie Ross. To Ottoline Morrell, he seemed 'in a terribly jumpy condition talking incessantly and jumping in his thoughts . . . terribly self-centred and spoiled and his head very swelled.' At tea, he said, 'Don't be artificial,' adding, as a softener, 'Oh I suppose it's shyness that makes you like that.' She thought him torn between love of success and despising it.[81] In the Ministry of Munitions, housed in the old Hotel Metropole, Churchill, who had learned several of the *Counter-Attack* poems by heart, kept him for an hour. An intense admirer of physical courage, the minister tried to convert this protesting hero, speaking to him about the progress (particularly in sanitation) brought about by war which he declared to be a 'normal' occupation of man, like gardening. Churchill told Sassoon – who thought the politician's rhetoric had been aimed mostly at satisfying himself – that he wanted to take him to France at the end of the month.

Heinemann said that *Counter-Attack* had sold more than 3,000 copies and the economist Maynard Keynes took Sassoon to see Massine dance in *Cleopatra*, for which Bloomsbury was out in force: Mark Gertler, Roger Fry, Lytton Strachey, Duncan Grant, Clive Bell, Ottoline Morrell. This inspired the poem 'To Leonide Massine in "Cleopatra"', a resuscitation through the dancer's 'doomed and perfect' beauty of the young who had gone off to fight. Massine's stage death cannot, however, replicate those 'who sleep in ruined graves' beyond recall. Then he addresses himself at the end, still in the high language of Swinburne or Lionel Johnson:

> O mortal heart
> Be still; you have drained the cup; you have played your part.[82]

During an interlude amid all this acclaim, he had lunch with a brother-officer, the now one-armed Ralph Greaves who claimed that war had at least given nobility to their lives – far more than the aimlessness of peace would do. Neither could have imagined how true this was to be.

Sassoon's head ached badly after the social rush and he welcomed the quieter scene at Half Moon Street, from where Ross was to leave soon for Australia to advise the Melbourne Art Gallery, thus escaping the persecution of the last year. In Half Moon Street, Scott Moncrieff called, accompanied by the young Noël Coward, both annoying to Siegfried – Coward through his effusiveness and Scott Moncrieff because of what he had written about Sassoon's war poems. At the evening's end, Ross came to the front door and held Sassoon's hand, looking at him in exhausted sympathy. The next day, while resting before dinner, Robbie died of a heart attack. On 12 October the *Nation* published Sassoon's formal eulogy, 'To Robert Ross', a poem discreet about its subject, the man who had given a new freedom to his poetry and his life, whose 'loyal love' had 'deathless wings':

> That rise and triumph out of night.
> So, in the days to come, your name
> Shall be as music that ascends

When honour turns a heart from shame
O heart of hearts! O friend of friends![83]

He returned to Lennel, then left it for ever on 17 October, having been given four weeks' leave after another medical board at Craiglockhart. At Weirleigh, still mourning Ross, his brain seemed to him to dwindle to the size of his dog Topper's. He nonetheless managed, perhaps after a visit to a village church with his mother, to write 'Memorial Tablet', marked 'Weirleigh November 1918'[84] in a manuscript, a war poem of the type that Ross had inspired. The speaker is a dead soldier once 'nagged and bullied' by his squire to fight under the scheme of voluntary enlistment set up by Lord Derby in 1915:

> *my wound was slight*
> *And I was hobbling back; and then a shell*
> *Burst slick upon the duck-boards: so I fell*
> *Into the bottomless mud, and lost the light.*

Later the squire in his pew gazes smugly at the man's name on the roll of honour without any idea of those hellish 'two bleeding years I fought in France'. Sassoon makes the village hierarchy an accessory to the slaughter at Passchendaele, the dead man asking ironically at the end, 'What greater glory could a man desire?' than his name on the war memorial 'in proud and glorious memory'.[85]

*

IN LONDON, THE rush began again. On 5 November, the frenetically social Marsh introduced him to a colonel, an Oxford archaeologist, who had apparently done wonderful things in the Middle East. At the Savoy, with Eddie, he found the small, fair-haired young-looking T. E. Lawrence and discussed Doughty and Henry James, Marsh overflowing with appropriate anecdotes. Sassoon at one moment exclaimed to the quiet Lawrence, 'What I can't understand is how you came to be a Colonel!'[86] Lawrence, who had asked to meet the author of *Counter-Attack*, felt charmed by the question, but Sassoon was not yet mesmerized by one of the most compelling influences of his life. The next day he went again to the Ministry of Munitions to see Churchill, who was 'full of victory talk', sounding, Sassoon thought, like the leading article of a newspaper, opposed to the idealistic Woodrow Wilson and intending (his audience surmised) that a victorious Britain should increase its power, with Germany skinned alive.[87]

He felt relieved to leave London to go, for the first time, to Max Gate, near Dorchester, to see Thomas Hardy. Sassoon had heard many stories of Hardy, Hamo Thornycroft speaking of a delightful simplicity, Gosse describing 'true Thomas's' unmemorable conversation, Ross recounting the first Mrs Hardy's irritation at the flattering of her husband. Muddling the trains, he arrived late in a horse cab at the modest red-brick house where both Hardys – Thomas in his seventy-ninth year and his much younger second wife Florence – seemed shy, perhaps, Sassoon thought, because of the flamboyant Glyn Philpot portrait of which he had, with characteristically naive narcissism, sent them a photograph. Sassoon's military record probably also impressed his host – who had once said how proud he would have been to have the right to be called captain – although Hardy's poems on the Boer War and his drama about the Napoleonic era, *The Dynasts*, show war as tragic rather than glorious.

To Sassoon, these small quiet people in candlelight represented the utopia of heartfelt writing, of shunned publicity, of 'human homeliness' and feeling as opposed to cerebral frigidity, of wholesome country life against city sophistication. The verdict of Emma Hardy, the writer's first wife, on her husband ('a great writer, but not a great man')[88] would have shocked Sassoon, who ignored much of Hardy – such as his interest in technology, his determined secretiveness, his susceptibility to the flattery of fashionable women and his sometimes devious or coldly commanding domestic behaviour. His admiration heightened by Hardy's verse collection *Moments of Vision* in 1917, Sassoon came as a worshipper, feeling 'very large and hearty',[89] and they spoke of Browning, Shakespeare, Shelley and

Keats, Hardy telling his delighted listener that good poetry must be written from the heart. The even quieter Florence was transfixed by their visitor, only alarmed by a rumour that he was considering standing for Parliament. 'Imagine, a son of the Sassoon family and cousin of the Rothschilds, a Labour member!' she thought. 'My head spins.'[90] During these bright, frosty days at Max Gate, Sassoon felt he had met the modern Shakespeare.

From Dorset, Sassoon went to see Toronto Prewett, who was studying at Oxford University, and took the Canadian to Garsington. Ottoline Morrell arranged for Sassoon to go to lunch the next day on Boar's Hill in Oxford with John Masefield, who introduced him to his neighbour, the septuagenarian Poet Laureate Robert Bridges. The Laureate, who detested the Germans, gruffly asked, 'What did you say his name was – Siegfried Digweed?' Bridges showed them photographs in a newspaper of some German socialists, declaring, 'Did you ever see such a parcel of pudding-faced dullards?'[91] Sassoon wondered if this was aimed at him as a radical young writer.

At Garsington, the Morrells had a literary house party: Aldous Huxley the novelist, the printer and conscientious objector Francis Meynell and his pianist wife. Meynell brought the news of the Kaiser's abdication and Lady Ottoline, desperate for love or at least emotional sympathy, thought that the Sassoon 'I knew lies out in France dead – and the one who was here is a vain young animal – dashing along – successful – conceited – and self-sufficient', hating the idea of unkindness but 'himself extremely cruel'.[92] She told Virginia Woolf he was 'terribly spoilt. I never want to see him again – so coarse, so ordinary, so just like other conceited young guardsmen. I felt he had been seeing odious people who had changed him completely.'[93] Siegfried Sassoon would never live up to her romantic idea of him, especially when he tried to be both friendly and distant. The charge of self-absorption was made against him regularly for the rest of his life, often by those to whom their hero could never give enough.

On the morning of 11 November Sassoon walked in the water

meadows near Garsington while the church bells rang to celebrate victory. In London, that evening, he found the capital erupting in wet, dull weather, and a friend of Robbie Ross, Richmond Temple, who had been in the Royal Flying Corps, asked him to stay in a flat near Bond Street, then to dinner with a couple called Bigham in Cheyne Walk. The host, a 'small, meagre and prim' civil servant, and his wife had also invited the writer Enid Bagnold, an American woman journalist (Mrs Helen Campbell), an 'effeminate' musician called Navarro, the lawyer Hugh Godley and Cosmo Gordon-Lennox; and, to the war-hating poet, the 'good dinner' and 'sympathy with the mob flag waving' of these non-combatants seemed hateful – one of the guests had only seen war service with the Central Liquor Control Board. This was, he decided, 'a loathsome ending to the loathsome tragedy of the last 4 years'.[94]

TEN

Love and politics

HOWEVER TRAGIC THE war may have been, it transformed Siegfried Sassoon from the awkward, apparently irrelevant young writer
of 1914 into a spokesman for a whole way of thinking, even for a
generation.

The man who had panicked in front of Rupert Brooke now
thought that he could, under certain circumstances, dominate Robert Graves, not least through Graves's fear that his wife Nancy
found Siegfried attractive. Their positions had changed. The Graves
whom Sassoon had met in 1915, experienced in battle and intellectually self-confident, had even become a slight hero-worshipper of
Siegfried and his Military Cross. Those who had been Sassoon's pre-
war mentors – Edmund Gosse and Edward Marsh – could be in no
doubt about his position as a poet. But, as critics of *Counter-Attack*
had said, he now needed to decide how to write in peacetime. In
fact Sassoon had, perhaps unwittingly, already set off in a certain
direction. In 1914, he had thought of travel, of Schoenberg and
continental Europe, only for the trenches to prompt a perpetual
contemplation of England, a pastoralism effective in its contrast
with the Western Front and his men's ordeal: a country of hayricks,
fox-hunting, sunrises over sown fields, singing larks and piano music
drifting on to lawns through open drawing-room windows. This
was not necessarily what he wanted. Sassoon, from Limerick in

1918, had written to Ottoline Morrell that he hoped to work if not, as he had previously told Edward Carpenter, with the workers (or 'the Giant Labour'), at least on behalf of them.[1] But the war seemed to have made him even more of an English gentleman, a lover of country landscapes, someone fastidious in his dislike of what he thought vulgar, a man of chivalry and kindness, affronted by bullying and injustice, reserved, disdaining ostentation and self-advertisement. This nobility restricted another part of Siegfried Sassoon – the intensely emotional, idealistic man who yearned to be a great lyrical writer.

His poems show both the clash and the change. 'Reconciliation', written soon after the armistice, appeared in the *Herald* on 16 November 1918. This short, quietly passionate poem asks a British mother who lost her son not to hate the enemy, for if she visits the boy's grave she may see the mourning German mothers of the men who killed him before being killed themselves.[2] Then the war ceases to be the overwhelming subject, and the next two poems are by a man involved in the first serious love affair of his life.

*

ONE ASPECT OF Sassoon was not Byronic: his sexual chasteness. This, however, changed, partly because of Dent and Theo Bartholomew's anxieties about a young artist called Gabriel Atkin, then living in Margate and suffering from 'incessant alcoholism'. Bartholomew wanted Atkin to study at the Slade School of Art, yet feared he might go wild in London. Dent thought that Sassoon would be a good mentor. Bartholomew – who had found Siegfried agitated on a recent visit to Cambridge – agreed, perhaps feeling that an introduction to someone sexually free to the point of profligacy might calm the agitation. So he fed the poet 'a lot about Gabriel'.[3] On 26 November, back in London after his first meeting with Atkin at Margate, Sassoon wrote ecstatically to Bartholomew, 'Have you heard from Gabriel since I went there? He is one of the divinest things that have happened to me. I am going to see him again.'[4]

In the word 'divinest' there is a note of the 1920s: a decade of art, of pleasure, representing for some a return to the 1890s and the world of Wilde. Certainly there was a distinct whiff of *fin de siècle* about Gabriel Atkin. Born at South Shields in 1897, and therefore some nine years younger than Siegfried Sassoon, he went to Durham University and art school in Newcastle. Christened William Park Atkin – for some reason he took the name of Gabriel – he had Anglican clergymen among his uncles, a grandfather who had painted 'greatly admired'[5] watercolours of the Tyne valley and a background of Tyneside respectability with possible links to Leigh Hunt, the poet and friend of Byron. His talent was suited to watercolour, usually of landscapes or groups of people, at first in northern England, and, after the war, on the continent: his style decorative and pleasant, with a feeling for café life and caricature. Osbert Sitwell thought Atkin's work had charm, sensuality and visual imagination. The art critic and painter Roger Fry bought one of his pictures, praising him in print.

Gabriel Atkin enlisted at the start of the war and, like Sassoon, went to Cambridge for part of his training. On 25 February 1917, Dent approached him in the Pre-Raphaelites' room of the Fitzwilliam Museum and they became friends. The artist was attractive, charming, pliable, reckless and a good pianist with a passion for Italian opera, although the critical musicologist did not 'at all' like his 'pseudo-pre-Raphaelite watercolours'.[6] Stationed in Essex and later at Margate, Atkin longed for London ('the whole exotic delicious atmosphere of London sends me mad'),[7] while chasing pick-ups in east-coast resorts or dreaming of the Rossettis at the Fitzwilliam and Dent's crème de menthe.

In February 1918, Gabriel Atkin met an actor called Cassidy, who thrilled him with stories of the world of Robbie Ross. By March he was quoting Sassoon's 'scarlet Majors at the Base', and at the end of that month Bartholomew introduced him to 'Enrico' Festing Jones, once Samuel Butler's companion and another friend of Robbie's. But Dent and Bartholomew fretted about 'the child'.[8] By October Atkin was involved with a young aristocrat and drinking a new Portuguese liqueur while wearing a silk dressing-gown – a vignette from Noël Coward or Ivor Novello. The sexual and alcoholic prospects seemed illimitable for, as he told one of his lovers, W. J. H. Sprott, 'although I have no constitution at all, I have an infinite capacity for coping with this sort of thing'.[9] There were rumours of compromising photographs in circulation. He dreaded returning to Newcastle.

By 30 October 1918, Dent and Bartholomew had spoken to Gabriel about Siegfried Sassoon. To Atkin, who may have seen the Philpot portrait, the war poet looked 'most attractively Byronic', but his military duties kept them apart. On 5 November, Atkin thought of becoming a Roman Catholic ('I like the atmosphere and I like the smell')[10] but feared the confessional. Two days after the Armistice, still in Margate, he regretted missing Sassoon; then at last, on 24 November, Atkin told Dent, 'Siegfried is the most amazing gorgeous person in the universe. He is the most wonderful thing that has ever happened. I'm not going to talk . . .' But 'life is intensely wonderful. I'm wildly happy and I want to burst into song. I've got a pound of chocolates by my bedside, a pink shaded candle, 2 Abdulla cigarettes, Georgian Poetry vol III, and eternal happiness.'[11] He excused himself to Sprott. The affair was 'willing and it was unforeseen – I couldn't help it,' it had made him 'dotty and inarticulate', although 'you know how much I love you' and 'I never give my devotion and then recant it.'[12] By 27 December, Atkin told Dent that he had given up promiscuity.

Sassoon's poems of this time are more about lovers' separation, of isolated selves, than about fulfilment. In 'Parted', the poet lies alone listening to a town – its midnight bells, drone of noise – while 'longing for you', the only source of life. 'Lovers' is about the sleeping lover at his side; in 'Slumber-Song' (written at Weirleigh in December) the lover is serene, again in sleep, the verses building around him.[13] Atkin needed to be changed, Sassoon thought, to bring about an ideal, and he felt he could guide this frail, delightful creature towards seriousness. It was a kind of narcissism – an almost aesthetic experience, watching himself bring order to chaos, like the making of a work of art – and the wish to help or heal seemed to be reciprocated, Atkin telling Sprott that 'I have a great trust in resting his tired head after this godless war.'[14] In December, Sassoon told Marsh, 'I am happier than ever I was before.'[15] He supervised Atkin's time in London in December, introducing him to Marsh, Glyn Philpot, the Asquiths, Lady (formerly Mrs) Colefax, Pinto, Graves, his great-aunt Mozelle and the Sitwells. Now the artist wanted to enrol at the Slade after demobilization and 'to work like hell'.[16] He told Sprott that 'I am bound hand & soul to Siegfried' and 'I'm going to be serious', although 'I have never been a noble character.'[17] The spur was that 'Siegfried Sassoon is wonderful, marvellous, fine. He makes me feel such a worm by his absolute excellence.'[18] But this conflict between moral determination and guilt-ridden but incurable weakness proved to be a bad basis for romance.

*

THEN SASSOON WENT back to politics. While playing golf at Rye, he had a letter from Max Plowman asking if he would speak for the Labour politician Philip Snowden at Blackburn in the forthcoming general election. Lloyd George's coalition government had put up a VC against the pacifist Snowden; an acknowledged war hero like Sassoon could contradict the charge of lack of patriotism. Encouraged by his golfing partner George Wilson – his decent, fair-minded old teacher from Henley House who wanted all points of view to be represented in Parliament – Sassoon accepted, and then went hunting in Sussex to be teased by other sporting friends about his radicalism. To Marsh, he wrote, as if to forestall criticism – and after arranging to bring Atkin to dinner at the Savoy Grill – that Snowden seemed 'honest and brave – though I don't agree with (or understand) his point of view entirely. Forgive me Eddie – I'm daft.'[19] Not only daft but brave: Snowden was one of the most unpopular men in England in the triumphalist December of 1918.

From Blackburn station he was taken, in uniform, to begin the campaign, hesitantly addressing meetings against conscription and against a vengeful attitude to Germany. Shocked by the grey, hopeless landscape yet thrilled by his own and Snowden's idealism, Sassoon felt enraged by government propaganda against him as 'a stage-soldier who'd never been near the war, but had been got down by the Pacifists!'.[20] At the final meeting he quoted Hardy ('In our hearts of hearts believing'), having used Whitman in previous speeches, and in his diary wrote of 'a new phase of my life', of being 'inflamed to an ardour which cannot fail me'. At last he had 'escaped – for ever – those reactionary and self-indulgent influences to which I was bred and educated. I have offered myself to the people and they have accepted me. Will I live to be worthy of their trust? Who knows?'[21] Snowden got only a fifth of the votes cast and went down heavily to defeat.

After Christmas, Rivers came to Weirleigh and teased Sassoon about campaigning for Labour one day and mixing with grandees in London the next. The doctor, a socialist, advised a course of study in Oxford, congenial to Sassoon because of its proximity to Garsington; political economy would be useful if he wanted to work for the Labour Party. Prewett and Graves were already there and Masefield and Bridges near by. He was, he thought, a political poet.

*

AT WEIRLEIGH, THE stables were empty, the lawn unkempt, and Theresa disapproved of many of her son's new friends and influences. Hardy she did not admire, preferring Kipling; Graves she disliked; she loathed Gabriel Atkin, who imagined that her icy silences meant that she 'disapproves wildly of my art';[22] and saw pernicious Garsington pacifism in Lytton Strachey's *Eminent Victorians*, a mockery of her favourite age. Rivers, almost alone, she respected. Oxford was a relief for Siegfried after his mother's censoriousness. Ottoline Morrell had found him a sitting room and two bedrooms in Merton Street, overlooking Christ Church meadow, expensive at £192 a year ('about half my income'). He sent off for a demobilization form, Rivers promising to testify that Sassoon was unfit for duty, for 'I refuse to garrison Ireland, which is entitled to self-determination under our peace terms.'[23]

In Kent, he wrote more poetry: 'Picture-Show' (later the title of his privately printed volume of June 1919); 'Middle Ages' (about a clash of arms in a dark wood, a bloody throwback to his pre-war medievalism); 'The Dark House', like de la Mare in its menace, with a lover who steals away through a rain-soaked garden. 'Miracles' evokes a peaceful dream and a confused waking. The war reappeared in 'A Last Word', which mocks the jingoistic games player who finds his pre-war superiority reversed by Sassoon's MC and 'three wound stripes' in contrast with the athlete's 'four years home service'. The poem has a sense of manliness proved at last to the public-school type from whom he had previously had to hide his homosexuality and his poetry. On 9 January 1919, in the *Labour Leader*, he published 'Cold Steel' about 'my mother' hanging what is presumably the dead Hamo's sword on the wall of Weirleigh: about how, while 'hating cruel things', she admires militarism and Tory politics. 'The Imperfect Lover', written at Weirleigh on 22 January, asks, presumably of Atkin, 'I never asked you to be perfect – did I?' In 'a little kingdom of our passion' there was perfection before each reached the other's soul, the lover finding the poet's 'gloomy, stricken places', 'ghosts' and 'my atmosphere of devils' – a hint perhaps of controlled sadism:

> *Since, if we loved like beasts, the thing is done,*
> *And I'll not hide it, though our heaven be hell.*

'To a Childless Woman', also from early in 1919, he compared later to the unashamed emotion of Charlotte Mew, a poet whom he admired. The poem is a vision of a woman in 'dumb and wintry middle age', possibly a nun praying to the Virgin Mary, 'the enhaloed calm of everlasting motherhood'. Sassoon wrote, 'I too have longed for children,' an intimation of what he might always lack, this having been brought home to him in January when Nancy and Robert Graves's first child, a daughter, was born.[24] They asked him to be the girl's godfather.

*

AT GARSINGTON SASSOON talked frankly to Ottoline Morrell of how he had been 'utterly miserable' about his homosexuality for years but now felt 'much happier – as he meets others of the same way'.[25] Post-war life certainly showed him to be more daring in this respect, as in his open friendship with Atkin, who was slipping again into drunkenness and extravagance, and as in his appearance at a fancy-dress ball as a Tartar prince, his face made up by Glyn Philpot. Also at Garsington was the American philosopher George Santayana, who went back to Oxford with Sassoon in Philip Morrell's farm milk-float, Santayana thinking the poet had 'bitterness and moral chaos beneath',[26] partly because his Jewishness must estrange him from the essentially aristocratic, if sometimes bohemian, world he had chosen. The confusion showed in another swing away from social convention. In London, at dinner, Marsh spoke slightingly of the recently murdered German communists Karl Liebknecht and Rosa Luxemburg, and Sassoon flared up in a revival of his political self. At the start of February, dining at the Reform Club, he saw Massingham, editor of the *Nation*, and volunteered to go to Glasgow to report on industrial unrest.

The visit lasted three days. John Langdon-Davies, another socialist, in Glasgow to find out if the fleet might mutiny, thought that the poet was unsuited to political agitation. In their hotel, a salesman told Sassoon how much he admired his poetry and then took them both to see his wares: rows of prams stored in a vast basement. Later, at a local meeting of the Socialist Labour Party, a woman shouted, 'Mr Sassoon, we are glad of your sympathy of course, but you will never understand us, Mr Sassoon. For you, Mr Sassoon, never took Marx in with your mother's milk.'[27] Sassoon, abashed, asked Langdon-Davies to write the articles and take the money. His attempt to be a revolutionary was drifting into farce. In London, at the 1917 Club – to which Snowden had got him elected – he heard someone say of him, 'I've heard he spends a hundred a year on scent.'[28]

The trouble was that social lionization and pleasure mixed badly with a flaunted red tie and Labour sympathies. There was a clash when Osbert Sitwell descended grandly on Oxford to see his brother Sacheverell at Balliol and brought the novelist Ronald Firbank – then living behind drawn blinds in the High Street – into Sassoon's life. At the Oxford Musical Club, Prewett introduced Siegfried Sassoon to the young composer William Walton, and Sassoon introduced Walton to the composer's eventual mentors, the Sitwells. Actively homosexual undergraduates like Beverley Nichols, the future journalist, showed a sexual freedom that jolted Sassoon's puritan instincts. The purpose of the war – and his opposition to it – had gone. Firbank, in particular, with his fantastic art and epicene life, was an affront to the trenches yet as rebellious in his way as Sassoon.

Oxford was a strange mixture: dons who had been too old to fight and undergraduates too young, eager to hear him read his poems. Certainly there was no shortage of admirers, Atkin noting after one visit to Merton Street that 'it is a little like being at the court of Louis XIV'.[29] But Sassoon felt that 'I never seem to stop talking and can't write or do anything I want to.'[30] While there, he wrote some unmemorable work: 'The Goldsmith', an infantile poem about craftsmanship in ancient Crete, and 'Devotion to Duty', where 'the king' scans 'the G.H.Q. dispatch' before it is revealed that he is the biblical David hearing of Bathsheba's husband's death. The more inspired 'Aftermath', perhaps prompted by leaving the army, returns to the war with long Swinburnian lines and a repeated question ('Have you forgotten yet?') about bad memories which he feels must be heeded if it was not all to happen again. Near the end of his time in Merton Street, he wrote 'Cinema Hero', mocking the escape from an unheroic world offered by unreal cowboy thrills at 'the pictures'.[31] On 11 March came his official military discharge. Judged unfit for service because of his wound, Sassoon left with the rank of captain, which he used for the rest of his life, reminding the world that he had proved himself in the trenches.

*

ON 13 MARCH, he told Robert Graves that he had agreed to be literary editor of the new Labour-supporting *Daily Herald*, which would take him to London at least two days a week. This 'cushy job' paid quite well – £5 a week and extras. Sassoon now felt obliged to find at least £300 to help his brother Michael, back from Canada and broke with two sons to support. And the *Daily Herald* suited his political mood. 'I hate the bloody British Empire,'[32] he told Marsh, disgusted by the scramble for colonies at the Paris Peace Conference. Heinemann, Theresa and Marsh disapproved of his connection with such a radical publication. But Sassoon thought he could do some good in the job, particularly by getting first-rate writers as his reviewers, partly to help them financially – people of the calibre of Graves, Forster, Havelock Ellis, W. H. Davies, Walter de la Mare, Bertrand Russell.

Among these were two important members of the group that sustained and supported him in his forthcoming battles against modernism: H. M. Tomlinson and Frank Swinnerton. Older than Sassoon, Tomlinson by some thirteen years, Swinnerton by two, 'Tommy' and 'Swinny' – these diminutives reflecting their clubbable natures – came from poor backgrounds. Tomlinson's father was a foreman in the London docks and Swinnerton's a copperplate engraver in the London suburb of Wood Green.

Tomlinson left school at thirteen to work in a shipping office before becoming a journalist. With a yearning for sea-borne adventure acquired during his docklands childhood, and a passion for botany, zoology and geology, he wrote about exotic journeys in articles and books that made his name before 1914, when he became a war correspondent on the Western Front. Swinnerton arrived in Fleet Street in his fifteenth year to join a magazine called the *Scottish Cyclist*, then progressed to jobs in publishing and a long career as an immensely productive writer of novels, articles, memoirs and reflections. Both were often in the Reform Club, where Sassoon was also a member, usually in a group that might include Arnold Bennett, Sir Hugh Walpole, John Galsworthy or H. G. Wells.

Tomlinson and Swinnerton valued clear narrative and writing that did not feature only, or appeal only to, rarefied lives and intellectuals. Both were great admirers of Thomas Hardy and Arnold Bennett and suspicious of Bloomsbury; both thought that James Joyce's *Ulysses* was 'an Irish ramp'.[33] Both men were small; Tomlinson's looks seemed to reflect his adventurous life with a rugged face and deafness worsened by the war; Swinnerton was dapper, twinkling, with a neat beard and pince-nez that he often dropped into his drink. Neither Tommy nor Swinny was a homosexual. Both corresponded with, and almost always agreed with, Sassoon over the next four decades. With each, he felt large, slightly protective as a result of his unspoken authority over them.

At the *Daily Herald*, the associate editor Gerald Gould and the editor George Lansbury were delighted to have Sassoon's name in the paper, and an efficient secretary, Miss Clephane, nursed him. The pacifist book-designer Francis Meynell sent out an eight-page pamphlet entitled *A Literary Editor for the New London Daily Newspaper*, and included four of Sassoon's poems. This breach of copyright annoyed Heinemann, who insisted on the destruction of all undistributed copies. Sassoon's first *Daily Herald* piece – in his column called 'Literary Notes' – appeared on 2 April. The tone is self-deprecating, vaguely radical and amateur. He reviewed a play called *War Is War* by William Archer, best known as Ibsen's translator, about German atrocities in Belgium, describing it as 'a piece of crude and belated propaganda', and praised Herbert Read's poems *Naked Warriors* for being 'the horrid truth' about war. Reviewing Rudyard Kipling's latest book of poems (*The Years Between*) he said, 'Kipling has written some great books but this is not one of them'; Alec Waugh's essays were said to contain 'some pleasant little papers'. On 30 April he tackled some novels, announcing, 'I am no judge of fiction.' On 21 May Sassoon declared that 'Literary Notes' should deal 'only with authentic literature', then drew attention to the new periodical the *Owl*, edited by the artist William Nicholson, Robert Graves's father-in-law.[34] Later in the year he welcomed another literary magazine, and a very different one, *Coterie*, whose editorial board included a phalanx of modernists and opponents of the Georgians: T. S. Eliot, Richard Aldington, Aldous Huxley and Wyndham Lewis. 'What a relief it is to find poets being witty,' he wrote, 'instead of maundering on about botany and the weather, washed down (or out), with what might have been their emotions (only they got them from Daddy Wordsworth, who really knew what he has getting excited about) . . . Anyhow I'm longing to see what they'll do next.'[35]

Arthur Waugh, the man of letters and the father of Alec and Evelyn, complained of the flippancy of the 'Literary Notes'. But the job was demanding: writers besieged Sassoon for work and certain publishers refused to advertise in the left-wing *Herald*. He tried to propitiate Heinemann by reviewing a high proportion of his firm's books. Then, in May, came some privately printed verses that included pastoral poems about the Kent landscape and a letter from their young author, Edmund Blunden, another war veteran who had won the Military Cross. Blunden ended his letter 'with gratitude not only for your vivacious criticism in the *Herald*, but also for your great efforts throughout the war to bring the ferocity of the trenches home to a public more disturbed about rations than Passchendaele'.[36] Sassoon wrote encouragingly, they met and the greatest friendship of his post-1918 life began.

*

IN THE MIDDLE of April 1919, he had an experience of religious intensity when, one sultry night, the poem 'Everyone Sang' came to him in a few minutes, like a revelation. To Sassoon it symbolized release – sexual and emotional – from the test of the war into hope for a better world. The motif of birds winging endlessly across the sky – and the song too without end – carries a sense of a utopia without thought or responsibility, an effusion of words representing a search for something joyful to replace the tension of the trenches. Ralph Hodgson's 'Song of Honour', printed in Marsh's *Georgian Poetry 1913–1915* and admired by Siegfried and Theresa, is an earlier poem with a similar vision, Hodgson's seen at night on a hilltop where it seemed 'as if the whole world knelt at prayer' except for the poet. And in 'Song of Honour' birdsong spreads into a hymn to all creation exemplifying what is right and good. 'Everyone Sang' also seems a touching wish for hope and virtue. Whether it is good poetry or not is another matter; and Graves – and others – mocked its predictable language and naive excitement.[37]

The poem 'Prelude to an Unwritten Masterpiece' is darker with its recurring dream – 'some complex out of childhood; (sex of course!)' – of being chased through an orchard into a wood, a reflection perhaps of psychoanalytical talks with Rivers, until the end, in a veering away from seriousness that became even more typically Sassoonian, when the poet imagines a reader saying, 'Why can't you cut it short, you pompous blighter?'[38]

In a sense, this was what Sassoon was doing with his poetry: cutting it short, or retreating into small-scale publication of it. By 3 May, he had the proofs of *Picture Show*, his privately produced collection of which 200 copies were printed by the Cambridge University Press under the supervision of Theo Bartholomew. Once more he was shunning commercial publishers. There were thirty-four poems, several about the war (including 'Concert Party', 'Night on the Convoy', 'The Dug-Out', 'Battalion Relief', 'I Stood with the Dead' and 'Memorial Tablet'), as well as the elegy to Ross, a tribute to Rivers ('To a Very Wise Man', its ending reminiscent of the telephonic exchange with 'little' Orme in 'To Any Dead Officer'), some love poems and 'Everyone Sang' and 'To a Childless Woman'. Private publication avoided the critics, but Sassoon greatly valued some judgements. Hardy declared the book 'your best thing yet',[39] de la Mare also praised it and Gosse liked the way its 'beauty' contrasted with some of the poems' violence.[40] But, in the *Cambridge Magazine*, E. C. B. Jones (Mrs F. L. Lucas) deprecated the clichés in the love poems and the triviality of a throwback to pre-war hunting days called 'What the Captain Said at the Point-to-Point'.[41] Now the poems about the war seem the strongest part of the volume. 'Falling Asleep', written while staying with the Loders in 1919, sets the tone for much of the post-war poetry, where peacetime sounds of a quiet house, distant hounds, bird calls and music prompt drifting thoughts of beauty, then of a story about a soldier and the sunlit faces of his marching men, all fading into September darkness:

> *Waiting for sleep, I drift from thoughts like these;*
> *And where to-day was dream-like, build my dreams.*
> *Music . . . there was a bright white room below,*
> *And someone singing a song about a soldier,*
> *One hour, two hours ago; and soon the song*
> *Will be 'last night': but now the beauty swings*
> *Across my brain, ghost of remembered chords*
> *Which still can make such radiance in my dream*
> *That I can watch the marching of my soldiers,*
> *And count their faces; faces; sunlit faces.*[42]

By 24 July, *Picture Show* had sold a disappointing thirty copies in four weeks.

Already he was beginning to seem slightly out of date, a little too much at ease among the old, perhaps finding them more amenable than writers of his own generation or younger. In June, Sassoon went again to Max Gate to give Thomas Hardy a seventy-ninth-birthday tribute by younger poets, forty-three poems written out by their authors on handmade paper, with a foreword by the Poet Laureate Robert Bridges. Soon afterwards, this time with Sydney Cockerell, he visited the ancient anti-imperialist poet and Arabist Wilfrid Scawen Blunt, at Newbuildings, Blunt's house in West Sussex where, suddenly exuberant, Sassoon climbed a tree in quick, long-limbed movements. The next month, back with the admirers of modernism, he was taken in for ten days by Osbert Sitwell to convalesce after an agonizing attack of sciatica. Norman Loder called at the Sitwell house in Swan Walk, to be horrified by the Cubist paintings and early-Victorian décor. 'Whatever are you doing here?' he asked. 'Who are these Sitwells?'[43] He was relieved to hear that Osbert and Sacheverell had both been officers in the Grenadier Guards.

Sassoon did urge Marsh to be more adventurous in the next volume of *Georgian Poetry*, advising the inclusion of Edith Sitwell, the Australian W. J. Turner and more of his own new poems, not the 'mud and blood'[44] of the war. When *Georgian Poetry 1918–1919* came out in November, it had nine poems by him – six overtly connected to the war – with 'Everyone Sang' at the end of his section. Marsh ignored the Sitwells, but W. J. Turner, Siegfried's new friend and influence, was in with seven poems.

A curious mixture of sophistication and ignorance – Sassoon once claimed that Turner had never heard of Keats or Chaucer[45] – Walter Turner, born in 1884 in Australia, had arrived in England in 1907. The next year, he went to Dresden to join a firm of merchants and became vastly impressed by German and Austrian culture. He returned to London in 1913 to work as a professional writer, with frequent visits to the continent. During the war, when he served in an artillery unit in Kent, Turner began his long career as a music critic and had six poems in Marsh's *Georgian Poetry 1916–17*. In April 1918 he married Delphine Dubois and, after demobilization, involved himself with Graves and William Nicholson in the *Owl*. Turner sensed that Siegfried Sassoon, although impressed by his energy, adventurousness and knowledge of music, found him crude. The character Blow, based on Sassoon, in Turner's novel *The Duchess of Popocatapetl*, thinks Airbubble, who is Turner, a 'cad' and 'extraordinarily raw'; certainly Turner deprecated English literary gentility. Yet in October Sassoon took Turner to Garsington and, a month later, while standing with the Australian on a station platform after visiting de la Mare in Hertfordshire, suddenly admitted his homosexuality to his new friend.

*

IN HIS REVIEW of *Coterie*, a new literary quarterly, in the *Daily Herald*, Sassoon wrote that 'probably the most interesting poem in the book is one by Wilfred Owen, who was killed in action a week before the Armistice'. The news of Owen's death had taken some weeks to reach Sassoon and, when it did, his post-war life, with Atkin and the Blackburn election and lionization in London and Oxford, had been so hectic that the tragedy seems to have merged with the memories of all those others to whom he had been close, not even yet made appreciably different by 'little Wilfred's' poetry. Now Owen, proud during his life to have been 'held peer by the Georgians', left their hands when the Sitwells launched a series of anthologies called *Wheels* as a rival to Edward Marsh's *Georgian Poetry*. In November 1919 the fourth *Wheels*, with a print-run of only 1,000 copies – far fewer than Marsh's sales – was dedicated to the memory of Wilfred Owen and had seven of Owen's poems, including 'Strange Meeting', as well as work by all three Sitwells and Aldous Huxley and illustrations by the Vorticist William Roberts. Edith Sitwell had written to ask Owen's mother if she and her brothers might publish the poems.

In the *London Mercury*, J. C. Squire dismissed Owen, but Sassoon's old tormentor Middleton Murry thought that the poem 'Strange Meeting' was more impressive than anything in Marsh's anthology, telling Katherine Mansfield, 'It's what Sassoon might have done, if he were any real good.'[46] Edith Sitwell, who had never met Wilfred Owen, wanted to edit a selection of his poems, but Sassoon, stirring himself at last, insisted that Owen had wished him to do this. Mrs Owen sent any manuscripts she could find; then the rush of Sassoon's life intervened. In January 1920 he went to New York, leaving the material with Edith Sitwell, having done no work on it, although the printers had been promised the text by February.

As if to show his own wish to break out, Sassoon's 'Promenade Concert' appeared in the *New Statesman* on 11 October. The poem is humorous at first about the orchestra under Sir Henry Wood:

> *Shall I compose an ode for Wood and Wind?*
> *I shall do no such thing. I'll puff my pipe.*

Then, as the music swells, 'my intellect's ennobled by emotion' – a desirable process for Sassoon – and the sound mingles with love:

If someone that I love were here tonight
I could compare this crowded hall with life.
It is your heart, your heart that I would sing to . . .
O someone that I love, stand up and crown me![47]

On 30 October, Heinemann published *The War Poems of Siegfried Sassoon*, sixty-four poems of which twelve – including 'Concert Party', 'Night on the Convoy', 'Aftermath' and 'Everyone Sang' – had not been in *The Old Huntsman* or *Counter-Attack*, although nine of them were in the privately printed *Picture Show*. The book was, Sassoon hoped, his farewell to war poetry, and – for poetry – it sold well: 2,000 copies were printed and another 1,000 in January 1920. But this time the reviews were not so widespread. In the *Daily Herald* H. J. Gillespie praised the book's realism and truth more than the poetry.

*

IN NOVEMBER 1919, Siegfried Sassoon stayed with Norman Loder and his wife Phyllis near Cirencester, falling from a horse owing to the effect of sciatica on his grip, and had to listen to inane talk about strikes and politics and how the war had at least taught the French to wear comfortable boots. By late autumn, he had abandoned Weirleigh for sunless, furnished lodgings in Hugh Street, near Victoria station. The poetry took on a slightly sardonic, satirical tone, as in 'Promenade Concert'. 'Early Chronology', published in the first number of Squire's *London Mercury*, is based on the anthropologist Elliot Smith whom Sassoon had heard in Rivers's rooms in Cambridge:

> *Professor Brown with level baritone*
> *Discoursed into the dusk.*
> > *Five thousand years*
> *He guided us through scientific spaces*
> *Of excavated History . . .*[48]

Weirleigh. It originally had a tiled spire that was taken down.
Siegfried Sassoon thought that the house lacked 'dignity'.

Finchcocks, near Weirleigh: an example of 'the mellow old
mansion in a park' that Sassoon longed for as a child.

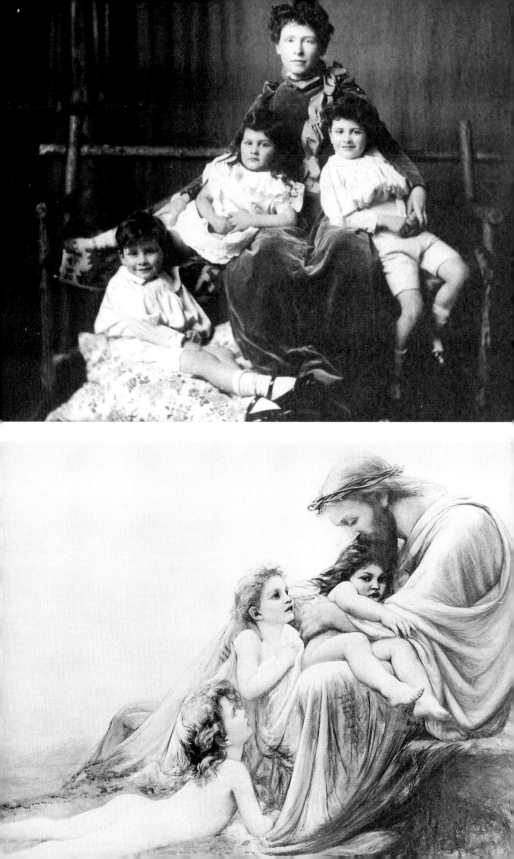

Opposite top.
Theresa Sassoon with
her three sons.

Opposite bottom.
Theresa's painting of
Christ for which she
used the boys as models.

Alfred Sassoon.
His mother gave him
two Stradivarius
violins when he showed
promise as a musician.

The sculptor Hamo
Thornycroft, Theresa's
brother. In addition to
memorial statues of the
great, he sought a new
'democratic' art.

The young cricketer. Siegfried Sassoon is holding the score book.
Tom Richardson, the groom and Sassoon's childhood hero, stands second left.

Matfield in the early 1900s.
The Sassoons were isolated from the agricultural depression of the time.

Theresa Sassoon in the garden at Weirleigh with a friend.
Siegfried dreamed of this childhood playground all his life.

Norman Loder out hunting.

Hamo Sassoon,
younger brother
and confidant.

At the Trinity College, Cambridge, Boat Club Ball, June 1906.

Edward Dent,
musicologist and opponent of
jingoism and sentimentality.

Sydney Cockerell.
Steeped in pre-Raphaelitism,
he befriended Sassoon in 1915.

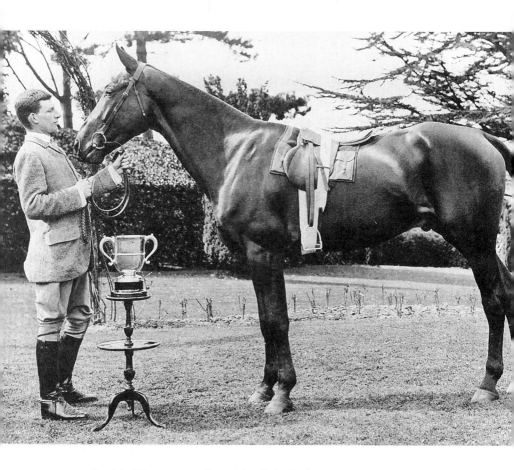

Siegfried Sassoon and Cockbird, his beloved pre-1914 hunter and winner of races. 'What a chameleon I am,' he wrote of riding in 1922, 'it excites me more than anything in my London life.'

The somnolent academic monologue is real, but compared to T. S. Eliot's evocation of the Mephistophelean Bertrand Russell discoursing in 'Mr Apollinax' the poem seems dreamily vague.

Then the war returned. *Clarté*, started by Henri Barbusse to unite intellectuals of France and Britain against militarism, made Sassoon its British secretary. There was a meeting at the House of Commons of about thirty people, with speeches by Shaw, Wells and Zangwill and a suggestion by Sassoon that everyone should read Hardy's *The Dynasts*. His connection with the movement did not last. More preoccupying was Gabriel Atkin, whom, in the late summer, Sassoon had neglected as a punishment before feeling 'much happier'[49] about him. But by 5 December, Atkin told Theo Bartholomew he was dying from drink and dissipation. The librarian believed this to be mere drama and thought that 'S.S. must attend to it.'[50] By now Sassoon had another preoccupation. Back in August, he had written to Florence Hardy from Cambridge, where he was visiting Rivers, 'I have promised to go to America next January – for 12 weeks. It will probably be rather a bore, but I thought it would be a change, (and they offered me quite a large sum!).'[51] A lecture tour seemed a way to escape and to make money, not only for himself but to help his friends who, imagining him to be rich – because of his name – turned to him often. Now he was giving money to Graves, Atkin, Prewett and a new beneficiary: W. J. Turner.

So an American tour loomed as hopes of the perfect love affair faded. Graves, having refused to lecture in the United States, told Mr Pond of the lecture bureau that Sassoon would be excellent there. Rivers urged Sassoon to go, saying he too would be lecturing in Baltimore in February. Atkin might come over but, above all, the trip promised an escape from 'post-war complexities'.[52] Sassoon planned to abandon 'the conventional style' and 'merely talk and read my poems.'[53] But his inaudible reading at Harold Monro's Poetry Bookshop persuaded him to go to the Central School of Speech Training and Dramatic Art where the Principal, Miss Elsie

Fogerty, offered tutoring that included a session when he recited to an Albert Hall empty except for four cleaning ladies.

His living arrangements changed again. Hugh Street had become too depressing so Sassoon lent Turner £1,300 to help him buy a house at 54 Tufton Street in Westminster and took two small rooms there himself; he also arranged for Turner to succeed him temporarily as literary editor of the *Daily Herald*. On 10 January 1920, the *New Statesman* published Sassoon's Hardyesque poem 'The Passing Show', about a middle-aged couple in Leicester Square, the 'pinched and grey' wife grumbling about her shabby, cheerful husband's drinking, watched by a 'tall, young soldier' with a pretty girl. The soldier turns to kiss his girl's 'happy face'. The implication is that their young love will one day resemble the other couple's disappointment.

Then, on board the Dutch liner *Rotterdam*, he settled alone into a first-class cabin. The man with whom he had been meant to share had cancelled his trip. The silence was a relief. Lying in bed, Siegfried Sassoon read Trelawny's *Records of Shelley and Byron*, awaiting his own Byronic debut in the United States.

ELEVEN

Byron in America

ON 28 JANUARY 1920, Siegfried Sassoon arrived in New York, suffering from excruciating toothache, to face slushy snow and a hotel he instantly disliked. Reporters came to interview him, to show that he was already known on this side of the Atlantic. Certainly there was expectation in some literary circles. *The Old Huntsman* and *Counter-Attack* had been published in the United States, and the poet and critic Louis Untermeyer had written of their author as the most interesting English poet since Masefield and Brooke.

In a preface to the American edition of *Counter-Attack*, in December 1918, Robert Nichols, well known for his theatrical lecture tours, evoked a figure more of anthropological than of literary interest, a mixture of Byron, Heathcliff and one of the lesser primates: 'tall, big boned, loosely built . . . pale or with a flush . . . a heavy jaw, wide mouth with the upper lip slightly protruding and the curve of it very pronounced like that of a shrivelled leaf (as I have noticed is common with many poets)'. Suddenly this could, remarkably, transpose into 'a sullen falcon'. His slow speech had the 'troubled thickness' of 'a deep grief', his large hands wandered aimlessly, then clutched at his knees or at the edge of a table, and he breathed hard. When Sassoon read his poems aloud, he seemed to do so to himself. What he liked best, according to Nichols, was to talk or 'shout' about hunting or open-air mornings, about the poetry of Shelley, Masefield or especially Hardy, usually with a desperation brought about by the remembered pain of the war.[1]

But Pond of the lecture bureau now said he had been able to book only two engagements in February because the country was saturated with British authors. Sassoon would have to get his own work, even though Pond, now on the verge of bankruptcy, had guaranteed travelling expenses and a minimum of twenty-five lectures at one hundred dollars each. Sassoon began the process of making himself known: first a taxi journey with W. B. Yeats ('so nice and dignified among all this obscene publicity')[2] to a reception at the National Arts Club, then the Poetry Society of America's dinner at the Hotel Astor: 250 people and a four-and-a-half-hour meal without alcohol – as the United States endured the constitutional ban on intoxicating liquors – followed by three hours of speeches. Sassoon spoke for fifteen minutes and read three of his war poems, then an encore with 'Everyone Sang'. He talked of his toothache and praised Thomas Hardy. A relieved Pond said that it had gone well.

Sassoon's hotel room was stifling and his teeth tormented him; while in the United States he visited the dentist nineteen times. He was sleeping badly and there were more interviews, one with Louis Untermeyer. Even a League of Nations lunch was a relief, with the chance to hear the Irish republican leader Eamon de Valera debate against Sir Horace Plunkett and St John Ervine and see how 'extremists are the only people who get anything done'. The east wind blew 'colder than anything I've known'.[3] On 2 February he moved to an apartment in Westover Court, on noisy West 44th Street in the theatre district, up three flights of stairs with a lift, looking on to a giant neon sign advertising Wrigley's Spearmint Gum – 'Don't argue but stick it in your face.'[4] The fastidious Sassoon wished it had been telling people to read the poems of Thomas Hardy.

No one else smoked a pipe, and Hugh Walpole seemed to be the only popular English writer on the lecture circuit, mostly because of his experiences in Russia. Sassoon dreaded selling himself. He saw

Louis Untermeyer again (a Jewish 'good-hearted impulsive sort of man')[5] and Louis's wife Jean became intrigued by this 'tall, sinewy', shy, captivating English poet with 'pain'[6] in his face (perhaps it was those teeth). With the Untermeyers, he heard the pianist Richard Buhlig, remembering Buhlig's playing of César Franck in London in 1913, and met Vachel Lindsay, Robert Frost and the liberal publisher Ben Huebsch. The Untermeyers took him out to the country, Sassoon innocently slipped his hand into Jean's in the back of the car, then climbed trees, rode a horse bareback and delighted their infant son. Untermeyer and Huebsch helped him get engagements and, when alone in the city, he used Sydney Cockerell's introduction to Belle da Costa Green, librarian at the Morgan Library, and, as if coming in from 'a desert',[7] saw the manuscript of Pope's *Essay on Man* and a lock of Keats's hair and his last message to Fanny Brawne, which made Sassoon cry.

On 6 February he travelled by train through deep snow to Philadelphia and the women's college, Bryn Mawr, to face an audience of about 300 girls, aged from eighteen to twenty-two, all in bright-coloured dresses 'like a flower garden'. Moved to see so many young people 'all listening to my war horrors', he spoke for fifteen well-prepared minutes, read about twenty poems, then, in response to demand, nine more. About a third of the way through he pointed at a portrait of the college's founder and said, 'I can't help thinking that that old gentleman is looking at me all the time.' The girls laughed, lightening the atmosphere, and Sassoon wondered if his programme was 'almost too much for a sensitive audience'. Afterwards a girl asked why he had omitted 'Suicide in the Trenches'.[8] An observer wrote to tell Cockerell that the poet had been sympathetic if, at times, almost incomprehensible.[9] This was to be the usual impression: mumbling incomprehensibility lit up by a sense of integrity and idealism.

Back in New York, the English writer Laurence Housman warned Sassoon that his 'pacifist utterances to interviewers'[10] were unpopular. But the telephone never stopped. Frank Crowninshield, editor of *Vanity Fair*, offered one hundred dollars for a 1,700-word article on war poetry; _Vanity Fair_ printed his piece on Thomas Hardy; the _New York Times_ offered fifty dollars for a book review; and on 15 February Louis Untermeyer's piece in the _New York Herald Tribune_ had the headline 'Wilting Poet. Back from War. Speaks in Trumpet Tones.'[11] Any homesickness was cured when, over dinner, the English poet John Drinkwater reminded him of the pathetic literary feuds of London. The appearance of the broken-down old 'Mister' Harnett from Limerick, in New York to try to salvage his business affairs, jarred also with Sassoon's surge of histrionic idealism.

He dined with the writer John Jay Chapman and his wife ('a delightful couple: quite first rate'),[12] who had lost their favourite son in the war. Chapman – a short, stocky, bearded figure with thick brush-like dark hair and a hook instead of his left hand, which he had thrust into the fire when young as a penance for having struck someone – was a classical scholar and friend of William James. Chapman thought that the war had been righteous and heroic, with great 'spiritual benefits'; if only it had lasted three times as long for the Americans. Later the openly sexual jazz dancing in the Biltmore Hotel shocked Sassoon, who thought it 'a good answer to Chapman's theory that the U.S.A. is better for the war'. But one jibe had stuck – the American's description of his war poetry as 'a pathological exhibit'. Sassoon noted, 'I am beginning to want Rivers to come and talk to me – my sheet anchor of wisdom and common-sense liberalism.'[13]

*

A NEW FRIEND was at the Biltmore party: Sam Behrman, who also had an apartment in Westover Court. In his diary for 6 February, Behrman wrote of seeing the Englishman – 'a serious young man but a fresh complexion' – at the opera; on 9 February he noted 'a quite delightful talk'[14] with him. Sam Behrman – bespectacled, dark, rather small, seven years younger than Sassoon – had grown up in poverty as the son of a rabbi in Worcester, Massachusetts, before escaping to Harvard, then to hard years in New York where he did an MA in English at Columbia, before working in journalism to earn enough to fulfil what he thought of as his destiny, to be a playwright. Sent by the *New York Times* to interview Sassoon, he felt drawn to the courteous, initially shy but soon startlingly confiding poet. By 19 February, Behrman was writing of 'a wonderful talk' about the foolishness of exulting in the 'animal splendour' of courage and war.[15] The affection had changed to hero-worship, and Sassoon liked this young American's humour, anglophilia and admiration. The strange city was growing on him, even if he scorned its materialism. On 21 February he told Turner that in spite of toothache and indigestion, 'it is great fun', although the Americans asked too often about the war and international politics. 'All will be well if I can avoid falling in love.'[16]

Rivers came to New York on his way to lecture in Baltimore. Sassoon told him of the exchange with Chapman, and the doctor advised against arguing with a man of such passionate views. On 24 February, however, at a reading at the Cosmopolitan Club, with Mrs Chapman presiding, there was an unavoidable row. In a forty-minute introduction, he described the perversion of noble qualities in the trenches and the pain endured by shell-shocked patients at Craiglockhart. He followed this with seven poems. Former officers and the parents of sons killed in the war were in the audience, and someone hissed the line 'such men have lost all patriotic feeling'; but there was applause at the end nonetheless. Then Chapman leaped on to the platform, shaking his hook as he shouted, 'What is to become of Thermopylae?',[17] repeating his views on the ennobling war and Sassoon's 'abnormal state of mind'. When he had finished, he was jeered, and several people later remarked that Sassoon showed courtesy. Chapman wrote the next day, only half apologizing, saying that peacemongers and adoring women were exploiting the poet. Not all American women were captivated; the poet Edna St Vincent Millay said, 'I wonder if he would have cared so much if it were a thousand virgins who had been slaughtered.'[18]

What was he saying in those introductory words? Some notes in a manuscript diary, only partly published in his autobiographical

Siegfried's Journey, show the basis. The poems, he said, had been written for his soldiers, the true victims of the war, and he went back to Duhamel for his concept of their frailty and martyrdom. He had wanted also to attack the system; unless society gave up war, he thought, the Prussian system that taught 'militarism' to the children in schools was the best preparation for adulthood. As always, he made no mention of certain results of the enemy's way: the German atrocities in occupied Belgium, northern France and eastern Europe, or Germany's transformation during the war from a partly democratic society into a military dictatorship.

Nations, he thought, needed outlets for heroism; but not war in which noble courage and the human fear of being thought a coward, of failing, had been exploited by 'jingo' politicians and 'blood thirsty' journalists. War wrecked individual peace for the victor as well as for the vanquished; it had wrecked the calm that Sassoon sought (although he did not say this) at the centre of himself. Then he used the words that came more than ten years later at the end of *Sherston's Progress*: 'For only in the inmost silence of our heart do we know world for what it is and ourselves for what world has made us.'[19]

*

GABRIEL ATKIN WAS to come over in April when they might go to California together, and Sassoon sent Meiklejohn £110 to give the artist for the ticket and spending money. In New York, however, another Atkin loomed: the actor Glenn Hunter, born in 1897, nine years after Sassoon, and a Broadway romantic lead of the 1920s, then playing an adolescent boy in Booth Tarkington's play *Clarence*. After coming to New York at the age of seventeen in search of a stage career, and sleeping rough in Central Park and on railway stations, the slickly handsome Hunter was enjoying, in *Clarence*, 'the hit of his 23-year-old life'.[20] How Sassoon and he met is unclear, perhaps at one of the many teas, dinners or lunches. Behrman thought the actor – who clearly encouraged, then rejected his new admirer – 'talented, good looking and absolutely empty' and detested 'this thoroughly commonplace young man'.[21] Sassoon tried to explain himself. The trouble was that his poems took very little time to write, leaving hours for brooding over the 'private agony'[22] of his homosexuality. The strongly heterosexual Behrman was shocked, but in March wrote in his diary of 'a wonderful strange day. S.S. told me everything. Beyond the sun-lit shallows his mind is like a black form moved by turbulent currents.' Their friendship mixed laughter and frankness, the American usually listening, always the admirer. Sassoon read Behrman a poem about the King and Queen making love out of patriotic duty; another time he read some of T. S. Eliot's poems, Behrman finding that they 'flicked like whips'. Once, after talking to him until 3 a.m., Behrman tried to persuade Sassoon that he should write something in prose. The fascination was absolute: 'my mind riveted to S. these few days'.[23]

*

ON 10 MARCH Sassoon spoke in Philadelphia, where one old lady said, 'I feel as if I had been at the funeral of the world,' and a newspaper reported his denial that the Germans had committed atrocities: they had merely used that 'brutal efficiency' needed in war.[24] Many of the Europeanized Americans seemed straight out of Henry James – ruthless hostesses, urbane men of letters, the club men of the east coast, even the fiery Chapman. After Yale, he went to Vassar, the women's college, writing to Behrman, 'I don't know how I pull these shows off. To-night was a hell of a success, and I wore the mask of a white waist-coated and moderately genial young man. Funny Life!'[25] Only later, back in London, did he feel that these theatrical triumphs had got him 'nowhere'.[26] Americans, Sassoon found, knew little about the war and were stunned by some propaganda photographs of the trenches given to him by the artist Eric Kennington. At Lake Forest, near Chicago, Pond had fixed an engagement at a girls' school and Sassoon stayed for eight days with Horace Martin, an anglophile lawyer. Martin left Sassoon alone except to arrange some introductions for readings and take him to a concert by Pablo Casals, 'a small rather cruel looking man'[27] who seemed to despise his audience.

Sexual obsession gripped him. Towards the end of his life, Sassoon told his young friend Dennis Silk that he had always been very highly sexed, which had brought him great torment. On 21 March 1920, he wrote some lines in his notebook:

> *You have no words to say*
> *That can make lovers wise:*
> *Only your breath can blow*
> *Wild petals through my heart . . .*
> *And the world that I would know*
> *Is the world within your eyes . . .*[28]

Three days later, he told Sam Behrman that he was 'continually haunted'[29] by Glenn Hunter with posters advertising *Clarence* up in Chicago, and by 29 March he had still heard nothing from the actor. The people he met seemed 'like shadows – or suits of clothes walking,'[30] except for the poet Carl Sandburg, then labour editor of the *Chicago Daily News*, who showed him round. Deep-voiced, craggy, of measured utterance and simplicity, Sandburg, an itinerant labourer in his youth, reminded Sassoon of H. M. Tomlinson. Looking down with Sandburg from the top of a tall building on to the sprawling industrial city, Sassoon laughed at his own foolishness in coming here to say that war did not pay. At the end of March he arrived in Toronto for two days, to be guided by Frank Prewett, now back in his homeland, who thought him 'highly pleased with his adventures'.[31] But Sassoon told Marsh of his 'perfectly ghastly cardiac enterprise'[32] and withdrew his offer of a holiday for Atkin, using possible scandal as the excuse; but the infatuation with Hunter may have been at least part of the reason.

In Chicago, at the National Council of Jewish Women, Sassoon had his greatest effect yet when a member of the audience had hysterics at the back of the hall, and Behrman noted his return to New York, 'as delightful as ever. Looking wonderful . . .',[33] although later 'very uneasy and boyish and shy'.[34] Sassoon read at the Greenwich Village Theatre and Columbia University, Behrman transfixed by the performances now sometimes divided between Richard Buhlig's playing and Sassoon's poetry. Then Hunter upset him, Behrman cursing this 'rotten little bounder'. Searching for a distraction, Sam suggested that his English friend should write a novel, based partly on the Hunter affair. Sassoon said he would cancel another trip to Chicago and stay in New York to write. First he read his poems to more than 2,000 people of the Free Synagogue in Carnegie Hall. Seated between two rabbis, he declared that his audience could not know the reality of war. His God, he said, 'resided in the spirit of man' which he had seen in the eyes of dying men on the battlefield. Behrman commented, 'It was tremendous.'[35]

In Boston Sassoon worked on the novel, making its main character a concert pianist, rather like Richard Buhlig, but the story's background gave difficulties, added to by a nagging lust for Hunter, worse when away from New York and possibly increased by the book's homosexual content. 'Birdie' Stansfield, now a prosperous wool broker, appeared, a throwback to the trenches. At Harvard – where Sassoon stayed with the English socialist Harold Laski, who was teaching at the university – one member of the audience, the graduate student Willard Connely, found the poet's style 'cramped', his shyness awkward and his voice monotonous. The sympathy for Germans and objectors to the war irritated the young American, who despised the adoring women in the audience and wondered, 'Will Sassoon continue a good poet now that war is lacking?' At the end of the reading, the poet Amy Lowell announced, 'I love that man.'[36] At the dinner before, in the Harvard Union, a waiter had dropped a pile of dishes, making Sassoon and another veteran of the trenches dive instinctively under the table.

Sam Behrman thought that the beginning of the novel had 'extraordinary stuff in it'[37] and started to type it out. He helped Sassoon move into a larger apartment in Westover Court with a hired piano and laughed when the clumsy Englishman broke the glass barrier in a taxi by stretching out his legs, knocked a box of flowers off the balcony of a restaurant or offered forty-five dollars to buy a horse-drawn cab and its horse. Now Sassoon was astonishingly talkative (almost always about himself), reading Hardy's poems to his new friend and, still the chameleon, becoming, not always consciously, what Behrman seemed to expect – clumsy, impulsive, trustful and naive. Sam liked to hear of Siegfried's life: of him diving out of a tree as a child at Weirleigh, shouting, 'I am going to take a leap into the future,' before being knocked unconscious; how he had made Lord Brassey weep by playing Gluck; then his anger at Churchill's militarism, Marsh's reaction to Liebknecht's murder, D. H. Lawrence's betrayal of Ottoline Morrell in *Women in Love*; and stories of Weirleigh, Norman Loder and the dead Hamo, how Sassoon had patted the quarrelling Turners on their heads, telling them 'to be good'.[38] The American laughed at the occasional self-dramatizing ('after all I have only 20 or 30 years to live').[39] Siegfried told him how he had been transfixed on the subway by 'a perfectly commonplace man hugging and kissing a child – man poor, undistinguished in every way – only that in his life, lighting it for a moment. Perhaps it was because both, father and child, seemed condemned . . .'[40] Again the scene could come from Hardy.

The réclame continued; but by 12 May Sassoon 'wanted to be alone' although, needing the money, he still gave readings. Behrman noticed a lapse in dramatic tension. On 15 May, the *New York Evening Post* interviewed Sassoon, the journalist sensing suffering in this 'tall powerful youth' who said that 'My coming to America is only part of my campaign against war.' His August self-interview for *Vanity Fair* was lighter, 'A Poet As He Really Is': a portrait of an uncouth yet elegant figure in a batik dressing-gown, breakfasting off porridge and goat's flesh, whose effete life of bat-hunting and sport had been transformed into manliness by the war ('the man was terrific').[41] News from England – that Turner had let Tufton Street until July and that Theresa wanted a quiet summer – made him feel he was better off in the United States, in spite of prohibition and a 'longing'[42] for Gabriel. Hunter seems to have faded from his life, never marrying, having a last success, ironically, in a Broadway revival of the English play about the First World War, *Journey's End*; in 1945, Behrman sent the actor's *New York Times* obituary[43] to Sassoon, who did not refer to it in his letter of response.

*

RIVERS HAD GIVEN Sassoon an introduction to the 'psycho-pathologist' Dr John MacCurdy, who had a house in Pleasantville, about thirty miles from New York. Here, in the suffocating heat, Sassoon wrote some more of what Behrman called 'splendid' material[44] but, as Sassoon saw later, his new friend's 'critical faculty wasn't good then',[45] too admiring of slickness and over-writing, and the prose work had lost life. MacCurdy appeared at dinner and, sitting out afterwards in the moonlight, Sassoon joked, 'Oh what's the use of watching the moon. Let's go back home.' To Behrman, who was also there, the evening seemed beautiful but melancholy; for the next ten years, Sassoon said, he would gather 'impressions' and live 'freely', then settle down 'to do some great work'. His war poems consoled him, for 'when I am dead perhaps my poems will keep some young fellows from being tortured'.[46]

Sassoon went back to verse for 'Fireflies', parodies of poets from Marsh's Georgian anthologies: Drinkwater, D. H. Lawrence, W. H. Davies, de la Mare, Wilfrid Gibson, Graves and Masefield. Edmund Wilson published these verses in *Vanity Fair* in September and included one of Sassoon by Sassoon, written in a few minutes, a work of wry self-knowledge:

> *'Good evening; good evening!' the lecturer bowed,*
> *When we heard him last Monday in Carnegie Hall,*
> *Now the charm of his smile has caught on with the crowd,*
> *And he's promised to come here again in the fall.*
>
> *'I'm afraid he's a Red!' whispered Dora to Daisy,*
> *As he cursed the old men who in war-time were lazy.*
>
> *But the lilt of his eyebrow has sent both of them crazy!*[47]

He kept up the 'red talk', declaring at a New York musical evening that the communist trades unionist Eugene Debs was 'the only honest man in the country: that's why he's in jail'.[48] Yet he felt stronger for having known this harsh landscape, where even the birdsong was 'a little cruel', and the beautiful but 'rather soulless' New York and its brilliant light. When alone he played his grand piano or read Turgenev ('the perfect form and economy of effect').[49] Surely this trip must be the prelude to grander work, an escape, as he told Ottoline Morrell, 'from all the Georgians and their conventional poetic vocabularies' to 'do something which really expresses my own inside feelings'. As for the prose story, he had dropped it 'in utter disgust',[50] its homosexuality and stiffness making it unpublishable, and said he might try a play.

Sassoon still could not sleep. The *New York Times* printing presses were near his apartment building and vans came in and out all night. He wanted to leave in June but the boats were booked up until August and the indecisive Prewett might come with him, so in the oppressive heat he took up an invitation from Edward Warren to visit his house, Fewacres, near Portland in Maine. Thirty years older than Sassoon and again from the Henry James mould – a bachelor and collector of Greek art, rich, aesthetic, ruminative, the author of some private homoerotic verses – 'Ned' Warren, who had known Robbie Ross, offered simple comfort with riding, walking and no one else, only requiring his guest to listen to long monologues about art, literature and life, so self-absorbed that Sassoon could almost go to sleep unnoticed. Warren worked on his magnum opus – a learned but recondite defence of homosexual love – all morning, only wanting company for an afternoon walk and at dinner before bed at half-past ten; once they went to the Boston museum to see his Greek collection. An anglophile, with a house in Lewes, Ned clearly liked this good-looking poet, but the only physical challenge – for the host asked for nothing more intimate than the evening monologues – came when Siegfried Sassoon nearly drowned in a fast-flowing river.[51]

Sassoon told Pond that the agency owed him 500 dollars for

lectures, 80 pounds for boat fares and 150 dollars for train tickets. He would waive the travelling costs as Pond's advertising expenses must have been high. He gave Sam Behrman an inscribed copy of his *War Poems* (1919) with 'A Mystic as Soldier' handwritten in the front, Behrman noting, 'He couldn't have given me anything which would have delighted me more.'[52] There was a last meeting at the Cooper-Union; then, on the final night in New York, Behrman and he talked late, doubting they would ever meet again.

On 12 August, Sam saw him off on the liner *Imperator*, amid stupendous heaps of flowers and encircling steam launches organized by publicity agents for a party of film stars also on the ship. Sassoon shared a cabin with the publisher Ben Huebsch and, during the eight-day crossing, they became firm friends, Behrman and Huebsch remaining his two closest American contacts: both Jewish, different from the Jamesian grandees and lion-hunting hostesses. Sassoon ran round the upper deck, once swarming up a mast watched by an anxious Huebsch, who was unaware that his own slightly irritating, ponderous calm had prompted this. The film stars' promoters took over the sweepstake on the miles covered by the ship, there was a fight over the result, a riot broke out and Sassoon knocked down one of the Hollywood party. Meanwhile the violinist Mischa Elman practising Bach in his cabin near by – and the thought of Elman's continuing genius – seemed to mock him for he had little idea of what he would do in England. At Southampton, no one was waiting. In London, the Reform Club seemed dead and at 54 Tufton Street the Turners were away, as was Gabriel Atkin. Sassoon dreaded the old concealment at Weirleigh where he knew Theresa would want to hear 'everything at once'.[53] So he went with Ben Huebsch to Garlands Hotel.

*

WHILE IN THE United States, Sassoon had written poems about the histrionic poet Vachel Lindsay reciting, a Broadway performance of *Richard III* ('He died in clashing brass-ware, tired but tense'), the humorous 'An All-British Sonnet (Peace Celebration)' – mocking the war leaders – and 'Storm on Fifth Avenue' – nothing that showed a new direction or a definite break with the Georgians.[54] Now he went back to another part of his pre-war life, going cub-hunting in Northamptonshire and buying a horse that went lame by November.

The social rush returned as well, and he wondered if he had too many friends. Atkin was painting and had written a novel, turned down by Chatto and Windus, yet was still with 'silly people'; then, again, Gabriel failed Sassoon, once more 'incurable',[55] even thinking of going on the stage in what seemed like a ghastly resemblance to Glenn Hunter. Theo Bartholomew felt shocked by Sassoon's unreal hopes for Gabriel, though he was moved also by 'the essential fineness of S.S.'. It seemed 'painful, tragic'.[56] Maynard Keynes took up Atkin, obsessed by his physique; soon the economist's friends were complaining of the artist's louche habits.

Sassoon's living conditions were bleak. In 54 Tufton Street, his two small, red-and-white-painted second-floor rooms were without a kitchen; a window door led out to a small balcony overlooking some 'working-class dwellings'.[57] The Westminster house, built in 1919, was several feet below the level of the rest of the street and his sitting room had a small writing table and sofa, a couple of chairs, a small fireplace with a coal fire and a few bookshelves filled with the twenty-seven-volume edition of Pickering's Aldine poets bought in October. In fact everything about Sassoon's new quarters, except for the Aldine poets, seemed small and he had to keep his piano in one of Turner's rooms because the instrument could not be moved upstairs; he felt free to play it – and to use the kitchen – only when they were away. For the moment this fitted in with his anti-materialism and his scorn for possessions, and soon he evolved a strange routine: reading and writing until the small hours, a cup of tea brought to him by the daily woman late the next morning without breakfast, before he went to the Reform Club for lunch at 1.00. In the evenings, after dinner out or a concert, Sassoon usually talked to the Turners and any guests they might have. A later variation was to have a simple meal cooked by the daily in the late afternoon, perhaps grilled fish and a milk or steamed pudding.

In this oddly masochistic new life, better in theory than in practice, the war and its poetry surfaced when, in December, Chatto and Windus published *The Poems of Wilfred Owen*. Sassoon had written a short introduction, saying that more comment should be left to 'professional critics'; to him, the book showed 'profound humanity' and 'absolute integrity of mind' and he completely agreed with Owen's views on the war. Mrs Owen thought the piece was 'just what I would have wished. What he would have wished – and it is *true*.'[58] Later Sassoon said that Edith Sitwell had done all the editing and blamed her for omitting the poem 'The End' and line 10 of 'Strange Meeting'. The pain of losing Owen flared up, worse in the anti-climax of his return to London, and clouded his work on the proofs. He transcribed into his own copy fifteen poems from unpublished manuscripts, citing this later as evidence of trouble taken over this early, and ineffective, attempt to reveal the genius of his dead friend.

The book uncovered old wounds when, in their reviews of it, Scott Moncrieff, Robert Nichols and Middleton Murry mentioned the rumour of Owen's cowardice in 1917. On 12 March 1921 a letter refuting this appeared in the *Nation*, quoting Mrs Owen, purportedly from Edith Sitwell but in fact written by Sassoon. The dead poet's younger brother Harold, an artist recently out of the merchant navy, came to see him. Later Harold Owen complained of condescension, but Sassoon sent him to the painter William Rothenstein and to Eddie Marsh, telling Marsh that he hoped to raise £200 to help Harold and claiming to see in the watercolour landscapes the same sense of colour as in Wilfred's poems. Marsh, generously, offered ten pounds.

His own poetry returned to satire, not altogether happily for his indignation was much weaker than it had been during the war. 'Spontaneity', supposedly on how to write verse, is facetious, and 'Philharmonic' – on the transforming unintellectual power of Elgar's violin concerto – displays little more than charm. 'Lines Written in the Reform Club' (composed in December 1920) is still cosily facetious; he felt nowhere near his ambitions as a lyric poet.[59]

Turner, to whom Sassoon had handed over the literary editorship, wanted him to write for the *Daily Herald*, so in October he did a piece on Thomas Hardy. 'Sham poetry', Sassoon wrote, 'is as pernicious as sham religion,' and *The Dynasts* was great because it showed that 'men are alive only while they struggle'.[60] An awareness of the futility of effort, while still striving, was, he thought, the basis of nobility and tragedy, in Hardy's case made more moving by tenderness and pity. Others mocked Sassoon's own sense of being set apart, Prewett, still in Canada, writing to Ottoline Morrell about a Siegfried who was often charming yet seemed to think, 'I am a poet; poets are geniuses; genius is odd; therefore I am odd. Vanity, vanity . . .'[61] This was the greatness to which he aspired, and still hoped to reach.

TWELVE

'Why can't I create something?'

IN TUFTON STREET, the chimes of Big Ben tormented the insomniac Sassoon through the small hours. He had hoped that Walter Turner's energy might prompt his own but it seemed to mock him, and Turner said that he would go mad if he had as little to do as Sassoon. The atmosphere in the house became tense when Turner's marriage foundered. Some people wondered if the Australian might be partly homosexual, but he took up with a much younger woman, complaining that his wife Delphine was sexually cold. Sassoon wrote a poem about her unhappiness, wondering if he was sentimentalizing 'a calm face where nothing lurks concealed'.[1] Then Turner satirized the Sitwells and Lady Ottoline Morrell in print, laughed about a bad review of Thomas Hardy's poems, saying 'That's one for Siegfried,'[2] and complained that Sassoon used his money to control people. In 1925, Sassoon left Tufton Street, the relationship having soured.

Money lent or given is a feature of Sassoon's disjointed post-war years. Robert Graves, Harold Owen, Siegfried's brother Michael, Turner, the composer William Walton, Gabriel Atkin, John Law (his old soldier servant), 'Toronto' Prewett (now back in England): all these were helped; and, in November 1921, his great new friend, Edmund Blunden, asked for £25. That month Sassoon thought of selling some of his books, needing £150 to set Harold Owen up as an artist, £500 for Atkin's 1922 allowance and £100 for Prewett. Already in the last year Michael Sassoon had had £150 and Atkin £380, in addition to £530 given to other people and causes. Turner never repaid the loan that had allowed Delphine and him to live in Tufton Street.

*

ONE FIXED POINT in his life during this time was the Sitwells, who seemed inescapable in those places where aristocratic life and the arts met. In 1917, Edith Sitwell had written to tell Sassoon how much she and her brothers sympathized with his protest against the war and there was some mutual admiration, but he became irritated by their petty quarrels, their publicity seeking – which he thought copied from Whistler and Wilde – and their literary self-indulgence, sensing 'masked guns'[3] behind the elaborate courtesies, and, with Osbert, a fierce competitiveness. A part of the trouble was that their taste for the fantastic and for modernism – they admired T. S. Eliot and Wyndham Lewis – and their contempt for the Georgians, combined with a fascination with the baroque, made Sassoon feel old-fashioned, even dull. Osbert wrote chidingly:

> *We see in your birds and sheep*
> *An elephant or nigger minstrel.*[4]

Furious when, in November 1921, Sitwell – using the pseudonym 'Augustine Rivers' – mocked Graves, Turner and Blunden in *Wheels*, Sassoon broke with the family, and was annoyed that Robert Graves still saw them. Although he liked some of Edith's work, he thought the poetry of Osbert and Sacheverell was too aesthetic and lush, often frivolous, obscure or mere 'acrobatics'.[5]

In spite of the sporadic rows, Osbert Sitwell – a homosexual and, like Sassoon, reluctant to parade it – clearly intrigued him, arousing sadistic fantasies of vulnerability beneath the social ease and portly hauteur: strange visions of a naked, helpless, humiliated, overweight man. Sitwell sensed a wish to hurt, even a 'pleasure' in 'humiliating your friends'.[6] Another link was the nostalgia which suffuses much of the Sitwells' work and lives. Visits to Renishaw, the vast Sitwell house in Derbyshire, revealed an aristocratic obsession with family history and with their eccentric father Sir George, whom they mocked and feared. To Osbert, Sassoon often seemed touchy, whereas Edith, whose poetry he selectively admired, fell in love with him. Sensing this, he could tease her, even when she exploded, after he had criticized some of her work, 'Do you suppose I write poems instead of singing in my bath? . . . Do you suppose I toss these things off lightly, like yodelling?'[7] Such outbursts amused him, although her joke about Siegfried Sassoon and his later lover Stephen Tennant resembling 'the aged old Earl' and Little Lord Fauntleroy in the novel of that name was a little too close to the bone. But Osbert Sitwell, less easy to ridicule, always seemed to have the last word, if sometimes an extraordinarily pompous and self-important one, provoking in Sassoon the comforting thought that his sparring partner was not quite 'first-rate'.[8]

All this was a long way from Weirleigh. Theresa thought the Sitwells 'silly' and consumed by 'conceit'.[9] For most modern artists, she felt little less than hatred and never liked Siegfried's later war poems. Through numerous irritations, he still adored her, feeling wrenched by her martyrdom: her breakdowns and her struggle to bring up three sons; the loss of Hamo; Michael's penniless return from Canada with a wife she disliked; her eczema brought on by worrying. Sassoon knew she felt proud of his books and his fame, particularly his poems about nature and childhood and, later, his autobiographies. 'How fine she is,' he often thought, 'and how pathetic.'[10] Occasionally his emotion rose, almost unbearably, as at a concert where he watched her from a distance, or over lunch in London when 'wrecked looks' and country clothes could not hide her distinction; or at heartbreaking moments, like her anxious 'polite voice' to a waitress ('Salad? Are you bringing it?').[11] He was always, he felt sure, her favourite. It was important for him to feel this. Theresa, he knew, hoped to see him with a wife and children and must disapprove of his homosexuality, which was unmentionable between them even though he brought Gabriel Atkin and, later,

Stephen Tennant to Weirleigh. In July 1922, Sassoon was best man at Robert Nichols's wedding and, to his surprise, wept, and was amazed to see the bachelor Eddie Marsh in tears as well.

*

THE TRUTH WAS that the different parts of Sassoon's new life were hard to reconcile, as he searched for new inspiration and a structure to replace the war. With the Loders, for instance, at their house at Cirencester, he found hunting and riding in point-to-points a relief from literary London, partly because he did not have to think, even if it all seemed out of date, perhaps doomed, as he foretold in his poem 'Reynardism Revisited', published in the *Nation* in February 1922:

> *I wonder if these Nimrods really are*
> *Crassly unconscious that their Reynardism*
> *Is (dare I say it?) an anachronism.*[12]

Yet he dreaded the time when the country would be handed over to drag hounds, the foxes all shot, the characters of the rough point-to-point world gone.

Phyllis Loder was pretty, intelligent and a good pianist, and Sassoon sentimentalized her, as he did Delphine Turner, tolerating her complacent lack of curiosity. 'Perhaps we aren't meant to know,' she said once, when they were discussing intellectual matters, or 'What a pity it is Mr Turner doesn't play any games.'[13] To Sassoon, the Loders were like children. He flirted with Phyllis, thrilled to think what she would make of his homosexuality, then smiled secretly at his double life. 'What a chameleon I am,' he wrote of riding in races, for it 'excites me much more than anything in my London life',[14] a thrill not experienced since the war. In July 1923, while giving Phyllis lunch in London, Sassoon had a foreboding of tragedy. That autumn the Loders moved to Ettrington, near Stratford-on-Avon, and he never saw them again; the tragedy came when their son John died four years later. Sassoon abandoned hunting, losing interest in it until January 1931, after he had written the *Memoirs of a Fox-hunting Man*, believing later that this absence had let him create a utopia in his mind that might have been tarnished by more recent experience of its real people.

Music was the basis of another friendship – that with Frankie Schuster, a patron of Elgar and the heir to a Jewish banking fortune who took him to performances in England and continental Europe. Sassoon found the fussy, snobbish, spoilt Schuster slightly ridiculous, redeemed by his kindness and genuine love of music. He knew also that he brought something to Frankie who liked having a tame, well-known poet around. Schuster had another protégé: Anzie Wylde, a New Zealander who had lost a leg at Gallipoli. Perhaps the attachment had homosexual feelings on one side, but Anzie met the painter Wendela Boreel and married her, Schuster presiding over a grand wedding. Sassoon liked Wylde – a skilled player of the stock market – and found his lack of pretension a relief at The Hut, Schuster's luxurious house near Maidenhead. Wylde, like Turner, served as a confidant on sexual matters, hearing about most of Sassoon's affairs during the 1920s.

In 1921, Robert Graves wondered if too 'leisurely' a life was harming Sassoon.[15] The two Fusiliers were drifting further apart, Graves moving towards such theories as that of the White Goddess, an idea of feminine power as the basis of creativity. Nancy Nicholson was succeeded by the American poet Laura Riding, then by a series of muses, while his poetry diverged from what Sassoon had admired – and from modernism – into poems about love, myth and theory that showed impatience with almost all contemporary poets. In 1926, Robert Graves wrote, in a *Survey of Modernist Poetry*, under the influence of Riding, that Georgianism had become too 'concerned with Nature and love and leisure and old age and childhood and animals and sleep and other uncontroversial subjects', thus mentioning most of the themes of Sassoon's post-war work.[16]

Sassoon needed stimulus of the sort he had found in 1916. Atkin he saw often and sex fevers, as he called them, flared up at other times, but the flames were embers when they reached his poetry.

Visiting Walter de la Mare, he became fascinated by the poet's son Colin, and at Garsington the young David Cecil excited him. But it was to 'little' Blunden that Sassoon turned increasingly for literary sympathy, this time without the awkwardness of physical attraction. Small, gentle, sharp-nosed, with long, drooping hair, 'wonderful'[17] eyes and a thin body often breathless from asthma and wartime gassing, Edmund Blunden came from Kent, but from a different world from Siegfried Sassoon. His parents had both been teachers, each from a long line of country people, among whom, Blunden claimed, was Wat Tyler, the leader of the Peasants' Revolt. Devoted to his old school (Christ's Hospital) and to his regiment (the Royal Sussex, in which he had seen action on the Somme and at Passchendaele, where he won his Military Cross), Blunden loved English country beauty, tradition and landscape. His war poems, mostly written after the war, convey bad memories rather than immediate horror, but war brought to him, as to Sassoon, a feeling that he was one of the elect who had known unique, unrepeatable kindness, courage and comradeship. The trenches nearly broke this young, brave man. He went back to Oxford, with his wife Mary, where Robert Graves, then living near by with Nancy, was overbearing and tactless, attempting to control not only his poetry but his drinking habits. When they were together, Graves noticed Blunden 'shaking with nerves' during almost hysterical talk about the Western Front.[18]

Sassoon, some ten years older, encouraged Blunden. 'You must not overdo the archaic and quaint words,' he wrote in 1919, soon after they had met,[19] and the next year praised poems whose titles show Blunden's preoccupations: 'Almswomen', 'Perch-fishing', 'The Pike' and 'The Veteran'; these were, Sassoon thought, too spontaneous to be the work of 'a professional Georgian'.[20] After Oxford, Blunden moved to rural Suffolk, where Sassoon sometimes visited him and Mary, seeing his hard life as a penniless writer and Mary's involvement with another man. In 1922 Edmund Blunden dedicated *The Shepherd and Other Poems of Peace and War* to Sassoon. They had another passionately shared enthusiasm, book collecting, where Blunden had the more scholarly eye but far less money.

Sassoon introduced his new friend to Thomas Hardy, taking him in 1923 to stay at Came Rectory, once the home of William Barnes, the Dorset poet, and visiting Max Gate each day. Seeing Hardy and Blunden together, these two lovers of an increasingly elusive rural England, moved Sassoon almost to tears. Hardy compared Blunden to the young Keats; to help such purity of spirit in its struggle with the world seemed a form of absolution. Blunden had that frailty and struggling idealism to which Sassoon, the merciful knight, often responded. In April 1924, Edmund Blunden went for three years to teach English literature at Tokyo University without Mary – for their marriage had broken down – and Sassoon missed him badly. The friendship, although close, was perhaps not equal, partly because, over the years, Sassoon lent, or gave, Blunden a great deal of money. Years later, Sassoon allowed to be printed, by a friend of Philip Gosse, a Shakespearean spoof (written in 1934) called *An Adjustment* about an exchange of books that portrays himself as a duke and Blunden as a humbler figure, an unconscious reflection of how things were. And Edmund Blunden differed from Siegfried Sassoon in one important way; he married young and was, through three marriages and many affairs, a lover of women all his life.

Rivers was Sassoon's most trusted post-war guide. The doctor was joined by Henry Head, a pioneering neurologist and a comforting man who, with his literary wife Ruth, also had a parental role over the next decade. The world of Robbie Ross lingered in Ross's old landlady, the Cockney character Nellie Burton, and in Samuel Butler's friend Enrico Jones. With this mingled Sassoon's social and sexual lives: Gabriel Atkin; a clergyman called Cyril Tomkinson whose meandering homosexual fantasies could be too much; and a self-conscious group of aristocrats, artists, writers and aesthetes such as Lord Berners, the Sitwells and Stephen Tennant, all reminiscent of the 1890s, the decade that had formed Sassoon. Above it all loomed the creators, the men of mystical power, T. E. Lawrence and Thomas Hardy. And Hardy, John Masefield told Ottoline Morrell, loved Siegfried 'like a son'.[21]

*

In April 1921, thinking that he might have found 'a moral equivalent of war', Sassoon cancelled two reservations on the train de luxe to Venice for himself and Gabriel Atkin. England, he told Sam Behrman, was in a state of revolution. Massingham at the *Nation* had agreed that he should send a report, this time on the strike-ridden coal-fields of south Wales and Gloucestershire.

Sassoon's old soldier servant John Law, who worked with pit ponies in the area, guided him through a scarred landscape and human deprivation so shocking that, after interviewing miners and bosses, to be alone among the Rossettis in Llandaff cathedral came as an almost palpable relief. If the government suppressed the strike brutally, he thought, 'I may yet find myself leading revolutionary miners.' He reflected that this had surely been 'the most satisfactory week since I returned from America 8 months ago'. Then a scornful agent from the Miners' Federation broke the illusion, Sassoon seeing that he must seem a 'university chap' of the type that had exploited these people for generations. In three articles, he ridiculed the idea that the strikers had taken over from the Germans as Britain's enemy[22] but found it hard to argue the miners' case and, at dinner with the sceptical Meiklejohn and Atkin, floundered badly. Out of this came the poem 'The Case for the Miners',[23] reflecting an emotional certainty that he was right.

Sassoon's socialism was encouraged by Rivers, now the prospective Labour candidate for London University, but other friends certainly failed to share it. Gabriel Atkin, who – like a child – enjoyed provoking his mentor, got into a brawl at the Café Royal, before, in May, they went away together to Somerset. There Sassoon worked on his novel, or story, but the writing failed. In Holland, staying in a hotel with Mrs Tas, a rich woman whom he had met in New York, Sassoon became a polite, self-disguising guest; when, in

September, with Schuster, he saw Elgar conduct his own work at Hereford, he found the music full of the emotion that he longed to express in his own writing. 'Why can't I create something?' Sassoon complained on his thirty-fifth birthday on 8 September 1921.[24] He longed to find 'the still small voice that speaks to the secret heart alone'.[25]

Sassoon had time for pranks. He announced in the *Nation* that he had put a goldfish in the Tate Gallery fountain to remind his rich relations to do more to stop Millais's picture *Christ in the Carpenters' Shop* from leaving the country, and wrote to the *Saturday Review* suggesting that Walter Turner would write for the paper only if its circulation was more than 500. Gosse, who had recommended Turner to the editor, was furious. But in September 1921, when he went to Rome with Frank Prewett, whose fare he paid, the Colosseum made him yearn for public martyrdom. In Rome, Prewett developed acute gastritis and had to be treated for it, telling Ottoline Morrell that 'Siegfried has been angelic' and 'seemed suddenly to develop feminine tenderness and solicitude, just the qualities one supposed he lacked'.[26] And in October, a poem came, about two people in Rome: how, in the beautiful city, one 'wronged' the other's faith, as if Sassoon expected disillusion to follow.[27]

Siegfried Sassoon met his new inspiration through Lord Berners, when the rich, aristocratic composer and eccentric invited him to his flat in Rome. Among the guests was the young Prince Philipp of Hesse, a nephew of the last Kaiser of Germany, a heavily built man, aged twenty-five, of extreme urbanity and interested in classical antiquities. He seems to have been almost immediately attracted to Sassoon, writing of happiness 'like a precious jewel',[28] but had to leave for Venice after a few days. At the end of October, from one of his family's castles near Frankfurt, the prince wrote to Sassoon recalling 'your voice, Rome with all its beauty, the murmuring of fountains, some vague melody of Bach played by small untrained fingers'. The gods, he thought, had been 'very kind to us'.[29] But three days later Philipp of Hesse said that 'R', an English boy, was coming over to see him, and 'you know what that means'.[30]

Perhaps the relationship with R cooled. In any case the prince, who had been in the war, promised Sassoon 'a photograph of myself in uniform'.[31] Philipp of Hesse drifted from one person to another, responding to pressure and admiration. Earlier he had been to Rome with a friend called Maurice, yet he lived in Berlin with Princess 'Baby' Galitzine, a demanding American divorcee. With his dilettante reverence for writers, he was clearly impressed by this good-looking English poet.

*

IN APRIL 1922, meeting Robert Graves and T. E. Lawrence by chance near Piccadilly Circus, Sassoon became self-conscious, imagining they might be laughing at him. Asked by Lawrence if he was writing poetry, he answered defiantly, 'I sit up all night writing bloody balls.' Lawrence asked, 'Do you burn the balls?' to which Sassoon replied that he did, and stalked off. Graves said Lawrence thought him 'an absolute savage', but that day he felt more like 'a naughty child'.[32] He wondered if E. M. Forster and he had failed in not taking more risks with their writing, yet *Ulysses* repelled him after only a few pages. On 1 May 1922, he thought he had written only seventeen publishable poems since July 1919. The literary world did not console him, possibly because, as he told Virginia Woolf, 'I am not at all intellectual – in fact I have a very cumbersome mind.'[33] She liked Sassoon and wanted to publish his work at the Hogarth Press, but later she agreed with this self-analysis, writing of him, after a visit to Garsington, 'more brain, O God, more brain!'[34]

A hint of something mildly heroic arose when the *Maoriland Worker*, a socialist paper in New Zealand, was prosecuted for blasphemy after publishing 'Stand-to: Good Friday Morning', but the New Zealand Supreme Court threw out the charge. And in poetry, he often looked back now, once to that Roman idyll, in 'The Villa d'Este Gardens', a plaintive evocation of Byron, Landor, Liszt and Robert Browning. Other poems early in 1922 were the facetious 'On Being Urged to Write About Love'; 'Romantic Drama' – perhaps remembering his own lecture tour – about an ageing actor whose 'intellect was servant to my art', and another retrospective glance, this time to childhood in the unpublished 'A Child's Kingdom'.[35]

He wept helplessly in his dreams and had nights of sleeplessness, yet his poetry could never reach this pain. Gosse thought 'The London Museum' would have been as good in prose, and 'Sheldonian Soliloquy' is a charming mockery of a cultured concert audience.[36] Sassoon's journalism, like his published verse at this time, often appeared under pen-names such as Cyprian Oyde, S. Perides, Christian Mount, Simeon Hart or Sigma Sashun, as if he wanted simultaneously to publish, remain anonymous and avoid the risk of being taken seriously as well.

On the morning of 6 June 1922, Siegfried Sassoon was staying with Frankie Schuster at The Hut when Robert Nichols rushed into his bedroom with *The Times*. The newspaper reported that Rivers had died while preparing for bed in his rooms at St John's College, Cambridge – the cause of death, 'strangulation of the intestines'. Often Sassoon thought of his guide's last terrifying minutes alone and flinched at the imagined pain.

Elgar was there, at his most bluff, with Schuster and Glyn Philpot, and Sassoon almost wept in front of them in the garden, but bit his handkerchief and hit croquet balls, thinking, 'Rivers doesn't want you to blubber on the lawn, half-an-hour before lunch.'[37] He tried, but failed, to write a poem about this man whom he thought had saved him. At the funeral in Cambridge, the choir entered the chapel of St John's College already singing, and his memories and the pure voices made Sassoon cry alongside the medical men, Elliot Smith, Perry, Henry Head and his old New York host John Thomson MacCurdy. Afterwards Head declared that nothing mattered except life, and Sassoon remembered Bertrand Russell's belief in life as the source of all good.

*

A MONTH LATER, in July 1922, he was moving in very different company to that congregation in Cambridge when he set off again on a European journey. This time he went by car with Walter Turner, for whom he paid – getting in return the benefit of the Australian's knowledge of art and music. In Frankfurt, Sassoon thought he had found Philipp of Hesse's flat, but it turned out to be the wrong address. In Munich, where they joined Schuster and a group of music lovers that included the conductor Adrian Boult, a telegram arrived from Philipp to say he would come later than originally planned. A sense of half dread, half ecstatic anticipation seized Sassoon – an excitement at seeing, and being seen with, his lover combined with a fear of public shame. Finally, on 8 August, his 'Hoheit' arrived and they walked together in the park at the Nymphenburg palace.

Philipp was effusive, sometimes red in the face from drink or flustered by messages from Baby Galitzine. He said that he wanted to marry and to have children, but in their hotel he fondled the pillows and asked where Sassoon slept. The next morning he showed off some medals, including a favourite obscene one. Sometimes the prince called Sassoon Maurice by mistake, the name of the man with whom he had gone to Italy in April. Only occasionally did darkness fall over the good taste, as when he said that in politics 'one should meet violence with violence', or stayed up late exchanging dirty stories with trashy people, smoothly turning aside Sassoon's unsophisticated outbursts, one against self-indulgent people who owned too many castles.

Siegfried felt he was in love. He planned to pay for them to go to Italy, to end the subterfuge of creeping in and out of hotel rooms in the early hours, and as for the neurotic Baby, twelve years older than the prince, 'I don't mind at all,' he wrote in his diary. 'It seemed funny and incongruous but not unpleasant.' Once, at lunch, to show that he too had another life, Sassoon spoke of Gabriel Atkin.[38] He went with the Schuster group to Salzburg, Turner now loudly intrusive; then Philipp left with the Australian, arranging to be back in Munich in a few weeks. Schuster also left, for Berlin. Sassoon moved from Munich to Berchtesgaden and the mountains to think about the German who was now in Homburg with Baby.

Philipp seemed heavy and unimaginative, not as attractive phys-ically as Atkin, more interesting perhaps, yet coarse. Sassoon wanted to sting the prince into responsiveness by 'violent methods', to improve, even to save, him. He wondered if he was only one of a succession of lovers, yet copied some poems into a notebook to give to him. In the mountains, he walked, bicycled and dreamed of a war against the French, wondering if he should be a conscientious objector; he dreamed also of Weirleigh and of Osbert Sitwell as a worm-ridden corpse.[39] A birthday letter from his mother ended, 'God bless you, my dear'. He thought that surely he could reassure Theresa that they agreed over everything important, that he could even be honest enough with her to rid himself of some of his sexual shame; yet subconsciously he knew that this was impossible. Social-izing was restricted to one dinner with two intelligent Englishwomen before, on 9 September, he was back in Munich, ready for the prince.

Lord Berners was also there. At first Sassoon avoided him, but Philipp knew the eccentric composer. Although Baby stayed for a short time in Philipp's hotel, the affair began again, the prince giving Sassoon a birthday gift of a small Russian triptych he had carried during the war. They could not be easily alone together, for Germany, especially Bavaria, was now a fashionable destination. Indeed the Sitwells were in Munich, with William Walton, and talked to Berners but cut Sassoon. The prince drifted again towards trashy other travellers, showing himself to be a narcissist who surrendered sexually like Gabriel and lapsed into hero-worship; like Atkin too, he accepted money, this time for their trip to Italy. Sassoon, suffering a loss of confidence, suddenly feared that, without Berners, he might not be able to keep Philipp amused. In Munich he wrote two poems: 'Clavicord Recital', inspired by Berners's playing, and 'Solar Eclipse', written after seeing Poussin's *Apollo and Daphne* in the Alte Pinakothek; this was poetry about art, a lapse into what Sassoon called his Pre-Raphaelitism.[40]

They went to Italy in Berners's car, Philipp of Hesse bringing his servant – who travelled by train – and choosing the best restaurants, for which Sassoon paid. In Venice, the grand talk flowed, the prince mentioning 'my grandmother, the Empress Frederick',[41] and inveighing against Sassoon's socialism, and, once again, the English turned up: the Sitwells, Wyndham Lewis, Roderick Meiklejohn, Francis Meynell, the singer and composer Ivor Novello. Sassoon knew that he and Philipp must be the talk of smart London, yet surely (he thought) he could dominate these people through literary achievement and contempt. One evening, when the prince described him as 'a growling old bear with the heart of an angel inside', Sassoon recalled that Meiklejohn had once said that he was 'half-god and half-animal'.[42] In Rome, he declared his dislike of the effete, frivolous Novello, but Berners said one must make room for all types and Philipp added he had been brought up to be polite to everyone. Irritated, Sassoon thought Philipp was merely a man of culture; at least Gabriel Atkin painted. Both liked the back of Sassoon's neck, to Philipp the 'quintessence' of attractiveness.[43] The prince showed his prejudices, loathing the French and modern art, advocating a Europe ruled by its royal families. Sassoon imagined him in ten years' time: bald, self-indulgent, pontificating, surrounded – and paid for – by snobs. Philipp's bitterness about his family's downfall was a real danger, he thought.

Sassoon bought postcards of the martyrdom of St Lorenzo by Santacroce, which gave him a sexual thrill – reflected in the poem 'Martyrdoms'[44] – as did portrayals of St Sebastian, a beardless Christ, a prostrate Abel or an Isaac quailing before Abraham. In Naples, where the Fascists were marching, the prince said he constantly sought pleasure, refused to believe in human progress and thought brute force to be the only way to treat social unrest. Sassoon wondered how this could be combined with a worship of Goethe and persuaded him to read *Tess of the D'Urbervilles*. In Pisa, where Philipp left him, he felt love for the prince, who had 'always been so patient with me'.[45] They wrote to each other, the German declaring on Christmas Day from Schloss Friedrichshof, 'That letter was my Sig over and over again, always blaming himself and never thinking how bad his friends really are – I thought you were a perfect angel of patience for me during those wonderful days in Italy when I behaved myself so disgracefully and not a day passes now that I don't bitterly reproach myself for my bad conduct. But you know me and you know how I am and I hope you will forgive me in time!'[46] They never met again.

*

HIS *RECREATIONS*, a privately printed collection of poems, came out in June 1923. Sassoon, perhaps partly because of his former lover, had thought its design should resemble a book from the Darmstadt press, founded by a Grand Duke of Hesse, a relation of Philipp's, but Theo Bartholomew guided him towards a binding of blue paper-boards with a vellum spine and hand-made paper; each poem had an ornamental initial to the first line. Seventy-five elegant and expensive copies were printed by the Chiswick Press, and bound by Maltby of Oxford, to whom Ottoline Morrell had taken the sheets. *Recreations* has twenty-four poems, a mixture of the satirical, the frivolous and the quaint, together with vignettes of places like Broadway or the Villa d'Este gardens that had moved the poet, usually to melancholy, and the dreamy 'Falling Asleep' (one of three poems that are also in *Picture Show*) where time dissolves into nostalgia almost before it has been lived. Sassoon sent the book to his friends. Ralph Hodgson's response must have pleased him, although hinting at possible improvement ('I think you could do anything, given the spell'),[47] but Pinto saw 'only a fine technique and the languid interest of a half-amused spectator'.[48] Too many letters emphasized the book's charm. Prose failed to offer much either. There was an atmospheric piece about a billiard match for the *New Statesman* in January 1921, but when Sassoon showed his journal to E. M. Forster, the novelist thought that he was not a writer of stories yet might be able to use the material for auto-biography.

Bartholomew told him that he needed to fall in love. Osbert Sitwell warned that 'Your danger, I think, is to be lulled by your sleepy friends into an Olympian calm – as regards your writing.

Don't be lulled, and don't take their standards for granted. You are being "humbugged" a good deal.'[49] Lovers and protégés were letting him down: the chaotic Atkin, then Prewett – who had a job on the Garsington farm – wrote to say he had robbed Philip Morrell and Sassoon passed this on to the Morrells. Out of pity, he advanced the Canadian another £500 to buy a farm near Abingdon and subsidized the publication of his poetry. Toronto's early promise had not been fulfilled. At Cambridge Sassoon had met Richardson K. Wood, a young American studying at King's, but the affair was not love.

Tufton Street, before he left it, should have been more pleasant. Gabriel Atkin lived near by, in a flat on the Embankment, and Walter Turner attracted writers and musicians to the house. This was probably the height of Sassoon's friendship with Ralph Hodgson, who came often – someone very different from Siegfried in several ways: strongly heterosexual, an admirer of T. S. Eliot but not of Hardy and against fox-hunting, and an overwhelming talker, further showing up his dazzled listener's inarticulacy and uncertain opinions. Turner, who seems to have taken complete control, rented a tiny room downstairs to the poet Edward Shanks, thus filling the place up even more; and, in October 1923, went to Florence for ten weeks during which time Sassoon, having lent Turner the money to buy the house, found himself renting it for £5 a week to keep other tenants out.

When he was alone in Tufton Street, between 1 and 3 a.m. on 26 October, he wrote the first poem of *The Heart's Journey* sequence, an 'idyllic' revelation apparently inspired by memories of the Weirleigh garden. The style is new, so much so that Sassoon worried about it and tore up the first draft: transmitting an emotion compressed by strict rhyme and metre, the short words often interspersed with longer alliterative syllables that seem to linger in regret:

> *Song, be my soul; set forth the fairest part*
> *Of all that moved harmonious through my heart;*
> *And gather me to your arms; for we must go*

To *childhood's garden, when the moon is low*
And over the leaf-shadow-latticed grass
The whispering wraiths of my dead selves repass.

'For we must go' perhaps echoes Eliot's Prufrock – 'let us go and make our visit'. 'Towering Tom', as he was to call the American, affected him in spite of Sassoon's long guerrilla campaign against modernism. But in November 'My Memoirs' ('When I was a child, old Queen Victoria reigned') is not much more than doggerel.[50] Some recognition came when 'Aftermath' and 'Everyone Sang' were read on BBC radio on 11 November, Armistice Day. But he seemed irrevocably linked to the war.

*

ALREADY CONSCIOUS OF T. E. Lawrence's charismatic power, Sassoon became, during the autumn and early winter of 1923, enthralled by this mysterious figure. Lawrence, too, had been made by the war, in his case the campaign against the Turks in the Middle East, changing from a pre-1914 academic archaeologist into a guerrilla leader and a proponent of Arab self-determination (which he saw betrayed by the Treaty of Versailles). After the war, he went back to Oxford, to All Souls, and then, in an act of self-mutilation, enlisted in the ranks, first in the Tank Corps and later in the RAF, changing his name to Shaw. An ascetic, homosexual masochist, Lawrence put into his friendships a hypnotic, often wordless, sense of mystical understanding. Small, of immense vitality combined with an emotional and physical awkwardness that made him – like Thomas Hardy – hate to be touched, he seemed to reach beyond the material world. For Sassoon, who was often uncomfortable with reality, his aura was especially strong. Lawrence knew the lasting demons of battle. Partly to exorcize these, he wrote an account of the revolt in the desert, a huge book mixing the style of Gibbon and the King James's Bible with intensely evoked physical detail and action, showing that one could be both an intellectual and a hero of the kind depicted by Henty and other writers of late-Victorian boys' adventure stories. Sassoon, who read the manuscript of the third version of *The Seven Pillars of Wisdom* in November 1923, felt as if he had lived through an epic.

In December, Sassoon was reading Proust; then, one evening in the Reform Club, he took up Aldous Huxley's novel *Antic Hay*, hating its 'smart, priapic writing' so different from *Swann's Way* or *The Seven Pillars*. When Sassoon had been back at Tufton Street for five minutes, the house peaceful without the Turners, Lawrence, on a week's leave, arrived to see him, the one man with whom he wanted to talk. Struck by the contrast between the 'the infallible superman' of *The Seven Pillars* and this small, apparently frail figure, Sassoon felt 'enormous and protective', as he had with Hardy,[51] before this subsided into a sense of Lawrence's spiritual influence and power. It was not a sexual attraction but it overwhelmed him and, later that month, inspired by this visit to be fiercely self-critical of what he now saw as his insubstantial writing, he burned almost all the poetry that he had written since February. One whole evening had been taken up with doggerel about the politician F. E. Smith ('God's ghastliest Bounder') and the newspaper owners, Lords Beaverbrook and Rothermere – a trinity he particularly loathed – and sent to Ralph Hodgson ('I feel better for the expectoration');[52] now it seemed pathetically trite. He was still waiting for a transformation to happen, as the war had happened, and these heroes – Lawrence, Hardy and Rivers – made the gap between his ideals and his life seem even more distressing.

THIRTEEN

'The unknown want'

AMONG LIVING POETS, Sassoon saw Thomas Hardy as his great example. But Max Gate had become a shrine, Hardy representing genius at the end of its life, outside the inadequacies of the present, and this was part of the fascination for Sassoon, whose poetry would have benefited from more of Hardy's influence. 'Primitive Ritual', for instance, has a dire first line ('Look eastward with your mind-sight') and goes back through awkward word combinations and lifeless rhythm to his pre-war fairy-tale world.[1] His 'Reading Blunden's Poems' – revised in 1931 but never published – seems more heartfelt, evoking the Kent country yet too sentimental and dreamy for Hardy.[2]

Sassoon bought a picture by the Vorticist William Roberts and a portrait of Lytton Strachey by Henry Lamb, but when Ralph Hodgson preferred the idyllic cottage scenes painted by the Victorian artist Birkett Foster, he realized, slightly shamefully, that he agreed. In February 1924, he wrote a poem about William Shenstone, the eighteenth-century gentleman–poet – hardly an icon of the 1920s. A tour with Frankie Schuster to the Mediterranean in March, travelling in a grey Rolls-Royce driven by Anzie Wylde and staying in luxury hotels, seemed the wrong sort of contrast. Theresa came to The Hut, Schuster patronized her and Sassoon suddenly felt furious with the smart set, later seeing even Elgar besmirched by them when the composer put on a bluff, silly social manner. The Hut wrecked people, he felt; the actress Constance Collier, whom Sassoon met there, had 'shoddy and superficial opinions',[3] although later, away from Schuster, he came to adore her.

Sassoon could not now put literary fame against this faintly contemptible world, as his royalties of three pounds for 1923 showed. When some more prose sketches failed, he fell back again on satirical poetry. 'A Music Critic Anticipates Eternity', written in the south of France, has a facetious ending; in 'The Grand Hotel' the rich on Lake Como are 'poisoned by possession'; 'Afterthought on the Opening of the British Empire Exhibition' has the hymn 'Jerusalem' prompting thoughts of change in a 'war-memoried land'; 'A Guide to Elemental Behaviour' (later called 'Breach of Decorum') depicts chaos in 'Lady Lucre's' salon when someone calls Christ 'the world's greatest Socialistic teacher'.[4] Much of this post-war work slid into disappointment only weeks after its appearance. '*Recreations* seems so futile,' he told Robert Graves, 'a series of disgusts.'[5]

The draft of the prose work was dreary, dead without sex. Why write about sex at all? Sex racked him with anxiety and frustration. He seems to have fallen out with Richardson Wood, the American, a mean, spoilt young man, fond of fashionable psychological jargon.[6] Aldous Huxley pilloried Wood in the short story 'Hubert and Minnie': beautiful, narcissistic, immature, affected, passionless, with shy, evasive eyes.[7] Lord Berners told Sassoon that Philipp of Hesse had been lent two rooms in Rome by his latest mistress, making him feel relieved that he had lost contact with the prince. And Atkin had sent an account for expenditure connected to a recent exhibition for which Sassoon had promised to pay; at least it was less than he had expected. He felt that he needed a new sexual adventure: 'a weekend (anywhere) with an attractive man. It wouldn't matter if I'd never seen him before and never saw him again! That is a psychological fact. Ugly, but accurate . . .'[8] He slept badly, dreaming erotically about the young Prince of Wales. In Westminster Abbey, he thought of the choir boys having their bottoms smacked, then wept at the sight of the martyr-like cross-bearer, so like his idea of St Lawrence.

On a visit to his old tutor Mr Hamilton ('the Beet'), now Vicar of Windsor, who had married one of Sassoon's Donaldson cousins, he saw Theresa's huge picture *The Hours*, on loan to the Hamiltons. Its idealism, purity and link to his childhood prompted further guilt about lust for Colin de la Mare. At the end of July 1924, Sassoon did another of those calculations of his generosity. The total came to about £320, and a new person had joined the list: John Philbin, to whom he had given £30.

*

ANOTHER FRIEND, Richmond Temple, now in public relations, thought that Siegfried Sassoon's life was too cramped and gave him an astonishing gift: the Gwynne, a two-seater 8-horse-power motor car worth £220. This seemed immensely generous until Sassoon found out that the vehicle had been given to Temple after he had advertised the model. The Gwynne made Sassoon's friendship with John Philbin, a likeable American mining engineer, probably a homosexual, who turned up penniless at The Hut.[9] Philbin could handle the new car, unlike Sassoon, who collided with a dog cart near Maidenhead and knocked a bicyclist on to the pavement. So Philbin drove its owner down to Weirleigh before Sassoon took his first motoring trip alone into the past: to Sevenoaks and the New Beacon School for an Enoch Arden day of anonymous solitude when self-pity mixed with a sense of relief at having escaped from his constricting youth. Later in August, he and Philbin went to Garsington, then they were off in the Gwynne again, this time westwards: to Marlborough (where he asked after O'Regan, his old English teacher); to Stonehenge; to Sutton Veny, where they stayed with the William Nicholsons; and to Sherborne and Dorchester. They called at Max Gate, to find T. E. Lawrence there on his motorbicycle, over from Bovington Camp. Later they went to Lawrence's cottage, meeting his friend Russell – whom Sassoon assumed was 'T.E.'s' sexual partner – then through the Wylye valley, to Abbotsbury and H. M. Tomlinson, who had rented The Old Coastguard Station; this pastoral England seemed a world away from modernism. In Bournemouth, they met Schuster and his party, and Sassoon shared a room with Philbin, who 'doesn't attract me physically'.[10]

The Gwynne had him now. 'It is less trouble than a horse and much more mobile,'[11] he told Graves. After instigating an appeal, through the Royal Society of Literature, to give the Poet Laureate Bridges a clavicord for his eightieth birthday, he went west again, this time with Gabriel Atkin: to Henley, Cheltenham, the Forest of Dean, Brecon, Manorbier, Swansea, Hereford, Stratford-on-Avon, then back to London. The poetry reflected this new freedom – still gently satirical, as in his July tease at the smug crowd at the Oxford–Cambridge cricket match ('The Blues at Lord's'), and endlessly self-examining, as in 'Eyes', written that same July and revised years later, about how a sense of youthful self-regard falls away as one gets older. In 'Grandeur of Ghosts', written at Garsington in August, he is pained by flippant talk about his heroes:

> *They have spoken lightly of my deathless friends,*
> *(Lamps for my gloom, hands guiding where I stumble,)*
> *Quoting, for shallow conversational ends,*
> *What Shelley shrilled, what Blake once wildly muttered . . .*

But the car journeys led, on 4 August, to 'Stonehenge'; then, on the 6th, he wrote the unpublished 'The Cerne Giant' about local 'maidens' being thrilled by the huge chalk figure's 'immemorial erection'. The landscape inspired him. The poem 'A Ruined Castle' came out of the Welsh borders and evoked the dead who, after the war, still haunted Sassoon; 'At the Grave of Henry Vaughan' is a heartfelt tribute to the quietist seventeenth-century poet who had also been a soldier. In 'With de la Mare at Carey Castle', inspired by a visit to Walter de la Mare in his holiday cottage in Pembrokeshire, two poets stand 'at the edge of time' – a de la Mare glimpse of the supernatural spirits of the place.[12]

On 6 September, Sassoon headed towards Malvern, to visit

Henry and Ruth Head, and on to Hereford and Ross-on-Wye for music with Schuster, Philbin and Adrian Boult. This rural world seemed an enchanting combination of order and tradition: the Malvern Hills, Ludlow Castle, yew hedges in a country-house garden, the churches, cathedrals at Hereford and Worcester. Music swelled his emotion: English pieces like Parry's 'Blest Pair of Sirens', Elgar's Cello Concerto and *The Kingdom*, then Brahms's *Requiem*, Rossini's *Stabat Mater*, part of *Messiah*, Holst's *Hymn of Jesus*. On 12 September, Schuster and Philbin left for London; Sassoon drove alone to Ludlow again, then to Church Stretton, over Wenlock Edge, in Housman country, 'feeling moody and sexual', sentimentalizing Berchtesgaden and Munich into an English idyll.[13] The hotel at Church Stretton reminded him of a trip from Liverpool in September 1915, possibly with David Thomas or Bobbie Hanmer – a vague, beautiful memory.

In bad weather, he went on to Shrewsbury, avoiding Mrs Owen who would have interrupted this solitary journey of discovery, and found that Shropshire brought back a boyhood cricket match at Weston Park. At Lichfield, he lit a match to look into the fuel tank of the Gwynne, causing a small fire, and in the hotel a young billiard marker and some sparkling red Burgundy prompted lustful thoughts. Memory pulled constantly at him, through the Atherstone country: that odd engagement to Bobbie Hanmer's sister who had eloped with a married master of foxhounds, then Longthorpe, near Peterborough, where, staying with the Loders five years before, he had written 'Falling Asleep'. At Wisbech, half a bottle of port prompted 'Apocalyptic Indiscretions', mixing lust and aestheticism in a cry against passionless intellect:

> *In me the cave-man clasps the seer,*
> *And garlanded Apollo goes*
> *Chanting to Abraham's deaf ear.*
> *In me the tiger sniffs the rose.*
> *Look in my heart, kind friends, and tremble,*
> *Since there your elements assemble.*[14]

Norfolk brought a pert woman hitchhiker, and the grand country houses of Blickling and Holkham, followed by an Enoch Arden moment at Edingthorpe where Theresa had taken them in the summer of 1897: the autumn landscape seemed now like a Birkett Foster woodcut or a John Clare poem. He passed churches and the Broads where he had been in 1901, reaching Norwich on a grey day and feeling like Cobbett on a modern rural ride through a country unspoilt by 'cinemas, char-a-bancs', industry and 'Newspaper Syndicates'.[15] Here the past moved him, the tradition of landscape painters, fallen castles and abbeys, antiquarian clergymen, landowning families, partridge shooting, the stream of provincial English rural life imagined in placid nostalgia. Through Dereham, Castle Acre and Downham Market, he went to Ely and the 'clerical atmosphered'[16] Lamb Hotel where he had half a bottle of Moselle at dinner and later, in his room, heard someone below playing Schumann and Grieg, relieving the place's dowdiness. Sassoon had travelled 724 miles from 6 to 17 September and had only £2 10 shillings left. He headed back to London, stopping off at Cambridge to inspect his portrait by Glyn Philpot, which was now hanging in the Fitzwilliam Museum.

*

IN TUFTON STREET, the old life returned: concerts, Atkin at dinner with Bartholomew, Schuster. On 18 October, the *New Statesman* printed 'Evensong in Westminster Abbey', the result of more than eight months' work, a ponderous poem about being stifled by the abbey's history and liberated by organ music.[17] Sassoon thought 'London life doesn't suit me.'[18] But that month he was elected a Fellow of the Royal Society of Literature and another love affair had begun.

Seven years younger than Sassoon, the actor, composer and popular musician (his great hit had been the wartime 'Keep the Home Fires Burning') Ivor Novello had carefully coiffed, effeminate good looks and a flattering manner, and was one of the most admired performers of his day. Robert Graves remembered him during the war in an ambience of incense, cocktails and silk dressing-gowns.[19] On 29 September Sassoon went alone to see Novello's show *The Rat*, going backstage afterwards, but noted, 'Didn't see I. Novello.'[20] Then, on 2 October, Novello had lunch with him at the Savoy. On the 3rd, Sassoon wrote, 'Left letter (half serious) at theatre enclosing snapshot and suggesting Sunday for meeting again . . .'[21] This dragged on for some months, Sassoon the suppliant, Novello the pursued. Later Sassoon, perhaps ashamed of the experience, destroyed some of his diary for this time, and recalled 'fake sun tan, curling cigarette smoke', the mirrors and unshaded bulbs of a dressing-table, vanity and laughter: 'what an unblinking little hell it was!'.[22] In December, Jean Untermeyer, visiting London, found him awkward in Tufton Street, greeting her almost tongue-tied, his arms hanging limply and a 'curious helpless look'.[23]

Another friendship was quite different. On 18 December 1924, Sassoon sent a postcard to a twenty-year-old actor called Glen Byam Shaw whom he had met with Constance Collier. The card is an odd communication, with sadomasochistic overtones – a reproduction of Benvenuto Cellini's sculpture of Perseus holding a knife in one hand and the head of Andromeda, severed at the neck, in the other. The writing mixed green and red inks. 'How green of you not to know anything about Benvenuto Cellini. This is' [now in red ink] a red letter day in your life because you are beginning to find out that he was an old Italian sculptor.'[24] On 24 December, Sassoon sent a picture of a praying knight by Pintoricchio: 'this young Knight is praying that you may be happy . . .'[25] Novello was a link, for Glen had suffered from a friendship, perhaps a love affair, with him. As if echoing a possibility of something new, if not necessarily better, over Christmas at Garsington late one evening, having been reading Gorky's memoir of childhood lent to him by Ottoline Morrell, Sassoon wrote what he called later his first post-war poem with 'my mature mode of utterance' or 'cello voice'.[26] This is 'Alone', admired by Cavafy[27] and both a reflection of disillusion and a beautiful meditation on two selves – the solitary and the social – in a life 'endured and known'. The inspiration, he told Sam Behrman, had been inexplicable, a religious moment for which 'I can take no personal credit'.[28]

> 'When I'm alone' – *the words tripped off his tongue*
> *As though to be alone were nothing strange.*
> 'When I was young,' *he said*, 'when I was young . . .'
>
> *I thought of age, and loneliness, and change.*
> *I thought how strange we grow when we're alone,*
> *And how unlike the selves that meet, and talk,*
> *And blow the candles out, and say good-night.*
> Alone . . . *The word is life endured and known.*
> *It is the stillness where our spirits walk*
> *And all but inmost faith is overthrown.*[29]

*

EARLY IN 1925 Sassoon went again with Schuster to the south of France, where Atkin was now leading a bohemian, drunken life. Having taken refuge in Proust, a writer not guaranteed to raise one out of morose introversion, he found, back and sleepless in Tufton Street, that R. H. Mottram's novel *The Spanish Farm* dragged up bad memories of the war. Prison-visiting at Pentonville – taken up to widen his world – deepened his depression, and the homosexual hero of J. R. Ackerley's play *Prisoners of War* brought yearnings for a more honest life.

The ninety-nine copies of his next, privately printed, book of poems, *Lingual Exercises*, sent out from the press on 30 March, raised him up when Edith Sitwell wrote enthusiastically and Hardy said he thought the book Sassoon's best, particularly liking 'To an Old Lady Dead',[30] written about Philip Morrell's mother whose corpse Sassoon had seen in Oxford. Desmond MacCarthy gave *Lingual Exercises* a good review in the *New Statesman*. But Robert Graves warned against a Shropshire Lad tendency[31] and H. G. Wells observed that 'much of your verse is really prose material . . .'[32] In May Heinemann published Sassoon's *Selected Poems*, which contained nothing, except six from the privately printed *Picture Show*,

that had not appeared in the *War Poems* of 1919. The book sold
1,408 copies by the end of the year and reminded its readers of
Sassoon the hard-edged rebel. But two 1925 poems go back to a
softer satire, one mocking interest in the royal family's shooting
activities in Africa and the second inspired by Lord Astor's complaint about high taxes.

A weekend at Taplow, the country house on the Thames reigned
over by the Edwardian hostess Lady Desborough, brought smart,
cultured talk and underlying ruthlessness. Philip Sassoon, his ornamental cousin, fluttered through the salons; also there were Edward
Marsh and Desmond MacCarthy, both irritatingly socially adept.[33]
Sassoon sensed he would be dropped when some new celebrity came
along. A skidding incident in the Gwynne near Runnymede in July,
after which he changed a tyre at midnight with a jack raised by a
volume of Dorothy Wordsworth's *Journal*, made a slight break in
his protected life. On 13 July he set out again from Bray in the
Gwynne, Atkin joining him at Maidenhead station, and by the end
of the month, when he got back to Tufton Street, they had covered
1,000 miles, through Salisbury, Blandford, Dartmoor, Fowey and
Falmouth.

Atkin was good, drinking too much but 'very meek', Sassoon
told Blunden, 'busying himself with water-colour painting and
poster-designing, while I stalk the coves and cliffs.'[34] The empty
lanes and freedom made Tufton Street seem even more difficult; the
Turners quarrelled ceaselessly, the daily woman who had prepared
his oddly timed meals left and an apparently permanent fun-fair on
the waste ground near by shattered the night's silence. Delphine
Turner was miserable because of her unfaithful, bombastic husband,
who was a bad and ungrateful driver of a car for which Sassoon
had helped to pay. Ottoline Morrell and Nellie Burton promised to
help the poet find somewhere better to live; so he set out once more
in the Gwynne, to stay with the Heads in Dorset; and then on to
Max Gate. The Heads took him over to see Henry Head's sister,
who was married to General Pinney, inspirer of the poem 'The
General', and the chameleon Sassoon came out, talking politely to

Pinney – whom he had once thought little less than a murderer – about hunting, cricket and infantry warfare. In September, he picked up Cyril Tomkinson before going on to Hereford and into Wales and back through Bridgnorth and Stratford, running over – and killing – a sheep near Betws-y-Coed, for which he had to pay the shepherd, whom he had also knocked down. Sassoon enjoyed the drama when one of the wheels came off near Dunstable.

He reached towards the 'unknown want', the phrase of Walt Whitman's that had obsessed him since he had first read it before 1914 and whose spirit was reflected in his poem 'Alone'. In 'All Souls Day', written in the early hours of 24 September, the soul, 'a starlit sentry' – like Henry Vaughan's 'winged sentry' – is confronted by mysterious shapes of doomed companions, reminiscent of the war dead.[35] There was a sense that people were waiting. On 6 October a parody of 'Everyone Sang' appeared in *Punch*, mocking Sassoon for not publishing public editions of his work. On the same day, he had a response to a postcard he had written to Glen Byam Shaw.

*

THE FRIENDSHIP HAD a slow-burning start. Early in 1925 Sassoon sent the young actor a postcard of a huge bed in the Residenz at Würzburg, and the suggestive message, 'Best bedroom 54 Tufton Street'.[36] In September, he sent from Gloucestershire one of a London policeman directing traffic. 'The police are a splendid body of men,' it began, and went on, 'Since leaving London I have been more or less happy, so have been unaware of being alive. Have several times wondered whether to send you a post-card, and now I have found this marvellous picture of vanished London.'[37] Glen Byam Shaw answered, saying he wanted to see Sassoon again.

From a family of four brothers and one sister, whose father John Byam Shaw, an artist adept at angels and knights in armour in the style of Burne-Jones, had died in 1919, Glen had natural charm and sweetness. A 'nervous'[38] child and a failure during his schooldays at Westminster, he never forgot this insignificant start (to which friends ascribed his modesty). On leaving school, he joined a repertory company and began a career in the theatre. He had good looks, subdued glamour and an inclination towards hero-worship; he was also emotional, quietly loyal and an excellent listener. When Sassoon fell in love with him, the young actor responded gently, anxious to learn from a famous poet. The older man felt constrained, perhaps because of the boy's age or physical reluctance, and the relationship seems to have been only occasionally sexually complete.

At their first dinner together at the Reform Club, and afterwards at Tufton Street, Sassoon told him about the cruelty of Novello ('our mutual friend'); afterwards he sent Glen a copy of *Lingual Exercises*. For Glen, the evening had been 'something I shall never forget'. He felt sure that Sassoon could help him as 'most Stage people are bloody', although 'I love acting and everything to do with the Stage more than anything else.' Glen lived with his mother and sister in Campden Hill Gardens, near Holland Park, and knew of rooms to rent near by, in Campden Hill Square, where J. M. Barrie had written *Peter Pan*. 'I want to say lots of things, but I daren't because you are a great poet,'[39] he declared.

Glen was in repertory at Oxford, playing (among other parts) Oswald in Ibsen's *Ghosts*. 'I miss you very much (Does that surprise you?),' Sassoon wrote on 26 October. 'I have walked into your dear heart and I am now sitting there and feeling as safe as the bank of England. What an unromantic comparison; as safe as a Chubb Safe – will that do any better? Laugh, anyhow, – just to please me. (I am easily pleased, as I took so much time and trouble to explain to you last night, – wasn't it funny, all that long-winded explaining?) Does all this sound silly? I don't care if it does: I am only trying to talk to you, and I don't claim to be a brilliant talker.' He thanked Glen for 'sitting here and restoring my faith in the niceness of life and emptying all the nastiness out of the window . . .' Novello had once propositioned Glen in a car. Sassoon said, 'Life isn't like that really; you only struck a nightmare patch of it, where standards of decency don't exist, and everything is a sham and an evasion of sincerity.' He ended, 'If *you* are good, life is good. Having thus addressed the congregation the clergyman gathered up his notes and pronounced the benediction . . .'[40]

Sassoon took the rooms in Campden Hill Square, renting them for £750 a year from Harold Speed, a snobbish painter whose bad art could be seen in the flat downstairs. The place was quiet, with a view over west London, near both Glen and Gabriel Atkin, who now lived in Ladbroke Grove. Speed agreed to the removal of a partition, which created a larger living room, and Siegfried Sassoon sat by a gas stove, on the top floor, hearing the distant buses on Holland Park Avenue and the low, rather reassuring rumble of trains on the Great Western Line about a mile away. In this new peacefulness, his piano often had Bach on the stand, a view of old Exeter by the mid-Victorian artist J. B. Pyne hung above the chimneypiece and a convex mirror reflected Sassoon himself sitting in his chair, a red-shaded lamp at his side. Above the writing desk was a picture that he had bought by the early-nineteenth-century painter Julius Caesar Ibbetson, of Masham market in Yorkshire with 'a glowing twilight atmosphere'.[41] It was vaguely nostalgic.

Sassoon told Glen about Atkin, 'to prove to you that I am capable of keeping an eye on people I am interested in, and don't drop them after a few months of copious letter writing'. The letter's last words were 'I wish I could give you a good hug.'[42] Glen answered, from the Oxford Playhouse. 'I have been thinking of you a lot. You know that don't you, you old coon?' he said. 'I imagine you toddling off to your Beethoven, something in G something. I'm sure I should love it just as much as you, though I shouldn't understand it or be able to make clever remarks about it . . . Please write. I'm happy. So are you. Hurrah!'[43] By 6 November, Sassoon was saying, 'I trust you with all my soul now.' He enclosed a poem he wrote the night before Glen left.

> *Though you have left me, I'm not here alone;*
> *For what you were befriends the firelit room;*
> *And what you said remains and is my own*
> *To make a living gladness of my gloom.*[44]

In a cinema one afternoon Sassoon saw Marsh, Novello and
Constance Collier and felt how much better it was to be with Glen,
to share abstruse jokes with the young actor and make a private
world of favourite books like *The Diary of a Nobody* or characters
from Sean O'Casey's play, *Juno and the Paycock*. Sassoon taught
Glen Byam Shaw to drive and on 19 December took him to
Weymouth and to Max Gate to meet Hardy. Hearing that his uncle
Hamo had died, he turned to the boy; the night following the arrival
of the news of Hamo Thornycroft's death was the first time that
they slept together. During his first week in Campden Hill Square,
Sassoon went round to Gabriel Atkin's lighted flat but left without
ringing the bell, and, some days later, delivered a note asking Gabriel
to dinner – but there was no answer, 'to my great relief'.[45] In
January 1926 he sent Glen a postcard of the Cerne Giant, the
Wiltshire chalk figure with the huge erection.

*

THE POEMS THAT were to be published in *The Heart's Journey*
volume of 1927 mounted up, quiet poems suited to his new life in
this quiet place: 'To a Room', an introspective meditation on 54
Tufton Street, after 'Strangeness of Heart', inspired by some lines
from Landor about the sadness of the day when the poet no longer
responds to the blackbird's song. In December 1925 he wrote 'To
My Mother'[46] and 'The Power and the Glory', an early intimation
of religious feeling, he thought later.[47] There was further consolation
in *Jean-Christophe*, the long novel by Romain Rolland about the
life and growth of a musical genius, lent to him by Constance
Collier, which gave him 'courage' to 'go on my way alone as far as
possible'.[48]

The Graves family, with Robert Graves's new inspiration, the
American poet Laura Riding, left for Cairo where Robert was to
be professor of English at the university. Sassoon gave him money
and a car for Egypt and on 8 January 1926 went to the London
docks to say goodbye. He had dinner with Gabriel Atkin and Gabriel
came back to Sassoon's room: the same 'flaccid companion'.[49] Mary

Voules, Atkin's new protector, said that Gabriel spent money like a maniac. Then, in early March, Atkin found his room in flames, and almost everything destroyed except the piano. The artist left for Antibes, Sassoon noting, 'What a relief.'[50]

At night the sexual cravings could be terrible, aggravated by the Reverend Cyril Tomkinson's voyeuristic talk. Part of the trouble was the restraint that Sassoon imposed on his relationship with Glen. On 26 February, he explained why he could not come to see the young actor at Oxford. 'What you must think of me had best be left unimagined. But, as you already know, I am no ordinary man, & all this week I've been in a state of mind which made it impossible for me to see anyone. I don't regret it, as it always means that poetry will be produced, & such has been the case . . .'[51]

He saw his old army comrade Ralph Greaves, now a reader of music for the Oxford Press, and the stammering, one-armed Greaves, struggling in the civilian world, said he missed the war days: 'it was a man's life'. Sassoon thought, 'I know what he means but don't agree.'[52] The war returned again when the old medical officer Captain Dunn wrote to ask him to contribute to a history of the Second Battalion of the Royal Welch Fusiliers. The past seemed a possible escape from a solitude that was, nonetheless, good for poetry. 'To an Eighteenth Century Poet', suggested by reading Cowper's 'tranquillities' and written on 26 January, shows an affirmation of poetry's immortality; an exhibition of Sargent's pictures led to 'On Some Portraits by Sargent', a satire on the work of 'this brilliant hireling of the rich'.[53] After the meeting with Ralph Greaves came 'To One Who Was With Me in the War', coinciding with his start on the piece for Dr Dunn. This poem has a sense of the ultimate falseness of talking about a tremendous experience without its reality. Published in the *New Statesman* on 22 May (signed Sigma Sashan), it released, as he told Blunden, 'a long pent-up emotional accumulation'.[54] March brought a hopeful poem inspired by spring in Kew Gardens. 'A Last Judgement' is much stronger, about the death of Don Juan, a puritan vision of hell's punishments, written not long after the fire in Atkin's room.[55] In

March the *North American Review* published his short story, about the pianist – 'The Meritritzky Concerto' – a reminder that he was unsuited to this medium.

Sassoon looked through his diaries and read some war books, 'thrilled' particularly by Herbert Read's memoir *In Retreat*, in preparation for the piece for Dunn.[56] He wrote to Cottrell to renew contact, but heard that the old quartermaster had died.[57] How different from an evening with Constance Collier at Wyndham's Theatre when Ivor Novello hurled himself at his former admirer, exclaiming, 'Isn't he an old pet?'[58] Marsh was now infatuated with 'Ivor'.[59] Atkin had already had £50 that year and, back on the drink in France, owed Sassoon about £160. The relationship with Glen was different, Sassoon thought: 'less intense', and 'he has treated me far better than any of the others'.[60]

He found a chance of dramatic, even Byronic, political involvement when, in May 1926, the General Strike, led by the coal miners, brought the possibility of revolution. 'You old coon,' Glen wrote to Sassoon from Leeds where he was on tour, 'I suppose you will stick up for those bleeding miners etc. God damn them I say, and let him bless you while he's about it . . .'[61] Sassoon felt 'a tornado of emotions'[62] prompted by the urge to help other outcasts like the strikers. This, he thought, may have been 'connected' to his sexuality, which was repressed by 'social taboo', and even to the lack of critical interest in his *Satirical Poems*,[63] published by Heinemann in April.

Siegfried Sassoon and Osbert Sitwell made an unlikely pair of radicals. But, after dinner at the Reform Club on 8 May, they went to the *Daily Express* office in Fleet Street to see Beverly Baxter, the newspaper's editor, determined that the case for the strikers should be heard, and, finding he had gone home, rushed to Baxter's flat in Chelsea. Here they found Mr and Mrs Sacheverell Sitwell and the composer William Walton, none of whom was especially experienced in settling industrial disputes. Osbert Sitwell urged Baxter to persuade his employer, Lord Beaverbrook, to curb Winston Churchill, the member of the government most fiercely against the strikers, but Baxter wanted the total humiliation of the trades unions.[64] 'That's right,' Sassoon shouted. 'Shoot them down! Shoot them down! You're like all the rest.' He then sought to appeal to the editor's vanity, reminding him that engagements in the war were not won by corps commanders but by 'the initiative of company officers in the trenches'. As they left, Baxter seemed to think about this but, recalling the incident in his memoirs, refers to Sassoon as a 'gallant eccentric'. Later Sassoon realized that he had had 'nothing to guide me except war analogies and my instinct against settling disputes by violent methods.'[65]

The brief political foray was succeeded by an intensely social summer, 'a perpetual fête galante',[66] with Garsington, then a concert where Walton's *Portsmouth Point* overture – dedicated to Sassoon – seemed too much like inferior Stravinsky. The Desboroughs asked him to their other huge house, Panshanger in Hertfordshire, and Lady Desborough put a girl dressed up as a boy next to him at dinner. 'Did they do it to test his sex?'[67] Ottoline Morrell, another guest, wondered. Sex and anti-striker sentiments spiced up the talk, Lord Desborough announcing that one of his cows was a lesbian.[68] All this left little time for writing, Sassoon thought ruefully. Glen asked him not to go with Philip and Ottoline Morrell to continental Europe: 'wire and say you're ill'.[69] The boy helped him to pack and then left, doomed to be on tour in a mediocre play by Novello.

*

THE TRIP WITH the Morrells and their daughter Julian also included a homosexual couple: Robert Gathorne-Hardy and his friend Kyrle Leng. A younger son of the Earl of Cranbrook, Bob Gathorne-Hardy later became secretary to the writer Logan Pearsall Smith and was youthful looking, an admirer of Sassoon's poetry and a bibliophile. Sassoon had encouraged Ottoline to ask him to join them. During a journey marred by rows between the Morrells and their daughter, Sassoon dreamed of Glen, then had a flirtation with Robert Gathorne-Hardy before Leng and Gathorne-Hardy left the party at Versailles – perhaps because of this. 'I wanted you to stay with me,' Sassoon wrote to Gathorne-Hardy. But Leng's troubled face 'made me talk about my "strict moral code" which must have sounded frightfully priggish'.[70] Sassoon, alone with the Morrells, became lonely. 'Darling Glen how I long for you to be with me,'[71] he wrote from Verona, and to Gathorne-Hardy, from Bologna, he said, 'This letter is only a craving for companionship.'[72] He felt repelled by the luxury, disappointed by lack of adventure, yet dreaded a return to uncertain poetic inspiration in spite of Glen. 'He would much rather have been alone,' Ottoline thought. 'Indeed he seems to live in a state of crossness.'[73] Once they talked about religion. Philip and Julian said they believed only what physical circumstances told them, whereas to Sassoon 'the enigma of life' could not be settled so easily.[74]

On his return to an 'unsatisfying' Weirleigh, happiness came from memory. The Marchant sisters, Matfield neighbours from his childhood, came to tea. In Theresa's studio were the pictures she had painted thirty years ago, but nothing new.[75] Sassoon wrote a prose fragment, 'An Inquiry', about a visit to Weirleigh.[76] The Sitwells put him to shame: Osbert had a new novel coming out and was off on a tour of the United States, Sacheverell had written his autobiography at the age of twenty-nine and Edith's poems seemed to pour from her. Sassoon had sleepless nights thinking of Glen, who went to Cardiff on the Novello tour. On 7 October, Siegfried Sassoon had dinner with Osbert Sitwell, who had sent him his novel, a clever rendering of trivial material. On 8 October he was 'alone all day; hair cut at Trumpers; dined at Kensington Palace Hotel. Piano tuner came in afternoon. Worked at a sort of story which will probably end in nothing and even now seems futile.'[77] Thus began the *Memoirs of a Fox-hunting Man*.

FOURTEEN

The fox-hunting man

THE BOOK MOVED slowly and there were many stumbles. Osbert Sitwell and Glen Byam Shaw, to whom he had talked about his hunting memories, had urged him to write these down. E. M. Forster too had seemed interested, and Sassoon claimed that Dr Dunn's request for war material had prompted thoughts of autobiographical writing. Also he needed something; the bursts of poetry left too many empty hours for dreams or the itch of sexual frustration and puritan guilt about idleness. Then there were those recent drives through an unspoilt rural England whose brief reality he wanted to prolong in his imagination.

The work began as spoof reminiscences of a retired sporting colonel living in Cheltenham. But on 9 October 1926, Sassoon destroyed these and, using the past to escape a tormenting present, wrote about a boy growing up in Kent. In the process, he created, in parallel with an autobiography, a utopia purged of his own awkward boyhood, his homosexuality, his Jewishness, his wish to be a writer, Theresa's mental fragility and the socially demeaning, hideous Weirleigh. Sassoon seals up this beautiful world, as he seals up parts of his true self. *Memoirs of a Fox-hunting Man* has a sense of completeness. Until the war, there is scarcely a whisper of anything outside the easy, *rentier*'s life of the narrator. He is born into solitude, an only child, an orphan, looked after by a maiden aunt, perhaps an oblique reflection of how he had been set apart by poetry and a love for men.

A routine evolved: no rough drafts, just edging forward, writing late at night in pencil that was inked over later in revision. Usually back from dinner at the Reform Club or a restaurant in Kensington – if he had not been asked out – by around ten o'clock, Sassoon made a pot of strong tea, sat in his armchair and lit his pipe. At his elbow was a green-glassed reading lamp, on his knee a sketcher's notebook. He wanted to simplify everything, sometimes sitting for an hour and a half without writing a word.

The names are changed: Siegfried Sassoon becomes George Sherston, the Christian name solidly English, the surname taken from two villages: one in the Cotswolds, where he had hunted with Norman Loder, the other (called Sherston Magna) in north Wiltshire, an acknowledgement of Glen for it is the ancestral home of the Byams. Sometimes the changes go no distance: Mr Moon, the tutor, to Mr Star, or Gordon Harbord to Stephen Colwood, after the house where Gordon had lived. Then there are those chosen, as with Dickens, to reflect character or occupation: the nasty Croplady and Jaggett, the chatty Buzzaway, the carrier John Homeward. Over it all hangs the sense of a pure young knight, like those early photographs of Uncle Hamo in armour, the late-Victorian public-school ideal, embarking on a beautiful journey that stalls in the morass of the Western Front. The book was, he wrote later, an 'allegory of an "innocent" generation being shown reality'. On the last page Sherston, hearing a bird sing beyond a destroyed wood in the trenches, stands 'deprived of everything he valued'.[1]

Sassoon drew on his own reading: Surtees for the hunting scenes, the precisely dissecting first-person narrative of Proust, the story of a young man's spiritual and intellectual education in Romain Rolland's *Jean-Christophe*. The result was not only a literary work but an addition to the slow-growing myth that those who fought in the First World War had suffered an avoidable tragedy, not worth the pain. This began in his own and others' poetry. Now Siegfried Sassoon made it more powerful in his new book, originally a refuge from chaotic reality – from Gabriel Atkin, haunting war memories, guilt about Glen and fear of an empty future.

On 10 October a letter came from Glen suggesting dinner. Sassoon did not answer, noting, 'I want to be alone, and my relationship with G. is really a false one, as it ought to include sexual relief, and doesn't! . . . I want to vanquish sex.' Although exhausted, he already had 'a sense of success'. But two days later Glen and he had dinner together and went to a variety show. Like Osbert Sitwell, in whom Sassoon had also confided, Glen showed excitement about the book. So far they were the only two who knew of its existence.

Sassoon read Glen part of the memoirs for the first time and they stood the test. He had now written 6,300 words in the last six days. Could he reach 80,000 words? Glen thought he could, so 'I shall continue to write the book, if only for him. That it is neatly, delicately, and amusingly written I cannot doubt.' The years of journal writing helped, and his isolation brought back a clear view of characters like Tom Richardson, Gordon Harbord and Norman Loder. On 17 October he worked till 4 a.m., though plagued by 'sexual cravings' after champagne at the Reform Club. Then, unusually, he went on after his 12.45 breakfast of kipper and coffee, introducing 'Denis Milden' (based on Norman Loder) for the first time. Sassoon, his spirits dipping, worried if it was merely an escapist drug to make 'the past a more profound reality than the present'.[2] Three days later, he dined with Osbert Sitwell. After listening for an hour while Sassoon read the first 10,000 words, Osbert said they were unique and should go on for at least another 90,000 words. Sassoon begged him not to talk about the book, fearing its death if too many people asked how it was going.

The mental suspense was extraordinary: the dread each day that he might stall, and then being drawn into the book's world again. To read his satirical poems at the University College Literary Society was an intrusion. That night, however, he did another 450 words, finishing the first part, 13,500 words long. He had tried to avoid sentimentality, sophistication and the diffuseness typical of a first-person narrative. On 22 October, after a haircut at Trumper's and dinner at the club, he 'wrote the first page of the Flower Show match'.[3] 'Gosh how tired I feel!' he told Glen. 'Am longing to read you some more.'[4] The next day, he took a break at Easton Glebe, H. G. Wells's house in Essex where Wells said something that perhaps influenced the character of George Sherston: how 'for nations, as for individuals, modesty is the greatest source of power'.[5]

Near the end of October, still on the Flower Show match, Sassoon thought the book seemed 'very trivial' but 'to stop would be to admit defeat'.[6] Avoiding Weirleigh, whose gloomy reality might interfere with writing about a sunlit childhood, he dined on 31 October with Osbert again and read the latest 8,000 words. Sitwell liked them, 'so I suppose it is all right' – although some had sounded 'rather tame', not nearly as exciting as when they were being written.[7] Early in November he went briefly to Weirleigh, felt depressed and brought back his old hunting diaries.

Sex plagued him. On 29 October, after a block, an evening with Edmund Gosse released another 800 words before some books on flagellation in a shop window and Gosse's stories about Swinburne brought sexual cravings. Then, during dinner with his landlord Harold Speed, a pianist and a pupil of his, 'a very pretty boy',[8] caused another spasm of desire. In the Reform Club, the homosexual world surfaced again when Beverley Nichols appeared and Sassoon recalled an impudent review by Nichols of *Satirical Poems* in the *Sketch*. When passing Barker's store in Kensington High Street, he saw a dummy in the window that looked like Gabriel Atkin.[9] A message from Mary Voules about Atkin's remorse over his past behaviour infuriated him, prompting the shameful thought that 'I get a sort of sadistic pleasure from knowing that I am giving pain to G.A. And if revenge is worthwhile, I am certainly having it on him.'[10] Sassoon had not written to Atkin for months. That night he wrote another 900 words of his book. Later some of Gabriel's drawings, brought back by Miss Voules from Nice, touched him, especially one of a group, Atkin with his hand on Sassoon's shoulder, looking up tearfully at him, the weakness there in a drooping mouth and sad eyes. The works seemed charming, witty, like illustrations from a Firbank novel, yet brightly trivial: café scenes on the Riviera, young men, disapproving aunts, watercolours of Mediterranean exile. Sassoon recalled the happiness of 'the erotic delirium of eight years ago'.[11]

He thought again of his divided life, how he hated the snobbish, affected talk of Lord Berners, even of Osbert Sitwell, yet they both understood him. This was partly a question of background, of education – of homosexuality, culture, privilege and taste. He knew that these restricted him. They were barriers against what he really wanted to write about: the social condition of the country and the exploited poor he had seen in the army. The memoirs suddenly seemed limp, yet halfway through November he glimpsed the whole book in his head for the first time and knew it meant months more of solitude. He thought of a new title: *A Tale That Is Told*, better than *Memoirs of a Fox-hunting Man* because at least a third of the book would be about the war. Now George Sherston, the narrator, had become a slightly priggish aesthete, interested in the Pre-Raphaelites.

Obsession made him vague. His hat blew off in the street and he left it there; he forgot his tie for the Reform Club; and he scribbled on the club's dining-room order form a sentence about the village carrier, John Homewood, turning the corner and the past going with him: a glimpse of the book's end. Then Sherston dropped his aesthetic pretensions, and the narrative came back on course, to be blown off again when he picked up Hardy's *The Woodlanders* at the club, finding its style more stilted than his own but the detail much more real. On 21 November he could not work, an accumulation of insomnia and low spirits,[12] then after dinner with H. F. Thompson, a childhood friend, talk about the memoirs led to another 500 words. He told Glen, as if insuring against failure, that the book now seemed 'the most dreary piffle ever put on paper, but you must judge for yourself'.[13]

At the start of December, attending a Russian ballet performance

of works by Lord Berners and William Walton, Sassoon felt the
strain of moving in two worlds: those of this predominantly social
occasion and the memoirs.[14] Three days later, he had dinner with
the Gosses and said he was writing 'A sort of novel'. Gosse – who
in 1918 had wanted him to write a long story about English country
life – cried out, 'Verse. I want you to write verse,'[15] and advised
against taking the narrative into the war. Edith Sitwell, when she
came to his flat, was shown the manuscript but not allowed to read
it. Sassoon brought Gosse the manuscript of T. E. Lawrence's *The
Seven Pillars*, about which the old man had shown great curiosity.
'A little light reading,' Sassoon said. 'Your own?' the man of letters
asked.[16]

*

AFTER 1 DECEMBER 1926, Sassoon abandoned the book and
claimed to have thought little about it until he lent the manuscript
to E. M. Forster in March 1927. He did, however, read more
extracts to an approving Glen. Now the transcribing of the poems
for *The Heart's Journey* took up his time. He wrote in his diary that
the thought of the book 'disgusts me, in spite of Glen's assurances
that I *must* go on'.[17] In the middle of the month, he read the
memoirs to Sam Behrman, in London for a performance of one of
his plays, thinking them 'very flat and tame'.[18] Behrman's hero-
worship was always stimulating and Sam introduced him to the
theatrical producer and millionaire bibliophile Crosby Gaige, who
offered to bring out *The Heart's Journey* in a special edition
designed by the American typographer Bruce Rogers.

Mrs Hardy wrote to say she had heard Thomas Hardy, talking
to himself about the obtuseness of critics, mutter, 'I wrote my poems
for men like Siegfried Sassoon.'[19] This seemed a good thought with
which to leave for Brighton to spend Christmas there with Schuster.
At the end of the year, he was with Glen in London, noting, '1926
was, for me, almost a year of chastity,' with only few lapses in 'the
usual everlasting conflict'. But 'on the whole I did well'.[20] Sassoon

realized, however, that Gabriel Atkin's return, and its consequent sexual temptations, was potentially fatal. 'Gabriel is the thread on which my book is written.'[21]

In Dorset, with Glen, he saw Thomas Hardy and the Heads and in the hotel 'neither of us wanted to fall asleep. In these two days Glen has given me all that I have looked for these last twelve months.'[22] On 20 January 1927, he dined again with the Gosses and, during talk of the Sitwells, Gosse suddenly asked, 'Would you like to marry Edith?' Astonished, Sassoon answered, 'I don't think poets ought to marry one another.' 'Perhaps I shouldn't have asked you that question,' Gosse said. 'But don't let it deter you if you are really fond of her.'[23] Tentatively, Sassoon gave the old man the manuscript of his unfinished prose work. Five days later, he felt depressed by a bad concert and a fall in the street that had torn his trousers. Then came Gosse's first letter about *Memoirs of a Fox-hunting Man*. 'I have read Parts I and II and I write provisionally to say I am delighted with it so far. There is no question at all you must go on steadily.' The memoirs would, Gosse thought, be 'an extraordinarily original book' without any of the 'fantastic' ('the usual cheap trick of the age'). The hunting scenes were superb: the one in Part I 'one of the best things of the kind in the language'. There should be more; 'beat all the Surtees and Beckfords'.[24] He would write again.

This meant that Sassoon must go on. At first he felt no excitement, merely anger that the public might be more excited by these 'memoirs' than by his poetry. He might burn the manuscript, but Gosse had it. A longing for peace suffuses the poem 'Everyman', written on 27 January, about grappling with life, the fist raised in defiance, then the relief of oblivion.[25]

Gosse wrote again that day. He still had not finished reading the manuscript but was now less ecstatic. Sassoon, he said, must 'positively rewrite' a section describing his hero's life at Cambridge where Sherston seemed so feeble, slack and 'inefficient', uninterested in anything, that it was hard to imagine him capable even of being a good rider. The moment Sherston left Cambridge, Gosse thought, the charm of the writing returned – an example, surely, of Sassoon's own view of his university days. To Gosse, the groom Dixon was the best figure in the book, potentially 'a great creation'.[26] He should be brought back into it more strongly.

Sassoon thought this showed an essential belief in his work, and that he must cut out the conflict, central to his own life, between sport and the hero's artistic development. He adopted Gosse's suggestions, and wrote to Glen, needing reassurance. Then Gosse wrote again. 'You seem to forget the whole purpose of your book is to portray a hunting man' and 'hunting must be the centre of the picture'. Moreover, a second cricket match was dangerously like a copy of the first. Sassoon seemed to have made no preliminary sketch of what he wanted to say, a return to those aimless days before 1914. 'You must pull yourself together, and make this, as you well can make it, a really good book. Remember, no satire and no sneering! Hunting has to be its subject and Dixon has to be the central figure.'[27] But for Sassoon the 'gusto' seemed to have vanished.

On 8 February, the Beethoven quartet op. 132 at the Wigmore Hall strengthened him. His brusque manner was starting to offend – Lord Berners told Ottoline Morrell he now found Sassoon pompous and rude – but that night he wrote the euphoric lyric, 'A Flower Has Opened in My Heart' in less than half an hour, and felt a poet again, though he also mused that 'intellect isn't used at all'.[28] This affirmation of springtime peace and country serenity, a miracle of inexplicable inward light, of 'clear song and wild swift wing', seems, at its end, more a yearning than an achieved state of mind. Again frustration welled up. 'Why can't I write about life?' he wondered.[29] The past always seemed stronger. Another poem – 'I Accuse the Rich' (published in the *New Leader*) – was hectoring propaganda.[30]

On March 8, Sassoon gave E. M. Forster the manuscript of his prose book and his latest poems. He respected the novelist's literary judgement. Forster wrote afterwards chiding Sassoon for his self-centred and anti-social life, avoiding judgement on the memoirs. To T. E. Lawrence, however, the novelist was lukewarm about the 'unhappy and remote' poet's manuscript: 'quiet, charming stuff about village cricket matches. Unfinished and likely to remain so.'[31] Sassoon was nervous of Forster, who made him feel clumsy, even stupid. After the publication of *Memoirs of a Fox-hunting Man*, 'Morgan' was much more generous in his praise.

At a concert, the Delius piece *Sea Drift* – with its words about the 'unknown want' – made Sassoon cry, its effect mixed with news from Miss Voules that Gabriel had heart trouble brought on by drink and sexual excess as a male prostitute in Nice. Sassoon had once read Atkin one of Walt Whitman's poems on which the piece was based and the music revived 'those first days of rapture, so brief, but for me so intense. I was drunk with physical passion then, as I'd never been before, or ever since.'[32] He felt inspired to write his two-verse lyric 'In the Stars We Have Seen the Strangeness of Our State', the vast sky a metaphor for life darkening with age yet still bright.[33] Towards the end of May, Sassoon gave Miss Voules a cheque for £500 and sent her to France to bring the sick Atkin home.

On 14 April he drove into a lamp post in Hyde Park, the car – a Morris Oxford that had replaced the Gwynne – turned over and Sassoon broke a rib. At first he went to Nellie Burton in Half Moon Street, then for longer to Schuster at The Hut. While Sassoon was recovering, his aunt Rachel Beer, who had been in an asylum at Tunbridge Wells for years, died. The funeral – which Siegfried was still too immobile to attend – showed the Thornycroft superiority, Theresa thought, for the Sassoons looked 'so very ordinary'. He knew that Mrs Beer's money would change his life. Theresa was left nothing and he had to help her at Weirleigh which, as she wrote, 'cannot be run on less than 4 servants indoors and 3 men in the garden'.[34] The Hut showed how money brought 'slackness'[35] and too much cosy triviality. At least it would allow him to be generous to his friends. To Glen, acting in Glasgow, he wrote, 'I distrust this money and am afraid of being corrupted by it,' but he added, 'will you want your children sent to Eton or Harrow?'[36] The lawyer said that Michael and Siegfried would get £40,000 each from Rachel; in the event it was nearer £50,000.

The war dreams came back, a sign of 'repressed emotion and unhappiness'.[37] A brief surge came at dinner with Gosse who described a recent evening with a literary society at Oxford where the modern writers most admired were Eliot, Joyce, the Sitwells and Sassoon. Back at Bray, Schuster was irritating, Anzie talked too much about the Stock Exchange, and the house's change of name – from The Hut to The Long White Cloud – seemed to emphasize its unreality. He came back to London to find Glen angry that Schuster had snubbed him at The Long White Cloud.

*

ON 22 JUNE 1927, the infant son of Sacheverell Sitwell and his wife Georgia was christened at Lambeth by the Archbishop of Canterbury, another sign of the family's apotheosis. One of the guests at the dinner afterwards, also attended by Sassoon, was a figure worthy of Aubrey Beardsley: Stephen Tennant. Aged twenty-one, Tennant was a younger son of the late Lord Glenconner and his widow Pamela who, after Glenconner's death, had married Lord Grey of Falloden, once Sir Edward Grey, a Liberal politician and the Foreign Secretary when war broke out in 1914.

Sassoon had seen Tennant thirteen days earlier, at a dinner given by Osbert Sitwell, but had not been introduced to this extraordinary, effeminate young man. Much later, he felt sure that they had met the year before, when he, Stephen and Lord Berners had walked together from the Chelsea Town Hall, from a performance of the Sitwells' *Façade*, to a party given by Lady Colefax. Tennant, never one for details, did not remember this.

Tall, thin and narrow waisted, Stephen Tennant endlessly appraised his own looks. His hair was 'subtly but artificially dyed a dark gold, the texture is very fine and silky'; his nose high and narrow; his eyelashes long and 'stained a darker brown than is natural'; his mouth 'well-shaped, the colour of dark ham, or deeper red when I colour it'. Cream and powder covered his skin, except if he was sunburned when he left it a natural colour; his eyebrows were 'plucked back from the centre' and 'well-shaped and dark'. He thought that 'my buttocks and my shoulders are well-shaped and my neck very long and graceful'. But his best feature, he felt, was his hands: 'long, white and thin with almond shaped nails' above strangely narrow wrists; 'the beauty of my hands is daily encouraged with almond milk and lemon creams and other pomades'. Tennant was very self-conscious, afflicted with an 'innate shyness' under a vivacious social manner that he tried to control, for 'I hate glee and enthusiasm which is always jejune'. He thought that uncontrolled laughter coarsened his face. Addicted to rehearsing expressions alone in front of a glass and trying on elaborate clothes, he knew that 'some say I am beautiful'.[38] Sometimes he wondered if he was heartless; 'my mother used to say that my eyes were like cold sea-water'.[39] As an aesthete, he had one religion: that beauty was eternal, 'the still small voice that has been heard by man ever since the morning of the world. We hear it in the words of poets, in music, and we see it in the eyes of those we love.'[40]

Georgia Sitwell had told Sassoon that, although they had not been introduced, Stephen had wanted to see him again. Conscious of this, Sassoon talked more than usual at the dinner after the christening, before the party went on to a music evening in Berkeley Square – mostly 'a contemptible crowd, frivolous and self-indulgent'. Tennant, however, fascinated him: affected manners, 'an ultra-refined voice', consumptive and fragile but witty, intelligent, apparently enthralled. The Sitwells liked Stephen; perhaps the frivolity might be changed. Glen Byam Shaw said that he had been at Westminster school with Tennant. Sassoon wondered if the young man could love; he seemed too narcissistic, too beautiful.[41] He loathed the idea of such young beauty being sullied by a London world of intrigue, silly bitchiness, venality and betrayal.

*

Edward Marsh, patron of the
Georgian poets.

Stockwell ('Buffalo Bill')
in an unusually humorous
mood on a donkey.

In the back row (second left) with the Royal Welch Fusiliers
at Litherland in June 1915.

'Good-morning; good-morning!' the General said.

Rawlinson with his staff.

Maxse.

Pinney.

The Victims.

'Tommy dead; and Bobbie Hanmer in Salonika . . . they fade, with their bright hair and happy eyes.'

David Thomas
(Tommy)

Bobbie Hanmer.

The Manor House, Garsington.

Craiglockhart: 'Dottyville'.

Lady Ottoline Morrell.
She wrote of Sassoon,
'He thrills me.'

'Little Wilfred': Wilfred Owen
with a friend's son at Leith,
Edinburgh, July 1917.

Rivers – 'You understand my
thoughts', Sassoon wrote.

'Toronto' Prewett dressed as an Indian brave at Lennel.

Gabriel Atkin. Sassoon thought: 'He is one of the divinest things that have happened to me.'

Thomas Hardy and Edmund Gosse: 'Grandeur of Ghosts'.

Henry and Ruth Head. Sassoon turned to them after Rivers's death.

With Robert Graves at Garsington.

With Walter Turner, who suspected that Sassoon thought him 'a cad'
and 'extraordinarily raw'.

Edward Warren,
connoisseur of the homoerotic
and Sassoon's host in Maine.

'Frankie' Schuster,
patron of musicians and owner
of the Long White Cloud.

ROBERT GRAVES CALLED at Campden Hill Square. Sassoon showed him *The Heart's Journey* and Graves said he thought Sassoon had 'a strangely virginal mind'. As a desperate-looking Graves left, another victim of the literary grind, Sassoon felt a sudden immense compassion and kissed his astonished old friend on the 'knobbly' forehead, exclaiming, 'dear Robert!'[42] Graves thought Stephen Tennant 'an appallingly artificial young man'. Sassoon realized, with a shock, that he felt more at ease in the febrile social world of the Sitwells and Tennant than with Graves.[43]

The past came again, with a trip to Kent with Glen Byam Shaw to see Ellen Terry, that icon of the late-Victorian stage. 'Who's the other boy?' she asked Glen, delighting Sassoon, who thought the visit 'the most wonderful episode in the history of our friendship'.[44] The last few weeks had left an impression of 'unhurrying happiness', the only blot the approach of middle age. In July, before Glen went to act in a play in New York, he, Sassoon and Frankie Schuster set off for France. After arriving in Calais, they drove north-east in Sassoon's car through the landscape of the war. At the rebuilt Menin Gate – now a mere 'sight-seers' centre' – in Ypres, the names of the unburied British dead carved on the stone made him cry and he wanted to explore the trenches with Glen, but Schuster's presence made this impossible. That night Glen cried as well; it was a comfort 'like nothing I'd known before I met him'.[45] Out of this came a poem, reaffirming wartime anger, about the gate and those 58,000 carved names – 'the unheroic Dead who fed the guns' – accentuating the gap between their reality and this complacent memorializing.[46]

They drove on to Bayreuth, Sassoon finding this 'undeniably the most perfect holiday' and 'G the most adorable companion'.[47] 'Speasey' was a name he gave Glen, a Byam Shaw family nickname (it was sometimes 'Speisy' or 'Speazey'). At Bayreuth, Schuster's social overdrive started to irritate him, and Sassoon and Glen longed to get away from the old man, but they went to operas, concerts and parties, through Munich and Hesse, Prince Philipp now only an idealized memory. Glen returned to England and Schuster left to stay in France with a rich connection of Siegfried's, Mrs Meyer Sassoon. At the end of September, Sassoon drove on alone to meet the Sitwells, Burton and the German impresario, critic and translator Max Meyerfeld in Berlin, a city he found ruthless, expensive and decadent. With Osbert and Sacheverell he went to Dresden, then to Prague and Tabor, Linz and Vienna to join Sir George Sitwell and his 'pathetic'[48] drunken wife Lady Ida, who had been in prison for debt.

The talk, much of it competitive, often about the Sitwell enthusiasm for the baroque, exhausted him. On the way back, the war landscape deepened his gloom: the dead trees, shelled ground and memorials both fascinating and dire. In Campden Hill Square, Glen broke down about going to the United States; 'in comforting him I was in an emotional Elysium', Sassoon wrote. 'I am always happiest when he turns to me as his protector and reminds me of his youth and sensitiveness.'[49] He gave Glen the freedom to have love affairs and, weeping again, prayed on his knees for the boy to come back safely.

An old comfort returned. Edmund Blunden was back from Japan, with a new companion, Aki Hayashi; Siegfried Sassoon avoided involvement in the break-up of Blunden's marriage and welcomed his dear friend. There was also the book. On 4 October, at Osbert Sitwell's urging, Sassoon looked at it again. That night he wrote another 1,000 words, discovering 'my idea of happiness; to be working at my prose book again'.[50] Now he was writing it for Glen. By 10 October he had done 3,500 words of prose, a 'terrific sweat'. Then a letter came: an invitation to stay at Wilsford, with Stephen Tennant, the country house in Wiltshire where the young man lived with his mother, Lady Grey.

The Sitwells, Tennant said, had been asked as well. 'Will you hate Wilsford?' Osbert Sitwell wondered. 'It may be nice for two days, though not for a lifetime. Both Stephen and Cecil [Beaton] are in delirious form and excitement is beyond bounds.'[51] Sassoon took fright; perhaps he should refuse, yet he felt fascinated so accepted the invitation. While driving to Wilsford, he missed a turning near the village and thought, 'For two pins I'd go straight back to London. How can I face all those bright young people?'[52] Arriving at about eight o'clock in the evening, exhausted after the late nights and insomnia that had accompanied his writing, he found a grey house on the edge of the village of Lake in the valley of the River Avon, near Salisbury.

*

STEPHEN TENNANT WAS linked by birth to political power and aristocratic England. Lady Oxford, the wife of the former Prime Minister, Asquith, was his aunt; his stepfather, Lord Grey of Fallo-den, had been the Liberal Foreign Secretary from 1906 until 1916 – the longest continuous holder of that office in modern British history and, according to Lloyd George, one of those most responsible for the First World War; at the start of the century, his uncle, George Wyndham, had been the Conservative Chief Secretary for Ireland.

Tennant's parents, however, were very different from each other, in their family histories and their temperaments. His mother, born Pamela Wyndham, had been a Soul, from that cultured, aristocratic group that clustered round the Conservative politician Arthur Balfour; her family had estates in Sussex, Cumberland and Yorkshire and her father, a younger son, built a country house called Clouds – a name suited to this rarefied, ethereal world – at East Knoyle, near Wilsford. In contrast, the Tennants' fortune had been founded in Glasgow during the early years of the nineteenth century on the manufacture of bleach. Stephen's grandfather, Sir Charles Tennant – the last family member to be energetically involved in the business – had built a castellated mansion in the Scottish borders and owned a large house in Grosvenor Square. The social ascent of the Tennant family was complete when Stephen Tennant's father Edward became the first Lord Glenconner in 1911. But 'Eddie' proved a dull husband and the beautiful and self-consciously cultivated Pamela took up with Sir Edward (later Lord) Grey before Tennant's death in 1920.

Wilsford, designed by the fashionable architect Detmar Blow, reflected Pamela's taste, that of Arts and Crafts, and of the William

Morris style that had inspired her own childhood home of Clouds. Built of grey local stone and knapped flints, seventeenth century in appearance, the house has an older garden of yews, holm oaks and hedged-in lawns that can seem claustrophobic, a barrier against the world. Blow and Pamela created a charming pastiche, ostensibly complacent yet perhaps reflecting anxiety in its desire to look back, to escape from contemporary life. Wilsford invited fantasy, its kingdom a fairyland where anything could be dreamed. But there had been suffering and foolishness as well. Pamela loved her children and made them a part of her narcissistic performance, props for her beauty and the theatre of her own life, publishing their sayings, as she published her own poetry and the quaint remarks of the people of Wilsford village. She lost her adored eldest son Edward, or Bim, in the battle of the Somme. Her daughter Clare, another beauty, became cold and unresponsive to her.

Bim had written poetry and was manly. Stephen, Pamela decided, must be an artist, hence his effeminacy and curious physique, like some throwback to *fin de siècle* aestheticism, to the world of Wilde. At the age of fourteen, Tennant had held his own exhibition of fashion drawings, one of which was bought by Queen Alexandra. He studied at the Slade and designed the dresses for his elder brother Christopher's wedding. But his mother did not see some sides of him, how from an early age he had hung around the army camps on Salisbury Plain in search not of sex but of admiration. Indulgent and protective, she may, however, have sensed that he was frail mentally and needed the comfort of attention, that his often silly, self-conscious outrageousness was an attempt to conceal invalidism and shame.

Pamela was not there. The party was Stephen's in this house with servants and the seclusion to pursue the extreme aestheticism that governed his life. A Swiss manservant showed Sassoon to his room, Lady Grey's bedroom on the ground floor, where a wood fire smoked slightly and the atmosphere was 'friendly and aristocratic'. At dinner, the other guests were Mrs McLaren, a disciple of Osbert Sitwell; Sacheverell Sitwell and his wife Georgia; the sisters Baby and Zita Jungman, from the world of Evelyn Waugh's 'Bright Young Things'; the composer William Walton, apparently 'violently excited'[53] over Sassoon's memoir; the photographer Cecil Beaton; Osbert Sitwell and the young artist Rex Whistler. Sassoon, sensing Tennant's interest, talked a lot, his host's eyes seldom off him.

During the after-dinner charades, Stephen, Beaton, Rex Whistler, Georgia Sitwell and Zita Jungman dressed as nuns in sheets, then discarded these (in the dark) and appeared in pyjamas, to dance to music from a gramophone, Tennant eventually putting on an evening dress of Georgia's. The puritan Sassoon felt uncomfortable, yet sexually moved, extraordinarily so, and later, when Tennant came to his room to see if the fire drew properly, could only say, 'I'm glad to have seen you enjoying yourself.' Sleepless until four o'clock, he wandered alone in the garden and nearby churchyard to the sound of owls hooting in the veiled moonlight.

The next morning, at breakfast, Stephen Tennant admired the 'morose blues' of his jersey and tie; then, continuing the Arcadian theme, some of the party (but not Sassoon) dressed up to be filmed wearing costumes inspired by Watteau while Stephen handed out basketfuls of artificial flowers. Tennant's huge black eyelashes cast 'ladders of shadow' on his pale face, while Beaton directed the charade and Osbert Sitwell, coy in front of Sassoon, murmured that he 'felt the revolution brewing'. At lunch, the guests were still in costume; afterwards Sassoon drove Tennant, Mrs McLaren and Osbert to tea with Lytton Strachey near Hungerford. Sitwell asked Sassoon if he liked Stephen's motoring costume of a leather and grey fur coat, to which Sassoon replied, 'I like everything about Stephen, so far.'

The writer Edith Olivier, a spinster neighbour and friend of Lady Grey, came to dinner and once again most of the party dressed up. Sassoon, in his ordinary clothes, sat next to Stephen, who wore a Russian-style dress encrusted with pearls, a turban on his head, and seemed fascinated to hear of Siegfried's Enoch Arden complex. After a film show, of Tennant in more fantastic clothes at his stepfather's house in Northumberland, the boy danced again, an

immense white and silver train flapping behind him, before the lights went off for hide and seek. During the game, Stephen begged Siegfried to take him for a drive later and came at 3.00 to Sassoon's room in his motoring clothes, his lips still bright with lipstick. Before they set out, he looked in a mirror and addressed his face: 'You know what you've got to do.'

They went to Stonehenge, about twelve miles, and stayed out until dawn, Tennant making 'the most passionate avowals and simply intoxicating my senses'. Almost running out of petrol on the way back, they crept in through the garden door before Tennant flitted away, his white shoes bright on the grass. The next morning they drove together to London, Tennant asking Sassoon about his poetry and saying he had never been so happy, before being dropped at a ladies' hairdresser in Berkeley Square.

This was love, mixed with guilt as, for Siegfried Sassoon, it always would be. 'He now seems to me the most enchanting creature I have ever met,' he wrote in his diary, back in Campden Hill Square, 'but I am torn by my sense of what Glen would think of me if he knew. I told S.T. that he must be very secretive about seeing me, and suggested that he only comes to see me here. This seemed what he wanted.'[54]

FIFTEEN

Stephen: love and anger

SASSOON KEPT WHAT had happened secret, although those two nights had changed his life. To Osbert Sitwell, he described the Wilsford weekend merely as 'very unsettling' before Sitwell declared Stephen to be 'quite virginal', a state that seemed hard to reconcile with the hours in the car. In Campden Hill Square, Harold Speed's servant said that a Mr Tennant had called. Sassoon had already sent Stephen a card of a photograph of Nellie Burton, Osbert and Sacheverell Sitwell and himself, taken in Berlin.

Tennant's note was written on the desk's blotting paper. He asked if he might come to tea with Sassoon the next day, adding, 'I hope you have recovered from the emotions of the week-end. This is the most lovely room I have ever been in.' To Sassoon this was 'everything I could have desired'. He had not wanted to see Tennant that evening because he knew the boy was going to a party given by Lady Colefax and loathed the thought of him tainted by the society hostess. 'It is not easy to write the words,' he put in his diary, 'but here they are. "I am glad Glen is in New York."'

On 19 October 1927, Stephen Tennant came to Campden Hill Square, wearing a dark-blue suit – tall, silky fair-haired, a pale powdered face, large clear grey deer-like eyes, very feminine. He produced a pocket mirror and combed his hair, inspecting his half-inch-long eye lashes in silence as Sassoon played the theme from the first movement of Rachmaninof's third piano concerto. Then Tennant talked fast and nervously. His mother watched over him and he loved her, so the relationship had to be kept secret. Osbert, above all, must not know. Tennant said he felt like a lecherous vampire, interrupting Siegfried's work. Sassoon told him about Glen Byam Shaw, and Tennant said, 'I suppose he's a lovely creature – all actors are – is he dark or fair?' 'He is darker than you are,' Sassoon answered, to which Tennant said, 'Thank God.' Sassoon said that Glen had been at school at Westminster with Stephen. Tennant was glad to hear that Byam Shaw would be in the United States all winter. 'I know it is awful of me,' he said, 'but I adore being a siren.' He confessed that this new friendship with Sassoon left him 'almost swooning with happiness'.[1]

In his family's house in Smith Square, Stephen Tennant's room had silver sequins and sham pearls decorating the bed, silver curtains, a dark-blue ceiling with a gold star in its centre, a green parrot in a cage and an Epstein bust of Stephen – all suffused with the smell of tuberoses, scent and white lilies. The place was extraordinary, rather frightening. 'I wish Speazey weren't in New York,' Sassoon thought suddenly. Tennant spoke of Siegfried's 'shatteringly beautiful face' and wished they had slept together at Wilsford, to which Sassoon answered, 'But I want you to respect me Stephen.'[2] Did Tennant think him an old fogey? How serious was he? The Sitwells seemed to treat Stephen as an adorable joke. Osbert Sitwell declared slyly that all Tennants were riddled with consumption, for which doctors said 'that copulation is the best cure'. The gossips were already talking about the Wilsford weekend – Ottoline Morrell (who had heard from Lytton Strachey), the Sitwells, Beaton – and laughing about this absurd couple: the craggy war hero and the precious, shrieking aesthete.

*

A ROMANCE WITH Stephen seemed to offer so much of what Siegfried Sassoon wanted, not least the chance to save someone – as he had hoped to save Gabriel Atkin and those innocents in his company during the war – who looked like a sacrificial young man from the narrative pictures and stained-glass windows of his Victorian boyhood. In addition, Tennant's intense perception of beauty and joy in small and great things moved Sassoon – who, a later friend thought, valued beauty more than almost anything else. He valued also the elegance of Wilsford and the boy's links to an aristocratic England and to its country life. During the war, Sassoon had felt attracted to young soldiers but, unlike Ackerley or Forster, took no working-class lovers. Fastidious, rather snobbish, he liked Stephen's background.

For him, Stephen Tennant's childlike, pure vision seemed to redeem the selfishness, petulance and narcissism. Quickly Sassoon, romanticizing a strong physical desire, made a myth out of Tennant, complete with monsters, in the form of Beaton and other temptations, and good influences like Edith Olivier, and believed that he could change him. But the outrageousness covered wounds – hence the boy's wild energy and the resulting exhaustion: the desperate evoking of overwrought visions of Marseilles *matelots* for his never-finished novel *Lascar* or the pressing of dried flowers between the pages of lushly written journals before hours of catatonic sleep. Art, Stephen thought, was the only way to preserve 'the wonder of youthful happiness',[3] as Siegfried Sassoon attempted to do in his poems. Tennant's drawings are merely eccentric and charming, his writing flashy but unsustained. He tried to put art into each moment, but the art turned too often into frivolity, silliness and petulance, unchecked by lack of money. Tennant's health and temperament constrained him, but within the world he made there were few constraints. Sassoon tried to shape a new person who could not be. With his spasmodic, hard glimpses of reality, Stephen eventually saw that their future was impossible, that Siegfried's possessiveness would get worse, grimmer and more boring. He could not be serious, for the serious truth about himself was too bleak to contemplate for long.

Sassoon thought that he must restrain Tennant's wish for consummation for 'as long as that act is postponed I can remain on my dignity, if a display of that awful attitude becomes necessary'.[4] Stephen's letters were already gushing, one beginning, 'My heart's best beloved' and another, from a cold Wilsford in early November, saying, 'I am resting and relaxing luxuriously thinking of nothing – or rather of one vast beautiful thing that warms my heart mind, body and soul.'[5]

He told Sassoon he had been at a fancy-dress party that summer dressed as the Queen of Rumania and been kissed by a Norwegian diplomat. Sassoon deplored this, recalling the wrecked Gabriel Atkin. Tennant had what Gabriel lacked; he was an aristocrat known and liked by the people who made Gabriel an outcast. Gabriel's only superiority was as an artist, but soon Stephen showed that he had, at least, literary and artistic appreciation, admiring Sassoon's two latest sonnets, one written to him ('I found you in a loveless masquerade') that has a sense of succumbing to sorcery. Tennant told him he was virginal yet had submitted to other people's advances because they pleased his vanity.[6] Looking at the scarlet lips, the darkened eyelashes and eyebrows, the pink made-up cheeks, Sassoon saw in the frail body the frenetic movements of the consumptive; there was 'death in that beloved face'.[7] A poem written during these days already turns the romance into an idyll of the past, as if it was doomed:

> Remember how you called me kind and strong,
> And how you made my rugged branches flower:
> Remember how the blossom lit the tree
> And how our secret world was wild and free.[8]

He took Stephen to meet Theresa, writing beforehand of this 'charming young man' who 'has the merit of being a step-son of your favourite politician',[9] the countryman Lord Grey. Surprisingly she seemed to like him, although inveighing against men who wore make-up. Tennant thought Weirleigh haunted by loneliness and Sassoon's lost childhood. On the way back to London, they skidded on some tram lines and Stephen whispered, 'It's all right my darling.'[10] Sassoon began to visit Stephen Tennant's trichologist

Miss Strathearn, near Berkeley Square; then Edmund Blunden came round to meet Tennant, apparently also liking him. Obsessed now with the present, Sassoon abandoned *Memoirs of a Fox-hunting Man* to write thousands of words in his diary about this intoxicating new love affair and, in December, drove Stephen to Max Gate and to the Heads at Forston, Hardy remarking that Tennant walked like the young Swinburne.

Sassoon met the person Stephen loved more than anyone, more even than his mother: his old nanny Rebecca Trusler, who had also worked for the Kiplings, the Burne-Joneses and the Lutyenses. Nanny was a reminder of so much, not least in the brooch she wore that had been given to her by Stephen's brother Bim who had been killed on the Somme: a tiny replica of a piece of artillery from the First War, encircled by the words 'Béthune 1914–1916'. She spoke often of her time with other families, saying that all great artists were vague; how Sir Edward Burne-Jones was a very untidy man like Mr Rudyard Kipling, and as for Lady Oxford (Margot Asquith, wife of the former Prime Minister), 'Whatever people may say about her, she's got a heart as big as a brick.'[11] A short, sturdy, grey-haired, direct woman, familiar with Hardy's novels, even now she rocked Stephen in her arms when he was tired. 'I am very glad to meet you because you are a great friend of Stephen's,' she said, looking Siegfried Sassoon straight in the eye. He looked firmly back, saying, 'I am,' and felt that she understood everything.[12]

Stephen was, he decided, his girlfriend whereas Glen was a boyfriend; it was Glen's cheap packet of cigarettes against Stephen's gold cigarette case containing a powder puff. And when he took Sassoon to lunch with Lord and Lady Grey, Stephen had the demeanour of a demure girl amid the tasteful talk. Tennant adored his mother, but her love could be concealed by poise and the effort of disguising sadness. He recalled her weeping at her desk as she wrote a memorial volume about Bim: 'the terrible phenomenon of a grown-up person crying – always so fearful for a child'.[13] She was well read, beautiful, used to getting her way. As Lord Grey also knew his English poetry, there was much quoting at the lunch, yet

Sassoon thought that Stephen made the most interesting remark, about how bad Wordsworth could be. He could never like this slightly chilling woman who obsessed her son, but Lord Grey seemed 'a perfect dear',[14] not like a politician, the epitome of an English gentleman: a naturalist and ornithologist, a lover of Northumberland, fly-fishing and literature. In the glow of Grey's modest charm, Sassoon failed to see the man who, through his policy of promoting secret ties with France, had taken Britain into the First World War.

*

HE CALCULATED WHAT he had given away in 1927: £150 to Miss Voules, £250 to Theresa since October, £21 to the composer William Walton for a sciatica cure and £25 for the copying of his concerto, £50 to Edmund Blunden. Then he bought some presents: an onyx pendant encircled with brilliants for £62 from Cartier for Stephen; for Blunden, first editions of Leigh Hunt and Defoe, facsimiles of Gray's *Elegy* and the 1820 Keats poems. Blunden said there had been no sexual relations between him and his Japanese friend Miss Hayashi, and, as if in approval, Sassoon sent the poet a hamper from Fortnum and Mason as well. Then he left to spend Christmas at Weston in Northamptonshire, the home of Sacheverell and Georgia Sitwell.

In the eighteenth-century house, Cecil Beaton, Elizabeth Ponsonby, Dick Wyndham, William Walton and Stephen engaged in constant dressing up, cross-dressing, drinking, acting games, the making of home movies and the eating of large meals. His room icily cold, snow making the roads impassable, a trapped Sassoon crept most nights into Stephen's bed, his puritanism rebelling against the ranks of lipstick-stained glasses, full ashtrays, empty bottles, the mess left for servants to clear up. On Boxing Day Frankie Schuster died after an operation for a gastric ulcer and Sassoon missed the funeral, thinking, 'I don't feel his death as much as I feel not feeling it.'[15] The memoirs were stuck. 'I seem to be losing interest in my career as a writer,' he wrote to Glen Byam Shaw.[16]

After Christmas, he started another poem: 'there is no happiness like it'.[17] On 5 January 1928, he began the memoirs again, shunning an Albert Hall costume party attended by Stephen Tennant, recalling Atkin's drunkenness at similar evenings. Now he stayed often at Smith Square, avoiding the servants, but by 11 January had written 4,000 words. Stephen read these and 'adored'[18] them. The next day Tennant came to Campden Hill Square at noon, waking his friend with the news that Thomas Hardy had died. Sassoon played Beethoven's funeral march from the *Eroica* symphony on the piano and wept before going to see Gosse, who seemed almost stimulated by talking about the funeral arrangements.

He stayed at Wilsford with Stephen (and Edith Sitwell) and drove to Max Gate, where Florence, in tears, said she had never known death could be so grim; then she added that Hardy had looked beautiful. The funeral in Westminster Abbey had been arranged by Sydney Cockerell and J. M. Barrie, who had scarcely consulted her. Barrie had brought Hardy's heart, preserved before the cremation, and he and Florence had taken it to Stinsford church – where it was to be buried in the graveyard – during the morning service. To Sassoon, the double burial was gruesome, inappropriate for the modest Hardy. Arriving late at the Abbey, he failed to reach his privileged seat and watched the pall-bearers – among them Cockerell, Barrie, Gosse, Kipling, the Prime Minister – and the interment of the ashes from afar. He wept when going home; then the tributes brought further anger: Robert Nichols's insensitive words to him after the service, a 'trivial and pert little poem'[19] by Humbert Wolfe, a crude, self-promoting article by Robert Graves; 'I have never felt hatred for R.G. before.'[20] Worse, Stephen's interest in it all seemed silly and prurient, like his chatter about what clothes to take on a trip to the Bavarian Alps. Sassoon tried a tribute in poetry – a pompous elegy called 'Catafalque' – but *The Times* rejected it and the *New Statesman* turned down what he thought was a better effort. The best of his Hardy poems, 'At Max Gate' – contrasting the twinkling, fireside figure with the hidden, darker Wessex wizard – was not published until 1950.[21]

He wrote another eight lines about his hero, still not quite good enough:

> *When Hardy died and pens (who'd bored him) prattled,*
> *My soul rebelled. Blindly I was embattled . . .*[22]

Florence Hardy turned to Sassoon, wanting him and Gosse to edit Hardy's letters. Sassoon thought it a pleasant prospect and said he would help with any Hardy biography, but later the widow's adoration turned sour when she recognized herself as the pathetic wife of a great writer in Somerset Maugham's novel *Cakes and Ale*, these details possibly fed to Maugham by Stephen Tennant. Upset, she told Ottoline Morrell that Hardy had seen Siegfried as an amusing boy too often accompanied by 'tiresome young men'.[23]

On 21 January, Stephen left for the Bavarian Alps where it was believed that the air might help his lungs. At the end of the month, Sassoon went back to the book, adding 600 words in just under two hours and, on 3 February, the day of Field Marshal Haig's funeral, another 1,100 words. Two days later, Sam Behrman came to Weirleigh, welcomed by Theresa ('a great person', Sam thought, 'full of wisdom and understanding and serenity')[24] who, at the end of their visit, looked agonized when Siegfried said they were not staying, reminding Behrman of the illimitable love of Bazarov's parents for their son in Turgenev's *Fathers and Children*. Surprising praise for the manuscript had come when he had read bits of it to Graves and Laura Riding and they judged it 'first rate, like Defoe'.[25] On 10 February, after doing another 1,000 words, he felt 'half dead'.[26] From Bavaria, Stephen wrote, 'Oh darling! What wouldn't I give to feel your arms round me!'[27] He flirted by telling Sassoon how he had gone to a carnival ball dressed in green silk, 'painted like Jezebel',[28] and had sunbathed in just a dressing-gown or a snakeskin belt. Stephen wrote of his devotion to 'darling, darling Galahad'.[29] Sassoon gave William Walton £20 to join Stephen in Germany.

By 24 February, he had written 16,000 words since the end of January. Tennant reported that Willie Walton seemed to have fallen in love with him, but this barely disturbed Sassoon. He sent £100 to Glen Byam Shaw in the United States, to help pay for an operation, and felt safe about Stephen ('it was very clever of me to send W. out there');[30] his loyalty to Glen seemed symbolized by his determination to finish the book. Stephen wrote to say that if Sassoon failed to come out he would be back in less than three weeks. Clearly the book was a race against this return. Nothing was 'alive' in his mind except the need to finish and then revise it; 'is it worth the trouble?'[31] On 26 March he did 1,200 words in three hours: 'almost too good to be true!'[32]

Some letters about *The Heart's Journey* pleased him: from Edmund Gosse, from J. C. Squire, from Ralph Hodgson and Edith Sitwell. Then Florence Hardy wrote to say that the poet Charlotte Mew had killed herself. Sassoon greatly admired Mew's poetry for its unashamed emotionalism and directness; it was, he thought, the very opposite to the cerebral obscurities of the Eliot–Pound revolution. They had met through Sydney Cockerell and he had tried to help this small, obviously unhappy woman whose work had been praised by critics as diverse as Hardy and Virginia Woolf. The news of her death was terrible, especially Mew's last wish to the doctors that she dreaded being brought back to the world. Shattered, Sassoon forced out a further 700 words. He bought another twenty copies of *The Heart's Journey*, leaving only 205 on the market; his book would at least be rare. The publishers had not advertised it, he complained; but, dreading the critics, he had refused to send out any review copies.

On 2 April, Sassoon noted that he had done 2,000 words in the previous two nights. The death of Dick Tiltwood, based on David Thomas, was painful to write and self-doubt kept creeping in. 'The book I have written seems a very cramped affair – everything too much tidied up,' he thought. 'But life is so large and untidy that there was no other way of doing it.'[33] The end came on Easter Sunday. On a mild, overcast morning, with a thrush singing from a leafless tree in Campden Hill Square, Sassoon finished *Memoirs of a Fox-hunting Man*. He sat back, then boiled himself an egg before setting off in his car to The Long White Cloud, now owned by Anzie Wylde, stopping at Runnymede where the church bells rang for an early service.

*

A LETTER ARRIVED from Stephen Tennant in Paris about wild shopping: scent, a dressing-gown patterned like pink leopardskin, shirts 'like frosted Devonshire cream'. More ominous was Stephen's meeting with the young Russian painter Pavel Tchelitchew – 'so heavenly, and so amusing and so clever'. Sassoon, furious, thought Tennant 'a glaring example of the behaviour of the rich people I loathe and despise'.[34] He wrote to Stephen, telling him to give to the Lord Mayor's fund for the Distressed Mining Areas, to which he had already sent £105 in the name of Edith Sitwell. Taking the last instalment of the memoirs to be typed, Sassoon still felt worried about them. Sick of Heinemann, he had arranged with Richard de la Mare of Faber and Gwyer to publish the book anonymously. On 18 April Dick de la Mare wrote ecstatically about the first 21,000 words, and later offered a £100 advance, saying that he wished to publish the book in September

Back in London for his brother David's marriage to the actress Hermione Baddeley, Stephen Tennant came round, admitted to a flirtation with Tchelitchew and launched into stories of the wedding: smashed glasses, drunkenness at the Gargoyle Club, rowdiness and decadence. Shocked, Sassoon realized that he liked hearing about these people and enjoyed the thought of rescuing Stephen from them. Tennant went insatiably to parties, usually dressed up, once in a sailor suit and gold earrings, his face painted, with promises, often not fulfilled, to come to Campden Hill Square at dawn. And Glen seldom wrote from New York. Was Stephen 'just vain and shallow'?[35] Sassoon could see that 'I am being eaten up by jealousy.'[36] Glen wrote at last to say, 'There is so much to tell you that I can't write, but I think I shall be home soon.' A letter came from Stephen, covered in large crosses, reporting on a 'heavenly day'[37] in

Bournemouth with Edith Sitwell, and saying he longed to be with him. He drove with Tennant to another party, noticing how the boy held his hands up as if praying because it made them deathly white. Stephen never drank alcohol; admiration was his drug.

At the start of May, they went off together, this time to Oxford and then on to Weston. As so often, there was something that spoiled their return to London: stories of drunkenness at the Gargoyle Club, of David Tennant's pyjama party where many of the guests were sick. The boy's hysterical vitality was amazing, linked, Sassoon thought, to an inability to achieve sexual satisfaction.

They were now having what each wanted to be a full physical relationship, but Stephen could not fully take part because of his inability to reach orgasm. Sassoon and he became quickly aroused and Tennant eagerly pleased his lover, before Sassoon tried, often for an exhaustingly long time, to help Stephen to achieve ejaculation. There seems to have been little anal sex. Later the fragile Tennant complained that Siegfried had sometimes been rough, and this may have come from Sassoon's exasperation at failing to satisfy him. 'I fear there is something wrong,' Sassoon wrote, but 'I am, I think, more infatuated with him than ever before.'[38]

He felt the dull weight of middle age. To read Gide's *The Counterfeiters*, recommended by Stephen, in the cramped atmosphere of the studio at Weirleigh, made him see how far he still had to go to leave the world of his upbringing. Tennant was brave, Sassoon decided, to vaunt his taste, to be so shamelessly artificial. He contrasted this with his own caution, particularly here at the scene of so much concealment. *The Counterfeiters* made him want to write a rambling homosexual novel, yet still the fear of scandal, of hurting his mother and others, held him back. Osbert Sitwell said that Stephen had misbehaved with a sailor near Wilsford, and that the local policeman had gone to Lord Grey. Sassoon made Osbert admit this was a lie. At lunch with Henry Festing Jones, born in 1851, he enjoyed talk about the Pre-Raphaelites, now out of fashion, thinking, 'I am happiest, really, with elderly people, because they

can talk about the past.'[39] If only, Sassoon felt sometimes, some of these could be immortal, for when they went his own youth seemed to be slipping away even faster.

On 15 May, when he called at a nursing home in Welbeck Street to ask after Gosse, there for a prostate operation, a nurse came out and said that the old man had died about ten minutes before. Sassoon went to a Queen's Hall concert – the 'Mass of Life' – and, dreading crude sympathy, avoided Robert Nichols, who was in the audience. Gosse would never read the completed prose book; he and Sassoon would never edit Hardy's letters together. Five days later he and Tennant went to see the Sitwells in Carlyle Square, Sassoon thinking what a bad effect Osbert had on the boy; and when standing with H. M. Tomlinson at Gosse's funeral, he recalled how Sitwell disliked the simple Tommy. After an earlier evening at Hanover Terrace, he had written 'One Who Watches', sensing death's nearness to the great figures of his youth, 'those in whom my loves must die' until they stayed only 'hoarded like happy summers in my heart'.[40] Sassoon had wanted to please Gosse. They had often agreed, for Sir Edmund had decried the modernist icons – Eliot, Pound and Joyce – and had sympathized with the kind of writer that Sassoon wanted to be. If their relationship, for the younger man, had always been touched with awe, he also felt that a great guide and supporter had gone.

*

AT A CHARITY matinée, Beaton came dressed up as Gainsborough, Eddie Marsh as Thackeray and Tennant as Shelley, an incredible apparition, neither man nor woman. Sassoon's puritan distaste for the London summer extravaganza came out in a poem of April, 'Doxology De Luxe', asking for the rich to 'be damned for evermore'.[41] At the start of June he took Stephen to see Walter de la Mare; then Glen Byam Shaw rang. He was back from America.

Tennant said he was longing to see the actor. 'I think he regarded it as a sort of duel for supremacy over me,' Sassoon wrote. The night of their meeting, Glen announced his presence in Campden

Hill Square by sounding the horn of Sassoon's car, and Stephen leaned out of the window to shout, 'Siegfried is just coming down.' At the door Glen looked surly and mystified. Sassoon said, 'You'll find Stephen Tennant in there.' After three-quarters of an hour of difficult talk, with Stephen conciliatory and Glen antagonistic, Sassoon and the two young men got into the car. Glen drove and they dropped Stephen at Smith Square before Sassoon went to the Byam Shaw house with Glen. The actor spoke amiably about his replacement, and the reason for this soon came out: he was in love 'for the first time in his life'[42] with Angela Baddeley, an actress whose sister had married David Tennant.

For Sassoon, there was scarcely a hint of jealousy, for the obsession with Stephen filled his life, often in a surge of joy. Hearing Vaughan Williams's 'Shepherds of the Delectable Mountain' at a concert, he felt a mystical uplift that became a sudden wish to write the 'Modern Pilgrim's Progress' for 'this godless age'. And Stephen had taken a step towards seriousness, signing up for lessons in woodcarving, taking a box every night at the Russian ballet to watch Stravinsky conduct those works that symbolized the age's appetite for experiment. Once, at Smith Square, the boy put Lord Grey's soft hat on Sassoon's head. Sassoon saw a battle between Stephen's Lord Grey side – gentle and civilized – and that of Cecil Beaton – trivial and hard. One night, when the three of them were together, Glen spoke frankly to Tennant about vanity and the boy seemed cowed. How different was Ralph Hodgson, who in Campden Hill Square pitied the rich and their empty acquisitions, interspersing his opinions with singing old songs like 'Drink to Me Only' during a Georgian evening, earthy in language and lacking in artifice, 'English to the bone'.[43]

Sassoon copied out a poem written at the end of March called 'The Paris Telephone Directory', not sharp enough to be satire.[44] He wanted to pillory this high-bohemian world of gossip, backbiting, jealousy and trivia, yet he went to Wilsford after an evening in Stephen's box at the ballet. William Walton, Arthur Waley (the translator of Chinese poetry), Beryl de Zoete (Waley's companion) and Edith Olivier were there. The valet William filmed them and they escaped in a painted caravan drawn by two cart-horses through country that reminded Sassoon of a Turgenev novel. The next week, at Smith Square, Lady Grey fetched Stephen's published book of drawings, *The Vein in the Marble*, to show Sassoon before helping herself to caviare. Edith Olivier was an ally who had described Sassoon to Lord Grey as 'a safe man'.[45] All the while he felt time passing, vitality ebbing, and believed that 'without Stephen I should have no sense of youth at all'.[46]

Ralph Hodgson wrote about the manuscript of the memoirs, 'You don't know how good it is. It's nature (human) with a pen. I hope it is going to be of great length . . .'[47] Thrilled, Sassoon took Hodgson to see de la Mare at Taplow where, in an explosion of talk, Hodgson said, with Sassoon agreeing, that scientists were the modern seekers after truth, not the Churches, particularly not the Roman Catholic Church. Then a party at St George's Baths, given by Brian Howard and other Bright Young Things brought fury when Stephen disobeyed him by going. Lady Grey asked Edith Olivier to beg Sassoon to stop Stephen from attending his brother David's rowdy fancy-dress party. He failed and instead waited outside the house near the Adelphi, hearing the sounds of drunkenness and fighting; 'mostly theatrical people', a patrolling policeman said. Eventually Tennant emerged in a tight pink costume covered in Nottingham lace; 'the evening almost made me dislike Stephen'.[48] But at Wilsford, when he showed Siegfried the pool where he kept terrapins and lizards and a toad called Madame Blavatsky, the anger softened and, that night, Sassoon lay awake, thinking, 'Quiet rain is whispering in the trees now, – my heart is at peace.'[49]

*

HE HAD MOVED on from the Morris Oxford car, through a Chrysler, to an almost new Packard bought from Anzie Wylde, driving all of these machines in a dangerous mixture of daring and vagueness as he pursued Stephen's hectic life. In the north, leaving

Renishaw, the Derbyshire home of the Sitwells, after the usual trivial family dramas, he went towards Falloden in Northumberland, Lord Grey's country house, seeking out the house of Gabriel Atkin's aunt near Newcastle on the way – a semi-detached, comfortable-looking place – then speeding off, realizing that he might see Atkin. Falloden was far from Gabriel: a plain Georgian mansion in wild country, with Lord Grey dressed in ancient tweeds, feeding ducks and speaking about the local bird life. Even Stephen seemed calm, Lady Grey less affected, and Grey 'glorious in his limitations'[50] – a Wordsworthian combination of literary and country interests, one of the greatest fly-fishermen of his generation, then giving a glimpse of worldly distinction when he spoke of being the Chancellor of Oxford University.

For Sassoon (and even for the very Tory Theresa, usually scornful of Liberals), Lord Grey of Falloden was everything that an English politician should be: unintellectual, country-loving, modest, a quoter of Wordsworth. He felt amazed when, later, Osbert Sitwell questioned the wisdom of this man whose secret diplomacy before 1914 was at least as responsible for the consequent slaughter as any of the generals. Grey and Falloden represented one part of what Sassoon wanted of England: modesty, rural beauty, unostentatious comfort, the world of a country squire rather than that of a grand aristocrat. Yet, partly because of Stephen Tennant, he moved increasingly among grand country houses, extravagant behaviour and wild spending, very different to the modesty of his earlier days or the Thornycroft creed of decency and unpretentious hard work. With Stephen, he felt the complication of these divided feelings: love and desire but also disapproval and shame at his own, new way of life.

The Greys plotted with him to save Stephen from public scandal and possible arrest. Rowdy, often homosexual, elements of the Bright Young Things had offended the more staid London hostesses and filled the gossip columns; and the threat was that the boy might be suspected of illegal 'real immorality'.[51] Lady Grey felt that he must leave the country. Sassoon was happy to arrange, and pay for, a trip to Italy to see the Siena performance of the Sitwells' *Façade*.

*

SO SIEGFRIED SASSOON set out in his red Packard for the continent. He drove alone through Arras, past a sinister ruined fortress near Montmédy – dream-like, wrecked in the war, engendering Pre-Raphaelite visions of ghostly decay – to Munich, where he met Stephen, Nanny and Tennant's valet William. A good review of *The Heart's Journey* in the *Manchester Guardian* arrived by post, and on 5 September, Sassoon left Munich in the car with Stephen, Nanny Trusler and William taking the train. They were bound for the Haus Hirth, a guest house in the mountains at Untergrainau, near Garmisch, owned by Walther and Johanna Hirth.

The Hirths had suffered in the great German inflation. Walther, once owner of a Munich newspaper, had sold it after the war and seen the money vanish with the collapsing currency. Their house, a characteristic Alpine chalet, became popular with the British. Walther – short, broad, with a childlike face and longish greying hair – wore leather shorts and white stockings, revealing huge knees. He spoke odd, quite charming English, saying, in praise of generosity, that 'I am in all ways a Communalist.'[52] Johanna, the daughter of a doctor from Darmstadt, looked younger; tall, rather beautiful, she spoke better English and had been married to a German count who was killed in the war. The Hirths charged guests only £1 a day but there was a certain formality; in the evenings all the guests except Sassoon and Walther wore dinner jackets. The servants had been told that he was England's greatest poet. Sassoon and Tennant got out their books; Stephen had *Of Human Bondage* and Sassoon Wordsworth's *Prelude*, Dickens's *Great Expectations*, Forster's *Aspects of the Novel*, Edward Thomas's *Literary Pilgrim in England*, Wasserman's *Christian Wahnscheffe* and the *Oxford Book of English Prose*. Sassoon was given a room in a small house on a hill above the garden. The atmosphere was cosily domestic, with ducks, geese and several dachshunds which the childless Hirths worshipped.

At dinner, when they drank to a united Europe, Walther claimed that the Germans had committed no wartime atrocities and expressed his dislike of the French; to his wife's embarrassment, he was in the process of becoming an admirer of the Nazis. On 8 September, Sassoon's birthday, a huge cheesecake decorated with forty-two candles appeared at breakfast.

The next day they left for Italy, flowers piled high in the car by the Hirths. Once again William and Nanny went on by train, leaving Sassoon to do the valeting, and in Cremona, he noted, 'Packing and unpacking S's things occupies me a lot – about 30 bottles and cold cream jars to unwrap.' Yet he told the Heads, 'Sometimes I wonder if it can be true that I am so happy.'[53] In Siena, they joined the Sitwells and their group – William Walton, Constant Lambert, Beryl de Zoete – too late to see *Façade*. The idyll dissolved when Stephen, a bad sightseer, complained that Sassoon was 'horrid' to him[54] and a Sitwell drama erupted at Montegufoni, the castle bought by Sir George, as Edith took furious offence that they had missed *Façade*. Beryl de Zoete borrowed £11 from Sassoon who, in addition to paying all the bills for Stephen, gave Georgia Sitwell 500 lire as well. 'Sometimes I would give a lot to be alone,' he told Glen Byam Shaw on 23 September. 'And there are times when I long for Speasey.'[55] The friendship with Glen had survived the actor's engagement. At first Angela had thought Sassoon sinister, but she soon liked him, even loved him.

Stephen and he left for Bologna and Padua and, near the end of the month, Venice, where they met up with Nanny and William. Irritation flared up once more when he spoke of Theresa's misery in the city forty years before during his father's affair with Constance Fletcher, and Tennant responded with a few glib phrases and silly exaggerations. And the matter of payment still grated. After all, Stephen had an allowance of £8,000 a year.

*

FOR SASSOON, THE success of *Memoirs of a Fox-hunting Man* lit up the late-summer and early-autumn months of 1928, then darkened into dissatisfaction. Theresa, who read it just before publication, greatly admired the book, even his 'half-portrait' of her as Aunt Evelyn. 'It is a masterpiece of prose,' she wrote. 'How you have preserved in a sort of amber made up of sunlight of the past years of dear old simple English life. That happy human time that is gone.' Aunt Evelyn was 'just what a boy would see' and how good Dixon was, just like 'dear old Richardson'.[56] He was relieved. In Aunt Evelyn he had drawn 'only a very faint portrait of a very small part of your character' and it was 'the greatest joy to me when you enjoy my writings'.[57]

Publication day was 28 September. The day before, Walter de la Mare wrote to Sassoon about the work's 'ease and quiet and lovely Englishness';[58] there was only one doubt: might it have been better to end before the war? In a slightly bleak Venice, Sassoon bought the *Observer*, to read two columns of praise by J. C. Squire. By 6 October they were back at Haus Hirth to a mixture of English and German guests, and Nan Tennant, Stephen's jolly spinster aunt. Dick de la Mare reported that the first edition of 1,500 had run out before publication. Evans of Heinemann said that 1,173 copies of *The Heart's Journey* had been sold between 11 September and 2 October, attributing this to a good review by the poet Humbert Wolfe. The *Daily Mail* disclosed the identity of the anonymous author of *Memoirs of a Fox-hunting Man*. Surely, Sassoon thought, this was the work of Robert Graves's journalist brother Charles. But it was all 'excellent publicity'.[59] 'I am delighted with Miss Sitwell's review,' Theresa wrote on 4 October. 'It is really understanding.'[60]

This success made Haus Hirth seem even more delightful. From pinewoods below mountains powdered with snow, butterflies came into the guest house, small birds twittered in the nearest tree, there were trout to eat from the hill streams and a deep bell from the church at Untergrainau mingled with the softer bells worn by grazing cows in the Alpine meadows. Letters arrived about the memoirs – Ruth Head telling Stephen of the reviews, Burton comparing Sassoon to Shakespeare – then suddenly, to Sassoon, the prose book seemed a sham, containing 'almost none of the things I would like to write', denying the most important parts of him.

Stephen and Nanny went on to Paris by train. On a drive alone through France, this shame about cowardice and concealment deepened when Sassoon read Maugham's *Of Human Bondage* – a book that broke illusions – and his joy faded as, familiar with every aspect of Stephen, he wondered if even this thrill had gone. He thought that Tennant might leave him this winter and, at his age (he was forty-two), 'I can't expect that any more exquisite young men will fall in love with me.' He realized that he dreaded losing him. In Paris, Stephen was waiting, as was a telegram from Dick de la Mare about the offer of a £350 advance from an American publishing firm for the memoirs, now increased to £500; seven other American publishers had bid for it. The silly young people like Brian Howard and Meraud Guinness who crowded round Stephen showed Sassoon respect, but Tennant, wildly extravagant, apparently uncontrollable and saying that he hated fox-hunting, launched into a round of crazy shopping and night clubs.

The memoirs were in their fourth reprint; 3,000 copies had been sold. Buying the *Nation*, Sassoon saw a review by Raymond Mortimer, implying that George Sherston was too impersonal, without sensual feeling or a sense of physical growth. The piece seemed, Sassoon thought, typical of Bloomsbury, of which Mortimer was a devoted disciple – sterile, trivial, backbiting, afraid of life, the exact opposite of what he wanted to write. And Mortimer's 'lecherous little mind' was 'nosing about after revelations of homosexuality'.[61] Sassoon and Stephen moved to a hotel in Versailles. The boy had a temperature, but then he recovered, gushing again in chic talk that seemed to go with his made-up face, the constant refrain that something was 'heavenly' or 'too grim for words'.[62] Separate rooms, with Nanny's room between them, at least gave Sassoon some relief. So far only two reviews had been annoying: Mortimer's and a piece by Robert Graves in the *Daily Mail*, mocking the author's attempts at anonymity.

But he felt the gulf between what he wanted to achieve and what he had done, and a poem of 12 November laments how 'delight today and death tomorrow' mean only 'despair'.[63] To others, he concealed his doubts. 'O Speasey, your old Mr Sassoon is at last having the delirious success which he has secretly longed for all these years of diary keeping,' Sassoon told Glen on 27 October. 'Bores from all over England'[64] were writing to him about hunting. The good notices still came in, one by J. B. Priestley, another in the *New Statesman*, and he sent Theresa a further £100 for 'I suppose you will be getting short again by now.'[65] On 15 November, Sassoon heard that the memoirs had sold 850 in the previous week and now 400 in only two days. During sleepless nights, he made notes for a possible sequel, called, for the moment, 'The Autobiography of an Officer'.

On 17 November he took a telegram to Stephen Tennant, joking as he passed it over, 'More messages from Mummie.' In a sense he was right, for it read, 'Lady Grey seriously ill internal haemorrhage return at once Doctor Kemp.'[66] Apparently calm, Stephen, with Nanny and William the valet, set off for London by train. Left behind, Sassoon thought, 'S. will now need me more than ever before.'[67] The next day, on his way to England by car, he saw near Pontoise a small green parrot – extraordinary to find one this far north. Lady Grey had kept parrots. At the Reform Club and Campden Hill Square, he found heaps of letters, including one from Stephen Tennant at Wilsford where Lady Grey had died aged only fifty-seven: 'I smell the narcissi and violets as from a thousand miles away and although my spirit is strong, my body is not brave. I seem to be in a dark hideous nightmare.'[68] The funeral took place at Wilsford, with a memorial service on the same day at St Margaret's Westminster. Sassoon went to neither; funerals and memorial services, he claimed, always upset him too much.

He called at Smith Square to find Stephen Tennant sitting in bed: made up, very beautiful. Tennant's mother's death meant that the house was to be sold and the silver room abandoned. On a table were Lady Grey's psychical journals, in which she had recorded her attempts to reach her dead son. After letting Sassoon out through a side-door, Stephen ran after him in bare feet, clutching a white fur-lined dressing-gown around his body, to beg him to be careful when he drove to Weirleigh the next day. Sassoon read some vivid notes on the battle of Arras that Dr Dunn had given him and stayed awake all night. He gave Theresa, who was sad when he left, a copy of his poem 'To My Mother', published as a pamphlet by Faber in its Ariel series in September, with an illustration of a mother and child by Stephen Tennant: a celebration of selfless love and also, obliquely, physical passion.

*

TEN THOUSAND COPIES of *Memoirs of a Fox-hunting Man* had been sold by the end of November. Nineteen-twenty-eight was the year of the war book. Edmund Blunden's memoir, *Undertones of War*, published at the end of November and venturing only by inference into the pre-war world, had already sold out its edition of 1,500. By 7 December Sassoon had written 1,700 words of his next volume. He went to Wilsford at the weekend with Stephen; it was cold, with a magnificent sunset and little sadness. Tennant danced alone, dressed in black, to the gramophone, and Sassoon chose some books from Lady Grey's library for Stephen to keep: Gilchrist's life of Blake, Hogg's Shelley, Robbie Ross's study of Aubrey Beardsley (inscribed to Lady Grey by the author), H. M. Tomlinson's *The Sea and the Jungle*, a first edition of Stephen's favourite *Henry Brocken*. Three days later he took Tennant to King's Cross station, to catch the night train for Falloden. The valet William carried a parrot in a cage and, on the platform, watched by astounded passengers, Stephen knelt to say, 'It's all right Poll darling,'[69] to receive an answering squawk.

People pressed in on Sassoon from all sides: letters from friends not seen for years like Dorothy Hanmer (who thought Dick Tilt-wood must be based on her brother Bobbie, when in fact the character was mostly David Thomas, with hints of Hanmer), sugges-tions like that from Victor Gollancz that he should write an anti-war novel for the benefit of the League of Nations Union, a dinner with Anzie Wylde where all the other guests were bores. He and Tennant went to King's Cross again for Stephen was going north to Glen, his family's home in Peebles, for Christmas. To Sassoon, the dark station 'was made almost beautiful, certainly aesthetically significant, by my emotions about S., my perfect companion and beloved one. His sweetness to me since we came back from abroad has been heavenly, and I am deeply grateful to life for giving me such happiness.'[70]

On the last day of 1928, feeling harassed, he went to William Nicholson's studio in Apple Tree Yard to talk about the artist's pictures for an illustrated edition of *Memoirs of a Fox-hunting Man*, to find, with Nicholson, the small, neat figure of Max Beerbohm. Sassoon felt awed, tried to play up to this hero of the nineties with epigrams, saying of Osbert Sitwell: 'Everything he touched turns to publicity.'[71] If only, he thought, it might be possible to have some hours alone with this immaculate master. The Beerbohms came, early in January 1929, to tea at Campden Hill Square. Stephen Tennant – whom they seemed to like – was also there, and Max and Florence asked Sassoon and Tennant to call on them at Rapallo. Even better, Beerbohm agreed to read the manuscript of the new book when it was finished.

SIXTEEN

*'I ask for nothing but to be
near him always'*

THE ACCLAIM FOR the memoirs was overwhelming, with only
a few exceptions like Robert Graves – who called the anonymity a
publicity stunt and criticized the book's evasions – Raymond Mortimer and 'a famous fool'[1] in the *Manchester Guardian*. This made
Siegfried Sassoon think better of the book. What *Memoirs of a Fox-
hunting Man* had, he thought, was 'youngness',[2] excitement without
material ambition, that joy of seeing things for the first time.

The boom in war books was at its height. Nineteen twenty-
seven saw, among others, T. E. Lawrence's *Revolt in the Desert* and
Max Plowman's *A Subaltern on the Somme*; in 1928 – in addition
to Sassoon's *Memoirs* and Blunden's *Undertones of War* – there was
the last volume of Ford Madox Ford's trilogy of novels, *Parade's
End*. These accounts of suffering, sensitive young men inspired pity
and anger among many readers then and later. Ford's hero is
haunted by the line of George Herbert, 'Sweet day so cool, so calm,
so bright, the bridal of the earth and sky': a vision of serenity in the
chaos of the trenches. Such dreamy longings – and the sense of a
hard, overwhelming enemy – mix with doom and despondency in
many of the more literary memoirs of the First World War, making

it hard to recall the total defeat of the German army in November 1918.

Sassoon's own quest in the memoirs was for a version of an English myth. He caught a surge of English nationalism: Vaughan Williams, Elgar and Delius, the Georgians' rural landscape, and, during his childhood, Morris's Arts and Crafts movement; then, in the war itself, Brooke's conquest of a foreign field 'that is forever England'. This vision, often imbued with a pastoral nostalgia, may have been, for most people, a fantasy. The English were leaving the land, and the soldiers of the First World War came mostly from the slums of industrial cities that made the army sometimes a scarcely greater ordeal than their bleak civilian lives. But the end of fantasy can bring pain. Sherston looks back to his boyhood 'when I understood so little of the deepening sadness of life, and only the strangeness of the spring was knocking at my heart'.

George Sherston, the book's narrator, is Siegfried Sassoon with almost all the unusual, some might say the most interesting, bits left out. We get the diffidence, the self-deprecating humour, the love of country life, the sporting courage and the sensibility, without the sexual torment, the Jewishness, the poetry or Robert Graves. Sherston is no literary man; books are bought mostly for their aesthetic appearance and almost his only mention of contemporary writing is a reference to Edmund Gosse's autobiography, *Father and Son*. George Sherston has no brothers or sisters. He is an orphan brought up by a spinster Aunt Evelyn, a meeker character than Theresa, and they live in isolation in the weald of Kent. There is no precise description of their house but it seems a more considerable, and more attractive, place than Weirleigh.

Names are changed but the real characters of Sassoon's boyhood are there: the groom Richardson; the Harbord family; his first hero, Norman Loder; David Thomas, whose death had turned Siegfried into a warrior. Sometimes the originals saw behind the veil and complained. Cockbird's real owner, a Mr Newgass, wrote that Sassoon had traduced him as 'Tony Lewison', a bad rider and a lacklustre man. The prose is simple, with few metaphors, and some reassuring clichés. Visible objects are observed with what one reader saw as 'pre-Raphaelite' precision (Sassoon took pride in one sunset 'which I recovered quite exactly')[3] to reflect youth's preoccupation with 'trivialities'.

Everything filters through George Sherston's naive, slightly puzzled self. The narrative is slow, rather meandering, sensual enough to evoke a physical atmosphere, and has a soft, glowing quality; the *Memoirs* must be one of the most charming books ever written. Ideas or hints at restlessness or intellectual curiosity are absent. The hermetic world of the *Fox-hunting Man* is complete. Few people of a different class from the narrator intervene, unless they are servants like the groom Dixon or the housemaid Miriam. From earliest childhood George is kept away from the village boys or the sons of local farmers, and hop-pickers from the East End of London are shadowy 'merry' Cockneys. Ashford – the nearest large town – seems miles away, a strange place where there is a brewery and men are hanged. There is no rebellion against this world's values; only once does a parson shout at the hunt, 'Brutes! Brutes!' Because Aunt Evelyn and George do not rely on farming for their livelihood, they are protected from an agricultural depression that had lasted since the 1870s. The humour is gentle with only the occasional hard glint, as in the snobbish account of an unreliable and caddish officer called 'Pardon Me', mocked for his greed and lack of social poise.

The reader knows Sherston, without being intimate with him, and accepts his usually unexplained surges of feeling, as when he looks at the reproduction of Watts's *Love and Death* whose 'secret meaning' induces 'a vague emotion of pathos'. George cannot talk about this to the fox-hunters or to Denis Milden, whom he shocks by saying, when Milden shouts to say that he has seen a fox, 'Don't do that; they'll catch him.' Yet for this outsider, and Sherston does seem slightly outside much of what he describes, boyhood becomes a utopia of hunting achievement, social acceptance, manliness proved, cricketing success and races won. Sometimes a grown-up, more complex world looms – in Canon Colwood (Gordon Harbord's father), 'a naturally nervous' repressed man, the lonely, slightly bogus Colonel Henson, the rough Croplady, Jaggett and Pomfret or the unpopular Parson Yalding – but it soon passes. There are long, empty days, but they are mostly sunlit.

The war begins in a similar idyll. George feels excitement on first joining the army, secure in doing what he ought to be doing. There is another ideal friendship, this time with Dick Tiltwood, based on David Thomas with perhaps undertones of Bobbie Hanmer (born of 'generations of upright country gentlemen'), its chasteness and sentimentality worthy of a late-Victorian novel of public-school life. The book ends on Easter Sunday 1916, two weeks before the Somme offensive, when Sherston, after the deaths of Tiltwood and Dixon, expresses the victim's pain that haunts the memoirs: 'As for me, I had more or less made up my mind to die; the idea made things easier.'

The view of the First War in *Memoirs of a Fox-hunting Man* matches Sassoon's war poetry written after November 1915: that of innocence betrayed, of waste. This legend of a series of pointless disasters may ignore the treaty obligations to a neutral Belgium, the unforeseeable effects of mass machine-age warfare, even the final victory. In its vision of equal guilt, it seems to exonerate pre-war German policy and the harsh occupation of Belgium and northern France. But its literary beauty is strong enough to filter history through emotion and to make a lasting myth.

*

LETTERS STILL POURED in, more than 300. Julian Dadd remembered Sassoon's wartime conduct that 'has helped to give me a moral stiffening many times in my life when I have most needed it';[4] Lady Lindsay-Hogg wrote to protest about the portrait of the horrible 'Bill Jaggett', obviously based on her son; his old Cambridge friend 'Gussy' Guilford, now working unhappily for the BBC in Manchester, said he still had a copy of Sassoon's poem about King Edward I that had failed to win the Chancellor's Medal.

Early in January 1929, in the house in Smith Square that was about to be sold, Stephen Tennant suddenly said, 'I've some bad news,' and produced a letter about the doctor's anxiety after recent tests on fluid from his lungs. When he read it, Sassoon broke down, partly, he thought, from self-pity yet also moved by Stephen's 'heartbreaking loveliness and gaiety'.[5] Tennant, usually brave, also collapsed, saying, 'What does it matter whether I am tired as long as I am happy – I don't suppose I shall live.'[6] For comfort, Stephen read his two favourite writers: Willa Cather and Emily Dickinson, with whom he thought he had a psychic communion. Sassoon ordered him a diamond that cost £180, thinking that if the disease was catching, 'infection' was worth this 'Paradise'[7] that seemed such a contrast to the Somme bombardment, which he had reached in his sequel to *Memoirs of a Fox-hunting Man*.

At the end of January, Tennant went to Haus Hirth, with a pile of suitcases, Nanny and the valet William. Now there came a new threat: Nanny's own failing health. Stephen, terrified, told Ottoline Morrell that 'my love for her is the greatest thing in my life – the one huge selfless force in me'.[8] A new treatment began for his own condition, the collapsing of the infected lung supervised by a Dr Kaltenbach. He read Sassoon's letters and thought of Heathcliff and Cathy on the moors in spring.

In London, another part of Sassoon's past fell away when he heard of the suicide of Nevill Forbes, whom he had not seen since June 1917. Before the war, he had confided his homosexuality to Forbes, the brilliant musician and linguist. Forbes, like Ross, had possibly been broken by post-Wilde intolerance. Sadness and reflection, however, were softened by the continuing acclaim. At the beginning of March, Sassoon heard he had won the James Tait Black Memorial Prize for the best novel of 1928, worth £180. Then Marsh wrote that he had been asked if Sassoon would accept the Hawthornden Prize, which meant more money. To Marsh he suggested that T. E. Lawrence should make the presentation, or, if Lawrence refused, E. M. Forster: 'another shy man I admire immensely'.[9] In the event, Lawrence would not break his anonymity (as a soldier in the Tank Corps he had escaped his celebrity) for the presentation, yet called Sassoon 'the ideal Englishman'.[10] The acclaim seemed to spur the writing; by 2 April he had reached 49,000 words of his book. The British sales of *Memoirs of a Fox-hunting Man* approached 19,000.

By this time, Sassoon had another young friend: Rex Whistler, with whom Stephen had studied at the Slade. Whistler, charming, gentle, a brilliant natural draughtsman, was fascinated by the older man. Towards the end of February, when they stayed together with Edith Olivier in Wiltshire, he sensed Rex's captivation – which survived a soaking when Sassoon, as usual vague at the wheel, drove him into a pond. He found Rex desirable but drew back. Stephen Tennant remained an obsession that increased when, on 5 April, Sassoon arrived at Haus Hirth.

*

THE HIRTHS HAD, he felt sure, saved Stephen's life. He arranged for £500 to be sent from his bank for an extension to the house and a new roof; Stephen said he would match it. Edith Olivier, there with some other English guests, thought how well Sassoon seemed, generous with his money, different from 'the rather grim alarming aloof poet of London', now saying 'again and again how happy he is'.[11] Tennant's power over him was immense; 'I ask nothing but to be near him always.'[12] And Stephen wrote, 'I did not sleep last night but tossed and turned feeling my hot happy face blushing and sighing and remembering kisses that still seemed to be assuaging the longing of weeks.'[13] To Tennant, Siegfried's face seemed 'carved and suffering and most noble', his good looks 'phenomenal', the 'exotic' eyes evoking 'the glow and glitter of Persia'.[14] The weather was strange – clouds 'like being in an ermine muff'[15] – and Tennant's mood febrile with storms of hysteria about the invalid Nanny and himself.

On Walther's birthday, Stephen handed him a tile from the broken roof inscribed by Sassoon to mark the gift; the Hirths were overcome. But the endless cheeriness of Haus Hirth could grate; 'good nature can be so mindless', Stephen wrote. Everything inside the place began to seem ugly or banal: the crudely carved wood, the bland prints of British naval heroes in the sitting room, the dark, heavy food and too much laughter, a lace-curtain good cheer. Sometimes Tennant yearned for the acidity of Bloomsbury, its 'stiletto, the delicate withering superiority'.[16] Johanna fussed; she thought Stephen was losing weight. Once a week he went into Garmisch to see the doctor, and Nanny wanted to keep Sassoon from tiring her grown-up child. On Stephen's birthday, 21 April, Sassoon gave him the only poetry he had written since coming to Untergrainau, ten lines beginning:

> *Because today belongs to you by birth,*
> *For me no other day can ever bring*
> *The wild flower wonderment of wakening earth.*
> *And so, till now, I have not seen the spring.*[17]

Other gifts were an emerald ring, and Gerard's late-sixteenth-century *Herbal*, to interpret the wild flowers – gentians, orchids, lilies of the valley, Solomon's Seal, primulas, fritillaries encircled by butterflies. On good days they walked together or Sassoon went out alone, damming a stream or crossing flower-filled meadows in a return to boyhood; and Stephen cursed himself for being 'vain, selfish, pleasure loving and frivolous – unto the empty are all things empty'.[18] Sassoon always carried everything – spades to make dams, coats to lie on, spare jerseys – but still found peace elusive. Surely bodily recovery must come from the healthy life and everything should be here to make him happy – except the threat that Stephen might die.

They spoke of Charlotte Mew's poetry and her tragic life, of Blunden's *Undertones*, and Stephen wrote in his journal, 'what a profoundly sweet creature he is: beautiful, loveable, kind and strong'.[19] Tennant thought that it was the wartime rebel Sassoon that others found fascinating, a heroic alternative to the timid acceptance of most people's lives. Rex Whistler arrived. Sassoon still felt tired and had only done 2,000 words of copying from the first draft of his prose book at Haus Hirth. William Walton, also there, played his violin concerto on the piano; then Edith Olivier left and

Walton went to Paris. At the end of the month Sassoon finished Edmund Blunden's *Undertones of War*, fearing that his own war memoir could never match this. He was only sleeping with the aid of drugs given him by Johanna Hirth and tried to write poetry but failed. Still he had no real energy, except to add up what he had given away in the last year, more than £2,000: £500 for the Hirths' roof, £500 for his mother, £260 for Glen's car, £105 for the Miners' Relief Fund, £160 for Stephen's diamond ornament, another £750 for Glen (half the cost of his house in Putney). Then the smaller sums: £62 for Walton, £22 for Burton, £60 for a picture by William Nicholson for Stephen, scarves and earrings for Edith Olivier.[20] 'Giving people things feels as if it absolves me from the effort which my friends demand from me . . . I sort of pension them off with presents,' he wrote, in a shaft of shameful self-knowledge.[21]

Sassoon went with the Hirths to see a house at Breitenau, a mile away on the road to Garmisch, without running water, on a small island in the river. In the third week of May, Siegfried Sassoon, Nanny, Stephen's aunt Nan Tennant, the valet William and Nanny's English nurse moved there, to make an even more hermetic world. Stephen's room was on the third floor, shared with his parrot Poll, and Sassoon had a bed in the library by the front door. The place was dark, cramped, melancholy in feel – for Stephen, reminiscent of Strindberg or Chekhov – an odd, creaking house, with its owner, Frau Schneider, living in the annexe, a house of bad taste and dispiriting cosiness. But beyond the bland and oppressively dark deodars lay an Alpine spring. Again boyhood returned as they fished tadpoles and newts out of a pond for Stephen's aquarium, for which a glass tank had been ordered from Munich. In the evenings, the boy recited Emily Dickinson's poems, Sassoon showed Tennant his war diaries and read *Undertones of War* aloud, which thrilled Stephen, or played the grand piano, also sent from Munich. They saw a German right-wing group, the Stahlhelm, holding a field day near by in uniform and Stephen noted, 'the German soldier is beautiful'.[22]

To Sassoon, the boy's hunger for life and love was heartrending.

When he read Stephen's diary, its ecstatic language made him not only fear for this fragile yet rapturous sensibility but regret his own constricting caution. One night they walked along the valley in the moonlight, Tennant wearing a mauve silk velvet dressing-gown, and Sassoon, enraptured, knew 'I can't control him (or myself) on such occasions'.[23] In the hospital, the X-rays showed improvement. No wonder the memoirs seemed flat; original writing – as opposed to copying – was almost impossible and the thought of London grim after this 'paradise of crystal air and branching green and timelessly talking water'.[24] He wanted to take Breitenau for another month, rejoiced that Labour had gained seats in the British general election and read bitchy bulletins from Cecil Beaton. He heard how Robert Graves's inspiration Laura Riding had taken up with a man called Phibbs – with whom Nancy Graves had also been involved – then had tried to kill herself by jumping from a window, followed by Graves's own more cautious leap from a lower floor. How much better to be in these Bavarian meadows even when Stephen shrieked abuse, thinking that Sassoon had lost his parrot after letting go of the string that acted as its lead. Later Tennant felt remorse and they were reconciled, 'but I can never atone for my beastliness'.[25]

In the first week of June, Sassoon did 5,000 words of fair copying and approached the story of Mametz Wood, feeling that to write this was 'like mental penal servitude'.[26] Stephen was sexually demanding, seeking a release that never came. He was thrilled by his own hero and by the war stories of a writer of genius: the roar of shells and the guns, the poet saying how he loathed 'the agony and often boredom' of remembering it for his book but must go on. Sassoon's physical presence transfixed him. 'I never tire of watching his face, his wonderful hands and beautiful expressive body,' Tennant wrote. 'Sometimes his face is lined and ravaged and his eyes are bright and hollowly oriental, his frowning and brooding face is lovely too but best I love his clear still look which comes when we are in the woods – by our river, in pine scented mossy glades, or on hillsides in June sun and winds, then he is most wonderful.'[27] For Sassoon, the paradise, described euphorically in letters to friends like Glen, slipped too often away, love and beauty rubbing against an imperfect reality that made him see that the idyllic could perhaps only come in his writing.

He refused to go back for the Hawthornden Prize ceremony, angry at what looked like a stunt – probably got up by Eddie Marsh – of having the sporting philistine Lord Lonsdale present it. To Marsh, he said he must be with Stephen for 'it is a matter of life and death'.[28] At the end of June, there was another scene: Stephen petulant, then howling that he was superficial and hopelessly spoilt, and 'swinish' too. Sassoon longed for Glen's calm sweetness, and Tennant now yearned for a southern city, with stifling narrow streets, bars filled with husky sailors, the Mediterranean lapping over sun-warmed stones. Stephen thought how different they were, even in small things like Siegfried's immaculately tidy room and the mess in his own. But he wrote that 'it's a great honour that I am allowed to make him happy. What a queer story – I so notoriously idle, empty and vain – frivolous and (so London says) hard and shallow . . .'[29] At the start of July, Nanny and her nurse went back to London, and Sassoon felt relieved, having feared that the old lady might die at Breitenau. He moved upstairs, nearer to Stephen.

Now he too found the Hirths exasperating: the saccharine chatter about the dachshunds, the Princes of Hesse and the weather: the sweet routine of Uncle Walther and Tante Johanna. The food had gone into decline: half-cooked rice, dishwater soup, cold slabs of ham, overripe plums, strawberry ices that tasted of soot. Sassoon managed 8,650 words of copying in nine days before Stephen made another scene, ending in self-reproach at stopping his friend from working. He longed to finish the book, yet the river, the bonfires, the dammed streams and swimming in the cold torrents were 'primevally exciting'.[30] Through it all welled up intense moments of physical desire for his extraordinary companion.

Edith Olivier and Nellie Burton reported on the Hawthornden Prize presentation, at which Blunden accepted the £100 cheque for Sassoon. Lord Lonsdale – whom Burton admired 'more than any other man living'[31] – made a meandering speech and there had been the usual London malice: the Sitwells angry at not having been asked, Walton gossiping about Sassoon and Stephen, Meiklejohn's grumbles that he should have come back. Then Stephen's elder brother wrote that Nanny had had a stroke and was asking for them both, so they must return.

*

ON 29 JULY, they arrived in London. Nanny lay in bed in Christopher Glenconner's flat near Sloane Square, and Stephen went in for only a few minutes before emerging in choked-back tears. Then they both went to the Hyde Park Hotel, where Sassoon unpacked six Bavarian scarves and the 45,000 words of fair-copied manuscript: the outward signs of four months away. They knew that they were back in Britain when a woman shouted at them from a passing car, presumably because of the very effeminate-looking Tennant, 'You two revolting bits of filth!' Reading his diary, Sassoon felt it far removed from the joy of memory that was already gilding the past. Stephen believed himself to be 'on the edge of a nervous breakdown'[32] before going alone to Wilsford, where he was soon thinking, 'Oh why isn't Sieg here?'[33]

Visiting Theresa, Sassoon knew that he could not live at Weirleigh, embroiled in its tedium, yet it belonged to him 'more than any other place on earth can ever do', with its sense of that real and imagined past out of which he increasingly made his writing.[34] Theresa fussed, raising other memories: of his prolonged adolescence and her intolerant attitude to sex; of ignorance, repression and bigotry. The peaches were woolly, having been kept too long – different from the profusion of Wilsford. And from Wilsford, there came a howl for help. 'Every day is more unendurable than the last, without you,' Stephen wrote. On 15 August Sassoon heard that Nanny had died; with Lady Grey also gone, he felt, with a sense of power and responsibility, that he was now the only person who could save Stephen Tennant.

Stephen seemed resigned. They went together to the trichologist

Miss Strathearn, then to see Ottoline Morrell – in increasing pain from cancer of the jaw – and back to a hotel near Buckingham Palace where Tennant was staying. That night Stephen came to Campden Hill Square, saying that without Sassoon he would kill himself. The boy was too agonized to go to Nanny's funeral, returning to Wilsford with a new stock of lizards, snakes, tortoises, worms, orchids, a rare green tree frog and a Tchelitchew picture, a gift from Siegfried who later joined him, feeling like a husband as they saw the bailiff together. Wilsford was now Tennant's domain, for he had rented it from his brother David, and in the library Sassoon found Wordsworth's copy, with his signature, of Benjamin Haydon's *Lectures on Painting*,[35] explaining this to Stephen, who had no idea that the book was there.

He had done 3,000 words of fair copying of what he called the 'Autobiography of an Infantry Officer' since leaving Germany. One night he woke in tears after a horrifying war dream in which Stephen had been condemned to death in the trenches. Blunden came to Wilsford and Sassoon watched his two friends, fascinated by Stephen's aesthetic awareness, different to that of the war-obsessed little poet to whom the holes of a rabbit warren resembled the rutted aftermath of the Somme. Stephen had many of his meals upstairs, leaving the other two together. To Blunden the place seemed 'a sort of earthly paradise – trees, birds, flowers, dogs, reptiles, fishes and all!'[36]

On 8 September, Sassoon wrote of enjoying, with William Walton and Stephen, his best ever birthday: a picnic, gifts from Stephen of a pipe cleaner, a magnifying glass and an auburn-coloured dressing-gown. In the hall, he told Tennant (who wrote of it afterwards) 'things too lovely to repeat. He put his mouth over mine crushing it – some kisses seem to draw the very soul out of one's body – his do mine. I feel all my heart swooning at the touch of his mouth – my soul dies a hundred million deaths when his breath is on my face and neck.'[37] Sassoon gave Tennant an edition of Parkinson's seventeenth-century *Herbal*, and then reflected that to many people this was a relationship of 'nameless horror and unmentionable vileness'.[38] Stephen's German doctor from Heidel-berg, Dr Hansen, came to see his patient. 'Oh you look beautiful,' were his unethical first words during the consultation, and, when they walked round the garden, he kissed Tennant, murmuring, 'Do you remember when I held you in my arms in Bavaria?'[39] Hansen said that Stephen's lung was better. Sassoon claimed to have no jealousy of the German, but felt relieved when Rex Whistler and William Nicholson arrived. And writing about the war revived the sense of his own ageing. Sassoon thought that he coughed too much, a sign of physical decline, 'and I am disillusioned about sexual intercourse. It has become a tiring business . . .'[40]

In London, he looked at old love letters from Gabriel Atkin. How lifeless his memoirs seemed compared to these; with Stephen, he knew 'perfect happiness',[41] but first love was incomparable. Perhaps he should start a new affair with someone who knew nothing of his fame, to whom he could gradually reveal this and be free of the exhaustion of trying to satisfy Stephen Tennant. Back at Wilsford, Tennant's passion was 'stronger than ever'.[42] As the boy himself wrote, 'I worship him. I am madly and utterly in love.'[43] They were to go south that winter for the warmth, to Rapallo to see the Beerbohms and on to Sicily. There was a flare-up over a bottle party Tennant wanted to go to in London; then Sassoon gave him some Redouté prints, a book of Steinlein drawings and a seventeenth-century bestiary, and peace returned. And Stephen showed his love by going round to Fabers with Rex Whistler to persuade Dick de la Mare to scrap the William Nicholson frontispiece of the illustrated *Memoirs of a Fox-hunting Man* – an unflattering portrait of the imaginary George Sherston.

Doubts about the next volume gripped Sassoon when he saw, at Glen's suggestion, Sean O'Casey's play *The Silver Tassie* with its symbolic war scene that made the *Infantry Officer* seem unimagina-tive. Sassoon offered to take over Osbert and Sacheverell Sitwell's overdrafts from the bank 'as a sort of mortgage' that would cost him about £5,000. 'I suppose I did it because I like getting power over people,' he noted in his diary. 'And Edith's remarks about me "being mean with money" have rankled in my mind.'[44] Then, as he struggled with the usual emotional mixture – anxiety about work, guilt at the real motives for his generosity, both euphoria and doubt over Stephen – the blow came. Blunden had a review copy of Robert Graves's memoir *Goodbye to All That* and wrote to warn Sassoon of its author's 'bombastic and profit-seeking display of your private affairs'.[45]

Sassoon went round to Jonathan Cape (Graves's publisher) and asked for the book. On the way to have his hair cut, he read bits of it with horror. Robert Graves had been brooding about Sassoon, having expected more financial help. Now, reeling from the débâcle with Laura Riding, Phibbs and Nancy, he had written *Goodbye* to make money, in as controversial a way as possible. He had a loose attitude to accuracy, believing that it could be sacrificed to reach a higher truth. What infuriated Sassoon was a description of Theresa, admittedly not named, trying to reach the dead Hamo through automatic writing – 'one of the most hurtful things I've seen in print.'[46] Then Graves's portrait of him gave an impression of instability; the lone taking of a trench was 'pointless'; and his wild war poem, written in hospital in 1918, is quoted without per-mission. This was 'Mad Jack', a shell-shocked candidate for Craig-lockhart. The book seemed egotistical, inaccurate, condescending, journalistic and falsely tough, the swaggering narrator different from the prim, shaky wartime Graves. *Goodbye to All That* revelled in unpleasantness, as in the descriptions of soldiers' lechery and the resurrection of Owen's reputed cowardice. Graves appeared as Sassoon's saviour in the protest turmoil of 1917. He left out the fact that Sassoon had made him swear on the Bible that he would never be court-martialled; he challenged Sassoon's position as the discov-erer of Blunden; and he usurped much of the material of the *Infantry Officer*. Sassoon wrote a furious letter to Jonathan Cape and showed this to Osbert Sitwell, who said the book should be kept away from Theresa. During this 'torture', he could not sleep, thinking of how to get back at Graves, perhaps by calling in a loan of £150 made in 1926. Edmund Blunden and he went through the book meticulously, annotating some 250 of its 448 pages[47] with corrections and jibes, some infantile, against its author. Sassoon, urged on by Blunden, whose dislike of Robert Graves had begun at Oxford in 1918, decided that *Goodbye to All That* should not be published in its present form.

He saw Jonathan Cape, a large, quiet-voiced, amenable man who said he would cut the passage about Theresa and Sassoon's verse letter to Graves, leaving blanked pages. Cape said he had not read the book, that Graves was in Spain and that only a few copies had gone out, mostly abroad and to reviewers. Sassoon warned Theresa not to read *Goodbye to All That*, which was 'very bad', the author 'slightly crazy'.[48]

*

ON 14 NOVEMBER, Siegfried and Stephen, with the valet William and Poll the parrot, left for Paris, seen off by Glen Byam Shaw and Dick de la Mare. Sassoon's fury subsided. The Graves book now seemed absurd, as they lived richly: expensive dinners, hired cars, scent and gifts for Stephen: an emerald ring worth £80, an order for a diamond star (£100) and a toy bulldog ('he loves to have such toys on his bed'). André Gide called, after a letter of introduction from Ottoline Morrell. He was polite and serious in this encounter with another writer. Sassoon felt 'rather juvenile'[49] but enjoyed the talk about Gosse, Wilde and Ross. At least he and Stephen were now sharing hotel bills, but he was glad to leave Paris, always a dangerous city for the wild Tennant, for Italy on 22 November. In the train, howls came from Stephen's compartment, then a storm of petulance, because the boy had crushed his new emerald ring in the cover of the wash basin.

In Rapallo they called on Max Beerbohm at the Villino Chiaro, finding his mannered, subtly malicious wit and reminiscences rather like those of Robbie Ross – whom Max quietly derided – and admiring his pale-green scarab ring, the *fin de siècle* voice and indigo-blue distempered drawing room with a photograph of Aubrey Beardsley. Later that evening, Sassoon embellished his own copy of *Goodbye to All That* with inappropriate headlines from the weekly edition of the *Daily Mirror* and other magazines. Tennant accused him of 'not being lecherous enough'; 'perhaps he is getting tired of me', Sassoon thought glumly, but still felt that he must save Stephen from 'danger and defilement'.[50] Anger about *Goodbye* rose again; the book showed no gratitude to Ross or William Nicholson, certainly not to Sassoon himself. The *Daily Mail* said that Graves's book had sold 2,000 copies in the first five days since publication.

They acted upon Ottoline Morrell's suggestion that they call on W. B. Yeats, who had a flat in Rapallo. Yeats told the story of Laura Riding's attempted suicide and Graves's broken marriage, asking why *Goodbye* had been so successful. Neither he nor Mrs Yeats seemed to have read the *Fox-hunting Man*. They saw Yeats again. This time he derided Hardy's poetry – too like 'first drafts' – then read them some of his own work, including 'Sailing to Byzantium', which Sassoon thought beautiful. When the poet said he had smelt roses or violets from the spirit world, Tennant declared that his mother had often been almost stifled by the scent of extraterrestrial gardenias.

At the Villino, Beerbohm dripped charming malice, abominating George Moore, saying that Galsworthy's books were good on uncles but bad on sex and love, and that Wells wrote novels 'like collapsed blancmanges', chaotic but with 'enjoyable passages'.[51] *Goodbye to All That* he thought 'ably written' with 'no sense of beauty but an unerring nose for ugliness' – within six months it would be forgotten. Encouraged, Sassoon transcribed some more of his own book: 950 words one night, 650 the next.

Stephen and Sassoon talked of the memoirs, sometimes about the war, Tennant marvelling at his 'wide deer-like eyes, the lovely lids and brow structure – the full carved lips and strong nose with its long nostrils – the red shining hair . . .'[52] On 4 December they left for Naples. Four days later, Sassoon wrote a poem, 'perhaps a fairly good one', but hysteria and accusations of neglect left him little time for his manuscript. Stephen tired easily and his beauty routine took hours 'but it is his way of living, and can't be changed'.[53]

Graves still rumbled in the distance. Burton wrote that everyone was talking about *Goodbye*, news came that it had sold 30,000 copies, Julian Dadd thought its author's trench experiences had left him mad, but the person whose objective view Sassoon wanted was E. M. Forster. He did some more fair copying, 750 words on 14 December. The war had come back to him, yet more forcibly, in *Goodbye*, in his own memoirs and when he read the German Ernst Jünger's evocation of battle's transforming, even redemptive, power in *Storm of Steel*.

There were more scenes with Tennant. 'I alternately cried and screamed and abused him and then wept,' Stephen admitted; then came 'heavenly reconciliation'.[54] On 18 December, in cold weather, on the way to Sicily with Tennant, the valet William and the parrot Poll, Sassoon suddenly longed to escape from Stephen's demons, to explore life. Jünger's book had made him think that struggle and its satisfactions were better than this mind-numbing luxury. The last time he had been in these waters was in 1918, on the way from Egypt to the Western Front. In Palermo, the routine began again: Stephen hysterical if left, cautious sightseeing, the rapid onset of exhaustion.

On Christmas Eve, Tennant described the scene to Blunden: he himself writing letters in one room, Sassoon playing Chopin on the gramophone in another, often coming in to talk or dance clumsily to the music; the whole place smelling of his pipe. 'I wish you could see it,' Stephen wrote, describing his thin white velvet dressing-gown to the desperately poor poet. 'It's like mother-of-pearl and Devonshire cream – if you could mix them.'[55] For Christmas, Sassoon gave Tennant a diamond and platinum star bought in Paris and the manuscript of a poem written in Naples: 'I Looked on That Prophetic Land'.[56] In 1929 he had won two literary prizes and had a bestseller, and he now heard that the Royal Society of Literature had given him its Benson Medal. But reading *War and Peace* made

him feel that there was no greatness yet to what he had written. As the year ended, Stephen drew Sassoon, thinking, 'He is like a god of beauty.'[57] Tennant had oil rubbed into his scalp by the valet William; then, unusually, Sassoon underwent the same process. 'It's a delicious treatment,' Stephen noted, 'soothing and refreshing and very scalp feeding.'[58]

*

THE NEW DECADE was different to the 1920s. The mandarin antics of the Sitwells and the small group where the arts and society met were eclipsed by a political awareness aroused by economic crisis. Extremism in continental Europe, and civil war in Spain where the two totalitarian systems – communism and fascism – clashed directly, made many artists and intellectuals believe that they had to take sides.

Siegfried Sassoon was not a political writer. His protests against the war had their origins more in emotion than in a wish for radical change. During the post-war decade, he seemed often a poet of noble intentions but, to other contemporaries, increasingly unadventurous. Wyndham Lewis put Sassoon into *The Apes of God*, his satire on the smart literary London world, published in 1930, but as a subsidiary character; and Bloomsbury angered and frightened him by its intellectual iconoclasm and frankness. Reflecting an uncertainty about the present, his post-war poetry is often melancholy and nostalgic, effectively fierce only about the old horrors of the war, as in 'On Passing the New Menin Gate', far removed in spirit from Eliot and Pound's modernist dismissal of traditional form or a coherent past.

The titles of Sassoon's poems of 1929 show this backward glance. In March came 'Farewell to Youth'. 'Mysteries', 'Childhood Recovered' and 'War Experience Footnote' followed in April; 'Acceptance' in May and 'The Heart's Paradise'. In June he wrote 'We Shall Not Sleep' (a reflection of his Enoch Arden wish) and 'My Past Has Gone to Bed' in August. The last two poems of the year – 'A Guidebook to Oblivion' and 'Presences Perfected' – were similarly old-fashioned in style, unlike the fractured world of Eliot or the

Auden generation's left-wing urgency.[59] In the 1930s, young poets like Spender, MacNeice and Day Lewis respected Sassoon's war poems and his pacifism – and his friendship with Wilfred Owen – but were not much interested in his recent work. This increasing enthusiasm for Owen could be irritating to him. He inspired a new edition of the poems, prepared and introduced by Blunden in 1931, that would bring 'little Wilfred' to the next generation. But when Stephen Spender came to see him, Sassoon, tired of questions about his one-time protégé, snapped that Owen's accent had been an embarrassment.

The First World War haunted its surviving poets. Robert Graves wrote a bestseller about it and left England for a new life in Majorca, set apart from modernism. Disengaged from the political debates of the 1930s, he wrote love poetry – his didacticism coming through even in this – and historical novels, becoming preoccupied by theories about myth, creativity and the power of the Feminine or White Goddess. Edmund Blunden, although he hated some memories of the trenches, felt that there had been a potency of life then that never quite returned. In 'The Watchers', he wrote,

> *When will the stern, fine 'Who goes there?'*
> *Meet me again in midnight air?*
> *And the gruff sentry's kindness, when*
> *Will kindness have such power again?*

Sassoon's nostalgia was different from this, a longing more for the inspiration, even for the anger, that had once seized him, for a true linking of words with thought, belief and emotion. Instead he made a quieter, more soothing alternative, a utopia unknown in reality, a past world of beauty and order, raised by the music of his prose.

*

ON 7 JANUARY 1930, Siegfried Sassoon and Stephen Tennant left Palermo for Agrigento. The manuscript preyed on him, 'a dead-weight on my mind – which is too much tethered to be able to work with any freedom or clearness'.[60] It should not be like the German bestseller, *All Quiet on the Western Front*, in which too much horror or stress on 'physical functions'[61] dulled the effect. He persuaded Stephen to let him work in the mornings. In the afternoons, they collected shells or visited the sights.

They had another row; 'he's such a clumsy darling' in argument, Tennant noted, thinking also that 'I hate this place. I could scream with boredom but I look very rested, fresher and that's everything.'[62] The view from the hotel was beautiful: almond trees, Greek temples, a sunlit sea, and Sassoon also thought that his lover's face looked 'younger and healthier than it has done since September'.[63] They went on to Syracuse, Etna rising above the landscape, and quarrelled again, Tennant uttering the dread words, 'I shall make separate plans,'[64] but again there was reconciliation. Letters penetrated their enclosed world; Osbert Sitwell said that Gabriel Atkin had taken up with the 'drug taking' novelist Mary Butts, and Forster told Stephen he disliked *Goodbye to All That*, finding the tone forced, 'as if he was practising being formidable'.[65] At first Sassoon tried to exorcize the book by writing doggerel verses about its author; then he wrote to Graves on 7 February ('Dear R.G.'), trying to give a calm summary of his rage.

The book, he said, had haunted him since leaving England. In fact two months before, if he had seen Graves, he might have tried to knock him down. He had failed to get in touch since November 1927 for many reasons, among them his fury over Graves's high-handedness with Gosse and insensitive attitude to Hardy's death (*Goodbye* was disrespectful to Hardy as well). Then Graves had written an unfriendly review of the *Fox-hunting Man*. Sassoon had, he said, been preoccupied with Stephen's health and with finishing the second volume of memoirs about the war, a work which made *Goodbye* seem even more crass, hitting him like a Zeppelin bomb. Moreover it omitted to mention that Sassoon had only agreed to go before the medical board in July 1917 after Graves had sworn on the Bible that there would be no court martial. The book had other inaccuracies and crude passages, inflating casualty figures, dwelling unnecessarily on brothel visiting and exaggerating the role of its author; Dr Dunn, an impeccable witness, had found it unworthy. But if Graves was making money, this was good, and he might also like to know that 'I made a new will last year' and he would benefit 'to the extent of £300 a year tax paid'. The point of the letter was 'to relieve my mind'; no reply was needed. 'But I do implore you not to write anything more about me.'⁶⁶ The letter shows anger at the trespassing on holy ground: Hardy, Gosse, Graves's claim to have known Rivers well, the imputation that Robbie Ross had had black blood (presumably to neutralize Ross's spreading of similar rumours about Nancy Graves), the repeating of the charge of cowardice against Owen.

Relieved, Sassoon decided to put Graves back in his book, and 'I will write about him as if he'd died in 1916.'⁶⁷ He went to bed for seven days with a bad throat, yet wrote easily at last. But, on 26 February, a letter came from Majorca. Tennant, although shocked ('it's a gross dirty letter – using such words as Fuck with relish'), saw Graves's point. They argued; 'he [Graves] is hurt and sullen at S. ignoring him,'⁶⁸ Stephen thought.

The unrepentant letter hit out at Sassoon's 'inverted vulgarity', arguing that brothel visiting had not been very obvious: 'it doesn't take long to fuck' – something about which neither Sassoon nor T. E. Lawrence seemed to know much. There was another sexual jibe at Sassoon's 'homosexual leanings' and his jealousy of Nancy for disturbing their friendship. Graves declared that lack of money had forced him to write *Goodbye*; if only Sassoon had helped 'you would not have had the Zeppelin bomb'.⁶⁹ Sassoon should learn to be himself more in his writings. Why had he failed to send Graves *The Heart's Journey*?

Typically, Sassoon felt guilty. He had thought of offering money the previous June before hearing of Laura Riding's suicide attempt, and by then Graves had written half his book. At first he tried to forget the letter, showing Stephen some poems he was sending to Blunden, and, as therapy, scraped lime off the backs of shells, wishing that Rivers was alive. But Robert Graves still lurked, a reminder that 'I have always when offended by him, wanted to dominate him and humble him.'[70] So, on 2 March, he wrote another letter to Graves, taking up the points: the breaking of Hardy's privacy, his preoccupation with Stephen Tennant precluding anything else last year. He raised the phrase about fucking ('not a pretty remark, Robert'); the time needed to fuck, Sassoon declared, depended on 'the taste, capacity etc of the participants'. He protested again about the inaccuracies relating to the war and the raising of Owen's reputed cowardice. Sassoon denied the charge that he had ever found Graves attractive and reiterated his anger about the references to Theresa's attempts to contact the dead Hamo. The *Fox-hunting Man* he defended as a 'carefully thought out and constructed' narrative and said he had not sent Graves *The Heart's Journey* because he believed his old friend thought of him as 'a back-number (poetically)'. The letter ended, 'yours – I really don't know what', but he attempted to dilute the quarrel with humour in the heading 'Souraccuser'[71] instead of Syracuse.

Goodbye to All That featured in a lovers' row set off by the death of D. H. Lawrence, whom Tennant admired. Defending Graves's book, Stephen said that Sassoon's work had lacked fire and energy since 'the marvellous war poems' and that 'too much care and deliberation' sterilized it; 'I was very rude about his poems.' Sassoon answered haltingly that now he had found 'a haven of calm and spiritual tranquillity – and this was shown in *The Heart's Journey*'. But to Tennant a poet must strive; someone of forty-three should not sit back; such 'chimney corner philosophy sickens me' and 'nothing is solved until we die'. He disliked Siegfried's effusive admiration for Max Beerbohm's epigrams; 'well, they are Max's generation, not his, he's a young man'. The row died when Sassoon said he wanted only to be with Stephen, not to fight battles, not even to write. Tennant noted that Siegfried had 'suffered so, poor darling, he's been so grand and brave and turbulent – and here am I callow and glib . . . but I know I am right – he is a young man, he should support his generation'.[72]

*

IN FOUR DAYS at the start of March, Sassoon rewrote 4,000 words, worried now that 'my book somehow lacks vitality'.[73] Stephen was painting flowers, admiring shells and telling Ottoline Morrell of his great happiness, even after another scene.[74] From Syracuse, they went out sometimes by car or on donkeys and Sassoon thought 'if S. weren't childish and had self-control, he wouldn't be the adorable companion he is'.[75] The poem 'In Sicily' is a tribute to this:

> *Because we two can never again come back*
> *On life's one forward track, –*
> *Never again first-happily explore*
> *This valley of rocks and vines and orange-trees,*
> *Half Biblical and half Hesperides,*
> *With dark blue seas calling from a shell-strewn shore:*
> > *By the strange power of Spring's resistless green,*
> > *Let us be true to what we have shared and seen,*
> > *And as our amulet this idyll save.*
> > *And since the unreturning day must die,*
> > *Let it for ever be lit by an evening sky*
> > *And the wild myrtle grow upon its grave.*[76]

He had decided to end the book with the medical board at Liverpool; was this decision based on inertia or artistic taste, he wondered? On 31 March, on the balcony of the Grand Hotel in Syracuse, Siegfried Sassoon finished *Memoirs of an Infantry Officer*. Then another Lawrence caused another row. Stephen Tennant wondered why T.E. had not submitted to the Turkish bey who had made homosexual advances to him, and Sassoon raged against these 'bottle party standards of morality'.[77] Tennant wept before the usual reconciliation.

At the start of April, at Rapallo, Max Beerbohm demolished much of contemporary art and writing: Eliot ('a dried bean' and 'a case of the Emperor wearing no clothes'), D. H. Lawrence ('a diseased mind'), E. M. Forster (unreadable), Wyndham Lewis, the abstract art of Ben Nicholson. 'The jaded are in the saddle as never before,'[78] Beerbohm said; Walter de la Mare was among the rare signs of hope. He read the manuscript of the *Infantry Officer* and praised its poignancy and style; so pleased was Sassoon that he wrote an alexandrine sonnet to Max. Tennant's birthday present arrived from Paris – a ring of a dark sapphire set in brilliants and platinum – but there were more scenes, Stephen howling, 'You'd better go and live with the Beerbohms,' and saying that the young writer Peter Quennell had called Sassoon 'a sanctimonious self-pitying martyr'. These rows ended in exhaustion, Tennant saying proudly, 'Don't you think I'm good at quarrelling?'[79] A poem, written on 26 April, 'The Heart's Reward', conveys Sassoon's melancholy, less rapturously than in 'In Sicily':

> Can life be comforted by omens of decay, –
> Discovering in a head whose hairs are going grey,
> Calm consolations led by wisdom on their way?
>
> Will happiness be mine when the restless body tires,
> And wearied of the wine of dangerous desires,
> I turn toward the heights that shine with unbefriending fires?[80]

He felt exhausted by Stephen Tennant's ardour and the failure of his own efforts to bring him complete sexual satisfaction. 'I am too old for a perpetual honeymoon.'[81] But in Paris, where they stayed outside the city at Saint-Germain, Sassoon, now feeling weak and ill, reassured himself that this love affair had been 'immeasurably the most happy and complete one in my life' in spite of its sexual difficulty. He could protect the young man only because Stephen was in love with him.[82] Tennant teased him about 'Pavlik' Tchelitchew but at night they were reconciled to the sound of rain, Sassoon dreaming of Richardson, the groom who had been his childhood hero, and of Weirleigh.

SEVENTEEN

Elected silence

BACK IN ENGLAND, illness struck. By the second week of June 1930, Stephen Tennant had been diagnosed as suffering from worsening tuberculosis and Siegfried Sassoon took the boy in his arms and wept. But Tennant said that he wanted two weeks alone at Wilsford.

This meant a crack in the idyll – at the moment just a crack – for Sassoon was growing very attached to the Wiltshire paradise. The gardeners there, Beryl and Eileen Hunter, lent him a horse, a cob called Bruno. He liked the schoolgirlish Hunter sisters – the solid Beryl and the dark, more impulsive Eileen – both lovers of horses and country life, both adoring of him, rather gushing, so that he nicknamed them 'Really and Truly'. But Wilsford was Stephen's kingdom. Two Syracusan donkeys grazed in a paddock, reminders of Sicily, and the garden overflowed with honeysuckle, lilies, anchusa and white borders beneath enclosing yew hedges; all this was inseparable from Stephen Tennant. The place seemed an England beyond the present when, after solitary rides over the Wiltshire downs, Sassoon rode towards the manor past deferential villagers or walked with Stephen over its lawns, running back to fetch him a coat if there was a hint of cold. The atmosphere fascinated him: the traces of Lady Grey's world, of the Souls, of a pitiable Lord Grey – in his eyes the epitome of honour and decency overwhelmed by the age's barbarism – and the tragedy of Bim's death bringing images of a self-confident, elegant country blown apart by the First World War. A tank on nearby Salisbury Plain brought back the trenches, inspiring the poem 'Mimic Warfare' on how different mock battles were to the reality.[1] In 1930, Stephen's beauty seemed to merge with what had survived at Wilsford to create an earlier, sweeter life before the rumbles of an economic crisis and a literary revolution. Sassoon told Fabers that the printers must reproduce Stephen Tennant's drawings, regardless of expense, for the Ariel edition of his poem 'In Sicily', inspired by their travels together.

Sassoon left Wilsford and then returned. Tennant's wish for solitude seemed to pass and, from a wheelchair, he said faintly, 'We do have such fun, don't we?'[2] Sassoon spent £125 on an illustrated twenty-volume study of shells[3] for him and read aloud those children's books that Tennant loved: Mrs Molesworth, E. Nesbit, a novel called *The Schoolboy Baronet*. Stephen gave Siegfried a silver ring – two hearts with 'Christ thee my Comfort be' inscribed inside – given by him once to Lady Grey; then Chandler, the doctor, and Lord Glenconner, Tennant's elder brother, agreed that Stephen should rest as if he were in a sanatorium for at least a year. But he did not seem to get better and when bad news came about his good lung, Sassoon, near hysteria, got in touch with a Dr Snowden who had a sanatorium close by at Ringwood. Snowden came and advised hearty eating and rest, saying afterwards of the patient, 'Thank God I wasn't born with a temperament like that.'[4] Stephen gained thirteen ounces, but Glen Byam Shaw warned Siegfried that he himself would break down if he kept up this obsessive attendance on an invalid. One night Sassoon watched Stephen asleep in the Stone Parlour, a poster advertising the *Daily Telegraph*'s serialization of the *Infantry Officer* on one wall, the boy's face 'marble white'[5] as if dead – a scene similar to that where Proust's narrator watches over the captive Albertine. At Wilsford the observer was trapped, not the sleeping object of his love.

Like Marcel in *In Search of Lost Time*, Sassoon wanted to isolate Tennant. Stephen's socialite brother David was kept away;

friends like Beaton, Rex Whistler and the Sitwells felt excluded, and Glen Byam Shaw reported Osbert Sitwell's comment that Tennant had been much more amusing before he had taken up with Siegfried. On 23 September, Sassoon left Wilsford again. The patient had said that he wanted to be alone for ten days and, wallowing in orchids and idleness, thought shamefully, 'I suppose I am completely decadent.'[6]

*

'EVERY PAPER ACCLAIMS S.S.'s book. 2nd impression ready,'[7] Stephen Tennant wrote in his journal on 10 September. Earlier, Sassoon had despaired of the proofs of the memoirs. The book seemed too Cranfordish, too cosy, not enough like Remarque's gritty *All Quiet on the Western Front*, and Fabers had chosen *Memoirs of an Infantry Officer* as its title, not his choice, *Memoirs Continued*. But reviews in the *Times Literary Supplement*, *Manchester Guardian*, *News Chronicle*, *Everyman* and other publications were good, and in the *Daily News* Blunden gave his usual praise. Robert Graves preferred the book to the *Fox-hunting Man*, having previously thought the 'puppet' Sherston too weak; now, as if in answer to Graves's criticism, this was 'Sassoon himself writing, whatever he calls himself'.[8] This was true, in fact, for much of the book is based on diaries.

As in the *Fox-hunting Man*, the names of real characters are changed: E. J. Greaves – as in the first volume – is 'Old Man' Barton and Julian Dadd still Julian Durley. Stockwell becomes Kinjack, Orme is Ormonde, Captain Dunn is transformed into Captain Monro, Ralph Greaves is Wilmot. Away from the front, the Brasseys are Lord and Lady Asterix and Theresa, in part, still Aunt Evelyn. Ottoline Morrell and Garsington do not appear at all. Graves is introduced as David Cromlech (the Welsh for a grave): tactless, defensively exuberant, oddly prim. Litherland is Clitherland.

The book begins at the Fourth Army School at Flixécourt in the spring of 1916 and ends with the narrator's protest and arrival at Craiglockhart (Slateford in the book) some fifteen months later. It includes incidents that inspired many of the war poems. 'Natural talking is the thing,'[9] Sassoon wrote of his narrative method, as in the *Fox-hunting Man*; 'emotion provides the engine power' and 'I see myself as a hero and martyr – (not as a clear thinker).'[10] The spirit is that of sacrifice. Sherston looks at some of his brother officers and thinks, 'I couldn't save them, but at least I could share the dangers and discomforts they endured.' In his notes for *Memoirs of an Infantry Officer*, Sassoon compared the protest of 1917 to his high emotion on joining up in 1914; in 1917 also 'I felt the desire to suffer.'[11]

Sherston is the amateur, invariably childlike, at first unquestioning, the same 'somewhat solitary-minded young man'. 'I suppose these brass-hats do know a hell of a lot about it all, don't they?'[12] he asks another officer, just before the first day of the Somme. He only hints at sex (as when a soldier falls asleep against him or in his handling of a dead young German), feels wild 'exultation' after the rescue of Corporal O'Brien (whom Sassoon allows to keep his real name), knows that time will deplete his courage and feels his public-school self cut off from the mysteriously stoical soldiers he commands. He has only a hazy notion of anything outside England. He looks back to a beautiful, gentle past and seems so self-deprecating and gentle that one feels the protest could never have come off without a push from Tyrrell (Bertrand Russell) and Markington (Massingham).

Much of the book's power is in the contrast between this sweet personality and the ordeal that he has to suffer. One of its most vivid scenes is a description of a division's return from the Somme when Sherston feels that he has seen 'an army of ghosts', perhaps as the war might be 'envisioned by the mind of some epic poet a hundred years hence'.[13] There is a sense of tremendous, implacable forces, as in Hardy's *The Dynasts*. *Memoirs of an Infantry Officer* seems haunted, not by fear but by regret, pity and decency. This haunting induces a melancholy and, at times, angry desire for what has gone, even if it never existed.

The unanimity of critical praise soon broke. In the *Adelphi*,

Herbert Read, who had won the Military Cross on the Western Front, wrote that the book had too much delicacy, art and tenderness and failed to condemn the war enough.[14] Pinto said he preferred the *Fox-hunting Man*, which seemed more of an 'organic whole';[15] moreover the *Infantry Officer* again missed out entirely how Sassoon became a poet. Robert Graves, in the *Clarion*, quoted from Sassoon's letter to him about *Goodbye to All That* and congratulated himself on having forced an abandonment of the 'novelistic distortion' of the *Fox-hunting Man*. Of himself as the tactless Cromlech, Graves wrote that there was only one character on whom Sassoon was harder: himself. He disputed Sassoon's assertion that 'Cromlech' had lied to get 'Sherston' before a medical board in 1917 for he had known that there would never be a court martial, having (he claimed) consulted 'the War Office authorities'. But *Memoirs of an Infantry Officer* was 'a very good book indeed'.[16] After this review, Sassoon was so irritated that he felt he never wanted to see Graves again. He read his old friend's new book, *But It Still Goes On*, telling Blunden he found it 'deadly dull'.[17] David Cassilis is obviously based on him: a vain, homosexual, pipe-smoking architect always 'under restraint' and in love with the Graves-like character, Dick Tompion, who tells Cassilis 'you're a constant pain in my belly'.[18]

On 7 October, in London, Sassoon heard his sales: 27,000 for the *Fox-hunting Man* in its 7s 6d edition and the *Infantry Officer* 24,000 already. At the Reform Club, dining with Max Beerbohm and William Nicholson, who urged him to take the memoirs into the post-war years, he saw Gabriel Atkin, who was with Roderick Meiklejohn. Atkin looked anxious, healthy but coarsened in appearance. Sassoon avoided introducing his old friend to Beerbohm; and Gabriel set off thoughts of idleness and its dangers. He could never be happy, he thought, being idle. But Stephen tethered his mind. Sassoon sent presents to Wilsford, small humorous objects, postcards, including one of Emma Hamilton on which he wrote, 'She's not unlike someone I spend week-ends with. Anyway she knows all about bee sting mouths.' Dr Snowden said that Tennant need not go away for the winter. Stephen wrote in his journal that he missed 'my Kangaroo' with his 'coppery' hair, 'like a drift of dark red beech leaves',[19] but felt 'much better alone. I meet Nanny every night in dreams and wake up so comforted and happy.'[20]

*

SASSOON RETURNED TO Wilsford. After four days the invalid lost a pound in weight, and Stephen, claiming that this was because of over-excitement, asked Siegfried to leave. Back in Campden Hill Square, Sassoon completed a poem about transient happiness before being summoned again and told, with hysterical force, that this time he must stay for ever. He thought that this fever and fragility – and its tenderness and suffering – intensified their love. But his Christmas message to Tennant seems to envisage solitude: a card on which he drew a man in a Wiltshire landscape and copied out the last two lines of his poem 'December Stillness' ('December stillness, crossed by twilight roads, / Teach me to travel far, and bear my loads').[21]

Wilsford still felt a home to him; he even started going out on Bruno with the local hunt. But an enemy surfaced, from within. A Nurse May had arrived to look after Stephen Tennant, and she detested Siegfried Sassoon. With hatred in her face, she accused him of keeping the boy from his family; suddenly Sassoon saw that she was repelled by their relationship, by him reading to Tennant alone at night and the obvious intimacy between them. Tennant lost three-quarters of a pound, and when Sassoon remarked on this, Nurse May said contemptuously, 'Yes poor boy: he ought to have some visitors.' Towards the end of January 1931, Dr Snowden, perhaps encouraged by her, said Sassoon should leave the boy for two or three weeks.

He left the next day. He bought a hunter called Silvermane and arranged for the mare to be sent to Wilsford, a small outbreak of independence for Stephen loathed the sport. Stephen wrote to ask him to stay away for a further ten days, so Sassoon went to a hotel near Wilsford, telling the invalid where he was. Tennant took the

news calmly, saying, 'Shall we go away together when I'm well?'²²
Then he said that he wanted to be alone for another fortnight.

At Weirleigh, Theresa said, 'Leave him to stew in his own juice,'
adding that she preferred Blunden. Sassoon worked on a short story
about a feckless character based on David Tennant but found its
realism too hard, or upsetting, to sustain.²³ The presentation to him
by Walter de la Mare of the Benson Medal at the Royal Society of
Literature seemed nothing beside Stephen's elusiveness. Another
letter arrived; Tennant wanted him to stay away for another three
or four weeks; Sassoon must 'grin and bear it' and 'do some writing
or something'. While staying with Edith Olivier at Wilton, he rode
over to Wilsford and looked through the window. Stephen stared
out furiously, saying, 'I told you not to come and see me for three
weeks.'²⁴ Sassoon collected Forster, who had been staying at Wilsford, and the novelist said Stephen was upset that Sassoon had tried
to see him at all but avoided more talk about the rift. Stephen sent
him a pot of caviare, as if scattering bait for a fish.

Edith Olivier became a comforter and an intermediary, strangely
innocent and kind. Some fourteen years older than Sassoon, also the
confidante of Cecil Beaton and Rex Whistler, whom she adored, she
wrote romantic novels and books about Wiltshire, becoming mayor
of Wilton (where her father had been the rector). But she lived
perhaps most fervently through the dramas of her younger friends.
Others tried to help. William Walton suggested a break in Ascona,
the romantic Swiss village on Lake Maggiore, where the composer
was staying, at Sassoon's expense, with his German lover Baroness
Imma von Doernberg. The novelist Rosamond Lehmann said Tennant had told her that Sassoon was 'far away the most important
person in his life'.²⁵

In Ascona, on yet another holiday, Sassoon saw only William
Walton and Imma von Doernberg ('a charming creature'). He read
– Aksakoff's *Years of Childhood*, Gordon Craig's *Irving* and the
Leavises' journal *Scrutiny* with essays on Eliot, Joyce and Lawrence
– and walked by the lake, damming pools, as at Breitenau, among

wild flowers and butterflies, pleased to hear from the Hunters that Nurse May had been replaced by a Miss Turnbull. Still unable to write, he started to transcribe his 1925 diaries, thinking of turning these into a new book called *Memoirs of a Literary Man*.

*

IN MAY, DUCKWORTH published his anonymous parodies of the civil servant and poet Humbert Wolfe, called *Pynchbeck Lyre*. To Sassoon, Wolfe's bad, and surprisingly popular, verses were infuriatingly mediocre and he disliked the way that this figure (whom Osbert Sitwell called 'Humbug' Wolfe)[26] had managed to get these and his opinions so easily into print. He had, however, been reluctant to allow the publication of this small book, the literary equivalent of shooting at a barn door, which, although often funny, did little for his literary reputation even if it sold 600 copies within the first three days. Harold Nicolson revealed the author's identity in the *Evening Standard*. 'Requiem' shows the tone, both of Wolfe and of his parodist:

> *Swing tripe, swing tosh! You need no longer worry*
> *About your sales; now Nemesis is drumming;*
> *No need to sing of Switzerland or Surrey,*
> *Or ask when immortality is coming.*
> *Scrawl slowlier, fountain pen; put by your bosh.*
> *Prepare to be forgot. Swing tripe, swing tosh!*[27]

Bulletins came from Wilsford: from Rosamond Lehmann, the Hunters, Edith Olivier and the new nurse Miss Turnbull, to whom Sassoon gave a car. The Hunters in particular relayed every nuance – Miss Turnbull's row with the secretary Miss Osborne, Rex Whistler's remark that Tennant was right to avoid the possessive Sassoon – making the place seem like a little princely court with its bitchiness and petty rivalries. Rosamond Lehmann thought Tennant hysterical and more self-absorbed than ever – with that 'curious, shrewd, imperious, cold side' – saying that he still loved Sassoon but 'you exhaust him'. She wondered if he had had a delayed nervous breakdown caused by the deaths of his mother and Nanny Trusler and urged Sassoon to be patient for 'I left loving him as much as ever . . . He is sick in mind and body.'[28]

For Sassoon, another holiday of twenty-four days at The Long White Cloud at the end of July was 'a complete failure',[29] followed by an equally disappointing trip to Cannes with Anzie Wylde and Anzie's boisterous friends. On 12 August he had a letter from Tennant; 'I want you to love and believe this letter. And I want you to trust me. I don't want you with me just now, but if you will be patient and try to trust my judgement everything will be alright . . .'[30] Two days later another letter came, starting 'My darling, I am so happy to get your letter.'[31] Miss Turnbull wrote that her patient had a slight temperature, felt depressed and could not go to Cannes, which Sassoon had suggested.

Sassoon decided to take up the offer of Rosamond Lehmann's husband Wogan Philipps to rent him Ipsden House, near Abingdon, described by Lord Berners as 'a mixture of gloom and charm'.[32] On his way there from Weirleigh, he stopped in London, to find a letter from Eileen Hunter. Stephen had ordered the Syracusan donkeys, Denis and Gilbert, to be got rid of because their braying had disturbed his afternoon nap.

At Ipsden, sitting with the silky grey Dandie Dinmont dog called Sheltie that came with the house, Sassoon read Stephen's rapturous journal of their time together and obsession seized him. With this came another anxiety; the country, and most of the western world, was gripped by an economic crisis, apparently insoluble unemployment and the prospect of socialism. Sassoon, ostensibly a socialist, felt he should welcome radical change yet began to wonder how he might cope with the loss, through heavy taxation or even revolution, of his private income and the ability to support not only his friends, like Blunden, but a fretting Theresa as well.

He went over to Wilsford, crept up to the big house but did not see Stephen. The Hunters suggested he should find somewhere in Wiltshire, near yet far enough away to be separate. William Walton came to stay at Ipsden, and after the composer left Sassoon played

some of his *Belshazzar's Feast*. In the middle of 'praise ye the gods
of Gold', he had an idea for a poem – 'Mammoniac Ode' – pleased
at this first sign of inspiration since May and a poem about red
roses, written at Ascona.[33]

The Hunters found him Fitz House in Teffont Magna; coinciden-
tally Sassoon had admired it when driving past with Glen Byam
Shaw the previous September. Built in the sixteenth and seventeenth
centuries of local stone, with mullioned windows and a clear chalk
stream full of trout running between the house and the road, its low-
ceilinged dark rooms making it seem 'almost a cottage',[34] Fitz House
was rented to a Colonel French who had it on a long lease from
Lord Bledisloe. Fourteen miles from Wilsford, quite near Wilton and
Edith Olivier (who had once lived there briefly with her sister), the
place seemed peaceful but not isolated – a good example of English
vernacular architecture that included a thatched fourteenth-century
tithe barn and a converted seventeenth-century wool store attached
to the main residence.[35] The Colonel was asking £3 3s a week, or £4
if the two servants and one gardener were included. Nan Tennant
rang from Wilsford to say that Stephen's temperature was back over
100 and that he had told her that Sassoon got on his nerves.

He went north for a week, for the first performance of Walton's
Belshazzar's Feast in Leeds, and stayed at Renishaw, feeling that the
money he had given Walton for four months in Ascona had been
used well. At the end of October, he was back, prowling round the
walls of Wilsford, to hear the invalid Stephen talking to Rex
Whistler about a workman, 'he was so shy and sweet'.[36] This was
Enoch Arden come to life: the hidden watcher with that sense of
power in concealment, sadism and masochism mixed, the superiority
of observing and the inferior role of forgoing pleasure. Alone in Fitz
House, ashamed, Sassoon drank half a bottle of champagne and
broke down, sobbing, 'Stephen, Stephen what are you doing to
me?'[37]

He brooded on unflattering stories about Lady Grey: her ordering that all the cockerels in the village should be killed because their
morning crowing woke her, her snubbing of the local gentry. This

unfeelingness had infected Stephen who, following the expulsion of the donkeys, had recently commanded that a cow should stop lowing. A trip by car to East Anglia with Ralph Hodgson raised Sassoon up through Hodgson's joy in English provincial life and history. But on their return, after hearing from Edith Olivier that Stephen still refused to see him, he dreamed of the boy and burst into tears.

Sometimes the bonds slackened. While following the South and West Wiltshire hunt in his car, Sassoon met the master, a hunting character called Ikey Bell, an admirer of the *Fox-hunting Man*. Bell offered to lend him a horse and asked Sassoon to stay the night. The deference of this hard-bitten man and of another guest – who seemed like Geoffrey Harbord – and five hours in the saddle made him feel years younger. Also out were more reminders of his past: someone he had hunted with in Cork in 1918, an ex-officer of the Royal Welch Fusiliers and other readers of his books. At Fitz House, the servant Lapworth smiled approvingly at the mud-covered hunting clothes. In Liverpool to collect an honorary degree – where the university's Chancellor Lord Derby also praised his books – Sassoon met Yates, once the quartermaster of his old regiment's Second Battalion. A fan, Doris Westwood, obviously in love with Sherston and his creator, was writing to him. Unmarried, from Sutton Cold-field, she lived through the *Memoirs* and wrote bleak novels that featured her idea of Siegfried Sassoon. Although they never met, he confided in her about Tennant. Doris Westwood, the huntsmen and the Liverpool ceremony showed that his work was still popular and powerful.

The torture returned when Sassoon spent Christmas Day with the Hunters, giving the gardeners a portable radio and talking about the war with their old father who had been torpedoed in a hospital ship. Eileen and Beryl, enthralled by him and the Wilsford dramas, listened aghast to his complaints about Stephen's cruelty. For Tennant, Sassoon put into an envelope a photograph of himself on his mare and a piece of paper on which he had written three Shakespeare quotations about friendship, perplexity and loving 'too well'.

He went up to the manor to leave this and the gift of a diary for Nan. Nan Tennant appeared – invincibly jolly and sensible, probably thinking Siegfried mad – and spoke of Stephen's feverish attacks, before accompanying him through the warm twilight to the gate of the Hunters' house. No answer came to the Christmas message but later he found a Christmas card at Campden Hill Square, its envelope addressed by Edith Olivier, 'To Siegfried from Stephen. Best wishes for 1932', the first sign from Tennant since 8 September.

*

FOR HIM AS a poet, the year had been disappointing: lukewarm reviews for the *Pynchbeck Lyre* parodies; 'Mammoniac Ode' written in late summer, then the revival of a poem begun in 1924, another weak satire called 'The Utopian Times', for an anthology illustrated by Rex Whistler. In October he wrote 'Break Silence', about mocking nocturnal voices. The long 'To a 17th Century Platonist' came in December, inspired by reading a volume by John Norris, bought on a book-hunting trip; the poem imagines Norris – 'an odd ingenious friend' – as a serene presence in the house and stayed unfinished until November 1932.[38]

The book buying went on – in Salisbury, Bournemouth, Ringwood – and the therapy of polishing the bindings and reading his purchases. When Theresa fell ill with 'ovarian troubles', he visited her in hospital at Tunbridge Wells and called at a local bookshop, picking up first editions of Coleridge, continuing his passion for the Romantics: Wordsworth, Shelley, Leigh Hunt, Keats and Lamb – Blunden's period. He almost broke down when he saw the old lady recovering from her operation, some violets from Weirleigh by her bed and the photographs that he had sent her of Liverpool cathedral. She asked about Silvermane and kept pressing his hand, a pathetic display of courage and tenderness.

At Fitz House, Sassoon copied out and revised five old poems for his next collection, to be called *Vigils* – a book that he planned of about twenty short poems, dating from 1926, often intense, he

Prince Philipp of Hesse, the Kaiser's nephew who apologized for his own 'bad conduct'.

Edmund and Mary Blunden.

Fun at Garsington, with Lord Berners and Julian Morrell.

Sassoon at Haus Hirth, with Stephen Tennant and Bach.

Lord Grey of Falloden:
'human – simple yet profound'.

Lady Grey, Stephen Tennant's
mother. Sassoon found her chilling.

Siegfried and Stephen in the garden at Wilsford.

Glen and Angela Byam Shaw in the car given to them by Sassoon.

Ralph Hodgson. Sassoon thought
him 'English to the bone', although
Hodgson chose to live in Ohio.

Osbert Sitwell:
not quite 'first rate'.

In fancy dress for the Wilton Pageant.

Heytesbury. When he bought it in 1933, Sassoon thought he was 'walking calmly into the first volume of a Trollope novel'.

Hester Gatty.

Edith Olivier,
Siegfried and Hester.

With George:
'the best thing
life can give'.

Geoffrey Keynes:
'an unfailing friend'.

The squire of Heytesbury.

'The Great Dictator', taken by George.

With Geoffrey Keynes's grandson while receiving an honorary degree at Oxford in 1965. Dennis Silk is to the right, behind Sassoon, with Haro Hodson on the far right.

Hester on Mull.

George Sassoon.

thought, but lacking 'impetus and richness'.[39] For the first time in two or three years, he felt inspired to write poetry, but needed peace. At the start of February, he heard that Stephen had been forbidden to move since a haemorrhage on 21 January 1932. The next evening he wrote thirteen lines: 'Time will be memory' – 'top notch',[40] he thought, although they were never published – one line reviving the memory of 'legends of youth' and its search for 'love the invisible, sense of spring . . .'[41] Whitman came into his mind: those mournful lines 'O past, o happy hope, o songs of joy!', ending: 'Never more.'

The Hunters told him that Stephen seemed almost catatonic: unshaven, not seeing Nan, tired even of orchids, reading only the latest edition of the *Amateur Aquarist and Pondkeeper*. Still Sassoon dreamed of him, sometimes wild dreams after rereading Tennant's erotic diaries which seemed a revolt against his own dreary life. He sent extracts from the Browning love letters, about Elizabeth Barrett Browning not being as ill as she thought. The envelope was returned to Beryl Hunter by the nurse, who said, 'Mr Tennant isn't yet up to reading letters.' At Wilsford he saw Stephen again through the window, corpse-like yet serene, perhaps made up, and asked for Nan who told him that the boy was still an invalid, with deadened feelings. Back at Fitz House, he drank a small glass of champagne, then wept: 'Stephen doesn't care.'[42] Suddenly it seemed better if Tennant were dead.

His writing edged forward: a first draft, on 20 February, of 'The Hour Glass', to be revised in November, another lament for time passing. On 28 March came the poem 'Prehistoric Burial' about the burial mounds above Wilsford; and he knew ecstasy again in the 'extraordinary experience' of catching fugitive memory in written words.[43] Sam Behrman came to Fitz House and they went together to Wilsford, to see the Hunters, Behrman noting how they adored Sassoon. Wilsford's invalid was, Sassoon said, perfectly well; at this the Hunters looked embarrassed. When the American exclaimed how beautiful the place was, Sassoon answered, 'Yes. It is beautiful. It's like *The Turn of the Screw*,' and, according to Behrman's later account, a flamboyant young man appeared, intimating familiarity with the house's occupant, for Stephen had left his kingdom occasionally, exciting police attention by outrageous behaviour in Salisbury.

Another visit from Ralph Hodgson to Fitz House led to Lady Violet Bonham Carter, daughter of the former Prime Minister, Asquith, and an acquaintance of Hodgson, having them both to lunch at Stockton, an Elizabethan house she and her stockbroker husband, Maurice Bonham Carter – once Asquith's private secretary – rented near by. Earnestly intelligent, gushing, highly political and conventionally well read, Violet Bonham Carter became a confidante, her children offering some sense of family life to the isolated Sassoon. Soon Diana Cooper was telling Glen Byam Shaw that Violet was 'madly in love'[44] with the poet. Visiting Cecil Beaton at Ashcombe, Beaton's idyllic retreat on the Wiltshire downs, was worse: a silly gathering with the Sacheverell Sitwells and others. As a socialist, Sassoon, ashamed enough of his selfish thoughts during the economic crisis, felt horrified by the much more openly selfish, pleasure-obsessed Sitwells. His poetry shows a sense of dissolution. In 'Thoughts in 1932' he jogs across Wiltshire, conscious of a decline from late-Victorian England into 'The Black Thirties'; then, above Stonehenge, he hears the drone of war planes. On 21 June, influenced by Hodgson's philosophy, he wrote 'Credo', about heaven experienced in life and living, and on 7 July 'Human Histories' on the millions of nameless dead, 'lost lineaments of human histories'.[45]

Sassoon cultivated Violet Bonham Carter because of her link to Stephen through her stepmother Lady Oxford, Asquith's second wife, who before her marriage had been Margot Tennant. Violet described how Stephen, walking with the aid of sticks, admitted to pretending at times to be weaker than he was and had failed to respond when she mentioned Sassoon. Again he sent Tennant some extracts from the Browning letters, adding in his own hand, 'July 19 1930. S gave me a silver ring. July 19 1932. Never a word.'[46] Then Violet Bonham Carter reported that Stephen had seemed stronger and talked of Sassoon. 'He used to be a friend of mine,' Tennant said, 'but we had a quarrel.' Violet told him that Sassoon was near by because of Stephen. 'Oh no, surely not on my account' was the response. She praised Sassoon and Stephen Tennant began to speak lovingly of his old friend, prompting her to say, 'of course you'll be seeing him soon', to which Tennant agreed and gave her a spray of gentians to share with his once beloved S.S. Sassoon felt ecstatic; 'what an unholy power S. has over me',[47] he thought.

Two days later the joy ran out. The Hunters told him of Stephen's plans for parties and trips to Brighton, of how Beaton had been at Wilsford; it was the bad old world again. A glum poem, 'The Quiet House', of this time speaks of 'long empty afternoons' in a place 'where the sweet voice of love has never spoken'. 'First and Last Love' is about youthful curiosity and a love clung to through 'rigorous' lonely nights. He made an early draft of 'The Merciful Knight', inspired by the couplet quoted to him by Ralph Hodgson from Camden's *Remains Concerning Britain*, 'Betwixt the stirrup and the ground / Mercy I asked, mercy I found.' Finished in March 1933, the poem – a Pre-Raphaelite fairy-tale vision of a knight of long ago – tells of finding salvation in an instant's thought or action, of how this instant can become a lasting lesson:

> *Mercy from long ago, be mine that I may know*
> *Life's lastingness begun.*[48]

When Violet Bonham Carter told Sassoon that Stephen Tennant had seen Dr Riddock, who had been recommended by Henry Head, he was delighted. Riddock had suggested a clinic for nervous cases at Penshurst in Kent. Finally on 17 August a note came from Wilsford. 'Will you come to tea with me? Wednesday? Or Thursday? Tell me a fine day so that we can have tea in the garden. One thing you will like will be the ripe corn on the ridge. Tomorrow would be nice, wouldn't it? But you won't be able to write an answer. I will wait till I hear, with love from Stephen.'

Sassoon came to Wilsford on the hottest day of the summer, and the housekeeper showed him to the ilex tree in the garden. When

Tennant arrived in a bathchair, he seemed calm, his face fuller, unhealthy and not made up. As usual, his hands were cold, and he spoke about the garden, abandoning the bath chair for a divan, under an umbrella, where he sipped some milk and soda water. Sassoon thought he was pretending to be weaker, a defensive act. Stephen asked his visitor not to talk so fast and showed no interest in life outside Wilsford. Sassoon teased and petted him. He said 'a few sweet nothings' and gave Stephen a book, *Kangaroo Land*, by a clergyman about the Australian gold fields of the 1850s. At the end Tennant seemed upset when Sassoon said he was going away for two weeks. Two days later they had tea – again in the garden – and this time Stephen talked more freely, saying that the 'nerve doctor' had told him he was subconsciously unhappy, and Sassoon noted a complete 'reconquest of my feelings'. Tennant said he regretted his behaviour. Sassoon wrote, 'I can only record that the nightmare is over.'[49]

Eileen Hunter had begged Sassoon not to have his life wrecked by Stephen again. But soon he was sitting once more in the hall at Wilsford, praising the Hunters, to which Tennant answered, 'They are very kind, but they don't know how to look after my bull-frogs.'[50] Back at Fitz House, a telegram arrived – 'Where are you? Stephen' – then another saying that he wished to mark Sassoon's forty-fourth birthday. At tea, Stephen gave him eye lotion, cold cream, bath essence and flower and shell drawings done in Sicily and seemed solicitous, even loving.

This was paradise. Not even *New Signatures*, the anthology of young poets, with work by Auden, Spender and others, disturbed Sassoon greatly; he thought the poems 'clever and adroit', influenced by the cinema, modern only like posters of machines and modern American architecture. More painful was a comment by Leavis: 'Mr Sassoon does not call for much attention.'[51] On 11 September he wrote a most unAudenish poem about lonely growth and undiscovered fulfilment, and again felt anxious about his work. Ten days later, he had finished eight alexandrines – the final draft of 'The Hour Glass' – once more a reflection on time. Then he read a few sentences of Bacon in an anthology and felt his head clear. By half-past midnight he had written a poem, perhaps a prelude for *Vigils*, 'Lone Heart Learning', about a solitary search for truth, worth and peace – lines, he thought, with 'music and movement'.[52] The inspiration survived the arrival of a piano at Fitz House which he had feared might distract him. In October he produced the light 'Two Old Ladies', a vision of childhood; then 'Babylon', his 'Ozymandias' about the fall of temporal empires, perhaps inspired by Walton's *Belshazzar's Feast*. He wrote 'Words for the Wordless', to be revised later, on 27 October, almost envying the safe secrets of the dead. His book-hunting produced 'Metamorphosis', about a pedestrian translation of Ovid crossing time to be read years later by Siegfried Sassoon in a Wiltshire village.[53]

*

ON 2 OCTOBER, a letter came from Swaylands, the clinic at Penshurst. It contained a few lines: 'Here I am in this huge hospital lovely Oaks from my window – beaming nurses peep in – Dr Ross once called me "my dear" which made me much less lonely – he is so kind – I keep your letters under my pillow to ward off loneliness.'[54] The treatment was for 'protective obsession'[55] and infantilism. Sassoon went to Oxford for a week to see Blunden, then moved on to Penshurst, where he found Tennant affectionate. Dr Ross revealed that Stephen had refused to see Sassoon at Wilsford because Nurse May had said the excitement might kill her patient.

In Wiltshire, he went out more, trying to show independence from Stephen yet still curbed by his own puritan nature: to dances and fancy-dress parties with the Mitford sisters, Rex Whistler, Cecil Beaton or the more comfortable Edith Olivier, moving among the Bright Young Things who now flickered in an atmosphere of economic and political crisis. At Weirleigh, Theresa said, 'I suppose Stephen Tennant is just the same. That type needs to be under medical control.'[56] Stephen suddenly looked better, although claiming to be too tired for visits which Dr Ross said over-excited the patient. Lady Martin, a neighbour at Weirleigh, told Sassoon his mother had said of Stephen, 'I hear he is in a lunatic asylum – the best place *for* him.'[57]

Back at Fitz House, he transcribed *Omar Khayyám*, partly as therapy, copying FitzGerald's different texts in red, green, brown and blue inks on to coffee-coloured paper. When Stephen asked to see his latest poems, Sassoon rebelled. These were too serious for the frivolous invalid; only Blunden and Hodgson had read them. After lunch with the Hunters on Christmas Day, he had a telephone message to ring Swaylands before five o'clock; by the time he read it, the hour had passed. On Boxing Day he received a telegram asking him to come immediately, and on New Year's Eve another telegram arrived, perhaps a cry for attention because Glen Byam Shaw was staying at Fitz House. Sassoon wrote that he would be there on 10 January, thinking that 'for once he isn't getting his way'.[58]

On 7 January 1933, he wrote, 'The possibility of writing poems is literally all I have to look forward to.'[59] And, in the first years of a febrile decade, Sassoon's poetry, while still glorying in solitary pleasures, sounds a warning. In 'The Facts', of November 1932, glimpses of the jungle beneath civilization's façade make 'this thought-riddled twentieth century day' bleak. 'November Dusk' evokes the thrush's evening cry from a leafless walnut tree, like 'the world's farewell to sight and song'.[60] The unpublished 'Rumination by a Wood Fire'[61] mixes hissing logs, cricket scores, the falling pound and old books into joy in his own solitude. 'An Unveiling', in the *Spectator* on 3 March 1933, reflects a terror of gas and bombed cities; at its end comes Owen's 'old lie' – 'Dulce et decorum est . . .' 'It is, I suspect,' Sassoon told Blunden, 'somewhere near my wartime standard.'[62]

His nerves combined with vagueness to make him hit the kerb while driving, break a glass, throw a match into a full wastepaper basket and set it alight. He fell off his horse and broke his arm, and soon afterwards had a letter from Stephen Tennant. 'I am most dreadfully unhappy because you don't want to visit me,' it said.

'This morning Dr Ross said "surely he would leave his work for one day." The emotional blackmail intensified. 'Could you spare one day? Love from Stephen.'[63]

Sassoon wrote to Ross to say that work prevented him from coming until the following week. Then Ross reported that Stephen's temperature had risen. Sassoon thought resignedly, 'Even now I cannot imagine life without him.'[64] At Swaylands, Stephen said that Ross had promised to treat his inability to have an orgasm which (the doctor claimed) was only a nervous condition. Sassoon thought, 'I have always known it was S's most serious difficulty, in fact it has been the tragedy of his life.'[65] The nurse said he was a very difficult patient, and one doubts if the treatment succeeded. Sassoon bought the boy a toy kangaroo – a gift from 'Kanga' – and Ross said Stephen had a high temperature that often went with tuberculosis and must be kept in bed for weeks. A farewell prolonged by Stephen almost made him miss a train back to London; and a remark – 'Isn't it fun spreading out coats for picnics?'[66] – showed a childlike Tennant who had once enchanted him.

At the start of February, at the Queen's Hall, Sassoon again heard *Sea Drift* by Delius. The piece that often set off poetic yearnings this time inspired the decision, taken later in Wiltshire while playing the piano after tea, to continue the Sherston series as 'poetry seems to have died out in me lately'.[67] He found Craiglockhart difficult to write about, but reached 6,000 words in ten days; then he boiled over after colliding with a bus near Wilsford, manhandling the driver and trying to intimidate the local policeman. Witnesses took the driver's side and a summons to appear at Salisbury magistrates' court deepened his self-pity. Stimulated by an article in the *Spectator* by Norman Angell, he wrote two anti-war poems. But the motoring trouble infuriated him. Playing the piano one night, he found himself near to tears. His own overwrought emotions were heightened by political dramas that even he noticed: the Sino-Japanese war, the failure of the disarmament conference, the Nazis in Germany, then the debate at the Oxford Union – when undergraduates voted against fighting under any circumstances for King and Country by 275 to 153: that, Sassoon thought, at least showed a desire for peace.[68]

On 3 March his four 'peace poems' were published in the *Spectator*, probably 'quite inaudible in the European hullabaloo . . . All this worrying about the next war has completely knocked my prose writing on the head.'[69] He even saw his conviction by the Salisbury magistrates for the motoring offence as a sign that Nazi methods had arrived in Britain. Fined £5, he complained to Glen Byam Shaw, 'How many of them suspected that I have written poems in the last 2 months which will be glorious long after Salisbury Town hall has been pulled down and carted away?' He told Glen also that the Nazis were the effect of injustice to Germany by other nations, especially the French, yet thought, 'Fascist bullying infuriates me. I cannot believe that any good will come of it. To-day they boycott the Jews.'[70] A newspaper reported that the Prince of Hesse, recently Göring's host in Rome, had been made governor of Hessen-Nassau. Of this news that Philipp, Sassoon's former lover, had sold out to the Nazis, he noted, 'Excuse me smiling.'[71]

On 19 April Sassoon wrote to the Archbishop of York in protest at his letter to *The Times* condoning war under certain circumstances. Temple answered that disputes should be referred to the League of Nations but Christians should sometimes resort to force 'for the sake of justice as defined by the most impartial tribunal'.[72] Sassoon replied that 'like most poets' he was 'a man of emotions and intuitions rather than ideas' yet knew that war, particularly a war of modern technology, was never worth it. He played *Sea Drift* again. If only Rivers was alive. The thought of war seemed like the end of the world.

The poetry of 1933 reflects the international crisis. 'Antiquities', written in January, is about the decline of empires into tourist sites and ruins. Then came the prophetic works: 'A Premonition', on the National Gallery after a gas attack; 'News from the War-After-Next', portraying a Hitler-like dictator and anti-Christ; 'The Ultimate Atrocity' of bacterial bombing; and 'Messengers', a glimpse of a terrible future. In the unpublished 'The Christian Objective', Sassoon shows the devil rejoicing in the Archbishop of York's words. The second batch of peace poems published in the *Spectator* on 31 March – the first had appeared on 3 March, under the collective title 'The Road to Ruin' – was headed 'The Path of Peace'. Less apocalyptic, it started with Sassoon's own favourite, his fairy tale of 'The Merciful Knight'. In April he wrote the unpublished 'A Foreseeing', probably referring to Hitler and the Nazis and reviving memories of the First World War dead. 'At the Cenotaph', inspired by Ribbentrop laying a wreath, continues this theme, imagining 'The Prince of Darkness' at the Cenotaph, then 'as he walked away I heard him laugh'.[73]

*

STEPHEN HAD REFUSED to see him and Ross wrote to say that Tennant was very ill. Masochistically, Sassoon went to Wilsford and wandered through the idyllic gardens. A card arrived at Easter, with a message in pencil: 'A happy Easter, love from Stephen.'[74] On 18 May, a terse answer came from Ross. 'Dear Captain Sassoon. I understand that you wish me to write to you about Mr Tennant. He is physically rather better than he was, but he still says that he does not wish to see anybody. Yours sincerely J. A. Ross.'[75]

He wrote a long letter to Stephen, headed 'Something to read', and its last sentences showed his despair.

O Steenie, I have given you the last four years of my life. I was giving you my life all the time, even when you refused to see me or send me a message. I ask nothing of you now; only that you should be aware of the significance of what I am doing and have done, for you ... When I returned from London on Wednesday, I found that 3 large yellow roses had burst into bloom on the wall of this house. The first roses. Automatically, I picked them and put them in a glass beside the photograph of you and me at Versailles. That was my little act of faith in you. Does that melt your heart? With love from S.[76]

One night he had a 'psychic' experience between insomnia and sleep, seeing a white, slightly evil, beautiful, sexless face staring at him. At Wilsford, Beryl Hunter wept at his continuing obsession, and another letter came from Dr Ross. Stephen had asked him to say that 'since your last visit his feelings towards you have not been what they were. He says that you upset him and make him feel ill, and that he cannot see you again.'[77] Ross had told Violet Bonham Carter that Stephen feared Sassoon might shoot him. This seemed a spiral of craziness and self-absorption, exacerbated when Robert Graves asked, from Majorca and apparently forgetting the upset caused by *Goodbye*, 'I want to know whether you still have money in any quantity, and accessible, and if so whether you can lend me some. I need about a thousand pounds . . .'[78] Stupefied, Sassoon put the letter to one side but gave Blunden the first year's rent on his house and Burton £25 for a bridge in her garden and two weeks' holiday in Dieppe with Robbie Ross's niece.

Change came unexpectedly, brought about by a pageant at Wilton that celebrated the tercentenary of the death in 1633 of the poet George Herbert, an ancestor of Lord Pembroke, the owner of Wilton House. The actors were a mix of the famous, some local grandees and friends of the organizers, and Edith Olivier persuaded Sassoon to take part. Rex Whistler played Inigo Jones (architect of Wilton), Dean Inge from St Paul's played John Donne, Lord and Lady Pembroke took the roles of their ancestors; Sassoon agreed to be the Marquess of Hamilton, a nobleman in the retinue of King James I. Many people said that Siegfried Sassoon looked superb in his rich black and gold costume; he had always enjoyed dressing up, unless the occasion seemed too silly. The pageant itself was a series of *tableaux* in fancy dress evoking the atmosphere of an age, with music of the time. During rehearsals, a swan rose from the river and Sassoon thought of Stephen raised above humanity in white, his favourite colour: 'a supernatural omen of my love.'[79]

Among those involved in the pageant, playing King Charles I, was a young man called Richard Gatty, a relation of the Morrisons, a family who owned the neighbouring estate of Fonthill. Sassoon, introduced probably by Edith Olivier – who knew the Gattys through the Morrisons – spoke to Richard's sister Hester, 'a charming young lady who is a niece of Julia Horatia Ewing!', the children's writer. 'Miss G looked delightful in a lavender coloured silk dress (Charles I period).'[80] He put down a sprig of oak he had been carrying, and she kept it as a memento of a writer and a hero. That night Sassoon had dinner with David Cecil, the writer and Oxford don, and his wife Rachel, the daughter of Desmond MacCarthy, obviously a happily married young couple. To his surprise, he found that he had enjoyed the last three days.

The change continued: Ottoline Morrell visited him, zany but stimulating, and, towards the end of June, a new friend entered his life. The bibliophile and surgeon Geoffrey Keynes, brother of the economist Maynard Keynes, had been close to Theo Bartholomew, the Cambridge librarian who had advised Sassoon about his privately printed books of poems. In 1933, when Bartholomew died, Geoffrey Keynes wrote his obituary. He sent it to Sassoon, who asked him to Fitz House to advise on a new limited edition of his poems. Soon the veil of shyness lifted, for Sassoon immediately liked this 'very nice man, richly intelligent about books and life', only about six months younger than he was and slightly military in his abrupt, decisive way of talking.[81] Thinking that, as a doctor, Keynes might understand, he told him about the recluse at Swaylands.

Wilton, Keynes, the parties, the admiration and a resurgence of poetry offered at least a sporadic escape from self-pity. Thoughts of the pageant lingered; he sent a photograph of himself in fancy dress to Blunden. On 6 July he drove for dinner to Mells, a manor house in the Mendip Hills in Somerset, and enjoyed the Pre-Raphaelites on the walls and the old-fashioned, cultivated atmosphere created by its owners, Lady Horner and her daughter Katharine Asquith. He went to London, to stay with Geoffrey and Margaret Keynes in Hampstead. Margaret, one of Charles Darwin's granddaughters, was welcoming, Keynes showed him his book collection and they went to two ballets, meeting Lady Oxford who gave a remorseless analysis of Stephen's character that disconcerted Sassoon. Geoffrey

Keynes was a new light – 'a delightful man, and evidently likes me very much' – who had served as a doctor on the Western Front, revered creative artists, particularly poets, and wished for nothing better than to help, even to serve, them.[82] Sassoon was astonished at his own happiness during this summer, so much better than in 1932 or 1931. Edith Olivier now spoke of Stephen as if he were dead.

The obsession could rear up again. At Taplow Court, with the Desboroughs who had a large house party – the Bonham Carters, the Winston Churchills, Philip Sassoon and others – he lay sleepless, thinking of Stephen, now back at Wilsford after 305 nights away. Churchill, whom Sassoon had avoided since 1919, fearing seduction by his charm, prophesied war within twenty years and seemed to look forward to it although he had 'a son who would probably be killed'.[83] Philip Sassoon nervously asked him to Lympne, his house in Kent. Then he went north, to join the Keynes family in a rented holiday house near Alnwick in Northumberland. At Falloden, he found the blind, mournful Lord Grey who said of Stephen's mother, 'Anyhow Pamela was spared seeing my collapse,' and of Stephen, 'He would have *killed* her.'[84] Sassoon knew this was a last visit; the decrepit Grey could not live much longer. At their holiday cottage, the Keynes children played in the garden, someone practised the piano. It was a cheerful atmosphere: young people, closeness, laughter.

At Lympne, Philip Sassoon's house, Siegfried found Lord Berners; Lady Desborough; Rex Whistler, painting a mural in the hall; Penelope Dudley Ward, with whom Rex was in love; Noël Coward. Another guest, Anthony Eden, said he hoped for a crisis before the winter between Germany and Austria so that the League could turn on the Nazis; if not, there would be war in ten years. 'I gathered that he is something important,'[85] Sassoon noted of the then Parliamentary Under-Secretary at the Foreign Office. Cattiness surfaced after Rex left, the feline host and Berners complaining that he had not been amusing enough. The visit gave Siegfried Sassoon a vague hankering after high life, partly because he had been a success.

In London, Geoffrey Keynes showed him more treasures – pages from the manuscript of Darwin's *Origin of Species*, photographs of Rupert Brooke who had been at Cambridge with Keynes; Blake drawings; a 1542 herbal – and they went again to the ballet. A collector not only of books but of people he admired, Keynes, although married, had a strong strain of romantic homoeroticism that allowed for extra frankness with his new friend. In June 1933, writing to Sassoon about the ballet, he admitted that 'For [Serge] Lifar [the Russian–French dancer], I cherished the Grand Passion for several years, and one of the High Spots was when I helped him take off his clothes in his dressing room after Apollo. I don't suppose you were so foolish . . .'[86] And, a month later, after Sassoon had stayed with him in London, 'Your visit made me feel all nice . . .',[87] particularly when they had discussed ballet dancers. Sassoon showed him his diary of the affair with Tennant, and in July Keynes wrote of his interest in 'the story of two splendid lovers'.[88] Often the surgeon and bibliophile turned up at Fitz House, and later at Heytesbury in the company of young men with whom he had been camping or travelling; Margaret Keynes was not usually included in these expeditions.

Back at Fitz House, Sassoon sensed he had returned to nothing. He needed love; his poetry, he decided was passionless, his new collection, *Vigils*, too contemplative and valedictory: like a farewell to youth. The Hunters said that Stephen Tennant had ordered his brother David from the house for talking to the nurse in the library. That night Sassoon dreamed of Stephen again, a desperate dream. It was, he thought later, one of the worst times of his life. Geoffrey Keynes came down on 2 September. Sassoon urged him to try and see Stephen, so Keynes presented himself at Wilsford, saying he was the brother-in-law of the dancer Lydia Lopokova, Maynard Keynes's wife. Extraordinarily, he was admitted for twenty minutes, noticing Tennant's shaking hands but impressed by his knowledge of the ballet. Sassoon sensed some light. His spirits were also raised by the calligraphy of the privately printed edition of *Vigils* designed by

Stephen Gooden and produced under Keynes's supervision.[89] A routine began again: dinner with neighbours, riding, revising his poems.

On 5 September, he saw a young woman in a pink dress sketching near Fitz House, opposite the village school. She had been there the evening before when he had observed her 'nice' face, thinking it vaguely familiar. After he had left his car in the garage, she came over to introduce herself as Hester Gatty, reminding him that they had met at the Wilton pageant; Sassoon thought he had forgotten this because now she wore no make-up. He asked her to dinner, delighted to be reminded that she was a niece of the writer Julia Horatia Ewing whom Stephen and he admired. He noted a sense of unhappiness. The twenty-seven-year-old Hester Gatty was staying alone at the Black Horse in Teffont. To his surprise, he thought her attractive. 'Anyhow,' he thought, 'she is not likely to forget her evening with me, as I was at my best all the time, and we got on so easily.'[90]

EIGHTEEN

Hester: 'A flower has opened in my heart'

HESTER GATTY HAD been born in March 1906, some nineteen
years after Sassoon, the daughter of the colonial judge Sir Stephen
Gatty – once the Chief Justice of Gibraltar – and his second wife
Katharine who came from the rich Morrison family, the owners of
the Fonthill estate near Teffont. Sir Stephen, after the death of his
first wife, had married again, aged fifty-five. He died in 1922, when
Hester was only sixteen.

Sir Stephen Gatty's father was a clergyman, one-time vicar of
Ecclesfield in Cheshire and later sub-dean of York, and his mother a
writer of children's stories. His elder brother became, as Garter King
at Arms, the head of the College of Heralds; another brother,
Charles, wrote books and moved preciously through London draw-
ing rooms as a cultivated bachelor. But the best-known writer in
the family was Sir Stephen's sister, Julia Horatia Ewing, author of
Jackanapes, a Victorian children's story of courage and sacrifice.
Siegfried Sassoon liked another Gatty connection: that with Alexander Scott, Nelson's chaplain on the *Victory* and the father of Sir
Stephen's mother. The ethos of the Gattys was Victorian. As a child
Stephen Gatty had played charades with Tennyson at Farringford

and the Morrison textile fortune transformed Fonthill, Lady Gatty's childhood home, into a house of comfortable, pompous nineteenth-century prosperity after the darkly eccentric millionaire collector William Beckford had abandoned it in 1825.

Hester's childhood summers were spent mostly on the island of Mull off the west coast of Scotland, in a house at Lochbuie, first rented and then owned before it was sold in 1914 for fear of German U-boats. The Gattys, rich through Sir Stephen's marriage to Katharine Morrison, had two other houses, in Richmond, Surrey, and Ossemsley Manor near Christchurch in Hampshire. Hester was educated by governesses while her brothers, Richard and Oliver, went to public school and to Oxford, Oliver becoming a scholar and science tutor at Balliol. She did the London season as a débutante, worked as secretary to a scheme for helping unemployed young people, then fell in love with her unresponsive first cousin, Simon Morrison, and had a nervous breakdown. When Sassoon met her, she seemed delicate: Pre-Raphaelite and ethereal, a romantic who had suffered. Mull remained the place she loved best, for its grand landscape and for its isolation.

Hester had joined a literary group of about twenty young women called the Scratch Club that met in each other's houses. Some members of the Scratch Club became professional writers, like the biographer Georgina Blakiston and the novelist Jan Struther, later the author of *Mrs Miniver*; men who attended irregularly included Evelyn Waugh, Cyril Connolly and John Betjeman. Nancy Cunard and the black American actor and singer Paul Robeson came once, but only once. In December 1924, the Society published an anthology called *Ventures in Verse*; and the *Morning Post*, in an article headed 'The Muse's Kindergarten', praised Hester Gatty's two pieces as being 'full of the Celtic world-sorrow'.[1] By 1933 she had turned from poetry to painting, yet had been impressed enough by Sassoon at the Wilton pageant to set off on the sketching trips to Teffont.

*

THAT FIRST EVENING at Fitz House, Sassoon found out not only that Hester Gatty's mother had known Lady Grey but that her uncle, Charles Gatty, had written about Lady Grey's brother (and Stephen Tennant's uncle) George Wyndham, the Conservative politician, once the Chief Secretary for Ireland. Hester knew and disliked David Tennant; then they spoke briefly of Stephen. The next day she sketched in the Fitz House orchard; perhaps flustered, he went to Lake in the afternoon and ran into a car on the way. In the evening, again over dinner, he discovered that her breakdown had lasted for three years, ending only the previous year. On 7 September 1933, Sassoon took Hester over to Wilsford, where he learned from the Hunters that Lord Grey had died early that morning. Lady Gatty arrived at Teffont to fetch Hester and the girl's last longing look made him wonder if he had been too kind to her; 'it is almost alarming the way I draw people to me and then withdraw into my solitude'.[2]

He played Tchaikovsky's sixth symphony in melancholy regret and visitors came: Geoffrey Keynes, William Walton and Osbert Sitwell with Edith Olivier. Edith and Osbert had seen Stephen; both said he seemed well. Edith Olivier gave a party to which Sassoon went, seeing Evelyn Waugh ('very drunk, most unpleasant and vulgar'), and enjoyed it, dancing for the first time since 1921; 'it was such a contrast to my usual austere solitude'.[3]

At the start of October, Hester Gatty came over from Fonthill where she was staying with her aunt, Lady Morrison, and Sassoon drove her back to her home, Ossemsley Manor in the New Forest, a large ugly Edwardian house, where he met Hester's deaf, kindly mother, Lady Gatty. Hester intrigued him, she seemed out of place in Ossemsley's opulence, needing a world with more soul – a world which he could give her, yet 'how could she ever be happy with such an ultra-queer character as I am?' He imagined what he should say: 'look here, I am 47, and I have never had a love affair with a woman. The best thing you can do is never to see me again.' He knew she liked his fame. As for him, 'it is the nearest thing to love that I've felt since 1930 knocked me on the head'. He could feel attracted to women, although far less strongly than to men. Dorothy Hanmer, Delphine Turner, Phyllis Loder, Imma von Doernberg, perhaps Rosamond Lehmann: all these had attracted him, partly because of their admiration – a soft, slightly perplexed admiration, different from the hard celebrity-seeking of Lady Desborough, Violet Bonham Carter or even Ottoline Morrell – or their need for help, and partly because they were beautiful. Dorothy Hanmer had, at the start of the war, shown a way to respectability, to what he thought people wanted from him and what he wanted from himself. Hester might be the same, and might need help as well, so that he could see his healing power in her, as he had hoped to see it in Stephen. The act of helping her, and of pleasing her sexually, seemed suddenly arousing, even a possible redemption. Then might come a family, decency, a name passed on, the opposite of Wilsford.

The Hunters had sent him a calendar on which his poem 'Vision' was quoted: 'I love all things that pass.' The verses seemed suddenly what he must not be: retrospective, regretful, passion a glowing memory rather than a bright fire. Two days later, on the way to dinner at Mells, he decided he should marry Hester.

He went to London, possessed by the idea of love and of making Hester happy. They met at the National Gallery and although she had been going back to Ossemsley that evening Sassoon persuaded her to stay until the next day. They spoke of Stephen and Wilsford. When her taxi drew away at the end he exclaimed, 'Angel' – and stared into her grey-blue wide eyes. The next afternoon they went to Salisbury by train together in a first-class compartment that he had reserved. She said that he did not yet know her true self; then Sassoon kissed her, saying that she represented paradise, and watched her face transform, a reflection of his effect. At Salisbury, she left in her mother's car for Edith Olivier's house at Wilton and he drove to Teffont 'feeling like the king of the world'. That evening he had dinner with Edith, seeing Hester superb in a dark reddish dress with long diamond earrings. He thought, 'O Hester, you must redeem my life for me.'[4]

After breakfast the next day, he played the piano, almost crying with joy. He had cryptically told Edith Olivier of his feelings and went back that afternoon to Daye House, her home in the park at Wilton, staying there with Hester until 11.30. That swan at Wilton had been Stephen leaving him, Sassoon thought, not a reflection of what they had known together. 'In those 6 hours all the sadness and discomfort were smoothed out of her face and it seemed as though a new life had come into her eyes,'[5] he wrote of Hester, seeing again an apparent triumph of his healing powers. In this new heterosexual romance, he studied himself as closely as the object of his love.

Hester went to Ossemsley, wanting to tell her mother at once. At Fitz House, Sassoon played Bach, again near to tears. He went to London again, first reading an ecstatic letter from Lady Gatty; one from Hester ('divinely lovely')[6] he kept for the train. At Waterloo she met him. 'Where shall we go?' she asked. They went to the Tate Gallery and sat in front of Stanley Spencer's huge painting *Resurrection*, thinking it not really good but not caring one way or the other. And there was a coincidence; he said that after he took her to Wilsford he had heard her voice calling to him at night, and she replied that she felt sure she had been thinking of him then. Afterwards she wrote, 'If I send you my love, it is not big enough for what is here. I think that love itself is in me.' He sat clutching the letter, almost hysterical and half crying. The affair seemed 'like believing in God'.[7]

What did Hester find in Siegfried that made her love for him seem so vast? Her passion was intense. Laurence Whistler thought that Hester had a strongly sexual femininity, subdued by her Gatty Victorian upbringing and still latent when she and Sassoon met. To others, like her friend Miriam Rothschild, she seemed in need of protection and perhaps he – as an older man – may have inspired subconscious hopes of a replacement for a dead father. Then the mystique of Siegfried Sassoon, his fame as a writer and as a war hero, must have seemed alluring. He was attractive, poetically handsome, gentle and sympathetic in manner yet with a strongly masculine presence. Hester went after him; the sketching trip to

Teffont was an attempt to take further their first meeting at the Wilton pageant. And to both, marriage gave a romantic way out of an emotional cul-de-sac: his impasse with Stephen Tennant, and the bleak aftermath of her nervous breakdown.

As with Stephen, Sassoon wanted to protect her from the world. He was angry when they lunched at Claridge's and saw Osbert Sitwell, Nancy Mitford, Cecil Beaton, Tilly Losch and Randolph Churchill – some of the greatest gossips that he knew. The Hunters told him that Stephen did not want to see anyone until the spring. Far now from this, he took Hester to St Paul's, where they looked at one of his uncle Hamo's monuments, and, back at Lowndes Square, he met Oliver, her brilliant brother. Hester was physically fragile, her doctor advising that she should not have a child for the first two years of marriage.

They planned to marry at the end of April and he set about telling his friends. The Hunters he knew would be happy, with a twinge of regret; 'it means the end of so much for them'. At Daye House he introduced Hester to Glen and Angela Byam Shaw, saying, 'I am very happy. This is the reason.'[8] He prepared his mother by asking her neighbour, Mrs Hussey, who knew Hester, to mention it to Theresa. Not until 25 October did he write to her: 'I have the most joyful news for you, and my only fear is that the excitement it causes will be bad for you.' He mentioned Hester's links to Mrs Ewing and to Nelson's chaplain and her beauty, 'dignity', intelligence, good sense, sweetness of character and understanding of music and poetry. One more 'sordid' detail for 'I know you like facts': 'Hester has about £2,000 a year of her own.'[9] Then he took her to Weirleigh where Theresa said she was the daughter-in-law of her dreams.

Searching for somewhere to live, they looked at a house that Sassoon had once admired. In September he had driven past it with the Hunters and said that if he had two lives he would like one as an 'easy-going country gentleman. And this is where I'd like to do it.'[10] A large, barrack-like, grey-stone Georgian mansion, surrounded by fine trees, set back from the village of Heytesbury in the

Wylye valley, it was a much more substantial property than Fitz House or Weirleigh, with 90 acres of parkland and 130 acres of woods. His decision to buy it was, perhaps, a reflection of his experience of country-house life at Wilsford where, despite Stephen's moods, Sassoon had found an English paradise; now he would show Tennant that he could make a paradise of his own, this time a genuinely eighteenth-century one, not an Arts and Crafts pastiche. The owner, Captain Jump, was asking £20,000, which seemed a colossal sum, but Hester had her income and there was the money left to him by his aunt Rachel Beer, whose portrait he hung in the new house's library.

Cecil Beaton told Stephen about the engagement and Tennant burst into tears; people must not abandon him, certainly not people to whom he had given his love. Hester wanted Siegfried to write to Stephen Tennant and exorcize this ghost. Sassoon too felt a presence between them. Stephen had now told Edith Olivier that he felt 'very angry and jealous'. The letter was hard to compose:

> *My dear Stephen, I have always wished and strived for your happiness and well-being, and I hope that you will wish for mine. Let us, at any rate, forget the unhappiness of the past 2 or 3 years, and be thankful for the wonderful harmony which we shared before that.*
>
> *You are, I hope, beginning, a new life of recovery and health, and I send you my heart's blessing, that you may find all that can truly compensate you for what you have endured through your long illness and solitude.*
>
> *I cannot say more than that, can I? – not now. S.S.*

After writing this, Sassoon lay on his bed for two hours, 'feeling like death'.[11] On 14 November came Stephen's response:

> *My dear Sieg. I thought I heard you calling me – I dreamed that you said my name urgently, tell me if you did, – but I expect it was only my fancy. It was this morning, and also something like it yesterday. Oh Sieg, I went to Stonehenge on*

Saturday! – and put my hands on the grey lichens, – and somehow the happiness had the quality of terribleness that all deep emotion has. And all round the undulating downs in chilled silver air. Would you let me still to be your friend? I always would anyway wether [sic] you wished it or not, Edith tells me how happy you are. Love Stephen.

Sassoon answered,

My dear Stephen. When you have made someone into a Stonehenge it is not altogether easy to bring them back to life again. But I accept your letter in the spirit in which it was written, rejoicing that you are well enough to visit our venerable Wilts monument, past which I have ridden so many times in the past 2 years. I am glad also that you wish me to remain your 'invisible friend', and look forward to the time when you feel able to face 'visibility'. My tenancy here ends on January 28, but 'letters will be forwarded' if you feel like writing to me before 'spring breaks through again'. S.S.[12]

The letter seems to mix a slight triumphalism towards his former torturer and a reluctance to say goodbye. On 6 November notice of the engagement appeared in *The Times*. By the 20th they had decided to bring the wedding date forward to 16 December, at Christchurch, near Hester's home.

Sassoon knew his friends would be amazed. 'I have given you all a surprise, haven't I?'[13] he wrote to Roderick Meiklejohn. He sent Ralph Hodgson a photograph of Hester, saying how she loathed 'smartness', played the piano well, had a gentle voice and belonged 'to the "pre-make-up" period'.[14] To Geoffrey Keynes, he said how lonely the last three years had been; also how sure he was that he and Hester were 'made for one another'.[15] Edith Olivier told Henry and Ruth Head of this 'quiet serene beauty' with 'a very good brain and a very lovely nature'. Now at last 'Siegfried' looked 'well and un-nervy' and spoke of curing Hester by happiness.[16] Ruth Head exclaimed, 'O Siegfried, the joy of thinking you HAPPY' after 'your utter loneliness'.[17] To Burton it was wonderful that Sassoon was rid of Stephen, whom she compared to Lord Alfred Douglas. Stephen was often in tears, saying he felt completely alone; and other women like Violet Bonham Carter and Lady Desborough felt bereft. Blunden expressed pleasant surprise and Osbert Sitwell, saying how delightful Hester had looked at Claridge's, wished him happiness in this 'appalling world'.[18] Ottoline, meeting Hester, told Sassoon that she was 'a perfect darling';[19] then T. E. Lawrence came to Fitz House and approved.

But E. M. Forster wrote chidingly, as if Sassoon was betraying his kind, and what people said among themselves was often different to the ecstatic letters. Some saw in Hester a resemblance to Stephen Tennant (although photographs scarcely show this); and Ottoline Morrell, in her journal, found her 'delicate' and 'rather unremarkable', probably not 'very passionate' and thought that 'Happiness won't feed his muse.'[20] When they spoke of the Sitwells, he said, 'You see Ottoline, I couldn't take Hester among them. It would be desecration.'[21] Virginia Woolf joked to her nephew Quentin Bell about 'S.S.'s defecting' and how this had upset other homosexuals, particularly 'the lilies of the valley':[22] the writers Stephen Spender, William Plomer, W. H. Auden and J. R. Ackerley, all of whom lived in Maida Vale. Robert Graves asked, 'Is this story about you true, or a newspaper stunt? Good luck anyway.'[23] Sassoon's answer to him was the 199th letter he had written since 1 November. Edith Sitwell told her sister-in-law Georgia that the rescue of Hester from a nervous breakdown was 'bosh' as a basis for marriage.[24]

Fabers published *The Road to Ruin* on 9 November; 3,000 copies were printed of these seven poems about the possible catastrophe of another war and reviewers wrote of declining powers. For the moment, Sassoon had little time to brood. In the second week of December, he recorded that Heytesbury had been bought for £13,000. Staring at his new domain, he felt he was 'walking calmly into the first volume of a Trollope novel'.[25] The wedding arrangements were made, Sassoon mildly put out to discover that the vicar had not heard of him.

The ceremony, on 18 December, was a muted affair but with a full choir and a team of bell-ringers. Theresa, still unwell, stayed away. Glen Byam Shaw was the best man, and the only steadying drink the bridegroom took beforehand was a glass of milk. The guest list was restricted to about twenty close friends, among them Rex Whistler, T. E. Lawrence (who came on his motorbicycle Boanerges), Geoffrey Keynes and Hester's old French governess, who whispered to Sassoon that he should be firm with his wife. When he and Glen arrived at Christchurch Priory, the first person they saw was Lawrence, now Aircraftman Shaw, standing by the door. In the cool sun, Hester wore a white satin dress, a lace veil and a Russian crown-shaped tiara; light flooded the church through its long windows, and friends of the Gattys wrote that the groom had 'a wonderful face' and seemed 'so engaging and intriguing'.[26] The couple went straight to the Hyde Park Hotel in London, then to Tunbridge Wells for Christmas to be near Weirleigh. Theresa had written, 'I do not want to be greedy – but I do want to see as much of you both as I can . . . Goodbye beloved. May God's blessing be on you both . . .'[27] Then they returned to Fitz House, where, at the start of January 1934, Sassoon wrote in his diary, 'Hester makes life so easy and unintrospective that I scarcely know I'm alive.'[28]

On 26 January, E. M. Forster, who two years later pronounced himself 'half in love'[29] with Hester, saw them off from Tilbury on a honeymoon that took them first to Algeciras in Spain – which Hester had loved since her childhood in Gibraltar – and on to the same places, even to the same hotels, visited by Sassoon and Stephen Tennant on their odyssey of three years before. They were at Algeciras until 27 February, then Malaga, Algiers, Naples, Palermo, Syracuse, Genoa, Rapallo and the Beerbohms (for two weeks) before Saint-Germain until 15 May, and back at Heytesbury three days later to find a cricket match in progress on the pitch in the park. The world outside intruded seldom, sometimes unpleasantly. A review of *The Road to Ruin* in the *Times Literary Supplement* upset Hester by criticizing the poems' 'faint sarcasms' and the impression of 'a voice speaking too far from the mouthpiece of a telephone';[30]

Sassoon suspected Middleton Murry. The *London Mercury* also disliked these 'embittered war poems', much less effective than earlier work like the 'Menin Gate'.[31]

*

SASSOON HAD CHOSEN Sicily to make a new set of memories, and Hester seemed to be a healer. He drew caricatures, they looked at sites, she wrote home ecstatically and Sassoon did his utmost to please her in their lovemaking, to meet what he saw as marriage's obligations and to be gentle with her frailty. In the hotels they shared a room; at Heytesbury this was not to be, and at first Hester accepted it as a writer's need to work at night, to keep odd hours of solitude.

Sassoon had already reassured Ralph Hodgson that six indoor servants would not change him and that he wanted the place to be 'an earthly paradise for my few real friends to see me in' with everything the same as at Fitz House, 'only nicer'.[32] He took up cricket again and, as owner of the ground, adopted the local team, Edmund Blunden later joining him in these matches, even bringing an eleven of his own over from Oxford. Visitors began to come: Forster, Glen Byam Shaw, Geoffrey Keynes, Sassoon's and Hester's family, Edith Olivier and the Hunters. By 30 June, Sassoon craved to be alone, and drove thirty-five miles on a route that included Wilsford. Hester and Heytesbury seemed now to be his calm 'fortress'[33] but he thought sometimes of the tormenting excitement of the Tennant affair. Violet Bonham Carter was heavily patronizing to Hester. When Blunden came, Sassoon regretted not being able to have long talks alone with his friend, whose new wife, Sylva Norman, he found pretentious and intrusive. Soon he saw Edmund as being such an important part of Heytesbury life – with his love of cricket, gentle literary talk and understanding of Sassoon's poetry – that he christened one of the huge trees in the park Blunden's Beech.

'I am too comfortable,' he thought – without turmoil or challenge. And Hester's emotional and physical demands – not so much sexual as the constant wish for signs of his love – were wearing and made writing hard. Every evening she liked to tuck Sassoon up as she termed it. There were moments of childlike bliss, as when he bowled to her on the lawn or saw the dog Sheltie and his wife both running towards him, and these were comfortable, sentimental moments, not passionate, and inspired poems not of great love but more of gratitude for having been rescued. Heytesbury had stables and a groom, and Sassoon, by September, had a mare to ride, a quiet creature, not as exciting as Silvermane, 'that beautiful fanatic'[34] of Wilsford.

Their bedrooms were separate. Downstairs, Heytesbury had the full country-house array of dining room, drawing room, library and nether regions for the servants and kitchen quarters, with a garden tended by five men. The place was like a small kingdom – his childhood dream of a home like Finchcocks had come true. It seemed a worthy replacement, or rival, for Wilsford. But was he too old to have started out on all this? Hester took against William Walton and imagined people like Hilaire Belloc were bored by her, although she worshipped T. E. Lawrence. When she went for a night to Ossemsley in August, Sassoon felt relieved. That month Ottoline Morrell came and thought them great friends rather than lovers, rather too pleased to be out of touch with the world. Surely, she thought, it was fatal to live in a vast, isolated house.[35]

He loved the beauty: a clear August night with a full moon, motionless trees throwing shadows over the long lawns and park; the peace. After visiting Lord and Lady Heytesbury, whose family had once owned the house, he even thought of writing a historical fantasy about his new home. Hester wanted to make a studio to paint in next to the library, so he found a new work room on the top floor. She bought a pony, indicating to Sassoon that his solitary rides would soon be no more. In October he hunted again, and once the hounds went near Wilsford, that 'memory haunted country'.[36] One night in November he dreamed of a cold, inhuman Stephen, and all the next day felt depressed.

In December, Sassoon and Hester broke their isolation by going to London where, after a performance of Walton's unfinished first symphony, they dined at Wimborne House with the full complement of bright people. He thought his wife, in a grey dress and her grandmother's golden head-band, the most beautiful person there; Osbert Sitwell said that Somerset Maugham had been completely charmed by her. That month he felt had been their happiest yet, and 'to have made a success of the first year is all that matters – (and to have escaped from the entangling past)'.[37] On the last day of 1934, he contemplated the future. He had eleven servants (six inside and five outside), a dog, two mares and a wife so was not alone as he heard the bells of Heytesbury church. Yet, during this, 'the most consistently happy year of my life', all his talks with Hester, or all the amusing ones, had been about the past. 'I am re-creating, not creating – life in my mind.'[38]

What had he written during this time that mixed bliss and uncertainty? At the end of October he finished two Armistice Day poems which he sent to *Time and Tide* and the *Spectator*; writing was 'the only thing that matters to me at present',[39] the justification for his life. The post-war poets – Auden, Spender and the great figure of modernism, 'Towering Tom' (T. S. Eliot) – were pushing him to the margin, however much he might dismiss them in conversation with Blunden, Hodgson, Tomlinson and others. Some of his poems were domestic – like 'Property' ('Upstairs among my books . . .') – or affirmations of the power of poetry. 'Ode' meditates on man's search for the eternal, 'Gloria Mundi' shows autumn's transitory beauty, 'Thanksgiving' celebrates Sassoon's rescue by Hester, and 'The Gains of Good' is about the strength of virtue. In December came another lament for lost youth, 'Long Ago'. 'Possibly Poem', of the same month, is a take-off of modernism, an attack on its obscurity. On 27 December he wrote 'Anno Domini', on age again and that paradox of wanting serenity yet fearing its effect on his work.[40]

Not even he, in his kingdom of Heytesbury, could escape the threat of war and political chaos. Sassoon read with horror about the Nazis, and his poem, 'The Writing on the Wall', published in the *Left Review* in October 1934, is an allegorical view of their inhumanity. 'Alarums' evokes the panic; 'Asking for It' condemns the arms race; 'Memorandum' contemplates humanity's giving way to its bad instincts; while 'Again the Dead' resembles those laments for the slaughtered youth of the Great War.[41] In 1935, he became more involved with the Peace Pledge Union, formed a year earlier by Canon Dick Sheppard, the rector of St Martin-in-the-Fields church in Trafalgar Square. Attracting such disparate figures as Lord Cecil of Chelwood, Norman Angell, the philosophers C. E. M. Joad and Bertrand Russell, the communist Harry Pollitt and an estimated 100,000 members by 1936, it appealed to men of military service age to renounce war. The Peace Pledge Union was moved by the dread that the next conflict would be worse even than the last, particularly for civilians, and culminated in the Peace Ballot of 1934–5, organized by the League of Nations Union, which showed an anti-war feeling and dislike of rearmament. Sassoon contributed the poem 'Asking for It' to the collection *We Did Not Fight 1914–18, Experiences of War Resisters*, with essays by David Garnett, Bertrand Russell and Norman Angell.

In July 1935 he agreed reluctantly, and only on condition that Blunden performed as well, to read at a peace meeting in the Albert Hall where his rendering of 'Have You Forgotten Yet?' was electrifying: 'one of the most impressive things I have ever heard',[42] Dick Sheppard told Hester. At the end of 1936 in Birmingham Town Hall, at a meeting attended by 3,000 people with 1,500 in an overflow room, Aldous Huxley, the Labour politician George Lansbury and the retired solder Brigadier General F. P. Crozier spoke under an immense red banner inscribed, 'War will cease when men refuse to fight',[43] raising the iniquities of nationalism and the Versailles Treaty, the 'mad' armaments race and the uselessness of the League of Nations without pacifism and an economic union of Europe. Sassoon read his poems for ten minutes, and performed in the same month at a gathering in the Albert Hall. By then his pacifism was faltering in the face of reports from Nazi Germany. 'It is a pretty murky time for non-resisters, isn't it?'[44] he told Sheppard.

But the campaign shaped politicians' behaviour and the emergence of the policy of appeasement in the 1930s.

*

THE DOMESTICITY OF Heytesbury covered Sassoon like a warm blanket. One occupation, showing how much time he had on his hands, was the drawing of Max Beerbohm-type caricatures of the Sitwells, depicting Osbert as a grotesque, conceited personification of authority, a cross between grand aristocrat, circus ringmaster, heavyweight boxer, racehorse owner, emperor, bishop and pope while Edith watches in wilting arrogance. In the middle of January 1935, he felt pleased by a poem about dreams of youth and wrote two others in February, but spent much time decorating manuscripts in watercolours. Now Sassoon often took dinner in bed, to make time for late writing. Then he started a prose fantasy based on life at Wilsford, reaching 20,000 words, but found it intolerable to write about bad memories. He sold a poem celebrating George V's silver jubilee to *Harper's Bazaar* – 'a counter-blast to pacifists' – and refused to sign an anti-royalist letter in the *Left Review*.[45]

On 17 May 1935, Sassoon heard of T. E. Lawrence's motorcycle crash. At first it seemed that Lawrence might survive; then, on the 19th, he died. Sassoon could not bear to speak of the tragedy to Hester and stamped out of the room. That night, near dawn, he felt a hand touch his head, followed by a flood of reassurance; it must have been a man, he thought, because Hester would have laid her hand there longer. On the way to the funeral, Sassoon told Hester, who said she had felt the same; he believed that it was evidence of T.E.'s supernatural powers. At the village church at Moreton in Dorset, near Lawrence's last home at Clouds Hill, the mourners included Florence Hardy and E. M. Forster, with Winston Churchill crying by the grave. Sassoon rebuked three photographers who came too close. He wrote a poem about Lawrence, sending it to Marsh, who thought rightly that the lines were better unpublished, and, when Geoffrey Keynes questioned him relentlessly about T.E., began to fear the same picking over the dead as had happened with Hardy.

More sorrow came when Anzie Wylde, his friend since the early Schuster days, dropped dead in the south of France.

A. W. Lawrence (T.E.'s brother) rang to say he wanted Sassoon to help the producer Korda with a film of *Revolt in the Desert*, if only to keep Robert Graves out of it. Lawrence's old comrade, Colonel W. L. Stirling, became involved and Korda promised a fee of £2,000. Sassoon wanted to stress the mystical side and to keep the lyricism of *The Seven Pillars*, but in July, at a meeting in London with Alexander and Zoltan Korda and their scriptwriter Lajos Biro, the scheme started to fall apart when Biro wanted only a simple outline. Sassoon's efforts at scriptwriting seem to have been eccentric, with much of the narrative spoken off the screen and the Arab characters talking in Arabic. By September his involvement was dwindling. The last drawing in his outline notes is of the Arab Auda saying, 'The Kordas can go and f— themselves,' to which Lawrence answers, 'Good!'[46] All this interrupted his struggle to finish the next Sherston volume, which Hester typed for him.

Sometimes he dreamed agonizingly of Stephen, who wrote plaintive letters, one blaming himself, for 'I can never find words to express how fine you were.'[47] Sassoon had written him such a kind letter; 'in the desolation of my loneliness it was like food to the starving'. Stephen measured everyone against him now.[48] Hester offered to leave him for three months or more if it would help his writing; quickly he said he needed only an occasional couple of solitary days. Then, in September 1935, she became pregnant and had a miscarriage. She went away, first to Ossemsley and then to London, for over a month, from 7 November until 16 December, to let him work.

In spite of the memoirs, poetry was still the part of his writing that Sassoon cherished most, now often poems of nostalgia and pastoral yearning or poems about the past's echoes in his present life, the titles showing their atmosphere: 'In Heytesbury Wood', 'A Pilgrim's Progress', 'Vigil in Spring', 'Eulogy of My House' and 'On Edington Hill'.[49] In September he produced 'T.E.L.' about light and life withdrawing until Lawrence becomes 'this legend mask of stone'.[50] Sassoon's fear of another war is manifest in 'Here on His Way to Eathundun, King Alfred Passed' when he wonders if Wiltshire was madder then than now as aeroplanes drone overhead. In 'Silver Jubilee Celebrations', he satirized Kipling's speech to the Royal Society of St George when he claimed the country must 'arm or perish'.[51]

The publication of *Vigils* by Heinemann in November 1935 was the first public airing of his poetry – apart from the short, polemical *Road to Ruin* – since *The Heart's Journey* of 1928. The reviewers generally ignored it or were harsh, although Edmund Blunden offered a counterbalance in a 'quite perfect review'[52] in the *Listener* that saw the book as a return to an older tradition than the war poems: one of 'beautiful though tentative' evocations of boyhood and a response, like Vaughan's, to an invisible vastness. In a letter to Sassoon, Edith Sitwell called the book 'truthful, bare, controlled, and fiery and deeply moving'.[53] *Vigils* has an atmosphere of gentleness and middle-aged melancholy, of pastoral charm and beauty, that seemed to many a regrettably ethereal response to the terrifying times. The poems predate Heytesbury and marriage and include an elegy to Rivers and 'In Sicily', inspired by the weeks there with Stephen. The dissonances, learned from Hardy, pile up: 'reillumes', 'sigil', 'trophydoms', 'tragi-tone', 'inbreathed', 'firstling', 'armamental', breaking, but not lifting, the collection's slightly mournful spirit.

*

ON 9 JANUARY 1936, Siegfried Sassoon finished volume three of his Sherston memoirs and felt raised up by 'my lovely heart-breaking book which is like life – laughter and tears'.[54] Fabers, obviously pleased, gave him an advance of £750 and (with the help of a new literary agent, J. Pinker) he obtained a $4,000 advance from the American publisher Doubleday. Forster, at Heytesbury for a fortnight, recovering from a prostate operation, seems to have been only quietly favourable, disappointing to its author who longed for his good opinion. By 3 March Hester was in her sixth week of another pregnancy, anxious after the previous miscarriage and not wanting to see people.

Two weeks later, Sassoon had started to make notes for a book about his childhood, having tried a counter-attack on the forces that had disparaged *Vigils*. This, appearing in the *Spectator* on 31 January, is a facetious article about modernism in which the writer reads his ancient 'Aunt Eudora' poems by Auden, Empson, Ronald Bottrall and Rex Warner and thinks 'how I wish the young poets of 1935 would try to express themselves less artificially'.[55] The piece was followed by another, this time called 'Educating Aunt Eudora'; for Sassoon, modern poetry drove 'unliterary' readers away through its obscurity, didacticism, obsession with Freud and frantic attempts to depict the 'machine age'.[56] Michael Roberts, poet and editor of the influential *Faber Book of Modern Verse*, wrote 1,150 words in protest and Sassoon replied that 'I am a pre-machine age poet, and therefore hopelessly old-fashioned. Schubert-minded, I crave tunefulness!'[57] He followed this with another article in June. Three new poets gave him hope through their traditional 'tunefulness': Christopher Hassall, Ruth Pitter and Rex Whistler's brother Laurence. When Laurence Whistler's collection was treated roughly in the *Spectator* by Michael Roberts, Sassoon wrote to the magazine to protest. But his own work suffered too. W. B. Yeats's eccentric *Oxford Book of Modern Verse* of 1936 inveighed against war poets in its introduction and included only two pages of Sassoon and three of Thomas Hardy against seventeen of W. J. Turner and sixteen of the editor's friend, Dorothy Wellesley.

The Beerbohms came to Heytesbury, Max's urbanity making all other guests seem crass. Now Sassoon wanted to get on with his memoir of childhood, 'my only escape from boredom and enforced activity'.[58] The omens seemed good for *Sherston's Progress*, the title changed from the earlier *Further Experiences of George Sherston*. Fabers printed 15,720 and the advance sales reached nearly 11,000; the book was the *Evening Standard* 'Book of the Month' and a

Book Society Choice, and extracts appeared in *Nash's Pall Mall Gazette*.

There was bound to be excitement about the successor to the bestselling *Memoirs of a Fox-hunting Man* and *Memoirs of an Infantry Officer*. *Sherston's Progress* begins where the *Infantry Officer* had ended, with the arrival of its hero at Craiglockhart (called Slateford). Rivers is its dominant figure whose moral power, as Sassoon wrote earlier, had pursued him 'like the Hound of Heaven'.[59] He hoped to contrast his own, or Sherston's, 'crudity and incoherence of thought' with the doctor's 'exactitude', tolerance and patience. Rivers meant an end to the fear of prison and hospital. He could not be bluffed, though. From the first meeting, Sassoon – and Sherston – trusted and 'loved' this infinitely patient man. So Rivers becomes almost divine, the only character in the Sherston memoirs whose name is not changed, a symbol of 'reality and integrity in all that muddle'[60] of the war.

The book, begun not only from 'need of money' but to fill those low hours in Fitz House, then continued 'to show H. what I could do',[61] had been hard to write and has an episodic feel, as though the words were not coming as easily as before. George Sherston is still the same sweet, credulous narrator, seeking enlightenment, and *Sherston's Progress* has as its epigraph the quotation from *Pilgrim's Progress*, 'I told him that I was a Pilgrim, going to the Celestial City.' The possibilities for seriousness were great in describing the protest and his possible shell-shock but Sassoon diminished these by 'forced facetiousness',[62] to show Sherston's modesty and humour, which contributes to making the book less powerful than its predecessors. He had dreaded it being boring; the Mister and the Irish hunting scenes were, he thought, its best part. For Palestine and the first weeks of the return to France, he abandons fresh composition and uses his diary entries, slightly sanitized, with hints of sexual interest usually removed except 'Howitt' asleep 'with his moody sensual face and large limbs'; the entries about the soldier Linthwaite, to whom Sassoon had also been attracted, leave out anything too suggestive. Again some of the changed names have links to the originals: Linthwaite becomes Stonethwaite, Pinto is Velmore, the name of the street where he lived in the 1930s. Owen is left out completely. There is no poetry, and a rare glimpse of serious contemporary writing comes when Sherston reads Barbusse at 'Slateford' and Duhamel in France.

Despite the 'forced facetiousness', the book has an edge, as in the description of the wounded in France and even during the scenes in Ireland where one jolly landowner's village is merely 'an assortment of stone hovels in very bad repair' and the narrator thinks that the Mister would have been equally welcoming to Field Marshal von Hindenburg as to the British officers. At the end, Sherston is in hospital in London after his last wound, 'my mind in a muddle': a quiet finale with the observation that, if war continued as part of progress, the Prussian militarist way was best. Then comes the arrival in the ward of his saviour to whom Sherston, childlike, says, 'Oh Rivers, I've had such a funny time since I saw you last!' The last words are quietist: 'it is only from the inmost silences of the heart that we know the world for what it is, and ourselves for what the world has made us'.

Howard Spring in the *Evening Standard* thought the three volumes of memoirs gave Sassoon 'a place unique in English letters',[63] in the *Times Literary Supplement* Blunden praised 'the watchful quietness of spirit'[64] and in the *Observer* Ivor Brown attacked modernism, saying that Sherston showed that 'perhaps, even today, there is some life in sanity still'.[65] Others wrote enthusiastically, Forster saying that he too had liked the Irish bits and found in the war scenes one great erotic excitement: the description of a young officer asleep that 'happened to ring my bell'.[66] From County Limerick, Mrs O'Kelly gave news of the Mister: 'old now and his old house is crumbling around him and he wanders the roads fuddled and poor'.[67] But there were dissenting voices. In the *Morning Post*, Graham Greene, later a non-combatant in the Second War, jibed at Sherston cleaning his golf clubs at Craiglockhart during the battle of Passchendaele and called the book padded out, facetious and cliché-ridden.[68] Ottoline Morrell hated it: 'so jocular, "schoolboyish" and flippant' except for the 'real and sincere' hunting scenes in Ireland.[69] To John Brophy, in the *Sunday Times*, the prose was platitudinous and Basil de Selincourt, in the *Manchester Guardian*, disliked the 'over-refinement' of a style too literary for the horrors of the war.[70] In the *Listener* Christopher Isherwood was hostile, not openly rude.

'These people – sophisticated as they are –', Sassoon grumbled to Ruth Head, 'hate Sherston for being simple.'[71] Rivers, he felt, was 'the solution of the whole 3 volumes' of memoirs, 'as he was in my own life up to 1922' and afterwards through Sassoon's memory of him and his imagined reactions and advice. He admitted he might have 'overdone'[72] the clichés and the facetiousness in the search for a natural style, particularly in the Craiglockhart ('Slateford') scenes, which he had found very hard to write. The book sold over 12,000 in four weeks.

He still had that dread of the next war, 'like the idea of the end of the world'.[73] Hester had been left £5,000 by her aunt Dorothy, and in October they went to London, having rented 18 Hanover Terrace in Regent's Park, next to the Gosses' old home, because her doctor had said they should be within reach of expert medical help. On 30 October, Siegfried and Hester's son was born, Glen Byam Shaw sitting with Sassoon downstairs during the birth. The next day he wrote in his diary, 'Nothing more to worry about now. Hester and I have our little son and we are completely happy.' This was, for him, 'the best thing life can give'.[74]

NINETEEN

'A bullying barbarian of a world'

SASSOON TOLD THE Heads that the baby looked very like him: 'quite extraordinary. His mouth was firmly closed and his face had a most resolute expression, as though he knew that life wasn't going to be easy, in spite of his good fortune in being heir to Heytesbury House and a heredity of "all the talents".'[1] His only worry was that he would be too indulgent a father. The child was to be called George (as in Sherston) Thornycroft (Theresa's maiden name) and Dick Sheppard christened him on 28 November 1936 in St Martin-in-the-Fields. Edith Olivier was godmother, Blunden joined Max Beerbohm, Glen Byam Shaw and one of Hester's brothers as a godfather, and the increasingly frail Ottoline Morrell attended. Two days later, the fifty-year-old Sassoon carried George in a cradle through the front door of Heytesbury.

*

IN 1936, THERE had been a pause before a rush of poetry at the year's end. In July, 'A Message for Time' (later called 'Midsummer Eve') wonders if time destroys or wisely preserves in memory, and in October 'A Prayer from 1936' finds relief from the threat of war in music. In December, after the birth of George, came the euphoric 'To My Son', wishing for a possible hero's life; and then 'Earth and Heaven', about harmony arising from good deeds. 'Outlived by

Trees' goes back to immutability at Heytesbury, given more hope now by its infant heir.[2]

In the New Year, Sassoon heard of the suicide of Julian Dadd, racked by overwork and memories of the war. Recollected horror took him to Bristol on 13 January 1937, to read nine of his poems at a meeting of the Peace Pledge Union. Happily there were better, if sometimes gilded, memories. By 23 March he had given 27,000 words of his memoirs of childhood to Hester to type, telling Blunden that the book, to be called *The Old Century*, deliberately avoided 'unflinching self-revelation'.[3]

In April Hester and Siegfried went to Rapallo and saw the Beerbohms on most days, listening to Max's mellifluous malice, deflating aphorisms, memories of the 1890s and disdain for the present. The German writer Gerhard Hauptmann, also in Rapallo, thought Sassoon charmingly boyish. Hauptmann's son said the Nazis would not last, as Hitler had cancer of the throat, and Beerbohm, putting flippancy aside, declared that Britain must stand up to them. Max read the early chapters of *The Old Century*, thinking them 'like going into a garden at 6 o'clock on a summer morning': childhood as it was to a child. He added, 'Don't be afraid of being too long. Write whatever seems to you amusing and interesting.'[4] That August, Sassoon, to confirm what he had already written, went back to Edingthorpe, the Norfolk village where Theresa had taken them when he was eleven years old.

By September, the old complaint had returned – he was not alone enough – added to now by his wife's irritating preoccupation with George. Hester wanted to go off on her own and paint, and suddenly he had a dread of what might happen if she left him: the isolation, a return to the darkness of those lonely days in Fitz House, tormented by Stephen Tennant. On his birthday, there was champagne and a present of carefully chosen rare books from Hester. Sassoon seemed almost reluctant to unwrap the books, fell asleep after dinner and refused to make love to her ('I dreaded emotion').[5] She wept the next day and they had lunch separately: she upstairs and he in the dining room. In November he worked every night from midnight to 5 a.m.; by 21 December, part one of *The Old Century* was being set up in type. The book was to be dedicated to Max Beerbohm.

At the end of 1937, he assessed the new, young poets. Auden was often repellent but had 'a real poetic gift', MacNeice 'has some poetry in him, I think';[6] far better were Ruth Pitter, Laurence Whistler and Christopher Hassall, all boycotted by fashionable critics. His own work of this year included an embarrassing – and mercifully unpublished – 'Coronation Ode'[7] and 'Ideologies', a facetious poem about how 'experimental' notions are ignored by history. He wrote the usual evocations of landscape and place: the completion of 'Midsummer Eve', then 'A Remembered Queen', about Queen Matilda's twelfth-century chapel near Heytesbury. In 'Wealth of Awareness', he stands alone in contemplation on the lawn on a summer night; 'Old World to New' imagines how he would seem to the far future;[8] the unpublished 'Ancestral Admonition'[9] addresses a great-grandson at Heytesbury. In August Sassoon wrote an elegy to Dick Sheppard, who had died ('here's heaven on earth for friends beloved and dead').[10] Then, in 'Meeting and Parting'[11] – one of his most heartfelt poems – he describes meeting George's eyes, the eyes of a child 'doomed to live' who will stand at Sassoon's deathbed, and asks for forgiveness. In January 1938, Sassoon sent an article on poetry to the *Listener* at the urging of the literary editor J. R. Ackerley – a broadside against modernism, mentioning Laura Riding as a particularly absurd example. Ackerley had thought of getting a response from T. S. Eliot[12] but then found Sassoon's piece too general to print. He tried to mediate on behalf of the moderns. 'Auden was in here the other day,' Ackerley wrote, 'and wants to meet you. He admires your work very much and wishes you did more.'[13]

*

SASSOON, DELIGHTED BY a visit of the Beerbohms to Heytesbury in January, was making his own fortress, for the moment his work on *The Old Century*. The last chapters were hard to write; he told

Blunden that he might reprint his 1906 poems to fill up space. The disturbed world made him even more determined to write with healing serenity.[14] He might ignore the Spanish Civil War, but Germany was different. 'I'm really scarcely a Jew at all,' he told H. M. Tomlinson, 'but I should be one if I were a German and George would have his passport torn up if he were an Austrian Sassoon.'[15] A horrific thought crept over him: perhaps Britain should prepare for war. Then he went back to the jingle of hansom cabs in the recollected calm of 1907. Blunden liked the book's 'exquisite' first chapters, even if the unpoetic George Sherston 'had taken charge a little'.[16] Max Beerbohm, Glen Byam Shaw and H. M. Tomlinson admired them as well, and Theresa loved this 'quite wonderful book, and beautiful', like a Turner watercolour, tactful too about her, giving 'enough to show that there was a sad story'.[17] E. M. Forster also seemed impressed by this trip into a more easeful age, but the novelist's view of Sassoon's work became increasingly coloured by tact and affection, putting him among those writers 'lost'[18] and tempted into nostalgia.

In 1938, Hester, fearful of her health, decided that she did not want another child, a matter of sadness and later brooding for Sassoon. They went abroad in April, to Rapallo for four 'elysian'[19] weeks when Beerbohm checked *The Old Century*'s punctuation. By June, Sassoon believed that the book was his masterpiece and Gwen Raverat's woodcut for the title-page of an idyllic riverbank scene seemed perfect for it. Harder to write than the Sherston books, especially the end, it depressed him slightly with its lost utopia. 'What a peaceful world it was!' he wrote to Geoffrey Keynes. 'And what a bullying barbarian of a world it is now!'[20] That month he wrote of his reliance on alcohol in the evenings and 'a lack of anything to 'get up for'.[21]

Occasional messages came from Wilsford: the Hunters' report of wildly extravagant redecoration, requests from Stephen Tennant for visits, protestations of unhappiness, advice ('don't forget to bathe your eyes regularly with Optrex'),[22] a letter of admiration about *Sherston's Progress*. Stephen dreamed of visiting Heytesbury and getting into a bath that had been run for Hester. For Tennant, *Sherston's Progress* brought back how hearty Sassoon could be, how he had once thrown bread and teased him in Siena 'until I nearly cried'.[23] Tennant's albums are full of cut-out newspaper photographs or his own drawings of boxers, sailors and muscular men in swimming trunks; they are full too of wild flowers painted or preserved, of narcissistic overwrought prose dashed down in seclusion where eccentricity slid into madness. Over it all hangs the promise of the sprawling, disjointed *Lascar*, his unfinished novel of the Marseilles sea-front, enormous tattooed *matelots* and dreams of hot, erotic fulfilment.

When Sassoon sent him a copy of *The Old Century*, the book made Tennant want happiness for its author as he recalled 'the stricken look that sometimes comes into your eyes'.[24] To Stephen, it seemed a 'distillation of solitude' yet 'heavenly', its author resembling a 'dreamy little boy'.[25] Sassoon answered that Stephen had unknowingly contributed to it through his sensibility and perception of beauty in small things and his 'sense of fun'. Nostalgia for the past was not sad; not until it had been lived did life become golden. This stirred Tennant who wrote again, this time of his pride that 'unlike you, I don't hoard and roam in the past – or feel gratitude (gratitude is bunk . . . for old-hearted people) . . .'[26]

Friends comforted Stephen, William Walton telling of vanity at Heytesbury where Sassoon had shown him the proofs saying, 'Look at that passage – Osbert couldn't write it, Sachie couldn't write it.' Walton agreed that Hester slightly resembled Tennant – 'but flat (like flat beer)'.[27] Early in 1939, Tennant sent a postcard to Sassoon from Rhodes complaining, 'I shut you out for 2 or 4 years – you have shut me out forever.'[28] In the summer of that year, an article in the *Sunday Express* reached Heytesbury about Wilsford, the 'Bachelor Manor any woman would long to possess', where Stephen had ordered statues of twelve Nubian slaves and wanted to import Arab servants. The journalist saw its interiors that had been done up by the fashionable decorator Syrie Maugham, Somerset Maugham's wife: white carpets, white walls, white taffeta meant for débutantes' 'frocks', white feathers on the chandeliers, white flowers. With this came a sea motif, a reflection of *Lascar*: lobster baskets as lampshades, fishing nets draped over the banisters. Stephen's bed was covered in pale-blue satin; on the wall were two fourteenth-century stone windows bought in Bath, and there were mirrors everywhere. Sassoon kept the clipping as a memento of self-obsession.[29]

*

IN JULY 1938, when Hester and George and the nanny set off for Norfolk and the sea, Sassoon hoped to be alone, but their hotel was unsatisfactory and they returned after two nights. He had a compulsion now to heal the past; if only he could bring his selves of 1930 or 1932 into the present where Heytesbury and George might work their magic on those painful years. Sometimes to escape Hester he locked himself away. She said his mother and he were both tyrannical but offered to go off with George for six months; again Sassoon answered that the occasional six hours would be enough, seized by the old dread of what might come out of his consequent isolation. Drink calmed him, as did her sadness, when she implored, 'Be kind to me.'

He thought of leaving – but for where? Perhaps Palestine, to find that buried part of him, his Jewishness. But no: 'Heytesbury churchyard seems a more likely choice.'[30] Sometimes he was cruel, then felt remorse, and the quarrel ended by their making love, a way of comforting her, which left him exhausted. To rekindle his feelings, she would put on her best velvet evening dress and gold tiara to have dinner with him alone. In August Ralph Hodgson, over from Japan, came to stay for more than two weeks. The visit was tiring but wonderful; Hodgson's vitality electrified Sassoon – brilliant talk of dog shows, mastiffs, poetry, low-life sporting figures, art and life. This was 'one of the most extraordinary men I've ever known'.[31] T. H. White, staying at a nearby inn to work his falcons on the Downs, came over several times, adding to the rumbustious atmosphere. To White Sassoon seemed rather like a borzoi hound: 'beautiful, aloof, melancholy', also 'slightly selfish, slightly touchy, slightly possessive, slightly inaccessible', yet 'a saint-like person'.[32]

The Old Century was published in September 1938. The book reflects the time in which it was written – the late 1930s, the economic crisis and threat of another war – and Sassoon's own difficult life. His marriage seemed in trouble and interest in his poetry in decline. To write it, he went to his favourite room at Heytesbury, the music room on the first floor – a quiet room, small compared to the grand ground-floor rooms, yet elegant, reminiscent of one of the book's inspirations, Max Beerbohm. *The Old Century* has none of Beerbohm's malice and piercing wit but rather Sassoon's gentler humour and self-deprecation. The book is, as its author said, quiet and peaceful, written to delight people in bad times, with the ugliness of life left out. He was proud of the 'triumph of self-discipline', perhaps 'the most difficult feat I could have attempted', the opposite of 'those savage war-poems'.[33] Blunden thought it almost too private.

Ostensibly a straight autobiography, the book tells of Sassoon's life up to his twenty-first birthday. Originally he had wanted it to end in 1900, when he went to his first school, then on saying goodbye to Mr Gould, his housemaster, but the publishers thought both of these made the book too short. Certainly the section called 'Seven More Years' is less lyrical, with a few exceptions like his reading at Marlborough of Hood's poem 'Bridge of Sighs', described as a return to childhood intensity. There is no wallowing in the boarding-school atmosphere as in memoirs by Cyril Connolly or Robert Graves, perhaps because Sassoon decided to leave out sex, one of the most powerful features of adolescence. Instead, his early years, a hermetic, innocent world, seem the most deeply felt part of *The Old Century*. Not even the unpleasant nanny Mrs Mitchell nor Alfred Sassoon's absence, illness and death nor the visits of the formidable Wirgie and Aunt Lula who is eccentric to the point of madness tarnish the gold for long. The crazy Mrs Beer comes from London, outside the magic of Weirleigh.

The lulling narrative has exquisite set-pieces, beginning with what Sassoon thought to be 'the most perfectly articulated piece of prose poetry I have ever produced', a description of himself as a child with his mother at the watercress well near Weirleigh, then of watching Theresa as she sketches a man (here perhaps a rare reference to his Jewish roots) 'like someone out of the Bible', perhaps Abraham, scattering seed in the early spring landscape of the weald of Kent. These are familiar images of life's beginning: water welling up from a spring, seed thrown on to a field. What retrieves them from their familiarity, as so often with Sassoon, is the gentle intensity of their simplicity and detail, used only occasionally to reflect pain. An entertainment devised by his mother does let him obliquely show Theresa's character and fate in the stifling, small-scale life forced on her by her husband's flight and early death. Trying to break Weirleigh's long evening silence, she starts a poetry society and involves the local women in *tableaux vivants*. During one meeting of the poetry society, Siegfried (aged ten) and his brothers hide behind a canopy in a space above the fireplace; and, in a mixture of friendly writing and almost physical evocation, he shows childhood security and fearless excitement – the turning up of the oil lamps, Theresa's humming of the Keel Row while preparing the room, the tickling dust of the hiding place – as the wind rages outside. Guests declaim poems in cosy absurdity, then one of the boys sneezes and the 'little wretches' are thrown out. Sassoon imagines this being followed by indulgent laughter before tea and crumpets in 'that dawdling homespun world of long ago'.

The danger is that he becomes too sentimental. In another passage of which Sassoon was particularly proud – the description of his return some forty years later to Edingthorpe where Theresa had rented the rectory in 1897 – this danger is not entirely avoided as the past blends with the present, darkening at a lychgate built in the churchyard since his last visit as a memorial to someone killed in the First World War, the same year as his brother Hamo. Yet here, alone in the book, more than in the descriptions of his absent father's occasional return to Weirleigh, softening memory almost reaches a hard truth, inspired partly by Kipling's short story 'They' about the spirits of dead children. For the most part Sassoon stuck to the belief of Robert Louis Stevenson – whose flowing, dandified prose partly inspired his own – that art must not 'compete with life' or 'the dazzle and confusion of reality'.[34] This, he said, was what he aimed for in *The Old Century* and its successor *The Weald of Youth*. And the book is not only the story of his first years but a separate work of art, like one of those serene landscape paintings which Sassoon admired: an expression of personal nostalgia but also an evocation of beauty that had only partly existed but could still anaesthetize the present, where the phrase 'my twenty first birthday was a notably unobtrusive one' means not tedium but relief compared not only to what was to come but to an agitating, less satisfying, real past.

The reviewers, on the whole, were kind. In the *Sunday Times*, Desmond MacCarthy likened its enchantment to 'the morning of life', as in Hardy's poem 'The Self Unseeing', but added, referring to Sassoon's decision to leave Cambridge, 'it was lucky, however, that he had five hundred a year'.[35] In the *New Statesman*, David Garnett – who had spent much of the First World War in comfortable Bloomsbury protest working on a farm – admired 'this beautiful and charming book' which was, however, less powerful than the Sherston memoirs' portrait of the 'mixture of physical courage and moral cowardice' of that generation who fought in the trenches. The *Times Literary Supplement* declared the Edingthorpe passage to be surprisingly modern in mingling the present and the past in the way of J. B. Priestley's theories of time.[36] A dissenting note came in the *Manchester Guardian* from Basil de Selincourt, who thought the book 'poetically exquisite' but 'rather thin'.[37] Malcolm Muggeridge in the *Daily Telegraph* complained of the overpowering niceness of everyone and the occasional affectedness of the writing in this 'anaemic fairy story belonging to a remote past and with no bearing on the so ominous present'.[38] Sassoon remained convinced that the tone was right, declaring that he did not care if reviewers mocked phrases like 'land of nod' that had been carefully vetted by Beer-bohm and himself.

*

THE LANDSCAPE OF the present became even darker. Sassoon supported Chamberlain over Munich, and dreaded the coming to office of Churchill, whom he thought a self-seeking warmonger. The German anti-Jewish hysteria made him feel helpless, as if he was reading *The Old Century* aloud to a Nuremberg rally. But he still could not believe war would come. Meanwhile he needed a quarter of a bottle of whisky to send him to sleep at night. Hester was chainsmoking, hoping for guidance from the dead T. E. Lawrence and obsessed with the international crisis. Sassoon thought: 'I get dull and heavy and lose faith in my achievements. Perhaps Shenstone was right:

> *Poet and rich! 'Tis solecism extreme!*
> *'Tis heightened contradiction!'*[39]

The poetry of 1938 stays mostly domestic and personal, as if escaping the threat of war. 'A Local Train of Thought' is about an apparently changeless peacetime before the familiar sound of a train disappears. 'Thoughts in 1938', written in November, describes reflections on an ancient drove road at a time of omens of war; 'A Blessing' is inspired by George, as is the unpublished 'Childhood's Eden' about early years rushing by before nostalgia for those 'long-lost innocent skies'. 'Heart and Soul' declares that love does not die with age and the past but grows dearer, before a grim, jarring last line: 'holpen both by ghosts from the gloom'. The beginning of 'Brevities'' was mocked by Marsh ('I am the man who, with a luminous look') and has another unfortunate couplet:

> *I am that man who with a furrowing frown*
> *Thinks harshly of the world – and corks it down.*

In November came the unpublished 'Second Birthday', about George's wonderful ignorance of 'Evil's giant despair'. There were also some cosy lines about one of his favourite pictures, the Pyne view of Old Exeter: a glimpse of order and a safe past.[40]

An unexpected inducement to assess his views on the craft of poetry arose when he was asked to lecture at Bristol University in March 1939 for a fee of £20. Ruth and Henry Head helped; both were well read and shared his taste, apparently more now than Blunden, who had been lukewarm about Sassoon's recent poems. 'Direct utterance' was what he sought in poetry, he decided; this and visualization, or what Thomas Hardy called 'mindsight'. Sassoon wanted immediate impact, something seen and felt at the first reading, achieved usually through four means: Content, Tone of Voice, Visual Effect and Music. What the 'modernists' offered were dry statements, unintelligibility, a flat conversational tone, under-emphasis, artifice without emotion, lack of music. Housman's 'Tell Me Not Here, It Needs No Saying' seemed to him to be the perfect poem: intellectually simple but universal, at once musically enchanting yet slow to reveal its full meaning, intense, every word counting, verbally surprising yet with 'friendly and unaffected' images, compact diction and apparent artlessness, 'seeming to come from the source of tears'. Housman's own lecture on poetry guided Sassoon, maxims like 'Poetry is not the thing said but a way of saying it' and 'Meaning is of the intellect, poetry is not.' Sassoon had a 'life-long and instinctive abhorrence of contrived similes' and 'shyness of metaphor. Indirect approach to direct utterance seems to be what I want.'[41]

By the end of 1938 *The Old Century* had sold just over 10,000 copies – not enough to earn the £1,000 advance. Fabers had promised a £1,000 advance each on three more volumes of autobiography, and by 18 January 1939 Sassoon was making notes for the next volume and wanting solitude. The next day Hester accused him of leading 'too easy a life'.[42] He suffered increasingly from the indigestion that had plagued him since the trenches and dreaded loneliness, revealing a contradiction; he needed solitude yet feared it. He seldom slept before 3 or 4 a.m.

Hitler annexed Czechoslovakia, smashing the terms of the

Munich agreement. Sassoon envisaged the disintegration of Heytesbury life, now threatened also by plans for a road through the park.
Ruth Head died and Sassoon hoped that Henry, increasingly stricken
with Parkinson's Disease, might soon follow her. He wrote to Marsh
offering his services if war came, saying that he would 'give the last
drop of ink in my fountain pen to defend our liberties and decencies
from what Hitlerism means'.[43] He asked Marsh to show the letter
to Churchill; and Churchill put it in his pocket. Now Sassoon
opposed any more negotiations with the Nazi 'gangsters'.[44]

The warrior could surface. As a Fellow of the Royal Society of
Literature, Sassoon sat on the Society's academic committee, a group
of 'the great and the good' that, among other duties, supervised the
annual award of the Benson Medal for literary achievement. Furious
when it looked as if this might go to an absurd figure called Terence
Fytton Armstrong – who also went under the names of John
Gawsworth and the King of Redonda (a rock off the Caribbean
island of Montserrat, which he claimed to have inherited) – Sassoon,
urged on by Marsh (who was backing Christopher Hassall for the
award), tried to block Fytton Armstrong (or Gawsworth), who had
plagued him in the past for his autograph and advice, then resigned
his fellowship when, in April 1939, for the first time, two medals
were given: to Fytton Armstrong and to Hassall.[45] To Sassoon, it
seemed yet another example of the craziness of London literary life.
How much better off he was at Heytesbury.

On 7 June, a huge bough of a beech tree crashed down during a
cricket match, and he wondered if this was a bad omen. There was
an idyllic interlude, at Oxford, where he and Hester went with the
Heytesbury cricket team to play Blunden's Merton side, the Bar-
nacles, and the day seemed to Sassoon 'like the good old England
holding its own against the modern pandemonium'.[46] Hester dressed
up for dinner one night, wanting him to waltz with her to a tune on
the radio, and, although staying in his chair, he felt a revival of
physical attraction. Half an hour later she was upset, for she had
read his diary and seen the evidence of exasperation – a faltering of
love.

Friends like Miriam Lane (formerly Rothschild), who had known Hester before her marriage, noticed a change. The Pre-Raphaelite fragility had been transformed, perhaps by love, into something much more robust; Siegfried, even if taxed by the effort, had aroused her sexual love and joy. She became more energetic and demanding, wishing to possess him much more fully; the nightly separation, his odd hours of working, frustrated and upset her more as their sexual relationship faded because of his homosexuality. To Sassoon, she began to seem a threat, an oppressive presence, wanting to know all the time what he was thinking or doing, and once horrifying him by suggesting that she might play for the Heytesbury cricket team. She wanted more part in his work, to discuss writing and books in a way that he found affected and irritating. This was no longer a pale, pining creature wanting to be healed or saved, the girl who had reminded one friend of Millais's picture of the ethereal, suicidal Ophelia.

George became his great and entrancing hope, shown in the July poem 'In the Rose Garden'. That month he also wrote about growing spiritual feeling, a yearning for the simplicities of belief, called 'The Word Faithful'. These poems never made their way into any of Sassoon's collections yet they renewed his joy in verse.[47] The historian Lewis Namier came to visit: a brilliant man, Sassoon thought, but exhausting in his enumeration of the follies of Chamberlain. And Namier was a foreigner, a Polish Jew, and 'I don't feel comfortable with him.'[48] These intimations of catastrophe disturbed him, as when H. G. Wells had stayed and said the world financial system was on the brink of collapse. He began to feel that this time, in war or economic crisis, he might not pass the test.

*

ON 14 AUGUST 1939, at about quarter-past ten in the evening, Sassoon sat in his upstairs room, sending off copies of *Rhymed Ruminations*, his new, privately printed book of poems. He had addressed an envelope to Hilaire Belloc when a small piece of earth came in through the window. Thinking it was Hester joking, he looked out to see Stephen Tennant wearing a whitish mackintosh and white shoes. On being told of his arrival, Hester flared up, but then she calmed down, and even enjoyed Stephen's ingratiating and funny conversation, mostly about books and people. Tennant stayed for about an hour and looked well, fatter, with odd expressionless eyes, as if drugged. Sassoon felt that Stephen might want to harm the marriage; at the end, the visitor asked Hester to Wilsford: 'Siegfried, of course, will be too busy working.'[49] In those words, Sassoon believed he glimpsed hatred for her, but Hester remarked on Stephen's intelligence and charm. Tennant thought that his old friend had once or twice smiled conspiratorially, easily enticed into memories of Rapallo and talk about Christopher Isherwood. He found Hester puffy under the eyes, haggard; 'she would be good looking if she were less raddled'. She seemed frenetic, lacking in 'douceur'.[50]

The next visitors were easier: Cockerell and Blunden with his wife Sylva. Blunden, still pro-German, speaking of the essential decency of the people and the reasonableness of the Nazis. Sassoon, although disagreeing, also loathed the idea of young Germans being killed, people from the country of the Hirths. He thought of Rivers and saw in an evening view of the Wylye valley the atmosphere of Masefield's chilling poem 'August 1914'. On 1 September Hester came into Sassoon's bedroom after hearing that the Germans had attacked Poland. For him, the shock was less than expected for 'as we had to fight them sooner or later we may as well get it over and done with'.[51] Sydney Cockerell stayed on, having left his invalid wife in Gloucestershire. When war was declared Sassoon wished briefly that he had been killed by that bullet in July 1918. What remained of his old, cherished world must now be blown apart, even this calm Heytesbury where he could hear hounds bark in a distant kennel and owls utter their ghostly cries.

TWENTY

'In George I seem to live my life again'

Sassoon reread his war poems, thinking this war seemed horribly like a rerun of 1914: Winston Churchill at the Admiralty, the start of propaganda, then probably a long war of bloody attrition. Someone from the Ministry of Information wrote to say that he was on a list of authors who might be of use; a hint came that Heytesbury could be requisitioned as a military school. The first evacuees arrived: three pregnant mothers who were welcomed by Hester and put in the servants' quarters. By 22 September 1939, sixteen extra people were in the house: the refugees, Mrs Dengle (his old daily from Campden Hill Square) and her grandson.

Friends already had wartime duties. Geoffrey Keynes became a consulting surgeon in the RAF and Glen Byam Shaw an officer in the Royal Scots, having volunteered at the advanced age of thirty-five. Sassoon thought that Glen would never regret enlisting. 'I know what I should have lost if I hadn't gone back in 1918,' he told the actor. 'And what I gained, in self-respect, was something I've been thankful for ever since . . .'[1] But at Laurence Whistler's wedding in Salisbury cathedral, he wept, thinking that Laurence too might soon be in the fighting. Even the home front became like

1914, with Sydney Cockerell and Hester very warlike, obsessed by the news.

Towards the end of September, after a brief absence, Cockerell returned with 200 books and manuscripts which he asked if he could leave for safe-keeping at Heytesbury. This extraordinary collection included the sixteenth-century manuscript of Cardinal Bembo's poems, the twelfth-century St Albans Golden Psalter (the last book William Morris had handled before his death), Dante Gabriel Rossetti's *The White Ship* and the manuscripts of Thomas Hardy's *The Three Strangers* and Swinburne's *Astrophel*. The Golden Psalter dated from when Queen Matilda had lived near Heytesbury; briefly such a continuity of Englishness and beauty seemed to diminish the war. Some three years later, another aesthetic delight arrived: the picture collection of Sassoon's lawyer Anthony Lousada, also sent for safety. This included works by Sisley, Boudin, Joshua Reynolds and Wilson Steer, and an exquisite still life by Manet.

The expense of Heytesbury, in these threatening times, made Sassoon think that he would have to write another book. By 25 October, he had started a new volume of autobiography, writing, a week later, 'oh the happiness of being able to "do it again" '.[2] Hester suggested that she should take George away for a few days. Sassoon responded perversely, feeling she was abandoning him, but had meals alone on the second floor, sometimes bolting the door. By 15 November, exhausted, he had reached 10,000 words of what was to be called *The Weald of Youth*. By the year's end, the mood changed to melancholy, partly because of these 'falsifying memoirs', too much whisky and hot water at night and, above all, the failure to write something 'candid'.[3]

So he sought refuge in George, often bathing the child and taking him out for walks, preferably without Hester. Now Sassoon thought that only his son could bring him peace. And the poetry shows a continuing puzzlement about the present, as in 'Doggerel about Old Days' ('Will someone tell me where I am – in '39?') or 'Old Music' (where the past resembles a mellow violin) and 'Youth and Maturity' (unpublished) about dead great men. 'A Moment's Memoirs' (also unpublished), sparked by seeing the local hunt, brings back old adventures. The privately printed edition of *Rhymed Ruminations*, limited to seventy-five copies, had gone out in July 1939. In August came 'Mid-August Meditation' (also unpublished), about finding peace 'at moonless midnight' in spite of the dictators; then 'Fifty Years Between Us', also entitled 'To a Child', again unpublished, another lament about getting old.[4]

*

THE WAR BEGAN to impinge: soldiers on exercises near by, tanks practising attacks, the evacuees in the stables, huts going up, a part of Great Ridge Wood burned for charcoal. Some of his servants left to join the forces and it was difficult to find replacements. Hester often did the cooking and the cleaning, and Sassoon scrubbed tables, laid fires, brought in logs and cleaned shoes. This work, new to them both, added to the tensions. But on 16 March 1940 Sassoon gave his wife a goblet with these lines from an earlier poem engraved on it by Laurence Whistler:

> *A flower has opened in my heart –*
> *What flower is this, what flower of spring;*
> *What simple, secret thing?*
> *It is the peace that shines apart,*
> *The peace of daybreak skies that bring*
> *Clear song and wild swift wing.*

Whistler thought, years later, that there was still much love between them then.

In April, Sassoon saw Glen (who was on leave) in London with Angela and their children, and afterwards Hester had a tantrum for, understandably, she was jealous of the Byam Shaws. The Germans invaded Norway and Denmark, Holland and Belgium were overrun, northern France threatened and Churchill became prime minister; 'heaven help him to be equal to the task',[5] Sassoon prayed. The sound of anti-aircraft guns awoke the warrior in him; then Hester said that he had been referred to on the radio as the poet 'who thought the names on the Menin Gate worth nothing'.[6] So this was what he seemed to be now – a discredited pacifist.

On 19 May, perhaps in answer, Sassoon sent an eight-line poem to the *Observer*, probably inspired also by Churchill's broadcast: a call to arms, like those high-flown verses he had written before disillusion in the trenches but this time more solemn and inert. Geoffrey Keynes's gloom about the French army infuriated him and he blew up after his friend accused him at Heytesbury of 'facile optimism'.[7] Even the brave Dr Dunn wanted some sort of negotiation, seeing communism as the greater enemy. When news came of France's surrender, Sassoon thought that the French had collapsed because 'they are (with all their civilised intelligence) a rotten old nation, for whom food, money, and copulation are supremely important, and politics a discreditable game'.[8] He knew the danger that he faced from a German invasion because of his Jewish name, but Sam Behrman's suggestion that the Sassoons should come to the United States seemed 'too like running away'.[9] If the Germans came, he must die with dignity; at least Hester and George could revert to being Gattys. When the enemy reached Heytesbury, 'I shall put on my old R.W.F. tunic and go for them bald-headed.'[10]

His poem came out in the *Observer*; already he had sent another.[11] Then Hester's brilliant brother, Oliver Gatty, died from burns after an explosion in a field near Cambridge while working on an experiment connected to Air Raid Protection. 'Wonderfully brave' at first, she collapsed into his arms and 'feeling so sorry for her made me love her and broke down the barriers'.[12] For a moment he thought Hester and he were still 'wonderfully happy together';[13] if only she could be less restless, less obsessed by the news. Her concern seems understandable when searchlights lit up the night and bombs fell close by – one, at the end of October, in the park at Heytesbury, an hour after midnight, dislodging tiles from the roof and killing a rabbit which was auctioned in the village.

Sassoon's closeness to his son took on an almost mystical tone and he thought that 'in George I seem to live my life over again'.[14]

Hester felt excluded. She tried to make Siegfried love her, yet again he backed away, even if 'it seems that copulation is the sole solution to her problems'.[15] She said often how she longed to be loved by him, how he meant even more to her than George. A part of the problem was that he wanted Hester as an adjunct to himself: someone to run the house, to be Mrs Siegfried Sassoon, a great poet's wife, ornamental, not untidy (which she was), docile, adoring and frail.

He began to loathe her often reasonable demands for love and closeness. These, he thought, were childishly wilful: signs that she was 'neurotic and over-emotional', someone who 'has been given in to all her life by a weakly amiable mother'. His puritanism rose up; Hester, he thought, 'has had everything that money could buy'[16] and, as an only daughter, too much adoration. The irony is that Hester too reached back to childhood in her idea of Siegfried, cherishing for years Gerhard Hauptmann's remark when they met with Max Beerbohm at Rapallo that he seemed as if he had only just grown up. George, the boy and heir, became even more of an obsession for him, mixing delight with an aching love: 'to be loved and wanted, by one's heart's desire', Sassoon thought. 'Can that be analysed or measured?'[17] Yet to lose Hester was to be alone, for, if she left, George must be shared with her, bringing the loss 'of all my hopes of happiness'.[18] He told his wife that the only solution to her unhappiness was to have another child; she refused again, anxious for her fragile health. In September, he sent off the final proofs of *Rhymed Ruminations* for Fabers' commercial edition of the book without showing them to Hester.

Besides George, Sassoon had his books: the Victorian Dorset clergyman William Barnes's dialect poems; the letters of Lady Ritchie (Thackeray's daughter); a life of the Edwardian cricketer Lord Hawke; the letters to Sydney Cockerell, collected in the volume *Friends of a Lifetime*; Henry James's letters; then old favourites like Jane Austen, Trollope, Robert Louis Stevenson, Dickens and Edward FitzGerald's ('dear Fitz') letters about Suffolk of the 1870s, 'a perpetual Sunday afternoon compared to the present day':[19] all these made different worlds. His mother's vast picture *The Hours* arrived, left to him by Mr Hamilton, his old tutor. This, he thought, with Theresa's watercolour of *The Sower*, was what he wanted from his own work: simple, deeply felt idealism, as good as early Watts, redolent also of Elgar's music, an echo that had lasted his whole life.

When *Rhymed Ruminations* – a collection of forty-two poems (thirty-three of which had been in the privately printed edition of the previous year) – was published, none of the critics took Sassoon's point that it should be read as a 'considered sequence'.[20] The review in the *Times Literary Supplement* mentioned a 'contemplative retirement',[21] with only flashes of the First War anger, and in the *Spectator* Richard Church said that these often beautiful poems were nostalgic and traditional but never startling.[22] For Stephen Spender, in the *New Statesman*, this 'shy, wealthy, slightly embarrassed, attractive, problematic figure' seemed to have retired into a beautiful shell of parenthood, money and poems that were often precious and 'spinsterish'. The recommendation of the book to those who wanted 'a rest from the war'[23] infuriated Sassoon, who thought, wrongly, that Spender had not tried to join up to fight. But the poems of 1940, the year that his country was in perhaps its greatest ever danger, mostly deserve this. 'The Child at the Window', for instance, is about George watching from the house as his father came across the lawn after a ride – three sweet six-line verses suffused by gentle melancholy, even though Sassoon claimed that they had been influenced by the wrenching emotion of Charlotte Mew. In 'Progressions' youth and manhood dissolve into memories, and the unpublished 'A Bedtime Story'[24] has George asking for a story while searchlights glow outside and bombers fly over an apparently peaceful garden. In January 1941 Sassoon told Glen Byam Shaw that *Rhymed Ruminations* had sold 2,000 in spite of the nasty reviews, 'Auden worshippers to a man'. Sassoon went back to *The Weald of Youth* which had been lying in a drawer for almost a year.

*

ON 22 JUNE the Germans attacked the Soviet Union. Sassoon had sent the first nine chapters of *The Weald* to Fabers but had heard nothing. Some visitors appeared, not many, but generally pleasing, although they added to Sassoon's wartime dread by inspiring thoughts of the dangers they might face: Rex Whistler (stationed near by in the Welsh Guards), his nephew Hamo Sassoon – Michael's son – on leave at the end of August. Glen Byam Shaw might be sent to Persia, Hamo waited for orders and Sassoon worried about them both. *The Weald* yielded 300 words a night of drudgery amid bleak news of German successes. Hamo was called to Egypt and the fighting; Sassoon felt desolate. Briefly in London to discuss a possible film about the Sassoon family with his cousin Arthur Sassoon, he thought that the blackout made the city look much grimmer than during the last war. Later, while up to see the Byam Shaws, he saw the ruins of the bombed Raymond Buildings, his home in 1914. In 1941, Sassoon wrote only one poem he thought worth publishing, and that not until *Common Chords* of 1950: 'Man and Dog',[25] suited to the magazine *Country Life*, about walking with Sheltie.

Max Beerbohm's talk on the radio about music halls of the 1890s delighted him by evoking a lost England, and on 4 April 1942, Easter Sunday, at 4 a.m. – the anniversary of finishing the *Fox-hunting Man* in 1928 – he wrote the last word of *The Weald of Youth*. The end had been hard. While writing about Marsh – lately bombed out of Raymond Buildings – he recalled with a shiver how that monocled eye had flashed with impatience at young Siegfried's blundering talk. The book was too tidy to convey that early turmoil, but now he could write only about tranquillity. After no more than a week's break, he began the next volume and wrote 6,000 words on Robbie Ross's generosity, breaking off for a poem about cloud shadows on the Downs. In June 1942, his beloved Sheltie had to be put down, blind and in pain, and, as with T. E. Lawrence, he thought he heard the dog some weeks later.

Hester smoked too much, was exhausted by George and shouted at Sassoon when he went to say goodnight to the child. Now Rex Whistler and she seemed to unite against him, talking endlessly about the war. E. M. Forster came to stay, making Sassoon feel 'how utterly cut off I am from the world of people who think for themselves', and refused to condemn Auden's wartime departure for America. Forster avoided comment on the proofs of *The Weald of Youth*, but the novelist was, Sassoon reassured himself, too intellectual, too cultured – like Marsh, another visitor, still urbane enough to prompt further rueful thoughts of the isolation of Heytesbury. What its squire wanted now was for someone to ask him to do something useful: quite what, he did not know. To propose himself risked refusal or humiliation, perhaps even a response from the authorities that showed they had never heard of him. A lowly role, as a fire watcher or member of the Home Guard, was not how he saw himself. So Siegfried Sassoon stood aside from the war, sometimes dreaming of talks with Churchill before waking to another empty day.

On 5 August, he came back from posting a letter with George to find Stephen Tennant in the house with Hester. A now fat Tennant stayed for two and a half hours, eating a lunch of boiled egg, bread and treacle and figs and cheese, and talked of books and writers. Later Hester even urged Sassoon to be kind to this extraordinary person. Afterwards he thought of the great tracts of 'insignificance' in people's lives, how 'once in a lifetime, perhaps', people 'are fully alive, living above themselves, discovering powers they hadn't been aware of'.[26] Had those mad years with Stephen shown him life more intensely than at any other time apart from the First World War? Tennant wrote in his own journal, 'He needs me.'[27]

Autumn proved a paradise: incandescent skies, gold and green colours across stubble fields, sun through morning mist. On 22 September, Stephen Tennant came again, now more menacing, apparently challenging Hester when he said that he had no respect for Christian marriage, while the six-year-old George sat watchful on a sofa. To Sassoon the small boy and the ageing aesthete were both children, but Stephen, as Rex Whistler had said, was also 'a sort of devil'. Sassoon told Glen Byam Shaw (to whom he had dedicated *The Weald*), 'I hope there will be no more visits. Yesterday's worried and upset me.'[28]

*

THE WEALD OF YOUTH, published on 15 October 1942, had a frontispiece photograph of its author, shy and dreamy at Canterbury in November 1914 with a scarf loose at his neck. Now Sassoon thought that the book was first rate 'within its limits'[29] and liked the wood engraving by Reynolds Stone on the title-page of a rider in a gentle landscape. Fabers printed 10,000 copies, and good reviews followed in the *Daily Mail* and the *Daily Sketch* and letters of praise, from, among others, E. M. Forster and H. G. Wells ('a most valuable documentation for our age').[30] The *Times Literary Supplement* thought this account of 'a young man with £600 a year of his own and a soul' – and (unlike most poets) not tormented by love – showed 'the pattern of our time'.[31] Blunden provided the expected praise, this time in the *Spectator*, and there was a 'not unfriendly but quite superficial and smartly stupid'[32] review in the *New Statesman* by V. S. Pritchett. To others, the book seemed as distant in spirit as Trollope or Horace Walpole. When Graves told Marsh that *The Weald of Youth* was 'a little too elderly and urbane'[33] and when, in the *Observer*, Peter Quennell decried an 'orgy of amiability',[34] it is hard to disagree with them. By 27 November, the book had sold 8,000 copies.

The Weald of Youth takes Siegfried Sassoon from the age of twenty-three, in 1909, up to the beginning of the First World War, its title coming from the line 'Weald of youth, a remembered world', in his recent poem 'Heart and Soul'. Written 'with immense difficulty', the wartime and domestic interruptions compounded by Max Beerbohm's dilatoriness in returning the proofs, the book is only slightly less lyrical in atmosphere than *The Old Century*, although it describes some of the most difficult years of its author's life. *The Weald* should have been a record of extraordinary characters – the piratical Crosland, the feline Gosse, Wirgie again, Marsh and Rupert Brooke – but even here memory has a benign glow and few shadows.

Sassoon cannot bring himself to be harsh; Crosland becomes absurd yet avuncular, without the anti-Semitism and his unscrupulous pursuit of Robbie Ross; there are hints of Marsh's oppressive urbanity – but only hints – and one can sense – and only sense – Sassoon's humiliation at Brooke's hands. Sex is again left out: there is nothing at all about Edward Carpenter or those hours of frustration at Weirleigh; and, horrified when a doctor saw symptoms of syphilis in his account of Rachel Beer, Sassoon changed it. He is also discreet about family life, not mentioning the tensions over Michael's marriage or Hamo's homosexuality. Neither *The Old Century* nor *The Weald of Youth* deal at all with Theresa's breakdowns. So we are back in a delightful dreamland.

Sassoon felt proud of the oblique approach. He had hoped, he told a correspondent, that the time in Gray's Inn came across strongly for this had been 'a sort of belated adolescence'. Although he treated those months 'more or less humorously',[35] he had meant them to show strong feeling. E. M. Forster's lack of interest in the proofs was typical, he thought, for the book lacked the 'violent sensationalism' that the novelist seemed to need to compensate for his 'sensitive and ultra-refined nature'. In fact, even when the trenches are just across its borders, *The Weald of Youth* is another utopia, an escape from marital darkness, horror at another war and a sense of declining interest in its author and his poetry. This is true even at its end when, in exquisitely modulated nostalgia and honeyed melancholy, Sassoon writes of a last peacetime bicycle trip across the weald with what seems to be a restrained joy not only in possible sacrifice but also in a sure and simple future – very different to his own realities in the early 1940s.

*

REX WHISTLER CAME again and Hester clearly adored him. Sassoon did not mind, merely noting, 'I love Rex, but he isn't restful.'[36] News arrived that his nephew Hamo, although wounded, was safe in hospital in the Middle East. On 17 December, Hester cried for most of dinner; Sassoon locked his bedroom door. Then, the next day, he recalled that it was their wedding anniversary, which she had forgotten. Yet, thanks to a visitor, the Christmas of 1942 was the best of the war. Isidore Lubin, an American economist recommended by Sam Behrman, came to Heytesbury, bringing razor blades, silk stockings, raisins and fascinating talk. As Roosevelt's emissary, Lubin had seen Churchill and others, and Hester, riveted, proved that 'at her best she always makes a delightful impression'. Sassoon realized that 'nice Jews make me feel more comfortable than anyone else'.[37] But the poems of this year still seem stuck in sterile self-examination: 'The Hardened Heart' in April, about youth and disillusionment, 'On Scratchbury Camp' – in his favourite alexandrines – inspired by watching summer clouds at an ancient Downland fortified site.[38]

The truth was that the marriage was hurtling towards catastrophe. Sassoon had slept separately from Hester since their arrival at Heytesbury in 1934, and, after George's birth, their lovemaking had died, at first with the occasional rare resurrection, then completely. For someone like Sassoon, who by his own admission was highly sexed, this self-imposed celibacy – for he seems to have had no other lovers during this time – darkened an increasing sense of solitude and desperation, added to by his homosexuality. Inevitably, his son, doted on by both parents, became a part of the battle between them. Out of control, George erupted, threatening the refugee children with an axe, and Hester despaired. The boy had two gifts that led to a new rivalry: a pony sent by Dorothy Hawkins (formerly Hanmer, to whom Sassoon had once been unofficially engaged) – on which his father hoped to teach him to ride – and a bicycle produced by Hester. Sassoon's resentment surged: George seemed keener on the bicycle than the pony.

There was still his past achievement. He tried to see sex through this and to persuade himself of the merits of his own celibacy, writing in his diary of how 'the transience of direct sexual experience' was 'an obviously finite theme' – much better to express 'sexual vitality' through 'one's work' so that 'the memory of one's great moments remains proud & happy'.[39] Sassoon still seemed to equate sex with brief pleasure and lasting shame, a reflection of his unhappiness with his homosexuality and perhaps the lack of joy, for him, in this part of his marriage.

His writing, as if to reflect his own need to remember its success, still brought attention. Admirers, serving in the army near by, came over – among them Oliver Dawnay, a young Guards subaltern, and the landscape artist Edward Seago, now a camouflage officer, who knew about ballet and stage design. These reminders of fame pleased him, more so than other requests, mostly refused – to speak to the Eton College Literary Society, to be a guest of honour at a Foyle's literary lunch or to read at an evening organized for the Free French by Osbert Sitwell, attended by the Queen and her daughters.

Occasionally he was a public man, opening a British Council exhibition in Warminster of Modern French pictures and wondering, perversely, why he did this so seldom: 'I always make such a success of it, and feel refreshed by being made much of.'[40] *The Weald* had sold over 10,000 copies and was even doing well in the United States. In March, he learned that the new two-shilling edition of the *Fox-hunting Man* had sold nearly 30,000 copies. Poetry came again at the start of April, when he wrote sixteen 'tolerable lines'[41] about polishing the brass candelabrum, left to him by Nellie Burton, and his poem 'Go, Words, on Winds of War' on the German war guilt was published in the *Spectator*.[42]

Hester felt excluded when, in June, he was asked by his cousin Lady Cholmondeley (Philip Sassoon's sister) to dinner in London to meet the poetry-loving General Wavell. She lost her temper, saying she was sick of his 'boring friends'.[43] Sassoon thought of Glen Byam Shaw fighting in the Burmese jungles, where he had been wounded, of the darkness of the world. Then Lady Cholmondeley rang to ask Hester to the Wavell dinner, but Hester now wished Sassoon to have a change of scene on his own. The change was a disappointment. At the Cholmondeleys' huge house in Kensington Palace Gardens, the other guests were Wavell, Desmond MacCarthy, Sir Ronald Storrs and Ivor Brown, editor of the *Observer*, but the evening never took off. A shy Wavell seemed desperate to speak of poetry and his anthology – *Other Men's Flowers*, to be published in the autumn – but Lady Cholmondeley, now a senior officer in the WRNS, directed the conversation in too 'helter skelter'[44] a way, jumping topics like her gadfly brother Philip.

At last Blunden came to Heytesbury, with his new companion, the much younger Claire Poynting. The day before, Hester had been in tears because of another row with George, walking round the house at three o'clock in the morning, wearing a fur coat over her night dress. Claire seemed sensible: 'homely . . . – just right for E.B.',[45] but Sassoon never liked sharing Blunden and soon he was imagining how she might become 'a rather disagreeable fat little woman'.[46] Naturally Claire was shy and Sassoon also awkward at first, but he loosened up enough to recite the whole of 'Everyone Sang' while standing by the dining-room table. Heytesbury, to Claire, was redeemed from gloom by Hester's presence and the Gatty furniture that Sassoon's wife had brought to the house.[47] A student of English at Oxford, Claire listened to the two poets talk about literature, enthralled by the range of minor writers whose works they knew.

*

BY NOW, HESTER was ill, in pain with heart trouble, smoking too much, terribly nervous, drinking strong coffee. Her cooking became more eccentric. She gave Sassoon a letter enumerating her complaints about his behaviour, then threatened a judicial separation and wept in his room until late, recovering the next day to apologize. In August she seemed to be better but became angry again, talking once more of leaving. She asked when he would like her to go, and he answered, 'After lunch.'[48] She wept again at dinner, her nerves calmer a few days later after Rex Whistler had asked her to a ballet in London. Sassoon felt relief when she left the house, although she had asked him to ignore her earlier tirades. The next day she was back, asking if he would mind if she loved someone else. It was Rex. Sassoon thought, 'I don't blame her at all,' knowing that he was 'as much to blame as she is' for the death of love and the ending of sexual relations between them. Rex and she were both thirty-eight, twenty years younger than he was. 'George is all I have to live for at present,'[49] he decided.

The news came that Italy had surrendered to the Allies, and the evacuee children were to be replaced by American troops. Sassoon rode or walked alone all this time, to those places of enchantment at Heytesbury: Jubilee Slope, Heaven's Gate, Scratchbury Camp. The last volume of autobiography took off again and work raised him up. By 20 October he had finished part one of the book – 16,500 words – and a week later was 1,800 words through a new chapter. By 6 November the American troops were arriving.

Hester came back from seeing Rex, looking younger and happier. When she announced that she wanted to send George to boarding school he opposed this, knowing how much he would miss the boy; another row broke out, Hester yelling at George, and she wept uncontrollably at dinner. Sassoon's indigestion returned, clouding his work. The chapter about Craiglockhart and Owen was particularly hard to write. He had moved to the music room, his favourite in the house, but there were more scenes, turning his stomach again to agony, and the cook left. On 24 December Hester took George to Lady Gatty's until the 27th. Sassoon sheltered in the music room, dreading his wife's return.

The poetic introspection had continued. In February 1943, he completed the second draft of 'Microcosmos', started in 1932, a self-portrait of an artist, referring perhaps to his Anglo-Jewish inheritance: 'I am the fantasy which race has wrought'. 'Early March' is another *Country Life* poem. 'Getting Queer in Wartime' – an unfortunate title – was, understandably, not published; again it was about Heytesbury's woods and his own obsolescence. George inspired 'The Child on the Lawn', also unpublished. 'Gone' is a melancholy lament for lost happiness which Sassoon also rightly kept to himself.[50]

In November 1943, he wrote to H. M. Tomlinson about faith and his belief in the 'persistence and survival of loveliness'. He had hints of help 'from outside', sometimes on the edge of sleep, a presence or a voice like that of the dead T. E. Lawrence and, once, Max Beerbohm's sister Dora, a nun; he had the sense also of Rivers. To accept God unconditionally was, he thought, 'dangerous' because it precluded the search. For 'one must battle on – doubting and hoping, and awaiting the corroboration required!'[51]

TWENTY-ONE

The hardened heart

BY 22 JANUARY 1944 Sassoon had written 3,100 words of the new book, finding it a relief from the present. Heartbroken when George set off as a boarder for five days a week to the nearby Greenways School, he consoled himself by rearranging his books on the library shelves, moving those with cheerful titles to where he could see them: volumes like *Bliss*, *Victory*, *The Ascent of Man*, *A World of My Own* and *Diamonds and Precious Stones*. By the middle of March, the next volume of autobiography had reached 22,000 words.

Towards the end of April, Hester announced that she was leaving for ever, to live with her mother, and Sassoon hardened, vowing not to have her back. He would stay on at Heytesbury without her money, looked after by the cook, Mrs Johnson. His unhappy wife pushed an eight-page letter under his bathroom door while he was shaving which said that he was endangering George by not supporting her efforts to control their son. Then she seemed to reconsider her decision to go. When Sassoon stayed adamant, she offered to have another child and said she had no wish to marry Rex Whistler. A parting would be shameful for her. She would be 'overwhelmingly grateful' if he relented. In this she was probably right: the stigma of the failed wife was still strong at that time, as it had been for Theresa more than fifty years before.

She took a voluntary job in Salisbury, and came back to get some clothes. Sassoon felt stricken by hopeful memories and a reluctance to be harsh. But he blamed Hester, his bitterness and anger rising again. Above all, she should have given him another child, not now but six years before. Theresa wrote to say, 'Thank God you have done this,' claiming to have disliked Hester from early on, seeing her as 'utterly self-centred – so utterly selfish . . . incapable of real affection. People like her cannot live with anyone related to them in any way.'[1] Theresa saw her darling Siegfried, as he saw himself: a victim.

Often he rode to Greenways to see George and talked to the school's owner, Mrs Hancock, who had sons at the war, lending her £8,000 to ensure the establishment's future and George a school near home. The boy's time alone with him at Heytesbury was 'quite perfect'.[2]

In the middle of May 1944 a 'decent sonnet'[3] for *Country Life*, for a fee of three guineas, made him rejoice in writing poetry again. More troops and Hester came; he was still like flint, 'deliberately disagreeable to her'.[4] Edith Olivier tried to mediate. Sam Behrman, on a visit, advised a friendly separation, not a divorce. When his increasingly distraught wife told him of her new post-war plans – a London flat, a rented house by the Seine for painting, frequent visits to Heytesbury – Sassoon prepared for months, even years, of warfare. She wept, saying that she loved him yet could not 'live with a man who is writing prose books all the time'.[5] Lady Gatty offered to pay for the conversion of a part of Heytesbury into a self-contained flat for her daughter so that Sassoon and she could be separate yet see George. Sassoon refused. And now the school, Greenways, and its owner, Mrs Hancock, became a new battlefield.

Hester wanted George to go to the academically demanding Winchester and therefore thought that he should move to a more academic prep school. Instantly Sassoon asked Geoffrey Keynes to put the boy down for Oundle, a school near Peterborough where Keynes sent his own sons, partly to thwart her and also because Oundle was strong in science, at which George showed promise.

Hester then erupted in a not unjustified suspicion that Mrs Hancock, a widow who had turned to Sassoon for sympathy after losing a son in the war, was after him and spread such wild rumours of her sexual activities with a local butcher and various American soldiers that the owner of Greenways threatened to sue for slander.

*

IN JULY 1944, Rex Whistler, Hester's hope of happiness, was killed in Normandy. Sassoon had known that Rex's courage would put him in danger. Now all jealousy or anger about Hester and the artist vanished in sorrow at 'the worst pain I've felt since the war'. He comforted Edith Olivier, who had adored Rex, but he shunned the memorial service in Salisbury cathedral for 'it would only harrow me'.[6] Apart from this, the war news grew better, although a flying bomb was shot down only 500 yards from Weirleigh, breaking the windows of his old home. Over the previous five months sixty American soldiers had been at Heytesbury, twenty-five of them sleeping there and a thousand camped in the park. Sassoon confronted five drunken American soldiers in the front hall and one evening in the woods he heard moaning: a woman with a man, like those sounds in the country near Craiglockhart in 1917, a counterpoint to his own erotic dreams that made him think of the 'devitalised quality of my verse and prose written of late years . . . No risks taken . . . not even genuinely unhappy.'[7]

In the war's last full year, 1944, Sassoon wrote poetry as well as autobiography. In April came the unpublished 'Nirvana', about an escape from marriage's battlefield into an imagined calm; in May 'A Glimpse of Fitz' (also unpublished) showed the comfort that he found in Edward FitzGerald's letters. The Housmanesque 'Valediction to Youth' of June, with its expression of gratitude that 'I'm no longer young', also stayed unpublished.[8]

But the memoirs occupied him most of the time and he claimed never to have written a book he had liked so little: too ordinary, without atmosphere, just a string of incidents. The writing brought back the First World War and those unanswerable questions: could

he have stood more of the trenches without breaking down, had the
protest been a form of cowardice, had all that time out of the line
diminished his right to be remembered as a brave war poet? The
book upset Sassoon, yet he needed the money to live at Heytesbury
without Hester's support. Every evening he worked on the manuscript, the past coming often now in reports of death, like those of
the Hunter twins at Wilsford and that strange histrionic man Robert
Nichols. Sassoon dreaded the evening effort, 'yet I am miserable if I
don't get something done every night',[9] and it meant a break in the
'unutterable dinginess of the present'.[10] He wrote in the library – a
tall, white and gold room, 'walled in with good books'.

Assaults came from the outside world on his attempts to create
an idyll, such as a sneering article in the *Listener* about Rupert
Brooke, for Sassoon a writer as synonymous as Owen with a
moment in history, 1914 as against 1918 – both parts of his sacred
past. Such 'silly cleverness' made him 'sick'.[11] A New York anthology of war poetry annoyed him because Owen was more heavily
represented than Sassoon – 'the canonisation of Wilfred is still in
full swing', he told Blunden. 'It has become a sort of intelligentsia
cant'[12] – and the selection included non-combatants like Auden and
Geoffrey Grigson and again belittled Brooke. In March, Fabers sent
him a cheque for six months' royalties for £266. *The Weald of
Youth* was out of print, as was *Memoirs of an Infantry Officer*, but
the *Fox-hunting Man* had sold nearly 5,000 in its five-shilling edition
and the 2s 6d *Selected Poems* 12,000 copies in four years.

By the middle of April 1945, he was exhausted after four happy
weeks alone with his son. The main topic between them was 'leetle'
(or little), as George called his mother, Sassoon joking about her.
Hester came over fourteen times in twenty-eight days, saying that
after Rex's death, she had nothing to live for except George. She
still wanted to return to Heytesbury and went on paying the wages
of the outdoor staff. On Victory in Europe day he wrote of a perfect
time 'alone in my lovely house with my joyous and loving little
son'.[13] On 1 April the *Observer* published his poem 'Easter 1945'
that voiced his yearning for a better world. On 6 May, another

poem in the same newspaper seems a partial return to an old anger, an answer to those who said the war had been won in the arms factories – 'Won by production was it?' Surely the 'ardent or afraid' fighting men in the air or on sea or land were the true victors.[14]

His failed marriage was the main intrusion. A lawyer friend, Judge Sturgis, advised him to have George made a ward of court. Lady Gatty wrote to say that Hester was willing to try again and not impose herself on him while he was working; 'most women would not have acted so patiently.' Did Sassoon realize that he needed Hester's money to live at Heytesbury? And Hester was moving to a house in Winterbourne Dauntsey, near her mother, so she must have her furniture and pictures. In November 1945, a van collected these, leaving a barren Heytesbury and its resentful squire who, later, broke into some more tea-chests that she had packed and put their contents back in the rooms, causing his wife to observe that 'there is a very definite oriental streak in him that hops up at times that I cannot, & never could get used to . . .'[15]

But she kept on changing her mind, saying that she had fallen in love with him again and wanted to have another child, a little girl. She claimed that the Blundens had been wonderful to her, as had E. M. Forster and Geoffrey Keynes. She said she was thinking of writing a book about painter-poets, helped by Blunden. Were Sassoon's friends betraying him, he wondered? He removed all Blunden's books from the library because of 'his feeble compliance towards H.'[16] And Hester would not leave. In London, she waited for him at the dentist with a 'queer crazy look' in her eyes; then she produced a letter from her sister-in-law that said, 'Perhaps in time Siegfried will improve . . . but he is obviously far from right at the moment,' an imputation of mental instability repeated when Hester told Mrs Hancock that shell-shock and his head wound meant that he was 'not always responsible for his actions'.[17] Sassoon turned to whisky for the first time since 1941. After Hester, in the presence of George, threatened to name the owner of Greenways as a co-respondent in any divorce, Sassoon lost his temper and she cried again, 'If only you would give me another baby.'[18] When Mrs

Hancock said that she was thinking of marrying an ex-rubber planter called Gibbons, Sassoon urged her to accept him as soon as possible. Hester declared again that she would love him until she died.

Sassoon tried to enlist his friends. To Cockerell, he said that Hester was 'a borderline mental case',[19] and used the same phrase to Blunden. In fact each questioned the other's sanity, Hester repeating the charge of lingering shell-shock. She wrote later of this time, when Sassoon had told her brother Richard that she was mad, as 'one of the worst periods of my life', its 'torture' making her go to a doctor to get a certificate as proof of her sanity and 'the promise that I would be able to call on him as a witness if it was ever necessary'.[20] Sassoon repeated his threat to have George made a ward of court and Hester threatened in any legal battle to make 'full use'[21] of the affair with Stephen Tennant. Then she collapsed, saying tearfully that she wanted to dedicate the book she was writing to him. The next day he burned photographs of her at the Wilton pageant and a letter from the clergyman about their marriage service.

*

FABERS WERE PRINTING 20,000 copies of *Siegfried's Journey*, at ten shillings and sixpence each, and offering an advance of £1,000, so he felt rich. He read the proofs, admiring the book's concision, but thought that it lacked 'saturation of feeling and spontaneous felicity'.[22] News of the massive Labour victory in the general election pleased him because many Tories from the class he had loathed in the First World War had gone. Yet he knew now that there was no hope of lower income tax to help towards the cost of Heytesbury.

Then Glen Byam Shaw telephoned, back from the war, and towards the end of the month he and Angela came to Heytesbury, Glen limping from his wound. The old friendship flared up beautifully and they went to Minehead for ten days: the Byam Shaws and their two children and Sassoon and George, on whom 'my whole life depends – on him, for whom all my previous life has been a preparation',[23] as the boy moved away from childhood, inspiring a love in his father that was more complex and heartbreaking even than before.

A trip to London – to a play with the Byam Shaws, at which he gave a copy of *The Weald of Youth* to the actress Edith Evans, followed by a chance meeting with Osbert Sitwell and lunch at the Reform Club – made him see, back in the silence of Heytesbury, that he should try to write something as 'I have literally nothing to do all day.'[24] Yet Sassoon feared that the dropping of the first atomic bomb on Hiroshima made his style and literary inclinations seem obsolete. As if in answer, he wrote a sonnet on Belsen. He knew that he had only five more years before George went on to public school and adolescent independence. Then he would be sixty-four. 'I must exploit myself as a Grand Old Man of English Literature, I suppose!'[25] At least Geoffrey Faber had written to say that he loved *Siegfried's Journey*; and it became a Book Society choice, which meant an additional £450.

He thought he had no real friends except for Glen and Angela Byam Shaw. Even Edith Olivier was encouraging Hester to think the marriage might be retrieved. Blunden wrote an awkwardly phrased but friendly letter. 'Your friends know your nature and your necessities and however they may and must wish that your marriage had proved a triumph they will never lay blame on you because it did not,' Sassoon's greatest friend said. 'You stand unaltered; we look to the future and to your gaining a new "place of rest" and increasing your gift to all who read and think . . .'[26] In fact several people who knew him well – Blunden (despite this letter), Laurence Whistler, Miriam Lane, his later friend Haro Hodson – said that Sassoon was more to blame for the marriage's breakdown than his wife. As she supervised the moving of her furniture from Heytesbury, Hester begged again to be allowed to come back, giving him an eight-line poem about her love resembling an extinguished fire that might be revived. Alone for Christmas with George, and bicycling with the boy after lunch in the winter sun, Sassoon thought it 'the best Xmas day I've ever had at Heytesbury'.[27]

But his first winter alone in the huge house became an ordeal in some of the coldest weather of the century: frozen pipes, then floods in the cellar after a thaw, and Hester coming through the snow to see if she could help. He had managed twelve lines of verse 'in my minor prophet vein'[28] on the state of the world. And Patric Dickinson of the BBC wrote to say he wanted to broadcast some of Sassoon's poems in January 1946. Might he talk on the radio about Wilfred Owen? Irritated, he answered no. In 1945, the year of victory, Sassoon was asked for public poems. Belsen seemed 'this ultimate pollution . . . beyond the latitudes of human thought':

> *But how to live it down? How to redeem*
> *The heart of humankind – that maniac face*
> *Marred by abominations? How undream*
> *Gas chambers and the torturer's foul embrace?*

Sassoon thought time alone could bring 'decontamination'. On 9 November he produced 'Litany of the Lost', about the tyranny of invention and human weakness, with the repeated last line of each verse: 'Deliver us from ourselves.' Later that month he wrote 'Sanctuary', one of those cries for rest where the trivial falls away and he finds 'my shriven self, my source of song', also 'the lost commander of my life' who is 'love remade, love-lit, and more than lover'.[29]

*

HIS WRITING FACED a light as harsh as the old dazzle of modernism. The poetry of the Second World War was different from that of the previous one, not least because of the different atmosphere of the conflict itself. Instead of the immediate battles and passionate recruitment of 1914, there were, for the British, months of phoney war until May 1940 when the serious fighting began. And Hitler and the Nazis seemed very different adversaries from the imperial Germany of the Kaiser. Alan Ross, a young poet who had enlisted in the navy, wrote, 'No one seriously thought the war would have been better unfought or was being gratuitously prolonged by bungling politicians and generals, so acceptance rather than protest on the Sassoon and Owen level was the only valid response.' This made for poetry 'of less vehemence and satiric force'[30] – more realistic, less obviously emotional, less romantic in its rendering of suffering and pain. There were fewer British poems of combat, an exception being those by Keith Douglas, an Oxford contemporary of Sassoon's nephew Hamo, who had a Byronic relish for fighting. But Douglas does not linger over suffering or wounds or death, and the satire is not angry, as in Sassoon's 'The General' or 'Base Details', but pitying. His 'Aristocrats', about officers absurd in their blockheaded chivalry, was inspired by a colonel who left £3,000 to the Beaufort hunt. Such people seemed no longer threatening but pathetic and moribund. The way was set for the post-war realism of a society emerging after Labour's election victory of 1945, a move away from modernist obscurity but also from pastoral nostalgia.

At first this was not obvious at Heytesbury. *Siegfried's Journey* did well, perhaps because its soothing prose and undemanding sentiment contrasted with the ordeals of post-war austerity. The book's success was, Sassoon thought, a snub to the Gattys. To Howard Spring in the *Sunday Graphic*, its beauty came from 'the spirit'[31] behind the words rather than an artful style, although Spring remarked on the odd self-satisfaction at having abandoned idealism for the more uncritical attitude of maturity. Edward Shanks in the *Daily Dispatch* found the book full of 'exquisite portraits'[32] with, at its centre, this young man who mixed shyness and certainty. In the *New Statesman*, Raymond Mortimer thought that 'everyone inter-ested in 20th century letters'[33] would read it. For Edith Olivier, it brought to mind what Henry Lamb had said of Rex Whistler's paintings: 'He sees more light – and *represents* more light – than any other painter . . .'[34] Other letters arrived, including one from Forster, chiding his friend for being so preoccupied by domestic upheavals and ending 'Damn Hester' and 'Damn George',[35] which depressed its recipient for the rest of the day. To Sassoon's cousin, Mary Donaldson, the memoir had a longing for oblivion. 'Why do you sound so aged, Siegfried?'[36] she asked, still spry at seventy-two.

Helen Waddell saw in *Siegfried's Journey* a self-awareness combined with an awareness of others that made him resemble George Meredith, and 'I think you both know something of what Emily Brontë meant when she said anguish.'[37]

There was occasional acidity. The *Times Literary Supplement* found the book too introspective and bland – Owen, for instance, 'floats'[38] tantalizingly. In *Time and Tide*, Ifor Evans wrote that the book had few signs of 'awareness of anything that had happened in the world since 1920'.[39] Harold Owen objected to its 'complacence' and its patronizing portrayal of Wilfred as 'docile or humble' which failed to show how formidable he could be. Owen also recalled a similarly patronizing letter to him from Sassoon after the war; 'go on being the gallant little fellow that you are'.[40] The *Irish Times* thought the memoir repetitive and self-satisfied,[41] and one American reviewer criticized the 'self importance' and 'mannered attitude' of a book 'mellow to the point of decadence'.[42] In the *New Yorker* Edmund Wilson remarked on its 'narcissistic fatuity' and felt irritated that the author now saw his brave position during the First War as merely the result of impetuous immaturity. To Wilson, Sassoon seemed to have reverted to a fox-hunting 'well-bred British schoolboy' and 'one would like to see him shot in the rear with the arrow of one of his own satiric poems: the kind he wrote in 1916'.[43]

The book has a sweet reflectiveness, quite possibly because its author again had sought a sunlit alternative to his own wartime turbulence. Beginning in August 1916, with Robbie Ross's visit to him in hospital at Oxford, *Siegfried's Journey* ends in 1920 with its hero apparently clueless in Trafalgar Square after the American lecture tour. His time at the front and any hints of sexual involvement are left out, with neither Atkin nor Glenn Hunter mentioned. Sometimes the narrative seems like a smooth journey past smiling friends and mentors like Ross, Lady Ottoline Morrell, Rivers, Hardy, Wilfred Owen, Winston Churchill, Osbert Sitwell, T. E. Lawrence and Sam Behrman. The more abrasive Graves and Dent do not appear, nor do Bartholomew and the Cambridge homosexual circle. Even the protest of 1917 is made soothing by Sassoon's conclusion that he had been mistaken and the war should indeed have lasted until victory, his way perhaps of smoothing over the turmoil and doubt that these memories still evoked in him. The Craiglockhart passage alone carries a hint of a darker world, although he ignored Blunden's advice to quote from Owen's poetry.[44] He describes the background to some of his own famous poems, and there is some delightful, musical prose in the descriptions of visits to Max Gate and to the ancient poet Wilfrid Scawen Blunt in Sussex which, Sassoon said, evoked his idea of a civilized past. To him, the domestic tension had made the book's writing a miracle. Perhaps this, and its effect on his concentration, may be another reason why *Siegfried's Journey* seems rather too short to cover those years which were among the most eventful of his life.

He felt old, plunged into a week of depression after flu, even though the *Atlantic Monthly* was buying two excerpts of *Siegfried's Journey* for $1,000. The BBC broadcast nine of his poems read by the actor Felix Aylmer, making him think, 'I really am a very good poet.'[45] In the middle of January, he received a letter from Harold Nicolson – who had reviewed *Siegfried's Journey* favourably – to say that he had been asked by the publishers Constable to approach Sassoon about writing a biography of Meredith based on the Buxton Foreman archive that the firm had recently bought.

Lonely, with George at school, he felt comforted by the thought of this new book. The idea had come, he was sure, through Helen Waddell, the medieval scholar who lived with a Constable director, Otto Kyllmann, an old acquaintance of Meredith – and he knew Helen Waddell through Mrs Hancock ('Greenways again!'); another reason could have been the passages about Meredith in *Siegfried's Journey*. Offering a £750 advance, Michael Sadleir of Constable said he wanted a 'plainly written, unbrilliant, straightforward account of G.M.'s life and career'.[46] Sassoon saw it as a return to the world of Helen Wirgman, who had known Meredith well, even

to Weirleigh, for Theresa had sent a huge wreath to the writer's funeral.

*

HESTER ASKED HIM again to consider having another child. Sassoon, frightened now of the courts, asked his lawyer, the urbane, art-loving Anthony Lousada, to come to Heytesbury to be briefed on possible mediation with the Gattys over Hester's threatened legal action to gain custody of George.

On the first night, he spoke to Lousada about the marriage and George's resentment of Hester's fussing. While Lousada was there, Hester came over, her fifth visit that week, and the lawyer noted how Sassoon, although 'obviously upset', was 'distantly polite and seemed resigned'. Soon there was a sound of running, shouts of 'Daddy!' and George, back from Greenways, rushed in, only to look displeased when he saw his mother. To Lousada, George was 'a quick intelligent boy', apparently 'perfectly normal', and Hester an interruption in the close relationship between father and son. Her attempt to kiss the boy goodbye ended in a struggle. As she left, George shouted, 'Don't come tomorrow. You're not to come. We must have some time by ourselves. You mustn't keep coming over.' Lousada noted that Sassoon never reacted when George spoke roughly to Hester.[47] The Gattys now urged Hester to get a divorce on grounds of desertion. At Heytesbury she dropped her hat, and Sassoon noticed it had been bought in Paris in May 1938 when they were happy together. Regret struck him for the collapse of hopes of family life in this beautiful place. On Lousada's advice he wrote asking her not to come to Heytesbury and she appeared with his letter, handing it back in hysterics, saying that she still hoped for reconciliation.

George Meredith seemed a way out. Sassoon even saw the first Mrs Meredith's desertion of the novelist and of their son Arthur as comparable to the way Hester had treated him and George. He went to Cambridge to talk to G. M. Trevelyan, the Master of Trinity, about Meredith, and to London, to the Constable offices to read the papers, to see Geoffrey Keynes, Blunden, Helen Waddell and Otto Kyllmann and have lunch with H. M. Tomlinson; he then went to the ballet with Keynes. Hester, now jealous of his friendship with Helen Waddell, came to Heytesbury to paint. George and Sassoon went over to see her new house, The Grange, thinking that she was away – but she came out to ask them into the 'pretty and old-fashioned' but not cheerful place. Heytesbury, he thought, seemed 'a palace'[48] compared to The Grange for what it offered George: the heaven of a country childhood, better and more free than his own had been at Weirleigh. Now he could make those utopian memoirs a reality. Rolf Barber, a master at Oundle and friend of Mrs Hancock, came over to Heytesbury from Greenways to ride, and Sassoon saw this 'very nice and intelligent man'[49] of thirty-two as a possible help with George's future.

News came that H. G. Wells was dead – like the death of Voltaire, Sassoon thought. This seemed a reminder of how out of the world he was, and the mood made him 'zestless'[50] about the proofs of his *Collected Poems*. A programme that he had compiled for the radio on Meredith sounded satisfactory, with Alec Guinness reading the poems. But he was getting more reclusive, he felt, and could not imagine writing more good poetry. Then, in the proofs of the *Collected Poems*, *The Heart's Journey* and *Vigils* sections encouraged him, and the *Satirical Poems* inspired thoughts of taking the memoirs further into the 1920s. The seclusion remained unbroken when he stayed away from a fiftieth-birthday dinner given for Blunden at the Garrick Club, still angry at his friend's sympathy for Hester, sending wine and a poem that ignored these tensions:

> Ah what avails the unctuous phrase,
> Ah what the honeyed line,
> To laud those unassuming ways
> Which, Blunden, E. are thine?[51]

On 15 November Blunden was at Heytesbury, admiring the early chapters of the Meredith biography. This, and his thoughts for a review in the *Listener* of a book on fox-hunting, evoked a better time: 'the golden age' from about 1825 until 1918. And the past was enlivened by one living glory. Writing to a new correspondent, the publisher Rupert Hart-Davis, Sassoon looked back to the poem 'Meeting and Parting' as 'the most significant thing I've ever written'[52] because of its celebration of his son.

TWENTY-TWO

Heytesbury's solitary squire

SASSOON WORKED HARD on Meredith at Heytesbury through the freezing winter, to be interrupted one day in January 1947 when Stephen Tennant arrived in a hired Rolls-Royce. He looked even odder than usual – hennaed hair, a painted face, sliding at forty-one into middle age apparently forgetful of his once perfectionist narcissism – and Hester, who appeared during the visit, was not charmed this time, saying afterwards that the plump, excited, 'entirely selfish' visitor was bad for their son.[1]

By 18 March, he had written over 80,000 words. Work had become 'a godsend', taking his mind off 'the dreariness'[2] of solitary domestic life. His literary earnings for fifteen months since January 1946 came to a surprisingly good £5,600 and on 19 May, after keeping the manuscript of Meredith for two weeks, Mr Kyllmann of Constable telegraphed, 'Have read first eleven chapters you have done it magnificently.'[3]

*

HESTER SAID THAT the other boys were teasing George about his father's frequent appearances at Greenways. Their son was clearly suffering from the marriage's breakdown, spoilt by Hester yet contemptuous of her. Sassoon felt the tragedy and his own guilt, when Ince, the Greenways headmaster, said he thought that the boy

should stay at the school for weekends and not have the disruption of a divided but indulged home life. Miserable, Sassoon exclaimed in his diary, 'O the loneliness of those weekends.'⁴ Yet puritan realism made him feel that this was right. His own boyhood returned when he played in a cricket match at Greenways for the staff against the boys. Then on 11 July, at a quarter-past eight in the evening, Michael Sassoon rang to say 'in his funny off-hand way' that 'Ash passed out at ten minutes to seven.'⁵

Outwardly, Sassoon scarcely faltered, desperate to avoid a collapse that might seem weak to his wife. He resolved to miss the funeral, fearing that he would be overcome, and tried to think of practical matters like the end of his £400 annuity to Theresa, of a possible £1,000 a year more from her trust fund, perhaps £10,000 from the sale of Weirleigh; now there was no need to rush the memoirs. She was ninety-three; and he had (he told himself) long prepared for this. He had avoided Weirleigh, fearful of seeing an old, exhausted woman, although she had stayed lively until the end despite being plagued by eczema, and because the doctor had said that the excitement brought on by a visit might give Theresa a heart attack. Sassoon had also dreaded talking to her about Hester. He scorned his wife's wish to attend the funeral as 'typical'⁶ and selfish, forbidding her to go.

Slowly emotion forced its way through. He thought of Ash's humiliating struggles without his father, of her breakdowns during his childhood and youth. Her priorities, good and silly, had stayed with him. He had welcomed her approval of his friends and played up to her mild snobbery and prejudices. Theresa had mixed conservatism with courage and intelligence and given him a love which he had hated to betray. Much of his life – the initial wonder of his marriage, his awkwardness about homosexuality, his writing about an ideal world – had been an instinctive wish to be what she wanted or, at least, not to hurt her. Sassoon told Glen Byam Shaw of the 'horrid' thought of her 'drawing room being dismantled and the old place sold'.⁷ He never went to Weirleigh again.

*

ON 19 AUGUST 1947, just after he had written ten alexandrine lines called 'Innovations', Hester rang to say she and George were going to Mull, the island off the north-west coast of Scotland, to stay in a hotel near her old childhood haunt of Lochbuie. From there, they telephoned ecstatically about catching mackerel and walking over the high hills. This, she told Sassoon, was where she wanted to die. He agreed to let George stay another week, refusing to come up himself but still feeling the obsession with his son. His resentment swelled in solitude: anger at Edmund Blunden for seeing her, fear that she was stealing George.

Blunden, however, wrote a good review of the *Collected Poems* in the *Spectator*, 'temperate and understanding',[8] Sassoon admitted. He praised this volume which covered the years from 1908 until 1940 and seemed too short to do justice to 'the variousness of the poet's mind'.[9] The book sold 5,000 copies in five weeks but failed to achieve as much attention as its author had hoped, although Churchill sent a telegram saying, 'I am delighted to hear from the Bloody Young Bolshevik again. Thank you so much for the book.'[10] Cecil Day Lewis disliked the blurred music, prettily phrased quietism and 'exquisite and nostalgic fancy' of the later work that seemed minor and inert alongside the 'brave ardent irrational verses' of the war.[11] In the *Times Literary Supplement*, H. M. Tomlinson praised the mix of 'happy innocence' and 'cool understanding',[12] and in the *Fortnightly Review* Richard Church, a fellow pastoral poet, saw a descent into a gentle world of elegiac but private 'rich middle-class leisure'.[13]

Disappointed, Sassoon started to make notes for a successor to *Siegfried's Journey* that took his story through the early 1920s. But, waking in the middle of the night, he felt that these were 'false and trivial'. How much better to write 'an uncompromising "show-up" of life'; but the public wanted the 'same old stuff – the anodyne against depression'. The energy needed for the book was drained by the war against Hester. This now took the eccentric form of buying expensive pictures to show his independence of his wife and her possessions that she had removed from Heytesbury. The Bristol gallery of Frost and Reed benefited from this mood, selling him, among other works, a Panini for £300, a Vernet, a Turner watercolour of a ruined abbey (for £70), a de Wint for £85, a Dutch flower picture by J. Metz for £325 ('I mean to show her what I can do!'),[14] a seventeenth-century view of Amsterdam by William Trost, a scene of cattle and sheep by Tilder, and a Norfolk landscape of barges and windmills by Edward Williams. Morland. Soon he had spent £1,890 making the walls of Heytesbury his, not hers, and hung with 'mind resters',[15] far from the turbulence outside.

A solitary Christmas meant more brooding. Out of this came fifteen lines about the child that Hester had refused to give him, in Sassoon's mind a boy who would have been born in 1938. These were partly inspired by Rudyard Kipling's short story 'They', reread by him after Theresa's death in her marked copy from Weirleigh, as well as by Charles Lamb's 'Dream Children' and the memory of Thomas Hardy's dark assertion that the happiest people are those who have never been born. The melancholy of Kipling's tale of the dead children, coupled with fear of a gradual estrangement from George as the boy grew up, surged over him, especially when he found a photograph of his son on the lawn at Heytesbury between the pages of his mother's copy. George's beautiful childhood years should have been prolonged by a younger brother who could have broken the self-absorption of an only child. Sassoon realized this would have meant sharing his son more but to the benefit of the boy. Perhaps they were too close and this was bad for both of them, although the love ruled his life. Sometimes, in the garden, he imagined a figure under the beech tree and a summer sky, watching him in ghostly calm:

> O child I shall not know – heart-haunting cry
> Troubling the midnight silence in a thought
> That like a footstep pauses, passes by
> The door which might have opened, might have brought
> The face which never lived and cannot die.[16]

Other poems show strain and pessimism. The depressing 'Solitudes at Sixty' was written in August; 'In Time of Decivilisation', redolent of Hardy's 'In the Time of the Breaking of Nations', echoes with melancholy and the wish for mental tranquillity; and in December he wrote 'Hypnogogic Inventions', about mind pictures seen on the verge of sleep.[17] The memoirs stalled with his 1920s bewildered self and the need for honesty about the love affairs. The threat of nuclear war and the apparent end of inherited privilege made it all seem merely a trivial, rarefied 'education of errors'.[18] Gradually he abandoned the volume.

The 1948 New Year's honours list was, to Sassoon, another infuriating sign of the world's incomprehensibility and decay. T. S. Eliot's Order of Merit meant that modernism's triumph was now complete; then Vita Sackville-West, a mediocre poet, had been made a Companion of Honour, probably through the influence of her husband Harold Nicolson, who had recently become a socialist. When G. S. Fraser in the *New Statesman* gave Christopher Hassall's poems a bad review, Sassoon wrote to protest and looked up Fraser's own poetry, to be shocked by the simile 'like a schoolmaster denouncing masturbation'. He made a blacklist of critics: Fraser, Geoffrey Grigson, Roy Fuller, all employed at the *Listener* by J. R. Ackerley, its literary editor, whom he thought had been fatally seduced by literary fashion. After looking through his notebooks, he thought he had only written about 450 lines of good poetry over more than seven years: a miserable harvest. In February 1948, Sassoon managed 'a neat little pedestrian poem',[19] later published as 'Old-Fashioned Weather'. Ackerley at the *Listener* sent one of two poems back without comment and the other in proof with a note querying the sense of the last two lines.

Weirleigh was to be split up for sale, the agent saying the house had 'nothing to recommend it'.[20] The property fetched £8,000 and Sassoon's sadness was for what he had made of this grim, ugly house and its garden and view over the weald rather than for its reality. Other pleasures dwindled. Now he no longer felt welcome in the Heytesbury cricket team – perhaps not surprising as he sometimes walked back to the house when bored with fielding, leaving his team with only ten men. Music lasted, as with Elgar's ninety-first-birthday concert on the BBC: the violin concerto, 'Falstaff' and three part songs, unashamedly emotional, bringing back the days of Schuster and the 1920s. Hester oscillated between threatening divorce and claiming that she adored him. Then, in June 1948, two younger visitors penetrated the gloom: Richard Seymour, a bachelor clergyman of forty-three with a parish in the East End of London, and the young artist and writer Haro Hodson.

The sensitive, tall and athletic-looking Seymour had been corresponding with Sassoon for some years. Quickly, Sassoon confided in this admirer so that when Hester arrived the clergyman was distant with her. The younger Haro Hodson – he was still a student at Oxford after serving as an officer in the war – came as an admirer of Max Beerbohm and a friend of Mrs Gibbons (formerly Hancock). Hodson, who had already had several drawings published in magazines, had never read anything by Sassoon but was going to Rapallo and – at the suggestion of Mrs Gibbons, who knew his parents – collected the proofs of *Meredith* from Heytesbury to take to Beerbohm to check the punctuation. Intrigued by old people's reminiscences, darkly handsome, charming and a good listener, Hodson wrote poetry in the traditional style himself. In the library at Heytesbury, Siegfried Sassoon greeted him in a navy-blue jacket, holding a kettle; then Hester entered, with a face like 'a ravaged medallion',[21] obviously antagonistic. Hodson liked the humorous and gentle manners of his host but felt disconcerted by the jerky movements, the averted eyes and the waffling talk's sudden illumination by a sharp, direct gaze, as if from below, in spite of Sassoon's height. Soon poetry, Haro's looks and a shared admiration for Max Beerbohm began a friendship, and – for the older man – a platonic love affair.

*

THE BBC OFFERED fifty-five guineas for a talk about Wilfred Owen and Sassoon agreed to write but not read it. While toiling at this, he thought, 'I have, more and more, believed that he would have been incalculably valuable to me. His death made a gap in my life which has been there ever since.'[22]

He was reminded of the extraordinary course of his life since 1918 by wild letters from Stephen Tennant, often from hotels in Bournemouth, Paris or Venice, rebuking him for avoiding him, criticizing his writing for being 'pedestrian and conventional', without 'compulsive divine unrest',[23] and reporting that Lord David Cecil thought Siegfried extremely conceited. But, ultimately, nothing could distract him from the ache of George's absence on Mull with Hester, not even the advance copies of *Meredith*. Finally, on 19 August he left for the island, annoyed that Hester stayed on for several days in the hotel at Torosay, which was not what he had wanted. To be with his son in this beautiful but rain-sodden place was enlivening, though his indigestion reared up horribly. Geoffrey Keynes diagnosed a duodenal abscess, saying it needed an operation. By 19 October Sassoon was in hospital in the Central Middlesex at Park Royal, Acton.

Through the autumn and early winter came the generally good reviews of *Meredith*. Bonamy Dobree complained in the *Spectator* about the lack of footnotes and references, and Lady Milner, who had known Meredith, was harsh in the *National Review*, but the *TLS* praised this 'poet's estimate',[24] even though it had few new facts and little psychological investigation. When an academic criticized this absence of research in a letter to the paper,[25] Sassoon responded briskly, saying, 'I feel that those who pursue such researches among documents in public record offices would do well to digest another of Meredith's sayings to his friend Clodd: "Chiefly by that in my poetry which emphasises the unity of life, the soul that breathes through the universe, do I wish to be remembered; for the spiritual is the eternal." '[26] Sales went well: nearly 5,000 in the first week. Sassoon told the novelist L. P. Hartley that he felt that the book was what the publisher had asked for, 'a commonsense, unbrilliant performance. I am not a clever man.'[27] This seemed to be echoed in the United States, where *Time* called it 'simple and unpretentious',[28] and in the *New York Times*, an English professor at Princeton liked the amateurism and the clash of Sassoon's quiet approach with Meredith's flamboyance but not the inability to explain Meredith's 'psychological subtlety'.[29] The *Atlantic Monthly* expressed irritation at Sassoon's 'communing with the gentle reader'[30] and his self-deprecation, but praised the book's enthusiasm.

In fact Sassoon had taken trouble over parts of his research, analysing closely the texts of different editions of Meredith's poems. But the biography seems artless in its pleasant enthusiasm, protestations of its author's inadequacy ('all this is most unpalatable to me who am no critic'), and sentences that begin, 'I hear them saying to one another . . .', 'having conducted Meredith to his forty-fourth year . . .' or, in reference to a critical essay by Virginia Woolf, 'bowing gratefully to a gifted lady . . .' Clearly Sassoon is uneasy when writing about the diffuse, densely written novels of 'an intellectual experimenter' and prefers the poet of 'The Lark Ascending', other nature poems or 'Love in a Valley'; the tragic 'Modern Love', with its romantic hope and disillusion, reminded him rather too much of what had happened with Hester. Sometimes one senses a personal note, as in the description of Meredith's 'fathomless and immeasurable' feeling for his son Arthur, only for sadness to take over when Arthur prefers to be independent. Disliking the idea of a Freudian biography, Sassoon avoids psychological analysis, producing a fairly smooth narrative of what was, after the first marriage's failure, a not very exciting life. What he appreciates is the energy and feeling for nature, landscape and the open air in a writer who was an early mentor of Thomas Hardy and 'can make us remember what it felt like to be young'.[31]

*

HESTER WROTE TO Geoffrey Keynes to say that if Sassoon's stomach trouble was cancer she would like to know but her husband should not be told because 'he has almost an obsession about growing older and being ill. He can't bear the idea.' She was desperate to help. 'There is nothing I would not do for him.'[32]

The operation failed to find a long-term solution, but the hospital brought him happiness: doctors and nurses who acknowledged his fame, time to read, a good review of *Meredith* by John Betjeman. Lamb's letters, Shakespeare, Jane Austen, Henry James's notebooks, *Middlemarch* and Browning were all at his bedside and, when Hester appeared with some chrysanthemums, the doctor, having been warned by Geoffrey Keynes, refused her admittance, saying that the patient needed a complete rest. Haro Hodson was allowed in, Sassoon suddenly leaning forward to give him a glancing kiss. Other visitors included Nan Tennant and J. R. Ackerley. Towards the end of his time at Park Royal Sassoon went to Walter de la Mare's house in Twickenham, to be delighted by another of his heroes, a reminder of a living world of poetry that was apart from 'Towering Tom' Eliot.

Haro Hodson was told about certain friends: Geoffrey Keynes ('you will like him. He is brusque and plain-spoken, but an unfailing friend . . . A complete extrovert, but he adores young men, and will adore you . . . Of very fine quality. But on the surface, liable to appear insensitive'); Angela Byam Shaw ('She is so non-actressy – just a lovely human being'); H. M. Tomlinson ('a great prose writer and a great human being'). On poetry, Sassoon said he himself was 'essentially sculptural' like his mother, who had been a designer rather than a painter. He did not like 'flaking impressions, momentary moods, hit or miss effects of word arrangement'; in modern poetry there was too much 'chancing your arm' stuff, not enough 'exact'[33] meaning. He told Haro that Hester had heard a rumour, probably false, that 'the O.M. committee at the palace' had wanted to give him the honour but a hitch had let it go to Eliot instead. (Betjeman told Laurence Whistler that Sassoon would have got the Order of Merit and the laureateship if he had not been 'queer'.)[34] Hodson spoke of hunt balls and hunting, bringing memories of youth, and Sassoon longed to help this talented, good-looking young man, saying, 'O Haro, try not to think of me as so terribly old as all that (you don't, I know) because the strange thing is that I can still feel so young inside'.[35]

Back at Heytesbury, the problems of the rich crowded in when his woodman, his cook and his head gardener quarrelled and gave notice. Hester announced that she had not only bought a lodge on Mull but had rented 4,000 acres of rough shooting as well, another method, Sassoon thought, of luring George away. George seldom left his thoughts and 'if my health goes, what shall I have to offer him? The only solution for my mind is work to occupy it.'[36] The poetry of 1948 was, as Sassoon wrote, often about 'the impact of growing old in a decivilised world . . .' 'Old-Fashioned Weather' brought observations of life at Heytesbury; 'Praise Persistent' asked if attempts to reach the unseen in prayer were heard at all. 'Ultimate Values', written after coming out of hospital, is about memory enduring in the 'simplest human utterance of the dead'.[37] 'Arty people,' he wrote to Haro Hodson in January 1949, 'They make me sick'[38] – his temper no doubt worsened by a review of his *Collected Poems* in the American magazine the *Nation* that called the book 'safe-and-sane, milk-and-water, old-hat British'[39] work. On 7 March he wrote a poem, 'Resurrection', and felt pleased by it, noting again, however, that his poetry was now mostly about himself growing old in isolation.[40]

An exception, not because of its excellence but through its reflection of Sassoon's views on the First World War and doubts about himself, was 'A Falloden Memory'.[41] Written in March 1948, it shows his admiration for the former Foreign Secretary, Lord Grey of Falloden, 'human-simple yet profound', but, at the end, blind, deprived of the world of birds and the Northumberland landscape that he had loved. Sassoon had been reading G. M. Trevelyan's biography of Grey which treated his life as the tragedy of a noble, decent, unintellectual man, almost entirely ignorant of Europe when he became foreign secretary in 1906. To Trevelyan, and to Sassoon, Grey's story was that of the traducing of a selfless country-loving, war-hating public servant by ignoble great-power rivalry, militarism, political guile and historical inevitability. Sassoon would never have thought that this fine gentleman, either by failing to make the unofficial British alliance with the French clear to the Germans and to the world (even to his cabinet colleagues) before 1914 or by avoiding a continental commitment altogether, had been one of those most responsible, if only obliquely, for the slaughter on the Western Front. To Sassoon, Grey remained a beautiful British ideal, like George Sherston – someone who was called away to public service (in the way Sherston had nobly joined up in 1914) from his cherished peaceful, natural world – not at all the more complex, misguided, perhaps sly operator portrayed by later historians.

Trevelyan's defence of Grey changed further Sassoon's perception of his own actions. Even his own protest now seemed of doubtful merit when he read about pre-1914 diplomacy and German war aims and studied Trevelyan's account of Grey's high-minded, well-intentioned attempts to deal with these. 'Had I know some of this in 1917,' he wrote in his diary, 'I could never have "protested" against the continuation!'[42] Such second thoughts about the most celebrated action of his life, already latent after the memories brought back by *Siegfried's Journey*, deepened his melancholy.

*

In April, Hester took George to her new house on Mull, Ben Buie, and telephone calls and letters came from the north, showing the boy's happiness. Sassoon's intense feelings made him think that he should write about his son, because 'except for George, my life is at a dead end of loneliness and monotony'.[43] His stomach still gave him pain, as did irritation at the praise given to Osbert Sitwell's fourth volume of autobiography, *Laughter in the Next Room*, which, to him, seemed much too loose in construction, too bland about people still alive, its prose oddly insensitive and over-ornate. What was Sitwell but 'a self-made writer'? Edith Sitwell had become 'tiresome and pompous' and Sacheverell a 'very selfish'[44] socialite.

The success of Osbert Sitwell's series of memoirs – which had begun in 1945 with *Left Hand Right Hand* – became a new obsession, added to by Constable's rejection of his own suggestion that he should edit a volume of Meredith's verse, flaring up again when, on a trip to London, Sassoon saw Osbert in a bookshop and found him friendly, fat and pink, exuding delight in attention. Sitwell answered his letter of congratulation, regretting Sassoon's literary timidity ('so lacking in you in other directions') and his dislike of modernism, 'for every generation has eyes of its own . . .'[45] The BBC asked him to choose some of his poems and others by Wilfred Owen to be read on the radio. Still suffering from indigestion, Sassoon asked Christopher Hassall to do it (and to read them as well), afraid that what was wanted was not his prose nor his later work but the short war poems and 'Everyone Sang'.[46]

When her mother died, Hester came in tears to Heytesbury. The rich, old lady had settled £25,000 duty paid on George from which Hester would have the income to pay for the boy's education and, in addition, £150 a year more for herself than at present. Surely, Sassoon thought, this would keep her quiet. A new cook, Miss Benn, arrived with a giant poodle called Caesar and he liked her. Then one evening he listened to a concert – Delius's piano concerto and *Sea Drift* – music that, by its romantic feeling, seemed 'the essence of my creative being' and heightened his love for George 'which I control drastically'; the old 'high-strung self-dramatist' was still there. Above all, he felt young. Looking in a mirror at twilight, Sassoon saw someone 'unbelievably young for nearly 63', more like forty, even though death touched him through his friends: Edith Olivier in 1948, a confidante as great as – and even more unquestioningly devoted than – Lady Ottoline Morrell, who had died in 1938. Mornings at Heytesbury were often 'exquisite' yet incapable of disguising yet 'another great long *empty* summer day before me!'[47]

*

A SHARP-EYED VISITOR watched the hermit of Heytesbury. J. R. Ackerley knew that E. M. Forster disapproved of the way Sassoon ('a highly unsatisfactory character') had treated his wife, yet Ackerley accepted an invitation to visit Heytesbury with his adored

Alsatian bitch, Queenie. Exhausted by looking after an aunt and a neurotic sister, Joe Ackerley found 'an earthly paradise': a kingdom apart. Sassoon, 'self-centred and self-absorbed', dressed in old, tattered clothes that sometimes showed white smooth skin, looked beautiful, even when his worn face and averted eyes showed torture as he spoke, almost inaudibly, of 'his past fame, his present neglect, his unhappy marriage, his passionate love for his son'. To Ackerley, the grumbling of this deservedly famous writer seemed absurd, so unlike the serene Edward FitzGerald whom Sassoon admired. How much better to be like Forster, still lively with curiosity about people and things, still selfless and sympathetic, although ten years older than Sassoon. His host's obsession with George ('this schoolboy love') was also worrying; if anything happened to the boy, Sassoon would go mad. When George grew up, the intense relationship would end. Ahead lay 'disaster' and loneliness, then death.

Ackerley was joined at the house by James Kirkup, the twenty-eight-year-old son of a joiner from South Shields, gentle, courteous, a modernist poet but one who liked many of Sassoon's favourite writers. Siegfried appeared at lunchtime, disappearing in the afternoon to do odd jobs, to cut down thistles or undergrowth, probably (Ackerley thought) imagining that each felled plant was Hester. After tea, he let loose a flow of grumbling talk until bedtime, broken only by a stroll after supper. Kirkup dreaded missing the bus that would take him away from this depressing scene, yet admitted that their host had 'really opened my eyes to the virtues of traditional poetry'.

The guests noted the routine of tea: the boiling of the kettle in the library, the host talking so much that he forgot it had boiled. Hester came almost every other day, and Sassoon was sharp with his wife, Ackerley seeing misery in her 'pale, lined, ravaged face, dark lines beneath her eyes' and her mewing cry of 'Siggy, Siggy' as she searched for him. Sassoon said later that she had alienated many of his friends: Forster, Blunden, Rex Whistler, 'whom she fell for and would not leave alone'. When Hester opened the fête in the park – her speech written by the vicar – Sassoon watched in fury from a window. Although her manner was 'nervous, ingratiating, squirming', Ackerley pitied Mrs Siegfried Sassoon. He wondered if Siegfried feared blackmail when she said that a neighbour had talked of Sassoon's affair with Stephen Tennant.

Joe, too, was a homosexual. Sassoon told him about finding a soldier asleep in a ditch near the house – 'a wonderfully good-looking chap, most beautiful mild gentle sort of boy' – and how he had not asked him back. Would Forster have behaved like this, Ackerley thought? No, Morgan would have welcomed the boy into his drawing room and probably more. After hints that he was drinking too much, Ackerley bought his own cheap wine, thinking, 'The rich are very odd,' especially when Sassoon had recently paid almost £300 for a picture by Copley Fielding – 'just like that'. In the village pub, a local said that 'the Captain' was 'a decent old stick' and suggested that Ackerley should bring the squire of Heytesbury down there. Why didn't Sassoon mix more, Ackerley wondered? The irony was that Sassoon thought, condescendingly, that he was helping poor Joe by relieving the loneliness of a pathetic existence.

It was the same on another visit, some two years later: the self-pitying monologues, the complaints about having nothing to do. Ackerley told Sassoon that what kept most people going was curiosity about others. He pitied this 'sorry and dreary figure' on his beautiful estate. The self-obsessed Sassoon, he thought, got no fun out of life because he gave none, although essentially 'a dear man'. Now his humour was invariably sardonic and bitter as he lay idle on a sofa, perhaps recalling his glorious, young past.[48] Ackerley wondered if even George gave him happiness. As if countering this, Sassoon complained in his diary of a 'vaguely devitalising' semi-alcoholic Joe, trapped in the 'typical intelligentsia opinions' of E. M. Forster. Ackerley, having asked to see some poems for the *Listener*, never mentioned them again.

Sassoon went to Mull in August 1949, and Hester was there all the time, George making scenes and often in tears. Back at Heytesbury, she left him three poems, four lines of one of them showing her despair:

Soul, blinded with your own spilt blood,
Battered, my soul, to the last forced breath,
Crushed by heaped cruelty, wild winged hate,
Soul, are you dying? Is courage too late?[49]

Already he was filtering Mull through his transforming memory, recalling picnics, boating, damming pools, fishing for mackerel, offset by the bad bits, the midges and the scenes. Of George, he wrote, 'I see him, always moving actively, against that background of water and mountains – always seeming part of the place,' but then, in the house, crying from strained nerves, shouting at his mother, 'Go away' or 'Leave me alone.'[50] Ince, the headmaster, wrote to Hester suggesting she make a complete break with Sassoon for George's sake. Bearing the letter, she came to Heytesbury and threatened suicide, before saying that she was thinking of starting a market garden.

Ince and Sassoon thought that Hester should agree to a year's absolute separation and have George for half the holidays. But she said a legal separation would not leave her free to divorce him. The headmaster believed that the relationship between George and Sassoon was too intense and that they should be more apart during the school term. Hester signed the agreement. Sassoon agreed not to go to the school so often and that they would attend plays and functions there alternately.

To combat the craving for his son, he took up the abandoned autobiography again. Then his poetic impulse took on a new tone. 'Resurrection' in March had brought back a hope of real poetry, 'almost as though I had been "helped" ', but not quite good enough. A precursor of the later religious poems, it imagines the day of judgement taking place while Sassoon walks in his woods, 'the marred and mystic me'. The unpublished 'Spectators' is about watching the stars and feeling that God might be less strange than unbelief. In October came 'Acceptance', about man turning in need to God; then, after Christmas, on 27 and 29 December, late at night, '2 quite respectable little poems – much more like the real thing at last!' – 'The Unproven' and 'Redemption' – the first about the inadequacy of science to explain mysteries like death, the second asking for some sign of heaven's 'all-hallowing and eternal day'.[51]

This movement towards a solitary, spiritual search explains why the world outside Heytesbury increasingly seemed 'unreal, a sort of dream experience',[52] as when he went to the Omar Khayyám Club dinner in London as Lord Samuel's guest. Sassoon found the peer charming, a fan of Meredith and deprecator of T. S. Eliot. Among the others there were Sir James Grigg (former Secretary of State for War), Michael Sadleir (the publisher), Lord Horder, the cartoonist David Low and Wilde's son Vyvyan Holland. Sassoon stayed with the Keyneses at Arkwright Road and saw Tomlinson and Swinnerton at the Reform Club. To his surprise, he had enjoyed it, particularly the recognition. A similar pleasure came at Warminster grammar school, where he presented the prizes and boys recited two of his poems, 'Alone' and 'Everyone Sang'. Again it was a success but still dreamlike when he thought of it in the isolation of his huge house. What seemed all too real was when George, while staying with Hester's brother Richard Gatty in Yorkshire, went down with sub-acute appendicitis. In a series of desperate telephone calls, Sassoon ordered Hester to take him to be operated on by Geoffrey Keynes in London.

TWENTY-THREE

The search

IN JANUARY 1950, Hester telephoned about George being so happy with her in spite of his appendicitis. Sassoon's discontent became greater when he read an article by a Cambridge professor that exalted Eliot and more so when he heard, in February, that *Meredith* had sold 4,500, fewer copies than the publisher had expected. He wrote some short poems, one published by Ackerley in the *Listener* and addressed to the Supreme Being who would probably fail to answer. Was his self-deprecation a form of vanity, he wondered? To the village, he was just Captain Sassoon, not an eminent poet, partly because of his public modesty. Yet he felt miserable at being ignored and his fantastic dreams, he thought, surely showed repressed creativity.

Hester still came often to Heytesbury. Towards the end of May, another visitor, recommended by Sassoon's old wartime comrade Vivian de Sola Pinto, resurrected the past: the young scholar Dennis Welland, from Nottingham University, who was writing about Wilfred Owen.

Siegfried Sassoon had dreaded the visit, fearing humiliation before Owen's rising reputation, but when Dennis Welland arrived – 'a very nice man (under thirty), genuine and unpretentious' – the conversation, although awkward at first, came to life, encouraged by Welland's accounts of Harold Owen's 'tiresome behaviour'.

Sassoon said that the anti-war poets had had little effect, that all he wanted was to see a third war averted and it would be done by the deterrent of huge armaments, not by pacifist poetry, although 'huge armaments are always used in the end'. Leaving with some letters, manuscripts of poems and copies of the Craiglockhart magazine, Welland thought that the monologue had been drenched with sadness, his host apparently still a prisoner of the war.

Sassoon also brooded on the meeting. To talk about Wilfred had lifted the deprivation briefly, even giving him a sense of Owen's presence, but 'O, the lost years – the lost work that he should have done.' This would certainly have been against the prevailing literary fashion, for Owen, 'though more profoundly imaginative and word-masterful than I', and he were the same type of poet.[1] His own recent verse, in the proofs of the collection *Common Chords*, to be privately printed by Robert Gathorne-Hardy and Kyrle Leng's Mill House Press, seemed 'merely an encumbrance to be got rid of'[2] compared to what he and Owen might have achieved together.

*

IN THE SUMMER of 1950, George was awarded one of three £60 scholarships to Oundle. Sassoon played cricket for Heytesbury and, with Hester watching, it felt fleetingly like the first happy years of their marriage. Confirmation that this had ended came in December, when they both signed a legal deed of separation. According to this, 'unhappy differences' had arisen, leading to a parting 'on or about' 1 January 1945; now Hester could live apart from Siegfried 'as if she were unmarried'. Neither would have any financial claim on the other and each agreed, no doubt to Sassoon's relief, not to 'endeavour to compel the resumption of cohabitation between the spouses or to enforce any restitution of conjugal rights'. On George, they said that they would agree access, mode of upbringing and education between them; one point that Sassoon, regrettably, did not observe was that neither of them 'will in any way seek to influence the mind of the child in any manner prejudicial to the other'.[3]

The problem was that she would not leave, or leave for long. Now adrift, Hester wanted to see him, imagining, without reason, that they could revive some part of what she had wanted, some family life with George. She stayed possessive of Siegfried, her jealousy flaring up at the slightest pretext, and told her family that he was a wonderful writer and a good person who had treated her badly. Her unhappiness showed in hysterics, a shrieking of abuse, but this would pass and she would be charming or pitiable, someone who had suffered. Her brother Richard Gatty and his wife Pamela became her confidants. To them, Sassoon seemed increasingly strange and daunting, a nervous, mumbling man, shattered (Pamela Gatty thought) by the First World War, living in a carefully structured personal world, anxious to talk not of writing but of cricket or fox-hunting, then suddenly showing playfulness and joy, as in the past, by climbing trees, doing somersaults on the lawn to impress George, putting hats on statues or trespassing into forbidden places while visiting the Gattys in Yorkshire. The boy Siegfried could still leap out from behind the wooden, awkward old man.[4]

Some guests came: Nan Tennant, now almost seventy, a witness of the Stephen years, the young clergyman Richard Seymour. Sassoon reviewed Osbert Sitwell's latest volume of autobiography, *Noble Essences*, for the *Listener*, irritated by the mocking portrait of Gosse and a chapter on Owen, whom Sitwell had scarcely known. Two years later, he had a discomfiting lunch in London with the sleek, successful Osbert, a baronet since Sir George Sitwell's death in 1943 and now capable of repaying an old loan of £7,500.

He visited George at Oundle in November and took his son to see the brilliant scientist Miriam Lane, an expert on fleas and originally from the banking family of Rothschild, who lived near the school in an extraordinary lost domain where plants and animals ran wild. Although Miriam had known Hester since girlhood, Sassoon turned to her more and more for advice about his son, once proposing that she take the boy temporarily into her family to provide the stimulation not available from the unscientific minds of

Hester and himself. George cried at the end of the visit, because he was being bullied at school. Hester wrote to say that the bullies had called George and Sassoon 'dirty yids'.[5]

At the start of December 1950, an envelope came from the Prime Minister's secretary marked 'urgent and confidential'. Sassoon delayed opening it for half a minute. This could not be the Order of Merit, for there were no vacancies, but he might be made a Companion of Honour (CH), a worthy second; the letter turned out to be the offer of a CBE, a Commander of the Order of the British Empire. Almost immediately, he began to brood. This was not enough. E. M. Forster had been offered a knighthood (which he had refused), Elizabeth Bowen had got the CBE the previous year, as had C. Day Lewis and the old manager of Bumpus bookshop. Sassoon thought of refusing, then drew back, not wanting to insult the King. Eliot loomed again – the memory of his OM – still there when the manuscript of Dennis Welland's work on Owen arrived. Sassoon thought that 'as usual the subject depressed me profoundly'. He missed what Wilfred Owen might have become – a constant ally amid Sassoon's broken literary friendships with Bob Nichols, Graves, Turner, the Sitwells. Wilfred had been 'a kindred poet', although 'of more powerful intellectual genius'. Together, they might have defeated the Eliot school: a recurrence of Sassoon's fantasy.[6] Owen might have the OM; together they could mock this offer of a CBE.

To Welland, Sassoon wrote neat pencilled comments. Defending the phrase 'my little friend' in *Siegfried's Journey*, so annoying to Harold Owen, he said that H. G. Wells had called him 'little Siegfried'. He had wanted to show that Wilfred had seemed humble; in fact this relationship between 'brother poets' had been 'ideal', never solemn. The botched 1920 edition of Wilfred's poems had been almost entirely the responsibility of Edith Sitwell, who should not have included the famous preface which Owen would surely have cut; only after the book's publication did Sassoon have a chance to study the manuscripts. The poems were capable of standing on their own – Sassoon did not like prefaces to books of poetry. His own preface to the 1920 edition had been rushed as 'the whole business was utterly painful to me'. The Sitwells had not publicized the book enough because they were so preoccupied with their own careers. In *Noble Essences*, Osbert Sitwell had been malicious in quoting from Sassoon's letter to him about Owen and the obvious joke about Wilfred being 'quite good'[7] at poetry.

To the charge of jealousy, spread particularly by Middleton Murry and Scott Moncrieff, he said that he had introduced Owen to Ross and thus to the London literary world. Sassoon defended Rupert Brooke – surely Brooke's 'rhetoric' was appropriate for 'national emergencies' – and countered the notion that Brooke had been 'remarkably immature and incurably romantic' with the comment, 'not so much anti-romanticism please! Anti-romantics are liable to be Bores.' To Dennis Welland, the dilemma of the war poets was that, after reading the romantic writings that had inspired their youth, they had met a jarring, hideous reality. Death, Welland shrewdly observed later, had at least freed Owen from a war that had condemned Siegfried Sassoon to imprisonment in the past as he tried to come to terms with its lasting horrors.[8]

The unpublished poem 'An Incident in Literary History' – which begins 'Sassoon and Owen – names that found their niche' and ends by suggesting that his own last thirty years had been a disappointment – shows that at times Sassoon wondered too if it might have been better if he had been killed in the war.[9] In his diary, he tried to evoke an Owen who had lived on after 1918. 'I can imagine him as a sort of farmer – or doing some sort of social (youth) educational work,' he wrote. 'But not as a professional literary man . . . Helping young men would have been his vocation, apart from his poetry. And I don't think he would have married.'[10] He told H. M. Tomlinson how he had helped to save Owen's manuscripts for the British Museum Library by an appeal, giving £100, and had then persuaded Blunden to take on the editing of the 1930 edition. One feels this letter was written at least partly to reassure himself.[11] In

October 1959, on hearing his own First War poem 'The Death-Bed' read on the radio, Sassoon thought that the lines were still worthy of what Owen had once said about them, and wept.

*

FRANK SWINNERTON THOUGHT that the CBE was 'not good enough' and should be turned down; Swinnerton himself would refuse it. Bennett and Wells had refused knighthoods, as had Galsworthy. Sassoon heard that William Walton and Desmond Mac-Carthy had been knighted, that there were 104 other CBEs – 'poetry sharing its recognition with the manager of the Gas Works'.[12] But, in three days, he received thirty-three letters of congratulation and at Heytesbury station the ticket collector said, 'Excuse me asking – is there any cash attached to it?'[13] Kelsey Fry, the doctor in the RWF who in 1916 had pinned his own MC ribbon on to Sassoon, also had an honour; their photographs appeared in *The Times* alongside each other. He kept the news of the CBE from Hester, but when she read of it in the New Year she too felt disappointed.

He had agreed to Robert Gathorne-Hardy's printing of *Common Chords*, partly to tease Geoffrey Keynes who had a proprietary attitude towards the production of Sassoon's privately printed volumes. Now, thinking the poems 'so pedestrian and moralizing and lacking in transparency and spontaneity of imagery', not to mention 'wit and cheerfulness',[14] he dreaded the critics.[15] Briefly Gathorne-Hardy's admiration had cheered Sassoon up; perhaps there was 'a real music' in the poems.[16] But gloom soon descended; never had he looked at proofs 'with such a lack-lustre eye'.[17] One hundred and seven copies were hand-printed: a hundred on buff paper (fifteen shillings each) and seven on white parchment (five guineas each); one parchment copy went to pacify Geoffrey Keynes. The indolent Gathorne-Hardy failed to produce the book until August 1951, although giving the publication date as 1950.

All except four of the eighteen poems were in print for the first time, and the tone was meditative, even mystical, a foretaste of *The Tasking* of 1954. Too often, however, a banality of language and thought clouds the sincerity of these brave hopes for the possible immortality of the soul in an evil world. 'Contemporary Christmas' shows the problem:

> *Bells, that on this immaculate morn*
> *Rung in redeeming Christ reborn,*
> *What tidings brought you then?*
> We did our best, *the bells reply,*
> To broadcast, as in years gone by,
> Peace and good-will to men.

Common Chords has one sharp character study, in the poem 'At Max Gate' where old Thomas Hardy twinkles in his chair, courteously patting his dog, apparently serene, revealing nothing of his creative turmoil or pain.[18]

Another book of Sassoon's poems came out in 1951, also privately printed, entitled *Emblems of Experience*, designed by Geoffrey Keynes and printed by Will Carter's Rampant Lions Press at Cambridge. Sassoon considered *Common Chords* the better collection, 'less heavy and more lyrical',[19] although Keynes had outdone himself in the design of *Emblems*, as if to see off Gathorne-Hardy, with ornate printing and calligraphic capitals. Seventy-five copies were printed of *Emblems of Experience*, each one numbered in red and signed by Sassoon; ten had red initials painted by the artist Kenneth Breeze. *Emblems of Experience* had twenty poems – again, private poetry about memory, nature and spiritual quest. To Helen Waddell, the translator of medieval Latin lyrics who had inspired the poem 'Awareness of Alcuin', the collections seemed redolent of the seventeenth century, of Vaughan; and Edward Marsh thought, 'Nobody has so well rendered the ambiguity of the times we live in.'[20] In *Emblems of Experience*, Marsh admired most the poem about Edward Grey ('A Falloden Memory'), yet said how old the poems made Sassoon seem.[21] A flattering letter came from John Betjeman, beginning 'Dear and our best living poet',[22] praising what he called the two best books of verse since the war. *Time and Tide,* at John Betjeman's instigation, published the facsimile of three of Sassoon's poems in its issue of 6 December 1951.

In January 1951, after a visit to Geoffrey and Margaret Keynes at their house near Newmarket, Sassoon went down with flu and Hester arrived to look after him. In February, she went to Mull but at the end of the month he was still spending much of the time in bed before finally getting up to go to London for his investiture. Geoffrey Keynes took him to Buckingham Palace and he stood for half an hour, dressed in a blue suit – not, like most of the others, in a black tail-coat. His name was read out, sounding like 'Dr Sickfreed Sassoon', and as George VI put the CBE round his neck, the King said, 'I am glad to see you here. I suppose you are as busy as ever.' To this, Sassoon dropped his voice and let loose a histrionic, 'God bless you,'[23] clutching the hand of the startled monarch.

Early in March, he gave a talk at Oundle to about fifteen boys and three masters: hesitant, sometimes mumbling, although one master thought it 'the real thing'. But loneliness gripped him, coupled with a torturing desire that rose and fell during the long sexual abstinence that had existed since the early years of his marriage. At about this time, having met Haro Hodson by chance in London, Sassoon went to Hodson's flat in Wigmore Place. Elizabeth Mavor, whom Haro Hodson was to marry, arrived a few minutes later to find him there, an old and uneasy visitor, wearing a green eyeshade. To her, the room had a strange, intensely sexual atmosphere, as if the older man had been kissing Hodson; repelled, she wanted to leave yet stayed on, eventually sharing a taxi with Sassoon. He got out first at the Reform Club, after muttering, 'You must look after Haro,'[24] and gave her five shillings for the fare which, almost physically upset, she threw out of the taxi window when Sassoon had disappeared. He seemed like a man in hell, she thought, someone exuding a primitive sense of horror and pain.

The sense of George drifting away deepened the depression. The boy was noisy, playing the accordion, shutting his father out through a passionate interest in wireless, photography and science, the Thornycroft and Oliver Gatty inheritance. In August, after

George had left for Mull, Sassoon wrote, 'One suddenly becomes old when he goes.'[25] By 26 September, he had taken up the fourth volume of autobiography again and a month later had written more than 3,000 words, feeling that he was using his mind at last. By the end of November, after he had given another talk at Oundle, part one was finished, some 22,500 words. But early in December, having added another 2,500 words, Sassoon felt he was going stale.

At the start of 1952, Stephen Tennant came, his first visit for five years – plump, amusing, now forty-five, hair dyed yellow and the tuberculosis in remission, where it apparently remained for the rest of his life. At the end of January Tennant was back, carrying an enormous pot of cream, Sassoon careful of this 'highly intelligent and cultivated'[26] but heartless man. Blunden also returned. Sassoon had responded to Laurence Whistler's suggestion that the old friends should meet again, though he had shocked Whistler slightly by saying of his beloved Edmund (with a sigh), 'All right, you'd better tell him to come back',[27] as if talking of a lesser being.

*

THE RECONCILIATION WITH Edmund Blunden coincided with the arrival in England of Dorothy Wallis, an Australian who had been sending Blunden and Sassoon food parcels since the war. A red-haired idolater of poets, she saw these two, particularly Sassoon, as men of heroic dimensions.

First at Heytesbury for a week in December 1951, when she and Sassoon became 'intimately known to one another', Dorothy Wallis, thirty-six years younger than her host, became a frequent guest through the early months of 1952. Only Edmund Blunden and the housekeeper Miss Benn knew of this new, close friendship – further strengthening Sassoon's reunion with Blunden which Dorothy Wallis, like Laurence Whistler, also advocated. Sassoon found that Dorothy had 'the reticence of integrity' and 'has brought me nothing but blessings', mostly in her absolute devotion. Where would he be without her? 'The thing [presumably their intimate relationship] is determined, dared and done. And I am immensely the better for it.'

For Dorothy it was clearly 'a dream come true'. When he told Blunden that he felt this admirer's life was 'in my hands',[28] there is at least an implication of passionate devotion, even a love affair, Sassoon's first sexual involvement in years. In May he wrote a short poem called 'The Moment': 'the sort of faith poem which will be ridiculed by intellectuals'.[29] In July, Dorothy Wallis went away for two weeks, with her mother to Belgium and then to Ireland.

Life descended into dullness and, yet again, he could not sleep. At the start of August George rang from Mull, asking to stay longer. In September, the boy returned to Oundle, 'now almost a youth' – he was nearly sixteen. Sassoon felt that his memoirs of the post-war years could never be published without terrible publicity or a dishonest concealment of the truth.[30] On 28 September, he recorded the writing of two short poems: spiritual autobiography again.[31] Then Dorothy Wallis resumed her weekends at Heytesbury, and he told Blunden, 'I have found a jewel this time, never doubt it . . .'[32] The only drawbacks were that she had a difficult mother, was not 'hypersensitive'[33] and knew little of cricket.

By 13 November, working most evenings, he had written about fifteen poems since the end of September. 'The Tasking' came on 20 December, and on 1 January 1953 he told H. M. Tomlinson that the previous year had been 'the most unworried . . . since I don't know when, in spite of world conditions'.[34] The spirituality of the new work brought a mystical experience one night, 'as though a door had opened and a signal had come through to my consciousness, uncalled for, unexpected and sustaining'. The feeling was physical but timeless. From this he produced the poem 'The Knowing'; such work seemed the only way now 'because I can't write about human realities'.[35] 'Another Spring', printed in the *Times Literary Supplement* in March 1953 over the initials S.S., shows, in addition to his paradoxical wish for privacy and enjoyment of acclaim, hope in this 'sense of spring': a hint of lifting shadows.[36]

Then they fell again. In March a row between Dorothy Wallis and his housekeeper Miss Benn, partly about the buying of a stove for George, became a crisis, Miss Benn threatening resignation. Mr

Durrant, employed on the Heytesbury estate, said to Sassoon, 'You've got two of 'em, Captain, and they're both red heads . . .'[37] Dorothy Wallis became 'pretty tough', ignoring Sassoon's 'gentle counsellings'.[38] His 'last love' had failed,[39] and, banned from Heytesbury, the distraught Australian turned for advice to Glen Byam Shaw, to be told that Sassoon, having made a decision, was implacable. Blunden, in his tactful way, regretted it, writing to Sassoon that 'you may not see what it means to D.W. after that wonderful start . . .'[40] Sassoon said that she had been domineering, failing to see that 'a man of 66 can't be 33'. She would have to return to Australia. Her loving but overbearing wish to help, perhaps also her sexual ardour, had alarmed him. For Sassoon 'nothing shall ever come between me and George. He is all I have left in life.'[41]

*

BUT GEORGE WAS growing up. From Oundle, his housemaster Arthur Marshall, later a journalist and television quiz-show contestant, wrote about the boy's bad behaviour, begging Sassoon to be firmer. George should not be allowed to experiment with explosives on Mull and at Heytesbury. 'I know what he means to you,' Marshall wrote, 'and I do wish that there were something agreeable that I could say about him, but there is nothing at all to which I can cling or which gives me any hope at all for this unhappy boy's future.'[42] When Sassoon wrote back, equally angry at what he saw as this lack of understanding of his son, Marshall cringed, writing, 'Do not think badly of me. My life is not a very pleasant one.'[43]

A part of the problem was that George found much of his schoolwork boringly easy. During GCE exams, he had a spare hour at the end of the French paper, so translated the comprehension into German and designed a new wireless. Then, while on Mull, he met a seventeen-year-old girl whom Hester described as 'intelligent and charming'. Sassoon felt 'heart ache' at this sign of the end of boyhood yet 'thankful for this evidence of normality'.[44] In September, the boy came back from Mull, obviously in love, complaining that Heytesbury was 'dull'.[45] What Sassoon had foreseen, in his clearer moments, as inevitable became black reality, the ending of the dream of his son as the last 'ideal friend' in a quest begun during his own boyhood. This had never been linked to the boy's worldly success, although Sassoon had welcomed this as well. He loved in his son what he feared he was losing – a child's innocent approach to the world – and beneath this lay the buried ache of desire that he rigidly controlled.

Sassoon turned in his pain to other admirers, pilgrims to Heytesbury: John Sparrow (a barrister and later Warden of All Souls), Sparrow's handsome friend Colin Fenton (a poetry-loving wine merchant) and Archie John Wavell, son of the field marshal. The quietly religious Wavell, a Black Watch major who had lost his left arm, was on an army course at Warminster, near Heytesbury, and, like his father, loved poetry of the traditional kind. Sassoon and he talked for hours, about literature and the possibility of salvation on earth, before Wavell rejoined his regiment in Kenya.

Another focus of Sassoon's effort to make a new life was Cambridge. That summer he went to watch cricket there and to stay with Geoffrey Keynes at Newmarket. At Fenners, the Cambridge University ground, Sassoon met Dennis Silk, a young friend of Blunden's who, like Edmund, had been to Christ's Hospital school, and was now an undergraduate and a brilliant batsman in the university team. Henceforth Cambridge – and the Garden House Hotel – became an alternative to isolation, even more so when, at the end of 1953, Sassoon became an honorary fellow of Clare, his old college, next to King's where George might go as an undergraduate. E. M. Forster was living at King's, and other friends were also in the city: Frances Cornford, an unmodernist poet whom Sassoon admired; the woodcut artist Gwen Raverat, who had designed some of the frontispieces for his books and was, like Frances Cornford, a Darwin and therefore related to Geoffrey Keynes's wife Margaret; Philip Gosse, a retired doctor and the son of Edmund. These he needed more after Edmund Blunden left England in September 1953 to be a professor at the University of Hong Kong. And Dennis Silk strengthened the Cambridge connection. Silk's father had been a missionary to Indians in California and became a High Church rector of the Sitwells' parish church at Renishaw before dying young. The young Dennis found in Sassoon a substitute parent, and soon he was often at Heytesbury, to stay and to play cricket for the village.

*

SASSOON STILL FELT that ache of loneliness, of disappointment that the great lyric poem would not come, that not enough people cared for his vision. *Sea Drift* on the radio, that mix of Delius and Whitman, again affected him, its unaccompanied chorus ('Stars that rise') bringing uncontrollable tears as he clutched at his chest, as if at his heart. The piece brought back 'all the past that has gone wrong', as well as the solitude, frustration and lack of a loved companion. Dorothy Wallis had failed him and George, his greatest love, was in love with someone else. He recalled the paralysed Delius during a performance of this masterpiece at Queen's Hall, oblivious to the attention for which Sassoon longed, those murmurs of recognition, 'what a wonderful looking man he is'.[46]

Three days later he felt ashamed of such thoughts, then read the *Times* obituary of Stockwell, his old commanding officer, and remembered his own 'foolhardy exhibitionism', a device, he thought, to cover up his shortcomings as an officer. 'But how wonderful to be able to do such things with youth's impetus.'[47] Was that part of his reputation a fraud? His wartime exploits seemed all that people wanted to know about him, yet he knew how little time he had been at the front, how he might have cracked if forced to endure more. His fame might be based on falseness, on a lie.

The fire had died. Dylan Thomas's last poems were, he saw, like a rediscovery of language, diminishing his own work. In December, George was in Mull, sending only a brief message to say he was well. Then the news came that Archie John Wavell had been killed in action during the Mau Mau rebellion against colonial rule in Kenya.

TWENTY-FOUR

'*At the end of all
wrong roads I came*'

ARCHIE JOHN WAVELL'S death – and George's love affair – seemed a chipping away of what Siegfried Sassoon had hoped might be consolations for old age and his unfashionable poetry. He went back to the collection to be called *The Tasking*: poems generally without metaphor, but also 'non-visual' – which 'I deplore'.[1] They are spiritually introspective, like parts of *Common Chords* and *Emblems of Experience*, giving off even more of a sense of solitude yet still, the poet thought, lacking the 'great' poem he had once dreamed of writing.[2] Geoffrey Keynes, aware of a nickname that Sassoon had given him because of his obsessive book-collecting, signed himself 'your ever faithful Jackdaw'[3] and took these to be printed, remarking that they seemed 'a bit different'.

Poems written in 1954 are part of the same quest. 'Faith Unfaithful', in March, 'summed up my sad condition',[4] he was to tell Dame Felicitas Corrigan, the Benedictine nun who was to be his spiritual confidante and biographer, in December 1959. Then silence fell until Easter 1957 and 'Deliverance', which was written after he had decided to become a Roman Catholic. Sassoon later chose 'An Epitome' as 'just about the saddest poem I ever wrote'.[5] Like other poems in *The Tasking*, it has a hard concision, but it also has too often the dissonant language of Thomas Hardy – as in 'mind-life's epitome / From infanthood to eld' – without Hardy's mastery of buried feeling. The last two lines are especially bleak in their conclusion:

> *Accept your soul.*
> *Be evermore alone.*[6]

He knew *The Tasking* gave off melancholy, even desperation, and feared that the poems might be too quiet and personal for most readers. In a dream, Wilfred Owen appeared to him and Sassoon told of the recent surge in his young friend's reputation, but Owen, against the background of Weirleigh, failed to ask about Siegfried's poetry.

*

MANY PEOPLE, HOWEVER, were interested in his past. In Cambridge, in October 1954, Sassoon read his poems at Clare College, through puffs at his pipe, many of the crowd of students staying on afterwards to speak to this survivor, both a war-hero and an opponent of war, whose awkward integrity impressed them. Among the audience was Nicholas Herbert, once in the schoolmaster Rolf Barber's circle at Oundle where he had heard Sassoon say that only those who had written poetry were fit to speak of it. To Herbert, a good-looking sensitive boy, Sassoon sent a postcard from the Garden House Hotel, writing just one urgent line, 'I so much want to see you.'[7]

The days in Cambridge had again revived him. 'I *was* a success at Clare,' he told Geoffrey Keynes. 'It was the best fortnight I've had since the war.'[8] A month earlier, a piece had appeared in the magazine *John O'London* about 'our best living autobiographer', in which Oliver Stonor described a visit to an idyllic Heytesbury. 'Do we, I wondered, make quite enough fuss of him?' Stonor asked, delighting his subject. With the article came a previously unpublished short poem, 'Neighbours', about continuity in Wiltshire from flint-sharpening ancestors to Sassoon's own descendants years away.[9] That summer, asked to lunch with the Royal Welch Fusiliers at their barracks near Swindon to see the presentation by the Queen of new colours, he was put in the front row for the parade.

The ceremony of the colours seemed like the return of Sherston. On the way home, Sassoon stopped at Marlborough and went into the chapel where he had sat as an unsuccessful boy fifty years earlier. Then he reread *Memoirs of an Infantry Officer*, his diaries for March 1916, Dr Dunn's history of the Second Battalion of the Royal Welch Fusiliers during the First World War, *The War the Infantry Knew*, and looked at the old trench maps, names like Delville Wood and Thiepval evoking those terrible but enlivening times. Voices came back, and the protest; he read again Blunden's *Undertones of War* and H. M. Tomlinson's account of his time as a war correspondent, *All Our Yesterdays*.

At Oundle, George was now a hero: bright, tall, a rebel who set up a radio station, made subversive broadcasts, had a girlfriend and blew up part of the science laboratory. For Sassoon, the school brought about another reunion, after more than twenty-five years. Robert Graves had sent his son William there and Sassoon and Graves, with their sons, met for lunch in the local hotel. This, followed by Sassoon's presence at Graves's Clark lectures at Cambridge in October 1954, made (in Sassoon's words) 'all the years and misunderstandings'[10] melt away, even if there was still 'the same clumsy, opinionated half-schoolboy, half-schoolmaster, irritating at times but very likeable'.[11] Graves, in the lectures (which Sassoon had refused to deliver the year before), referred to his old friend's 'extraordinary' years of 'poetic efflorescence' from 1917 to 1921.

George won a science scholarship to King's, but soon afterwards he failed the medical test for National Service because of sinus trouble, so Sassoon did not need to worry about his son being in danger. But the rebel was in the ascendant, wanting to escape from Heytesbury and from stifling paternal love. Suddenly, in May 1955, the boy married the golden-haired Stephanie Munro at Kingussie register office in Inverness, telling neither of his parents; it was the break from their possessiveness that he so desperately needed. Hester had hoped for a grander wedding, perhaps a career for George in the Foreign Office, and made her despondency clear – Sassoon, for once, taking her side. The young couple went to Mull and stayed with Hester before leaving for Cambridge at the end of September. A month later, in Cambridge, Sassoon met Stephanie, who turned out to be capable and unaffected, even related to a grand Scottish family, the Grants of Rothiemurcus, and she clearly looked on George as a kind of genius. Sassoon sat in the chapel at King's, praying for his son. By December 1956, he complained of hearing nothing from the couple as George continued on his quest for independence.

So, at Heytesbury, other young men continued to take the boy's place: sometimes the handsome Colin Fenton, Nicholas Herbert in June 1955, Dennis Silk for nearly three weeks in August when he accompanied Sassoon to Stratford, where Glen Byam Shaw was director of the theatre, to see some Shakespeare. Yet the loneliness remained. De la Mare and Beerbohm had died, Blunden was in Hong Kong, and the spiritual sustenance glimpsed with Helen Waddell and Archie Wavell had been dashed by Waddell's mental decline and Wavell's death.

Heytesbury, however, became even more of a place of pilgrimage, visitors greeted sometimes at the door by the old manservant Durrant, sometimes by the owner himself. Nicholas Herbert recalls that Sassoon's head inclined sideways as he spoke, the eyes scarcely ever meeting yours, giving a sense of something unresolved, though often alleviated by the flash of an intense glance. He and Herbert went out on drives, Sassoon applying his own Highway Code, taking to the fields for possible short cuts, often ignoring traffic lights. A guest was seldom asked about himself – the visitors were almost always men – and the host's talk usually became a monologue, accompanied by apparently uncontrolled movements, often in praise of the pre-1914 world. Sassoon's sense of humour was schoolboyish, and he liked to mimic, as if more at ease in other people's personalities. Haro Hodson wondered if the first meeting with Hester, at

Wilton, had been easier because they were both in fancy dress and able to forget themselves on that fairy-tale day. And Heytesbury itself was like a land outside the modern world: the garden and park overgrown, the house vast and silent, the telephone an ancient contraption that Sassoon loathed, television restricted to a set in the cook's quarters on which the 'Captain' watched Test matches with Durrant.

In 1954, the poet Charles Causley wrote to ask if he and Robert Waller, a BBC producer and poet, might record Sassoon reading his own work for the radio. They arrived at Heytesbury, to find a place that seemed abandoned. The bell had broken, so they knocked, whereupon Durrant came to the door, Waller wondering if this might be Sassoon's old batman from the First World War. In the grand library, Sassoon looked ten years younger than his age, wearing an old, loose suit and a silk stock, offering tea and speaking in an aristocratic voice, quick then halting. When he recited his own work, the poet and the poems 'seemed a perfect unity',[12] the voice deep, regretful, then uplifted as if aspiring to greatness. Later that year the 'splendid sea-captainish' H. M. Tomlinson drove over and Causley and Waller recorded a programme about Hardy, Tomlinson referring to the great man simply as 'Tom'.[13]

There was another solace: visits to Mells in Somerset, once the home of the Horner family and inherited by Katharine Asquith, daughter of its last ancestral owner and widow of the Prime Minister's son Raymond, who had been killed on the Somme. Katharine had converted to Catholicism, under the influence of the writer Maurice Baring. Also living at Mells was another convert, Ronald Knox, who had become a Jesuit priest.

In a sense, Mells was all that Sassoon had wanted Weirleigh to be, even more than Heytesbury, where he had had to make his own tradition instead of inheriting one shaped by a long history. The medieval village, on a spur of the Mendips, near Roman remains, had been monastic property until the Horners arrived in the fifteenth century and the towering church has an 'implication of priestly power'.[14] There were even Pre-Raphaelite connections through the last Lady Horner's friendship with Burne-Jones, whose pictures hung in the greystone gabled house alongside a collection of Italian masters. Some monuments in the church – the tablet by Burne-Jones, Munnings's equestrian statue of Edward Horner, a stained-glass window by William Nicholson – introduced the twentieth century yet seemed to show continuity and order. And Mells evoked not only history but the privileged, lost paladins who had been Edward Horner's friends and, like him, were killed in the First World War – those young knights of a fanciful, aristocratic tradition of chivalry and sacrifice whose myth was what they might have given to England: Julian Grenfell, Charles Lister, Patrick Shaw-Stewart, Raymond Asquith and Stephen Tennant's elder brother Bim. Sassoon had been driving to Mells in 1933 when he decided to marry Hester Gatty.

Katharine Asquith and Ronald Knox sensed that Sassoon might wish to become a Roman Catholic. He had, after all, apparently turned to his own spiritual state in his recent poetry, as if searching for a haven that was strong and authoritative. But Knox was scrupulous in not searching for converts, constrained also by a strong reserve, as if he existed 'behind a plate glass window'.[15] A classical scholar, devoted to Eton and Balliol, the institutions of his gifted boyhood, Knox, formerly the university Catholic chaplain at Oxford, said mass in the chapel at Mells every morning at half-past eight. He liked Sassoon, believing that every word of the poet's 'is worth keeping'[16] and thinking him 'more a First War man than anyone I know'.[17] Sassoon began to appreciate Knox's books, theology for amateurs in crisp, humorous – if sometimes facetious – prose. In Ronnie he saw a scholar and near-saint: an intellectual who enjoyed light conversation and gave gently if awkwardly 'with both hands',[18] charmingly fascinated by recondite details of old railway branch lines and train journeys, creating at Mells, with Katharine Asquith, 'a survival of a vanished civilisation'.[19]

*

SUCH RELIEF SEEMED important when the critics had another swipe at him. At first it all seemed harmless: a book of letters received by Sydney Cockerell from various people over the years, called *The Best of Friends*, the successor to a similar volume called *Friends of a Lifetime*, with twenty-four of Sassoon's letters included. This collection, however, irritated some with its cosy, complacent traditionalism, the *Listener* review portraying Sassoon as 'a sort of pompous Colonel Blimp' in his view of the last war.[20] Frank Swinnerton tried to console him, saying that the magazine 'represents the buggers of the Third Programme at their lowest',[21] but John Raymond, in the *New Statesman*, joined the hunt, writing how Sassoon 'smugly' patted himself on the back for not having seen a film since 1936.[22] The *Listener* review was by Herbert Read, the war poet and art critic, who sent Sassoon a 'sort-of'[23] apology, saying that lives like Rex Whistler's had been sacrificed because of the iniquitous Versailles Treaty and that the author of *Counter-Attack* should know this.

Sassoon, however, defended his heroes. In the autumn of 1956, perhaps urged on by Violet Bonham Carter who had loved Rupert Brooke, he objected to the publishing of what he felt were demeaning passages in an edition of Brooke's letters by Geoffrey Keynes. That summer also he recorded a broadcast on Max Beerbohm – whose voice was, he thought, that of 'the last civilised man on earth'[24] – declaring that Elysium was to be with Max at Rapallo on the roof of the Villino Chiaro, with the Mediterranean below. In October, Sassoon's reading of a selection of his recent poems was broadcast on the BBC's Third Programme. And on 9 November Fabers brought out *Sequences*, his first commercially published book of poetry since the *Collected Poems* of 1947, although the poems themselves had already appeared in the privately printed volumes *Common Chords*, *Emblems of Experience* and *The Tasking*.

As usual, old friends came out to help. H. M. Tomlinson said of *Sequences* that 'it goes on the shelf with Herbert, Vaughan, and Traherne',[25] while Blunden, in the *TLS*, compared the poet with Vaughan, and also praised the conversation poems – those describing Hardy at Max Gate or Grey at Falloden, and 'Cleaning the Candelabrum'. And surely, Blunden thought, there was ultimate optimism, as in 'The Best of It' asserting 'Life, that by no disaster is undone'.[26] In the *Listener*, Richard Church, who was among the limper of the neo-Georgians, wrote of Sassoon's retreat, comparing him to Cowper, yet thought the collection's mood too monotonous, a mood that made the reader think, 'Snap out of it.'[27]

The views of the younger critics reflected the changes in poetry since 1947. New poets like Kingsley Amis and Philip Larkin, and a group known as the Movement, led by Thom Gunn, John Wain and Donald Davie, had a distrust of metropolitan sophistication, T. S. Eliot, Pound and obscurity, prizing direct language and common sense. Sassoon shared some of their tastes, their Englishness and dislike of affectation. Larkin, for instance, greatly admired Hardy. But the Movement put the provincial towns of the north or the midlands in the place of a lost land of flower gardens, hedges and birdsong and mostly ignored Siegfried Sassoon, which was even worse, he thought, than getting bad reviews.

In the *Manchester Guardian*, Philip Larkin tackled *Sequences*. To Larkin, Sassoon's poetry seemed 'less sophisticated' than his 'Isherwoodian' autobiographies and 'at any rate latterly has registered more misses than hits'. But always, he added, there was depth of feeling. In *Sequences* the poet succeeded less with 'Eternity, Armageddon and the Universe', more with 'the immediate and colloquial', and the whole collection was 'intensely appealing'[28] in its gentle modesty. The review, a reflection of his personal, rather than poetic, appeal, stirred Sassoon to write to its author and ask to see his poems. Larkin responded with his latest collection, saying he had just reread the Sherston books with pleasure. Sassoon found the poems 'very accomplished', occasionally moving, even if one, as he told Blunden, was 'addressed to the most private part of his anatomy! . . . You may remember that R. Graves once did it.'[29] Larkin particularly pleased him by stating his dislike of 'symbolic poetry, or poetry full of quotations from other writers and other languages. I think sometimes it was an evil day when English poetry fell into the hands of the Americans and Irish. From which you may gather that Pound and Eliot and Joyce are not my favourite authors.'[30]

*

ON 9 JANUARY 1957, a letter arrived at Heytesbury from London, from a nun: the Reverend Mother Margaret Mary McFarlin, the Superior of the Assumptionist Convent in Kensington Square. An admirer of Sassoon's poems for more than forty years, she saw in *Sequences* a change, a yearning for God. The previous night Sassoon had dreamed of someone who understood his quest, 'someone kind who wanted to know if I was all right'.[31] Now Mother Margaret Mary, as he called her, became, to him, 'the greatest benefactor of my life'.[32]

Everything seemed to fit. There was even a link to Mells, for Ronald Knox had been a chaplain at Aldenham school where she had taught during the war. In April, Siegfried Sassoon came unannounced to the Convent in Kensington Square, asked for Mother Margaret Mary and was astounded to find the figure in the dream. She saw a tall, thin, elegant man in shabby clothes who spoke in almost incomprehensible bursts of words.

Born in 1905, Margaret Ross McFarlin, known to her friends as 'Madge', had grown up in Liverpool, the fourth child in an intensely Roman Catholic family of five: three girls and two boys, the children of a compositor. Educated at local schools and at Liverpool University, she did a thesis on British First War poetry – which had an especial poignancy for her because her brother had been wounded at the front – and, while a student, was a pacifist and a member of the Fabian Society. She admired Sassoon's war poems but, finding the anger and language crude, preferred Owen. She remained interested in his work, however, thinking the biography of *Meredith* uninspired because its author was only at his best when writing about himself.

In 1930, while teaching at the Convent of the Assumption at Richmond in Yorkshire, Madge McFarlin took her vows, although earlier she had wanted marriage and children. From 1932 until

1978, as Mother Margaret Mary, she was a teacher of English as well as a nun – the head or Superior of schools and convents at Kensington, Aldenham, Exton, Hengrave, Sidmouth, Richmond and Oxford. A beloved schoolmistress (who danced and laughed with her pupils), but no intellectual, she had humour, immense sympathy and spiritual self-confidence. The poetry of Hardy and Browning, and the religious devotion of Hopkins, Herbert, Newman and Vaughan, feature in the early letters between her and Sassoon.

Realizing that the philosophical side of religion bemused him, she directed her new correspondent to the mystical writings of St John of the Cross. She saw Sassoon no more than twenty times during the ten years of their friendship; and one of the themes that she tried to follow with him was that of love without possessiveness, the true love which he found hard to achieve. She gave him the Catholic aids to worship – a rosary, missals, crucifix and a small statue of Our Lady – and was surprised by how earnestly he wanted to submit. Mother Margaret Mary thought often of those words at the end of *Sherston's Progress*, 'it is only from the inmost silences of the heart that we know this world for what it is, and ourselves for what the world has made us'. To the nun, this was 'so right – and with that strange melancholy tone that haunts so many true things about life. Why is it, I wonder?'[33] This seemed to her to be what he sought: to reach those silences, not to understand intellectually what was there but to find emotional peace.

Sassoon's first answer to her was 'so uninhibited'[34] that he destroyed it, fearing that she might think him mad. Then, on 10 January 1957, he wrote how her 'message' had come 'like a blessing from above' or 'the answered orison'.[35] He had seen no one since the publication of his book and hers had been only the second letter, friends having written earlier about its three privately printed predecessors. By 23 February, he felt high emotion and, when reading Gerard Manley Hopkins's 'The Air We Breathe' aloud to Colin Fenton, almost broke down over the last few lines. By March he was writing of 'the inexpressible joy of that one-ness which has been created in these wonderful weeks' and his 'peace'. God had not yet revealed himself fully but Sassoon had hope of this revelation and lived only for it. How appropriate that the way had been unlocked by what someone else had seen in his poetry, the writing of which had, until now, brought his closest glimpse of the divine. Diffidence was one of his failings – though it was a strength as well, for modesty brought power. He was now no longer diffident about his worthiness of divine grace.

He addressed her as 'Dearest Mother' and said how 'this morning, after reading the Missal, I prayed for you for a long time, on my knees – such calm and healing for me'. He sent her some unpublished poems, examples of his search, written in 1953 and 1952. But why had he not been able to pray, when he had such 'hunger for holiness'? He had been imprisoned in his 'private religion' revealed through poetry, and when no poetry came, felt in 'darkness'[36] until her letter. On 1 April, he wrote of reading of a fire in the convent, of his anxious prayers from 'your faithful poet' for her, his rescuer.[37] On Good Friday and Easter Sunday, he wrote the poem 'Deliverance', having decided to become a Roman Catholic.

Authority was what he wanted, not the soft, apologetic Church of England. The Abbot of Downside surely would 'put the fear of God into me'. And Sassoon longed to be 'put in my place'.[38] 'Be ye as little children': he yearned for those reassuring words and 'never to be lonely and forsaken again'.[39] By the spring he wanted instruction, hoping that Ronald Knox might give it, but Knox was ill and felt that Sassoon needed someone else, not so close to him, not so shy. One possibility was Dom Hubert van Zeller, a monk at Downside, but then Zeller had to go to the United States. So Knox suggested another Downside monk, Dom Sebastian Moore, whom Sassoon had met at Mells in 1955, a tall man who rode a motorbicycle and seemed 'tremendously alive'.[40]

Born in India, Moore had been in the navy when he realized his vocation and entered the Dominican order in 1938; the way had been hard and in 1954 he suffered a breakdown. Sophisticated, articulate, musical and well read – with a First-Class degree from Cambridge in English – Moore inclined towards mysticism. An expert on the work of David Jones, and therefore knowledgeable about First War writers, he had read Sassoon's poetry, thinking it agnostic, a challenge to belief, and wondered if he might be too intellectual for the poet. At the end of May Siegfried Sassoon began to see him regularly at Downside, often dressed in cricket flannels for a knock-up afterwards in the school's nets. For the first meeting, Sassoon entered a parlour, hung with bland secular pictures, and waited before a young-looking man – a couple of inches taller than he – came in, displaying 'the direct regard' of integrity and piercing blue eyes: 'a really noble-looking man. I felt quite at ease at once.'

When he told Moore of the dream, then the letter, the monk exclaimed, 'But it's terrific!' Moore accepted this as authentic and most unusual. He said he would not be using the catechism as much as the gospels – especially that of St John – in the instruction, and understood Sassoon's difficulty with rational analysis. After two hours, they went together into the huge Victorian abbey church, 'the church of my dreams', Sassoon told Mother Margaret Mary, 'white and soaring and immensely long.' They met two or three times a week, Moore sometimes coming to Heytesbury ('I shall hire a car to bring him').[41] The monk said he could be received into the church before September. Knox had suggested 8 September.

To Sebastian Moore, soon known to his pupil as 'Sebbie', the sessions were almost too much fun, sparkling with reminiscence and jokes. He saw Sassoon's need for a loving authority he could rest in, not an intellectual authority of calm reason. Moore instructed indirectly, relying on self-expression on both sides, noting with amusement the displays of vanity; later, after reading his work to some Downside pupils, the poet said, not entirely ironically, 'Do they realise what lucky boys they are?' Like Mother Margaret Mary and, later, Dame Felicitas Corrigan, he tried to heal Sassoon's broken marriage but met the weary response that Hester should be seen as a wayward child.[42] For the moment, as if to prolong it, Siegfried Sassoon kept this solitary joy from his family and his friends.

At the end of June he was awarded the Queen's Gold Medal for

Poetry for 1957, *The Times* celebrating it in an editorial headed 'A Thoroughly English Poet'.[43] But in the midst of this there was sadness. Since January, cancer of the liver had weakened Father Ronald Knox and on 24 August he died. Towards the end of July, Sassoon had an intense moment of 'uplift', the climax of six extraordinary months, while he was driving to Downside, 'as though a new faculty had been added to my being',[44] mixed with sadness about Ronald Knox. On the way back to Heytesbury, he stopped, left his car and fell on his knees in a field. On 14 August, at Downside, he was received into the Roman Catholic Church.

*

SIEGFRIED SASSOON'S CONVERSION was not, like that of J. H. Newman, the result of long intellectual reasoning. Nor did the light come in a sudden burst, as experienced by St Paul. What happened had come slowly, encouraged by a slow falling away of much that had seemed worth while in his life, a process that began as far back as what he saw as the betrayal of his sacrificial idealism during the First World War.

At first poetry had seemed enough, especially during that war, when he had found a power and a purpose in writing far stronger than before or since. In the post-1918 decades, however, neither the poetry nor even the successful Sherston memoirs quite matched Sassoon's expectations; the results were often too quiet, not the lyric greatness that he wanted, or, in the case of the prose books, too retrospective, even dishonest, with much that had been essential left out. Sassoon had hopes of greatness, once even, as during his political involvement, of being a great leader or, at least, one of the great figures of his age. He had always felt, partly because of his mother's love, a sense of being of the elect and this was heightened by a self-imposed Byronic solitude that went with, and contradicted, a more prosaic quest for sexual peace and love. But while he rather liked the drama of being an outsider – his Enoch Arden complex as he called it – he had also wished, since his childhood at the unsatisfactory Weirleigh and as a Jewish schoolboy and fox-hunter, to be honoured, to be accepted. Rebellion was not natural to Sassoon and had been forced on him by the horror of the trenches. Throughout his life, he had sought simplicity and calm. Now he found this: a calm gently ruffled perhaps by quiet dreams but always protected by an all-powerful, benevolent mystery. The hopes of other times – as when his first love for Hester had seemed 'like believing in God'[45] – had come true.

Roman Catholicism brought authority – an end to questioning, the return of a certainty not known since the young Siegfried discovered that his father had left. It brought an understanding, and forgiveness, of everything about him that was wrong. In the Church, he belonged, at last, to a definable and (to him) an admirable world, an elect drawn together by religious mystery, by the idea of the unknowable which he believed was at the core of the most important part of his life: his poetry. The search for utopia – re-created in his prose books – ended with the monks, nuns and priests, the holy Catholics of his last years. Sassoon's Catholicism also had beauty and history, even glamour, exemplified by what he saw and loved at Mells, the Roman Catholicism of *Brideshead Revisited*. When his new faith began to manifest itself in inexplicable visions and mysticism as well, his joy in it became an ecstasy greater than anything that he had ever known.

*

HE WROTE TO only a few friends, such as Cyril Tomkinson, an Anglican clergyman, whom he told of his discovery of authority and 'continual peace and happiness' after three years of 'dark night'. Surely Rivers would approve.[46] Glen Byam Shaw, whom, with Dennis Silk, he told on his yearly trip to Stratford a month after the conversion, thought it 'miraculous' and Silk could only rejoice in what seemed to bring Sassoon so much joy. To them both he hinted at how confession, and subsequent absolution, soothed a sexual shame which still plagued him. Robert Graves and others thought, rather mockingly, that the rituals and theatre of Catholicism, its demand for sacrifice and emphasis on suffering, appealed to his homosexuality. Byam Shaw had longed for Sassoon to be at peace. Neither Hester nor George had been able to provide this ('it wasn't their fault that they couldn't'). Now the actor saw that this faith was the inevitable conclusion.[47]

There was one intrusion. On 21 September, a journalist from the *Sunday Express* breached the defences at Heytesbury and coaxed Sassoon into talking about his conversion, promising that nothing would be published. The next day, an article appeared, as if authorized, under the headline, 'Poet Siegfried Sassoon becomes a Roman Catholic', reporting Sassoon as saying, 'This is the most wonderful thing that has ever happened to me.' Even George did not know yet, Sassoon said. All his life had been a searching for religion – 'for a faith that I could accept'. The aspect he liked most was 'the complete authority of the church', and this was odd, the article implied, after his rebellious record in the First World War. He lived alone, as Hester, in Scotland, 'rarely visits me now'.[48] Cressida Ridley and Christopher Hollis, two neighbours, encouraged Sassoon to write to *The Times* about the intrusion and his letter appeared on October 1 about the 'entirely unauthorised' exhibition of his 'most sacred intimacies'.[49] *The Times* carried a reply from the editor of the *Sunday Express* the next day, declaring that the reporter had made no attempt to hide his notebook.[50]

The controversy spread the news; it was the first that George and Hester had heard of this earthquake in his life. E. M. Forster wrote to send his 'love and my wishes for your good . . . Love again dear Siegfried'.[51] Sassoon answered that he had often thought over the past months, 'whatever will E.M.F. think of me?'[52] Anti-Catholics sent vicious letters and Catholics expressed their pleasure; some friends, such as Geoffrey Keynes and Philip Gosse, were hurt they had not been told. The Blundens only guessed when, on leave from Hong Kong later in the year, at a lunch in Oxford, they saw Sassoon's rosary fall out of his pocket, although he did not refer to its presence; not until later did Edmund have confirmation, indirectly, from the *Sunday Express*. Laurence Whistler, although pleased to see Sassoon so happy, felt that his friend belonged to

Anglicanism, 'the church of your childhood', of liberty, beauty of language and 'sober and genial common sense'. Catholicism closed off so much through its dogmatism, Whistler thought.[53] Nicholas Herbert wondered if the conversion would rob Sassoon of the habit of questioning, central to much of his best work, and the agnostic Frank Swinnerton could feel no sympathy.

To Philip Gosse, who was considering conversion, Sassoon wrote of how he had been continually in tears during the months up to August, supposedly a sign of grace, and this had ended in complete physical calm. 'I'm very pleased indeed you have gone over to the Roman Church,' Robert Graves wrote. *Goodbye to All That* had recently been reissued. Graves felt that 'my admiration and affection displayed there for you came out very strongly when I reread it'.[54] How nice George had seemed at Oundle, he added. Sassoon answered that he had found faith not through submission to dogma but through prayer and help from 'a very holy Catholic'. The reason he had been so upset about *Goodbye* in 1929 was his 'great state of mental fatigue and worry with writing the Infantry Officer. All that you wrote about me was entirely generous – beyond my deserts.' He ended, 'bless you, old boy'.[55] The serenity now covered the past. He told Mother Margaret Mary of 'the most profoundly peaceful Xmas Day of my life'. He had read nothing, but listened to some Schumann songs on the radio. Peace formerly had been 'episodic and unreliable'; now it was 'permanent'. Siegfried Sassoon realized that 'I've never before known what *real* peace is . . .'[56]

TWENTY-FIVE

'*Trying to be like Our Lord*'

SASSOON SET UP a little oratory at Heytesbury and prayed there for an hour most evenings. In December 1957, his small crucifix, once Lady Gatty's, seemed to cloud over and shake; and two months later, while praying for her to be relieved from arthritis, he saw Katharine Asquith's face in obvious pain yet full of love, like a saint's. In March 1958 – the night before he wrote the poem 'Lenten Illuminations' – an almost life-sized curly-haired seraph, and then a little angel, luminous, with an arm raised, as if in answer to a plea,[1] appeared to him.

What were these visions, Sassoon wondered later to the nun Dame Felicitas Corrigan, 'nice little treats, I suppose – too physical to be graces?'[2] Sometimes on his knees, he knew serenity yet often felt obsessed by lust. He prayed to be delivered from his body and after ten or fifteen minutes this always worked; sometimes he did his first penance naked. He found it hard to avoid the narcissistic idea of Sir Galahad, reminiscent of those Victorian paintings of his youth, and wished to endure some real sacrifice or suffering yet suspected that pride must rob this of merit. He longed for Hester to be converted; his treatment of her was not on his conscience, for surely he had been 'only a door-mat for her waywardness, poor dear'.[3] Sassoon began to see literature and music through his faith. Elgar's *Serenade for Strings*, for instance. The long lyrical *andante* and its sense of rapturous upward movement reminded him that the composer had been born a Catholic, the religion of his own new-found joy. Dying seemed less upsetting (the recent deaths of Gwen Raverat and Ronnie Knox had been followed by that of H. M. Tomlinson).

Sassoon began a campaign to convert Miss Benn, his cook. When she accused him of being too trusting of a First War veteran to whom he gave money, he answered, 'Please don't be so angry with me – I am only trying to be like Our Lord!'[4] Primed with sherry, she massaged Sassoon's lumbago in his back for half an hour each evening, but towards the end of 1959 she resigned. Hester thought that the cook had changed 'from treasure to tyrant' and she moved in to look after Siegfried until Mrs Hardy arrived, a woman of about thirty with a six-year-old daughter. George told his father that he himself was not a Christian; Sassoon knew that this 'complete individual' could not submit to any authority. Having done little work at Cambridge, the boy now had a Third-Class degree, a house in Huntingdon Road and a good job at a scientific-instrument factory. Then difficulties in George's marriage brought him back to his father. George became 'quite older brotherish',[5] giving his view of Christ as an inspired prophet like Brahma or Confucius. 'Pray for us both dearest,' Sassoon asked Mother Margaret Mary, '– all out!'[6] A year later, while at Cambridge visiting George, Sassoon went to Hengrave, near Bury St Edmunds, where Mother Margaret Mary was now the Mother Superior, having moved from Kensington Square, and had 'a perfect day' of 'absolute peace'.

In the summer of 1958, the *Downside Review* published 'Lenten Illuminations'. The poem was printed in December by the Cambridge University Press in a private edition of thirty-five arranged by Geoffrey Keynes – who, confronted by this new affirmation of faith, said evasively that he kept an open mind on religion – and one of 2,200 by the Downside Press the next year. Preceded by Sassoon seeing a seraph during his nightly prayers, and written in three days, 'Lenten Illuminations' expressed, he hoped, his joy in conversion and had seemed to be guided by some other power.

Resembling in style 'To One Who Was with Me in the War', the poem begins on Ash Wednesday as he prays in Downside's chapel alone, as 'one addicted much to meditationment' (again the awkward diction of Hardy). His old unfaithful self enters, to see, in an especially clumsy phrase, 'faith revealed where towards he pilgrim'd without finding'. Previously he had felt moved in a Christian way only on Good Friday (as described in that First War poem 'Stand to: Good Friday') through the 'almost unbearable idea of how He [Christ] died', but, even in his 'purgatorial time', he had thought that God might eventually be revealed. He had, he thought, never been obedient enough to see the glory of Mary, 'Mother immaculate', until now, at last peaceful under 'inflexible authority'.

'Lenten Illuminations' seems to range back in influence as well as in evocation of past times: to Hardy, even to Tennyson, in the phrase, used of the candles in the abbey church, 'They are what they are' (reminiscent of 'That which we are, we are' from 'Ulysses', Tennyson's poem that had marked some of his early verses). And in this new faith, Sassoon had found his lost childhood, his utopia:

> *This is the time of year when, even for the old,*
> *Youngness comes knocking on the heart with undefined*
> *Aches and announcements – blurred felicities foretold,*
> *And (obvious utterance) wearying winter left behind.*

> *I never felt it more than now, when out beyond these safening*
> *walls*
> *Sculptured with Stations of the Cross, spring-confident,*
> *unburdened, bold,*
> *The first March blackbird overheard to forward vision flutes*
> *and calls.*

> *You could have said this simple thing, old self, in any previous*
> *year.*
> *But not to that one ritual flame – to that all-answering Heart*
> *abidant here.*

With 'Lenten Illuminations' was printed the short 'Sight Sufficient', on the need for faith through 'sightless seeing', for God's love was 'beyond blind thought'. However awkward the verse, both poems are moving in their simple, sincere joy.

*

THEY SHOW ALSO that through all this pleasant turmoil he remained a poet of decidedly unmodernist views. Early in 1959, Sassoon served on the committee chaired by the Poet Laureate John Masefield to choose the winner of the Queen's Medal for Poetry (which he had won in 1957) and successfully championed Frances Cornford, a writer of short, usually rhyming, verses, sometimes pastoral, often melancholy, adept at rhythm and the strong last line.

Meanwhile a project that furthered interest in his own work was under way. Despite Sassoon's anxiety about its potential for disturbance, Geoffrey Keynes began work on a bibliography and soon was at Heytesbury asking about forgotten articles and their dates and poems published years before which their author preferred to forget. This led to several explosions, usually kept to his diary, and even the deliberate concealment of a notebook in which he had kept such details for years. Keynes's relentless, and occasionally insensitive, quest for what he needed for his bibliophile research or to fill a gap in his extraordinary book collection, or for information on people (such as T. E. Lawrence) or subjects that obsessed him, often maddened Sassoon. This irritation could lead him to forget Geoffrey's admirable dedication to poetry and to poets and his devotion to his beloved Siegfried. The past came back also with Christopher Hassall's huge biography of Sir Edward Marsh who had died in 1953, reminding him how little there was of Marsh's world in his new Catholic life.

Sassoon became absorbed into Downside, playing cricket for the abbey team (called the Ravens) and talking to the other monks like the sculptor Dom Hubert van Zeller. Now his religion filled his life. In the summer of 1959, Hester's twenty-year-old niece (and

Sassoon's goddaughter) Jessica Gatty came to Heytesbury. Earlier, Sassoon had spoken to her while staying with her parents in Yorkshire, once, in a garden in the nearby town of Richmond, saying that a divine being must be behind such beauty. The Gattys became anxious about his effect on Jessica, disapproving of its emotional intensity.

*

IN 1958, RUPERT Hart-Davis, then aged fifty-one, proposed himself for lunch at Heytesbury.[7] Sassoon took to this pipe-smoking, cricket-loving, former Guards officer publisher whose literary tastes often coincided with his own. Like Geoffrey Keynes, and even Blunden, Hart-Davis also had that slight military edge. Rupert Hart-Davis may have been an admirer, and friend, of T. S. Eliot but he disliked most aspects of modernism, thinking Samuel Beckett 'unreadable rubbish',[8] and put Hardy above all twentieth-century poets. Beneath a bluff, humorous friendliness, this new visitor combined businesslike energy with critical appreciation. With Siegfried Sassoon, he quickly took on a role that he had with other writers like Max Beerbohm and William Plomer: that of adviser on matters such as copyright and the organization of what Sassoon called his 'literary remains'.[9] By 1967, the year of his death, Siegfried Sassoon saw Rupert Hart-Davis as 'a source of strength and encouragement'[10] beyond anyone else except for Mother Margaret Mary. In August 1961, he named him in his will as a literary adviser, along with Edmund Blunden, to his executors (Glen Byam Shaw and the solicitor Anthony Lousada) in the place of Geoffrey Keynes. This hurt Keynes, to whom Sassoon gave the fair reason that Rupert was a much younger man who should be around to help for many years. After his adored Siegfried's death, Hart-Davis not only kept what he thought were unsuitable biographers at bay but published selections from Sassoon's war poetry, his letters to Max Beerbohm and three discreetly and methodically edited volumes of diaries that begin in 1914 and end in 1926, before the affair with Stephen Tennant.

Dennis Silk was often at Heytesbury, fascinated by Sassoon's First War heroism, his rebellion and his deep knowledge of cricketing history. Silk found him generous and honest, the least urbane person he had ever met. Early in their friendship, Sassoon entertained him in the Garden House Hotel at Cambridge, once inviting the entire university cricket team as well. He asked the undergraduates to fire the names of first-class cricketers at him so that he could give their initials, showing an extraordinary memory. When a waiter spilt soup over one of the team, the boy cried out, 'Christ!' – to which Sassoon said quickly, 'Christ, J.' Sassoon tried to turn Silk against Hester, whom the young man thought sadly neurotic, consumed by adoration for George. Silk became a master at Marlborough, sometimes bringing pupils to Heytesbury, such as the future racehorse trainer Ian Balding – another athlete, a rugby player and jockey, whom Sassoon thought 'a modest, splendid boy'.[11] During Balding's future visits, Sassoon, unusually, became a listener, fascinated by the brilliant young rider's accounts of racing characters that evoked memories of pre-1914 point-to-points and the now sweetly nostalgic world of *Memoirs of a Fox-hunting Man*. Ian Balding also brought a girlfriend, the musician Heather Lewis, to Heytesbury, who delighted the poet by setting some of his verses, like 'The Chord', to music. Heather Lewis was one of the few women outside a religious order to become close to him in the last years; another was a Roman Catholic neighbour, Muriel Galsworthy, niece of the novelist John.

When Sassoon spoke intensely of T. E. Lawrence, Silk wondered if this was a glimpse of homosexual feeling. It was the only time he sensed it. In October 1959, the Roman Catholic actor Alec Guinness, who was to play T. E. Lawrence in Terence Rattigan's play *Ross*, came to Heytesbury for Sassoon's memories, finding his host shy, perhaps in love with the memory of Lawrence. Once, during one of many chaotic car journeys, Dennis Silk glimpsed the warrior. Sassoon had turned across the main road into the Heytesbury drive without signalling, as another car was overtaking him. The other driver swung clear, they both stopped and the man got out and said,

'You bloody fucking twat.' Squaring up to him, Sassoon replied, 'You can have it if you want it,' before the driver recoiled and walked away. Sassoon tried only half-heartedly to convert Silk to Catholicism, knowing that to be a Roman Catholic would wreck his chances of becoming headmaster at an Anglican public school.[12]

*

IN OCTOBER 1959 Siegfried Sassoon began a friendship with another Roman Catholic nun who was rather different from the sweet, unintellectual Mother Margaret Mary: Dame Felicitas Corrigan, a Benedictine at the Abbey of Stanbrook near Worcester, who had been put in touch with him by Sydney Cockerell, an old friend of Stanbrook's former abbess, Dame Laurentia McLachlan.

A musician who played the organ in the abbey, a biographer (of Helen Waddell) and the author of books on the psalms and the liturgy, Dame Felicitas, having read *Siegfried's Journey*, asked for a photograph of its author. Sending a recent one taken by George, he told her of his admiration for the work of Stanbrook's private press, run by the nuns, and enclosed his Catholic poems, 'Lenten Illuminations', 'Rogation' and the short 'For Grace in Me Divined'.[13] He asked Felicitas Corrigan about the visions he had seen – of the Madonna, of angels and of seraphs. Now he claimed to have cessation of thought while at prayer, on the verge of mystical transformation. She teased him. Surely the visions were a result of emotion, perhaps linked to the incubation of his poem 'Ask Your Angel – Ask That Vigilant Voice'. Were they, like Macbeth's dagger, the result of an overwrought brain? Was a life-sized seraph derived from the iconography of Christian art? Can a spirit be 'so circumscribed'? Above all, 'has an angel got arms'?[14]

On 25 June 1960, driven by his young Roman Catholic friend Brian Butler, Sassoon visited Stanbrook for the first time. There to greet him were the Lady Abbess and Dame Felicitas, the latter charmed by this 'tall, spare figure with the emaciated face of an El Greco saint and the pent-up energy of a hydrogen bomb'.[15] He was nervous and after vespers read to the nuns: some earlier poems, extracts from *The Old Century* and the recent 'A Prayer at Pentecost', his audience overwhelmed when he looked up as if gazing towards eternity. He spoke with Dame Hildelith, the abbey's printer, then, breaking the rules, lit his pipe. Delighted, Dame Felicitas inhaled the smoke, denied to her since entry into the convent some twenty-seven years earlier.

The nun later decried what she called 'the Sassoon cult', saying, 'He didn't delude me.'[16] Disapproving of what he said about Hester, she wondered if he was capable of love and its sacrifices, if his adoration of George came too much from his son's reflection of himself. He spoke to her of his homosexuality, more openly than to Mother Margaret Mary, whose sweetness he may not have wanted to test by mentioning this, to him, shameful state. When Mother Margaret Mary asked about the love poems of the 1920s, he was disingenuous, writing of 'lyric responses to a charming young person who befriended my loneliness with innocent companionship' and 'a sad record of an idealised episode which ended in disillusionment – one of my many errors of judgement!'[17] Later he told her that he had once known Ivor Novello 'quite well'.[18] Felicitas Corrigan thought that he achieved a degree of mysticism through prayer and faced his 'patent egocentricity' in his last years, that he had imaginative sympathy, which was why she wrote her study of him, *A Poet's Pilgrimage*.[19] To her, and to others, he gave his conversion a characteristically histrionic note, believing that there had always been a prophetic strain in him, the result perhaps of his Jewish antecedents. Indeed Catholicism seemed to make him more aware, at last, of his father's own hereditary religion.

Soon he liked to be at Stanbrook for his birthday and usually once more in the year. Dame Felicitas recalled him sitting in an armchair, putting away the handkerchief he had been twisting in his hands and lighting his pipe before letting out a flood of talk, young-looking, 'wonderfully handsome' in his quest for 'simplicity, sincerity and truth'. She looked often at a photograph of Sassoon taken in 1952 in the library at Heytesbury. To her 'all his Jewish ancestry is in his face and he looked like an Old Testament prophet, weeping and lamenting as he sits in the dust of which he is made. I find it rather a terrible photograph'[20] – the epitome, she thought, of twentieth-century man in search of faith, rejecting despair.

He had been delighted by the wish of nuns at Stanbrook to print an edition of his poems at the abbey press that would reflect what he saw now as his slow move towards the Catholic faith. Before the poems came a quotation from Hilaire Belloc, one with 'a key significance in the progress of my submission'.[21] How appropriate also that it had been written to an earlier convert, Katharine Asquith. Belloc's words showed Sassoon's need: the church as a home rather than what 'men fall in love with', a need 'to which corresponds in every outline the outcast and unprotected contour of the soul'. Important in this was Verlaine's sentence, quoted by Belloc, 'Oh! Rome – oh! Mère!' – in which Rome is seen as an answer and a protection, a source of illimitable, unquestioning love, like that of a mother for her child. How much more significant the faith was, Belloc thought, to the converted, 'those who come upon it from over the hills of life and say to themselves "Here is the town"'.

The Stanbrook Abbey volume was called *The Path to Peace*. It opens with some poems of solitary searching for an immortal power, followed by the bad years after the Second War and before 1957. The last section had been written since his conversion, starting with an extract from 'Lenten Illuminations'. 'Arbor Vitae' saw his own grace shown in a tree that, after winter, lived again in 'an awoken year':

> *So grace in me can hide –*
> *Be darkened and denied –*
> *Then once again*
> *Vesture my every vein.*

'Unfoldment' told of daffodils flourishing in the warmth of his room; so might prayer free him from his own 'dark being'. 'Rogation', in similarly awkward language, asked that wisdom and mystery, not reason, might guide him. Showing the influence of Gerard Manley Hopkins, the poem ends:

> *World watcher, armed and influent to befriend;*
> *Hope of humility, resistless Rood,*
> *Beyond our bodements bring beatitude.*

The last poem was 'A Prayer at Pentecost' (1960), addressed first to 'Master Musician Life' – for Sassoon, their dialogue was over – then to 'Spirit, who speaks by silences' that might remake him. Apart from the much longer 'Lenten Illuminations', the post-conversion poems are brief, ecstatic utterances, mostly of two verses ('Arbor Vitae' has four short ones).

The volume was hand-set at Stanbrook in an italic type. The edition was limited to 500 copies of which 20 were on handmade paper and bound in full vellum with hand-letters and gilded: 480 on thinner but also handmade paper, quarter-bound in vellum, with the initials hand-lettered. Dennis Silk had a few copies of 'Rogation' in a single leaf printed by the boys at the Marlborough College Press. To Dame Felicitas, Sassoon said that this poem was perhaps 'tabloid theology', yet it also had what he had failed to see when he wrote it, a cry for peace, for an irresistible power: the ten lines were 'the outcome of hundreds of hours of prayer and devotional meaning'. For him, 'these poems are my living heart!'[22] As with the other post-conversion writing, it is the personal delight and sincerity that impress rather than the poetic resonance or skill.

*

HE WISHED TO share all this, to resume the role of a powerful proselytizing poet that seemed to have left him in 1918. And when, on 29 April 1960, Sassoon received some poems – inspired, their author said, by reading (among other things) 'Unfoldment' in the *Tablet*[23] – he seemed to have found an ally and a disciple. They were about nothing less than 'the recovery of Christendom' and the longest of them – called 'Piers Prodigal' – had been written for the composer Gerald Finzi who was setting it to music when he died.

The letter came from Ian Davie. Born in 1924, Davie had converted to Catholicism in 1950 and was working for the Colonial Office as a spy-catcher in Hong Kong after war service in India and a degree in theology from Oxford. Almost becoming an Anglican priest before his conversion to Roman Catholicism, Davie wrote religious poetry, mystical, often pastoral, different both from the Movement poets and from modernism. Edmund Blunden, still a professor at Hong Kong university, had advised him to send his work to Heytesbury.

Sassoon fell upon these themes that had lasted his whole life: the Arthurian quest, a dislike of materialism, a sense of wonder and a delight in traditional England. Here was a young Catholic poet who, with his help, could turn back the juggernaut of fashion. He envisaged Owen all over again. The old dream that Wilfred and he might have held the line against modernism was replaced by another of a conquering partnership with this new young genius. Sassoon particularly liked the long 'Piers Prodigal' with its ending that evoked the early morning about which he had often written himself:

> *Stillness of woods: the earth's fresh daybreak smell:*
> *Rich fragrance such as rain-soaked gardens yield.*
> *And richer recompense that I should see,*
> *In clearest pools of mirrored day revealed.*
> *A gracious and consenting self – my own,*
> *Even the self that Christ would have me be.*[24]

He asked Ian Davie to Heytesbury, telling him from this 'oasis of peace and beauty'[25] – the opposite of the literary revolution that they were both fighting – that 'you couldn't have sent the poems to me at a better time'. Davie endured his first terrifying drive, in the ancient Humber with a black hood patched up with yellow plaster that shone in the sun, and Sassoon seemed not so much shy as awkward, scarcely talking at all about the First War although the visitor detected a slight jealousy of Wilfred Owen. Mother Margaret Mary, to whom he had sent the book, said all the nuns at Hengrave were praying for 'Piers Prodigal' to be published. Sassoon decided not to approach Rupert Hart-Davis – who published 'low Anglican'[26] poets like Andrew Young, R. S. Thomas and Charles Causley – but to act on Katharine Asquith's suggestion of the Harvill Press, where one of the directors was a Catholic. Harvill accepted the book and Sassoon wrote an introduction. On the publication of *Piers Prodigal* in October 1961, it filled an entire window of Hatchards, the bookshop in Piccadilly, for a day before being removed. Reviewers commented on its resemblance to the Georgians and sales were poor, leaving the hope of recognition in a more discerning future.

In 1962, Davie left the Colonial Service to become a schoolmaster at Red Rice school, near Andover, then at Marlborough where he was head of English. Both schools were not far from Heytesbury, which he visited quite often, sometimes with his pupils. Sassoon did not appear until lunchtime so guests had the morning to themselves before a monologue by the host, usually about poetry, rarely touching upon Hester, except to express weary indulgence, or George, whom he obviously adored. Once Davie, while walking in the garden, looked up at the house, and saw a young man in the window of Sassoon's bedroom. Later he asked his host who it was, to be told proudly, 'It's one of the things I can do.' But beyond this hint of narcissism and face-painting, Davie never felt any sexual threat and Sassoon spoke seldom of Stephen Tennant, only to say he was vain and stupid. He sometimes said to Davie, 'I hope you're writing more' – but never asked to see anything.[27] The dream had faded.

Ian Davie's work, however, retained its effect. In July 1960, Jessica Gatty stayed alone at Heytesbury. One evening she and her uncle Siegfried listened to Mozart's G minor quintet on the radio before he read her *Piers Prodigal*. At the end the girl burst into tears. Soon afterwards she began to visit Mother Clare, a nun at Kensington Square, for informal instruction in the Roman Catholic faith. In October 1961, Jessica Gatty was received into the Roman Catholic Church at Kensington Square and went back to the Sue Ryder home in East Anglia where she was working. 'Her submission is far the highest blessing I have received since my own conversion, and permeates my whole being,'[28] Sassoon told Ian Davie.

*

THE LACK OF literary recognition still rankled, even in his new-found serenity. Sir Alan Lascelles, once the Queen's private secretary, well read and musical, came to see him and said that, if Masefield died, Sassoon would be offered the OM. Lascelles was another new friend, this time a contemporary who had been with Sassoon at Marlborough – although neither recalled the other – and later a member of the legendary pre-1914 Oxford generation. He, too, had fought on the Western Front, winning the Military Cross, before becoming a courtier and private secretary to Edward VIII, George VI and Elizabeth II. In August 1960, Sassoon stayed with Lascelles at Sir Alan's house in The Old Stables at Kensington Palace. John Betjeman was there and said, 'I am nothing. You are a great poet.'[29]

Lascelles, who, unusually, preferred Sassoon's post-conversion work to the war poems – and also had that rather military air of brisk, commanding capability perceptible in Keynes and Hart-Davis – coaxed him into the London social scene where he saw his cousin Lady Cholmondeley again. She wrote to Siegfried Sassoon about a granddaughter who wanted to become a Roman Catholic and had just been sacked from her school for hitting the matron. What should she do, Lady Cholmondeley asked? Sassoon advised that universal panacea, the Convent of the Assumption in Kensington Square.

Supported by Rupert Hart-Davis, Lascelles persuaded him to attend a dining club called the Literary Society, once described as a meeting place for writers who want to be gentlemen and gentlemen who want to be writers. To Sassoon these dinners at the Garrick Club, even when he sat next to a friend like John Sparrow, were too worldly,[30] although everyone was kind. Once David Jones came to lunch at Lascelles's house – 'a pathetic, helpless-seeming little man –

ultra sensitive'[31] – and they discovered that Jones's battalion had relieved Sassoon's after his bombing exploit in 1916. The author of *In Parenthesis* wanted to talk about his own Catholicism but was too shy, and deaf, to raise the topic with this inaudible old man who clearly did not appreciate his work. Sassoon liked Tommy Lascelles and felt so at ease with him that he once turned a series of back somersaults on Lascelles's lawn to show how supple he still was, declaring that 'it was a routine procedure'.[32]

Now he had another comforter, in some ways a successor to Dorothy Wallis but with less sexual involvement: Lyn Humphries, the pretty, auburn-haired wife of the manager of the local tree nursery at Heytesbury. In her forties and fond of poetry, she had met Sassoon when collecting her daughter Frances from the big house where the girl had gone in search of the author of 'Everyone Sang', a poem the child had read in a book given to her by her mother. Sassoon had been kind to Frances, showing her books in his library; Lyn first charmed him by knowing the answer to a clue in the *Times* crossword puzzle. Soon she called quite frequently, invariably in the evenings, and knelt in front of him with her hand on his knee when he sat in an armchair or on the sofa; there was talk in the village of their relationship. Sometimes Lyn met others there, perhaps Haro Hodson or the amateur jockey John Lawrence, and Sassoon spoke often of famous people – Churchill or T. E. Lawrence or Elgar – the conversation taking on a ritual in which Lyn asked, 'Did you know him, Captain Sassoon?', to get the answer (at which they all laughed) 'Know him? He was a friend of mine.' Lyn's interest in cricket and poetry drew Sassoon closer to her. Of Hester he said simply, 'She came between me and my writing' or 'She would not let me see George,' speaking of her as if she was a naughty child.[33] When Hester visited she seemed kind and vague, untidy, rather beautiful, mildly jealous.

George and Stephanie parted; then, in December 1960, Stephanie gave birth to their daughter. Sassoon tried not to think about the divorce, taking refuge in prayer. During Christmas of 1960 and

January of 1961, Hester supervised the domestic scene at Heytesbury, with George accompanied by a new girlfriend, Marguerite Dicks, whom he would eventually marry. Meanwhile an Isaac Rosenberg 'boom'[34] had joined the critics' praise of Owen.

TWENTY-SIX

'My final test of endurance'

THE *TIMES LITERARY SUPPLEMENT* reviewed *The Path to Peace*, its critic noticing continuity: how like a poem of 1909 ('Come in This Hour to Set My Spirit Free') was to a poem of 1957 ('He Spoke. He Held My Spirit in His Hand'). The book had 'dignity, inwardness and sincerity',[1] but piety and sentimentality rather than greatness. In the *Sunday Times* Maurice Wiggin, who had visited Heytesbury, also noted an apparent changelessness, evinced even in its owner, a tall, thin active man in an old blue blazer and sand-coloured riding britches who talked of the Somme ('my finest hour'), his horses and the way that poems write themselves.

Sassoon had become even more of an object of curiosity, the attention still mostly on his youth and brave past. He agreed to read his work to the Newman Society, a Catholic group at Oxford, even though he felt bronchial and old. Here more than 200 people packed into a smallish room to hear the Edingthorpe section of *The Old Century*, poems from the First World War and others written since his conversion. This need for 'histrionicism', as he called it, arose again when he unveiled a memorial tablet to Walter de la Mare in St Paul's cathedral in December 1961, borrowing Lascelles's over-coat for the occasion and making Harold Nicolson think that he looked 'magnificent – like a Homeric bard'.[2]

In May 1961, Faber published another *Collected Poems* with

the additions from *Common Chords, Emblems of Experience* and *The Tasking*, printing 3,000 copies. This brought the reviewers out again and their familiar view of him: decent as a man, disappointing as a poet. In the *Spectator*, John Bayley remarked on the moving, amateurish quality of the war poems;[3] in the *Observer*, A. Alvarez was less kind, saying that the anger and savagery of these were his real achievement, not the lyric poems or the brave acts typical of an Edwardian gentleman–officer. Alvarez thought that Sassoon had no language to cope with the complexities of life after 1918.[4] At least the Roman Catholic paper the *Tablet* carried a long notice by Ian Davie: 'quite perfect',[5] Sassoon thought.

Some of his poems were printed in single sheets at the Stanbrook Press: short pieces emphasizing joy in submission and stillness of heart like 'Awaitment' and 'Before a Crucifix' about salvation through pain. In 'Compline' he seeks 'child simplicity', 'Proven Purpose' of September 1964 wishes for a still, unquestioning mind to receive God's will. In the same month 'A Prayer in Old Age' – called in manuscript 'An Orison for Old Age' – asks for no rest until the end of his experience of the temporal world:

> *I ask one world of everlasting loss*
> *In all I am, that other world to win.*
> *My nothingness must kneel below Thy Cross.*
> *There let new life begin.*[6]

*

WHILE SASSOON SOUGHT, and to some extent found, peace, interest in the First World War, and his part in it, became even greater. Since the 1920s, opinion had been hardening against the record of the military High Command, a process aided by such politicians as Winston Churchill and Lloyd George in their memoirs. The flood of war books that came at the end of that decade had the most effect; to many, it seemed intolerable that the sensitive, brave young writers of these years should have been subjected to such an ordeal, planned by supposedly uncaring, remote figures living in comfort miles behind the front line. The myth of an avoidable slaughter grew, feeding the demand for peace during the 1930s, exemplified by the Peace campaign of Dick Sheppard. After the Second World War, this gained even more force in popular histories that depicted the generals as grotesque, moustachioed buffoons, in doom-ridden television documentaries and imaginative works like the play *Oh! What a Lovely War* and Britten's *War Requiem* of 1961, based partly on Owen's poems. Sassoon himself was central to all this; *Memoirs of a Fox-hunting Man* and the war poems became school texts, set for O and A level or used to bring to life what had happened in the trenches.

He felt uncomfortable about such fame. His honest and constant self-examination never let him forget how limited his own time at the front had been or that the heroism had consisted of lightning moments of anger and exhilaration, never tested by long periods under fire; the interest, even adulation, seemed to him to be unearned. He told Mother Margaret Mary that he thought it wrong that the First World War had made his literary reputation; perhaps he had been supernaturally protected by missing all the worst ordeals of the battalions in which he had served.

But that time still obsessed him. Dennis Silk remembers listening for hours to stories of it, as if Sassoon needed the catharsis of reliving every moment of anxiety and pain, still brought constantly back into his life. An old comrade, Eric Bibby – who had been an officer with him on the Somme – called at Heytesbury, greeting Sassoon with 'Hullo Kangear', his First War nickname.[7] Blunden, visiting in August 1961, wanted to discuss some variants in Owen's poems he had seen in manuscript, but his host seemed uninterested, talking instead about the Western Front with Dennis Silk. In May 1963, Sassoon presented a picture by Richard Dadd, given to him by Lady Gatty (and originally owned by her father Alfred Morrison), to the Tate, in memory of the artist's three great-nephews. Two of these had been killed in the First War, the third being Sassoon's former comrade (who later committed suicide) Julian Dadd.

*

THE ONE FORCE strong enough to vanquish this was his faith. Sassoon minded that his family apparently failed to share the joy of this. Hester said that she did not find organized religion appealing and saw the natural world, in particular the landscape of Mull, as more worthy of worship for its power and beauty; George could never quite remember what went on at Stanbrook, or even the content of *The Path to Peace*, and thought that Jessica Gatty's conversion was a form of escapism. Sassoon concluded, a little angrily, that – with few exceptions like Dennis Silk or Alan Lascelles or Cressida Ridley – he was at ease only with Roman Catholics now. Mother Margaret Mary moved from Hengrave to the convent school at Sidmouth in Devon, nearer to Heytesbury, and brought some pupils there, her first visit to Sassoon's home. There was an anxious moment when Dennis Silk, now engaged to Diana Milton, brought Diana to Heytesbury. Luckily Sassoon found her 'charming, sensible, and gentle', someone who 'fitted in perfectly at once'.[8]

Age was weakening him. He suffered sporadic illness: rheumatism, aching teeth and gums, as well as the old digestive disorder. The winter of 1961 was icy and Hester stayed for more than six weeks, her house on Mull unreachable because of snow. Sassoon built up the library fire, cut small logs in his wood shed but spent much time in bed. When his gums were operated on – and his teeth removed – in Odstock hospital at the end of March 1962, he made the ordeal into a challenge for his faith as the pain was terrible. He read Belloc and Hopkins, Ronald Knox, Newman's sermons and the Bible and thought of Katharine Asquith's much worse suffering from arthritis. A religious poem – 'Before a Crucifix' – followed this, these short verses coming as if he was merely their recorder.

> *When ultimate earned afflictions overtake me,*
> *Lord, if it is Thy will to bend and break me,*

Grant sacramental purpose to prevail.
By Thine example, be this body broken;

Through Thee, some sacrificial strength awoken,
Where life's illuminings no more avail.[9]

More deaths came – of Ralph Hodgson, on his farm in Ohio, and of Sydney Cockerell – and more people wrote to him about the past. To Michael Thorpe, who wished to do a thesis at the University of Singapore on Sassoon's work, he said that he preferred attention to be given to his poetry written after 1918 and tried to put Thorpe off.[10] But, encouraged by the poet D. J. Enright – who taught him at Singapore – Thorpe continued with his research. Sassoon complained again of the interest in 'that ghastly war'[11] and refused to send Thorpe any of his manuscripts.

As in his faith, he valued now, even more, the simple in literature: the human episodes, humour mixed with pathos or emotion. Jane Austen, for instance, he liked for her mind but not for her heart. Henry James he thought too hard now; what he wanted was the scene in Trollope's *The Warden* of a worried, simple, good Mr Harding playing his cello. Charles Lamb had such things in him, as did Edward FitzGerald; after all 'we are all children in the long run'. Sassoon liked to think of the simple almost saintly souls in fiction: Pickwick, Mr Pooter, Colonel Newcome, Kipps, Don Quixote, Parson Adams in *Joseph Andrews*.[12] Prudence he scorned, for imprudence went with generosity. This inner life seemed to envelop Heytesbury. The novelist Anthony Powell thought, when he went there, that the house was outside the contemporary world.[13]

Soon after Christmas 1964, with Hester, George and Marguerite in the house, Sassoon had an internal haemorrhage one night from his old duodenal ulcer and collapsed on the way to the bathroom. He stayed on the floor in the cold, his family still downstairs, and eventually stumbled back to bed before saying his nightly prayers. Hester and George persuaded him to do something about passing Heytesbury on to the next generation in order to avoid taxes. Sassoon agreed to this but, still in bed most of the time, left all the arrangements to them. His important manuscripts he made over to George, recognizing that some would have to be sold to pay death duties. By the end of February 1965, he was resting much of the time on the library sofa with George's old school rug over his knees.

In the aftermath of Winston Churchill's death and funeral in January 1965, 'Everyone Sang' – seen, rather oddly, to epitomize the 1940 spirit – had been printed in *The Times* and the *Sunday Telegraph*. On 24 February, Sassoon heard that Oxford University was offering him an honorary degree, and, although pleased, he wondered how he could face the ceremony. In June, this took place; and Colin Fenton drove him from Heytesbury to All Souls, to stay with John Sparrow. Dennis Silk was in the crowd in the Sheldonian theatre; among others being similarly honoured were the Russian poet Anna Akhmatova and Geoffrey Keynes (Keynes thought that Sassoon looked tired, thin and bloodless). The public orator read, in Latin, the citation about 'this eminent artist in verse and prose', brave but protesting during the First War, about which he had been too often reminded. Sassoon, it said, disliked publicity but liked recognition, wanted seclusion yet had published several autobiographies: a man who had 'an instinct for getting the full flavour of an experience' and a devotee of cricket, 'a country dweller of the utmost urbanity'.[14]

That summer his digestion played up, perhaps partly because of summer visitors, and he missed his usual birthday visit to Stanbrook, not feeling well enough. On Remembrance Sunday, 11 November, several of his poems were broadcast, including 'Song Books of the War' which Churchill had liked to recite. He was alone for Christmas, 'a luxury'.[15] Hester thought of coming afterwards, but on 12 January 1966 he put her off. Although getting up every day for lunch and dinner, he did little else because the bad rheumatism in his arms and hands had now reached his left shoulder. In February he felt relieved when Blunden – to whom he had given £4,000 to help buy a retirement house in Suffolk – beat Robert Lowell in the election for the professorship of poetry at Oxford.

The winter was hard: rheumatism, exhaustion, the cellar flooding in December, the oil heater broken, no hot water for almost a month, then, in March, George so ill with glandular fever that Geoffrey Keynes put him into St Bartholomew's hospital in London. Sassoon himself went, again under Keynes's supervision, to have his prostate removed in Bath, by a surgeon who reminded him of Rivers. Some visitors delighted him: Glen Byam Shaw, Colin Fenton, Dennis Silk and George, to whom he felt close again, the loving boy of 1953 now back as a man of twenty-nine. Still there was no escaping the war. The man who worked the heat lamp to relieve Sassoon's arthritis turned out to have been in the same division as him in 1917, having gone out as a boy of less than eighteen, so they talked of this 'extraordinary intensive bond'.[16]

He read Michael Thorpe's critical study of his writing and felt grateful that Thorpe, now at the University of Leiden, had taken the trouble. But Thorpe's approach was too academic, missing his high spirits, Sassoon thought, and seemed to disapprove 'of the world I was brought up in'.[17] In a letter, he told Thorpe how he saw his own story: never a professional writer, *Satirical Poems* an exercise in the use of words to get rid of the war, his prose mannered until the *Fox-hunting Man* (natural through its 'diary' style), *Picture Show* transitional and imposed on him by Theo Bartholomew's wish, in 1919, to design a new collection of his poems. A new poetic voice came only in 1924 with 'At the Grave of Henry Vaughan', 'Alone', 'Stonehenge' and 'Grandeur of Ghosts', then *The Heart's Journey* and *Vigils*. Sassoon found his fame as a war poet 'a positive burden' and still loathed the war while admitting its fascination. Thorpe was right to see Sherston as more effective as a form of anti-war propaganda than 'outspoken indignation'; right also to admire *The Old Century* and its deliberate nostalgia. The reception of *Sequences* had been 'heart-breaking'. Thorpe liked *The Tasking* but not 'Rogation' or 'Lenten Illuminations'.[18]

*

THE BOOK WAS only one of the tributes as the poet completed his eightieth year. The Arts Council asked Charles Causley to discover what Sassoon might like and in early summer Causley came to Heytesbury with the Council's literature director, Eric Walter White, to find Sassoon picking jonquils by a stream. After tea, against the distant sound of a cricket match, he teasingly said, 'I'd like a bust.'[19] George took a photograph of his father in an overcoat, a scarf below his chin, looking downwards, the mouth slightly open as if about to utter some measured thought, his hair more dark than grey as he sat in the spasmodic sun. This appeared opposite the title-page of what emerged from the afternoon: a volume bound in green called *An Octave*, eight poems written since his conversion in 1957, printed in an edition of 352 numbered copies. Sassoon was given a hundred and the rest were offered to private subscribers (at two guineas) in a letter signed by the Poet Laureate John Masefield. The poets W. H. Auden, John Betjeman, C. Day Lewis, Roy Fuller, Robert Graves, Ted Hughes, David Jones, Philip Larkin, Herbert Read, Edgell Rickword and R. S. Thomas – not all admired by Sassoon – also signed. Other signatories were a truer record of his last years, friends like Rupert Hart-Davis, Edmund Blunden, Richard de la Mare, Geoffrey Keynes and Glen Byam Shaw.

The *Fox-hunting Man* was read on the radio and Sassoon was struck by 'the absolute *innocence*' of it all.[20] In the *Guardian*, W. L. Webb recalled reading the Sherston memoirs as a schoolboy in suburban Manchester, wondering now at their 'slightly masochistic nostalgia'. Perhaps, Webb thought, exhaustion after the war protest had led to a retirement into reticent autobiographies[21] and the touching, humble poems of the last years. The Stanbrook Abbey Press printed a fine edition of *Something About Myself*, the story written for his mother at the age of eleven, dedicating it to him with the comment that he had kept the heart of a child.

On his birthday he took communion from the Roman Catholic curate who came to the house, then had a quiet lunch and listened to a tribute on the radio, inappropriately on *Woman's Hour*, a sepulchral reading of 'The Death-Bed'. At half-past three the Silks and the Hart-Davises arrived, followed by two people from the Arts

Council with copies of *An Octave*. The Silks brought a cake with eighty candles and a leather-bound volume with tributes and messages written by friends such as E. M. Forster, Sassoon's brother Michael and many others, including Mr Armitage who managed the Heytesbury estate. Hester and George, from Mull and Cambridge, sent an enormous bunch of chrysanthemums. After receiving the manuscript book from Hart-Davis, Sassoon put it to one side. Hart-Davis presented it again; again it was pushed to one side. Four or five days later the Keyneses came and Sassoon produced the book, having only looked at a few of the pages.

On 13 September he was driven to Oxford, to see Mother Margaret Mary, now in charge of a students' hostel in Headington. Two days later he wrote to Alan Lascelles that the birthday book delighted him in its 'extraordinary mixture of distinguished and homely characters, as it should be'.[22] Sassoon received nearly a hundred letters about his birthday – including one from John Masefield who said that his poetry would help bring about a resurgence in religious faith – and thirty telegrams, and there were articles in *The Times*, *Telegraph* and *Guardian*. The radio put on another programme, with contributions from Dennis Silk, Glen Byam Shaw and Charles Causley. This concentrated too much, he thought, on the war poems and Blunden sounded tired.[23] By 11 October Sassoon had stomach pains again, brought on, he thought, by over-exertion.

*

STILL HE READ the old favourites: books that re-created a lost England: *Handley Cross*, *Framley Parsonage* (in a first edition), which reminded him of his mother's ideal of a secure mid-Victorian county world. The parish priest, Father McCarthy, came every Friday morning to celebrate mass in the house as Sassoon could not get to church, though the convert disliked the new mass, longing for the old words. The writer Tom Clarke, working on a television play about the protest of 1917, visited him but Sassoon said he did not want to be involved, calling himself not so much a pacifist now as a quietist. Clarke thought he seemed worried that people might think he was exploiting his wartime experiences.

His old powers of sympathy revived when, in February 1967, he wrote to Rupert Hart-Davis about the sudden death of Hart-Davis's third wife, Ruth Simon. But by May 1967 he was dozing much of the time. Still the OM – that group of twenty-four people who have to be of immense distinction, chosen personally by the sovereign – was on his mind since the vacancy created by the death of T. S. Eliot. Hart-Davis said that Lascelles had tried hard a year or two before, and now did not feel optimistic. In June, an old soldier, V. King, who at the age of sixteen had been with him on the Somme in the First Battalion Royal Welch Fusiliers, wrote about the memoirs. Sassoon told him how he had found commanding a company 'very tiring' and preferred 'doing stunts' in no-man's land. 'I suppose that, like me, you find the memories of 1916 etc inescapable,' Sassoon wrote. 'Until the recent revival of public interest in the war, I avoided talking about it as much as possible, except with those who were in it. Young people now *want* to hear about it.'[24]

Later in the summer Sassoon went into hospital in Warminster to have fluid drained off his stomach. Dom Philip Jebb, a monk at Downside and Hilaire Belloc's grandson, heard of this and bicycled twenty miles from the abbey, to find a corpse-like old man with an emaciated face and thin neck and a stomach grossly swollen with the tumour of cancer; then the corpse came to life, recognized the monk and asked how Kent was doing at cricket. They spoke of Belloc and of death. Sassoon said, 'I'm sorry for being in such low form but deep down I'm not. Is it wrong to look forward to being in Heaven?' The monk said, no, of course not. The patient held up his thin arm, saying, 'This is no longer a Raven's arm', referring to the Downside cricket team. He said he wanted to die at Heytesbury, and Jebb advised him to go home. Bicycling back to Downside through the woods of Longleat, the monk, usually lowered by death-bed visiting, felt uplifted.[25]

His doctor told him the truth: he had inoperable abdominal

cancer. Sassoon asked that Hester and George should not be told. By 22 August there was a night nurse and a day nurse on the way. Rupert Hart-Davis, who had heard from Mother Margaret Mary, persuaded Sassoon to allow him to tell Geoffrey Keynes. Sassoon was not in pain, only in intermittent discomfort. 'He knows everything,' Hart-Davis wrote to Keynes, 'and is utterly courageous and matter-of-fact about it.' Earlier Sassoon had asked Rupert if his poems were 'all right', to be told that they were. Then he had ventured further: had every one been a bull's-eye? To this Hart-Davis had to answer no, some had even missed the target altogether; and the dying poet laughed. Should they get Hester down from Scotland, Rupert wondered? Sassoon answered, 'Good heavens no. We're in enough trouble as it is.' Hart-Davis was asked to write to six of Sassoon's best friends in case they might be hurt if they heard the news from elsewhere. It should be kept, however, from Dennis Silk who was about to set off on a cricketing tour of Canada which Sassoon did not want to spoil for him.[26]

Heytesbury was ill suited to an influx for, as Hart-Davis noted, 'the idiotic thing is that in this enormous house there are only three usable bedrooms, apart from S's'.[27] Hester had had a stroke and was in hospital in Oban. George, still on Mull, felt he should be with her. On 26 August Jessica Gatty drove Mother Margaret Mary over from Oxford for her last visit. 'Thank God you had prepared me to see such a skeleton but he was still lucid,' she wrote to Hart-Davis, dreading the end for, as she told Ian Davie, even 'the bravest are assailed in the last moments by fears we cannot know'.[28] She and Jessica gave Sassoon lunch to allow the cook Mrs Day a break, before walking in the park on a fine late summer day. When they returned, he was restless and hot and asked for the nurse. Mrs Day and the nurse kept visitors away but 'why not let S. have joy till the near end?' Mother Margaret Mary hoped he would be released soon and they said 'au revoir'. She asked him 'not to leave us too long behind'. He thanked her for ten years of 'lovely friendship', saying, 'There was never a foot wrong.'[29]

On 1 September George, now at Heytesbury, took up a last

letter from Mr King. Sassoon read it, remembering a message that
the soldier had brought him in Mametz Wood. He was too weak
for communion yet held up his crucifix and declared, 'He is still
with me.'[30] To George, he said, 'This is going to be my final test of
endurance and I mean to put up a really good show.' Later he
weakened, speaking with difficulty yet smiling and making jokes
until quarter-past eight when he held the nurse's hand and died,
after a series of small heart attacks.

At Stanbrook, that evening at seven o'clock, Dame Felicitas
Corrigan felt an urge to make the Stations of the Cross and to pray
particularly for the dying. Mother Margaret Mary, in the convent
chapel in Oxford, thought 'something was happening' but did not
'quite trust telepathy'.[31] George had tried to telephone Mr King but
could get no answer, so wrote to describe the end. Sassoon's son felt
sure that 'the thoughts in his mind of the old days in the trenches
helped him over those last few hours. He was a great old man, and
I am proud to have had him for a father.'[32] He left out that the Irish
nurse had suggested George should get his accordion and that he
had played 'The Wild Rover' in the dead man's room, the high-
spirited Irish tune redolent of Sassoon's sporadic childlike leaping
joy, following Mr King's reminder of those days on the Western
Front that had made Siegfried as a poet and as a man.

Epilogue

THE DEATH CERTIFICATE described Siegfried Sassoon as 'Poet and author retired' and said that he had died of 'a secondary carcinoma of liver and peritoneum and carcinoma of the stomach'.[1] The next day, the Heytesbury cricket team stood for two minutes' silence before defeating a side that usually beat them. The funeral was fixed for ten o'clock in the morning on 6 September at St George's in Warminster, to be followed by burial at Mells, in the Anglican churchyard, near the grave of Father Ronald Knox.

About twenty people came to the private ceremony. Lyn Humphries arrived with Lord Heytesbury and the village doctor; Rupert Hart-Davis accompanied Angela Byam Shaw who carried her own bunch of roses and yellow flowers. Haro Hodson sat with Hart-Davis and Angela. Glen had come to Heytesbury after Sassoon's death yet could not get to the funeral; Hester was too ill to move from Mull. The address was given by Father Martin Salmon from Downside on the theme 'He who with such anguish sought peace'. The mourners then drove to Mells, through small sunlit fields, where, in the churchyard, Dom Philip Jebb officiated. Hodson saw the agent Mr Armitage in a bowler hat, looking like someone off a racecourse, and the lawyer Lousada; cows grazed in the next field under a drizzling rain while birds scattered near by. Afterwards, over drinks in the manor, Mrs Humphries wept and Rupert Hart-Davis said he planned to rescue the manuscripts and diaries from Heytesbury. Mother Margaret Mary had not been able to leave her convent for the service.[2]

A requiem mass was set for 11 October in London at the church of the Holy Redeemer in Cheyne Row. George Sassoon asked Rupert Hart-Davis to give the address but others insisted on a priest, so Martin Salmon spoke again, with suggestions from Hart-Davis. He evoked a many-sided man: shy and witty, hero and hater of war, public figure and recluse, poet and country squire. The peace of Sassoon's pre-1914 innocence had been taken from him by the war: 'years of butchery and boredom'. Rivers was mentioned and the memoirs and the trials before his conversion. No reference was made to George or Hester before a leap to Mother Margaret Mary and Ronald Knox, to Sassoon's young friend Dennis Silk and 'his beloved Doms' at Downside. Salmon concluded with a quotation from 'Lenten Illuminations'. He thought that Sassoon had 'found his grail'.[3]

The obituaries, the *Times* one written by Colin Fenton, concentrated on the First World War. In the *Observer*, Edmund Blunden, lamenting the end of fifty years of friendship, said that those who thought that Sassoon had lacked intellect were wrong, for he was 'one of the ablest men I have known'. His writings were, Blunden thought, 'Kentish', healthy and pastoral; and the religious element, obvious after his conversion, had permeated the war poetry as well. When the battle of Passchendaele began, Blunden had only Sassoon's poems, recently sent from home, from Kent, to give him hope: 'poems describing our war and in their way appealing for the multitudes about to face horrors I still feel and dream anew'.[4] One correspondent wrote of how, at last, the Somme was over. The Roman Catholic Christopher Hollis in the *Spectator* said that the war protest of 1917 showed no essential radicalism, just a loathing of the fighting: a conservative pacifism. Always Sassoon had thought that man unaided could not order his life. Hollis quoted the war line 'O Jesus make it stop' to show a wish for a higher power.

In 1970 Tom Clarke's play *Mad Jack* was shown on BBC1.

Clarke told the *Radio Times*, 'Sassoon was a desperately conventional man who wanted to be considered a Fox-hunting man. He did something absolutely against his own instincts.'[5] In 1973, Hester died, on Mull, having spent much time in the company of Jimmy Halliday, her shepherd at Lochbuie, and chain-smoking, not caring how she looked, rooted in the wild country, not 'in the world' but 'free to move in the things of the imaginative life',[6] as Sassoon himself had wanted to be. A year later, when Rupert Hart-Davis was asking around for Sassoon's letters, for a possible published collection, Glen Byam Shaw sent him his, and then commented on Hart-Davis's piece on their old friend for the *Dictionary of National Biography*, suggesting an addition to show how much George had meant to Siegfried. To Byam Shaw, Sassoon 'had two supreme happinesses in his life. 1st His son. 2nd His spiritual peace.' The publishing of the letters worried Byam Shaw. 'No Rupert I can't and I won't have anything to do with it':[7] the breaking of his old friend's privacy, and of what was to Glen an almost sacred friendship, seemed both a potential embarrassment and a betrayal.

Any biography was clearly difficult while Stephen Tennant still lived. Tennant did not die until 1986. In his last years, he was a recluse at Wilsford, his bed strewn with sea shells, sheaves of his own drawings and the manuscript of *Lascar*: fat and with turbulent orange hair, still proud of what he thought of as his shapely legs. He erupted occasionally into torrents of talk with selected visitors yet spoke seldom of 'Siegfried', whom he hinted had been impossibly possessive.

Sassoon had left £92,443 in his will. George struggled on in a decaying Heytesbury, attempting to keep the place up. In June 1974, beset by expenses and insurance losses at Lloyd's, he sold many of the books, letters and manuscripts from the library, the first of several sales. Four-fifths of this first sale, the biggest, went to the dealer Lew David Feldman, of the House of El Dieff in New York. In the United States, Feldman sold this on, to Columbia University, to the New York Public Library, to the Harry Ransom Center at the University of Texas at Austin and to other institutions, or to private collectors. Eventually the house itself, less attractive since a road had been put through its park in 1986, was sold too. Heytesbury is now divided into flats, with the landscape that Sassoon loved blighted by a huge mound of earth built to hide the almost constant traffic and to muffle its roar.

Hester had told her husband that he should understand the effect his fame had on George; perhaps a wish to escape had been partly behind their son's early marriage. Becoming a successful electronic engineer, George broke further away, learning Serbo-Croat, travelling often to Yugoslavia, writing about biblical history and the Kabbala. Easily irritated by Siegfried idolaters, he disposed of many of the papers in the face of disapproving reactions from Geoffrey Keynes and Rupert Hart-Davis, who sometimes must have seemed to him to resemble those bristling, military figures of authority lampooned in his father's poetry. Neither Keynes nor Hart-Davis, admirable in their work to perpetuate their hero's memory, seemed to be aware of the debts – at Lloyd's, or in connection with the huge, broken-down house – that had to be paid. They did not realize another, equally difficult inheritance: Sassoon's stifling love for his son. Eventually time softened the confusion, allowing George Sassoon not only to love his father, which he had always done, but to feel that he could understand him.

*

THE BOOKS HAVE survived, not only as literature but as a version of history. Although Sassoon took almost no part in the political or public life of his time after his protest of 1917, an exception being his public support during the 1930s for Dick Sheppard's Peace Movement, he became, indirectly, a political writer. Sheppard's campaign undoubtedly encouraged appeasement towards the dictators of Europe; but ironically, as this took hold as public policy, Sassoon, realizing the truth about the Nazis, began to draw back from pacifism. By 1939, he felt that war was the only way to stop Hitler. In *Siegfried's Journey* – the last volume of his autobiography, published in 1945 – he recanted his 1917 protest, writing that he now thought it had been necessary to fight on until the defeat of the enemy. But these paragraphs in a book that sold far less well than his earlier work lacked the resonance of the war poems or the Sherston memoirs. The man himself became a myth, inspiring not only novels and plays but an idea of how the trenches had really been.

Siegfried Sassoon's war has been explained many times, first by its advocates, then by the revisionists and by revisionists of revisionists. It reinforces the idea of an unimaginative, out-of- touch, incompetent High Command presiding over an avoidable slaughter: of innocence betrayed. Other literary memorials loom beside it – Owen's preface about the poetry being in the pity, Blunden's and Graves's memoirs, most of the war poets who feature in anthologies – and it leaves a sense, so strong in the 1930s, that another war must be prevented at almost any cost: that this had been the worst ever war. For the British in the Second World War, the fighting in the Far Eastern jungles, in Normandy in 1944 or in the Italian campaign were ordeals at least as great as those in the trenches, although involving fewer troops. But there is none of the sense of that innocence lost and exploited which still arouses anger over the Somme or Passchendaele. Sometimes it seems as if there is a national need for an epic, almost masochistic view of exhausted soldiers coping with horror, the British equivalent of the Russians at Stalingrad or the Americans fighting the Japanese in the Pacific, yet more helpless, more overwhelmed.

In the decades since Sassoon's death, historians have pointed another way, suggesting that the British army stuck it out, evolving from the small force that landed on mainland Europe in 1914, to enforce treaty obligations to neutral Belgium, into the main component of victory in 1918 without mutiny, recovering from terrible, bloody battles to defeat its supposedly invincible opponents, that the war was necessary to stop the domination of Europe by a militaristic regime and its unstable, weak 'supreme warlord', the

Kaiser. Then a new novel or film comes out, read or watched by thousands, even millions, and it seems as if the historians might as well have stayed silent.

Ronald Knox's remark about Siegfried Sassoon being predominantly 'a First War man' is right. Those four years shaped him and his writing for ever. That is not surprising, given that he had entered the army as a fastidious young idealist anxious to conform to a background that repressed what made him different: his Jewishness and his homosexuality. But Sassoon's war experiences were restricted to inauspicious times, to the prelude and start of the Somme in 1916, to the Hindenburg trenches in April 1917 at the time of the battle of Arras, just before the failure of the Nivelle offensive; then to the early summer of 1918 when the Allies were still reeling from the massive German attacks of March. Back in Britain, he heard of an apparently bloody, bad end to the Somme; after his first wound, the slaughter at Passchendaele dominated reports through the autumn of 1917. He missed completely – and was in a state of near-hysteria, then troubled convalescence, during – the last battles of 1918 when Wilfred Owen wrote from the front line that there was no place he would rather be.

Out of this, and the years that followed, Siegfried Sassoon created something quite different from historical truth. He transformed his own guilt, turbulence and pain into anger, satire and lyrical beauty, searching always for the utopia that, at the end, he found in faith. Much of his work shows, I think, a kind of chivalry in its idealism, respect for fair play, pity for the suffering, a cherishing of innocence and beauty amid discordant modernism and the ugliness of the machine age. This means, perhaps, an avoidance of tarnishing truth. Sassoon evokes a lost, decent England achieved only in the imagination, perhaps only in the imaginations of those a little outside this country of the heart. The myth is strong, even mesmeric, better and more honourable than most myths by which nations live, and the writings of Siegfried Sassoon have helped it to endure.

Notes

Asquith: Earl of Oxford and Asquith
Berg: Berg Collection at the New York Public Library
BL: British Library
Bodleian: Bodleian Library, Oxford
Brotherton: Brotherton Library, University of Leeds
Carbondale: Southern Illinois University at Carbondale
Columbia: Columbia University Library, New York
CUL: Cambridge University Library
Eccles: library of the late Viscountess Eccles (Mary Hyde) at Four Oaks
    Farm, New Jersey
Eton: Eton College, Windsor
GS: George Sassoon
HRC: Harry Ransom Humanities Research Center at the University of
    Texas at Austin
IWM: Imperial War Museum
Lilly Library: Lilly Library at Indiana University at Bloomington
McMaster: McMaster University, Hamilton, Ontario
Maryland: University of Maryland at College Park
NYPL: New York Public Library
PRO: Public Record Office, Kew
Rutgers: Rutgers University at New Brunswick, New Jersey
RWF: Royal Welch Fusiliers
Sheffield: Sheffield City Archives

Stephenson Harwood: Siegfried Sassoon's solicitors, Stephenson Harwood
Tulsa: McFarlin Library, the University of Tulsa
Yale: Beinecke Library at Yale University

CP: *Collected Poems*
FHM: *Memoirs of a Fox-hunting Man*
IO: *Memoirs of an Infantry Officer*
OC: *The Old Century*
PP: *Siegfried Sassoon: Poet's Pilgrimage* by Dame Felicitas Corrigan
SJ: *Siegfried's Journey*
SP: *Sherston's Progress*
WP: *War Poems*
WY: *The Weald of Youth*

Preface

1. Sassoon to R. Hodgson, 1 September 1930, Yale.

1: 'The daybreak world'

1. Note in R. Graves, *Goodbye to All That* (London 1929) p. 404 in copy annotated by Blunden and Sassoon, Berg.
2. Siegfried Sassoon, 'Sheldonian Soliloquy', *CP* (London 1971 edition) p. 160.
3. Sassoon to Mother Margaret Mary, 12 February 1957, CUL add mss 7935.
4. Sassoon to R. Graves, n.d., Carbondale.
5. Siegfried Sassoon, 'Notes for a Film Script', GS.
6. Mrs S. D. Sassoon is said to have referred to the Rothschilds as 'the hairy-heeled ones'. S. Jackson, *The Sassoons* (London 1968) p. 72.
7. Ibid., p. 71.
8. 'Notes for a Film Script', GS.
9. S. Bernhardt, *My Double Life* (London 1907) p. 282.
10. Notes for *OC*, GS.
11. Ibid.

12. H. Thornycroft to A. Cox, 17 November 1883, TII C T[H]93, Henry Moore Institute, Leeds.
13. Sassoon to Dame F. Corrigan, 12 September 1962, Corrigan papers, Stanbrook Abbey.
14. E. Manning, *Marble and Bronze* (London 1982) p. 93.
15. Sassoon to Mother Margaret Mary, 20 July 1957, CUL add mss 7935.
16. A. Wilton and R. Upstone, eds, *The Age of Rossetti, Burne-Jones and Watts* (London 1997) p. 65.
17. Notes for *OC*, GS.
18. H. Thornycroft journal, 11 March 1890, J5, Henry Moore Institute, Leeds.
19. BL add mss 46622/f. 14.
20. *OC*, pp. 15–16.
21. Ibid., p. 17.
22. Sassoon to Mother Margaret Mary, 8 April 1967, CUL add mss 7935.
23. Draft of *OC*, CUL add mss 9454/1/11.
24. 'Strangeness of Heart,' *CP*, p. 181.
25. *OC*, p. 15.
26. Siegfried Sassoon, *Letters to a Critic* (Nettlestead 1976) p. 22.
27. *FHM* (Faber Library edition 1932) p. 17.
28. Notes for *OC*, GS.
29. H. Wirgman to A. Thornycroft (Cox), n.d., TII C W2, Henry Moore Institute, Leeds.
30. H. Wirgman to A. Thornycroft (Cox), n.d., TII C W6, Henry Moore Institute, Leeds.
31. Notes for *OC*, GS.
32. *OC*, p. 19.
33. Ibid., p. 40.
34. Columbia, notebook 3.
35. *OC*, p. 75.
36. 'The Ripple', December 1897, Tulsa, copy in CUL add mss 9454/1/2.
37. *PP*, pp. 52–4.
38. Sassoon to Mother Margaret Mary, 4 February 1957, CUL add mss 7935.
39. *OC*, p. 85.

40. Clipping (n.d., probably 1927) in CUL add mss 8889/3/70.
41. *OC*, p. 87.
42. *WY* notebook, GS.
43. Ibid.
44. Notes for *OC*, GS.
45. Ibid.
46. *My First Horse* (London 1947) pp. 9–23.
47. Poetry notebook, Tulsa, copy in CUL add mss 9454/1/1.
48. Columbia notebook 5.
49. Columbia notebook 6.
50. *FHM*, p. 35.
51. Ibid.
52. G. Llewellyn to Sassoon, 5 October 1957, GS.
53. *OC*, p. 171.
54. Ibid., p. 175.
55. 'Notes for Autobiography', HRC.

2: 'Try to be more sensible'

1. *OC*, p. 187.
2. *OC*, p. 199.
3. See C. H. Sorley, *The Letters of Charles Sorley* (Cambridge 1919) p. 101 for praise of Gould.
4. *OC*, p. 209.
5. Interview with Hamo Sassoon.
6. Sorley, *Letters*, p. 252.
7. *OC*, pp. 212–13.
8. *OC*, p. 217.
9. Notes for *WY* and *OC*, GS.
10. *OC*, pp. 223–5.
11. Diary for 1903 and 1904, private collection.
12. *OC*, p. 230.
13. Diary 1903–4, private collection.
14. *OC*, p. 231.
15. L. MacNeice, *The Strings Are False* (London paperback 1982) p. 85.
16. *OC*, pp. 235 and 246.

17. OC, pp. 240 and 247.
18. Both in manuscript diary 1903–4, private collection.
19. Notes for *OC*, GS.
20. Columbia notebook 10.
21. Sassoon to E. Blunden, 6 February 1937, HRC.
22. *PP*, pp. 55–6.
23. *Cambridge Review*, 15 March 1906, p. 317.
24. Sassoon to E. L. Guilford, 12 July and 6 October 1906, BL add mss 62941.
25. OC, p. 262.
26. Sassoon to Mother Margaret Mary, 28 November 1958, CUL add mss 7935.
27. Sassoon to Mother Margaret Mary, 1 January 1959, CUL add mss 7935.
28. Sassoon to Mother Margaret Mary, 7 June 1962, CUL add mss 7935.
29. Sassoon to E. L. Guilford, n.d., BL add mss 62941.
30. C. Dakers, *The Holland Park Circle* (London and New Haven 1999) p. 257.
31. The poem was kept by Guilford and is now in the British Library, with his other letters from Sassoon. BL add mss 62941.
32. Sassoon to E. L. Guilford, 11 March 1907, BL add mss 62941.
33. H. Sassoon to Sassoon, 20 March 1907, CUL add mss 9375/860.
34. H. Thornycroft to Sassoon, 9 April 1907, CUL add mss 9375/861.
35. Sassoon to E. L. Guilford, 11 May 1907, BL add mss 62941.
36. OC, p. 271.

3: The weald of youth

1. Theresa to Sassoon n.d., private collection.
2. 'Notes for Autobiography', HRC.
3. Ibid.
4. *WY* manuscript, Columbia.
5. Ibid.
6. *WY*, p. 33.
7. Sassoon to L. Untermeyer, 11 October 1920, Lilly Library.
8. Copy at HRC.

9. WY, pp. 16–17.
10. Ibid., pp. 12–13.
11. Ibid., p. 13.
12. G. Keynes in his *Bibliography* (London 1962) says only twenty-five were printed.
13. E. Blunden, *A Selection of His Poetry and Prose* (London 1950), p. 314. Blunden's article on Sassoon's poetry was first published in the *London Mercury* of June 1929.
14. H. Thornycroft to Sassoon, 9 November 1909, CUL add mss 9375/867.
15. E. Gosse to H. Thornycroft, 14 May 1909, CUL add mss 9454/S/189.
16. A. Thwaite, *Edmund Gosse* (London 1984) p. 463.
17. E. Gosse to Sassoon, 5 December 1909, Rutgers.
18. Sassoon to Mother Margaret Mary, 15 March 1957, CUL add mss 7935.
19. *Academy*, 14 May 1910.
20. *Literary Post*, 11 May 1910, signed Hester Brayne. The two poems ('Two Sonnets') were printed in the *Academy* on 19 March 1910.
21. Notes for WY, GS.
22. C. Wallis to Sassoon, 2 October 1957, GS.
23. Sassoon to Sir A. Lascelles, 26 September 1966, Tulsa, copy in CUL add mss 9454/3/543.
24. 'The Investiture' CP, p. 80.
25. *Diaries 1915–1918*, ed. R. Hart-Davis (London 1983) p. 184.
26. Sassoon to R. Meiklejohn, n.d. 1917, HRC.
27. A. Gordon Taylor to Sassoon, 29 March 1930, CUL add mss 9375/822.
28. 'A London Diary', *Field*, 14 September 1967.
29. G. Llewellyn to Sassoon, 5 October 1957, GS.
30. WY, pp. 100–2. The party was given for the Dutch novelist Dr Van der Poorten-Schwarz who wrote under the name of Maarten Maartens.
31. WY, pp. 114–20, supplemented by notes for the WY, GS.
32. Sassoon to E. Carpenter, 27 July 1911, Sheffield ms 386/179.
33. Manuscript in the possession of William Reese.
34. Sassoon to E. Carpenter, 27 July 1911, Sheffield ms 386/179.

35. E. Carpenter to Sassoon, in C. Tsuzuki, *Edward Carpenter* (Cambridge 1980) pp. 147–8.
36. Sassoon to E. Carpenter, 2 August 1911, Sheffield ms 386/181.
37. E. Gosse to Sassoon, 6 December 1911, Rutgers.
38. Untermeyer notebook, Lilly Library.
39. E. Gosse to Sassoon, 30 June 1912, Rutgers.
40. Untermeyer notebook, Lilly Library.
41. 28 May 1912, Sidgwick and Jackson 17, Bodleian Library.
42. Sassoon to E. Gosse, 4 November 1912, BL Ashley A 3929/107.
43. *WY*, pp. 123–5.
44. *The Daffodil Murderer* (London 1913).
45. Ibid.
46. *WY*, p. 130.
47. *Athenaeum*, 22 February 1913.
48. E. Gosse to Sassoon, 13 February 1913, Rutgers.
49. 'A Brilliant Parody', *Cambridge Daily News*, 10 February 1913; *New Age*, 6 March 1913; *Manchester Guardian*, 9 April 1913.
50. C. Hassall, *Edward Marsh* (London 1959) p. 248.
51. Ibid., p. 26.
52. *PP*, p. 66.
53. E. Marsh to Sassoon, 22 February 1913, Eton.
54. Sassoon to E. Marsh, 27 February 1913, Berg.
55. 'England 1913', the untitled poem on lust and the soul, 'Cortège Macabre', 'Vision' and 'Of a Lady Wanting to be Wed' are all in the Untermeyer notebook in the Lilly Library. 'Prelude: the Troops' is in *CP*, p. 67.
56. *CP*, p. 44.
57. *WY*, pp. 143–5.
58. Sassoon to E. Marsh, 7 May 1913, Berg.
59. Sassoon to Mother Margaret Mary, n.d., April 1963, CUL add mss 7935.
60. E. Marsh to Sassoon, 14 October 1913, Eton.
61. Lord A. Douglas to Sassoon, 3 October 1913, copy at CUL add mss 9454/7/1/50.
62. Sassoon to E. Marsh, 23 October 1913, Berg.
63. Ibid.
64. *WY*, pp. 158–9.

65. Ibid., p. 164. Also draft of WY, GS.
66. Sassoon to Mother Margaret Mary, 1 May 1957, CUL add mss 7935.
67. Draft of WY, GS.
68. WY, pp. 178–82.
69. Ibid., pp. 184–190.
70. Draft of WY, GS.
71. *New Age*, 19 March 1914.
72. Sassoon to E. Marsh, 1 May 1914, Berg.
73. Sassoon to E. Marsh, n.d., Berg.
74. WY, p. 222.
75. Ibid., pp. 222–32; and draft of WY, GS.
76. Draft of WY, GS.
77. WY, pp. 243–6.
78. Sassoon to E. Marsh, 1 May 1914, Berg.
79. WY, p. 252.
80. Draft of WY, GS.
81. Sassoon to E. Marsh, n.d., Berg.
82. WY, pp. 268–70, and draft of WY, GS.
83. PRO/WO339/S1440/49289.

4: 'Grief can be beautiful'

1. G. Chapman, *Vain Glory* (London 1937) p. 27.
2. WY, p. 240. Wirgie had called the Schoenberg piece 'rather cater-waulesque'.
3. Sassoon to E. Marsh, 17 August 1914, Berg.
4. G. Harbord to Sassoon, 15 December 1914, IWM, SS4.
5. Sassoon to Mother Margaret Mary, 22 February 1958, CUL add mss 7935.
6. Diary, 6 August 1942. GS.
7. CP, p. 3.
8. Notes for WY, GS.
9. CP, p. 61.
10. FHM, p. 286.
11. G. Harbord to Sassoon, June 1915, IWM SS3.

12. Text of P. Liddle interview with V. King, Liddle Collection, Brotherton.
13. *CP*, p. 11.
14. Graves, *Goodbye to All That*, p. 229.
15. *CP*, p. 17.
16. Cockerell diary, 1 August 1915, BL add mss 52652.
17. Dent diary, 1 December 1915, King's College, Cambridge EJD/3/1/12.
18. B. Nichols, *The Unforgiving Minute* (London 1978) pp. 88–9.
19. Dent diary, 14 August 1915, King's College Cambridge EJD/3/1/12.
20. Ibid., 21 August 1915.
21. E. Dent to R. Maltby, 22 August 1915, CUL add mss 7973/M/81.
22. Dent diary, 15 August 1915, King's College, Cambridge EJD/3/1/12.
23. Bartholomew diary, August 1917, CUL add mss 8786.
24. Ibid., August 1920.
25. D. Thomas to Sassoon, 26 August 1915, CUL add mss 9375/834.
26. E. Dent to R. Maltby, 6 September 1915, CUL add mss 7973/m/84.
27. Sassoon to J. Bain, 12 May 1917, IWM, Special Misc U4.
28. Theresa to Sassoon, 17 August 1915, private collection.
29. A. C. Bayley to Theresa, 21 March 1916, private collection.
30. Sassoon to Theresa, both letters undated, private collection.
31. *Diaries 1915–1918*, p. 21.
32. J. C. Dunn, *The War the Infantry Knew* (London paperback 1997) p. 161.
33. Diary notebook, GS. Not in *Diaries 1915–1918*.
34. R. Graves to E. Carpenter, 30 May 1914, Sheffield ms 386/234.
35. Sassoon annotated copy of *Goodbye to All That*, p. 224, GS.
36. WY notebook, GS.
37. J. B. P. Adams, *Nothing of Importance* (London 1917) p. 57.
38. A small orange-covered copy, with 'Siegfried Sassoon, 1st RW Fusiliers Nov 1915, 2nd RW Fusiliers March 1917, 25th RW Fusiliers March 1918' written in the front (William Reese collection).
39. There are two early drafts in the Berg Collection, presumably sent to Marsh. Both have the first version of the last lines and one is dated 'March 7–10th'. The final version is in *WP*, pp. 16–17 and *CP*, p. 16 and is taken from the orange notebook (GS).
40. Manuscript at HRC.

41. *Diaries 1915–1918*, 10 December 1915, p. 26.
42. Ibid., 3 December 1915, pp. 22–3.
43. Diary, 17 December 1915, GS.
44. *WP*, p. 19.
45. *Diaries 1915–1918*, 10 December 1915, p. 26.
46. Ibid., 'Christmas', p. 28.
47. January 1916 notebook, National Army Museum, 9508–11–1.
48. For Cottrell, see Adams, *Nothing of Importance*, pp. 41, 247, 258, in which he appears as 'Jim Potter'. 'Red talk', in letter of P. Crawshay to Sassoon of 13 December 1928, CUL add mss 9375/163.
49. *Diaries 1915–1918*, 17 March 1916, pp. 43–4.
50. G. Chapman, *A Passionate Prodigality* (London 1933) p. 95.
51. *Diaries 1915–1918*, 8 April 1926.
52. *WP*, p. 63.
53. Adams, *Nothing of Importance*, pp. 131–2. *Diaries 1915–1918*, 22 February 1916, p. 39.
54. D. Langley, *Duty Done* typescript (RWF Museum), p. 47.
55. Adams, *Nothing of Importance*, pp. 131–2.
56. Ibid.
57. Graves to E. Marsh, 24 February 1916, *In Broken Images: Letters 1914–1946*, ed. Paul O'Prey (London 1982) p. 40.
58. 'A Testament' is printed in *WP*, p. 20. 'January', 'Druids', 'The Silver Stem' and 'Glory' are in the orange notebook (GS). In the Sherston memoirs, the character based on David Thomas is compared to Sir Galahad.
59. *CP*, p. 13.
60. O. Morrell to Sassoon, 26 January 1916, Maryland.
61. Graves to E. Marsh, 9 February 1916, Berg.
62. *WP*, p. 22.
63. 'Love', 'The Rainbow' and 'Pastoral' all in the orange notebook (GS).
64. *Diaries 1915–1918*, 23 February 1916, p. 40.
65. E. Marsh to N. Dent, 14 March 1916, CUL add mss 7973/M/24.
66. Burton to Sassoon, 18 November 1931, CUL add mss 8889/3/36.
67. Mrs Belloc Lowndes, *A Passing World* (London 1948) pp. 210–11.
68. *Diaries 1915–1918*, 6 March 1916, p. 40.
69. Diary, 16 March 1916, GS.
70. R. Graves to E. Marsh, 15 March 1916, Berg.

71. *CP*, p. 17.
72. Diary, 13, 15, 17 March 1916, GS.
73. Sassoon to E. Marsh, 16 March 1916, Berg.
74. *Diaries 1915–1918*, 19 March 1916, pp. 44–5.
75. Ibid., 28 March 1916, pp. 46 and 51.
76. *CP*, p. 19.
77. Manuscript in the Berg.
78. *CP*, p. 49.
79. *Diaries 1915–1918*, pp. 52–3.
80. 'To a Citizen Soldier', Dent papers. CUL add mss 7973/70.
81. Sassoon to E. Marsh, 3 April 1916, Berg.
82. Diary, 31 March 1916. GS.
83. Sassoon to E. Marsh, 19 April 1916, Berg.
84. Diary, 12 April 1916, GS.
85. Ibid., 15 April 1916.
86. *CP*, p. 24.
87. Diary, GS.
88. Ibid.
89. *CP*, p. 15.
90. Diary, GS.
91. Sassoon to H. Thornycroft, 18 May n.d., BL add mss 56099.
92. Diary, GS.
93. *Diaries 1915–1918*, 27 April 1916, p. 61.
94. *CP*, 35.
95. Ibid., p. 40.
96. *Diaries 1915–1918*, 20 May 1916, p. 62.
97. Ibid., 22 May 1916, p. 64.
98. *IO*, 35.
99. Ibid., p. 40.
100. Sassoon to E. Marsh, 30 May 1916, Berg.
101. *Diaries 1915–1918*, 1 June 1916, p. 70.
102. Ibid., 7 June 1916, p. 74.
103. Ibid., 9 June 1916, p. 77.

5: 'I am sure I shall get blown to shreds'

1. Dent to R. Maltby, 18 June 1916, CUL add mss 7973/M/106.
2. *Diaries 1915–1918*, 26 June 1916, p. 79.
3. *CP*, p. 33.
4. Diary, 26 June 1916, GS.
5. *IO* (London 1966 edition) p. 72.
6. Ibid., p. 75.
7. For the first day, see *Diaries 1915–1918*, 1 July 1916, p. 85.
8. Ibid., 2 July 1916, p. 85.
9. *CP*, p. 22.
10. *Diaries 1915–1918*, 4 July 1916, p. 88.
11. Graves, *Goodbye to All That*, p. 262.
12. *IO*, p. 93.
13. Ibid., p. 96.
14. *Diaries 1915–1918*, 16 July 1916, p. 94.
15. Sassoon copied this into his diary, with 'written 17 July, Mametz Wood' (Diary, May–June 1916, GS).
16. Sassoon to E. Marsh, 21 July 1916, Berg.
17. *Diaries 1915–1918*, 21 July 1916, p. 98.
18. *IO*, p. 119.
19. R. Graves to Sassoon, 12 May 1917, Berg.
20. *CP*, p. 28.
21. Manuscript, 6 July 1916, HRC.
22. Manuscript, 8 July 1916, HRC.
23. Manuscript, n.d. HRC.
24. *IO*, p. 122.
25. Sassoon to E. Marsh, n.d. August, Berg.
26. Diary, 2 August 1916, GS.
27. Sassoon to S. Cockerell, 12 August 1916, Berg.
28. Ibid.
29. O. Morrell journal, 17 July 1915, BL.
30. Ibid., 17 July 1915.
30. Ibid., 21 February 1916, March 1916, March 1916, April 1916.
31. Ibid., 18 August 1916.
32. R. Graves to Sassoon, 7 August 1916, Berg.

33. R. Graves to Sassoon, 18 August 1916, William Reese.
34. Sassoon to E. Marsh, 3 August 1916, Berg.
35. Berg Collection draft, different from *Diaries 1915–1918*, p. 102.
36. *Diaries 1915–1918*, p. 101.
37. Ibid., p. 102.
38. Manuscript, HRC.
39. *CP*, p. 29.
40. Ibid.
41. Ibid., p. 32.
42. Draft of *SJ*, GS.
43. *CP*, p. 34.
44. Draft of *SJ*, GS.
45. Owen to T. Owen, 26 August 1917, *Collected Letters*, ed. H. Owen and J. Bell (Oxford 1967) p. 488.
46. E. Gosse to H. Thornycroft, 31 August 1916, Brotherton.
47. R. P. Graves, *Robert Graves: The Assault Heroic* (London paperback edition 1995) pp. 160–1.
48. See S. Cottrell to Sassoon, 4 and 17 September 1916, J. Dadd to Sassoon, 19 March 1929, IWM SS1.
49. PRO/WO339/S1440/49289.
50. *SJ*, p. 21.
51. Ibid.
52. O. Morrell journal, 29 September 1916, BL.
53. Sassoon to E. Marsh, 21 October 1916, Lilly Library.
54. Sassoon to H. Thornycroft, 8 October 1916, BL add mss 56099.
55. Dent diary, 29 October 1916, King's College, Cambridge EJD/3/1/13.
56. PRO/WO339/S1440/49289.
57. J. C. Squire to Sassoon, October 1916, Columbia box 2.
58. 'The Tombstone Maker', *CP*, p. 27. 'Two Hundred Years After', *CP*, p. 23. 'A Ballad', *WP*, p. 56.
59. Orange notebook, GS.
60. *CP*, p. 23.
61. Quoted in *WP*, p. 57.
62. Graves, *The Assault Heroic*, p. 163.
63. 'Decorated', *WP*, p. 58. 'Arms and the Man', *CP*, p. 27. 'A Mystic as Soldier', *CP*, p. 15. 'The Poet as Hero', *WP*, p. 61.
64. *Cambridge Magazine*, 2 December 1916.

65. R. Graves to Sassoon, 30 November 1916, Berg.
66. PRO/WO339/S1440/49289.
67. *Diaries 1915–1918*, 27 December 1916, p. 109.
68. 'Secret Music', *CP*, p. 32. 'A Whispered Tale', *CP*, p. 21. 'The Distant Song', *WP*, p. 64. 'The March-Past', *WP*, p. 60.
69. *IO*, p. 145.
70. Sassoon to R. Ross, 30 January 1917, Eccles.
71. Sassoon to O. Morrell, 21 January 1917, HRC.
72. *Diaries 1915–1918*, 20 January 1917, p. 121.
73. Ibid., 20 January 1917, p. 121.
74. Sassoon to E. Gosse, 7 January 1917, BL Ashley.
75. *Diaries 1915–1918*, 23 January 1917, p. 124.
76. Ibid., 22 January 1917, p. 124.
77. Ibid., pp. 127–8.
78. 'Enemies', *CP*, p. 26. 'When I'm Among a Blaze of Lights', *CP*, p. 14. 'England Has Many Heroes', *Diaries 1915–1918*, 15 January 1917, p. 119. 'Blighters', *CP*, p. 21. 'Conscripts', *CP*, p. 30.
79. Sassoon to E. Gosse, 27 February 1917, Brotherton.
80. T. Hardy to Sassoon, 4 February 1917, Eton.
81. O. Morrell journal, February 1917, BL.
82. O. Morrell to L. Strachey, 16 February 1917, BL.
83. J. Dadd to Sassoon, 12 February 1917, IWM SS2.
84. *Diaries 1915–1918*, 15 February 1917, p. 131.
85. Sassoon to P. Morrell, 16 February 1917, HRC. The poem is in *Diaries 1915–1918*, 15 February 1917, p. 132.
86. *Diaries 1915–1918*, 11 February 1917, p. 131.
87. Sassoon to R. Ross, 22 February 1917, Eccles.
88. Diary, 25 February 1917, GS.
89. Sassoon to Theresa, CUL add mss 9454/3/589.
90. Sassoon to R. Ross, 8 March 1917, Eccles.
91. IWM SS1/1.
92. *CP*, p. 75.
93. 'The Optimist', *WP*, p. 74. 'In the Church of St Ouen', *WP*, p. 72. 'Return', *WP*, p. 73.
94. *Diaries 1915–1918*, 11 March 1917, p. 143.
95. F. Richards, *Old Soldiers Never Die* (London 1933) p. 221.
96. R. Graves, *Goodbye to All That*, p. 315.

97. *Records of the Royal Welch Fusiliers*, vol. 3 (London 1928–9) p. 275.

98. Sassoon to R. Ross, 18 March 1917, Eccles.

99. C. Edmonds (Carrington), *A Subaltern's War* (London 1929) p. 114.

100. E. Blunden, *Undertones of War* (London, Penguin edition 2000) pp. 103, 107–8.

101. Edmonds (Carrington), *A Subaltern's War*, pp. 35 and 19.

102. *Diaries 1915–1918*, 3 April 1917, p. 149.

103. Ibid., 3 April 1917, p. 149.

104. Sassoon to R. Graves, 4 April 1917, Carbondale.

105. *Records of the Royal Welch Fusiliers*, vol. 3, p. 277.

106. Ibid., p. 278.

107. Sassoon to O. Morrell, 11 April 1917, HRC.

108. *Records of the Royal Welch Fusiliers*, vol. 3, p. 280.

109. Ibid., vol. 3, pp. 281–2.

110. For this incident, see *Diaries 1915–1918*, 17 April 1917, p. 157 etc. Also *Records of the Royal Welch Fusiliers*, vol. 3, pp. 283–5.

111. *Diaries 1915–1918*, 16 April 1917, p. 156. The action is also described in *IO*, pp. 190–223.

6: 'The heroics of pacifism'

1. Sassoon to Theresa, 15 April 1917, Berg.

2. *WP*, (note) p. 76.

3. A. P. Graves diary, 28 April 1917, Berg.

4. Sassoon to R. Graves, 24 April 1917, Carbondale.

5. Sassoon to B. Russell, 23 April 1917, McMaster.

6. Sassoon to H. Thornycroft, 24 April 1917, BL add mss 56099.

7. Sassoon to O. Morrell, n.d. April, HRC.

8. *CP*, p. 69.

9. 'To the Warmongers', *WP*, p. 77. 'Wounded', *Diaries 1915–1918*, 24 April 1917, p. 160.

10. Sassoon to F. Hardy, 4 February 1927, Yale.

11. J. C. Dunn to Sassoon, 31 January 1927, CUL add mss 9375/2/242.

12. 'The General' is in *CP*, p. 75. Sassoon to O. Morrell, n.d., HRC.

13. Dunn, *The War the Infantry Knew*, pp. 331–40.

14. Sassoon to O. Morrell, 9 May 1917, HRC.

15. *IO*, p. 236.
16. Sassoon to Theresa, 12 May 1917, CUL add mss 9454/3/594.
17. Sassoon to J. Bain, 12 May 1917, IWM Special Misc U4.
18. *Morning Post*, 11 May 1917.
19. Sassoon to R. Meiklejohn, May n.d., HRC.
20. Diary, 13 May 1917, GS.
21. J. Dadd to Sassoon, 12 May 1917, IWM SS2.
22. Diary, May–June 1917, GS.
23. *Diaries 1915–1918*, 21 May 1917, p. 171.
24. Sassoon to H. Festing Jones, 23 May 1917, CUL add mss 8484.
25. *Diaries 1915–1918*, p. 169.
26. *TLS*, 24 May 1917.
27. Sassoon to H. Thornycroft, 26 May 1917, BL add mss 56099.
28. Sassoon to Theresa, 26 May 1917, CUL add mss 9454/3/596.
29. Sassoon to E. Dent, 29 May 1917, CUL add mss 7973.
30. *Cambridge Magazine*, 2 June 1917.
31. *Spectator*, 2 June 1917.
32. *New Statesman*, 9 June 1917.
33. *Nation*, 16 June 1917.
34. Sassoon to R. Graves, 29 May 1917, Carbondale.
35. 'The Hawthorn Tree', is in *CP*, p. 80. 'Death in the Garden', *Diaries 1915–1918*, 25 May 1917, p. 172. 'A War Widow', *Diaries 1915–1918*, 26 May 1917, p. 172. 'A Quiet Walk', *Diaries 1915–1918*, 1 June 1917, pp. 172–3. 'In an Underground Dressing Station', *WP*, p. 80. 'Supreme Sacrifice', *WP*, p. 81.
36. Sassoon to E. Dent, 2 June 1917, CUL add mss 7973.
37. Ms Columbia box 2.
38. PRO/WO339/SI440/49289.
39. Sassoon to A. Ridsdale, 6 August 1917, CUL add mss 9454/5/12.
40. A. Bennett, *The Journals*, ed. F. Swinnerton (London, Penguin edition 1984) p. 411.
41. O. Morrell journal, 10 June 1917, BL; see also *Ottoline at Garsington*, ed. R. Gathorne-Hardy (London 1974) pp. 181–2.
42. Bartholomew diary, 12 June 1917, CUL add mss 8786.
43. Dent diary, 13 June 1917, King's College, Cambridge EJD/3/1/13.
44. Draft of *SJ*, GS.
45. *SJ*, p. 51.

46. Ibid., pp. 51–2.
47. *Diaries 1915–1918*, 15 June 1917, pp. 173–4.
48. Draft of *SJ*, GS.
49. Diary, 18 January 1948, GS.
50. B. Russell to O. Morrell, n.d., HRC.
51. N. Stansfield to Sassoon, 15 June 1917, IWM, SS9.
52. J. Cottrell to Sassoon, 29 June 1917, IWM, SS1.
53. R. Graves to Sassoon, 30 June 1917, Berg.
54. T. Hardy to Sassoon, 27 August 1917, Eton.
55. Sassoon to Mother Margaret Mary, 26 December 1957, CUL add mss 7935.
56. *CP*, p. 84.
57. Sassoon to R. Graves, 24 June 1917, Carbondale.
58. Sassoon to R. Graves, 25 (?) June 1917, Carbondale.
59. *New Witness*, 28 June 1917.
60. *Diaries 1915–1918*, 19 June 1917, p. 175.
61. Ibid., 21 June 1917, pp. 176–7.
62. Ibid., 4 July 1917, p. 177.
63. E. Marsh to Sassoon, 27 January 1918, Eton.
64. Sassoon to R. Graves, 29 June 1917, Carbondale.
65. *CP*, p. 89.
66. Sassoon to J. Bain, 2 July 1917, in 2000 catalogue of James S. Jaffe Rare Books, Haverford PA, US.
67. R. Graves to Sassoon, 30 June 1917, Berg.
68. Sassoon to B. Russell, 4 July 1917, McMaster.
69. Draft of *SJ*, GS.
70. Quoted in letter from Sassoon to R. Ross, July 1917, typed copy in Lilly Library.
71. Sassoon to E. Marsh, 7 July 1917, Berg.
72. Sassoon to C. K. Ogden, 7 July 1917, Berg.
73. Sassoon to H. Cox, 7 July 1917, BL add mss 56099.
74. *IO*, p. 285.
75. E. Carpenter to Sassoon, 10 July 1917, CUL add mss 9454/4/3.
76. E. Marsh to Sassoon, 10 July 1917, CUL add mss 9454/4/8.
77. R. Ross to Sassoon, 8 July 1917, CUL add mss 9454/4/11.
78. H. Cox to Sassoon, 10 July 1917, CUL add mss 9454/4/4.
79. A. Bennett to Sassoon, 11 July 1917, CUL add mss 9454/4/1.

80. *In Broken Images*, p. 77.
81. J. Cottrell to Sassoon, 11 July 1917, IWM SS1.
82. E. Marsh to Sassoon, 10 July 1917, CUL add mss 9454/4/8.
83. H. Cox to Sassoon, 10 July 1917, CUL add mss 9454/4/4.
84. Sassoon to H. Cox, 11 July 1917, BL add mss 56099.
85. R. Graves to Sassoon, 12 July 1917, *In Broken Images*, p. 77.
86. J. Cottrell to Sassoon, 11 July 1917, IWM, SS1.
87. Sassoon to B. Russell, 11 July 1917, McMaster.
88. B. Russell to O. Morrell, n.d. July, HRC.
89. *IO*, p. 295.
90. Sassoon to B. Russell, 'Friday' n.d., McMaster.
91. *Diaries 1915–1918*, p. 178.
92. *IO*, pp. 297–300.
93. R. Ross to E. Gosse, 14 July 1917, BL Ashley A5739.
94. J. Dadd to Sassoon, 1 December 1929, IWM SS1.
95. Sassoon to O. Morrell, 17 July 1917, HRC.
96. H. Farjeon to his mother, n.d. July, BL add mss 56099.
97. *IO*, p. 304.
98. Sassoon to E. Carpenter, 9 October 1917, Sheffield mss 386/298.
99. Sassoon to E. Dent, 25 July 1917, CUL add mss 7973.
100. PRO/WO339/SI440/49289.
101. R. Graves to B. Russell, 19 July 1917, McMaster.
102. B. Russell to Mrs Swainwick, 20 July 1917, McMaster.
103. B. Russell to O. Morrell, 21 July 1917, HRC.
104. R. Graves to Sassoon, 27 October 1917, Berg.
105. Interview with Miriam Lane, to whom Churchill said this at a lunch in the 1950s. Mrs Lane, born Miriam Rothschild and a distinguished scientist, Fellow of the Royal Society and expert on fleas, knew Sassoon well after his marriage in 1933. She saw him often when his son George was at school at Oundle, near her home in Northamptonshire.

7: 'Dottyville'

1. Sassoon to O. Morrell, 30 July 1917, quoted in *Diaries 1915–1918*, p. 183.

2. R. Slobodin, *W. H. R. Rivers* (Stroud edition 1997) p. 78.

3. *SP*, p. 15.

4. Ibid., p. 87.

5. Sassoon to R. Ross, 25 September 1917, IWM SS8.

6. Sassoon to R. Ross, 26 July 1917, IWM, SS8.

7. E. Gosse to H. Thornycroft, 31 July 1917, Brotherton.

8. J. Dadd to Sassoon, 31 July 1917, IWM, SS2.

9. 5 August 1917, CUL add mss 9375/245.

10. H. G. Wells to Sassoon, August n.d., McMaster.

11. Sassoon to R. Meiklejohn, 1 August 1917, HRC.

12. *SP*, p. 22.

13. Ibid., p. 24.

14. Sassoon to R. Meiklejohn, 14 August 1917, HRC.

15. Sassoon to R. Graves, 8 and 10 August 1917, Carbondale.

16. Sassoon to R. Meiklejohn, 14 August 1917, HRC.

17. Sassoon to R. Ross 17 August 1917, Eccles.

18. Owen, *Collected Letters*, pp. 484–5.

19. *SJ*, pp. 58–60, and draft of *SJ*, GS.

20. To Stephen Spender. See P. Parker, *The Old Lie* (London 1987) p. 193.

21. Owen, *Collected Letters*, pp. 69–70.

22. Ibid., p. 255.

23. Ibid., p. 282.

24. Ibid., p. 300.

25. Ibid., p. 320.

26. H. Owen to Sassoon, 20 March 1946, Columbia, ms coll W. Owen.

27. Draft of *SJ*, GS.

28. D. Hibberd, *Wilfred Owen* (London 2002) p. 267; and Owen, *Collected Letters*, p. 487.

29. See D. Hibberd, *Wilfred Owen: The Last Year* (London 1992) p. 43.

30. Owen, *Collected Letters*, p. 581.

31. Ibid., pp. 486–7.

32. Ibid., p. 489.

33. Ibid., p. 492.

34. 'Dreamers', *CP*, p. 71. 'Does It Matter?', *CP*, p. 76. 'Banishment', *CP*, p. 86.

35. Owen, *Collected Letters*, p. 493.

36. Ibid., p. 494.
37. Ibid., p. 496.
38. *SJ*, pp. 61–2.
39. Owen, *Collected Letters*, p. 498.
40. Draft of *SJ*, GS.
41. Sassoon to R. Graves, 4 October 1917, Carbondale.
42. Draft of *SJ*, GS.
43. J. Cottrell to Sassoon, 16 October 1917, IWM, SS1.
44. Sassoon to O. Morrell, 11 October 1917, HRC.
45. *Goodbye to All That*, p. 326.
46. J. Stallworthy, *Wilfred Owen* (London 1974) p. 229.
47. Hibberd, *Owen: The Last Year*, p. 52.
48. Sassoon to R. Graves, 19 October 1917, Carbondale.
49. Owen, *Collected Letters*, p. 503.
50. A. Strong, *A Human Voice* (London 1917). The copy given by Sassoon to Owen is in the English Faculty Library, Oxford.
51. Hibberd, *Owen: The Last Year*, p. 56.
52. Owen, *Collected Letters*, pp. 504–5.
53. Ibid., p. 521.
54. O. Morrell journal, and *Ottoline at Garsington*, pp. 230–1.
55. J. Cottrell to Sassoon, 6 November 1917, IWM SS1.
56. *SP*, p. 67.
57. *SJ*, p. 67.
58. C. Asquith, *Diaries 1915–1918* (London 1968) p. 366.
59. Ibid., p. 379.
60. Ibid., p. 381.
61. Sassoon to E. Dent, 24 November 1917, CUL add mss 7973.
62. PRO/WO339/S1440/49289.
63. Sassoon to R. Graves, 7 December 1917, Carbondale.
64. *SP*, p. 97.
65. E. Marsh to Sassoon, 9 December 1917, Eton.
66. Sassoon to E. Dent, November n.d. 1917, CUL add mss 7973.
67. Sassoon to R. Graves, 7 December 1917, Carbondale.
68. Owen, *Collected Letters*, pp. 516–17.
69. Sassoon to O. Morrell, 4 December 1917, HRC.
70. J. Cottrell to Sassoon, 18 December 1917, CUL add mss 8889/3/141.
71. *Diaries 1915–1918*, 19 December 1917, p. 197.

72. Sassoon to H. Thornycroft, 21 December 1917, BL add mss 56099.
73. Sassoon to O. Morrell, 26 December 1917, HRC.
74. R. Graves to Sassoon, 20 November 1917, Berg.
75. R. Graves to Sassoon, November n.d. 1917, Berg.
76. J. Cottrell to Sassoon, n.d., RWF, 5353H.
77. Sassoon to O. Morrell, 26 December 1917, HRC.
78. Dent diary, 23 December 1917, King's College, Cambridge EJD/3/1/13.
79. E. Marsh to Sassoon, 19 December 1917, Eton.
80. Sassoon to C. Hassall, 12 July 1949, CUL add mss 8905.
81. E. Blunden, *London Mercury*, June 1929.
82. R. Graves to Sassoon, n.d. November 1917, Berg.
83. The 'Counter-Attack' or 'Craiglockhart' poems are in *CP* pp. 67–95, with the exceptions of 'A Wooden Cross' (*Diaries 1915–1918*, p. 185), and 'The Triumph' (*WP*, p. 127).

8: 'I must be strong'

1. Sassoon to E. Gosse, 14 January 1918, BL Ashley.
2. *Diaries 1915–1918*, 12 January 1918, p. 203.
3. Sassoon to T. Bartholomew, January n.d. 1917, CUL add mss 8487.
4. 'Journey's End', *Diaries 1915–1918*, 8 January 1918, p. 202. 'A Moment of Waking', ibid., 8 January 1918, pp. 201–2. 'In Barracks', *CP*, p. 95. 'Invocation,' *CP*, p. 88. 'The Dream', *CP*, p. 93. 'Dead Musicians', *CP*, p. 92. 'Together', *CP*, p. 95. 'Suicide in the Trenches', *CP*, p. 78.
5. Diary, January 1918, GS.
6. Richards, *Old Soldiers Never Die*, p. 271.
7. E. Marsh to Sassoon, 27 January 1918, Eton.
8. Ibid.
9. Graves, *Goodbye to All That*, p. 337.
10. R. Graves to Sassoon, n.d., Berg.
11. *SP*, p. 111.
12. Ibid., p. 135.
13. PRO/WO339/S1440/49289.
14. W. Heinemann to R. Ross, 21 January 1918, HRC.
15. E. Marsh to Sassoon, 3 February 1918, Eton.

16. Ibid.

17. Diary, 29 January 1918, GS.

18. 'Memory', *CP*, p. 105. 'Idyll', *CP*, p. 113.

19. Diary, 3 February 1918, GS.

20. 'Remorse', *CP*, p. 91.

21. *SP*, p. 142.

22. *Diaries 1915–1918*, 8 February 1918, p. 211.

23. Ibid., 13 February 1918, p. 212.

24. Notebook, GS.

25. *Diaries 1915–1918*, 22 February 1918, p. 216.

26. G. Harbord to Sassoon, 21 February 1918, IWM, SS3.

27. E. Dent to Sassoon, 20 February 1918, CUL add mss 7973.

28. *Diaries 1915–1918*, 28 February 1918, p. 218.

29. 'In Palestine' in ibid., 30 March 1918, pp. 226–7.

30. Ibid., 5 April 1918, p. 229.

31. 'Shadows' in ibid., 10 April 1918, pp. 232–3. 'The Dug-Out', *CP*, p. 102.

32. *Diaries 1915–1918*, 19 April 1918, p. 236.

33. Ibid., 12 April 1918, p. 234.

34. 'Concert Party', *CP*, p. 100. 'Flamingos', *Diaries 1915–1918*, 22 April 1918, pp. 237–8.

35. *Diaries 1915–1918*, 23–26 April 1918, pp. 238–9.

36. Sassoon to E. M. Forster, 1 May 1918, King's College, Cambridge EMF xviii Sassoon.

37. *Diaries 1915–1918*, 1 May 1918, p. 242.

38. 'Night on the Convoy', *CP*, p. 101.

39. Sassoon to O. Morrell, 9 May 1918, HRC.

9: 'Threshold of the dark'

1. National Army Museum 9508/11.

2. Sassoon to R. Graves, 15 May 1918, Carbondale.

3. P. Hoare, *Wilde's Last Stand* (London 1997) p. 111.

4. Sassoon to R. Graves, 15 May 1918, Carbondale.

5. Copy in RWF Museum archives, Carnarvon.

6. *Diaries 1915–1918*, 18 May 1918, p. 251.

7. Sassoon to O. Morrell, 16 May 1918, HRC.
8. Sassoon to R. Meiklejohn, 17 May 1918, HRC.
9. *Diaries 1915–1918*, 19 May 1918, p. 251.
10. Ibid., 24 May 1918, p. 257.
11. Sassoon to R. Graves, 29 May 1918, Carbondale.
12. Sassoon to R. Nichols, 2 June 1918, Bodleian ms Eng lett c7.
13. Notebook, GS.
14. 'Reward', *WP*, p. 122.
15. 'Colin', in *Diaries 1915–1918*, 12 June 1918, p. 267.
16. *Diaries 1915–1918*, 14 June 1918, p. 269.
17. Ibid., 15 June 1918, p. 270.
18. Poems in RWF museum, Carnarvon.
19. 'I Stood with the Dead', *CP*, p. 103.
20. V. de S. Pinto to sister, 21 June 1918, IWM SS6.
21. *Y Ddraig Goch*, the Journal of the Royal Welch Fusiliers, March 1968, vol. 17, no. 1, p. 13.
22. 'Spirit of the Bayonet' and 'To Any Father (Who Thinks War Splendid) . . .' are in red-covered notebook, GS.
23. O. Sitwell to Sassoon, 28 June 1918, Washington State University, Pullman.
24. *SP*, p. 249.
25. Letter from W. Stable in *Daily Telegraph*, 13 September 1967.
26. *Diaries 1915–1918*, 15 July 1918, pp. 273–6.
27. V. de S. Pinto to father, 14 July 1918, IWM SS66.
28. Blunden, *London Mercury*, June 1929, essay on Sassoon's poetry.
29. E. Gosse to Sassoon, 25 June 1918, Rutgers.
30. Notebook, 2 July 1918, GS.
31. Ibid., 1 July 1918.
32. Ibid., 17 July 1918.
33. Ibid., 23 July 1918.
34. Ibid., 25 July 1918.
35. Sassoon to W. Heinemann, 30 June 1918, HRC.
36. J. M. Murry to Sassoon, 12 February 1918, William Reese, New Haven.
37. *TLS*, 27 December 1917.
38. *TLS*, 11 July 1918.
39. *Nation*, 13 July 1918.

40. B. Russell to O. Morrell, 1 August 1918, HRC.
41. *Nation*, 27 July 1918.
42. R. Ross to O. Morrell, 15 July 1918, HRC.
43. *New Witness*, 18 October 1918; *Herald* (undated extract in Diary, GS); *Daily Chronicle*, 20 November 1918; *New Age*, 21 November 1918.
44. Sassoon to S. Cockerell, 6 September 1918, Berg.
45. G. Harbord to Sassoon, 9 September 1918, IWM, SS3.
46. *SP*, p. 275.
47. Sassoon to R. Nichols, n.d. July, Bodleian ms Eng lett c7.
48. PRO/WO/339/S1440.
49. PRO/WO339/S1440 49289, 22 July 1918.
50. Sassoon to R. Graves, 24 July 1918, Carbondale. The poem 'Letter to Robert Graves' is in *WP*, pp. 130–3.
51. Sassoon to H. Thornycroft, 'Sunday', BL add mss 56099.
52. Sassoon to R. Meiklejohn, 'Wednesday night', HRC.
53. Sassoon to E. Marsh, 18 July 1918, Berg.
54. Sassoon to O. Morrell, n.d. July, HRC.
55. *SJ*, p. 70.
56. O. Morrell journal, July–August 1918, BL.
57. Diary, August 1918, GS.
58. Ibid., 30 July 1918.
59. Sassoon to E. Dent, July–August, CUL add mss 7973.
60. Sassoon to E. Marsh, n.d. August 1918, Berg.
61. Sassoon to R. Graves, 28 June 1918, Carbondale.
62. Owen, *Collected Letters*, p. 567.
63. *SJ*, p. 71.
64. Owen, *Collected Letters*, p. 571.
65. Ibid., p. 570.
66. Ibid., pp. 578–9, 581–3.
67. 'Jesus in Heaven' in red notebook, GS. 'Great Men', *WP*, p. 134.
68. Sassoon to C. K. Ogden, 10 August 1918, McMaster.
69. Sassoon to R. Nichols, 15 August 1918, Bodleian ms Eng lett c7.
70. Viscount Esher to E. Marsh, 11 August 1918, Berg.
71. Sassoon to E. Carpenter, n.d. August, Sheffield ms 386/295.
72. E. Carpenter to Sassoon, 17 August 1918, Eton.
73. PRO/WO339/S1440 49289.

74. Sassoon to O. Morrell, 21 August 1918, HRC.
75. Sassoon to R. Meiklejohn, 22 August 1918, HRC.
76. Sassoon to O. Morrell, 4 September 1918, HRC.
77. August, Bodleian ms Eng lett c7.
78. *Diaries 1915–1918*, 10 August 1918, p. 118.
79. 'Vision', *CP*, p. 117. 'Ancient History', *CP*, p. 109. 'Wraiths', *CP*, p. 112. 'Limitations', *CP*, p. 121. 'Fancy Dress', *CP*, p. 110. 'Sunset at the Borders' in Nichols poems, Bodleian ms Eng lett c7.
80. Sassoon to O. Morrell, 27 September 1918, HRC.
81. O. Morrell journal, 5 October 1918, BL.
82. 'To Leonide Massine in "Cleopatra"', *CP*, p. 104.
83. As 'Elegy (to Robert Ross)', in *CP*, p. 107.
84. Bound copy of *Picture Show*, HRC.
85. 'Memorial Tablet', *CP*, p. 104.
86. *SJ*, p. 87.
87. *Diaries 1915–1918*, 6 November 1918, p. 280.
88. R. Gittings, *The Second Mrs Hardy* (Oxford paperback edition 1981) p. 54.
89. *Diaries 1915–1918*, 7 November 1918, p. 281.
90. Gittings, *The Second Mrs Hardy*, p. 95.
91. *SJ*, p. 94. It has been suggested that the Digweed name may have come into the Laureate's mind because a Miss Digweed appears in Jane Austen's letters and one of Jane's brothers married a daughter of Sir Brook Bridges (1767–1829).
92. O. Morrell journal, 10 November 1918, BL.
93. V. Woolf to V. Bell, 19 November 1918, *Letters of Virginia Woolf*, ed. N. Nicolson and Joanne Trautmann, vol. 2 (London 1976) p. 297.
94. Diary, 11 November 1918, GS; with *Diary 1915–1918*, 11 November 1918, p. 282.

10: Love and politics

1. Sassoon to O. Morrell, 4 February 1918, HRC.
2. 'Reconciliation', *CP*, p. 99.
3. T. Bartholomew to E. Dent, 16 November 1918, CUL add mss 7973/B/23.

4. Sassoon to T. Bartholomew, 26 November 1918, CUL add mss 8487.

5. G. Atkin to Sassoon, 3 August 1926, Berg.

6. Dent diary, 10 April 1917, King's College, Cambridge EJD/3/1/13.

7. G. Atkin to E. Dent, 12 June 1917, CUL add mss 7973/A/12.

8. T. Bartholomew to E. Dent, 5 April 1918, CUL add mss 7973/B/20.

9. G. Atkin to W. J. H. Sprott, n.d. 1918, King's College, Cambridge WJHS/3.

10. G. Atkin to E. Dent, 5 November 1918, CUL add mss 7973/A/29.

11. G. Atkin to E. Dent, 24 November 1918, CUL add mss 7973/A/31.

12. G. Atkin to W. J. H. Sprott, n.d. 1918, King's College, Cambridge WJHS/3.

13. 'Lovers' and 'Slumber Song', *CP*, p. 115.

14. G. Atkin to W. J. H. Sprott, n.d., King's College, Cambridge WJHS/3.

15. Sassoon to E. Marsh, 1 December 1918, Berg.

16. G. Atkin to E. Dent, 11 January 1918, CUL add mss 7973/A/34.

17. G. Atkin to W. J. H. Sprott, n.d. 1918, King's College, Cambridge WJHS/3.

18. Ibid.

19. Sassoon to E. Marsh, n.d. December, Berg.

20. Sassoon to O. Morrell, n.d. December, HRC.

21. Typescript of diary, CUL.

22. G. Atkin to W. J. H. Sprott, n.d., King's College, Cambridge WJHS/3.

23. Sassoon to R. Graves, 9 January 1919, Carbondale.

24. 'Picture Show', *CP*, p. 99. 'Middle Ages', *CP*, p. 111. 'The Dark House', *CP*, p. 112. 'Miracles', *CP*, p. 107. 'A Last Word', *WP*, p. 138. 'Cold Steel', in *Labour Leader*, 9 January 1919. 'The Imperfect Lover', *CP*, p. 116. 'To A Childless Woman', *CP*, p. 117.

25. O. Morrell journal, January 1919, BL.

26. G. Santayana, *My Host the World* (London 1953) p. 122.

27. Letter from J. Langdon-Davies, *New Statesman*, 22 September 1967.

28. *SJ*, p. 134.

29. G. Atkin to W. J. H. Sprott, n.d., King's College, Cambridge WJHS/3.

30. 'My dear Mr Pawling', 7 March 1919, Carbondale.

31. 'The Goldsmith' and 'Devotion to Duty', *CP*, p. 108. 'Aftermath', *CP*, p. 118. 'Cinema Hero' in *Picture Show*.

32. Sassoon to E. Marsh, 4 April 1919, Berg.

33. F. Swinnerton to Sassoon, quoting (with approval) H. M. Tomlinson, 22 April 1949, Berg.

34. *Daily Herald*, 23, 30 April, 21 May 1919.

35. *Daily Herald*, 31 December 1919.

36. E. Blunden to Sassoon, 3 May 1919, HRC.

37. 'Everyone Sang', *CP*, p. 124.

38. 'Prelude to an Unwritten Masterpiece', *CP*, p. 120.

39. T. Hardy to Sassoon, 19 July 1919, Eton.

40. E. Gosse to Sassoon, 5 July 1919, Rutgers.

41. 'What the Captain Said at the Point-to-Point', *CP*, p. 110.

42. 'Falling Asleep', *CP*, p. 123.

43. *SJ*, p. 164.

44. Sassoon to E. Marsh, 10 August 1919, Berg.

45. Sassoon to C. K. Scott Moncrieff, 19 January 1918, National Library of Scotland.

46. *Letters of J. Middleton Murry to Katherine Mansfield*, ed. C. A. Hankin (London 1983) p. 234.

47. 'Promenade Concert', in *New Statesman*, 11 October 1919.

48. 'Early Chronology', *London Mercury*, November 1919.

49. Sassoon to T. Bartholomew, 12 November 1919, CUL add mss 8487.

50. Bartholomew diary, 8 December 1919, CUL add mss 8786.

51. Sassoon to F. Hardy, 3 August 1919, Yale.

52. *SJ*, p. 172.

53. Sassoon to Mr Stuckey, 25 September 1919, Mugar Memorial Library, Boston University.

11: Byron in America

1. *Counter-Attack* (New York 1918) pp. 1–2.

2. Diary, 29 January 1920, GS.

3. Ibid.

4. *SJ*, p. 181.

5. Diary, 2 February 1920, GS.

6. J. Untermeyer, *Private Collection* (New York 1965) pp. 168 and 51.

7. Diary, 3 February 1920, GS.

8. Ibid., 6 February 1920.

9. Mr Pierce to S. Cockerell, 16 February 1920, C. Rothkopf, New York.

10. Diary, 7 February 1920. GS.

11. *SJ*, p. 182.

12. Diary, 10 February 1920, GS.

13. Ibid., 12 February 1920.

14. Behrman diary, 6, 7 February 1920, NYPL.

15. Ibid., 19 February 1920.

16. Sassoon to W. J. Turner, 21 February 1920, Berg.

17. S. Behrman diary, 24 February 1920, NYPL.

18. S. Behrman, *People in a Diary* (New York 1972) p. 116.

19. Diary, n.d., GS.

20. 'Who is Glenn Hunter?', *New York Times*, 9 November 1919.

21. S. Behrman to R. Hart-Davis, 14 March 1969, Tulsa, copy in CUL add mss 9454/6/1.

22. S. Behrman, *People in a Diary*, p. 9.

23. S. Behrman diary, 17 and 18 March 1920, NYPL.

24. *SJ*, p. 195.

25. Sassoon to S. Behrman, 19 March 1920, NYPL.

26. Draft of *SJ*, GS.

27. *SJ*, p. 196.

28. Notebook, GS.

29. Sassoon to S. Behrman, 24 March 1920, NYPL.

30. Sassoon to S. Behrman, 29 March 1920, NYPL.

31. F. Prewett to O. Morrell, 2 April 1920, HRC.

32. Sassoon to E. Marsh, 6 April 1920, Berg.

33. Behrman diary, 17 April 1920, NYPL.

34. Ibid., 18 April 1920.

35. Ibid., 26 April 1920.

36. Connely diary, HRC.

37. Behrman diary, 4 May 1920, NYPL.

38. Ibid., 16 June 1920.

39. Ibid., 11 May 1920.

40. Ibid., 7 June 1920.

41. *Vanity Fair*, August 1920.

42. Sassoon to R. Meiklejohn, 28 May 1920, HRC.

43. 'Glenn Hunter Dies; Stage, Film Actor', *New York Times*, 31 December 1945.
44. Behrman diary, 3 June 1920, NYPL.
45. Draft of *SJ*, GS.
46. Behrman diary, 15 June 1920, NYPL.
47. Sassoon to W. J. Turner, 9 July 1920, Berg.
48. Behrman diary, 16 June 1920, NYPL.
49. Sassoon to O. Morrell, 17 June 1920, HRC.
50. Ibid.
51. *SJ*, p. 215.
52. Behrman diary, 4 August 1920, NYPL.
53. Draft of *SJ*, GS.
54. 'First Night: Richard III', *CP*, p. 154. 'An All-British Sonnet (Peace Celebration)', in *New Republic*, 28 April 1920. 'Storm on Fifth Avenue', *CP*, p. 142.
55. Sassoon to S. Behrman, 13 December 1920, NYPL.
56. Bartholomew diary, 30 December 1920, CUL add mss 8786.
57. *Diaries 1920–1922*, ed. R. Hart-Davis (London 1981) p. 17.
58. S. Owen to Sassoon, 11 October 1920, Columbia ms coll Owen.
59. 'Spontaniety' in manuscript in Berg, dated 9 November 1920. 'Philharmonic' in *Recreations*. 'Lines Written in the Reform Club' was printed by Sassoon as a broadside for Christmas Day 1920.
60. *Daily Herald*, 27 October 1920.
61. F. Prewett to O. Morrell, 23 October 1920, HRC.

12: 'Why can't I create something?'

1. Black-covered 1921 notebook, GS.
2. 'Notes on 1920–25', GS.
3. Sassoon memoirs draft, p. 29, CUL add mss 9454/12 (b).
4. O. Sitwell to Sassoon, n.d. 1920s, HRC.
5. Sassoon to W. J. Turner, 7 August n.d., Berg.
6. O. Sitwell to Sassoon, 4 July 1923, Washington State, Pullman.
7. E. Sitwell to Sassoon, 22 March 1927, Washington State, Pullman.
8. Diary, 8 June 1942, GS.
9. Ibid., 16 May 1950.

10. *Diaries 1923–1925* ed. R. Hart-Davis (London 1985), May 1923, p. 31.

11. Ibid., 15 May 1924, p. 124.

12. 'Reynardism Revisited', *CP*, p. 139.

13. *Diaries 1920–1922*, 23 February 1922, p. 110. *Diaries 1923–1925*, 27 March 1923, p. 26, 5 July 1923, p. 45.

14. Diary, April 1922, GS.

15. R. Graves to Sassoon, n.d. March 1921 (letter begun in December), Berg.

16. R. P. Graves, *Robert Graves: The Years with Laura Riding* (London paperback edition 1995) pp. 44–5.

17. Thwaite, *Edmund Gosse*, p. 489.

18. R. Graves, *Goodbye to All That*, p. 363.

19. Sassoon to E. Blunden, 15 September 1919, HRC.

20. Sassoon to E. Blunden, 18 September 1920, HRC.

21. O. Morrell to Sassoon, 10 January 1923, HRC.

22. *Daily Herald*, 13 April 1921. *Nation*, 16 and 23 April 1921.

23. 'The Case for the Miners', *CP*, p. 137.

24. *Diaries, 1920–1922*, 8 September 1921, p. 81.

25. Diary extract, 10–13 September 1921, CUL add mss 9454/2/3a.

26. F. Prewett to O. Morrell, 9 October 1921, HRC.

27. Diary, after 1 October 1921 entry, GS.

28. Philipp of Hesse to Sassoon, 17 October 1921, CUL add mss 9375/390.

29. Philipp of Hesse to Sassoon, 28 October 1921, CUL add mss 9375/391.

30. Philipp of Hesse to Sassoon, 31 October 1921, CUL add mss 9375/392.

31. Ibid.

32. *Diaries 1920–1922*, 29 April 1922, pp. 150–1.

33. Sassoon to V. Woolf, 21 May 1922 or 1923, Berg.

34. V. Woolf to C. Bell, 23 January 1924, *Letters of Virginia Woolf*, vol. 3 (London 1977) pp. 84–5.

35. 'The Villa d'Este Gardens', *CP*, p. 143. 'On Being Urged to Write about Love', 'Romantic Drama' and 'A Child's Kingdom' are in 1922 notebook, GS.

36. 'The London Museum', *CP*, p. 149. 'Sheldonian Soliloquy', *CP*, p. 160.

37. *Diaries 1920–1922*, 6 June 1922, pp. 163–4.
38. Diary, 17 August 1922, GS.
39. *Diaries 1920–1922*, 2 September 1922, p. 230.
40. 'Clavicord Recital', *Nation*, 30 December 1922. 'Solar Eclipse', *CP*, p. 163.
41. Diary, 12 October 1922, GS.
42. Ibid., 15 October 1922.
43. Ibid., 26 October 1922.
44. 'Martyrdoms' became 'Since Thought Is Life, God's Martyrdoms Were Good', in *CP*, p. 178.
45. *Diaries 1920–1922*, 2 November 1922, p. 286.
46. Philipp of Hesse to Sassoon, 25 December 1922, CUL add mss 9375/403.
47. R. Hodgson to Sassoon, 21 June 1923, Bryn Mawr University, Philadelphia.
48. *Diaries 1923–1925*, 26 June 1923, p. 38.
49. O. Sitwell to Sassoon, 4 July 1923, Washington State, Pullman.
50. 'Song, Be My Soul; Set Forth the Fairest Part', *CP*, p. 175. 'My Memoirs', *Diaries 1923–1925*, 6 November 1923, p. 63.
51. *Diaries 1923–1925*, 16 November–9 December 1923, pp. 65–68.
52. Sassoon to R. Hodgson, 22 November 1923, Yale.

13: 'The unknown want'

1. 'Primitive Ritual' in *Lingual Exercises* (London 1925).
2. Unpublished, in Tulsa notebook, copy in CUL add mss 9454/1/4.
3. *Diaries 1923–1925*, 20 July 1924, p. 170.
4. 'A Music Critic Anticipates Eternity', *CP*, p. 157. 'The Grand Hotel', *CP*, p. 134. 'Afterthoughts on the Opening of the British Empire Exhibition', *CP*, p. 127. 'Breach of Decorum', *CP*, p. 135.
5. Sassoon to R. Graves, 6 June 1924, Carbondale.
6. Diary, 15 May 1924, GS.
7. Ibid., 6 June 1924.
8. Ibid., 13 June 1924.
9. Sassoon to R. Graves, 15 August 1924, Carbondale.
10. Diary, 11 August 1924, GS.

11. Sassoon to R. Graves, 15 August 1924, Carbondale.
12. 'The Blues at Lords', *CP*, p. 138. 'Eyes', *Diaries 1923–1925*, 5 July 1924, p. 152. 'Grandeur of Ghosts', *CP*, p. 182. 'Stonehenge' – as 'What is Stonehenge – It Is the Roofless Past' – *CP*, p. 179. 'Cerne Giant', *Diaries 1923–1925*, 6 August 1924, pp. 182–3. 'A Ruined Castle', *Diaries 1923–1925*, 23 August 1923, p. 191. 'At the Grave of Henry Vaughan', *CP*, p. 189. 'With de la Mare at Carey Castle', *Diaries 1923–1925*, 27 August 1924, pp. 192–3.
13. Diary, 12 September 1924, GS.
14. 'Apocalyptic Indiscretions' as 'In Me, Past, Present, Future Meet' in *CP*, p. 178.
15. *Diaries 1923–1925*, 16 September 1924, pp. 203–4.
16. Ibid., 17 September 1924, p. 205.
17. 'Evensong in Westminster Abbey', *CP*, p. 153.
18. Sassoon to R. Graves, 18 October 1924, Carbondale.
19. Graves, *Goodbye to All That*, p. 310.
20. Diary, 29 September 1924, GS.
21. Ibid., 3 October 1924.
22. Sassoon to G. Byam Shaw, 22 or 23 October 1925, CUL add mss 9454/3/14.
23. Untermeyer, *Private Collection*, pp. 171–2.
24. Sassoon to G. Byam Shaw, 18 December 1924, CUL add mss 9454/3/8.
25. Sassoon to G. Byam Shaw, 24 December 1924, CUL add mss 9454/3/9.
26. Sassoon to Dame H. Cumming, 27 February 1964, *PP*, p. 103.
27. See letter of K. Kavaphes (C. P. Cavafy) to H. Monro, 8 December 1925, Berg.
28. Sassoon to S. Behrman, 30 April 1925, NYPL.
29. 'Alone' – as 'When I'm Alone – the Words Tripped Off His Tongue' – *CP*, p. 180.
30. 'To an Old Lady Dead', *CP*, p. 184. This was also admired by Cavafy; see his letter to H. Monro of 8 December 1925, Berg.
31. R. Graves to Sassoon, 2 April 1925, Berg.
32. R. Nichols to Sassoon, 16 May 1925, Berg.
33. *Diaries 1923–1925*, 25 May 1925, p. 255.
34. Sassoon to E. Blunden, 25 July 1925, HRC.
35. 'All Souls Day', *CP*, p. 192.
36. Sassoon to G. Byam Shaw, 20 January 1925, CUL add mss 9454/3/10.

37. Sassoon to G. Byam Shaw, 9 September 1925, CUL add mss 9454/3/11.

38. G. Byam Shaw to Sassoon, 2 November 1947, CUL add mss 8889/3/120.

39. G. Byam Shaw to Sassoon, 21 October 1925, CUL add mss 889/3/43.

40. Sassoon to G. Byam Shaw, 26–8 October 1925, CUL add mss 9454/3/15.

41. *Diaries 1923–1925*, 25 September 1925, p. 286.

42. Sassoon to G. Byam Shaw, 26–8 October 1925, CUL add mss 9454/3/15.

43. G. Byam Shaw to Sassoon, 29 October 1925, CUL add mss 8889/3/45.

44. Sassoon to G. Byam Shaw, 6 November 1925, CUL add mss 9454/3/18.

45. Diary, 16 December 1925, GS.

46. 'To a Room' – as 'Farewell to a Room' – *CP*, p. 179. 'Strangeness of Heart', *CP*, p. 181. 'To My Mother', *CP*, p. 268.

47. 'The Power and the Glory', *CP*, p. 193; see also Sassoon to E. Sitwell, 28 March 1928, Berg.

48. *Diaries 1923–1925*, 13 December 1925, p. 301.

49. Diary, 6, 11, 14, 15 January 1926, GS.

50. Ibid., 10 March 1926.

51. Sassoon to G. Byam Shaw, 26 February 1926, CUL add mss 9454/3/35.

52. Diary, 20 January 1926, GS.

53. 'To an Eighteenth Century Poet', *CP*, p. 183. 'On Some Portraits by Sargent', *CP*, p. 152.

54. 'To One Who Was With Me in the War', *CP*, p. 186. Sassoon to E. Blunden, 20 July 1926, HRC.

55. The Kew Gardens poem is 'As I was Walking in the Gardens', *CP*, p. 176. 'A Last Judgement', *CP*, p. 196.

56. Sassoon to E. Blunden, 17 March 1926, HRC.

57. 25 March 1926, IWM, SS1.

58. Sassoon to G. Byam Shaw, 31 March 1926, CUL add mss 9454/3/38.

59. Sassoon to R. Nichols, 20 March 1926 (probably), Berg.

60. Diary, 1 May 1926, GS.

61. G. Byam Shaw to Sassoon, 7 May 1926, CUL add mss 9454/3/38.

62. Sassoon to E. Blunden, 20 July 1926, HRC.

63. Diary, 5 May 1926, GS.

64. Ibid., 8 May 1926.

65. Ibid. See also B. Baxter, *Strange Street* (London 1935) p. 121.
66. Diary, 29 June 1926, GS.
67. O. Morrell, journal, 22 May 1926, BL.
68. Diary, 23 May 1926, GS.
69. Ibid., 30 July 1926.
70. Sassoon to R. Gathorne-Hardy, 30 July 1926, Lilly Library.
71. Sassoon to G. Byam Shaw, 14 August 1926, CUL add mss 9454/3/51.
72. Sassoon to R. Gathorne-Hardy, 19 August 1926, Lilly Library.
73. O. Morrell journal, 26 August 1926, BL.
74. Diary, 4 September 1926, GS.
75. Ibid., 20 September 1926.
76. See manuscript at HRC.
77. Diary, 8 October 1926, GS.

14: The fox-hunting man

1. Sassoon to Mother Margaret Mary, 12 June 1966, CUL add mss 7935.
2. Diary, 17 October 1926. GS.
3. Ibid., 22 October 1926.
4. Sassoon to G. Byam Shaw, 21 October 1926, CUL add mss 9454/3/56.
5. Diary, 23 October 1926, GS.
6. Ibid., 27 October 1926.
7. Ibid., 31 October 1926.
8. Ibid., 9 November 1926.
9. Ibid., 2 November 1928.
10. Ibid., 17 November 1926.
11. Ibid., 30 November 1926.
12. Ibid., 21 November 1926.
13. Sassoon to G. Byam Shaw, 24 November 1926, CUL add mss 9454/3/59.
14. Diary, 3 December 1926, GS.
15. Ibid., 6 December 1926.
16. Ibid.
17. Ibid., 17 December 1926.

18. Ibid., 18 December 1926.
19. Ibid., 23 December 1926.
20. Ibid., 30 December 1926.
21. Ibid., 12 January 1926.
22. Ibid., 18 January 1927.
23. Ibid., 20 January 1927.
24. E. Gosse to Sassoon, 27 January 1927, Rutgers.
25. 'Everyman', *CP*, p. 224.
26. E. Gosse to Sassoon, 27 January 1927, GS.
27. E. Gosse to Sassoon, 2 February 1927, Rutgers.
28. Diary, 9 February 1927 GS. 'A Flower Has Opened in My Heart', *CP*, p. 195.
29. Diary, 18 February 1927, GS.
30. Ibid., 28 February 1927. 'I Accuse the Rich' in *New Leader*, 29 April 1927.
31. E. M. Forster to T. E. Lawrence, 30 March 1927, Bodleian.
32. Diary, 12 April 1927, GS.
33. 'In the Stars We Have Seen the Strangeness of Our State', *CP*, p. 180.
34. Theresa to Sassoon, n.d. 1927, private collection.
35. Diary, 4 May 1927, GS.
36. Sassoon to G. Byam Shaw, 3 May 1927, CUL add mss 9454/3/69.
37. Diary, 14 June 1927, GS.
38. S.T. journal, 26 June 1929, private collection.
39. Ibid., 28 January 1929.
40. Ibid., 17 January 1929.
41. Diary, 22 June 1927, GS.
42. Ibid., 27 June 1927.
43. Ibid., 1 July 1927.
44. Ibid., 13 July 1927.
45. Ibid., 25 July 1927.
46. 'On Passing the New Menin Gate', *CP*, p. 188.
47. Diary, 28 July 1927, GS.
48. Ibid., 13 September 1927.
49. Ibid., 1 October 1927.
50. Ibid., 5 October 1927.
51. Ibid., 17 October 1927, recounting O. Sitwell letter of 10 October.
52. Ibid., 16 February 1932.

53. O. Sitwell to Sassoon, 10 October 1927, Washington State, Pullman.
54. Diary, 15–17 October 1927, GS.

15: Stephen: love and anger

1. Diary, 19 October 1927, GS.
2. Ibid., 20 October 1927.
3. S. Tennant, 'The Room Beyond: A Foreword on Willa Cather', in Willa Cather, *On Writing* (New York 1949) p. xi.
4. Diary, 21 October 1927, GS.
5. S. Tennant to Sassoon, n.d. November and 5 November 1927, Berg.
6. Diary, 8 November 1927, GS.
7. Ibid., 17 November 1927.
8. Tulsa notebook, copy in CUL add mss 9453/1/3. 8 November 1927.
9. Sassoon to Theresa, 16 November 1927, Berg.
10. Diary, 21 November 1927, GS.
11. Ibid., 1 April 1929.
12. Ibid., 8 December 1927.
13. S.T. journal, 17 January 1929.
14. Diary, 12 December 1927, GS.
15. Ibid., 31 December 1927.
16. Sassoon to G. Byam Shaw, 31 December 1927, CUL add mss 9454/3/96.
17. Diary, 3 January 1928, GS.
18. Ibid., 11 January 1928.
19. Ibid., 14 January 1928.
20. Ibid., 28 January 1928.
21. 'At Max Gate', *CP*, p. 263.
22. 28 January 1928, manuscript at Eton.
23. O. Morrell journal, 14 December 1930, BL.
24. Behrman diary, 5 February 1928, NYPL.
25. Diary, 17 October 1927, GS.
26. Ibid., 10 February 1928.
27. S. Tennant to Sassoon, 18 February 1928, Berg.
28. S. Tennant to Sassoon, 13 February 1928, Berg.
29. S. Tennant to Sassoon, n.d. February, Berg.

30. Diary, 10 March 1928, GS.
31. Ibid., 25 March 1928.
32. Ibid., 26 March 1928.
33. Ibid., 6 April 1928.
34. Ibid., 12 April 1928.
35. Ibid., 23 April 1928.
36. Ibid., 25 April 1928.
37. Ibid., 26 April 1928.
38. Ibid., 4 May 1928.
39. Ibid., 8 May 1928.
40. 'One Who Watches', *CP*, p. 191.
41. Tulsa notebook, 12 and 13 April 1928, copy in CUL add mss 9454/1/3. Published in the *New Leader*, 4 May 1928.
42. Diary, 4 June 1928, GS.
43. Ibid., 26 June 1928.
44. 'The Paris Telephone Directory', in Tulsa notebook, copy in CUL add mss 9454/1/3.
45. Diary, 3 July 1928, GS.
46. Ibid., 7 July 1928.
47. Ibid., 9 July 1928.
48. Ibid., 20 July 1928.
49. Ibid., 30 July 1928.
50. Ibid., 18 August 1928.
51. P. Middleboe, *Edith Olivier* (London 1989) p. 77.
52. Sassoon to H. Festing Jones, 12 October 1928, CUL add mss 8484.
53. Sassoon to Heads, 'Thursday night', HRC.
54. Diary, 16 September 1928, GS.
55. Sassoon to G. Byam Shaw, 23 September 1928, CUL add mss 9454/3/111.
56. Theresa to Sassoon, 13 September 1928, private collection.
57. Sassoon to Theresa, 22 September 1928, Berg.
58. W. de la Mare to Sassoon, 27 September 1928, CUL add mss 9454/3/16.
59. Diary, 11 October 1928, GS.
60. Theresa to Sassoon, 4 and 17 October 1928, private collection.
61. Diary, 29 October 1928, GS.
62. Ibid., 7 November 1928.

63. Ibid., 12 November 1928.
64. Sassoon to G. Byam Shaw, 27 October 1928, CUL add mss 9454/3/ 115.
65. Sassoon to Theresa, 8 November 1928, Berg.
66. Diary, 18 November 1928, GS.
67. Ibid., 19 November 1928.
68. Ibid., 21 November 1928.
69. Ibid., 10 December 1928.
70. Ibid., 23 December 1928.
71. Ibid., 31 December 1928.

16: 'I ask for nothing but to be near him always'

1. E. Sitwell to Sassoon, December 1928 or January 1929, Washington State, Pullman.
2. Sassoon to R. Seymour, 16 December 1966, Rutgers.
3. Sassoon to Colonel W. S. Blackshear, 22 January 1954, HRC.
4. J. Dadd to Sassoon, 7 January 1929, IWM, SS2.
5. Diary, 9 January 1929, GS.
6. Ibid., 11 January 1929.
7. Ibid., 20 January 1929.
8. S. Tennant to O. Morrell, 25 February 1929, HRC.
9. Sassoon to E. Marsh, 12 March 1929, Berg.
10. E. Marsh, *A Number of People* (London 1939) p. 236.
11. E. Olivier journal, 7 April 1929, Wiltshire County Record Office.
12. Diary, 10 April 1929, GS.
13. S.T. journal, 6 April 1929.
14. Ibid., 12 April 1929.
15. Ibid., 7 April 1929.
16. Ibid., 12 April 1929.
17. To Tennant's delight, this poem – called 'April Birthday (To S.T.)' – appeared in the *Saturday Review of Literature* (New York) on 25 May 1929.
18. S.T. journal, 27 April 1929.
19. Ibid., 8 May 1929.
20. Diary, end of 1929, GS.

21. Ibid., 17 April 1928.
22. S.T. journal, 29 May 1929.
23. Diary, 22 May 1929, GS.
24. Ibid., 25 May 1929.
25. S.T. journal, 8 June 1929.
26. Diary, 15 June 1929, GS.
27. S.T. journal, 16 June 1929.
28. Sassoon to E. Marsh, 17 June 1929, Berg.
29. S.T. journal, end of July 1929.
30. Diary, 12 July 1929, GS.
31. W. Burton to Sassoon, 12 July 1929, HRC.
32. Diary, 5 August 1929, GS.
33. S.T. journal, 6 August 1929.
34. Diary, 10 August 1929, GS.
35. Ibid., 23 August 1929.
36. E. Blunden to A. Hayashi, 26 August 1929, Columbia Blunden box 3.
37. S.T. journal, September 1929.
38. Diary, 15 September 1929, GS.
39. S.T. journal, 19 September 1929.
40. Diary, 24 September 1929, GS.
41. Ibid., 9 October 1929.
42. Ibid., 21 October 1929.
43. S.T. journal, 21 October 1929.
44. Diary, 1 November 1929, GS.
45. E. Blunden to Sassoon, 11 November 1929, HRC.
46. Diary, November 1929, GS.
47. See R. P. Graves, *The Years with Laura*, pp. 132–3. Also the edition of *Goodbye to All That* edited by R. P. Graves (Providence and Oxford 1995) which has the annotations. The original annotated volume is in the Berg Collection. George Sassoon has another copy, annotated by Sassoon alone.
48. Sassoon to Theresa, 12 November 1929, Berg.
49. Diary, 18 November 1929, GS.
50. Ibid., 24 November 1929.
51. Ibid., 2 December 1929.
52. S.T. journal, 4 December 1929.
53. Diary, 8 December 1929, GS.

54. S.T. journal, 12 December 1929.
55. S. Tennant to E. Blunden, 24 December 1929, HRC.
56. In *CP*, p. 227 as 'Presences Perfected'.
57. S.T. journal, 31 December 1929.
58. Ibid., 1 January 1930.
59. 'Farewell to Youth', *CP*, p. 215. Mysteries' (unpublished), in Tulsa notebook, copy in CUL add mss 9454/1/4. 'Childhood Recovered' in *CP*, p. 213 as 'Down the Glimmering Staircase, Past the Pensive Clock'. 'War Experience Footnote' as 'War Experience' in *CP*, p. 216. 'Acceptance', *CP*, p. 247. 'The Heart's Paradise', in the *Nation*, 5 April 1929. 'We Shall Not All Sleep', *CP*, p. 218. 'My Past Has Gone to Bed', *CP*, p. 213. 'A Guidebook to Oblivion', *London Mercury*, May 1929. 'Presences Perfected', *CP*, p. 227.
60. Diary, 12 January 1930, GS. Agrigento was called Girgenti until 1927, and this is the name used in Sassoon's diary.
61. Ibid., 19 March 1929.
62. S.T. journal, 18 January 1930.
63. Diary, 18 January 1930, GS.
64. Ibid., 29 January 1930.
65. Ibid., 3 February 1930.
66. Sassoon to R. Graves, 7 February 1930, *In Broken Images*, pp. 197–201, original at Mugar Library, Boston University.
67. Diary, 9 February 1930, GS.
68. S.T. journal, 27 February 1930.
69. R. Graves to Sassoon, 20 February 1930, Berg.
70. Diary, 1 March 1930, GS.
71. *In Broken Images*, pp. 204–9. Original of 2 March 1930 in Mugar Memorial Library, Boston University.
72. S.T. journal, 3 March 1930.
73. Diary, 20 March 1930, GS.
74. S. Tennant to O. Morrell, 25 March 1930, HRC.
75. Diary, 22 March 1930. GS.
76. 'In Sicily', *CP*, p. 214.
77. Diary, 2 April 1930, GS.
78. Ibid., 10 April 1930.
79. Ibid., 23 April 1930.
80. In notebook, IWM SS4.

81. Diary, 29 April 1930, GS.
82. Ibid., 12 May 1930.

17: Elected silence

1. Mimic Warfare', *CP*, p. 201.
2. Diary, 17 June 1930, GS.
3. Reeve's *Conchologica Iconica* (1835–78).
4. Diary, 2 August 1930, GS.
5. Ibid., 5 September 1930.
6. S.T. journal, 28 September 1930.
7. Ibid., 18 and 20 September 1930.
8. R. Graves, *But It Still Goes On* (London 1930) p. 56.
9. *IO* manuscript, IWM SS4.
10. Ibid.
11. *IO*, p. 282.
12. Ibid., pp. 18 and 66.
13. Ibid., p. 112.
14. 'The Pity of War', *Adelphi*, October 1930.
15. V. de S. Pinto to Sassoon, 5 October 1930, IWM SS6.
16. 'Siegfried Sassoon by Robert Graves', *Clarion*, October 1930.
17. Sassoon to E. Blunden, 4 November 1930, HRC.
18. R. Graves, *But It Still Goes On.*
19. S.T. journal, 17 October 1930.
20. Ibid., 25 October 1930.
21. 'December Stillness', *CP*, p. 211.
22. Diary, 5 February 1931, GS.
23. Manuscript dated 17 February 1931, GS.
24. Diary, 6 March 1931, GS.
25. R. Lehmann to Sassoon, 8 April 1931, CUL add mss 8889/3/203.
26. P. Ziegler, *Osbert Sitwell* (London 1998) p. 143.
27. 'Requiem', in *Pynchbeck Lyre* (London 1931) p. 21.
28. R. Lehmann to Sassoon, 1 August 1931, CUL add mss 8889/3/207.
29. Diary, 31 July 1931, GS.
30. Ibid., 12 August 1931.
31. Ibid., 14 August 1931.

32. Ibid., 25 September 1931.
33. 'Mammoniac Ode', *CP*, p. 166. 'To a Red Rose' was published as an Ariel pamphlet by Faber on 8 October 1931, illustrated by Stephen Tennant, in spite of his exasperation with its author.
34. Diary, 28 September 1931, GS.
35. See 'Country Cornucopia' by George Plumptre, 19 July 1990, *Country Life*, for an assessment of Fitz House. I am grateful to the present owner, Major T. R. Mordaunt-Hare, and to his daughter for showing me the house and garden.
36. Diary, 31 October 1931, GS.
37. Ibid., 3 November 1931.
38. 'The Utopian Times', *CP*, p. 164. 'Break Silence', *CP*, p. 217. 'To a 17th Century Platonist', unpublished, in Tulsa notebook, copy in CUL add mss 9454/1/4.
39. Diary, 20 January 1932, GS.
40. Ibid., 5 February 1932.
41. In Tulsa notebook, copy in CUL add mss 9454/1/4.
42. Diary, 29 February 1932, GS.
43. 'The Hour-Glass', *CP*, p. 224. 'Prehistoric Burials', *CP*, p. 239.
44. Diary, 8 May 1933, GS.
45. 'Thoughts in 1932', *CP*, p. 231. 'Credo', *CP*, p. 226. 'Human Histories', *CP*, p. 223.
46. Diary, 19 July 1932, GS.
47. Ibid., 23 July 1932.
48. 'The Quiet House', unpublished, in Tulsa notebook, copy in CUL add mss 9454/1/4. 'First and Last Love' in *CP*, p. 211 as 'It Was the Love of Life, When I Was Young'. 'The Merciful Knight', *CP*, p. 221.
49. Diary, 20 August 1932, GS.
50. Ibid., 25 August 1932.
51. Sassoon to E. Blunden, 18 September 1932, HRC.
52. Diary, 23 September 1932, GS. In *CP* as 'An Emblem', p. 209.
53. 'Two Old Ladies', *CP*, p. 244. 'Babylon', *CP*, p. 223. 'Words for the Wordless', *CP*, p. 219. 'Metamorphosis', *CP*, p. 243.
54. Diary, 2 October 1932, GS.
55. Sassoon to V. Bonham Carter, 28 August 1932, Bodleian.
56. Diary, 19 November 1932, GS.

57. Ibid., 12 December 1932.
58. Ibid., 31 December 1932.
59. Ibid., 7 January 1933.
60. 'The Facts', *CP*, p. 171. 'November Dusk', *CP*, p. 245.
61. 30 November 1932, CUL add mss 9454/1/4.
62. Sassoon to E. Blunden, 22 December 1932, HRC. The poem is in *CP*, p. 204.
63. Diary, 12 January 1933, GS.
64. Ibid., 14 January 1933.
65. Ibid., 21 January 1933.
66. Ibid., 9 February 1933.
67. Ibid., 3 February 1933.
68. Sassoon to E. Blunden, 28 February 1933.
69. Diary, 3 March 1933, GS.
70. Ibid., 1 April 1933.
71. Ibid., 22 May 1933.
72. Archbishop Temple to Sassoon, 25 April 1933, Eton.
73. 'Antiquities', *CP*, p. 239. 'A Premonition', *CP*, p. 202. 'News from the War-After-Next', *CP*, p. 203. 'The Ultimate Atrocity', *CP*, p. 202. 'A Foreseeing' in Tulsa notebook, copy in CUL add mss 9454/1/6. 'At the Cenotaph', *CP*, p. 201.
74. Diary, 16 April 1933, GS.
75. Ibid., 18 May 1933.
76. Ibid., 19 May 1933.
77. Ibid., 26 May 1933.
78. Ibid., 30 May 1933.
79. Ibid., 5 June 1933.
80. Ibid., 9 June 1933.
81. Ibid., 26 June 1933.
82. Ibid., 10 July 1933. See also G. Keynes, *The Gates of Memory* (Oxford 1981).
83. Diary, 2 August 1933, GS.
84. Ibid., 14 August 1933.
85. Ibid., 19 August 1933.
86. G. Keynes to Sassoon, 26 June 1933, CUL add mss 8889/3/186.
87. G. Keynes to Sassoon, 16 July 1933, CUL add mss 8889/3/185.

88. G. Keynes to Sassoon, 20 July 1933, CUL add mss 8889/3/186.
89. Diary, 2 September 1933, GS.
90. Ibid., 5 September 1933.

18: Hester: 'A flower has opened in my heart'

1. *Morning Post*, 24 December 1924.
2. Diary, 7 September 1933, GS.
3. Ibid., 22 September 1933.
4. Ibid., October 6–7 1933.
5. Ibid., 8 October 1933.
6. Ibid., 11 October 1933.
7. Ibid., 12 October 1933.
8. Ibid., 23 October 1933.
9. Sassoon to Theresa, 25 October 1933, Berg.
10. Diary, 15 December 1933, GS.
11. Ibid., 31 October 1933.
12. Ibid., November 1933.
13. Sassoon to R. Meiklejohn, 10 November 1933, HRC.
14. Sassoon to R. Hodgson, 16 November 1933, Yale.
15. Sassoon to G. Keynes, 24 October 1933, CUL add mss 8633.
16. E. Olivier to R. Head, 24 October 1933, HRC.
17. R. Head to Sassoon, 25 October 1933, HRC.
18. O. Sitwell to Sassoon, 31 October 1933, Washington State, Pullman.
19. O. Morrell to Sassoon, 3 November 1933, Maryland.
20. O. Morrell journal, 25 October 1933, BL.
21. Ibid., 4 November 1933.
22. V. Woolf to Q. Bell, 21 December 1933, *Letters of Virginia Woolf*, ed. N. Nicolson and J. Trautmann, vol. 5 (London 1979) p. 262.
23. R. Graves to Sassoon, 21 November 1933, Berg.
24. E. Sitwell to G. Sitwell, December 1933, *Selected Letters of Edith Sitwell*, ed. R. Greene (London 1997) pp. 150–1.
25. Diary, 15 December 1933, GS.
26. Letters of December 1933 from 'Elizabeth' and 'John' in private collection.
27. Theresa to Sassoon, 16 December 1933, private collection.

28. Diary, 3 January 1934, GS.
29. P. N. Furbank, *E. M. Forster*, vol. 2 (London 1978) p. 181.
30. 'Some Recent Poetry', *TLS*, 15 March 1934.
31. *London Mercury*, January 1934.
32. Sassoon to R. Hodgson, 29 December 1933, Yale.
33. Diary, 7 June 1934, GS.
34. Ibid., 17 September 1934.
35. O. Morrell journal, 20 August 1934, BL.
36. Diary, 10 November 1934, GS.
37. Ibid., 17 December 1934.
38. Ibid., 31 December 1934.
39. Ibid., 30 October 1934.
40. 'Property', *CP*, p. 232. 'Ode', *CP*, p. 227. 'Gloria Mundi', *CP*, p. 251. 'Thanksgiving' in Tulsa notebook, copy in CUL add mss 9454/1/4. 'The Gains of Good', *CP*, p. 218. 'Long Ago', *CP*, p. 215. 'Possibly Poem', in Tulsa notebook, copy in CUL add mss 9454/1/5. 'Anno Domini', in Tulsa notebook, copy in CUL add mss 9454/1/6.
41. 'Alarums', in Tulsa notebook, copy in CUL add mss 9454/1/5. 'Asking for It', *CP*, p. 204. 'Memorandum', *CP*, p. 222. 'Again the Dead', *CP*, p. 220.
42. Reverend R. Sheppard to Hester, 15 July 1935, CUL add mss 9375/777.
43. *Birmingham Gazette*, 21 November 1936.
44. Sassoon to Reverend R. Sheppard, 22 October 1936, Lady Richardson.
45. Sassoon to E. Blunden, 6 April 1935, HRC.
46. Manuscript notes on the scenario entitled 'Arab No-Tes' in Maggs Catalogue, May 2001.
47. S.T. journal, 25 January 1936, Berg.
48. Ibid., 17 February 1936.
49. 'In Heytesbury Wood', *CP*, p. 234. 'A Pilgrim's Progress', in Tulsa notebook, copy in CUL add mss 9454/1/5. 'Vigil in Spring', *CP*, p. 210. 'Eulogy of My House', *CP*, p. 233. 'On Edington Hill', *CP*, p. 235.
50. Unpublished, in Tulsa notebook, copy in CUL add mss 9454/1/5, dated 9 September 1935.
51. 'Here on His Way . . .' in *CP*, p. 236 as '878–1935'. 'Silver Jubilee Celebration', *CP*, p. 236.

52. Sassoon to G. Keynes, 23 December 1935, CUL add mss 8633.
53. E. Sitwell to Sassoon, 22 December 1934, Washington State, Pullman.
54. Diary, 25 January 1936, GS.
55. 'Aunt Eudora and the Poets', *Spectator*, 31 January 1936.
56. 'Educating Aunt Eudora', *Spectator*, 14 February 1936.
57. *Spectator* 28 February 1936.
58. Diary, 18 July 1936, GS.
59. *IO* manuscript. IWM SS4.
60. Ibid.
61. Diary, 11 October 1949, GS.
62. Sassoon to C. Hassall, 4 April 1942, CUL add mss 8905.
63. *Evening Standard*, 3 September 1936.
64. *TLS*, 5 September 1936.
65. *Observer*, 6 September 1936.
66. E. M. Forster to Sassoon, 27 September 1936, Columbia ms coll Sassoon box 1.
67. Mrs C. O'Kelly to Sassoon, 30 September 1936, CUL add mss 9375/680.
68. *Morning Post*, 4 September 1936.
69. O. Morrell journal, 21 September 1936, BL.
70. *Manchester Guardian Weekly*, 11 September 1936.
71. Sassoon to R. Head, 9 September 1936, HRC.
72. Sassoon to R. Ellis Roberts, 9 September 1936, HRC.
73. Diary, 22 September 1936, GS.
74. Ibid., 1 November 1936.

19: 'A bullying barbarian of a world'

1. Sassoon to Heads, 3 November 1936, HRC.
2. 'Midsummer Eve', *CP*, p. 249. 'A Prayer from 1936', *CP*, p. 250. 'To My Son', *CP*, p. 251. 'Earth and Heaven', *CP*, p. 250. 'Outlived by Trees', *CP*, p. 233.
3. Sassoon to E. Blunden, 23 March 1937, HRC.
4. *Siegfried Sassoon: Letters to Max Beerbohm*, ed. R. Hart-Davis (London 1986) pp. 37–51.

5. Diary, 8 September 1937, GS.
6. Sassoon to H. E. Palmer, 19 December 1937, HRC.
7. 'Coronation Ode' in Tulsa notebook, copy in CUL add mss 9454/5ii.
8. 'Ideologies', *CP*, p. 244. 'A Remembered Queen', *CP*, p. 238. 'Wealth of Awareness', *CP*, p. 246. 'Old World to New', *CP*, p. 249.
9. 'Ancestral Admonition' in Tulsa notebook, copy in CUL add mss 9454/1/6.
10. *St Martin's Review*, December 1937.
11. 'Meeting and Parting', *CP*, p. 373.
12. Sassoon to H. M. Tomlinson, 3 January 1938, HRC.
13. J. R. Ackerley to Sassoon, 5 January 1938, Eton.
14. Sassoon to E. Blunden, 10 February 1938, HRC.
15. Sassoon to H. M. Tomlinson, 14 March 1938, HRC.
16. E. Blunden to Sassoon, 18 February 1938, HRC.
17. Theresa to Sassoon, 6 February 1938, private collection.
18. 'English Prose Between 1918 and 1939', in *Two Cheers for Democracy* (London 1951) p. 268.
19. *Siegfried Sassoon: Letters to Max Beerbohm*, p. 68.
20. Sassoon to G. Keynes, 2 June 1938, CUL add mss 8633.
21. Diary, June 1938, GS.
22. S. Tennant to Sassoon, 16 February 1938, Berg.
23. S.T. journal, July 1938, Berg.
24. S. Tennant to Sassoon, 16 September 1938, Berg.
25. S.T. journal, September 1938, Berg.
26. S. Tennant to Sassoon, 16 October 1938, Berg.
27. S.T. journal, November 1938, Berg.
28. S. Tennant to Sassoon, 13 March 1939, Berg.
29. *Sunday Express*, 4 June 1939.
30. Diary, 19 and 20 July 1938, GS.
31. Ibid., 11 August 1938.
32. T. H. White, *Letters to a Friend* (Gloucester 1984) pp. 240–1.
33. Sassoon to Lady Desborough, 8 October 1938, Hertford Record Office, D/ERV c2347/2.
34. R. L. Stevenson, *A Humble Remonstrance*, Swanston Edition of Stevenson, vol. ix (London 1912) pp. 151–2.
35. 'A Prelude to a Poet's Life', *Sunday Times*, 18 September 1938.
36. 'Mr Sassoon's First Years', *TLS*, 24 September 1938.

37. 'Boyhood', *Manchester Guardian*, 14 October 1938.
38. 'Poet's Memories', *Daily Telegraph*, 20 September 1938.
39. Sassoon to L. Whistler, 9 December 1938, L. Whistler.
40. 'A Local Train of Thought', *CP*, p. 240. 'Thoughts in 1938', *CP*, p. 241. 'A Blessing', *CP*, p. 252. 'Childhood's Eden' in Tulsa notebook, copy in CUL add mss 9454/1/5. 'Heart and Soul', *CP*, p. 247. 'Brevities', *CP*, p. 231. 'Second Birthday', in Tulsa notebook, copy in CUL add mss 9454/1/5. 'A View of Old Exeter', *CP*, p. 242.
41. Sassoon to R. Head, 21 November 1938, HRC.
42. Diary, 19 January 1939, GS.
43. Sassoon to E. Marsh, 3 May 1939, Berg.
44. Diary, 2 May 1939, GS.
45. See James Fergusson, 'Benson and Hedging', *R.S.L. Journal*, 2004, p. 72.
46. 18 June 1939, quoted in *Best of Friends*, pp. 66–7.
47. 'In the Rose Garden' is in the July 1939 diary, GS. 'The Word Faithful', in Tulsa notebook, copy in CUL add mss 9454/1/6.
48. Diary, 23 July 1939, GS.
49. Ibid., 15 August 1939.
50. S.T. journal, 14 August 1939, Berg.
51. Ibid., 2 September 1939.

20: 'In George I seem to live my life again'

1. Sassoon to G. Byam Shaw, 20 September 1939, CUL add mss 9454/3/250.
2. Diary, 3 November 1939, GS.
3. Ibid., 20 December 1939.
4. 'Doggerel About Old Days', *CP*, p. 255. 'Old Music', *CP*, p. 255. 'Youth and Maturity', 'A Moment's Memoirs' and 'Fifty Years Between Us' or 'To a Child', in Tulsa notebook, copy in CUL, Hart-Davis notebook, add mss 9454/1/6. 'Mid-August Meditation' in Tulsa notebook, copy in CUL add mss 9454/1/5iii.
5. Diary, 11 May 1940, GS.
6. Ibid., 14 May 1940.
7. Ibid., 24 May 1940.
8. Sassoon to Mr Bishop, 1 September 1940, Tulsa.

9. Sassoon to S. Behrman, 10 July 1940, NYPL.

10. Diary, 15 September 1940, GS.

11. These are 'The English Spirit', *CP*, p. 256; and 'Silent Service', *CP*, p. 257.

12. Diary, 6 June 1940, GS.

13. Ibid., 24 July 1940.

14. Ibid., 12 August 1940.

15. Ibid., 14 August 1940.

16. Ibid., 16 August 1940.

17. Ibid., 21 August 1940.

18. Ibid., 22 September 1940.

19. Sassoon to H. M. Tomlinson, 4 December 1940, HRC.

20. Sassoon to H. E. Palmer, 12 December 1940, HRC.

21. 'Peace Remembered', *TLS*, 2 November 1940.

22. 'Looking Backward', *Spectator*, 15 November 1940.

23. 'Poets of Two Wars', *New Statesman*, 7 December 1940.

24. 'The Child at the Window', *CP*, p. 252. 'Progressions', *CP*, p. 253. 'A Bedtime Story' in Tulsa notebook, copy in CUL add mss 9454/1/6.

25. 'Man and Dog', *CP*, p. 268.

26. Diary, 5 August 1942, GS.

27. S.T. journal, August 1942, Berg.

28. Sassoon to G. Byam Shaw, 23 September 1942, CUL add mss 9454/3/271.

29. Diary, August 1942, GS.

30. H. G. Wells to Sassoon, 23 October 1942, McMaster.

31. 'Education of a Poet', *TLS*, 31 October 1942.

32. Ibid., 8 February 1943.

33. R. Graves to E. Marsh, 19 October 1942, Berg.

34. P. Quennell, 'A Quiet Life', *Observer*, 15 November 1942.

35. Sassoon to Mrs O. Williams, 14 January 1943, Eton.

36. Diary, 14 November 1942, GS.

37. Ibid., 27 December 1942.

38. 'The Hardened Heart', *CP*, p. 264. 'On Scratchbury Camp', *CP*, p. 279.

39. Diary, 12 October 1942, GS.

40. Ibid., 18 September 1943.

41. Ibid., 3 April 1943.

42. 'Cleaning the Candelabrum', *CP*, p. 281. 'Go, Words, on Winds of War', in *Spectator*, 2 April 1943.
43. Diary, 13 June 1943, GS.
44. Ibid., 3 July 1943.
45. Ibid., 11 July 1943.
46. Ibid., 13 July 1943.
47. Interview with Claire Blunden.
48. Diary, 22 August 1943, GS.
49. Ibid., 3 September 1943.
50. 'Microcosmos', *CP*, p. v. 'Early March', *CP*, p. 278. 'Getting Queer in Wartime', 'The Child on the Lawn' and 'Gone' in Tulsa notebook, copy in CUL add mss 9454/1/6.
51. Sassoon to H. M. Tomlinson, 12 November 1943, HRC.

21: The hardened heart

1. Theresa to Sassoon, 3 May 1944, private collection.
2. Diary, 12 November 1944, GS.
3. Ibid., 20 May 1944.
4. Ibid., 25 May 1944.
5. Ibid., 2 November 1944.
6. Ibid., 29 July 1944.
7. Ibid., 31 August 1944.
8. 'Nirvana', 'A Glimpse of Fitz' and 'Valediction to Youth' are all in Tulsa notebook, copy in CUL add mss 9454/1/6.
9. Sassoon to G. Byam Shaw, 10 February 1945, CUL add mss 9454/3/288.
10. Diary, 11 January 1945, GS.
11. Sassoon to E. Blunden, 26 February 1945, HRC.
12. Sassoon to E. Blunden, 21 July 1945, HRC.
13. Diary, 8 May 1945, GS.
14. 'Easter 1945', *Observer* 1 April 1945. 'Lines (To Some Who Say Production Won the War)', *Observer*, 6 May 1945.
15. H. Sassoon to P. Gatty, n.d., CUL add mss 8276/61.
16. Diary, 1 November 1945, GS.
17. Ibid., 14 February 1946.

18. Ibid., August 1945.
19. Sassoon to S. Cockerell, 7 May 1945, BL add mss 52752/67.
20. H. Sassoon to P. Gatty, n.d., CUL add mss 8276/61.
21. Sassoon to G. Byam Shaw, 30 October 1945, CUL add mss 9454/3/293.
22. Diary, 12 July 1945, GS.
23. Ibid., 23 September 1945.
24. Ibid., 1 October 1945.
25. Ibid., 9 October 1945.
26. E. Blunden to Sassoon, 1 December 1945, HRC.
27. Ibid., 25 December 1945.
28. Ibid., 10 November 1945.
29. The Belsen sonnet is in Tulsa notebook, copy in CUL add mss 9454/1/6, as is 'Sanctuary'. 'Litany of the Lost', *CP*, p. 205.
30. Alan Ross, *Blindfold Games* (London 1986) p. 239.
31. 'Sassoon Flashbacks – Or How an Author Changes', *Sunday Graphic*, 17 December 1945.
32. 'Siegfried Sassoon Fills in the Blanks', *Daily Dispatch*, 29 December 1945.
33. 'Books in General', *New Statesman*, 19 January 1946.
34. E. Olivier to Sassoon, 16 December 1945, Columbia, ms coll Sassoon box 1.
35. Diary, 5 January 1946, GS.
36. M. Donaldson to Sassoon, 4 January 1946, CUL add mss 9375/226.
37. H. Waddell to Sassoon, 25 March 1946, George Ramsden, York.
38. 'A Poet Reviews His Journey', *TLS*, 5 January 1946.
39. *Time and Tide*, 2 March 1946.
40. H. Owen to Sassoon, 20 March 1946, Columbia ms coll W. Owen.
41. 'Heigh-Ho!', *Irish Times*, 2 March 1946.
42. 'Sassoon Memoirs Self-Important Record of Life with Literati', 23 March 1946, untitled clipping in GS papers.
43. 'Two Books That Leave You Blank', *New Yorker*, 30 March 1946.
44. E. Blunden to Sassoon, 25 September 1944, HRC.
45. Diary, 11 January 1946, GS.
46. M. Sadleir to Sassoon, 1 February 1946, HRC.
47. A. Lousada memorandum, 11 February 1946, Stephenson Harwood.
48. Diary, 31 July 1946, GS.

49. Ibid., 7 August 1946.
50. Ibid., 14 August 1946.
51. 'A Salutation', 1 November 1946, copy at HRC.
52. Sassoon to R. Hart-Davis, 2 May 1946, Tulsa, copy in CUL add mss 9454/3/379. The poem is in *CP*, p. 251.

22: Heytesbury's solitary squire

1. Diary, 6 January 1947, GS.
2. Ibid., 30 March 1947.
3. O. Kyllmann to Sassoon, 19 May 1947, CUL add mss 9375/983.
4. Diary, 14 May 1947, GS.
5. Ibid., 11 July 1947.
6. Sassoon to G. Byam Shaw, 18 July 1947, CUL add mss 9454/3/311.
7. Ibid.
8. Diary, 22 September 1947, GS.
9. 'A Poet's Variety', *Spectator*, 19 September 1947.
10. Diary, 12 October 1947, GS.
11. *Listener*, 16 October 1947.
12. 'The Poetry of Siegfried Sassoon', *TLS*, 1 November 1947.
13. *Fortnightly Review*, December 1947.
14. Diary, 13 December 1947, GS.
15. Sassoon to R. Hodgson, 25 February 1948, Yale.
16. 'A Child Denied', in Tulsa notebook, copy in CUL add mss 9454/1/6.
17. 'Solitudes at Sixty', *CP*, p. 276. 'In Time of Decivilisation', *CP*, p. 265. 'Hypnogogic Inventions', in Tulsa notebook, copy in CUL add mss 9454/1/6.
18. Sassoon to Mother Margaret Mary, 28 January 1957, CUL add mss 7935.
19. Diary, 21 February 1948, GS. 'Old-Fashioned Weather', *CP*, p. 277.
20. Diary, 28 April 1948, GS.
21. Interviews with Haro Hodson.
22. Diary, 30 July 1948, GS.
23. Ibid., 10 February 1948.
24. 'The Poet's Novelist', *TLS*, 18 September 1948.
25. From Richard Hudson, *TLS*, 4 December 1948.

26. *TLS*, 11 December 1948.
27. Sassoon to L. P. Hartley, 25 September 1948, John Rylands Library.
28. 'Everything But Simplicity', *Time*, 8 November 1948.
29. 'Tristram Shandy of the Biographers', *NYT*, 31 October 1948.
30. *Atlantic Monthly*, December 1948.
31. S. Sassoon, *Meredith* (London 1948) p. 115.
32. Hester to G. Keynes, October 1948, CUL add mss 8633.
33. Sassoon to H. Hodson, 30 October, 4 November, 9 November 1948, CUL add mss 9608.
34. Interview with Laurence Whistler.
35. Sassoon to H. Hodson, 16 November 1948, CUL add mss 9608.
36. Diary, 31 December 1948, GS.
37. 'Old-Fashioned Weather', *CP*, p. 277. 'Praise Persistent', *CP*, p. 269. 'Ultimate Values', *CP*, p. 277.
38. Sassoon to H. Hodson, 7 February 1949, CUL add mss 9608.
39. *Nation*, 15 January 1949.
40. 'Resurrection', *CP*, p. 270.
41. 'A Falloden Memory', *CP*, p. 280.
42. Diary, 11 March 1948, GS.
43. Ibid., 24 May 1949.
44. Ibid., 7 December 1947.
45. O. Sitwell to Sassoon, 24 May 1949, Washington State, Pullman.
46. Sassoon to C. Hassall, 7 June 1949, CUL add mss 8905.
47. Diary, 24 June 1949, GS.
48. Ackerley journal, Berg.
49. Diary, 21 September 1949, GS.
50. Ibid., 2 October 1949.
51. 'Spectators', in Tulsa notebook, copy in CUL add mss 9454/1/6. 'Acceptance', *CP*, p. 284. 'The Unproven', *CP*, p. 261. 'Redemption', *CP*, p. 271.
52. Diary, 16 November 1949, GS.

23: The search

1. Diary, 23–24 May 1950, GS. For Welland's account see 'Sassoon on Owen' by D. Welland, *TLS*, 31 May 1974.

2. Diary, 25 May 1950, GS.
3. Deed of Separation, 4 December 1950, Stephenson Harwood.
4. Interview with Pamela Gatty.
5. Diary, 12 December 1950, GS.
6. Ibid., December 13–16 1950.
7. See O. Sitwell, *Noble Essences* (London 1950) p. 98.
8. Welland, 'Sassoon on Owen'.
9. In Tulsa notebook, copy in CUL add mss 9454/1/6.
10. Diary, 17 August 1953, GS.
11. Sassoon to H. M. Tomlinson, 17 August 1953, HRC.
12. Sassoon to K. Hopkins, 2 January 1951, HRC.
13. Sassoon to R. Seymour, 10 May 1951, Rutgers.
14. Sassoon to R. Gathorne-Hardy, 9 February 1950, Lilly Library.
15. Sassoon to R. Gathorne-Hardy, 13 March 1950, Lilly Library.
16. Sassoon to R. Gathorne-Hardy, 31 March 1950, Lilly Library.
17. Sassoon to R. Gathorne-Hardy, 25 May 1950, Lilly Library.
18. 'Contemporary Christmas' in *Common Chords*, p. 14. 'At Max Gate',
    CP, p. 263.
19. Diary, 13 July 1951, GS.
20. E. Marsh to Sassoon, 8 August 1951, Eton.
21. E. Marsh to Sassoon, 10 January 1952, Eton.
22. Ibid., 26 September 1952.
23. Ibid., 28 February 1951.
24. Interview with Haro and Elizabeth Hodson.
25. Diary, 3 August 1951, GS.
26. Ibid., 29 January 1952.
27. Interview with Laurence Whistler.
28. Sassoon to E. Blunden, 18 April 1952, HRC.
29. Diary, 2 June 1952, GS.
30. Ibid., 24 September 1952.
31. Ibid., 28 September 1952.
32. Sassoon to E. Blunden, 10 November 1952, HRC.
33. Sassoon to E. Blunden, 1 April 1952, HRC.
34. Sassoon to H. M. Tomlinson, 1 January 1953, owned by the late Dr
    Lionel Dakers. 'The Tasking', *CP*, p. 291.
35. Diary, 17 January 1953, GS.
36. 'Another Spring', *CP*, p. 296.

37. Sassoon to E. Blunden, 6 February 1953, HRC.
38. Sassoon to E. Blunden, 26 February 1953, HRC.
39. Diary, 7 April 1953, GS.
40. E. Blunden to Sassoon, 8 May 1953, HRC.
41. Sassoon to E. Blunden, 11 May 1953, HRC.
42. A. Marshall to Sassoon, 22 March 1953, Columbia.
43. A. Marshall to Sassoon, 22 April 1953, Columbia.
44. Diary, 23 August 1953, GS.
45. Ibid., 15 September 1953.
46. Ibid., 13 November 1953.
47. Ibid., 5 December 1953.

24: 'At the end of all wrong roads I came'

1. Diary, 24 January 1954, GS.
2. Manuscript notes for *The Tasking*, GS.
3. Sassoon to P. Gosse, 6 April 1955, HRC.
4. Sassoon to Dame F. Corrigan, 9 December 1959, Corrigan papers.
5. Sassoon to Dame F. Corrigan, 5 August 1960, Corrigan papers.
6. 'Faith Unfaithful', *CP*, p. 294. 'Deliverance, *PP*, p. 173. 'An Epitome', *CP*, p. 300.
7. Sassoon to N. Herbert, n.d., Lord Hemingford.
8. Sassoon to G. Keynes, 28 May 1954, CUL add mss 8633.
9. 'Poet and Man of Action', *John O' London's Weekly*, 10 September 1954.
10. R. P. Graves, *Robert Graves and the White Goddess* (London paperback edition 1998) p. 240.
11. Sassoon to B. Huebsch, 24 March 1955, Columbia ms coll Huebsch.
12. C. Causley, 'Writers Remembered: Siegfried Sassoon', *Author*, Winter 1989.
13. Ibid.
14. Lady Horner, *Time Remembered* (London 1933) p. 194.
15. Sassoon to Dame F. Corrigan, 21 January 1960, Corrigan papers.
16. *PP*, p. 196.
17. H. van Zeller, *One Foot in the Cradle* (London 1965) p. 244.
18. Sassoon to Dame F. Corrigan, 18 February 1960, Corrigan papers.

19. Sassoon to S. Cockerell, 9 September 1955, HRC.
20. Sassoon to L. Whistler, 28 January 1956, Laurence Whistler.
21. F. Swinnerton to Sassoon, 6 February 1956, Berg.
22. *New Statesman*, quoted in W. Blunt, *Cockerell* (London 1964) pp. 340–1.
23. Sassoon to L. Whistler, 16 February 1956, Laurence Whistler.
24. Typescript of *A Tribute to Sir Max Beerbohm*, 28 June 1956, CUL add mss 8633.
25. Sassoon to H. Sassoon, 14 January 1957, GS.
26. 'Mr Sassoon in Contemplative Mood', *TLS*, 4 January 1957.
27. *Listener*, 27 December 1956.
28. P. Larkin, *Further Requirements*, ed. A. Thwaite (London 2001) pp. 163–4. Original piece in the *Manchester Guardian*, 30 November 1956.
29. Sassoon to E. Blunden, 6 January 1957, HRC. The Larkin poem is probably 'Dry Point' in *The Less Deceived* (Hull 1955).
30. Quoted by Sassoon in letter to E. Blunden, 6 January 1957, HRC.
31. *Independent* obituary, 2 May 2001.
32. Ibid.
33. Mother Margaret Mary to R. Hart-Davis, February 1968, copy in CUL add mss 9454/6/23.
34. Sassoon to Mother Margaret Mary, 31 March 1957, CUL add mss 7935.
35. Sassoon to Mother Margaret Mary, 10 January 1957.
36. Sassoon to Mother Margaret Mary, 31 March 1957.
37. Sassoon to Mother Margaret Mary, 1 April 1957.
38. Sassoon to Mother Margaret Mary, 4 April 1957.
39. Sassoon to Mother Margaret Mary, 5 April 1957.
40. Sassoon to Mother Margaret Mary, 29 April 1957.
41. Sassoon to Mother Margaret Mary, 29 May 1957.
42. Interview with Dom Sebastian Moore.
43. 'A Thoroughly English Poet', *The Times*, 29 June 1967.
44. Sassoon to Katharine Asquith, 'St Matthew', 1960. Mells papers.
45. Diary, 12 October 1933, GS.
46. Sassoon to C. Tomkinson, 16 August 1957, CUL add mss 7595/43.
47. G. Byam Shaw to Sassoon, 11 September 1957, Columbia ms Sassoon box 2.

48. 'Poet Siegfried Sassoon Becomes a Roman Catholic', *Sunday Express*, 22 September 1957.
49. *The Times*, 1 October 1957.
50. *The Times*, 5 October 1957.
51. E. M. Forster to Sassoon, 27 September 1957, GS.
52. Sassoon to E. M. Forster, 30 September 1957, King's College, Cambridge EMF xviii Sassoon.
53. L. Whistler to Sassoon, 30 October 1957, GS.
54. R. Graves to Sassoon, 28 November 1957, GS.
55. Sassoon to R. Graves, 7 December 1957, *In Broken Images*, p. 347.
56. Sassoon to Mother Margaret Mary, Christmas Day 1957, CUL add mss 7935.

25: 'Trying to be like Our Lord'

1. Sassoon to Mother Margaret Mary, 21 April 1958, CUL add mss 7935.
2. Sassoon to Dame F. Corrigan, 18 February 1960, Corrigan papers.
3. Sassoon to Mother Margaret Mary, 5 February 1958, CUL add mss 7935.
4. Sassoon to Mother Margaret Mary, 4 August 1958.
5. Sassoon to Mother Margaret Mary, 9 September 1959.
6. Sassoon to Mother Margaret Mary, 22 December 1958.
7. For an account of this meeting, see *The Lyttelton–Hart-Davis Letters*, ed. Rupert Hart-Davis, vol. 3 (London 1981) pp. 140–1.
8. P. Ziegler, *Rupert Hart-Davis* (London 2004) p. 135.
9. Sassoon to R. Hart-Davis, 21 February 1967, quoted in R. Hart-Davis, *Halfway to Heaven* (Stroud 1998) p. 78.
10. Ibid.
11. Sassoon to Mother Margaret Mary, 23 February 1958, CUL add mss 7935.
12. Interview with Dennis Silk.
13. Sassoon to K. Asquith, 23 November 1959, Asquith.
14. Dame F. Corrigan to Sassoon, n.d., typed copy in Corrigan papers.
15. *PP*, p. 192.
16. Interview with Dame Felicitas Corrigan, 1998.

17. Sassoon to Mother Margaret Mary, 31 October 1966, CUL add mss 7935.
18. Sassoon to Mother Margaret Mary, 6 July 1959.
19. Dame F. Corrigan to G. Keynes, 26 August 1973, CUL add mss 8633.
20. 'Siegfried Sassoon in pace 1 September 1967', in Corrigan papers.
21. Sassoon to Dame H. Cumming, 9 June 1960, National Art Library, V&A.
22. Sassoon to Dame F. Corrigan, 14 November 1959, Corrigan papers.
23. I. Davie to Sassoon, 29 April 1960, CUL add mss 9375/198.
24. 'Piers Prodigal' in I. Davie, *Piers Prodigal and Other Poems* (London 1961).
25. Sassoon to I. Davie, 26 May 1960, George Ramsden.
26. Sassoon to K. Asquith, 26 July 1960, Asquith.
27. Interview with Ian Davie, 1999.
28. Sassoon to I. Davie, 21 October 1961, George Ramsden.
29. Sassoon to Dame F. Corrigan, 13 June 1960, Corrigan papers.
30. Sassoon to I. Davie, 10 May 1961, George Ramsden.
31. Sassoon to Dame F. Corrigan, 5 August 1964, Corrigan papers.
32. Sir A. Lascelles to R. Hart-Davis, 15 June 1963, Duff Hart-Davis.
33. Interview with Lyn Humphries.
34. D. Welland to Sassoon, 4 October 1960, CUL add mss 9375/930.

26: 'My final test of endurance'

1. 'Poems of the Soul', *TLS*, 24 February 1961.
2. R. de la Mare to Sir A. Lascelles, 15 January 1962, Tulsa, copy in CUL add mss 9454/3/549.
3. 'Sassoon's Progress', *Spectator*, 23 June 1961.
4. 'Edwardian Swan Songs', *Observer*, 25 June 1961.
5. Sassoon to Mother Margaret Mary, 7 November 1961, CUL add mss 7935.
6. These are in manuscript – or versions printed at Stanbrook – with letters to Katharine Asquith, still owned by her family.
7. Sassoon to Mother Margaret Mary, 10 September 1961, CUL add mss 7935.

8. Sassoon to K. Asquith, 12 February 1962, Asquith.

9. *PP*, p. 224.

10. *Letters to a Critic*, 16 October 1963, p. 10.

11. Ibid., 17 August 1965, p. 11.

12. Sassoon to K. Asquith, 20 February 1963, Asquith.

13. A. Powell, *The Strangers All Are Gone* (London 1982) pp. 41–6.

14. 'Siegfried Sassoon CBE, Hon Fellow of Clare, 5 June 1965', in Asquith papers.

15. Sassoon to K. Asquith, 22 December 1965, Asquith.

16. Sassoon to Mother Margaret Mary, 19 January 1966, CUL add mss 7935.

17. Sassoon to R. Hart-Davis, 21 August 1966, Tulsa, copy in CUL add mss 9454/3/433.

18. *Letters to a Critic*, 12 August 1966, pp. 13–17.

19. C. Causley, 'Writers Remembered: Siegfried Sassoon', *Author*, Winter 1989.

20. Sassoon to G. Keynes, 6 September 1966, CUL add mss 8633.

21. W. L. Webb, 'Sassoon the Survivor', *Guardian*, 8 September 1966.

22. Sassoon to Sir A. Lascelles, 15 September 1966, Tulsa, copy in CUL add mss 9454/3/542.

23. Sassoon to Sir A. Lascelles, 15 September 1966.

24. Sassoon to V. King, 26 June 1967, Liddle Collection, Brotherton.

25. Interview with Dom Philip Jebb, Downside, 3 December 1998.

26. Hart-Davis, *Halfway to Heaven*, p. 83.

27. R. Hart-Davis to G. Keynes, 23 August 1967, CUL add mss 8633.

28. Mother Margaret Mary to I. Davie, 31 August 1967, George Ramsden.

29. Mother Margaret Mary to R. Hart-Davis, 27 August 1967, Tulsa, copy in CUL add mss 9454/6/18.

30. Dom W. Phillipson, 'A Tribute to Siegfried Sassoon', *Westminster Cathedral Chronicle*, October 1967.

31. Mother Margaret Mary to I. Davie, n.d., George Ramsden.

32. G. Sassoon to V. King, 2 September 1967, Liddle Collection, Brotherton.

Epilogue

1. Death certificate in the possession of G. Sassoon.
2. I am grateful to Haro Hodson for giving me a detailed account of the service and the reception afterwards at Mells.
3. Typescript in CUL add mss 9454/6/41a.
4. 'Sassoon – The Poet of Passchendaele', *Observer*, 3 September 1967.
5. *Radio Times*, 29 January 1970.
6. Hester to R. Gatty, n.d., Gatty collection, shown to me by Pamela Gatty.
7. G. Byam Shaw to R. Hart-Davis, 28 April 1974, Tulsa, copy in CUL add mss 9454/6/6.

Bibliography

MANUSCRIPT SOURCES

In addition to papers owned by his family or in private hands, the principal public collections of Siegfried Sassoon material in the United Kingdom are in the British Library (now also with the journals and papers of Lady Ottoline Morrell), the Cambridge University Library and the Imperial War Museum. There is additional material in the museum and archives of the Royal Welch Fusiliers at Carnarvon; the National Army Museum in Royal Hospital Road, Chelsea, London; the Bodleian Library, Oxford (the papers of T. E. Lawrence, Robert Nichols, Rolfe Barber, Violet Bonham Carter and Lady Colefax); the King's College Archives Centre at King's College, Cambridge (Edward Dent's diaries, Sassoon's correspondence with E. M. Forster and papers relating to Gabriel Atkin); the Brotherton Library at the University of Leeds (correspondence with Edmund Gosse and First War material in the Peter Liddle collection); the Henry Moore Centre at Leeds (the papers of the Thornycroft family); the National Art Library at the Victoria and Albert Museum (Dame Hildelith Cumming's correspondence with Sassoon); the Wiltshire County Record Office (diaries and papers of Edith Olivier).

In North America, the main Sassoon collections can be found at the Harry Ransom Humanities Center at the University of Texas at Austin; the Berg Collection in the New York Public Library (with notebooks and papers of Stephen Tennant); the Butler Library at Columbia University in

New York. Additional material is in the Beinecke Library at Yale University, New Haven (correspondence with Ralph Hodgson); the Southern Illinois University at Carbondale (correspondence with Robert Graves); Rutgers University in New Brunswick, New Jersey (correspondence with Edmund Gosse and the Reverend Richard Seymour); the New York Public Library (the papers and diaries of S. N. Behrman); Washington State University at Pullman (the Sitwell papers); McMaster University in Hamilton, Ontario (Bertrand Russell's papers); Wichita State University (papers of Gabriel Atkin). While I was writing this book, the late Kenneth Lohf left his British war poets collection, which he had kindly made available to me, to the Morgan Library in New York.

BOOKS BY SIEGFRIED SASSOON

Poetry

Poems (London 1906)
Orpheus in Diloeryum (London 1908)
Sonnets and Verses (London 1909)
Sonnets (London 1909)
Twelve Sonnets (London 1911)
Poems (London 1911)
Melodies (London 1912)
Hyacinth (London 1912)
Ode for Music (London 1912)
The Daffodil Murderer (London 1913)
Discoveries (London 1915)
Morning-Glory (London 1916)
The Old Huntsman and Other Poems (London 1917)
Counter-Attack and Other Poems (London 1918)
Picture Show (Cambridge 1919)
War Poems (London 1919)
Recreations (London 1923)
Lingual Exercises (Cambridge 1925)
Selected Poems (London 1925)
Satirical Poems (London 1926)

The Heart's Journey (London 1927)
Poems by Pinchbeck Lyre (London 1931)
The Road to Ruin (London 1933)
Vigils (London 1934)
Rhymed Ruminations (London 1939)
Poems Newly Selected (London 1940)
Collected Poems (London 1947)
Common Chords (Stanford Dingley 1950)
Emblems of Experience (Cambridge 1951)
The Tasking (Cambridge 1954)
Sequences (London 1956)
Lenten Illuminations (Downside 1959)
The Path to Peace (Stanbrook 1960)
Collected Poems 1908–1956 (London 1961)
An Octave (London 1966)
The War Poems (London 1983)

Prose

Memoirs of a Fox-hunting Man (London 1928)
Memoirs of an Infantry Officer (London 1930)
Sherston's Progress (London 1936)
The Complete Memoirs of George Sherston (London 1937)
The Old Century and Seven More Years (London 1938)
On Poetry (Bristol 1939)
The Weald of Youth (London 1942)
Siegfried's Journey (London 1945)
Meredith (London 1948)
An Adjustment (Royston 1955)
Something About Myself (Stanbrook 1966)
Letters to a Critic, with introduction and notes by Michael Thorpe
    (Nettlestead 1976)
Diaries 1920–1922, ed. Rupert Hart-Davis (London 1981)
Diaries 1915–1918, ed. Rupert Hart-Davis (London 1983)
Diaries 1923–1925, ed. Rupert Hart-Davis (London 1985)
Letters to Max Beerbohm, ed. Rupert Hart-Davis (London 1986)

BOOKS WITH ORIGINAL CONTRIBUTIONS
BY SIEGFRIED SASSOON

Poems by Wilfred Owen, with an introduction by Siegfried Sassoon (London 1920)

Great Names, ed. W. J. Turner (New York 1924). Sassoon contributed the piece on Thomas Hardy

Regimental Records of the Royal Welch Fusiliers by Major C. H. Dudley Ward (London 1928–9). Sassoon wrote long sections of the account of the second battle of the Scarpe in vol. 3, pp. 275–85, and two paragraphs on the physical experience of soldiering in a battle zone in vol. 4, p. 257

New Forget-Me-Not, decorated by Rex Whistler (London 1929) with the prose piece 'The Circus' by Siegfried Sassoon

Handley Cross by R. Surtees, a new edition introduced by Siegfried Sassoon (1930)

Hillingdon Hall by R. Surtees, introduced by Siegfried Sassoon (London 1931)

New Keepsake, decorated by Rex Whistler. Sassoon contributed 'The Utopian Times' (London 1931)

We Did Not Fight, ed. Julian Bell. Sassoon contributed 'Asking for It' (London 1935)

The Collected Works of Isaac Rosenberg, ed. Gordon Bottomley and Denys Harding, with a foreword by Siegfried Sassoon (London 1937)

The War the Infantry Knew, ed. Captain J. C. Dunn. Sassoon wrote 'A Subaltern's Service in Camp and Action' (12 March to 1 April 1917) in chapter 12 (London 1938, paperback edition 1997)

Poems from Italy, with an introduction by Siegfried Sassoon (London 1945)

The Saturday Book, ed. Leonard Russell. Sassoon contributed 'Footnotes on the Last Fifty Years' (London 1946)

My First Horse, ed. Peter Lunn (London 1947)

Tribute to Walter de la Mare on his Seventy-Fifth Birthday. 'Salutation from an old friend' (London 1948)

Fright in the Forest, a novel by Benn Sowerby, with an introduction by Siegfried Sassoon (London 1951)

Sport from Within by Frank Atherton Brown, with a foreword by Siegfried Sassoon (London 1952)

Collected Poems by Anna Gordon Keown, with a foreword by Siegfried Sassoon (London 1953)

Hunting Scenes from Surtees, with an introduction by Siegfried Sassoon (London 1953)

Safety Last by Lieutenant Colonel W. F. Stirling with a foreword by Siegfried Sassoon (London 1953)

Piers Prodigal and Other Poems by Ian Davie, with a foreword by Siegfried Sassoon (London 1961)

WORKS BY OTHERS

Ackerley, J. R. *The Letters of J. R. Ackerley*, ed. Neville Braybrooke (London 1975)

——. *My Sister and Myself: The Diaries of J. R. Ackerley*, ed. Francis King (London 1982)

Adams, J. B. P. *Nothing of Importance* (London 1917)

Amory, Mark. *Lord Berners: The Last Eccentric* (London 1998)

Asquith, Cynthia. *Diaries 1915–18* (London 1968)

Barbusse, Henri. *Under Fire* (London 1917)

Barnett, Correlli. *The Collapse of British Power* (London 1972)

Baxter, B. *Strange Street* (London 1935)

Beaton, Cecil. *Self-Portrait with Friends: The Selected Diaries of Cecil Beaton*, ed. R. Buckle (London 1979)

Becket, Ian F. W. *The First World War 1914–1918* (Harlow 2001)

Beerbohm, Max. *The Letters of Max Beerbohm 1882–1956*, ed. Rupert Hart-Davis (Oxford 1981)

Behrman, Sam. *Portrait of Max: An Intimate Memoir of Sir Max Beerbohm* (London 1960)

——. *People in a Diary* (New York 1972), published in Britain as *Tribulations and Laughter* (London 1972)

Belloc Lowndes, Mrs. *A Passing World* (London 1948)

Bennett, Arnold. *The Journals*, ed. Frank Swinnerton (London, Penguin edition 1984)

——. *The Letters of Arnold Bennett*, ed. J. Hepburn (Oxford 1968)

Bergonzi, Bernard. *Heroes' Twilight* (Manchester 1996 edition)
——. *Wartime & Aftermath* (Oxford 1993)
Bernhardt, Sarah. *My Double Life* (London 1907)
Blow, Simon. *Broken Blood* (London 1987)
Blunden, Edmund. *Undertones of War* (London Penguin edition 2000)
——. *Cricket Country* (London 1945)
Blunt, Wilfrid. *Cockerell* (London 1964)
Bond, Brian. *A Victory Worse than Defeat? British Interpretations of the First World War*, the Liddell Hart Centre for Military Archives lecture 1997 (London 1997)
——. *The Unquiet Western Front* (Cambridge 2002)
Borland, Maureen. *Wilde's Devoted Friend* (London 1990)
Bradford, Sarah. *Sacheverell Sitwell* (London 1993)
Bradley, A. C. et al. *A History of Marlborough College* (London 1923)
Brown, W. Sorley. *The Life and Genius of T. W. H. Crosland* (London 1928)
Caesar, Adrian. *Taking It Like a Man: Suffering, Sexuality and the War Poets* (Manchester 1993)
Campbell, Patrick. *Siegfried Sassoon: A Study of the War Poetry* (Jefferson, North Carolina 1999)
Cannadine, David. *G. M. Trevelyan* (London 1992)
Cecil, David. *Max: A Biography* (London 1964)
Cecil, Hugh. *The Flower of Battle: British Writers and the First World War* (London 1995)
Cecil, Hugh and Peter H. Liddle, eds. *Facing Armageddon: The First World War Experienced* (Barnsley 1996)
——. *At the Eleventh Hour: Reflections, Hopes and Anxieties at the Closing of the Great War 1918* (Barnsley 1998)
Chapman, Guy. *A Passionate Prodigality* (London 1933)
——. *Vain Glory* (London 1937)
Cockerell, Sydney, *The Best of Friends: Further Letters to Sydney Cockerell*, ed. Viola Meynell (London 1956)
Connon, Bryan. *Beverley Nichols* (London 1991)
Corrigan, Dame Felicitas. *Siegfried Sassoon: Poet's Pilgrimage* (London 1973)
——. *Helen Waddell* (London 1986)
Cunningham, Valentine. *British Writers of the Thirties* (Oxford 1988)

Dakers, Caroline. *The Countryside at War 1914–1918* (London 1987)
——. *The Holland Park Circle* (London and New Haven 1999)
Darton, J. Harvey. *From Surtees to Sassoon* (London 1931)
Douglas, Keith. *A Prose Miscellany* (Manchester 1985)
Duhamel, Georges. *The New Book of Martyrs* (London 1918)
Dunn, Captain J. C. *The War the Infantry Knew* (1938, and paperback edition of 1997)
Edmonds, Charles (Charles Carrington), *A Subaltern's War* (London 1929)
Edwards, H. I. Powell. *The Sussex Yeomanry and 16th (Sussex Yeomanry) Battalion, the Royal Sussex Regiment 1914–1919* (London 1921)
Eksteins, Modris. *Rites of Spring: The Great War and the Birth of the Modern Age* (London 1989)
Ellmann, Richard. *Oscar Wilde.* (London 1987)
Farmer, David, ed. *Siegfried Sassoon: A Memorial Exhibition*, with an introduction by Edmund Blunden. (Austin 1969)
Ferguson, Niall. *The Pity of War* (London 1998)
Fergusson, James. *More from the Obelus, books and papers from the library of Siegfried Sassoon and others* (London 1992)
Fitzgerald, Penelope. *Charlotte Mew and Her Friends* (London 1984)
Forster, E. M. *Two Cheers for Democracy* (London 1951)
——. *Selected Letters*, ed. Mary Iago and P. N. Furbank (London 1983)
Fryer, Jonathan. *Robbie Ross* (London 2000)
Furbank, P. N. *E. M. Forster: A Life*, vol. 1: *The Growth of the Novelist*, vol. 2: *Polycrates's Ring* (London 1977–8)
Fussell, Paul. *The Great War and Modern Memory* (Oxford 1975)
Girouard, Mark. *The Return to Camelot* (London and New Haven 1981)
Gittings, Robert. *The Older Hardy* (London 1978)
——. with Jo Manton. *The Second Mrs Hardy* (Oxford paperback edition 1981)
Glendinning, Victoria. *Edith Sitwell* (London 1981)
Gosse, Edmund. 'Some Soldier Poets', *Edinburgh Review*, October 1917, reprinted in Gosses's *Some Diversions of a Man of Letters* (1919)
Graham, Desmond. *Keith Douglas* (Oxford 1974)
Graves, Richard Percival. *Robert Graves: The Assault Heroic* (London paperback edition 1995)
——. *Robert Graves: The Years with Laura Riding* (London paperback edition 1995)

——. *Robert Graves and the White Goddess* (London paperback edition 1998)

Graves, Robert. *Goodbye to All That* (London 1929)

——. *But It Still Goes On* (London 1930)

——. *In Broken Images: Letters 1914–1946*, ed. Paul O'Prey (London 1982)

——. *Between Moon and Moon: Letters 1946–1972*, ed. Paul O'Prey (London 1984)

——. *Conversations with Robert Graves*, ed. Frank L. Kersnowski (Jackson and London 1989)

——. *Dear Robert, Dear Spike*, ed. Pauline Scudamore (Stroud 1991)

Hardy, Thomas. *Collected Letters*, vols 5 and 6, ed. Richard Little Purdy and Michael Millgate (Oxford 1978)

Hart-Davis, Rupert. *Praise from the Past* (York 1996)

——. *Halfway to Heaven* (Stroud 1998)

Hassall, Christopher. *Edward Marsh* (London 1959)

——. *Rupert Brooke* (London 1964)

Hibberd, Dominic. *Owen the Poet* (London 1986)

——. *Poetry of the Great War* (London 1986), an anthology edited with John Onions

——. 'Who were the War Poets Anyway?' in *English Literature of the Great War Revisited*, ed. Michel Roucoux (Amiens 1989)

——. *Wilfred Owen: The Last Year* (London 1992)

——. *Harold Monro* (Basingstoke 2001)

——. *Wilfred Owen* (London 2002)

Higgonet, Margaret Randolph, ed. *Behind the Line: Gender and the Two World Wars* (Yale 1987), essay on Rivers and Sassoon by Elaine Showalter

Hoare, Philip. *Serious Pleasures: The Life of Stephen Tennant* (London 1990)

——. *Wilde's Last Stand* (London 1997)

Hodgson, Ralph. *Poets Remembered* (Cleveland, Ohio 1967)

Horner, Frances. *Time Remembered* (London 1933)

Hyde, H. Montgomery. *Christopher Sclater Millard* (New York 1990)

Hynes, Samuel. *War Imagined: The First World War and English Culture* (London 1990)

——. *The Soldier's Tale* (London 1998)

Jack, Brigadier General J. L. *General Jack's Diary 1914–1918*, ed. John Terraine (London 1964)

Jackson, Stanley. *The Sassoons* (London 1968)

James, Lawrence. *Lawrence of Arabia: The Golden Warrior* (London 1991)

Jolliffe, John. *The Life and Letters of Raymond Asquith* (London 1980)

Jones, Nigel. *Rupert Brooke* (London 1999)

Kaye, Barbara. *The Company We Kept* (London 1986)

Keegan, John. *The Face of Battle* (London 1976)

——. *The First World War* (London 1998)

Kelly, D. V. *39 Months with the 'Tigers' 1915–1917* (London 1930)

Kennedy, Michael. *Portrait of Walton* (Oxford 1989)

Keynes, Geoffrey. *A Bibliography of Siegfried Sassoon* (London 1962); followed by David Farmer's 'Addenda to Keynes's Bibliography' in *Papers of the Bibliographical Society of America*, vol. 63 (1969) and 'Further Sassoon Addenda', vol. 73 (1979)

——. *The Gates of Memory* (Oxford 1981)

Lane, A. *An Adequate Response: The War Poetry of Wilfred Owen and Siegfried Sassoon* (Detroit 1972)

Langley, David. *Duty Done: 2nd Battalion The Royal Welch Fusiliers in the Great War* (Carnarvon 2002)

Larkin, Philip. *Further Requirements*, ed. Anthony Thwaite (London 2001)

Lawrence, T. E. *The Letters of T. E. Lawrence*, ed. D. Garnett (London 1938)

——. *Letters to T. E. Lawrence*, ed. A. W. Lawrence (London 1962)

Lee, Hermione. *Virginia Woolf* (London paperback edition 1997)

Lewis, Percy Wyndham, *The Apes of God* (London 1931)

Mack, John. *A Prince of Our Disorder: The Life of T. E. Lawrence* (1998 edition, Cambridge and London)

MacNeice, Louis. *The Strings Are False* (London paperback edition 1982)

McPhail, Helen and Philip Guest. *Graves and Sassoon* (Barnsley 2001)

——. *Wilfred Owen* (Barnsley 1998) in the series On the Trail of the Poets of the Great War

Manning, Elfrida. *Bronze and Steel* (Shipstone-on-Stour 1932)

——. *Marble and Bronze* (London 1982)

Mare, Walter de la. *Tribute to Walter de la Mare on his Seventy-Fifth Birthday* (London 1948)

Marsh, Edward. *A Number of People* (London 1939)
——. *Ambrosia and Small Beer*. Arranged by Christopher Hassall (London 1964)
Matfield and Brenchley Historical Society, *Siegfried Sassoon: A Centenary Celebration* (Matfield 1986)
Middleboe, Penelope. *Edith Olivier* (London 1989)
Millgate, Michael. *Thomas Hardy* (Oxford 1982)
Moeyes, Paul. *Siegfried Sassoon: Scorched Glory* (London 1997)
Morrell, Lady Ottoline. *Ottoline: The Early Memoirs of Lady Ottoline Morrell*, ed. Robert Gathorne-Hardy (London 1963)
——. *Ottoline at Garsington: Memoirs of Lady Ottoline Morrell*, ed. Robert Gathorne-Hardy (London 1974)
Muir, Percy. *Minding My Own Business* (London 1956)
Murry, John Middleton. *Letters of John Middleton Murry to Katherine Mansfield*, ed. C. A. Hankin (London 1983)
Nichols, Beverley. *The Unforgiving Minute* (London 1978)
Olivier, Edith. *Four Victorian Ladies of Wiltshire* (London 1945)
Owen, Harold. *Journey from Obscurity*, 3 vols (London 1963–5)
——. *Aftermath* (Oxford 1970)
Owen, Wilfred. *Collected Letters*, ed. Harold Owen and John Bell (Oxford 1967)
Panichas, G. *Promise of Greatness* (London 1969)
Parker, Peter. *The Old Lie* (London 1987)
——. *Ackerley* (London 1989)
Pearson, John. *Façades* (London 1978)
Pinnell, Andrew, ed. *Siegfried Sassoon: A Celebration of a Cricketing Man* (Bristol 1996)
Pinto, Vivian de Sola. *Crises in English Poetry* (London 1939)
——. *The City that Shone* (London 1969)
Powell, Anthony. *The Strangers All Are Gone* (London 1982)
Quinn, Patrick J. *The Great War and the Missing Muse* (Selinsgrove 1994)
Raphael, Chaim. *The Road from Babylon: The Story of Sephardi and Oriental Jews* (London 1985)
Rejwan, Nissim. *The Jews of Iraq* (London 1985)
Richards, Frank. *Old Soldiers Never Die* (London 1933)
Richards, Huw. *The Bloody Circus. The Daily Herald and the Left* (London 1997)

Rivers, W. *Conflict and Dream* (London 1923)

Robbins, Keith. *Sir Edward Grey* (London 1971)

Roberts, John Stuart. *Siegfried Sassoon* (London 1999)

Roberts, R. Ellis. W. R. L. *Shepherd: The Life and Letters* (London 1942)

Rolland, Romain. *Jean Christophe* (London 1904–12)

Ross, Alan. *Blindfold Games* (London 1986)

Ross, Robert. *Friend of Friends*, ed. M. Ross (London 1952)

Roth, Cecil. *The Sassoon Dynasty* (London 1941)

Rothenstein, William. *Twenty-Four Portraits* (London 1923)

Rutherford, Andrew. *The Literature of War* (London 1979)

Santayana, George. *My Host the World* (London 1953)

Seymour, Miranda. *Ottoline Morrell: Life on the Grand Scale* (London 1992)

———. *Robert Graves: Life on the Edge* (London 1995)

Seymour-Smith, Martin. *Robert Graves* (London 1982)

Sheffield, Gary. *Forgotten Victory: The First World War: Myths and Realities* (London 2001)

Silk, Dennis. *Siegfried Sassoon* (Tisbury 1975)

Silken, Jon. *Out of Battle: The Poetry of the Great War* (Oxford 1972)

Sitwell, Edith. *Selected Letters*, ed. Richard Greene (London 1997)

Sitwell, Osbert. *Laughter in the Next Room* (London 1949)

———. *Noble Essences* (London 1950)

Slobodin, Richard. *W. H. R. Rivers* (Stroud, 1997 edition)

Smith, Timothy d'Arch. *Love in Earnest* (London 1970)

Sorley, C. H. *The Letters of Charles Sorley*, ed. W. R. Sorley (Cambridge 1919)

Sorley, Charles Hamilton. *Marlborough and Other Poems* (Cambridge 1916)

Sox, David. *Bachelors of Art: Edward Perry Warren and the Lewes House Brotherhood* (London 1991)

Stallworthy, Jon. *Wilfred Owen* (London 1974)

———. *Singing School* (London 1998)

Stanbrook Abbey. *The Stanbrook Abbey Press* (Stanbrook 1970)

Stansky, Peter. *Sassoons: The Worlds of Philip and Sybil* (London and New Haven 2003)

Stephen, Martin. *The Price of Pity* (London 1996)

Sternlicht, Sanford. *Siegfried Sassoon* (New York 1993)

Stirling, W. *Safety Last* (London 1953)

Strachan, Hew, ed. *The Oxford Illustrated History of the First World War* (Oxford 1998)

———. *The First World War* (Oxford 2001)

Swinnerton, Frank. *A London Bookman* (London 1928)

———. *The Georgian Literary Scene* (London 1946)

———. *Figures in the Foreground* (London 1963)

Thornycroft, Rosalind (and Chloe Baynes). *Time Which Spaces Us Apart* (privately printed 1991)

Thorpe, Michael. *Siegfried Sassoon: A Critical Study* (Leiden 1966)

Thwaite, Ann. *Edmund Gosse* (London 1984)

Townsend-Warner, Sylvia. *T. H. White* (London 1967)

Trevelyan, G. M. *Grey of Falloden* (London 1937)

Tsuzuki, Chushichi. *Edward Carpenter* (Cambridge 1980)

Turner, W. J., ed. *Great Names* (New York 1926)

———. *Blow for Balloons* (London 1935)

———. *The Duchess of Popocatapetl* (London 1939)

Untermeyer, Jean Starr. *Private Collection* (New York 1965)

Vaughan, Edwin Campion. *Some Desperate Glory: Diary of a Young Officer 1917*. Foreword by John Terraine (London 1981)

Walsh, T. J., ed. *A Tribute to Wilfred Owen* (London 1964)

Walton, William. *The Selected Letters of William Walton*, ed. Malcolm Hayes (London 2002)

Ward, Major C. H. Dudley, *Regimental Records of the Royal Welch Fusiliers*, vols 3 and 4 (London 1928–9)

Webb, Barry. *Edmund Blunden* (London and New Haven 1990)

Welland, Dennis. 'Sassoon on Owen', *TLS*, 31 May 1974

Whistler, Laurence. *Laughter and the Urn* (London 1985)

Whistler, Theresa. *The Imagination of the Heart: The life of Walter de la Mare* (London 1993)

White, T. H. *Letters to a Friend* (Gloucester 1984)

Williams Wynn, Colonel R. W. and Major W. N. Stable. *The Historical Records of the Montgomeryshire Yeomanry 1909–1919* (Oswestry 1926)

Wilson, A. N. *Hilaire Belloc* (London 1984)

Wilson, Jean Moorcroft. *Siegfried Sassoon: The Making of a Poet* (London 1998)

———. *Siegfried Sassoon: The Journey from the Trenches* (London 2003)

Wilson, Jeremy. *T. E. Lawrence* (London 1989)

Wilton, A. and Robert Upstone, eds. *The Age of Rossetti, Burne-Jones and Watts* (London 1997)

Woolf, Virginia. *Letters* vols 1–6, ed. Nigel Nicolson and Joanne Trautmann (London 1977–84)

———. *Diaries*, vols 1–5, ed. Anne Olivier Bell and Andrew McNeillie (London 1977–84)

———. *Essays*, ed. Andrew McNeillie (London 1986)

Zeller, Dom Hubert van. *One Foot in the Cradle* (London 1965)

Ziegler, Philip. *Osbert Sitwell* (London 1998)

———. *Rupert Hart-Davis* (London 2004)

Index

Works by Siegfried Sassoon (SS) appear directly under title; works by others under author's name

'My Past Has Gone to Bed' (SS; poem), 350
'Mysteries' (SS; poem), 350
'Mystic as Soldier, A' (SS; poem), 117, 255

Namier, (Sir) Lewis, 416
Naples, 348
Nash, Paul, 60
Nation (journal): prints SS's 'In the Pink', 82; patriotism, 109; reviews SS's *Old Huntsman*, 140; SS introduces Owen to, 170; reports on conduct of war, 197; criticizes SS's *Counter-Attack*, 206–7; SS writes for, 266–7
Navarro (musician), 223
Nazism: SS's views on, 376–7, 396, 415; Beerbohm on, 405; Blunden praises, 417
'Neighbours' (SS; poem), 477
Neville, Lord Henry, 20
New Age (magazine), 53
New Beacon School, Sevenoaks, 22–3
New Leader (journal), 301
New Signatures (anthology), 372
New Statesman (journal): rejects SS poems, 116, 317; publishes SS poems, 239, 242, 282, 290
New Witness (journal), 148
New York: SS visits, 239, 243–7, 250–2, 254–5
New York Evening Post, 252
New York Times, 454
Newbolt, Sir Henry: 'The Vigil', 64
Newgass, Edgar, 42, 334
Newman, John Henry, Cardinal, 488
Newman Society, Oxford, 507
'News from the War-After-Next' (SS; poem), 376
Nichols, Beverley, 71, 232, 297
Nichols, Robert: reads at Sibyl Colefax's, 174–5; SS meets, 174; visits SS at Weirleigh, 176; SS asks to write to

Owen, 176; dislikes SS's 'Repression of War Experience', 187; SS requests elegy from in event of death, 196; SS sends poems to, 200, 214, 217; on shooting of SS, 203; friendship with SS, 208, 466; visits SS in Lancaster Gate, 211; writes preface to US edition of SS's *Counter-Attack*, 243; reviews Wilfred Owen's *Poems*, 257; wedding, 262; on Rivers's death, 269; at Hardy's funeral, 317; at Queen's Hall concert, 322; death, 436
Nicholson, Nancy (*later* Graves): engagement and marriage to Graves, 178, 185; attracted to SS, 224; children, 230; estrangement from Graves, 263; and Phibbs, 341, 346; Ross disparages, 353
Nicholson, William, 178, 234, 238, 279, 332, 340, 345, 355, 361, 481
Nicolson, (Sir) Harold, 364, 443, 451, 507
'Night Attack, A' (SS; poem), 106
'Night on the Convoy' (SS; poem), 193, 236, 240
'Night Piece' (SS; poem), 48
'Night and Rain' (SS; poem), 110
'Nimrod in September' (SS; poem), 55
1917 Club, 231
'Nirvana' (SS; poem), 435
Nivelle, General Robert, 126, 128, 159
'Noble Art, The' (SS; poem), 184
Norman, J. S., 23–4
Norman, Sylva (Mrs Edmund Blunden), 393
Norris, John, 368
North American Review, 291
Novello, Ivor: sees SS in Italy, 272; relations with SS, 282–3, 289, 291, 499; and Glen Byam Shaw, 283, 287; Marsh's infatuation with, 291
'November Dusk' (SS; poem), 374

Whistler, Rex: at Wilsford, 309, 345, 366; friendship with SS, 338–9, 373; and SS's claim on Stephen Tennant, 359, 364; Edith Olivier adores, 363; illustrates anthology, 368; at Wilton pageant, 378; paints mural at Lympne, 380; attends SS's wedding, 392; service in Second World War, 424; on SS as 'devil', 425; visits SS, 427; killed in Normandy, 435, 482; Henry Lamb on, 441; and Hester, 459

White, Eric Walter, 514

White, T. H., 409

Whitfield, Corporal Harold, VC, 197

Whitman, Walt, 67, 200, 205, 216, 229, 286, 302, 369, 475

Wiggin, Charles, 57, 192

Wiggin, Maurice, 507

Wilde, Oscar, 18, 45, 83–5

Wilhelm II, Kaiser, 145–6, 222

Williams, Ralph: 'Shepherds of the Delectable Mountain', 323

Wilsford (house), x, 306–11, 313, 317, 323, 331, 343–5, 357–8, 361–2, 369, 371–2, 377–8, 389, 408

Wilson, Edmund, 253, 442

Wilson, George, 29, 228

Wilson, Richard, 84

Wilson, Woodrow, 145, 221

Wilton: pageant, 378–9

Winchester College, 434

'Wind in the Beechwood, The' (SS; poem), 92, 115

Winnington-Ingram, Arthur Foley, Bishop of London, 116–17, 133

'Wirers' (SS; poem), 179

Wirgman, Helen, 18–19, 39, 41, 44–5, 61, 410, 426, 443

Wirgman, Theodore, 18

'Wisdom' (SS; poem), 65

'With de la Mare at Carey Castle' (SS; poem), 280

Wolfe, Humbert, 317, 328; SS parodies, 364

Woman's Hour (radio programme), 514

women: SS's poems against, 55, 180

'Wonderment' (SS; poem), 65

Wood, Sir Henry, 239

Wood, Richardson K., 274, 278

'Wooden Cross, A' (SS; poem), 179

Woodhouse, Violet Gordon, 212

Woolf, Virginia: praises SS poems, 59, 66; reviews SS's *The Old Huntsman*, 121, 139; Ottoline Morrell traduces SS to, 222; SS's confesses non-intellectuality to, 268; praises Charlotte Mew, 319; on SS's engagement to Hester, 391; on Meredith, 454

'Word Faithful, The' (SS; poem), 416

'Words for the Wordless' (SS; poem), 373

'Working Party, A' (SS; poem), 87, 138

'Wounded' (SS; poem), 135

'Wraiths' (SS; poem), 217

'Writing on the Wall, The' (SS; poem), 395

Wylde, Anzie, 263, 277, 303, 320, 324, 332, 365; death, 398

Wyndham, George, 307, 385

Wyndham, Richard, 316

Yates, 'Papa', 127, 367

Yeats, William Butler: with SS in USA, 244; SS visits in Rapallo, 348; edits *Oxford Book of Modern Verse*, 400

Yellow Book, The (magazine), 45

Young, Andrew, 503

'Young Men, The' (SS; poem), 76

'Youth and Maturity' (SS; unpublished poem), 419–20

Ypres, battle of (1917), 159

Zangwill, Israel, 241

Zeller, Dom Hubert van, 486, 495

Zoete, Beryl de, 323, 327